THE LAST MYCENAEANS
AND THEIR SUCCESSORS

OCTOPUS STYLE STIRRUP JAR, KOS

THE LAST MYCENAEANS AND THEIR SUCCESSORS

An Archaeological Survey

C.1200 – C.1000 B.C.

BY

V. R. d'A. DESBOROUGH

PUBLISHERS
Eugene, Oregon

Wipf and Stock Publishers
199 W 8th Ave, Suite 3
Eugene, OR 97401

The Last Mycenaeans and Their Successors
An Archaeological Survey, c.1200 - c.1000 B.C.
By Desborough, V. R. d'A.
Copyright©1964 Oxford University Press
ISBN 13: 978-1-55635-201-0
ISBN 10: 1-55635-201-8
Publication date 1/22/2007
Previously published by Oxford University Press, 1964

This edition reprinted by Wipf and Stock by arrangement with Oxford University Press.
First published in English by Oxford University Press in 1966.
Copyright© Oxford University Press, 1966.

PREFACE

THE writing and production of this book would not have been possible without the generous help of many people and institutions, and it is therefore only right and proper that I should acknowledge my indebtedness.

At the head of my list I place my family; their patient understanding, encouragement and assistance have been factors vital to the completion of the book.

I owe a considerable debt to the University of Manchester for its generosity in granting leave of absence and in providing financial assistance, and also to those of my colleagues who took over my commitments during my absence.

I most gratefully acknowledge the financial assistance I have received from the Pilgrim Trust Fund of the British Academy and from the Oxford Craven Fund.

It would have been inconceivable to undertake this research without making the British School of Archaeology at Athens my centre of operations; to its Managing Committee and officials go, therefore, my special thanks.

At all stages I have benefited greatly from the expert knowledge and helpful suggestions of others (though naturally the responsibility for all statements and opinions found in this work remains mine alone). I would like to mention the following: Dr. S. Alexiou, Professor A. Andrewes, Professor M. Andronikos, Professor J. Benson, Dr. H. Biesantz, Mrs. Birmingham, Professor C. W. Blegen, Mr. J. Boardman, Dr. H. W. Catling, Mr. J. N. Coldstream, Professor N. M. Condoleon, Professor P. Courbin, Dr. P. Dikaios, Mr. and Mrs. David French, Professor E. Gjerstad, Mr. D. E. L. Haynes, Mr. R. A. Higgins, Mr. Sinclair Hood, Mr. R. Hope Simpson, Mr. R. W. Hutchinson, Professor G. L. Huxley, Dr. S. Iakovidis, Dr. V. Karageorghis, Professor E. Kunze, Professor D. Levi, Professor S. Marinatos, Mr. R. Meiggs, Professor L. Morricone, Mr. R. V. Nicholls, Mr. M. Nicolaidis, the late Dr. J. Papademetriou as well as the members of the Greek Archaeological Service as a whole, Mr. P. Petsas, Dr. N. Platon, Mr. M. Popham, Professor P. J. Riis, Mr. C. A. Rodewald, Miss N. K. Sandars, Mrs. Seiradaki, Mrs. E. L. Smithson, Lord William Taylour, Mr. D. Theocharis, Dr. N. M. Verdhelis, Mrs. E. T. Vermeule, the late Professor Wace, and Mrs. Wace.

The typing of the manuscript has been an arduous business, and I am therefore specially grateful to Miss Norquoy and Miss Higgins, secretaries at the University of Manchester, for having undertaken this task.

I have also much appreciated the unfailing kindness of the Delegates of the Clarendon Press as well as the high quality of the work of all concerned in the printing and publishing of this book, both at the Aberdeen University Press and at the Clarendon Press.

V. R. d'A. D.

Manchester, 1963

ACKNOWLEDGMENTS

The author would like to record his gratitude to the following for permission to reproduce illustrations:

The Trustees of the British Museum: Pls. 1, 2, 7a, 9a, 15d, 17d, 18c and e, 20a.
The Visitors of the Ashmolean Museum: Pl. 22d.
The Syndics of the Fitzwilliam Museum: Pl. 18b.
The Director of the National Museum, Athens: Pl. 20b–d.
The Director of the Herakleion Museum: Pls. 6a, 22a and c, 23c.
The Director of the Patras Museum: Pl. 10.
The Director of Antiquities and the Cyprus Museum: Pl. 16b.
The Director of the University Museum, Philadelphia: Pl. 16a.
The Director of the Palestine Archaeological Museum: Pl. 19.
The Director of the Archaeological Institute, University of Heidelberg: Pl. 16d.
The Managing Committee of the British School at Athens: Pls. 11, 12, 17a and b, 18d, 24c and d.
The Editor-in-chief of the *American Journal of Archaeology:* Pls. 4c, 10.
The Publications Committee of the American School of Classical Studies at Athens: Pl. 20e.
Professor Benson: Pl. 4c.
Professor Marinatos: Pls. 8, 9b.
Mrs. E. T. Vermeule: Pl. 10.
Mrs. Seiradaki: Pls. 11, 17a and b.
Mrs. Alan Wace: Pl. 12.
Dr. V. Karageorghis: Pl. 13.
Mr. Z. Pierides: Pl. 18a.
Mr. Sinclair Hood: Pls. 18d, 24c and d.
Dr. N. M. Verdhelis: Pl. 24a.

CONTENTS

LIST OF PLATES	ix
LIST OF ABBREVIATIONS	xiii
INTRODUCTION	xvii
I. THE POTTERY	1
1. Late Helladic III B Pottery	1
2. The Breakdown of LH. III B and the Transition to LH. III C	4
3. Late Helladic III C Pottery	9
II. THE EVIDENCE OTHER THAN THAT OF POTTERY	29
A. *Evidence and Conclusions from Settlements, Tombs, and Places of Worship*	
1. Settlements	29
2. Tombs	32
3. Places of Worship	40
B. *Artefacts*	
1. Introduction and the Material from Hoards	47
2. Objects of Personal Use or Decoration	50
3. Pins	53
4. Fibulae	54
5. Household Utensils	58
6. Armour and Weapons	61
C. *External Influences*	69
III. THE PELOPONNESE	73
1. The Argolid and Corinthia	73
2. Arcadia	87
3. Laconia	87
4. South-west Peloponnese	90
5. Achaea	97
IV. NORTH-WEST GREECE AND THE IONIAN ISLANDS	102
1. Kephallenia	103
2. Ithaca	108
3. Summary	110
V. CENTRAL AND NORTHERN GREECE	112
1. Attica	112
2. Aegina	119

3.	Boeotia	120
4.	Euboea	122
5.	Phocis and Locris	122
6.	The Spercheios Valley	126
7.	Thessaly	127
8.	The Sporades	138
9.	Macedonia	139

VI. THE CENTRAL AND EAST AEGEAN — 147

1. The Cyclades — 147
2. The Dodecanese — 152
3. The Aegean Islands and the West Coast of Asia Minor — 158
4. Troy — 163

VII. CRETE — 166

VIII. THE EAST MEDITERRANEAN — 196

1. Cyprus — 196
2. The Southern Coast of Asia Minor — 205
3. Syria — 207
4. The Philistines and Philistine Pottery — 209

IX. ITALY AND SICILY — 215

X. SUMMARY AND HISTORICAL INFLUENCES — 217

1. c. 1300 to c. 1200 — 217
2. c. 1200 to c. 1150 or Later — 225
3. c. 1150 or Later to c. 1075/1050 — 230
4. The Land and Sea Raiders, and Absolute Chronology — 237
5. Mycenaean Civilization and the Implications of its Collapse — 241
6. The Evidence of Dialect and the Oral Tradition — 244

XI. EPILOGUE: THE EARLY STAGES OF THE PROTOGEOMETRIC PERIOD — 258

APPENDIX A. PROTOGEOMETRIC FINDS SINCE 1951 — 264

APPENDIX B. OCTOPUS STIRRUP JARS — 271

BIBLIOGRAPHY — 273

ADDENDA — 277

SITE INDEX — 281

GENERAL INDEX — 287

MAP: THE DISTRIBUTION OF EARLY CIST TOMBS AND PITHOS BURIALS — 289

LIST OF PLATES

Due acknowledgment for the respective permissions to reproduce many of the objects illustrated will be found after the Preface.

FRONTISPIECE Stirrup jar. *Boll. d'Arte*, 1950, p. 324, Fig. 99; Kos, Langada tomb 39.
Photo: Professor Morricone.

PLATE 1
(a) Kylix. *B.M. Cat.* I, 1, A 868; Ialysos tomb 12.
(b) Three-handled piriform jar, *B.M. Cat.* I, 2, C 460; Hala Sultan Tekke.
(c) Bowl. *B.M. Cat.* I, 1, A 1018; Kalymnos.
(d) Bowl. *B.M. Cat.* I, 1, A 956; Ialysos tomb A.
Photos: British Museum.

PLATE 2
(a) Stirrup jar. *B.M. Cat.* I, A, 913; Ialysos tomb 17.
(b) Stirrup jar. *B.M. Cat.* I, 1, A 911; Ialysos tomb 12.
(c) Stirrup jar. *B.M. Cat.* I, 1, A 928; Ialysos tomb 13.
(d) Stirrup jar. *B.M. Cat.* I, 1, A 929; Ialysos tomb 12.
Photos: British Museum.

PLATE 3
(a) Stirrup jar. *Asine*, p. 397, Fig. 260, 3; Asine tomb 5.
(b) Three-handled piriform jar. *CR*, vi-vii. 145, Fig. 170; Kameiros tomb 48.
(c) Stirrup jar. *CR*, vi-vii. 146, Figs. 171-2; Kameiros tomb 48.
(d) Stirrup jar. *CR*, vi-vii. 147, Fig. 173; Kameiros tomb 48.

PLATE 4
(a) Four-handled jar. *FLMV*, Pl. 37, No. 380; Mycenae.
(b) Stirrup jar. *FLMV*, Pl. 38, No. 393; Mycenae.
(c) Bowl. *AJA*, lxv. Pl. 105, Fig. 22 (=*BSA*, xxv, Pl. 7, c); Mycenae.
Photo: Mrs. Benson.
(d) Trefoil-lipped oinochoe. *FLMV*, Pl. 37, No. 382; Mycenae.

PLATE 5 Vases and small objects from Ialysos tomb 84. *Ann.* xiii-xiv, 391, Fig. 65.

PLATE 6
(a) Stirrup jar. *AE*, 1904, pp. 42 ff., Fig. 10 and Pl. 1; Mouliana Tomb B.
Photo: Mr. Popham.
(b) Stirrup jar. *Ergon* for 1959, Fig. 139; Naxos.
Photo: Professor Condoleon.
(c) Stirrup jar. *Ergon* for 1958, p. 28, Fig. 28; Perati tomb 65, No. 569.
(d) Stirrup jar. *Ergon* for 1954, p. 11, Fig. 10; Perati tomb 15β, No. 261.
Photos of (c) and (d): Mr. Iakovidis.

PLATE 7
(a) Kalathos with figurines. *B.M. Cat.* I, 1, A 950; Ialysos tomb 12.
Photo: British Museum.
(b) Kalathos with figurines. *Ergon* for 1961, p. 15, Fig. 11; Perati tomb 111a, No. 820.
Photo: Mr. Iakovidis.
(c) Jug. *Ann.* xiii-xiv. 321, Fig. 68; Ialysos tomb 84.
(d) Hydria. *Ergon* for 1959, Fig. 136; Naxos.
Photo: Professor Condoleon.

PLATE 8 Kraters. *AE*, 1932, Pl. 5; Kephallenia, Lakkithra tomb A.

LIST OF PLATES

PLATE 9
(a) Kylix. *B.M. Cat* I, 1, A 1008; Kalymnos.
Photo: British Museum.
(b) Kylikes. *AE*, 1932, Pl. 6; Kephallenia, Lakkithra tomb A.

PLATE 10
(a) Four-handled vase. *AJA*, lxiv. Pl. 2, Fig. 9, No. 8a; Prostovitsa, Achaea.
(b) Four-handled vase. *AJA*, lxiv. Pl. 1, Fig. 2, No 2; Lopesi, Achaea.
(c) Four-handled vase. *AJA*, lxiv. Pl. 1, Fig. 3, No. 3; Achaea.
(d) Stirrup jar. *AJA*, lxiv, Pl. 3, Fig. 22, No. 29; Achaea.
(e) Stirrup jar. *AJA*, lxiv. Pl. 3, Fig. 24, No. 35; Chalandritsa, Achaea.
(f) Bird Vase. *AJA*, lxiv. Pl. 4, Fig. 31, No. 45; Klauss, Achaea.
Photos of (b)-(f): Mrs. Vermeule.

PLATE 11
Pyxis patterns. *BSA*, lv. 33, Fig. 23; Karphi.

PLATE 12
Bowls and cup. *BSA*, xxv. 33, Fig. 9; Mycenae.

PLATE 13
Sherds. *BCH*, lxxxiv. 573, Fig. 125; Kition.
Photo: Dr. Karageorghis.

PLATE 14
(a) Stirrup jar. *Ker.* I, Pl. 10, No. 508; Athens, sub-Myc. tomb 98.
(b) Trefoil-lipped oinochoe. *Ker.* I, Pl. 24, No. 438; Athens, sub-Myc. tomb 19.
(c) Amphoriskos. *Ker.* I, Pl. 16, No. 460; Athens, sub-Myc. tomb 47.
(d) Bowl. *Ker.* I, Pl. 22, No. 434; Athens, sub-Myc. tomb 17.
Photos: German Archaeological Institute.

PLATE 15
(a) Lekythos. *Ker.* I, Pl. 13, No. 494; Athens, sub-Myc. tomb 84.
(b) Cup. *Ker.* I, Pl. 23, No. 437; Athens, sub-Myc. tomb 19.
Photos of (a) and (b): German Archaeological Institute.
(c) Lekythos. *Ergon* for 1960, p. 187, Fig. 209; Naxos.
(d) Cup. *B.M. Cat.* I, 2, C 721; Kourion.
Photo: British Museum.

PLATE 16
(a) Bottle. *AJA*, xli. Pl. 5, No. 25; Kaloriziki tomb 25.
Photo: University Museum, Philadelphia.
(b) Bottle. *AJA*, xli. Pl. 2, No. 82; Kaloriziki tomb 26 A.
Photo: Cyprus Museum.
(c) Bottle. *Ker.* I, Pl. 27, No. 507; Athens, sub-Myc. tomb 97.
Photo: German Archaeological Institute.
(d) Bottle. *Ker.* I, Pl. 37; Athens Acropolis, South-west Slope tomb B.
Photo: Archaeological Institute, University of Heidelberg.

PLATE 17
(a) Amphoriskos. *BSA*, lv. 21, Fig. 14, No. 9; Karphi.
(b) Kantharos. *BSA*, lv. 21, Fig. 14, No. 7; Karphi.
(c) Amphora. *Ergon* for 1958, p. 27, Fig. 27; Perati tomb 74, No. 590.
Photo: Mr. Iakovidis.
(d) Amphora. *B.M. Cat.* I, 2, C 754; Cyprus.
Photo: British Museum.

PLATE 18
(a) Stirrup jar. Zeno Pierides collection; Cyprus.
Photo: Dr. Catling.
(b) Stirrup jar. Fitzwilliam Museum, GR. 2 1960 (cf. *Archaeological Reports for 1961-1962, p.* 50, No. 15); probably Cyprus.
Photo: Fitzwilliam Museum.

(c) Stirrup jar. *B.M. Cat.* I, 2, C 696; Kouklia.
Photo: British Museum.
(d) Part of stirrup jar. *BSA*, liii-liv. 242, Fig. 28; Gypsades tomb VI A, 2.
(e) Stirrup jar. British Museum, 1939, 10-11, 1; Argos.
Photo: British Museum.

PLATE 19
(a) Stirrup jar. Ain Shems.
(b) Jug with strainer spout. Ain Shems.
(c) Bowl. Tell Far'a.
(d) Bowl. Tell Far'a.
Photos: Palestine Archaeological Museum.

PLATE 20
(a) Relief beads of glass paste. Probably Ialysos.
Photo: British Museum.
(b), (c) Relief beads, gold, traces of enamel. Mycenae tomb 88.
(d) Relief beads, gold, traces of enamel. Mycenae tomb 103.
Photos of (b)-(d): Mr. Tombazi.
(e) Necklace, gold. *Prosymna*, ii. Fig. 577. Prosymna tomb 2.
(Courtesy of the American School of Classical Studies at Athens.)

PLATE 21
Small finds from Kerameikos sub-Myc. tomb 108. *Ker.* I, Pl. 28.

PLATE 22
(a) 1. Bronze sword. *AE*, 1904, p. 30, Fig. 7: Mouliana tomb B.
2. Bronze sword. *AE*, 1904, p. 46, Fig. 11; Mouliana tomb A.
Photos: Mr. Popham.
(b) Part of bronze sword. *Pr.* 1954, p. 96, Fig. 5; Perati tomb 12, M 52.
Photo: Mr. Iakovidis.
(c) Bronze spearhead. *AE*, 1904, p. 30, Fig. 7; Mouliana tomb B.
Photo: Mr. Popham.
(d) Bronze spearhead. Ashmolean Museum, Cat. No. 1930. 18; 'Near Thebes'.
Photo: Ashmolean Museum.

PLATE 23
(a) Bronze shield-boss. *Ker.* iv, Pl. 37, No. M 49; Athens, Protogeometric tomb 24.
(b) Bronze shield-boss. *Ker.* iv, Pl. 37, No. M 13; Athens, Protogeometric tomb 43.
Photos of (a) and (b): German Archaeological Institute.
(c) Bronze shield-bosses. *AE*, 1904, p. 30, Fig. 7; Mouliana tomb B.
Photo: Mr. Popham.

PLATE 24
(a) Bronze helmet. *BCH*, lxxxii. 706, Fig. 26; Tiryns.
Photo: German Archaeological Institute.
(b) Bronze dress pin. In private possession. Unknown provenience; Attic sub-Mycenaean type.
Photo: Ashmolean Museum.
(c) Bronze dress pin. *BSA*, liii-liv. 257, Fig. 34; Gypsades tomb VII, 13.
(d) Iron knife, bronze rivets. *BSA*, liii-liv. 255, Fig. 32; Gypsades tomb VII, 12.
(e) Iron knife, bronze rivets. *Pr.* 1955, p. 106, Pl. 31, *b*; Perati tomb 38, No. M 85.
Photo: Mr. Iakovidis.

LIST OF ABBREVIATIONS

A. PERIODICALS

AA	*Archäologischer Anzeiger: Beiblatt zum Jahrbuch des Deutschen archäologischen Instituts.*
AAS	*Annales Archéologiques de Syrie.*
AASOR	*Annual of the American Schools of Oriental Research.*
AD	*Ἀρχαιολογικὸν Δελτίον.*
AE	*Ἀρχαιολογικὴ Ἐφημερίς.*
AJ	*Antiquaries' Journal.*
AJA	*American Journal of Archaeology.*
AM	*Mitteilungen des deutschen archäologischen Instituts; athenische Abteilung.*
Ann.	*Annuario della scuola italiana di Atene e delle missioni italiane in oriente.*
AS	*Anatolian Studies.*
BASOR	*Bulletin of the American Schools of Oriental Research.*
BBSA	*Bulletin of the British School of Archaeology in Jerusalem.*
BCH	*Bulletin de Correspondance Hellénique.*
Ber. R.-G.K.	*Bericht der römisch-germanisch Kommission.*
BJ	*Bonner Jahrbuch.*
Boll. d'Arte	*Bollettino d'Arte del Ministero della pubblica Istruzione.*
BPI	*Bollettino di paletnologia italiana.*
BSA	*Annual of the British School at Athens.*
CRAI	*Académie des inscriptions et belles-lettres. Comptes rendus des séances de l'année . . .*
Ergon	*Τὸ Ἔργον τῆς Ἀρχαιολογικῆς Ἑταιρείας κατὰ τὸ ἔτος . . .*
GRBS	*Greek, Roman and Byzantine Studies.*
Hesp.	*Hesperia; Journal of the American School of Classical Studies at Athens.*
ILN	*Illustrated London News.*
Ist. Mitt.	*Istanbuler Mitteilungen.*
JdI	*Jahrbuch des deutschen archäologischen Instituts.*
JHS	*Journal of Hellenic Studies.*
JIAN	*Journal international d'archéologie numismatique.*
JRGZM	*Jahrbuch des römisch-germanischen Zentralmuseums in Mainz.*
KX	*Κρητικὰ Χρονικά.*
LAAA	*Annals of Archaeology and Anthropology of the University of Liverpool.*
MA	*Monumenti antichi pubblicati a cura . . . dei Lincei.*
OA	*Acta Instituti Romani Regni Sueciae: Opuscula Archaeologica.*
Op. Ath.	*Acta Instituti Atheniensis Regni Sueciae: Opuscula Atheniensia.*

ÖJh	*Jahreshefte des Österreichischen archäologischen Instituts.*
PEFQ	*Quarterly Statement of the Palestine Exploration Fund.*
PEQ	*Palestine Exploration Quarterly.*
Pr.	Πρακτικὰ τῆς Ἀρχαιολογικῆς Ἑταιρείας.
PPS	*Proceedings of the Prehistoric Society.*
QDAP	*Quarterly of the Department of Antiquities in Palestine.*
RA	*Revue Archéologique.*

B. PUBLICATIONS

AC	J. D. S. Pendlebury, *The Archaeology of Crete.*
Aegean and Near East	*The Aegean and the Near East; Studies presented to Hetty Goldman* (Locust Valley, N.Y., 1956).
Aegina	A. Furtwängler, *Aegina, das Heiligtum der Aphaia.*
AF	*Arkeologiska Forskningar och Fynd* (Stockholm, 1952).
Aghios Kosmas	G. E. Mylonas, *Aghios Kosmas; an Early Bronze Age Settlement and Cemetery in Attica.*
Analysis	A. Furumark, *The Mycenaean Pottery: Analysis and Classification.*
Ancient Mycenae	G. E. Mylonas, *Ancient Mycenae, the Capital City of Agamemnon.*
Arte cretese-micenea	M. Borda, *Arte cretese-micenea nel Museo Pigorini di Roma.*
Asine	O. Frödin and A. W. Persson, *Asine: Results of the Swedish excavations.*
Ber. VI. int. Kongress.	*Archäologisches Institut des deutschen Reiches; Bericht über den VI. internazionalen Kongress für Archäologie* (Berlin, 1940).
B.M. Cat.	*British Museum Catalogue of Vases.*
CAH	*Cambridge Ancient History.*
Chronology	A. Furumark, *The Chronology of Mycenaean Pottery.*
Corinth	*American School of Classical Studies: Excavations at Corinth.*
CR	*Clara Rhodos; studi e materiali pubblicati a cura dell' Istituto storico-archeologico di Rodi.*
Cretan Collection	J. Boardman, *The Cretan Collection in Oxford.*
C.T.	A. J. B. Wace, *Chamber Tombs at Mycenae.*
CVA	*Corpus Vasorum Antiquorum.*
Délos	*Exploration archéologique de Délos: École française d'Athènes.*
Délos primitive	H. Gallet de Santerre, *Délos primitive et archaïque.*
Documents	M. Ventris and J. Chadwick, *Documents in Mycenaean Greek.*
Dorians	T. C. Skeat, *The Dorians in Archaeology.*
Δ-Σ	C. Tsountas, Αἱ προϊστορικαὶ ἀκροπόλεις Διμηνίου καὶ Σέσκλου.
E-A	C. F. A. Schaeffer, *Enkomi-Alasia.*
Ἐπιτύμβιον	Ἐπιτύμβιον Χρήστου Τσούντα (Athens, 1941).
Essai	E. Coche de la Ferté, *Essai de classification de la céramique mycénienne d'Enkomi.*

Eutresis	Hetty Goldman, *Excavations at Eutresis in Boeotia.*
Exc. in Cyprus	A. S. Murray and others, *British Museum Excavations in Cyprus.*
FD	*Fouilles de Delphes; École française d'Athènes.*
Fibules	C. Blinkenberg, *Fibules grecques et orientales.*
FLMV	A. Fürtwängler and G. Löschcke, *Mykenische Vasen.*
Fortetsa	J. K. Brock, *Fortetsa.*
Gournia	Harriet Boyd-Hawes, *Gournia, Vasiliki and other Sites on the Isthmus of Hierapetra, Crete.*
Graef, Akr. Vas.	B. Graef, *Die Antiken Vasen von der Akropolis zu Athen.*
Greek Pins	G. Jacobsthal, *Greek Pins and their Connexions with Europe and Asia.*
Hama	P. J. Riis, *Hama; Fouilles et recherches 1931–1938*, vol. ii, 3: *Les cimetières à crémation.*
Ker.	*Kerameikos; Ergebnisse der Ausgrabungen.*
Korakou	C. W. Blegen, *Korakou; a Prehistoric Settlement near Corinth.*
Levant	F. J. Stubbings, *Mycenaean Pottery from the Levant.*
Locriens	L. Lerat, *Les Locriens de l'Ouest.*
Mallia, Maisons II	A. Dessenne and J. Deshayes, *Fouilles exécutées à Mallia*, fasc. 2.
Malthi	N. Valmin, *The Swedish Messenia Expedition.*
Monuments	Hilda Lorimer, *Homer and the Monuments.*
MPI	Lord William Taylour, *Mycenean Pottery in Italy and Adjacent Areas.*
Nécropoles	H. van Effenterre, *Nécropoles du Mirabello.*
New Tombs	A. W. Persson, *New Tombs at Dendra, near Midea.*
Olympia	*Olympia; Ergebnisse der Ausgrabungen.*
Olynthus	D. M. Robinson, ed., *Excavations at Olynthus* (Baltimore, 1929–1952).
Palaikastro	R. C. Bosanquet and R. M. Dawkins, *The Unpublished Objects from the Palaikastro Excavations 1902–1906.*
Perrot-Chipiez	G. Perrot and C. Chipiez, *Histoire de l'Art dans l'Antiquité*, vol. vi.
PGP	V. R. d'A. Desborough, *Protogeometric Pottery.*
Phylakopi	D. G. Hogarth and others, *Excavations at Phylakopi in Melos.*
P.M.	W. A. Heurtley, *Prehistoric Macedonia.*
P. of M.	Sir Arthur Evans, *The Palace of Minos.*
Problems	E. Sjöqvist, *Problems of the Late Cypriote Bronze Age.*
Prosymna	C. W. Blegen, *Prosymna; The Helladic Settlement.*
P.T.	A. J. B. Wace and M. S. Thompson, *Prehistoric Thessaly.*
P.T.K.	Sir Arthur Evans, *Prehistoric Tombs at Knossos.*
Recherches	Y. Béquignon, *Recherches archéologiques à Phères en Thessalie.*
Royal Tombs	A. W. Persson, *Royal Tombs at Dendra, near Midea.*
SCE	*The Swedish Cyprus Expedition* (Stockholm, 1934 onwards).
Spercheios	Y. Béquignon, *La Vallée du Spercheios des origines au IVe siècle.*
Tarsus	Hetty Goldman, *Excavations at Gözlü Kule, Tarsus*, vol. ii.
Thermi	Winifred Lamb, *Excavations at Thermi in Lesbos.*

Tiryns	*Tiryns; Ergebnisse der Ausgrabungen.*
Verdhelis	N. M. Verdhelis, Ὁ Πρωτογεωμετρικὸς Ῥυθμὸς τῆς Θεσσαλίας.
Vrokastro	Edith H. Hall, *Excavations in Eastern Crete, Vrokastro.*
Zygouries	C. W. Blegen, *Zygouries; a Prehistoric Settlement in the Valley of Cleonae.*

INTRODUCTION

Much has been written in recent years of the period when Mycenaean civilization was at its height, but little either of the complex period of decline which succeeded it or of the period of subsequent transition and fundamental transformation out of which, in the fullness of time, the characteristic features of classical Greece were to emerge. The decline and the early stages of transition may be said to cover one hundred and fifty to two hundred years; it is with this time that my book is concerned, and I attempt, so far as is possible, to explain and clarify the course of events.

For the study of this period the historian finds that his conventional basic material, the contemporary written word, is denied to him. He has two classes of evidence on which to base his results: the archaeological material, and the oral tradition handed down to the Greeks of a very much later period, none of which was committed to writing until at least three centuries after the events with which it dealt.

In any historical research, the whole of the available evidence must be used, in so far as it is possible to do so. In this case, with two entirely different types of material, a common starting point must be established. The obvious one is the Trojan War, one of the focal points of the oral tradition on the one hand, and clearly confirmed, to my mind, by the archaeological evidence on the other hand; although it may not belong within the period of decline of Mycenaean power, it is one of its earliest symptoms.

The question then arises, which of the two types of material should be given priority? Is the oral tradition to be treated as a genuine account into whose scheme the archaeological data must be fitted, or are these data to be used as criteria to test the accuracy of the traditional stories?

Before this question can be answered, the oral evidence itself may be divided into two categories. First, information is given of certain major movements and consequent settlements, whether related to invasion or migration. These as such are in the main confirmed by the evidence of the distribution of dialects, as we have it, from the eighth or seventh century onwards. If we had no more than this, we could accept the fact that they took place, without knowing precisely when, or how, they were interrelated. The chronology and interconnexions are, however, also given, and in much detail, by the second category of the oral evidence; and with regard to this it appears to me that there is much scope for error, and that there is no way of testing the accuracy except by reference to the evidence of archaeology, however difficult this latter type of evidence may be to interpret correctly.

Consequently I intend to use the archaeological evidence as the basic material, at the same time assuming as true the existence of major movements of population as given by the tradition.

It may seem that, even so, undue space has been allocated to the archaeological side, but the reason for this is that no complete exposition exists of the material available for the twelfth and eleventh centuries. The nearest approximation to such an exposition is Furumark's monograph, *The Mycenaean III C Pottery and its Relation to Cypriote Fabrics*, in *Opuscula Archaeologica* iii; the analysis of the pottery is detailed and penetrating, but only the pottery is discussed, and only that of the Argolid, Attica, the Dodecanese, Crete and Cyprus (though these are the most important areas). Furthermore, the article was published in 1944, and so can take no account of the many important discoveries since then. Besides this, a valuable survey was published in 1962 by Å99lin, bringing together the evidence of the Mycenaean sites on the Greek mainland down to the end of the Mycenaean period and beyond, but this also fails to achieve the necessary completeness.

It has therefore seemed to me desirable to set out, without excessive detail, the whole of the evidence, including all such aspects of the Mycenaean and subsequent culture as come within the province of archaeology, over the whole area inhabited by the Mycenaeans or in touch with their civilization. It is only by presenting the evidence in full that one is justified in proceeding to any inferences of a historical nature.

It may still be argued that the time is not yet ripe for such a general survey, and it will be evident to the reader that certain aspects have not been treated as fully as they deserve, for which my own shortcomings are responsible. It is nevertheless my belief that the attempt has been worth making, and it is my hope that this book will be of value both to the archaeologist and to the historian.

CHAPTER I

THE POTTERY[1]

THE aim of this work is to examine, and so far as possible to clarify, the circumstances attendant on the breakdown of the Mycenaean power, the question of the survival of Mycenaean communities and ideas into later times, the extent to which non-Mycenaean elements made their appearance during and after the general break-up, and the circumstances under which the mainland of Greece and the islands of the southern Aegean reverted to conditions of relative normality. The evidence provided up to the present day by archaeological excavation will provide the foundation on which, it is hoped, some structure may arise, and in this evidence the pottery will form a major and chronologically determining factor. Thus, archaeologically speaking, the range of this book will extend from Late Helladic III B pottery, through Late Helladic III C and sub-Mycenaean, in each case with the relevant Late Minoan pottery running parallel, and finish with Protogeometric pottery. These styles of pottery, with the probable exception of sub-Mycenaean, represent distinct periods of time, and consequently the terminology will apply both to style and period. In the case of Late Helladic and Late Minoan, the abbreviations LH. and LM. will be used.

Of the several periods, LH. III B may be considered to form an essential introduction to the rest, and Protogeometric will be discussed in a brief concluding chapter.

1. *Late Helladic III B Pottery*

The pottery of this style covers, roughly, the period of the thirteenth century B.C., and was prevalent over the Mycenaean world, that is to say, throughout the Peloponnese, Attica, Boeotia, Phocis, and Locris; over much of Thessaly and the islands of the southern Aegean; in at least one major settlement on the west coast of Asia Minor, Miletus; in one settlement in South Italy, Scoglio del Tonno; and observable among trading posts—if they are not more than this—on the island of Cyprus and along the coast of Syria.

Within the central Mycenaean sphere of Greece and the Aegean this is a time of remarkable uniformity. The objects found, of whatever material, conform to a general pattern, and a similar statement, though there are occasional locally imposed variations, may be made with regard to settlement and burial architecture.

The uniformity of the pottery is of particular importance, as it has potentially great stylistic permutations, and homogeneity is not really to be expected.

---

[1] For Mycenaean pottery in general, the standard works are Furumark's *The Mycenaean Pottery: Analysis and Classification* and *The Chronology of Mycenaean Pottery*. More specialized studies include Furumark's *The Mycenaean III C Pottery and its relation to Cypriote Fabrics*, in *OA*, iii. 194 ff.; Stubbings's *The Mycenaean Pottery of Attica*, in *BSA*, xlii. 1 ff. and *Mycenaean Pottery from the Levant*; and Taylour's *Mycenaean Pottery in Italy and Adjacent Areas*.

The vases and sherds come either from settlements or tombs or sanctuaries. Sanctuaries are very rare, and may be left aside (cf. pp. 40 ff.); but a clear distinction must be made between settlements and tombs, both because there is a difference in popularity between vase types found in each, and because the evidence, as we have it published, is far better for vases found in tombs than it is for those found in settlements. There is as yet, to my knowledge, no good illustrated record published of a representative collection of LH. III B vases or sherds from any single settlement within the central Mycenaean sphere, while on the other hand the material available from cemeteries, such as those of the Argolid, Attica and Rhodes—not to mention the Cypriot tombs—is considerable and full. Also, certain important areas are not known at all from settlement evidence.

There are many different kinds of vase, but only a few are popular, and only a few are susceptible of much variation in decoration.

Bowls and kraters are fully and diversely decorated, and are typical of settlements, but not commonly found in tombs except for the amphoroid and other kraters found in Cypriot burials, which may be regarded as peripheral—these, incidentally, being frequently in a pictorial style which I shall not discuss.

These shapes are then mainly from settlements and so, bearing in mind the shortcomings of our knowledge of this type of evidence, it would be rash to attempt to demonstrate homogeneity from one district to another, or indeed to assess stylistic development. Only a few general remarks on bowls (Pl. 1c-d) need be made. The style of decoration is on the whole a clay-ground one, though there is a growing tendency in the latest stage to paint the inside of the vase. The main decoration is confined to the area between the handles, the rim and the lower part of the body being either banded or left clear. The prevalent system, for the main decoration, is that of panelling, with various rectilinear or spiraliform motives, or of antithetically arranged motives. Towards the end of the style, a thickening of the bands is at times to be observed. The present situation is carefully summarized in the publication recording a collection of settlement pottery from Mycenae.[1]

Most of the other types of vase can better be studied from the examples found in tombs. The most important is the stirrup jar (Pls. 2, 3d), not only because it is so favoured in LH. III B tombs, but also because of its enduring popularity in LH. III C. It has no standard shape, but the general scheme of decoration, and certain decorative elements, are widely accepted. On the body of the vase, the usual design is a succession of broad encircling bands of paint enclosing a varying number of very finely drawn thin bands; on the shoulder, the most common motives are a stylized flower, or some variation of this, and the multiple stem. Occasionally (perhaps a late development?), a subsidiary zone of decoration takes the place of the first group of fine bands below the shoulder. The draughtsmanship is generally excellent, as indeed is the case with other shapes. It is not easy to assess stylistic development or to distinguish regional differences. Much the same may be said of the kylikes (Pls. 1a, 9a), whether of the one or the two-handled variety, with their elegant slim shapes, and the octopus or whorl-shell decoration over the body, often continuing down on to the banded stem (these are the most common motives, but there are of course others, and very many kylikes are either plain or monochrome).

[1] *BSA*, lii. 217 f.

Other shapes must be dealt with more briefly. Three-handled piriform jars (Pls. 1*b*, 3*b*), both big and small, are common. These and the straight-sided pyxides, now gradually ousting the curved alabastra, have decoration on the shoulder. The little one-handled jugs were always popular, but they do not differ much in shape, and are as a rule either plain or decorated with bands only. The concave-sided tankard is a feature of LH. III B, banded round the middle, varied in decoration. So also is the long conical rhyton, equally varied in decoration. Rather less common are the plain feeding-bottles (spouted juglets), the cups, and the bowls with somewhat ogival profile known as kalathoi. Multiple vases and askoi are infrequent. Hydriai are more often found in settlements, and are plain, as is the ovoid amphora, a late development, and also a settlement shape.

To summarize on this style, it may be said that the technique and execution of the vases are of a high quality. The clay is as a rule finely prepared; a wash or slip is applied, and the paint is often slightly lustrous. Decoration is orderly and delicate; it is usually confined—apart from the encircling bands—to the upper part of the vase. There is no very great variation in motives (each vase type having its own characteristic designs) and normally these motives are given plenty of room—it is an open style. The tendency is strongly towards symmetry, and the motives used are often abstractions or conventionalizations of naturalistic designs. In such a formal, harmonious style it is inevitable that certain patterns should appear which can be called geometric; even so, LH. III B is essentially a non-geometric style, achieving a compromise between the too elaborate and the too simple. Its abstractions very possibly contribute to the fact that little change is to be observed throughout the course of the style.

The style is remarkably uniform wherever it is found in Mycenaean territories, so far as concerns the tomb evidence—settlement evidence being inadequate for comparative purposes. The same shapes appear, their distribution is on the whole the same, and the decoration is the same. Furumark states that within the central Mainland districts and the Levanto-Mycenaean region 'there are no variations of any real significance'[1] (he excepts of course the pictorial style). Outside these areas he places Rhodes in a separate category, as containing considerable quantities of typical LH. III B, but yet clinging to the LH. III A tradition.[2]

Stubbings's researches into Attic, Rhodian, Cypriot and Levantine pottery have not seriously modified Furumark's conclusions, though they provide a clearer picture of the local variations. Taylour's work on Mycenaean found in South Italy and Sicily shows how the knowledge of such local variations can lead to interesting hypotheses as to the origin of the pottery which made its way to this part of the world.[3]

The regional variations consist sometimes in the difference in relative popularity of a certain shape or decorative motive, but there are also instances of a shape or a decoration peculiar to a single area. In spite of such variations, there is still a considerable general homogeneity as between one area and another; there is no question, as is found in the succeeding LH. III C, of separate regional styles. The similarities are far more impressive than the differences.

[1] *Analysis*, p. 540.
[2] Op. cit. p. 541. See, however, Stubbings's comment in *Levant*, p. 20.
[3] See p. 1, n. 1.

From what is known of recently published settlement material in otherwise poorly known areas—for example, Iolkos and Neleia in Thessaly, and Miletus—there is no reason to alter this conclusion, though it must always be borne in mind that we are far from having a representative selection of pottery from any area, and that there do exist a few 'backward' areas where LH. III B had a strong provincial flavour.

It seems quite unnecessary to suppose that most of this LH. III B pottery was made in some central district and exported from there—in fact, there is good reason for believing that this was not so—but the style will have originated in some one district, and its ideas must have been accepted by, or imposed upon, potters of other areas, not only at the beginning but throughout the course of the style.

Stubbings writes: 'The III B style was, in fact, a creation of mainland Greece, which had entirely ceased to depend on Minoan design for inspiration.'[1] He therefore, as does Furumark,[2] places the origin of this style on the Mainland. This is obviously true, as the corresponding Minoan style is different, and that of Rhodes is slightly influenced by the continuing tradition of LH. III A; nor do there appear to be any other centres of sufficient significance in the Aegean which could have originated this style. The question is then, in which district of the Mainland did LH. III B originate? And it must be stressed that such a district must have been of considerable cultural prominence and prestige for other districts to have followed its lead and not to have developed independently after the original acceptance. Even cultural prominence as such would hardly be enough to account for the continued acceptance. The political centre of the Mycenaean world is to be sought, and to my mind it cannot be elsewhere than the Argolid, with Mycenae as the capital of the overall ruler. Both archaeologically and traditionally, Mycenae is the outstanding city, and the Hittite documents do not exclude the possible equation of the Mycenaean world with the territory of Ahhiyawa.[3]

2. *The Breakdown of LH. III B and the Transition to LH. III C*

It is obviously essential to be able, as far as possible, to determine the source and continuing inspiration of the LH. III B style, in order to understand the cause of its end and of subsequent developments. In the normal way, the continuation of a style will depend on its vitality, and after some time there will come a period of stagnation, and a fresh style will arise; art is not static. In this instance, however, assuming the Argolid to have been the centre of diffusion, other circumstances play their part, that is to say, those that resulted in the virtual destruction of the political dominance of this region. The relevant events are dealt with elsewhere (pp. 221 ff.), and it is only necessary to state here that some disaster overcame parts at least of outer Mycenae when LH. III B had been current for some time; that a second disaster, assigned to the end of LH. III B, caused widespread destruction in the citadel not only of Mycenae, but also of Tiryns; and that many Argive sites, of greater or lesser importance, were abandoned during this time. At the end of LH. III B, then, the Argolid suffered severe disaster and depopulation. The political

---

[1] *Levant*, p. 20.
[2] *Analysis*, pp. 539 ff.
[3] See most recently the analysis of Huxley in his *Achaeans and Hittites*. Il. ix. 69 (Agamemnon as βασιλεύτατος).

consequence is clear. The power of the Mycenaean overlord must have been broken, not only in the Argolid itself, but also over the whole Mycenaean world. Ceramically speaking, there are two effects to be considered. The effect of disaster following on disaster and of the conditions of major unrest will probably be reflected in the degeneration of the LH. III B style in the Argolid; and in so far as this is happening, and as the political dominance is removed, the style is likely to disappear, with greater or lesser rapidity, elsewhere. It is under these conditions that a gradual change from one style to another is probable, and also that the homogeneity will be seriously affected. Something new will arise, presuming there is not simply a progressive degeneration, and with the authority of the Argolid now fundamentally shaken, the elements of a new style may appear elsewhere than in the Argolid. Any new style, unless there are racial changes, is likely to be founded on the preceding one, but several new and distinct styles could emerge. At the same time, a period of transition between the old and the new is to be expected.

It is perhaps unnecessary to stress that in the development of a new style some new element must appear; in other words, a degeneration of a style cannot be called a new style. There must be new shapes, or new decorations, or at least a new way of using the motives previously current.

What, then, are the new elements which distinguish the emergence of LH. III C, and where in the Mycenaean world did they originate? There is an initial difficulty here, in that stratification evidence linking LH. III B with a new style is only very rarely found, and in particular is not yet available in the Argolid.

Furumark, in a fundamental article,[1] attempted to answer the first question without answering the second—and indeed, the first question must be answered before the second can be dealt with. He states his position and principles very clearly, both here and in his *Analysis*. He regards the emergence of LH. III C as a twofold process. On the one side there is what he calls conventionalization, and it is clear from what he says that this is no more than a deterioration of LH. III B. On the other side there is his 'stylization', which he explains as 'the process through which the other main class of Myc. III C 1 decoration, comprising the Close Style proper and the corresponding Rhodian decoration, was created'; and he claims that this was largely dependent on influences from LM. III B.[2] In so far as he is using only the criterion of conventionalization, it does not seem justifiable to speak of a new style; with stylization it is reasonable to do so, and there is no doubt that the principle of closeness in decoration, as opposed to the relatively open design of LH. III B, is something new.

It is not easy to know how to define one's terminology. If a group shows simply elements of deterioration, can one call it LH. III C? If a group shows in addition to this one or two new elements, can one still call it LH. III B? If one speaks of a transitional phase, which would be correct, then there may be difficulties in deciding at what point the transition ceases. If one tries to break the matter down into shapes and decorations, it will be seen that developments and change take place, not surprisingly, in an irregular fashion. The decorative system of the bowl may, for example, have retained its prior character appreciably longer than that of the stirrup jar (which would have an effect on

[1] *OA*, iii. 194 ff.   [2] *Analysis*, p. 549.

one's estimate of settlement pottery); the undecorated, or simply banded, types of vase may have to be left out of account unless their shape is materially altered.

These are the considerations which may have to be taken into account in any one district when there is a change of style; for them to be valid for other districts as well, there should be uniformity both in the degeneration of the old style and in the development of the new, and so far as LH. III C is concerned, there manifestly is not. In order to establish a relative order of commencement, new elements common to several areas, or at least linking one area and another, must be sought. The criterion of the appearance of a new motive or decorative system or shape in vases or sherds of the earlier style is always useful, provided one takes into account the possibility that the earlier style may have continued rather longer in one district than in another. It is altogether desirable to be able to make use of some innovation, characteristic of one particular region, which makes its appearance in other areas.

From these observations it will presumably be clear that, in between one district and another, what is stylistically later need not always be later in time—caution may indeed have to be exercised within a single region. This point may be particularly relevant in conditions of artistic deterioration or political stress. Finally, of course, it must always be remembered that the state of our evidence is neither full nor evenly spread.

A return may now be made to the questions concerning the early nature of LH. III C. It has already been stressed that closeness of decoration is an early characteristic; in the Argolid this is to be seen in the unmistakable and delicate Close Style, while the central and south Aegean are represented rather by the Octopus Style stirrup jars. These two systems differ radically from each other, but fortunately there is one extremely valuable cross-reference, in two Close Style stirrup jars of early type (Pl. 3a, c), the one from Asine tomb 5, in the Argolid, the other from Kameiros tomb 48, in Rhodes; they are so similar that they must be contemporary.[1] Their contexts are rather different, however; at Kameiros, the other vases seem to be typically LH. III B (Pl. 3b, d), while at Asine they are stylistically later, though two of them are jugs, and not easily datable. It seems likely from this that LH. III B survived slightly longer in the Dodecanese than in the Argolid, but one should still seek to find whether there are not other new elements in locally made Dodecanesian pottery which are associated with LH. III B. Furthermore, it may well be that the Close Style is not the earliest manifestation of LH. III C in the Argolid; here, most unfortunately, it seems that we have not sufficient evidence to be sure.

The analysis may be taken a step further on the basis of new motives of decoration or shapes which are common to most districts, and may be presumed (except in the case of the late diffusion of Granary Class pottery) to have been accepted at a fairly early stage, as each district tended progressively to go its own way, to the extent, for example, that there was little or no ceramic connexion between the Dodecanese and Achaea.

The chief decorative motives, in my opinion, are the concentric semicircles and cross-hatched triangles forming the main design on the shoulders of stirrup jars, and a variation of the semicircle motive, in alternate groups, upright and pendent, in a subsidiary zone below the shoulders of stirrup jars. The one shape is the amphoriskos.

[1] *Asine*, pp. 393 ff., Fig. 260, 3. *CR*, vi–vii. 138 ff., and 146, Figs. 171–2.

THE POTTERY

Of the decorative motives, that of the triangles does not seem to be quite so prevalent, and rarely appears in the earliest contexts, but with the semicircles it is different. The distribution is as follows. Semicircles on the shoulders of stirrup jars appear in early contexts at Athens,[1] and in the Dodecanese, at Ialysos in the (old) tomb 13[2] (Pl. 2c) and in tombs 64 and 83,[3] the context of that in tomb 64 being clearly LH. III B. The motive is also found in LM. III B contexts in Crete, on two stirrup jars from Milatos,[4] and on a very flat stirrup jar from Palaikastro.[5] The semicircles may be outlined with dots or just plain; there are very few in each group. No motive of this sort is to be recognized in any early context in the Argolid.

Alternating upright and pendent semicircles in a subsidiary zone are most prominent in Rhodes, with three instances in Ialysos tomb 83, and one each from (old) tombs 12 and 13 (Pl. 2c, d), and also in the Argive Close Style vase from Kameiros tomb 48 (Pl. 3c), which provides a cross-reference to the Asine vase, and so with the Argolid, where this motive does indeed appear in later Close Style vases from Mycenae.[6] There is also one sherd, of unknown context, from Mycenae, with this motive, where the decoration of the shoulder might be early.[7] In Attica, there are no demonstrably early examples, so far as I know, but the motive is found in the Fountain deposit.[8] From Crete, it may again be relevant to cite the Palaikastro stirrup jar, although its context is rather uncertain—but at least it is no later than LM. III B.

Of these two variations, that found on the shoulder is the more important, as persisting more or less throughout LH. III C in many areas; and as those districts where it is found in an early context are not known to have had any particular contact with the Achaean and Kephallenian series, it may be suggested that it was transmitted through the Argolid at an early stage; but that is no more than a suggestion.

Before considering the evidence of the amphoriskos, it may be advisable first to explain the origin of the Dodecanesian Octopus Style (Frontispiece), the counterpart of the Argive Close Style. This leads us back to Crete, and to LM. III B. The octopus is a decorative motive known throughout the Mycenaean world, but its use on stirrup jars is typical of Crete, developing in LM. III B into a type which is the clear origin of the Dodecanesian series. Furumark gives as the earliest example in Rhodes the vase from Ialysos tomb 84 (no. 6). He dates the tomb to his LH. III C 1 a-b, the vase itself standing 'very near to LM. III B 1 specimens'.[9] He makes a comparison with a vase from an LM. III B tomb at Kydonia;[10] a similar vase, much closer geographically, was found in an LM. III B tomb at Episkopi near Ierapetra;[11] and if the sherd illustrated in the Gournia publication is from a stirrup jar, it also may serve as a comparable example.[12]

From now on, these stirrup jars pursue a parallel course for a while, but the significant

---

[1] *Hesp.* ii. 365, Fig. 37 *f.*; 370, Fig. 43*a*.
[2] *B.M. Cat.* I, i, A 928.
[3] *Ann.* xiii–xiv. 271, Fig. 16; 314, Fig. 61.
[4] *AD*, vi. suppl., 156, Fig. 3 (not visible in the photograph).
[5] *BSA*, x. 225, Fig. 8b. Furumark, *Analysis*, p. 174, n. 8 considers this LM. III A 2.
[6] *Ann.* xiii–xiv. 314, Fig. 61; *B.M. Cat.* I, i, A 929, 928 (Stubbings, *Levant*, Pl. IV, 12 attributes A 928 to LH. III B). Cf. p. 6, n. 1 for Kameiros and Asine. *BSA*, xxv. Pl. X, g (Mycenae).
[7] *FLMV*, Pl. 35, No. 355.
[8] *Hesp.* viii. 390, Fig. 71, *o, p*.
[9] *OA*, iii. 224, cf. *Ann.* xiii–xiv. 317 ff.
[10] *AJA*, xlii. Pl. 28, 5 (= Matz, *Forschungen auf Kreta*, Pl. 56, 3 and Pl. 60, 3).
[11] *AD*, vi. suppl., 160, Fig. 9, middle.
[12] *Gournia*, p. 45, Fig. 25.

point is the original link between Crete and Rhodes. The material from tomb 84 (Pl. 5) is not noticeably LH. III B in character, and it certainly looks stylistically later than the groups with which the semicircles were associated and also than the Kameiros Close Style vase. Consequently, it is likely that the 'octopus' stirrup jar was a later development than the Argive Close Style, at least so far as the Dodecanese was concerned.

The most popular vase shape in Ialysos tomb 84 is not, as is customary in tombs, the stirrup jar, but the amphoriskos (Pl. 5); there are six of these, two- and three-handled, decorated in a pleasing open style. Furthermore, this shape is to be found in association with early pottery in tomb 66.[1] At least in Rhodes, the amphoriskos is one of the earliest manifestations of LH. III C, and throughout this period it is second in popularity only to the stirrup jars; it is thus possible that this innovation did originate in the Dodecanese, as an alternative to the small piriform three-handled jar. In the other areas already discussed, it cannot be shown to appear in so early a context [2]—in Crete it may not appear till rather later—but it is a constant concomitant of LH. III C.

We thus have the possibility of the amphoriskos originating in the Dodecanese, the certainty that the same area developed its 'octopus' stirrup jars from Cretan LM. III B originals, and the near certainty that the Argive Close Style was created in the Argolid, though taking over certain LM. III B motives. The origin of the semicircle motive is by no means so clear; in its variation for use in a subsidiary zone it appears in Crete only at an early stage; it is found on the earliest example of the Close Style in the Argolid; but it is more popular in Rhodes, where, however, it seems difficult for it to have preceded the Argive example at Kameiros. Neither for this motive, nor for that of the semicircles on the shoulders of stirrup jars, can one determine the originating area.

The outcome of this rather lengthy discussion is not on the whole very great, though one may make a few tentative suggestions. It seems that LH. III C elements began to appear while LM. III B was still untouched by the emergence of LM. III C, the significance of which is that LM. III B cemeteries were still in use after the second destruction in the Argolid.[3] The Dodecanesian Octopus Style started to develop rather later than the Argive Close Style, though it is probable that new elements had preceded it in this area. The LH. III B style may well have been less subject to deterioration in the Dodecanese than in the Argolid, though LH. III C elements could have appeared at about the same time as in the Argolid. So far as concerns the origin of a new style, the probability is that no single area can be indicated as providing it. It was diverse in origin from the beginning.

The one factor which, after the beginning of LH. III C, may have had more than local effect (apart from the Granary Class, whose diffusion may have been due rather to human dispersal) was the Argive Close Style (Pl. 4). It has a sort of conventional perfection and elaboration which must have been very difficult to imitate, as opposed to the rather carefree Creto-Rhodian octopods, but its principle of closeness is followed, in a rather inferior treatment, at least in the Peloponnese (cf. p. 15).

---

[1] *Ann.* xiii–xiv. 275, Fig. 20 (tomb 66); 319, Fig. 65 (tomb 84); cf. *OA*, iii. 200.

[2] Furumark (*OA*, iii. 197) includes two from Mycenae in his LH. III C1: *a* phase. Cf. *C.T.* tombs 515 and 527.

[3] Additional confirmatory evidence has recently been found in the tombs at Myrsini in eastern Crete (p. 178).

The conclusions, in relation to the disasters in the Argolid, may be summarized as follows. The second disaster, in which both Mycenae and Tiryns were involved, is said to have occurred at the end of LH. III B, and so presumably when deterioration had already set in (= sub-III B), but before the appearance of new stylistic elements (this is a preliminary and provisional judgment, of course). Fairly soon after, these new elements appear in the Argolid, the most important constituting the Close Style.

In Athens, the houses of the North Slope of the Acropolis contain both LH. III B and LH. III C pottery—and so does the Fountain deposit. They should then be dated after the Argolid disaster, but presumably not long after.

In the Dodecanese, there was no disaster nor threat of disaster, and a fairly vigorous new style appeared at about the same time as in the Argolid, but markedly independent of it. In Crete, it would seem that the troubles of the Mainland had no immediate effect.

The situation at the time of the major disaster at Pylos in Messenia is not so clear. At Pylos itself, the pottery is predominantly LH. III B, but a very small number of LH. III C sherds were also found.[1] Elsewhere in Messenia, the evidence is too slight for any connexion to be shown between the start of LH. III C there and its start in the Argolid.[2]

There come next the two major series of cemeteries in Achaea[3] and Kephallenia,[4] where the evidence seems to demand the supposition that there was a notable influx of population to these areas due, in my opinion, to disaster in other areas. The pottery from these cemeteries is almost without exception LH. III C. There are, however, LH. III B survivals, and if anything, more in Kephallenia than in Achaea; this would accord with the theory that many from Messenia fled to Kephallenia, many from the Argolid to Achaea. And so far as concerns the Argolid and Achaea, the connexion must surely be with the second destruction.

In most other districts, the evidence is too slender to warrant conclusions, or else is unpublished, although in Thessaly it would seem from preliminary excavation at Iolkos that the palace was not destroyed until after the beginning of LH. III C.[5] It is to be noted finally that the time of transition to LH. III C in the Mainland districts coincides in varying degrees of probability with destructions in the Argolid and at Pylos, and with danger to Attica, these probably being the occasions for the 'refugee' settlements in Achaea and Kephallenia, the earliest pottery of which contains some survivals of LH. III B. The similar 'refugee' settlement of Perati[6] in Attica may belong to a slightly later stage.

3. *Late Helladic III C Pottery*

The next stage to consider is the development of LH. III C in areas where this is possible, noting the similarities, differences and connexions between one area and another, thus building up some basis for a relative chronology.

The diversity of local styles is very marked, and in this we have a very different picture from that obtaining in LH. III B. To start with, a useful pointer may be derived

---

[1] Blegen, *AJA*, lxiv. 159.
[2] McDonald and Hope Simpson, *AJA*, lxv. 221 ff. Cf. pp. 93 ff.
[3] Vermeule, *AJA*, lxiv. 1 ff.
[4] Marinatos, *AE*, 1932, pp. 1 ff.; 1933, pp. 68 ff.
[5] Theocharis, *Ergon* for 1956, 1960 and 1961, and *Archaeology* xi (1958), 13 ff.
[6] Iakovidis, *Pr.* 1953 ff.; *Ergon* for 1954 ff.

from a rough analysis of the distribution of the most common vase shapes within five major groups of tombs, those of the Argolid (Asine and Mycenae), Rhodes (Ialysos and Kameiros), Kephallenia (Lakkithra and Metaxata), Achaea (several sites) and Attica (Perati). Of these, all but the first may be considered reasonably representative, as they produce at least 250 vases in each case. The total for Asine and Mycenae is barely a hundred, but this evidence cannot be omitted. I have not included the evidence from Cretan tombs here, as it is too scanty.

	Argolid	Rhodes	Kephallenia	Achaea	Attica (Perati)
Stirrup jars	45	33	25	50[1]	32
One-handled jugs	10	7	25	5	12
Kylikes	4	3	12	0.5	0.5
Straight-sided pyxides	—	4	4	9	?
Deep bowls	8	4	1.5	—	?
Amphoriskoi	10	25	5	8	17

All the figures are per cent. It must be stressed that they are only approximate for Achaea, and rather uncertain for Perati, being taken from brief preliminary reports.

The picture shows, then, considerable difference in the distribution of these shapes, of which the first five are LH. III B survivals, and the last an LH. III C innovation. It may be noted that deep bowls tend to be placed in tombs towards the end of the period rather than during its early stage.

One can now proceed to a rather more detailed analysis of the development and peculiarities of the style in each area.

In the Argolid Furumark[2] has identified three stages. Broadly speaking, the first stage is that in which LH. III B motives are still current, though somewhat debased and developing on the one hand into the splendid elaboration of the Close Style and on the other into a simplification which may be the forerunner of the Granary Class. The second stage, during which a third and final destruction took place at Mycenae, shows the Close Style and the simple Granary Class running side by side, with LH. III B features more or less forgotten. In the third stage the simpler style predominates, and the elaborate style becomes degenerate.

Principal interest centres on the Close Style and on the Granary Class. The Close Style *par excellence* is found mainly on stirrup jars and deep bowls, with rare examples on large jugs (Pl. 4a). Its quality and intricacy are such that one is tempted to suggest that most of, if not all, the pieces may have been the work of one potter. There is also what may be called a Close Style of inferior quality, where the execution is indeed good, but not up to the standard of the other.

This Close Style developed early, as already mentioned, and had a fairly wide distribution outside the Argolid; unfortunately, except for the earliest examples, it is very difficult to distinguish any internal stylistic development. It may not have survived long, if at all,

[1] Mrs. Vermeule (*AJA*, lxiv. 17) gives a much lower figure: 35 per cent.

[2] *OA*, iii. 196 ff.

after the final disaster at Mycenae. The Granary Class, on the other hand, is important because it does not appear until LH. III C is well into its stride, and because its simplicity finally prevails over the elaborate style and becomes the basis for later stylistic progress.

The principal shape on which the Granary Class manifests itself is the deep bowl (Pl. 12), and the basic system of decoration is dark-ground, though there are some bowls which have a light-ground effect. There are a number of variations on the dark-ground scheme, but before mentioning them a brief note is desirable on the type of bowl which is entirely monochrome, or which has only two narrow reserved bands below the belly. It is usually supposed that the Granary Class developed after the beginning of LH. III C, but monochrome deep bowls may well have an earlier history. A deposit of LH. III pottery from Mycenae, which the excavators claim is not later than the end of LH. III B, contains several sherds of these monochrome bowls.[1] This should mean that this type of bowl continues uninterruptedly throughout LH. III C, or until other variations become more popular, in the Argolid; but the settlement material is, as has been noted (p. 5), extremely meagre, and it is not easy to determine the full sequence. Evidence from another region may however be used to show the possibility that monochrome bowls appear early at least in LH. III C. In the Fountain deposit at Athens, the monochrome sherds are most numerous in the higher levels, but they do nevertheless occur at all levels, and could therefore be contemporary with the transition from LH. III B/C.[2] It is likely, therefore, that monochrome bowls should not be regarded as belonging necessarily to the Granary Class; the shape of the vase, and particularly the lip and foot elements, should be taken into account. The lip of Granary Class bowls flares more than on the earlier ones, and the foot is more pronounced and becomes at times slightly conical—this latter feature being a characteristic of certain other shapes of this class.

The scheme of decoration may then be monochrome, or there may be one or more narrow reserved bands below the belly, or else a reserved area is left between the handles, unfilled or—in the later stage, perhaps—with a horizontal wavy-line decoration; finally, for the dark-ground system, the whole vase may be painted over, with the exception of the lower body and the foot.

The one-handled cup (Pl. 12) may be treated similarly, or may be left clear of paint. So far as concerns the closed vases of this class, the amphoriskos tends to have greater areas painted over, and the wavy line may appear here also. The trefoil-lipped oinochoe and the lekythos in any case hardly precede the Granary Class as shapes, although there is one fine oinochoe (Pl. 4d) in the Close Style;[3] otherwise, these shapes mostly reflect the simple Granary Class features. The amphorae and hydriai of this class are apparently recognizable by a simple decorative motive on the shoulder or attached to the handle bases. As to stirrup jars, finally, there is no specifically Granary Class type.

In general, the Granary Class is that variation of LH. III C which is in vogue at the time of the destruction of the Granary and thereafter, and it is important to try to distinguish stylistically the pieces which precede this destruction from those which succeed it. This, however, is not easy to assess, though it is my impression that the popularity of the

---

[1] *BSA*, lii. 207 ff. and Pl. 43b.
[2] *Hesp.* viii. 366.
[3] *FLMV*, Pl. 37, No. 382.

wavy line belongs mainly to the post-destruction period, as also may the gradual movement towards a more conical foot, and the use of such shapes as the one-handled cup, the trefoil-lipped oinochoe, and the neck- and belly-handled amphorae. The lekythos and the amphora with collar neck seem certainly to be later.

It will be observed that I have assumed an Argive origin for Granary Class pottery; it would be difficult to prove this. Until its later stage, this pottery is more often found in settlements than in tombs, as its commonest shape, as has been said, is the deep bowl, and consequently it is not altogether safe to rule out such areas as the Dodecanese, Achaea and Kephallenia, the recorded material from which comes almost exclusively from cemeteries. On the other hand, the absence of any trace of the Granary Class (so far as is known) in the Achaean series, and the very slight evidence only in Kephallenia and the Dodecanese, make it very doubtful that it could have originated in any of these areas. Furthermore, it has been established by Furumark that it appears earlier in the Argolid than in the Dodecanese.

In Crete, this simple style is almost certainly introduced from without, and there is even less doubt about Cyprus (see pp. 23 f.). Perhaps one cannot yet exclude Thessaly as a place of origin, though the preliminary evidence from Iolkos is completely against such a supposition. Other areas, such as the South Peloponnese and Boeotia, could conceivably have been the original sources, but lack of evidence forbids any sort of conclusion. We must seek some area in contact with both eastern and western districts, and we are left virtually with the Argolid and Attica; I will confine myself to saying that the Argolid seems to me the more probable of the two. I shall therefore continue to assume that Granary Class pottery was created in the Argolid.

So much for the stylistic developments which may be said to originate in the Argolid. As to peculiarities in vase shapes, one can only say that, in the latest stage of the style, the trefoil-lipped oinochoe and the lekythos are apparently more popular in the Argolid than elsewhere, except in Attica.

LH. III C in the Dodecanese has also been divided into three phases by Furumark, and these are equated with developments in the Argolid, the first and last showing some influence from the Mainland, the second being mainly independent.[1]

The first phase shows the survival of LH. III B, the appearance of early LH. III C ideas, mainly of local origin, and the first stages—borrowed from Crete—of the octopus-type stirrup jar, which is to be the Dodecanese's only attempt to match the Close Style of the Mainland or the Fringed Close Style of Crete. Much of the decoration on other vases is in a pleasing open style. The second phase is marked by the loss of LH. III B elements, and by the full flourishing of octopus stirrup-jars (Frontispiece); so far as I can see, there is little else that characterizes it, and there is no parallel phenomenon such as the Granary Class. The third phase shows developments parallel to those in the Argolid, and Furumark points to some influence of the Granary Class on Rhodian pottery[2]—a matter which is very difficult properly to assess, the principal vase type of the Granary, as mentioned above, being the deep bowl, mainly found in settlements of which there is as yet no published record from the Dodecanese. In such elaboration as there was, there is a deteriora-

[1] *OA*, iii. 202 ff., 219.   [2] Op. cit. pp. 219 f.

tion, as in the Argolid, but the evidence for any growing predominance of a simple style is hard to gauge. It is on the whole not very easy to determine the chronological extent of this style in relation to other areas.

The development of LH. III C is thus not easy to follow in the Dodecanese, except perhaps in the octopus stirrup jars. It is worth noting, however, that a number of shapes are peculiar to this district, taken in conjunction with Naxos and Perati. Such are the jugs with strainer spout, which provide a link with Cyprus and Philistia, and the jugs with excrescent cup, both of which may have fictile or painted snakes round the body (Pl. 7c, d). Kalathoi with figurines on the rim (Pl. 7a, b) are known only to the central Aegean. Multiple vases and feeding bottles are more popular in this area than elsewhere. All these shapes appear early in LH. III C, so far as may be judged from the Rhodian tombs, and it is difficult to discover any stylistic development in them. The great popularity of the amphoriskoi, finally, and the possibility of the shape's having originated in the Dodecanese have already been noted.

For Attica, the main cemetery is that of Perati[1] on the east coast, and all that need be said at this point about its pottery is that it displays a remarkable fusion of Argive, Naxian and Dodecanesian elements; this fusion is particularly evident in an octopus-type stirrup jar (Pl. 6d) executed with Mainland Close Style motives on the shoulder.[2] There is evidence of the Granary Class, and this cemetery is probably in part contemporary with the cist tombs of Salamis and the Kerameikos (see pp. 115 f.). It must be remembered, however, that this is not a complete analysis; only a fraction of the material has yet been illustrated, and excavation continues.

As opposed to the cemetery of Perati, the settlement evidence is exclusively that of the Acropolis at Athens, in the fill of the disused fountain.[3] Beside the evidence this provides that a community still continued to live on the Acropolis, even though they no longer needed the underground fountain, the importance of the material arises from the fact that it constitutes the greatest amount of recorded and illustrated settlement pottery of this period. Nowhere in Greece or the Aegean is there anything to approach it. The great variety of decorative motives on bowls and kraters is particularly impressive, and, indeed, covers most of the known types of decoration, suggesting the possibility that there are more common factors in LH. III C than one might suppose from a study of pottery from tombs. On the other hand, the evidence of the Granary Class is somewhat less noticeable, and it is likely that the settlement on the Acropolis was primarily confined to the early part of LH. III C.

For sub-Mycenaean, we have of course the well known cemeteries of Salamis and the Kerameikos.[4] In these the victory of the simple style of the Granary Class is clear (Pls. 14, 15); its relation to the pottery of the Argolid will be discussed later (pp. 17 ff).

As to the pottery of the Kephallenian cemeteries,[5] it is not possible to discuss this in terms of stylistic development; the only such indication is that certain tombs probably started to be used later than others, judging from the fewer survivals of LH. III B. Certain

---

[1] See p. 9, n. 5.
[2] *Ergon* for 1954, p. 11, Fig. 10.
[3] *Hesp.* viii. 317 ff.
[4] Kraiker and Kübler, *Ker.* I; Wide, *AM*, xxxv. 17 ff.; Smithson, *Hesp.* xxx. 174 ff.
[5] See pp. 105 ff.

shapes and decorations are, however, more or less peculiar to this area. Kraters with side handles or vertical handles (Pl. 8) are prominent, sometimes with a high flaring or conical foot, a factor not likely to be connected with the rather similar tendency with smaller vases in the Argolid. These vases comprise 13 per cent of the total, and although they are no doubt known elsewhere, they were not, it appears, used at this time in tombs. Dippers are more common here than elsewhere, and the jugs with handle on the body are peculiar to this area. The remarkable continuing popularity of kylikes (Pl. 9b) will be seen in the distribution list given above, and the rectilinear decoration often applied to these vases is unknown outside this island and Ithaca.[1] There are also about fifty hand-made vases, probably not of Mycenaean inspiration (nor taken into account in the distribution list above).

Although stylistically it is difficult to assess development, a few vases suggest knowledge of the Granary Class,[2] and we know from the parallel and later settlement pottery of Ithaca that there was a survival until the time when the diffusion of Protogeometric pottery reached this part of the world.

LH. III C pottery in the Achaean cemeteries[3] is equally individual, and here it is even less easy to distinguish stylistic development, as the greater part of the material has never been illustrated. Early connexions with other areas are probable, and the Close Style had some effect. Links with the Granary Class are not readily discernible, and the occasional similarities between some of the vases and those of Attic Protogeometric may be only coincidental.[4]

As to the peculiarities in shape and decoration, large amphorae are characteristic of this region, and the four-handled variety (Pl. 10a-c)—6 per cent of the whole—must be regarded as a local product, and when found elsewhere within reasonably accessible range (there is one from Phocis[5]), must have been brought from Achaea or imitated from Achaean originals. A further remarkable speciality of the district is the bird-vases (Pl. 10f); there are only five, but they are of an advanced shape, not to be paralleled until those found in Cypro-Geometric, and those from Crete, of perhaps the same period as the Cypriote vases.[6] The relative isolation of Achaea, the lengthy intervening distance, and the probable chronological difference, seem to make it most unlikely that there should be any connexion.

For decoration, one may note that there is a greater tendency in this area than elsewhere to use fringed semicircles as a motive for the shoulders of stirrup jars. The system of covering much of the body of stirrup jars with regularly placed narrow bands (Pl. 10e) is also a characteristic of Achaea, known too in Kephallenia but less popular, and very occasionally found in the Argolid—in both cases there could be a connexion.

In Crete, finally, we have already seen (pp. 7 f.) that the start of LM. III C can with probability be placed later than the first appearance of LH. III C on the Mainland and in the Aegean. The development of this style may be divided into two main sections which

[1] *BSA*, xxxix. Pls. 8 and 9; *AE*, 1932, Pl. 6; *AE*, 1933, 80, Fig. 23.
[2] e.g. *AE*, 1932, Pl. 7, Nos. 80 and 85; Pl. 12, No. 185.
[3] Vermeule, *AJA*, lxiv. 1 ff., with reference to excavations by Kyparisses in *Pr.* 1925-40.
[4] *AJA*, lxiv. 17 f.
[5] Lerat, *Locriens*, Pl. 52.
[6] e.g. *SCE*, IV, 2, Fig. VII: 7 and 13; and *Fortetsa*, especially Pl. 106, No. 1518.

overlap. The earlier phase is that of which the Fringed Style (the counterpart of the Close Style) is the characteristic. On stirrup jars it takes the form of the octopus decoration (Pl. 6*a*), as has been seen, and also of the motive of the arc enclosing the triangle. For the rest, the flamboyant type of decoration in panels is chiefly found on pyxides (Pl. 11), tankards and kraters, and is not really suitable to other shapes. Deep bowls are rather too small for the intricacies of the Fringed Style, and here the examples known suggest the continuance of the LM. III B tradition.

The later phase of LM. III C—more usually called sub-Minoan—provides evidence of radical changes and innovations. The Fringed Style does persist on pyxides and on kraters and was also applied to the newly introduced kalathoi, in a rather emasculated fashion, but elaborate triangles now became common as the shoulder decoration of stirrup jars (Pl. 18*d*), while bowls gradually became deeper and show the technique of paint over the upper half of the body, leaving the lowest part and the now higher foot free (one of the Granary Class developments); and new shapes appear, such as the amphoriskos (Pl. 17*a*), the kalathos and the kantharos (Pl. 17*b*), all with the simplest possible decoration, occasionally including the wavy line.

In outlining stylistic development and change, where this was possible, I have so far stressed rather the elements which separated one district from another. There are also, however, numerous similarities, and instances where pottery of one area found its way to another, or else was imitated there.

There is of course a general fund of shapes and motives, deriving from the preceding LH. III B style, and persisting to a greater or lesser extent in all parts except Crete. Beside this, however, a very few features of LH. III C origin are also to be found widely over southern Greece and the Aegean. Mention has already been made of the concentric semicircles as a shoulder motive on stirrup jars, and to these may be added the hatched or (more often) cross-hatched triangles, similarly placed on stirrup jars; a motive which does not seem to belong to the earliest part of the style, but which I think must nevertheless substantially precede the destruction of the Granary at Mycenae. The only other factor to which one can point is a new shape, that of the amphoriskos, which surely replaces the small three-handled piriform jug, and does belong to early LH. III C. A more expert and deeper analysis might well identify further common factors, but these few are sufficient to show that there was no isolation at the outset. These features do belong to the early period, even though the triangle motive is perhaps not as early as the others. It would be hard, however, to point to any one shape or motive developed later which succeeded in permeating all areas in which LH. III C was still current. It is not of course possible to accept the factor of uniform deterioration of the style as a connecting link.

Apart from the common characteristics, there are many instances where elements of one local style are known to appear or to be imitated in other local styles. Sherds or vases of the Argive Close Style are to be found in Corinthia, Laconia, Attica, Delphi, Amorgos and the Dodecanese,[1] and approximations to it in Messenia, Achaea, Kephallenia and

---

[1] Corinthia: *Korakou*, p. 62, Fig. 86; Laconia: *AM*, lii Beil. vi (Amyklai); Attica: *Hesp.* viii. 368, Fig. 46, *n* and 390, Fig. 71, *e* (Athens); *Ergon* for 1954, p. 11, Fig. 10 (Perati); Delphi: *FD*, v. 9, Fig. 26; Amorgos: *B.M. Cat.* I, i. A 1029; Dodecanese: *CR*, vi–vii. 146, Figs. 171–2 (Kameiros).

Cyprus.[1] A wider and even more impressive range is to be observed in the diffusion of the octopus-type stirrup jars, coming in most cases from the Central Aegean (Frontispiece and Pl. 6), though some examples are perhaps traceable to Crete, the area in which this type originated. The known examples are listed elsewhere (pp. 271 f.), but, generally, there are few districts of the south Aegean where these vases are not found, and examples are also known further afield, at Delphi, at Pharsala in Thessaly, at Scoglio del Tonno in South Italy, at Pitane in Aeolis, and at Tarsus in Cilicia. The significant gap of the western Peloponnese and the islands lying off it would prevent our regarding this vase type as a truly common factor—and in any case it is not a style made or imitated, to my knowledge, outside Crete, the Dodecanese, Attica, Naxos and perhaps the Argolid where, however, it was not at all popular.

Both this Octopus Style and the Argive Close Style came to maturity early in LH. III C. So far as concerns the Close Style, the examples found outside the Argolid must surely belong to the time before the Granary was destroyed. With the Octopus Style one cannot be so certain, and connexions with Naxos and Attica will have persisted as long as the life of this style in the Dodecanese; but with the stylistic development not altogether clear, one cannot be sure about the pieces found further afield. The likelihood is that they belong to the time of early maturity. The evidence of both styles together would certainly indicate frequent and easy intercommunication within the south Aegean in early LH. III C.

The Granary Class has so far been used as a criterion for showing connexions at a later stage. Such links are to be observed in Attica, at Delphi, only slightly in Kephallenia and the Dodecanese, more strongly in Crete, and massively in Cyprus (a phenomenon which I shall discuss at a later point, see pp. 23 ff., 201).[2] There are, unfortunately, serious drawbacks in the use of this criterion. Absolute lack of evidence, and lack of settlement evidence, prevent us from knowing how much more widespread the influence of this pottery may have been, and how much fuller in districts known only from tombs. Furthermore, there are relatively few signs in the Argolid itself by which to distinguish the early and late phases of this pottery, and in consequence it is by no means easy to assess the period at which connexions occur in certain other districts, notably Kephallenia, and also perhaps the Dodecanese, though on Kalymnos the link seems clearly to belong to a late stage.[3] With Attica, there seems no reason to doubt strong continuing links, and the style has its effect—even as it does in part in Crete, where the original connexion may well come towards the beginning but was then perhaps discontinued.

Other connexions within a narrower sphere may be noted briefly: there are one or two links between the Achaean and Kephallenian styles, and the characteristic Achaean amphorae and four-handled vases found their way across the Corinthian Gulf, through Phocis and as far north as the southernmost part of Thessaly;[4] in the last instance a fairly

---

[1] e.g. *AE*, 1914, p. 105, Figs. 7 and 8 (Tragana in Messenia); *AJA*, lxiv. 17 and Pls. 1 and 2 (Achaea); *AD*, v. 102 f., Figs. 17 and 18 (Diakata in Kephallenia); *AJA*, lii. Pl. 58, *a* (Sinda in Cyprus).

[2] The pottery of the Salamis and Kerameikos cemeteries is clearly derived from the Granary Class, but examples are also to be found in the Acropolis Fountain deposit, *Hesp.* viii. 370, Fig. 49, *b* and *c*, and at Perati, e.g. *Pr* 1955, Pl. 32*b* (No. 446) and Pl. 33*a* (No. 470). Delphi: the Temenos tomb, *FD*, v. 11, Figs. 34–36; Kephallenia, see p. 14, n. 2; Dodecanese, see p. 12, n. 2; Crete, cf. e.g. *AE*, 1904, p. 29, Fig. 6 (Mouliana), and p. 179 (Knossos).

[3] *B.M.Cat.* I, i, Nos. A1021, 1023, 1024 (Pls. 15 and 16).

[4] See pp. 100, 130.

early contact may be indicated, but otherwise no chronological conclusions are possible. The very clear connexion between the Dodecanese and eastern Attica, certainly passing through Naxos, has already been indicated, as well as the early relationship between the Dodecanese and Crete. There are also contacts with the East Mediterranean, which will be discussed later.

So far, some suggestions have been put forward as to the time of commencement of LH. III C pottery in certain districts, and also as to the start of LM. III C in relation to LH. III C. During the early phase of LH. III C—down to the time of the destruction of the Granary at Mycenae—the evidence has tended to show that peaceful contact was maintained throughout much of the southern part of the Mycenaean world; and this may indicate some measure of recovery after the disasters on the mainland of Greece.

After the final destruction of Mycenae, we are faced with a different and difficult situation. It is obviously of great importance, for the general picture of our knowledge of events at this time and subsequently, and with regard to the matter of continuity or discontinuity of the Mycenaean tradition, to be able to determine the relative persistence of Mycenaean civilization in each area, but it does not appear that the Granary Class is a sufficient guide for purposes of cross-reference, except in Attica, in Cyprus, and to some extent in Crete.

In my opinion, some progress may be made by a consideration of the sub-Mycenaean and subsequent early Protogeometric material from Athens, in comparison with the material from the Argolid. In discussing this, I shall make use not only of the pottery, but to some extent also of objects of lesser chronological value which accompany the vases: the long bronze pins, the bronze fibulae of violin-bow and, more especially, of simple arched type, and the earliest iron objects.

The first step is then to determine the precise relationship between the LH. III C pottery current in the Argolid after the final destruction of Mycenae, and the sub-Mycenaean vases found in the cist tomb cemeteries of Salamis and Athens.

It was previously supposed that the vases of these tombs were almost all later than any of the latest Mycenaean material found in the Argolid, and they have been given the name of sub-Mycenaean or, by Furumark, LH. III C 2.[1] Kraiker, in his publication of the Kerameikos cemetery, has argued, with reason, that his vases must be later than those of the Granary at Mycenae, mainly because the Attic vases contain no further trace of the Close Style such as is visible in the Granary, and also because of the deterioration in quality.[2] In the Lion Gate stratification, however, there are two levels (X and XI) where the sherds are still predominantly Mycenaean, above the level of destruction (IX) which is clearly to be equated with the destruction of the adjacent Granary.[3] Furumark places the end of the Granary in his III C 1 b phase, and then identifies a later phase of fifty years' duration, III C 1 c, which precedes III C 2 (sub-Mycenaean), to which he also assigns a length of fifty years.[4] In his *Chronology*[5] he assigns some of the material from Asine House

---

[1] *OA*, iii. 195, n. 1, and 220 ff. It may be noted that Wace, *Aegean and the Near East*, pp. 130 ff. called sub-Mycenaean the pottery of Mycenae subsequent to the destruction of the Granary.

[2] *Ker.* I, p. 137.
[3] Wace, *BSA*, xxv. 29 ff.
[4] *OA*, iii. 202 ff. and 262.
[5] p. 78.

H and Tomb 1 to sub-Mycenaean, but in *Opuscula Archaeologica* iii, which appeared after the full published record of the Kerameikos cemetery, the only piece from the Argolid clearly identified as sub-Mycenaean is the cup from above Asine House G.[1] In consequence the material from the Kerameikos and Salamis graves is placed almost without exception later than any Mycenaean found in the Argolid. The difference between LH. III C 1 c and LH. III C 2 is a stylistic one, apparent in the deterioration of quality and in some variation of profile.

Without denying the possibility that Furumark may be right, it seems to me that a reasonable case can be made for the hypothesis that most of, if not all, the vases of the Kerameikos and Salamis cemeteries are contemporary with the latest stage of LH. III C in the Argolid.

First, it will be observed that the stylistic argument is based on a comparison of the material of one district with that of another, at a time when it is likely that there was much upheaval in the Mycenaean world. Although western Attica is not far from the Argolid, it is unsafe to assume that a parallel stylistic development was in progress in the two areas. The link between the two may have snapped temporarily, and in that case the potters of Athens and Salamis might have developed, or degenerated, along their own lines, leaving the Argives and others to maintain such ceramic standards as still existed.

Can any reason be given why they should have done so, apart from that of predilection and possible isolation? This cannot be known for certain, but it is in my opinion probable that a proportion of those buried in these cemeteries were newcomers from outside the main orbit of the Mycenaean world. This is a hypothesis which is also discussed elsewhere (pp. 37 ff.), and part of the argument concerns the use of cist tombs to the exclusion of chamber tombs, and a rather different distribution of vase types from that of previous custom. If the idea of a new racial element is acceptable, then the possibility of independent stylistic development is somewhat strengthened, even though the potters themselves may still have come from the indigenous population.

The custom of burial in cist tombs appears also, however, in the Argolid, and is there associated rather with Protogeometric and Geometric pottery than with anything earlier. Are we to suppose that this custom was taken over at the same time as on the west coast of Attica? The answer to this question, which is not necessarily concerned with the arrival of new peoples, leads on to another point. If the thesis of Furumark is accepted, then the sub-Mycenaean cist tombs of Athens and Salamis are later than any Mycenaean material in the Argolid; he gives a life of fifty years to these cemeteries—it can hardly be much less—and thereafter the Protogeometric style, associated with cremation, starts to develop, and spreads to other areas. But what is the position in the Argolid? Here, until recently, evidence for the period intervening between the latest Mycenaean and the first appearance of Protogeometric was very slight, and it was possible to assume a long interval of time of which we had no knowledge. Further excavation has, however, now taken place at Mycenae, Argos and Tiryns, and the results suggest that, although full continuity cannot be proved, the intervening gap was not very great. Mycenae affords no decisive information, although cist tombs of the Protogeometric period, and one containing two vases of the

[1] p. 211, Fig. 4, 3.

Granary Class, have been located.[1] Nor does Tiryns help to narrow the gap, though the earliest tomb of the later cemetery contained a stirrup jar,[2] and may thus take its place beside the previously excavated cist tomb 3, which produced an LH. III C (or sub-Mycenaean?) amphoriskos.[3]

The chief evidence comes from Argos (cf. pp. 80 ff.), where our knowledge has been increased by the excavation of both chamber tombs and (in a different area) cist tombs. The contents of the chamber tombs have not yet been fully recorded, but it is notable that the excavator has described as sub-Mycenaean the vases of several of the tombs,[4] and that these tombs have produced bronze objects of European origin, including long dress-pins, though at least two of these are different in type from the pins from the Salamis and Kerameikos sub-Mycenaean cist tomb cemeteries.[5] An arched fibula is also mentioned, a type not known in Athens before the sub-Mycenaean cemeteries.[6] For the cist tombs, on the other hand, two points may be stressed: that there seems to be no burial in which some vase was not found to show the influence of Attic Protogeometric; and that the continuance of the Granary Class tradition is observable in the bowls, both those with the wavy line and those with the lower area of the vase unpainted.[7] The important question is, how great a gap is there between the last chamber tomb and the earliest cist tomb? In my opinion, it is very small indeed. It looks as though there was some break—and I think the rather scanty settlement evidence tends to confirm this—but that the break did not involve any particular time lag. One cannot yet quite link chamber tombs and cist tombs. A near connexion is suggested by the discovery of a neck amphora, of a type which would I think in Attica be classed as early Protogeometric, in a chamber tomb of the Deiras cemetery.[8] Unfortunately, this amphora is a secondary deposit, found twenty centimetres above the floor, so the link is not yet proved. Nevertheless, it is a witness to the continued use of this cemetery at a time when a different area was in use for cist burials.

I would suggest then that the totality of this evidence—the picture will no doubt be clearer after full publication—leads to the conclusion that at Argos in any case, and possibly at other sites in the Argolid as well, we have virtually no gap in the sequence, and from this to the conclusion that cist tombs appear in the Argolid later than they do in Salamis and Athens. Consequently, chamber tombs were still being used in the Argolid after they had been replaced in west Attica by cist tombs. The problem then is not whether all sub-Mycenaean in Attica is later than all Argive LH. III C, as that is clearly not so, but rather what we are to call the vases from the late Argive chamber tombs which are contemporary with many, if not most, of the Attic cist tombs. That is a matter of terminology, and cannot be answered until the records are published, but I should be surprised if the latest pottery from the Deiras chamber tombs is very different from the latest pottery in

---

[1] *BSA*, xlix. 258 f. and Pl. 43.

[2] Verdhelis, *AE*, 1956, suppl., p. 4. This is a pit grave rather than a cist tomb and contained two burials; but the principle of multiple burial had been abandoned.

[3] Müller, *Tiryns* I, p. 128 and Pl. 16, 8. Cf. *PGP*, p. 208.

[4] Deshayes, *BCH*, lxxx. 361 ff. (tombs XVI–XVIII, XXII, one above XXIII, XXIX); lxxxiii. 771 (tomb XXX). See Pl. 18e for a very late LH. III C stirrup jar from Argos.

[5] Sandars, *BSA*, liii–liv. 236 f. The iron pins of Kerameikos sub-Mycenaean tomb 113 (*Hesp.* xxx. 175 f.) might suggest a later date, but not so its vases.

[6] *BCH*, lxxx. 365.

[7] e.g. *BCH*, lxxxi. 664, Fig. 55.

[8] *BCH*, lxxx. 362 and 363, Fig. 4.

the chamber tombs and houses at Asine which Furumark places earlier than sub-Mycenaean.[1] I shall continue on the assumption that all pottery found in chamber tombs should be called LH. III C, as still true Mycenaean, in contrast to the sub-Mycenaean of the Attic cist tombs which may indicate a new element of population.

One result of this is to bring the emergence of the Protogeometric style in Athens very close in time to the end of LH. III C in the Argolid. But this is not all, for the situation in certain other districts can be related either to the latest stage of LH. III C in the Argolid or to the transition from sub-Mycenaean to Protogeometric in western Attica. The areas concerned are as follows:

Corinthia. At Corinth the same sort of mixture of late Granary Class and Protogeometric has been found as in the earliest post-Mycenaean settlement at Argos.[2] It is therefore possible that the course of events in Corinthia was similar to that in the Argolid after the end of LH. III C, and so Mycenaean civilization may be said to have ended either at the same time as it did in the Argolid, or earlier.

Boeotia. As two of the cist tombs of Thebes[3] have produced vases like those of sub-Mycenaean Athens, it is possible that the same conditions held in this district as in western Attica, and that Mycenaean civilization disappeared, with the desertion of the chamber tomb system, earlier than in the Argolid.

East Attica. This district, as represented by the site of Perati, must be considered as quite separate from the western region. The great cemetery of Perati does not continue beyond LH. III C. It is extremely likely, however, that it was still in use after the sub-Mycenaean series had been inaugurated. To what extent the presence of slab-covered graves among the chamber tombs entails a link with western Attica is not yet known, nor is the pottery of much use, except in so far as it includes vases of the Granary Class. The iron objects (two knives (Pl. 24e) and what may be part of a pin) are evidence of lateness, but the discovery of four arched fibulae is even more decisive, for this type would seem only to have been introduced during the period of use of the sub-Mycenaean cemeteries.[4] It is probable, on the other hand, that the cemetery was abandoned before the rise of the Protogeometric style, or else there would have been some indication of its influence in the pottery of Perati.

Naxos. This island was linked with the Dodecanese and Perati to form a miniature Mycenaean *koine* during the LH. III C period. For the situation at the end of the period we have the following pointers. One of the chamber tombs contained a stirrup jar[5] which is similar to those of the Kerameikos sub-Mycenaean cemetery, and another chamber tomb produced an iron dagger.[6] The pottery of the Kaminia chamber tombs is recorded as being in general simple and late. It is then possible that LH. III C in Naxos persisted after the introduction of sub-Mycenaean to western Attica. On the other hand, a lekythos (Pl. 15c) of sub-Mycenaean type[7] was found in an area where there were cist tombs and

---

[1] *OA*, iii. 210 f.

[2] Weinberg, *Corinth*, VII, i. 3 ff. and Pl. 1; Broneer, *Hesp.* xx. 293 and Pl. 89a and b.

[3] Keramopoullos, *AD*, iii. 25 ff. (tombs 3 and 8). Cf. *PGP*, pp. 195 f.

[4] Iakovidis, *Pr.* 1954, p. 98, Fig. 10; 1955, p. 106, Pl. 31b (knives); *Ergon* for 1960, p. 21, Fig. 28 (pin?); *Pr.* 1954, p. 97; *Pr.* 1955, p. 102 (fibulae); and two other fibulae, unpublished, see p. 58.

[5] *Ergon* for 1958, p. 168, Fig. 176.

[6] *Ergon* for 1960, p. 191.

[7] Op. cit. p. 187, Fig. 209.

cremation burials, but no chamber tombs, and this would suggest that the chamber tomb cemetery had been deserted while sub-Mycenaean was still current in Athens, and before the full introduction of the Protogeometric style. This conclusion is strengthened by the material now available from Miletus, which suggests a move across the Aegean, probably touching Naxos but not necessarily the Dodecanese, at the time of transition from sub-Mycenaean to Protogeometric.

Western Asia Minor. The evidence from Miletus, as set out in the most recent publication, indicates a close link with Athens, in the earliest pottery connected with the re-occupation of the site after the Mycenaean settlement was destroyed. The sherds and vases are comparable to what at Athens would be transitional from sub-Mycenaean to Protogeometric.[1] Through this link it can also be established that the Mycenaean settlement must have been destroyed before the end of LH. III C in the Argolid, though one cannot say how long before.

The evidence of Assarlik on the Halicarnassus peninsula is the same as that of Miletus with regard to the appearance of pottery of sub-Mycenaean to Protogeometric type, and supports the hypothesis of a move across the Aegean at this time. No earlier Mycenaean settlement is known on this site.[2]

Chios. There was no immediate successor to the Mycenaean settlement at Emborio, and its destruction cannot be closely dated, although from the pottery it cannot have been far from the end of LH. III C as we have it in the Argolid (cf. p. 159).

The Dodecanese. There are no visible connexions with Athens, nor are they frequent enough with the Argolid for useful deductions to be drawn, though it is worth noting that only a very few vases can be classified as Granary Class,[3] which may mean either that the links were very few in the latter part of LH. III C, or that Mycenaean civilization came to an end in these islands rather earlier than in the Argolid. Comparison with the related districts of Naxos and East Attica would tend to favour the latter conclusion.

Thessaly. The concluding stages of Mycenaean civilization are still obscure for most of this area, and it is only at Iolkos—and even there with much hesitation—that developments in the south may be used as a guide to the course of events. According to the most recent reports,[4] the situation is that the palace of Iolkos was destroyed in early LH. III C; the adjoining settlement shows no sign of destruction, but it seems to have come to an end also in early LH. III C, while above it a substantial Protogeometric settlement was built, the cultural and architectural connexions between these two settlements being so close that a gap of not more than a generation is presumed to have occurred.[5] The ceramic problems involved in this state of affairs at Iolkos are considerable, but will no doubt be resolved with the full publication of the material; they are fully discussed elsewhere (pp. 135 ff.).

Connected with the disintegration of Mycenaean culture there are perhaps two groups of newcomers to the region. The first were those who introduced the cist tomb method of burial, and such tombs are found sporadically over much of Thessaly including Iolkos

---

[1] Weickert, *Ist. Mitt.* ix–x, Pls. 51–52.
[2] Paton, *JHS*, viii. 64 ff.
[3] See p. 12, n. 2.
[4] Theocharis, *Ergon* for 1960, pp. 55 ff.; *Ergon* for 1961, pp. 51 ff.
[5] *Ergon* for 1961, p. 59.

(pp. 38 f.); it is worth noting that a sub-Mycenaean lekythos was found in the earliest cist tomb at Theotokou,[1] and so should precede the rise of Athenian Protogeometric pottery. The period over which this group spread into Thessaly is not clear, however, nor is it known precisely when the second group arrived, newcomers who used hand-made pottery of Macedonian type and, at Marmariani [2] in north Thessaly, buried their dead in tholos tombs. In general, it is likely that there was a gradual infiltration into Thessaly from the north and west, with the district around Iolkos retaining its Mycenaean characteristics for a considerable length of time.

The relative course of events in the Argolid and in western Attica forms then a good starting point for an analysis of the situation in other districts, with regard to relative chronology and the definitive end of Mycenaean civilization. The regions discussed can all in greater or lesser measure, directly or indirectly, be connected with the Argolid of LH. III C times, or with sub-Mycenaean and Protogeometric Athens. The general area concerned is that of the central and southern Aegean; and the discussion on Cyprus (see below, pp. 23 ff.) will show how Crete also has connexions with the Argolid and with Attica. There remain, however, many districts where a link with the Aegean-facing regions is lacking at this time, and where the course of events remains uncertain. Such is the case for much of the Peloponnese. There is almost nothing from Arcadia, and the material from Elis, Messenia and Laconia is such as suggests almost complete depopulation in LH. III C, though recent finds are exceedingly promising for the period succeeding the Mycenaean (cf. pp. 95 ff.). Only in Achaea have we a reasonable corpus of LH. III C material, but unfortunately it has no related successor.[3]

Outside the Peloponnese, although one cannot trace connexions between Kephallenia and the Argolid after the Granary Class (and probably not late within the development of this phase), and although the LH. III C cemeteries have no known successors on the island, there is at least the evidence from Ithaca, where the material continues the Kephallenian ceramic series, and leads on into the time when the influence of Protogeometric is felt (cf. pp. 108 ff.). So here we do have continuity.

Finally, there is the district north of Boeotia, that of Phocis and Locris, where the only relevant evidence is that of the Temenos chamber tomb at Delphi,[4] whose contents show, it seems, connexions with the latest stages of the LH. III C style further south. After this, however, one does not know precisely what happened.

There remains for consideration the evidence from the island of Cyprus. Can it in any way clarify any of the uncertainties so far encountered, or lend weight to one hypothesis as against any other?

The island had connexions with the Mycenaean world in LH. III A and B, and recent excavations have helped by means of settlement stratification to confirm the course of LH. III C in the Aegean. The main site is Enkomi, where the sequence of events, covering the Late Cypriot III A and part of the III B periods, is briefly as follows.[5] The impressive

---

[1] *P.T.*, p. 211, Fig. 146 f.
[2] Heurtley and Skeat, *BSA*, xxxi. 1 ff.
[3] The earliest known evidence subsequent to the Mycenaean chamber tombs is the late Protogeometric pithos burial found near Derveni (*BCH*, lxxvi. 222; *AJA*, lxiv. 16 f. and Pl. 5). Neither the pithos manner of burial nor the pottery has any connexion with the preceding Mycenaean.
[4] *FD*, v. 6 ff.
[5] Dikaios, *Ber. V. Int. Kon. für Vor- und Frühgeschichte*, pp. 242 f.; Schaeffer, *Enkomi-Alasia*. Cf. pp. 197 ff.

and flourishing town of Enkomi V was built on the ruins of an earlier LC. II C settlement, wherein the Mycenaean pottery was not later than LH. III B. This town saw the sudden introduction by new arrivals of early LH. III C pottery, but it was destroyed after a short while, to be followed by the smaller and relatively insignificant settlement of Enkomi IV, whose connexions with the Aegean were slight. During the course of Enkomi III, however, at the beginning of Late Cypriot III B, there was a further influx of pottery from the Aegean, of a simple type whose characteristic motive was the wavy line, stylistically closely related to the later phase of the Granary Class, after the destruction of the Granary at Mycenae. This ware increased in quantity in the last two settlement levels, becoming predominant in Enkomi I. These settlements were probably short-lived, and the town was then finally deserted. After this, the evidence for the end of Late Cypriot III B and the earliest stage of Cypro-Geometric must be sought from other sites, and from tombs as opposed to settlements; and it is this material that forms the chief basis of the detailed comparative studies of Gjerstad and Furumark, wherein the connexions with the Mycenaean world are fully discussed.[1]

There were then two occasions when LH. III C pottery was introduced to Cyprus: in early LH. III C and after the destruction of the Granary. Of the earlier occasion all that need be said is that the fullest information comes from Sinda,[2] a site (not far from Enkomi) excavated by Furumark, where the bulk of the pottery belonged to his LH. III C 1 *b* phase and was connected with the Argolid, though it was preceded by a few LH. III C 1 *a* pieces, possibly imported from Rhodes. This pottery did not have any profound influence on the local Cypriot ware.

The second occasion is the more important one, both because the effect of the Granary Class pottery was very considerable and probably not confined to one point of time, and because it seems to afford some help in establishing the relative chronology of what is a rather chaotic period in Greece and the Aegean.

Using only the vases from the tombs, Furumark established a very strong case for deriving many shapes and decorations from LH. III C 1 *c*.[3] The subsequently discovered settlement material from Enkomi confirmed his conclusions. Very few of the sherds from Enkomi levels III to I have been recorded or illustrated, but there is evidence for deep bowls with wavy line decoration, the clay-ground system being more popular than the dark-ground, for a cup and a kylix with wavy lines, and for a vase which may best be described as a bowl-amphoriskos.[4]

The Granary Class seems the most obvious source, and a late date would be indicated by the wavy line motive. Conversely, it may be objected that this motive is not at all common in the Argolid, and that Granary Class vases are, at least so far as concerns deep bowls, in a dark-ground style. Such may be the case, but even so the clearest agreement between this material from Enkomi and that of the Aegean is to be seen in Asine House G, according to the pieces recorded by Furumark, and attributed by him to the

---

[1] *OA*, iii. 73 ff. (Gjerstad), 231 ff. (Furumark).

[2] *AJA*, lii. 531; *Arkeologiska Forskningar och Fynd*, pp. 59 ff.

[3] See n. 1.

[4] Coche de la Ferté, *Essai*, Pl. IX, 9–16; Schaeffer, *E–A*, p. 22, Nos. 21 and 24, and 367, Fig. 114; *Guide to the Cyprus Museum* (ed. 1961), Pl. X, 3.

transition of LH. III C 1 *b* to *c*, in other words immediately after the destruction of the Granary.¹ Here, a clay-ground wavy-line system is recognized on an amphoriskos, a cup, a jug, and a trefoil-lipped oinochoe; what remains of a collar amphora also has wavy lines, but one cannot say whether the rest of the vase was mainly unpainted. Furthermore, the Enkomi kylix with wavy lines may be compared with one from Asine House H—built over House G, and attributed to LH. III C 1 *c*—which also has wavy lines; unfortunately, the stem is missing, so one cannot tell whether it was smooth or ribbed.² To complete the picture, evidence of a deep bowl is desirable, and here as well there is a good example from Asine, though not from House G or H; this bowl has a double wavy line, enclosed by two broad bands, and has the lower body unpainted.³

On the basis of this evidence, it may reasonably be said that the pottery of Mycenaean type in Enkomi levels III to I finds its closest connexions in the Argolid at a time contemporary with, or soon after, the destruction of the Granary. It is not derived from any earlier Mycenaean pottery in Cyprus, and the conclusion that it was brought to the islands by people leaving the Argolid after the final disaster at Mycenae is very attractive.

To this material from Enkomi may now be added the sherds found in a well at Kition.⁴ These sherds (Pl. 13) are in the same wavy-line style, and from the fact that the well produced hardly any other type of pottery except this it may be concluded that the deposit was probably contemporary with Enkomi I. The material has been published in full (an enormous advantage) and a wider range of shapes is represented than at Enkomi, sherds of jugs, amphorae, and possibly of a krater having been found. No complete profile of any of these shapes was recovered, and so close comparison with the Argolid or elsewhere in the Mycenaean world is not possible, though the general types are known.

The settlement material is then reasonably close to LH. III C 1 *c* originals. In only one case can this be said of the pottery from tombs, and that is in the vases from an unrecorded tomb group found at Idalion.⁵ This grave, described as a small chamber tomb, contained vases which are almost exclusively of Mycenaean type, the shapes being different from those characteristic of settlements—stirrup jars, small jugs with handle to the lip, kalathoi, an askos, a ring vase, and a small collar amphora. The most common decorative motives are concentric semicircles (or loops) and triangles, with solid central filling. There is some resemblance to the sub-Mycenaean vases of Salamis and the Kerameikos, but these vases are less degenerate, and it is likely that the potter drew his inspiration from some other part of the Mycenaean world. Even so, this pottery reflects the very last stage of LH. III C, and as such may indicate later arrivals than those who first settled in Enkomi III. This group is thus of great importance, even though its precise position in the Cypriot series is not known.

Finally, there are the vases from tombs, whether of known or unknown provenience. The shapes current in LC. III/CG. are as follows:⁶ the stirrup jar (Pl. 18) (rare), the amphoriskos, the cup with high flaring foot (Pl. 15*d*), the bowl with two horizontal handles

---

¹ *OA*, iii. 209, Fig. 3, Nos. 10–14.
² Op. cit. p. 211, Fig. 4, 1A.
³ *Asine*, p. 303, Fig. 208, 1.
⁴ Karageorghis, *BCH*, lxxxiv. 570 ff.

⁵ I am most grateful to Dr. Karageorghis for permission to include this account of the material.
⁶ As well as the analysis given in the two articles mentioned in p. 23, n. 1, a very useful survey has been made by Daniel in *AJA*, xli. 63 ff.

and also with flaring foot, the trefoil-lipped oinochoe with high foot, amphorae of neck, belly (Pl. 17*d*) and collar variety, the one-handled jug with high foot (and occasionally with handle from shoulder to neck as in the lekythos), the kylix with ribbed stem, the kalathos, the spouted jug, the feeding bottle, the bowl with ribbon handles and the kantharos—this last, very popular shape being claimed by Daniel to be derived from the LH. III B amphoroid krater.[1] For decoration, the double wavy line is commonly found on cups, on the belly of amphoriskoi and belly amphorae,[2] and also occasionally on the neck of trefoil-lipped oinochoai and neck amphorae. For the rest, variations of rectilinear and curvilinear motives are used; the amphoriskos displays a fair number of differing motives of this sort. The bowl with horizontal handles has either two thick bands only, without further decoration, or geometric motives, as have the kylikes. Stirrup jars have variations of triangles on the shoulder (Pl. 18), and the belly amphorae may have a complex decoration. Jugs and oinochoai are most commonly simply banded below the neck, and kantharoi are usually plain. The general effect is of a clay-ground style. It will naturally be understood that there are also vases whose origin derives from the earlier local ware, but the shapes already enumerated provide the bulk of the ceramic offerings.

For a full discussion, the reader is referred to the articles cited above, but the following main conclusions appear to be justified: that this pottery, though not directly derivable from the Aegean, is indirectly so derivable, as having developed from pottery (such as that of Enkomi and Kition, and the Idalion group) which shows very close connexions with post-Granary LH. III C ware, and that its successful diffusion is due to the arrival of new settlers from the Aegean (in part from the Argolid) perhaps at successive stages between the destruction of the Granary and the end of LH. III C. Two further deductions may be made on the basis of these conclusions. First, it can safely be stated that the superficial resemblance of some of the shapes and decorations to those of the Attic Protogeometric style does not mean that this style had any influence on Cypriot pottery; on the contrary, it may be that the Attic potters were, for one or two features (for example, the high conical foot) indebted to Cyprus. As will be seen, the relative chronology would support this. Secondly, it is also unlikely that the Cypriot potters were inspired by the sub-Mycenaean vases of Salamis and Athens. There are parallels of shape and decoration, but the distribution of vase types, and the general style, are different. An additional factor is the absence of cist tombs in Cyprus, taken with the sudden and first appearance at this time of the true Mycenaean chamber tomb.[3] This last point confirms that the pottery owed its original introduction to actual settlers, and did not come in the way of trade.

The general picture thus obtained may be supplemented by evidence of more localized contacts between Cyprus and the Aegean. The first point depends on evidence other than that of pottery. It is reasonably certain that iron was first introduced to the Aegean from the East Mediterranean area, and so probably from or through Cyprus. At Enkomi, Schaeffer has stated that iron was first introduced in Enkomi IV, and he implies that after this it was in common use.[4] No details are given of these weapons and tools, but Dikaios

---

[1] *AJA*, xli. 68. I am not entirely convinced that the claim is correct.

[2] Comparison may be made with a belly-amphora from Perati, *Ergon* for 1958, p. 27, fig. 27, No. 590. Pl. 17*c*.

[3] *SCE*, IV, i. 30; *AJA*, xli. 57.

[4] *E–A*, p. 418.

found, in a room of level I of his excavations, part of an iron knife with bronze rivets.[1] This is not a usual combination, and it is therefore of some interest that four other such knives of this period should have been found in the Aegean, one in chamber tomb 5 at Vrokastro, one in tomb VII of the Gypsades cemetery near Knossos (Pl. 24d), and two in the Perati cemetery, one of which came from a pit grave and the other from chamber tomb 38 (Pl. 24e), where a cremation was associated with inhumations (cf. p. 61). Here we seem to have a link at least between Cyprus and Crete and east Attica, though not necessarily between east Attica and Crete, nor can contemporaneity be proved.

Returning to the ceramic evidence, however, we have rather more closely dated cross-references, on the one hand between Cyprus and Crete, and on the other hand between Cyprus and Attica (though in this case western, and not eastern Attica).

The link between Cyprus and Crete appears best in a peculiar decorative motive, a semicircle within a triangle, usually applied to the shoulder of a stirrup jar. In Cyprus, it is found on two stirrup jars and a belly amphora from a tomb at Lapithos, on a stirrup jar from Idalion and on one from Kouklia (Pl. 18c) on a spouted bowl-amphoriskos from Lapithos tomb 503[1], on two stirrup jars of unknown provenience (Pl. 18a, b), and in a rather degenerate fashion on an amphoriskos from Kaloriziki tomb 26A.[2] All the examples whose context is known belong to the later stage of LC. III B, and it may be noted that on other grounds the Lapithos groups may be placed earlier than the Kaloriziki tomb. It is probable that, as with the knives, a very short space of time is in question. In Crete, the clearest example of this motive is found on a stirrup jar in Gypsades tomb VI A (Pl. 18d), and another instance is probably to be recognized on a stirrup jar from the contemporary tomb VII (in which the iron knife with bronze rivets was found).[3] A rather debased version of the motive appears on stirrup jars from Fortetsa tomb Π and Agios Ioannis tomb VII (later than the Gypsades tombs mentioned).[4] Apart from these, a rudimentary example is known from Vrokastro, and the Liliana tombs produce two further instances.[5] A further connexion is to be observed in the elaborate triangle decoration which accompanies the above motive on most of the stirrup jars cited, whether in Cyprus or Crete. The conclusion from this is that Gypsades tombs VI A and VII are probably contemporary with the two Lapithos tombs mentioned, especially Ohnefalsch-Richter's group. And it may be added that this group need not be appreciably later than the final settlement at Enkomi level I, in which the iron knife with bronze rivets was found. As the Gypsades tombs belong within the sub-Minoan period (when the Fringed Close Style had virtually disappeared

---

[1] I am exceedingly grateful to Dr. Dikaios for permission to mention this knife. The only other knife of this type in the East Mediterranean, to my knowledge, is one from Hama, of probably similar date (Riis, *Hama*, II, iii. 124 and 237: G VIII 483 = 5 E 347).

[2] *Lapithos*: Ohnefalsch-Richter, *Kypros, The Bible and Homer*, Pls. 98 and 157.
  Tomb 503[1]; *OA*, iii. 106, Pl. 1, 18.
  Idalion: Dikaios, *Guide to the Cyprus Museum* (ed. 1961), p. 55 and Pl. 10, 4; (= *FLMV*, Pl. 14, 91?).
  Kouklia: B.M. Cat. I, ii. C 696 (decoration not visible on Pl. 4).

Kaloriziki: Tomb 26A; *AJA*, xli. 75, Fig. 8, motive 28 (= Pl. 1, No. 32).
Unknown provenience: (a) Fitzwilliam Museum, Gr. 2. 1960; (b) Zeno Pierides Collection, Larnaca.

[3] *BSA*, liii–liv. 242, Fig. 28 (VI A, 2); 241, Fig. 27 (VII, 5).

[4] Brock, *Fortetsa*, Pl. 132, 9; Boardman, *BSA*, lv. 140, Fig. 8.

[5] *Vrokastro*, p. 150, Fig. 89, H; Borda, *Arte cretese-micenea*, p. 29, Nos. 171 and 172 (Pl. 34, 2 and 3).

but certainly before the introduction of any Protogeometric influence) this period must then be in part contemporary with about the middle of LC. III B.

It is most likely that this motive travelled from Cyprus to Crete, but there is also evidence of a movement in the reverse direction, as a sherd of a Cretan vase was found in the well deposit at Kition.[1] This sherd is in a pictorial style, and comparison may be made with the krater of Mouliana tomb A, whose chronology is not easy to elucidate. It may well be that the appearance of this sherd at Kition clarifies the situation at Mouliana, for the deposit may be placed just before, or contemporary with, Ohnefalsch-Richter's tomb group from Lapithos, three vases of which have the decorative motive discussed above. The Cretan sherd may then belong to the beginning of sub-Minoan.

Further links are possibly to be found at this time. The settlement and tombs of Karphi, a site certainly founded after the beginning of the Cretan sub-Minoan period, contained several shapes characteristic of Cyprus at the transition from LC. III to CG. I, such as the askos and feeding bottle, and a straight-sided bottle [2]—a shape which will be discussed further as a link between Cyprus and Athens. The altar stand of the sanctuary at Karphi is probably of Cypriot inspiration.[3] Finally from Karphi, there is a kantharos,[4] by no means dissimilar to those found in LC. III B–CG. I A tombs; it is a shape which in each district might have evolved from the Mycenaean amphoroid krater, but the interval of time is rather long, and it is equally possible that a new shape is in question; in this case, the origin could be ascribed to Cyprus. Kantharoi are found on other Cretan sites—one in the Liliana cemetery, one in Fortetsa tomb XI (in a Protogeometric context), and in some quantity in the tombs of Modi, in West Crete, though many of the examples here have the flat base which is such a characteristic of Cretan vases.[5] In the other direction, in conclusion, there is evidence that the Cretan goddess with upraised arms found her way to Cyprus.[6]

Secondly, a link between Cyprus and Athens is possibly to be observed in a tall vertical-sided flask or bottle. In Cyprus, the shape is to be found only in graves which belong to the end of LC. III B, or are transitional to CG. I A—Kaloriziki tombs 25 and 26A (Pl. 15a, b), and Lapithos tombs 406 and 420 (though with a forerunner in Lapithos tomb 503¹, which lies well within LC. III B).[7] The type seems native to Cyprus, and consequently the two similar vases found in Athens (Pl. 16c, d) may have been imitations; the one comes from a late sub-Mycenaean tomb, and the other from a grave which is transitional to Protogeometric.[8] These vases are not in fact as close in shape and decoration as could be desired, and the possibility of a connexion depends much on the rarity of the shape; that is to say, if a rare type of vase makes its appearance in two or more areas over a short period of time only, and if these periods can be shown on other grounds to be roughly contemporary, then one

---

[1] Karageorghis, *BCH*, lxxxiv. 580 and 577 f., Figs. 129 and 130. Cf. Xanthoudides, *AE*, 1904, Pl. 3.

[2] Seiradhaki, *BSA*, lv, Pl. 11, *b*, upper right.

[3] Pendlebury, *BSA*, xxxviii, Pl. 34; Boardman, *Cretan Collection*, p. 133 and Fig. 49, B.

[4] *BSA*, lv, Pl. 11, *b*, upper middle. See Pl. 17*b*.

[5] *MA*, xiv. 637, Fig. 107 (Liliana); *Fortetsa*, Pl. 11, 164; *KX*, 1953, 485 f. (Modi).

[6] *BCH*, lxxxiii. 339 and 340, Fig. 4.

[7] *AJA*, xli, Pl. 2, No. 82; Pl. 5, No. 25 (Kaloriziki); *SCE*, IV, ii, Fig. V (Lapithos 406 and 420); *OA*, iii. 106, Pl. 1 (Lapithos 503¹).

[8] *Ker.* I, Pl 27, No. 507 (sub-Myc. tomb 97) and Pl. 37. Cf. du Plat Taylor, *PEQ*, 1956, 35.

may be justified in suggesting a link, always providing the areas are mutually accessible. The conditions are fulfilled here, and consequently it may reasonably be concluded that the end of LC. III B and the transition to CG. I A in Cyprus are contemporary with the transition in Athens from sub-Mycenaean to Protogeometric.[1] If the link has been interpreted correctly, then it follows that it is chronologically impossible for any LC. III B pottery to have been influenced by Attic Protogeometric, but quite possible for the former to have influenced the latter. It also follows that in Crete Gypsades tombs VI A and VII are earlier than the end of sub-Mycenaean in Athens.

This brief survey of the material from Cyprus has then produced interesting possible or probable conclusions. Groups of Mycenaeans moved to Cyprus on two occasions during the LH. III C period, first very early in the period, and second at some time after the destruction of the Granary at Mycenae. The second batch of arrivals may have been followed by yet further groups, and these movements take place during the earlier part of the Late Cypriot III B style. During the second part of this style, and perhaps into the beginning of Cypro-Geometric, the direction of ceramic influence (not necessarily entailing a movement of people) was reversed; evidence for this appears during the sub-Minoan period in Crete, and also in Athens at the time of transition from sub-Mycenaean to Protogeometric. Furthermore, it is possible that the Attic Protogeometric potters took one or two ideas from the contemporary Cypriot style. It is also probable that iron objects found their way from Cyprus to the Aegean during the whole of Late Cypriot III B. Finally, it seems reasonably certain that there was continuous contact between Cyprus and the Aegean during the later part of LH. III C and into Protogeometric.

[1] Probably *c.* 1050 B.C.; see p. 197, n 2. It may be added that a careful consideration of the Cypriot material and of its links with that of the Aegean seems to confirm my argument that sub-Mycenaean in west Attica is mainly contemporary with the latest stage of LH. III C in the Argolid and at Perati.

CHAPTER II

THE EVIDENCE OTHER THAN THAT OF POTTERY

Introductory Note

This chapter will be divided into three sections. The first will discuss the evidence of, and conclusions permissible from, settlements, tombs and places of worship, and will include a brief note on religious and votive objects whether found in tombs or shrines. The second section will be devoted to artefacts other than clay vases and terracotta figurines, and these will be classified according to their use. The third section will provide a summary of the intrusive elements. The material from Crete will for the greater part be left aside, as this island pursued its own way in most things.

I shall not enter into any full discussion of the material, unless it is a matter of some change or innovation occurring either at the end of LH. III B or during the course of LH. III C or immediately afterwards. In the case of the continuance of some well known and widely distributed custom or class of object, the main lines only of the relevant evidence will be given. Particular attention will, on the other hand, be paid to the question of survival beyond the Mycenaean age.

A. EVIDENCE FROM SETTLEMENTS, TOMBS, AND PLACES OF WORSHIP

1. Settlements

Although there are many areas of the Mycenaean world where the existence of a settlement can be deduced only from the presence of tombs or of surface sherds, the remaining districts provide ample evidence of the Mycenaean architects' and stonemasons' skill. The ability to work in stone at this period is indeed one of the outstanding features of Mycenaean civilization, and it is the strength and massiveness of this work which in part accounts for the survival of the many constructions.

For communication between settlements it is probable that there was a serviceable network of roads, at least in the central areas. This could be concluded from the use of chariots, and also from the obvious engineering skill of the Mycenaeans, but there is some positive evidence as well, both in the Argolid and in Messenia.[1] Although it is not possible to say when any road was built, the likelihood of construction during the LH. III C period may, on other grounds, be discarded.

---

[1] Wace, *Mycenae*, p. 109; McDonald and Hope Simpson, *AJA*, lxv. 257, n. 14.

Defence of settlements was a matter well within the scope of the Mycenaean engineer-architect. Fortifications are a well known feature of the two main sites of the Argolid—Mycenae and Tiryns—though there is no sign of them at Pylos. Across the Aegean, the settlement on Kos was unfortified, but Miletus was provided with a strong wall. At Athens, the Acropolis was surrounded by a wall, and so was the citadel of Gla in Boeotia. In Boeotia and north of this district, a different principle is to be observed, a wall enclosing an area much greater than that of the settlement. Perhaps even Gla is an example of this; certainly Eutresis has such a fortification, and so has Krisa in Phocis, and some sites in Thessaly. As opposed to Attica and the Argolid, where a smallish citadel was almost impregnably fortified, the defensive works of considerable circumference cannot have hoped to prevail against any strong organized attack, and may have been erected rather for temporary protection against small marauding groups from the mountains. One other defensive work may be mentioned, that of which a certain stretch remains south of the Isthmus of Corinth, and which was possibly intended to span the Isthmus.[1]

The actual construction of the walls was, as is to be expected, very solid, the Cyclopean type being the most popular technique, but ashlar work also found. As to chronology, one can be more precise than for the date of road construction, but even so there is much ground for divergence of opinion. Some defensive work must no doubt be assigned to the fourteenth century (LH. III A), but there was also much building, new work as well as strengthening, which can be dated somewhere about the middle of the thirteenth century. On the other hand, evidence of either new fortification or of repair has not yet been found during LH. III C.

The main work of the builder lay, however, not in fortification, but in houses. The most impressive of these were built for the kings, the palaces, a half dozen of which have already been discovered and excavated. Their principal architectural feature, as a rule, was a tripartite rectangular unit, a porch leading into an anteroom, this in its turn leading to the main chamber, the throne room wherein stood the hearth, a room used for religious and other purposes. The whole complex may be called the *megaron*, but the definition of *megaron* is more strictly applicable to the main chamber only, that is to say a rectangular room, with entrance at the end and not at the side, dominating the rest of the building. A *megaron* may therefore be found in houses of size and quality far inferior to those of the palaces, and indeed many houses, though not all, do have this feature; it is not always possible, owing to lack of evidence, to determine that a room is of this type. On the whole, however, the *megaron* is a distinguishing feature of Mycenaean architecture, as opposed for example to the Minoan custom, where although the rooms are rectangular, the entrance is almost always at the side (in other words, in the longer stretch of wall). The quality of construction varied in accordance with the wealth or rank of the occupant. At its best, it can compare favourably with much of the work of Classical Greece; at its lowest, it is still solid enough.

A long discussion would be needed to do justice to the architectural details and to the general technique of construction of Mycenaean houses, but this would only be of use if it

---

[1] References to the sites concerned will be found in the regional sections. For the Isthmus wall, see Broneer, *Antiquity*, xxxii. 81, Fig. 1 and 82.

transpired that there were significant changes in LH. III C as opposed to earlier periods, as there was with the pottery. The remarkable fact, however, is that we have practically no material for comparison. There is only one site in the Argolid with buildings whose erection can with certainty be attributed to this period, and that is Asine, where the houses are reasonably well built and adhere rather hesitatingly to the rectangular principle.[1] This is an almost isolated instance; some of the rectangular rooms of Grotta on Naxos might have been built after LH. III B, and so presumably may some of the houses of the Serraglio site on Kos, but one cannot tell for sure.[2]

Although, then, it is not possible to discuss architecture in the LH. III C period, it is well worth discussing why the evidence is so meagre. The first suggestion that could be made is that perhaps the inhabitants still used the perfectly satisfactory buildings which had been erected in LH. III B times, or even earlier. This is not a valid point, for on the Mainland (which provides the major part of our knowledge) the evidence shows that from Phocis southwards to the southernmost part of the Peloponnese there was very substantial destruction and desertion of settlements at or close to the end of LH. III B. So either the earlier buildings were no longer used, or they were no longer fit for use. Now, except for most of the southern Peloponnese, the remaining districts were still inhabited by Mycenaeans. It is possible to suppose that the survivors did just contrive to use what was left of the earlier buildings; but there is an added difficulty. There are three areas where the cemetery evidence proves a considerable influx of population in LH. III C (Kephallenia, Achaea, East Attica, pp. 98, 103, 115), and settlements must have been built to accommodate them. In no case has any such settlement been found. It may be claimed that this is a matter of chance, but if so it is remarkable; the more likely explanation is that there is little of significance to find in the way of good stone construction. Either it was not considered worth while to build extensively in stone, or else the leading architects and stonemasons had fled to other areas, inside or outside the Mycenaean sphere.[3]

This appears to be the situation in LH. III C on the Mainland south of Thessaly and in Kephallenia, and the extreme rarity of any stone construction for a period of centuries after LH. III C strongly supports the view that the skill had been lost. Is a similar situation visible in other parts of the Mycenaean *koine*? The islands of the Aegean, and the settlement at Miletus, escaped the Mainland destruction, and there is no reason to doubt that adequate stone houses were erected in LH. III C. Unfortunately, none of the settlements known (Phylakopi on Melos, Grotta on Naxos, Serraglio on Kos, Emborio on Chios, Miletus) has yet been recorded in sufficient detail for one to be able to attribute any constructions with certainty to this period. Except for the Naxian settlement, there was either catastrophe or desertion towards the end of LH. III C, and this may have resulted in a loss of the knowledge or desire to build in stone, even as on the Mainland.

Finally, there is Thessaly, where we are restricted in our knowledge to the fortress and palace of Iolkos. Here, the situation at the beginning of LH. III C may well have been

---

[1] *Asine*, pp. 74 ff.
[2] Condoleon, *Pr.* 1951, pp. 214 ff. (Naxos); Morricone, *Boll. d'Arte*, 1950, p. 322.

[3] One would nevertheless expect a substantial settlement at Perati on the east coast of Attica, closely linked with a still flourishing Central Aegean, but it has not yet been found.

much as in the Aegean. At some time during this period the palace was involved in a violent destruction, but it is of the greatest interest to note that in this case new and well-built stone constructions rose above the adjacent settlement (which was not destroyed) in the Protogeometric period.[1] In view of the almost absolute dearth of buildings of stone in other parts of Greece and the Aegean (excluding Crete) at this time it seems extremely likely that this is an example of the survival of the Mycenaean craft—a supposition confirmed by the evolution of the pottery series.

The situation in Crete differs from that of the rest of the Aegean world in various ways. There seems to have been no attempt to fortify any of the cities at any time during the Late Minoan period. As one must assume the Minoan masons to have been perfectly capable of building a fortification wall, the absence of defensive works suggests that there was reasonable internal harmony in Crete—a suggestion supported, at least down to the early stages of LM. III C, by the uniformity of the Minoan culture throughout the island—and that no particular danger was envisaged from outside. It is clear that in spite of disaster to the palaces the Cretans never lost their skill at building in stone; the best proof of this, in the LM. III C—sub-Minoan period which is contemporary with LH. III C, is the town of Karphi, certainly built by Minoans, though occasional examples of a *megaron*, in the sense of a room entered by the end (the short side), led the excavator to infer the possibility of intrusion by Achaeans.[2] New settlements were also built at about this time at Gortyn and Phaestos, and stone was the material used, although the construction is very poor when set beside that of the palace—for example, at Phaestos.[3] It is unfortunately apparently not possible to tell from these settlements whether it was a matter of Minoan survival or of Mycenaean intrusion.

In summary, this brief section stresses the considerable ability of the Mycenaean architect down to the end of LH. III B in contrast to the virtual absence of his works thereafter. The evidence of destruction and desertion of sites is the best witness to the disasters at or near the end of LH. III B on the Mainland south of Thessaly. It is likely that the art of construction in stone was lost or neglected in this area at the end of LH. III B, in the Aegean (except in Crete and perhaps in Naxos) at the end of LH. III C, but that it probably persisted in Thessaly, at least at Iolkos.

2. *Tombs*

Within the Mycenaean world, in the Late Helladic III A and B periods, the two kinds of tomb most commonly found are the tholos tomb and the chamber tomb, and in both the system is that of multiple burial. The chamber tomb is, indeed, characteristic of every district inhabited by the Mycenaeans. It is almost invariably, for convenience of construction, cut into sloping ground; the chamber in which the burials were laid is as a rule rectangular, and a narrow dromos or passageway, with walls tending to slope inwards, leads to the entrance to the chamber. There are variations of construction, but these

---

[1] Theocharis, *Ergon* for 1960, pp. 55 ff.; *Ergon* for 1961, pp. 51 ff.

[2] Pendlebury, *BSA*, xxxviii. 137.

[3] Levi, *Ann.* xvii–xviii (N.S.), 211, Fig. 2 (Gortyn); *Ann.* xix–xx (N.S.), 256 f., Figs. 86 *a* and *b* (Phaestos).

(which in part depend on the nature of the terrain) I do not intend to discuss, as they do not affect the situation in LH. III C. The tholos tomb is, as opposed to the chamber tomb, stone-built, with a circular chamber, in the floor of which pit graves may be dug, and a dromos which may also be stone-built. The shape of the chamber resembles that of the old-fashioned beehive. It is altogether superior to the chamber tomb, and no doubt usually housed the dead of the royal or noble families.[1] Its distribution is not on quite so universal a scale as that of the chamber tomb; it is known in most of the Mainland districts, and at Colophon in Asia Minor,[2] but no example has so far been found on any of the islands, with the exception of Crete (p. 173).

These are the two main types, and they represent, as has been stated, a system of multiple burial. The type of tomb which involves the system of single or double burial is much less commonly found. In Middle Helladic times, the slab-covered cist tombs designed for single or double burial were very common, but the continuous survival into LH. III of such tombs is to be observed only at Eleusis (p. 114). Elsewhere, there are only a few isolated LH. III examples, not necessarily implying continuity with earlier times. At Asine, three cist tombs are considered Late Helladic,[3] but of these there is reason to believe that LH. 12 may belong to Protogeometric times,[4] while the situation with regard to LH. 13 is obscure.[5] Only in LH. 11 (a child burial) is it clear that the contents are LH. III B, but this tomb lay in very close proximity to a Middle Helladic cist burial.[6] Two cist tombs at Dimini contained LH. III B vases and figurines, and one of these also produced a vase of native Thessalian ware—very rare in any LH. III B context.[7] LH. III B vases were found in a cist tomb at Emborio on Chios,[8] but this is almost the only indication on this site of contact with the Mycenaean world before LH. III C (pp. 158 f.). Most recently, cist tombs have been discovered at Kafkania, in the Olympia district, which may be Mycenaean.[9] In general, then, the evidence for cist tombs in LH. III, down to the end of LH. III B, is very slight indeed.[10]

The principle of single burial is also, however, to be observed in pit graves, similar to cist tombs in shape but not protected by stone slabs. Such graves, which usually, but not always, contained child burials, are known on four sites, two in the Argolid and two in Attica. In the Argolid, nine of these graves were found at Asine,[11] but their contents did not allow a more precise dating than simply Late Helladic. At Argos, on the other hand, a fair number were discovered, some very closely associated with chamber tombs.[12] It would seem that they are mainly to be dated to LH. III A, but some were used during the LH. III B period and one or two just conceivably in LH. III C. In Attica, four pit graves of LH. III B or of uncertain date were found in the cemetery at Voula,[13] but at Athens the

---

[1] Cf. however, McDonald and Hope Simpson, *AJA*, lxv. 258, n. 17.
[2] Goldman, *AJA*, xxvii. 67 f.
[3] *Asine*, pp. 354 f.
[4] *OA*, iii. 210.
[5] I can find no mention of this tomb elsewhere in the publication, nor is its associated vase illustrated.
[6] *Asine*, p. 129.
[7] *Δ-Σ*, pp. 150 ff. Cf. Skeat, *Dorians*, p. 9.
[8] Cf. *JHS*, lxxv. suppl., 20.
[9] *BCH*, lxxxv. 722.
[10] The four cist tombs of Kalbaki in Epirus, of LH. III date but outside the Mycenaean sphere, will be discussed later (pp. 37 f.).
[11] *Asine*, pp. 128 f., 354.
[12] Deshayes, *BCH*, lxxxiii. 768, Fig. 1 (the tombs with Arabic numerals).
[13] Papademetriou, *Pr.* 1955, p. 99; 1957, pp. 31 ff.

situation seems to have been much the same as at Argos, though no pit grave can be dated to LH. III C.[1]

The LH. III C period involves a number of changes, one of which may be noted straightway. We have seen that in LH. III A and B the tholos tomb and the chamber tomb had a very wide distribution. In LH. III C, the chamber tomb has still an almost universal distribution, and it is therefore remarkable that burial in tholos tombs is extremely rare. There are only two such cases, to my knowledge; the tholos tombs at Pteleon in south Thessaly, either built or re-used in LH. III C, and the tholos at Tragana in Messenia, which was re-used in LH. III C.[2] It seems reasonable to suppose, on this evidence, that the age of the monumental tomb is over, and that the situation is parallel to that observable on the Mainland south of Thessaly with regard to palatial constructions. There are, however, two districts of the Mainland where tholos tombs of the Protogeometric period have been found. In Messenia, one such tomb, of small dimensions, has been recorded,[3] but continuity of burial in tholos tombs throughout LH. III C is not yet satisfactorily demonstrable. In north Thessaly, the evidence for survival is much stronger.[4] It must be admitted that there is no evidence of a tholos tomb containing burials of LH. III C date—in fact, tombs of any sort of this period are almost entirely lacking; but the number of tholos tombs in use from the Protogeometric period onwards, together with the evidence provided by the well-built stone edifices of the earliest post-Mycenaean settlement at Iolkos,[5] suggest strongly that the Mycenaean stonemason's craft was preserved in this area.

The first change consists, then, in the virtual disappearance of the tholos tomb. Further changes emerge from a consideration of the geographical distribution of LH. III C tombs, as opposed to that of their predecessors. In this matter, certain areas are absolutely or relatively worthless for comparative purposes. Arcadia, Corinthia, the Megarid, Locris and most of the islands of the Aegean have produced no evidence, or hardly any, of cemeteries of LH. III date; these gaps, however, do not seriously affect the general picture. Areas where the tomb evidence is too slight and too localized include Thessaly, Phocis, Boeotia, Euboea, and the western coast of Asia Minor; all that can be said is that continuity of occupation into LH. III C is assured either by tomb or settlement material.

Of the districts which remain, a threefold division may be made: those where no particular change is noticeable, those where there was partial or considerable depopulation, and those which exhibit signs of an increase of population. The only district where one can be confident that, at least at the beginning of the LH. III C period, there was little or no change in the population pattern is the Dodecanese; the tombs both of Rhodes and Kos preserve a steady and unbroken continuity. Several districts, on the other hand, can be shown from the evidence of tombs (mostly supporting that of the settlements) to have been partly or extensively depopulated; in Messenia there are hardly any tombs datable to LH. III C, whereas earlier in LH. III they are thick on the ground, and surface investigation, as well as the rather meagre evidence from excavation, indicate the same situation in

---

[1] Hill, *The Ancient City of Athens*, p. 9, Fig. 3; Vermeule, *Hesp.* xxiv. 188, nn. 3 and 4; Travlos, Πολεοδομικὴ ἐξέλιξις τῶν Ἀθηνῶν, p. 23, Fig. 7.

[2] Verdhelis, *Pr.* 1951, pp. 141 ff. (Pteleon); Kourouniotis, *AE*, 1914, pp. 99 ff.

[3] Blegen, *AJA*, lxiii. 127.

[4] Heurtley and Skeat, *BSA*, xxxi. 1 ff.; Verdhelis, Ὁ Πρωτογεωμετρικὸς Ῥυθμὸς τῆς Θεσσαλίας, *passim*.

[5] See p. 32, n. 1.

Laconia, with the significant exception of the cemetery near Monemvasia, on the isolated eastern coast (p. 89). While the lack of tombs in these two regions suggests extensive depopulation, partial abandonment may be postulated in the Argolid; and whereas the cemeteries of some sites come to an end in LH. III B, LH. III C tombs are in use at Mycenae (though in far smaller numbers), at Argos and Asine, and probably at Nauplia and Tiryns (pp. 75, 79 ff.). In western Attica, finally, where the settlement evidence on the Athenian Acropolis proves continued inhabitation, the lack of tombs on nearby sites is a clear sign of depopulation, though not on quite so extensive a scale as in the southern Peloponnese (pp. 112 ff.).

As against this, eastern Attica, as represented by the vast and exclusively LH. III C cemetery of Perati, belongs to the third division, where the tomb evidence shows an increased population. The tombs of Monemvasia, mentioned above, may indicate a similar move to the east from central Laconia; and indeed the tombs and settlement at Asine may betray a parallel phenomenon (pp. 82 f.). It is also possible that the island of Naxos should come within this group, as the contents of the few chamber tombs are predominantly LH. III C (pp. 150 f.); but it would be as well to suspend judgment in this case until the full record of the settlement is published, and the discovery of further tombs. But the most impressive evidence of an increase in population, deducible solely from tomb material, is apparent in Achaea and in Kephallenia where, in contrast to the abundance of LH. III C tombs, burials of earlier date are rare. Thus, except in the Dodecanese, the present findings strongly suggest a considerable shift in population in the areas mentioned above.

It has been explained that the tholos tomb, previously popular, was only very exceptionally used in LH. III C times. The chamber tomb, on the other hand, suffered no such lapse from favour. Among all the areas where LH. III C cemeteries have been discovered, only in Kephallenia is there, from the beginning, a breakaway from the conventional construction of the chamber tomb (p. 104), a fact which may reflect the admixture of the Mycenaean strain with a non-Mycenaean native population which still used hand-made pottery (pp. 104 f.); and even here, the principle of multiple burial is retained. In every other area, the chamber tomb is the main type of tomb used in LH. III C times, and in certain districts no other type has yet been identified.[1] The continued use of this tomb, taken in conjunction with the similar types of offering therein deposited, implies the persistence of Mycenaean civilization in every district where it is found.

Leaving aside the evidence of western Attica, other kinds of tombs, known to have been built in the LH. III C period, are very rare. The tholos tomb of Pteleon in south Thessaly has been mentioned, as well as the re-used tholos tomb at Tragana in Messenia. A tomb near Aigion,[2] presumably LH. III C in date, is strikingly similar to the tombs of Kephallenia. One of the tombs recently excavated on Naxos is evidently a child's pit burial.[3] There is a curious 'double-compartment' cist tomb from Vardhates in the Spercheios valley, which will be further discussed below (p. 126). Apart from these, it is only at Mycenae, at Perati and possibly at Argos (p. 33) that we find burials in other than chamber tombs.

---

[1] The cist tomb cemeteries of Athens and Salamis will be discussed later, p. 37.

[2] Verdhelis, *AE*, 1956, suppl., pp. 11 f.

[3] Zapheiropoullos, *Ergon* for 1960, p. 189.

Mycenae provides the only examples known to the LH. III C world, outside Crete, of a pithos and a larnax burial. The pithos burial[1] was found in the Cyclopean terrace building, and the vases associated with it were assigned by Furumark to his LH. III C 1 *a* phase,[2] although a later stage is suggested by the high foot of stirrup jar No. 1, and by the airholes of both stirrup jars. Furumark considered stirrup jar No. 1 to be of Cretan origin;[3] and the pithos itself is more at home in Crete than elsewhere, although its use for burial purposes is very rare at this time (pp. 187 ff.). A possible link with Crete must also surely be indicated by the bath-larnax burial, since this is one of the most common types of tomb in the Late Minoan III period. This tomb was found in stratum XI of the Lion Gate deposit, and must therefore be later than the final destruction at Mycenae, a date confirmed by the associated pottery (which does not, however, display any connexion with Crete).[4]

Yet a third type of tomb, still datable to the LH. III C period, has been discovered at Mycenae. This was found in the Prehistoric Cemetery, and contained the skeleton of a baby, and two vases, one of which (a deep bowl with wavy-line decoration) is very close in style to others found in the latest III C contexts. It may be described as a cist tomb, in the sense that it is in the shape of a box made by the hollowing out of a single slab of stone.[5]

In each of these three cases the principle of multiple burial has been abandoned. Two of the tombs, and possibly all three, belong to the very end of the LH. III C series. After this, the characteristic tomb of Mycenae, and of other sites in the Argolid, is the cist tomb, that is to say an earth-cut grave usually lined and covered with stone slabs. There might perhaps be a connexion between these and the 'cist' tomb of the Prehistoric Cemetery and even the larnax of the Lion Gate, but it seems doubtful.

The tomb evidence of Mycenae comes from many parts of the site, but the cemetery of Perati is a compact unit. By far the greatest number of burials in this latter cemetery were made in chamber tombs, but there were a number of instances where multiple burial had been discarded. Such burials were either in pit graves covered over with stone slabs or (very rarely) in similar graves provided with shallow but quite distinct dromoi. These tombs were situated, as is only natural, on the crest of the hill, and it would be most useful to be able to establish their chronological relation to the chamber tombs, but for this full publication must be awaited.[6]

The evidence has so far tended to confirm what may be concluded from a study of the pottery and of settlement material, that the Mycenaean way of life continued to exist, if not to flourish, in most of the areas over which it had previously held sway. A considerable shift of population from one area to another may be deduced; and in spite of occasional exceptions—and these exceptions are not proportionately greater than in LH. III A and LH. III B—the chamber tomb remains the characteristic form of tomb for LH. III C; the exceptions appear to be no more than exceptions, and do not lead us to suppose that they represent any new intrusive racial factor.

---

[1] *BSA*, xxv. 406 f., Pl. 62.
[2] *OA*, iii. 197.
[3] Op. cit. p. 200.
[4] *BSA*, xxv. 36.
[5] *BSA*, xlix. 258 f.
[6] See reports in *Ergon* for 1958, 1959 and 1960.

The presence of such a factor in western Attica is, however, a possible deduction from the two large cemeteries of Salamis and of the Athenian Kerameikos,[1] which covered a period of time that was in part, as has been argued elsewhere (pp. 17 ff.), contemporary with the latest stage of LH. III C. But they differ entirely from all other cemeteries of this period in this vital point, that they contain no chamber tombs at all. They consist wholly of pit graves or cist tombs, the cist tombs (that is to say, pit graves lined and covered with stone slabs) being the more numerous, and the earlier.[2]

What then is the significance of these two cemeteries? One conclusion appears inevitable, that the people who buried here were not predominantly Mycenaeans, judging by the standard of the material characteristics of these people. The principle of multiple burial in chamber tombs had been so universal and persistent that it seems inconceivable that the elimination of this should not entail some radical change in the population. This does not mean that the Mycenaeans were not capable, of their own accord, of changing their burial customs, but such a change would surely be gradual, and reflected in other parts of the Mycenaean world.

At this point, it is necessary to ask whether the change involved new people coming from outside the Mycenaean world, or the emergence of a class of people who had previously lived in the Mycenaean world, but who had some inferior status. The type of tomb is an important factor in considering this question, but it cannot by itself give the answer. It is true enough that the cist tomb was widely used in Middle Helladic times, within the Mycenaean sphere, but the evidence does not warrant our making any direct connexion between the Middle Helladic tombs and those some eight hundred years later in date. The survival of cist tombs into Late Helladic times at Eleusis is of great interest, but neither these nor the very few cist tombs found on other sites (see back, p. 33) give promise of even a small-scale revival. It is also true that the cist tomb can be described as an improved version of the pit grave, and that there could be a fairly immediate chronological and geographical connexion with these graves. But in accepting the Salamis and Kerameikos cist tombs as the logical development of Athenian pit graves one would have also to assume, without proof, that the earlier pit graves belonged to some impoverished or subject element in the population, and that the disappearance of the chamber tombs meant that it had got the upper hand. The evidence of Perati, it may be noted, is of no assistance, as we do not yet know whether the slab-covered pit graves were earlier than any of the Salamis or Kerameikos cist tombs.

On the other side, demonstration that newcomers from outside the Mycenaean world were responsible for these two cemeteries should at least be able to be authenticated by the appearance of cist tombs of earlier date in the area of origin, and other cist tombs might perhaps be expected to be found on the route to western Attica. For the districts that lie beyond the Mycenaean orbit there is clearly earlier evidence only from the four cist tombs found at Kalbaki, near Iannina in Epirus.[3] The vases and most of the other objects deposited prove that the dead were not Mycenaean, but one of the tombs contained a short

---

[1] Wide, *AM*, xxxv. 17 ff.; Kraiker and Kübler, *Ker.* I; Kübler, *AA*, lxvii. 203 (= Smithson, *Hesp.* xxx. 174 ff.).

[2] Cf. *Ker.* I, pp. 9 ff.
[3] Dakaris, *AE*, 1956, pp. 114 ff.

sword of Mycenaean type, dated on stylistic grounds to late LH. III B.[1] So cist tombs do appear at about the right time and place to support the theory of intrusion from outside, but even so this is a solitary instance, and no more than a pointer. Also, no connexion with the Attic material appears in any of the pottery or small finds. Either within or on the fringes of Mycenaean territory, the curious tomb at Vardhates, in the Spercheios valley, might be a link in the chain, but the type of tomb is itself unorthodox and the vases, though in part LH. III C, are not precisely datable. The cist tombs of the Electran Gates cemetery near Thebes could comprise a final link, as some of the vases are of Mycenaean rather than Protogeometric character; but it is not possible to prove that any of these tombs are earlier than those of western Attica.[2]

If this were the only evidence, even taking into consideration the different pattern of small finds, the question of origin would perhaps have to remain an open one. There is, however, a considerable body of material which, although mostly post-Mycenaean in date, points to a northern origin for the cist tombs. The main feature is that of the distribution of cist tombs other than those mentioned, and is as follows:

Macedonia.   Kozani. *Ergon* for 1960, 99 ff.; *BCH*, lxxxv. 777 ff.
                 Vergina. *Balkan Studies*, ii. 89 ff.
                 Chauchitsa. *BSA*, xxvi. 1 ff.

The tombs of Chauchitsa cannot be dated with certainty earlier than the eighth century, but those of Vergina and Kozani must be in part considerably earlier (cf. pp. 143 ff.), especially those in which no iron objects or wheel-made vases have been found, and where the hand-made vases are associated with bronze objects of probably Danubian origin. The earliest burials could go back into the eleventh century.

Thessaly.   Retziouni.   *Verdhelis*, p. 52.
             ?Agrilia.   *Verdhelis*, p. 61.
             Palaiokastro.   *BCH*, lvi. 99; *PGP*, p. 313.
             Iolkos.   *Ergon* for 1960, pp. 58 f.; *Ergon* for 1961, pp. 55 ff.
             Theotokou.   *P.T.*, pp. 209 ff.
             Halos.   *BSA*, xviii. 1 ff.

Except at Theotokou, none of these tombs is later than Protogeometric, and the earliest tomb at Theotokou contained a sub-Mycenaean lekythos. The burials at Halos and Palaiokastro belong within the Protogeometric period, and so apparently do those of Iolkos, although the excavator considers that the links with the latest Mycenaean pottery are so strong that those who buried their children in these tombs must have found Mycenaean pottery still in use (cf. pp. 128 f.). Retziouni lies in the foothills of Olympus, north of Larisa, and the two tombs contained hand-made vases of the Marmariani type and a wheel-made amphoriskos which the excavator thinks may be sub-Mycenaean (cf. p. 133). The pottery associated with the tombs of Agrilia (on the lower slopes of Mt. Chasia, east of Kalambaka) is either local hand-made ware or (less frequently) Mycenaean of the

---

[1] Op. cit. pp. 143 f.

[2] Marinatos, *Ber. VI. Int. Kongress*, p. 334 (Vardhates); Keramopoullos, *AD*, iii. 25 ff. (Thebes).

latest period; until the vases are recorded, one cannot be sure whether these tombs should be connected with the others, bearing in mind the presence of a cist tomb of presumably LH. III B date at Dimini (cf. p. 33). In any case, it is possible that some of the Thessalian cist tombs are contemporary with the latest Mycenaean period.

Argolid.   Mycenae.   *BSA*, xlix. 259 f.; *BSA*, l. 240 f.; *BSA*, li. 129 f.
            Asine.   *Asine*, pp. 129 ff.
            Tiryns.   *Tiryns* I, pp. 127 ff.; *AE*, 1956, suppl., p. 4.
            Argos.   *BCH*, lxxxi. 663; lxxxiii. 762 ff.

Except for one probably sub-Mycenaean burial at Tiryns, all belong to the Protogeometric period, but the earliest are very close in time to the latest Mycenaean (cf. pp. 19, 81 f.).

Corinthia.   Corinth. *Corinth*, VII, i. 9 (Early Geometric).
             No comment is needed.
Achaea.   Chalandritsa. *Pr.* 1930, pp. 85 f.; *BCH*, lxxxv. 682.
            Pharai. *Pr.* 1954, pp. 400 ff.
Elis.   Ancient Elis. *Ergon* for 1961, pp. 186 ff.
            Kafkania. *BCH*, lxxxv. 722.
Messenia.   Nichoria. *BCH*, lxxxv. 697.

The Achaean tombs contained Geometric vases, but some of those from Chalandritsa were covered by a tumulus, apparently a northern feature,[1] and the dry stone technique and apsidal shape of one is paralleled at Nichoria, where the tombs are of the Protogeometric period. The tombs discovered at Ancient Elis are not typical cist burials, as they are pit graves simply covered, but not lined, with unworked slabs; the vases belong to the Protogeometric period, and may indeed be slightly earlier, according to the excavator's report. The Kafkania group awaits further exploration (see p. 92).

Apart from these tombs of the Mainland, others are known on Skyros, Andros, Tenos and Kos, and range in date from Protogeometric to Geometric; they are thus relatively later than those on the Mainland.[2]

Another type of single burial, in a pithos, deserves mention. It was a type of burial not entirely unknown to LH. III C (cf. p. 36), but its appearance in early post-Mycenaean contexts is in no way connected with Mycenaean practice. Pithos burials are found as well as cist tombs at Vergina,[3] where the links with the Mycenaean world were extremely slender. Of more interest, however, are those of the West Peloponnese, of Late Protogeometric date at Derveni in Achaea,[4] and Protogeometric at Palaiopyrgo[5] north of the Alpheios and at Nichoria in Messenia.[6] Nowhere else, to my knowledge, are pithos burials known of so early a post-Mycenaean date.

When this evidence is considered as a whole (see Map at back), it strongly confirms the conception of a non-Mycenaean origin for the single or double burial as opposed to the

---

[1] Cf. *AE*, 1956, p. 149.
[2] Cf. *PGP*, Site Index for references.
[3] *Balkan Studies*, ii. 91.
[4] *BCH*, lxxvi. 222; *AJA*, lxiv. 16 f. and Pl. 5.
[5] *AJA*, lxv. 226.
[6] *BCH*, lxxxv. 697.

multiple burial. One can be certain for the Macedonian tombs, and reasonably certain for those of the western Peloponnese, the southern part of which had been almost denuded of its Mycenaean inhabitants at the end of LH. III B. There may perhaps remain a suspicion of doubt in Thessaly and in the Argolid, but it is worth remembering that in the latter region, at Mycenae and Tiryns, the users of cist tombs had no hesitation in sinking them within the previous Mycenaean settlements.

A further consideration is the fact that the finds other than pottery associated with cist tombs are of a very different nature from those of the chamber tombs. This is only to be expected in Macedonia, but it is also the case when there was certainly or possibly connexion with the preceding Mycenaean culture, in Thessaly, Boeotia, West Attica, the Argolid and the western Peloponnese. It must also be remembered that the anthropological evidence from the sub-Mycenaean cemetery of the Kerameikos and from the Protogeometric cist tombs of Argos shows a notable increase in northern types of skull.[1]

It is therefore exceedingly difficult to avoid the conclusion that those who buried in cist tombs or pithoi were newcomers from outside the Mycenaean sphere, and this conclusion I shall accept as correct. It will also be reasonably clear from the above review of evidence that this is a matter not of one, but of several groups of intruders.

3. *Places of Worship*[2]

It is as a rule a simple matter, in Classical times, to identify a place of worship from the construction of a temple to the deity concerned, but in the Mycenaean age recognition may have to come rather through associated objects than through the remains of some building. This being so, it may be best to begin with a brief discussion of the objects of cult importance.

A distinction may first be made between objects which have to do with the cult of the dead, and those used as votive offerings in sanctuaries. Cemeteries produce the material for the cult of the dead, and this includes the following vase types of ritual significance: the kalathos with figurines on the rim (Pl. 7*a, b*), the jug with strainer spout or excrescent cup,[3] especially when associated with painted or fictile snakes (Pl. 7*c, d*), the rhyton for pouring libations and the composite vessel. Beside these, there are the terracotta figurines, whether of 'goddess' or animal type. All these must be presumed to be connected with the cult of the dead, inasmuch as they were found in tombs. The terracotta figurines were certainly also used as votive gifts in sanctuaries. There is evidence that the composite vessel was also used in such contexts,[4] and so also must the rhyton have been. For the other types of vase there is no sanctuary evidence, except that the kalathos as such, i.e. without figurines on the rim, was probably used for cult purposes other than those of the dead as much in the Mycenaean world as in Crete. Mention may also be made of the ring kernos, a vase which has several 'small vessels attached to the ring and communicating with its interior',[5] and

---

[1] Angel, *Hesp.* xiv. 322 f., 328; Charles, *BCH*, lxxxii. 306.

[2] This section takes no account of the situation in Crete, which differs much from that of the Mycenaean Mainland and Aegean. See pp. 187 ff.

[3] This and the kalathos are principally found in LH. III C in the central Aegean area, i.e. the Dodecanese, Naxos and Perati (see p. 13).

[4] *Asine*, pp. 298 and 299, Fig. 206.

[5] *Analysis*, p. 69.

as well as this is provided alternatively with plastic snakes, bulls' heads or birds. Only three are known, and one of them is from a tomb—the other two may or may not be.

This section is concerned with sanctuaries, and not with the cult of the dead as found in tombs, and consequently the vases so far only found in tombs may be set aside, though of course they may, for all we know (and that is not much) have been used in sanctuaries as well. In any case, these vase forms do not, except for the kalathos, seem to have survived LH. III C, though all with the apparent exception of the rhyton were used in this period, and one or two perhaps only in this period.

The terracotta figurines, found equally in tomb and sanctuary, constitute a class of their own, divisible into the human and animal categories. With very few exceptions the human figurines are made up of the three 'goddess' types, Φ, T and Ψ. Furumark has briefly discussed their development, and seems satisfactorily to have shown that the Φ type does not outlast LH. III B, but that the other two are both found in LH. III C contexts.[1] A more detailed study would be extremely valuable, and one has in fact been completed.[2] Here I will stress only two points, that these 'goddess' figurines vanish utterly at the end of the Mycenaean age, and that none has been found in any of the cist tombs of Salamis and the Kerameikos.

The animal figurines are mostly bovine, though some of them may represent horses. I have no comment to offer on their typology and development. The barrel-bodied beasts of Amyklai,[3] of LH. III C date, are perhaps the most interesting, as there might be some connexion with later objects such as the Protogeometric Kerameikos stag.[4]

Before discussing the few definite or possible instances of places or constructions of the Mycenaean age reserved for religious practices, it may be noted that there did exist a construction used for religious activity as well as other purposes, that is to say, the main room of the *megaron* of a palace. The clearest example of this is surely at Pylos,[5] with the libation channel running from close to the throne, and it is probable that all 'throne rooms' could be used for ritual purposes,[6] which would be quite in accordance with the tradition of the divine-born kings of Homer. Other parts of the palace as well might have some religious purpose. It is thought that the circular construction in the great court of Tiryns was an altar.[7] Wace claimed to have identified a separate shrine within the palace at Mycenae, but the evidence is not so convincing as it might be.[8]

It must be considered very doubtful whether the palaces, or any particular room in them, retained in later times any aura of sanctity. In view of the complete destruction and consequent desertion that overtook them, one cannot suppose that any special room was remembered as having been a cult spot. The palace as a whole would be known to later ages as the residence of the king and nothing else.[9] The only certain evidence of the site of a

[1] *Chronology*, pp. 87 ff. Cf. also Marinatos, *AE*, 1927–8, pp. 7 ff.; Mylonas, *Ancient Mycenae*, pp. 78 ff.; Alexiou, *KX*, 1958, pp. 208 f.
[2] By Mrs. David French.
[3] *AM*, lii, Beil. 6.
[4] *Ker.* iv. 20 and Pl. 26. See generally Ohly, *AM*, lxv. 67 ff. and Pls. 46 ff. on the material from the Heraeum at Samos.
[5] Cf. *AJA*, lxv. Pl. 53, Fig. 1.
[6] Everywhere where the hearth was, perhaps; cf. Mylonas, *Ancient Mycenae*, p. 53.
[7] Müller, *Tiryns*, iii. 137, 136, Fig. 64, and Pl. 5.
[8] *BSA*, xxv. 223 ff.; cf. Mylonas, *Ancient Mycenae*, pp. 61 f.
[9] Note the remarks of Blegen, *Korakou*, pp. 130 ff. with regard to the unlikelihood of a building at Tiryns being a later temple (cf. Müller, *Tiryns*, iii. 213 f.).

palace being used later for worship is at Mycenae, where a temple, of Hellenistic times, overlies part of the palace.¹ Its orientation is unusual, and has given rise to the supposition that it was deliberate, so as to place the temple over a remembered Mycenaean sanctuary; but this cannot be proved, and other reasons for the orientation could be adduced.²

The buildings or sites certainly or possibly used exclusively or primarily as places of worship are, as already stated, few, and are not all of similar type nor of equal importance. Our knowledge is restricted to one site in Triphylia, one in Laconia, two in the Argolid, two in Attica, one on Kea, and the sacred areas of Delphi and Delos.

The Triphylian site is that of Mouriatadha, a few miles from Kyparissia. In his recent excavations, Marinatos uncovered a building of *megaron* type, which he considers may have been a temple. This is not yet capable of proof, and the lack of any associated objects has so far prevented any attempt at precise dating. The identification as a sanctuary cannot therefore be considered as more than hypothetical. No later edifice was ever erected.³

At Amyklai, the Laconian site, there are no buildings associated with the Mycenaean and pre-Mycenaean material, but it is reasonably certain that this was a cult place. Seventy-five terracotta 'goddess' figurines were found, as well as several barrel-bodied horses or bulls of clay, one of which is decorated in the Close Style, thus proving that there was worship in LH. III C. A temple to Apollo was later built on this site, but the earliest post-Mycenaean material is the Protogeometric and Geometric pottery, the Protogeometric being of an individual type having no visible connexion with the Attic style. It must be borne in mind that there is no ceramic link between the last Mycenaean pottery and the Protogeometric material, and also that there is no proof that the site was used as a sanctuary in Protogeometric or Geometric times. Nevertheless, it does seem possible that in this instance the memory at least of the spot's being sacred survived.⁴

Of the two sanctuary sites in the Argolid, the shrine at Asine was in existence for a brief period of time only, and the spot was never again used for cult purposes.⁵ It is a household shrine, and as such is perhaps unique in the Mycenaean, as opposed to the Minoan, world. Comparison may in fact be made with Crete, not only on account of the type of sanctuary, but also because of the large terracotta head found in it, which has undeniable parallels in the Minoan series of goddesses with raised arms.⁶ There were also, however, 'goddess' figurines of the Ψ type, and the votive and other objects were generally Mycenaean. This shrine was built in LH. III C, and used only in that period.

The other site is close to Epidaurus, and here a sanctuary was built to Apollo Maleatas; most of the finds belong to Archaic times, but there was some Geometric pottery. Beneath the sanctuary, a considerable quantity of prehistoric material came to light, some of the pottery dating back to Early Helladic, and all main stages of Late Helladic being represented. As at Amyklai, the probability that this was a sacred spot in Mycenaean times was shown by the number of figurines both of human and animal type. Some of these figurines are datable to LH. III, though the preliminary reports do not say whether

---

¹ Wace, *Mycenae*, pp. 84 ff.
² Cf. Mylonas, *Ancient Mycenae*, p. 64.
³ *Ergon* for 1960, pp. 150 f.
⁴ Buschor, *AM*, lii. 1 ff; cf. *PGP*, p. 284.
⁵ *Asine*, pp. 74 ff., 298 ff., 308 ff.
⁶ Op. cit. pp. 308, and 307, Fig. 211; cf. Alexiou, *KX* 1958, p. 216, n. 127.

LH. III C was represented. There seems no reasonable doubt that the memory of the area as being sacred survived the fall of the Mycenaean civilization.[1]

One of the two Attic sites is not a sanctuary in the sense of an edifice; it is the Cave of Pan, situated above the Marathon plain. The use of the cave goes back to Neolithic times, and the character of the finds strongly suggests the existence of a cult. The first period of use continued uninterruptedly until the Mycenaean age, and then there was a break until the early fifth century. During this second period there is no doubt that worship took place in the cave, but this is not yet entirely certain for the first phase, nor is it known whether this first phase continued into LH. III C. There is no case here for supposing that there was any continuity of cult tradition.[2]

The second site is that of Eleusis, one of the great sanctuaries of later times. Here, below the level of the Peisistratid Telesterion, certain constructions were uncovered which indicate the possible presence of a Mycenaean sanctuary.[3] The earliest edifice was apsidal, and built in the Middle Helladic period. In LH. III, however, two impressive rectangular buildings were erected, the one being of *megaron* type. The whole was surrounded by a *peribolos*, separating it from other buildings. The finds consisted chiefly of sherds, covering most of LH. III, though nothing illustrated could with certainty be assigned to the LH. III C period. As well as the sherds, four terracotta 'goddess' figurines, two of which appear to be of the Ψ type, are illustrated.[4]

One would not, from the nature of the finds, inevitably conclude that this was a sanctuary, but the deliberate segregation of this building from others, and the placing of the Telesterion above it, suggest that it may have been one. With regard to the latter point, however, it must be borne in mind that no evidence came to light to show that this spot was used for any purpose at any time between LH. III and the sixth century. The gap is formidable.

It would obviously be a matter of some significance if one could prove that there was a Mycenaean shrine at Delphi. Evidence for such a shrine does exist, but it is not altogether easy to interpret. In the area of the main sanctuary, the temple of Apollo, a considerable quantity of Mycenaean sherds was found, all of which are said to be datable to LH. III B, and also fragments of a dozen figurines, six being 'goddesses' of Φ type, and the others bulls. It is not impossible that there was some small cult place here in Mycenaean times, though if this was so the area was not kept sacred, since even as late as the eighth century it was occupied by domestic dwellings only.[5]

The main evidence that a Mycenaean sanctuary was established at Delphi does not, however, come from the main sanctuary, but from underneath the foundations of the archaic sanctuary of Athena Pronaia; within one very small section a total of some one hundred and seventy-five 'goddess' figurines was amassed.[6] The circumstances of the discovery, however, indicate that the whole area was a disturbed one (for example, Geometric

---

[1] Papademetriou, *Pr.* 1948, pp. 90 ff.; 1949, pp. 91 ff.; 1950, pp. 194 ff. Cf. *Pr.* 1950, pp. 198 f., Figs. 5–7 for the figurines.

[2] Papademetriou, *Ergon* for 1958, pp. 15 ff.

[3] Mylonas, *AJA*, xl. 417 ff.; *Eleusis and the Eleusinian Mysteries*, pp. 33 ff.

[4] *AJA*, xl. 423, Fig. 10.

[5] Perdrizet, *FD*, v. 14 f., Lerat, *BCH*, lix. 329 ff.; *BCH*, lxxiv. 323; *BCH*, lxxxv. 357 ff.

[6] Demangel, *FD*, II, v. 13 ff. and 15, n. 2.

sherds were found below the Mycenaean), and there was no evidence of the existence of any building with which these figurines could have been associated. It has consequently been suggested that the material represents a group of offerings collected and buried at the time of the building of the archaic sanctuary.[1]

It must be admitted, then, that the evidence of Delphi leaves much to be desired; but two probable conclusions emerge. The one is that, from the great number of figurines which presumably came from somewhere on the site, there was some cult observed at Delphi in LH. III. The other is that the later inhabitants were aware of the religious significance of these animal and human figurines (or was it only a fortunate guess?). Continuous occupation on the site cannot be proved (Protogeometric sherds are rare), but it must have been a great temptation to later devotees to show that Apollo had been worshipped at Delphi from time immemorial.

Doubt has been expressed as to whether the edifice at Eleusis was in fact a temple; no such doubt seems possible in the case of the building still in process of excavation at Ayia Irini, on the island of Kea.[2] Much of the LH. III occupation has been lost through erosion, but one long and fairly narrow building was uncovered, containing 'considerable quantities of pottery in late Mycenaean styles (III C)'. The edifice had two rooms, one of which had benches along the side wall. The most significant finds were the fragments of large terracotta statues, identified as 'figures of female divinities or their attendants'. Various votive offerings were also recovered, and it seems clear, as the excavator states, that the building must have been a temple.

A further point of great significance is that after the collapse of this building 'a much smaller shrine was installed within the ruins'. No indication is given of the date of this shrine, nor is it yet known whether the small structures overlying this, with pottery ranging from Protogeometric to late Classical, were temples or shrines, but there must be a strong possibility that this provides evidence for the continuity of a cult of the Mycenaean period, and is thus of the greatest importance. It must warn us against undue dogmatism concerning other areas.

There remains the evidence provided by the island of Delos. In his recent work,[3] Gallet de Santerre has argued strongly in favour of continuity both of cult and settlement on the island, and much of the argument hinges on the acceptance of Delos as a religious centre in Mycenaean times. He shows that there was a prosperous LH. III settlement on this most unfertile island, and he attributes its prosperity to the existence of sanctuaries. Leaving aside the Hyperborean monuments, he identifies three buildings as cult places, the pre-Artemision Ac, temple $\varGamma$ and building H.[4] He explains that Mycenaean pottery, and nothing later, was associated with these buildings, as well as with the 'Palace', and that they were therefore built in Mycenaean times.

The qualifications of these three particular buildings to be considered sanctuaries are as follows. The pre-Artemision Ac was isolated from neighbouring houses, it was more massively and carefully built than they were, and it was larger than the ordinary house

---

[1] Lerat, *BCH*, lxxxi. 708 ff.
[2] Caskey, *AJA*, lxvi. 195; *Hesp.* xxxi. 278 ff.; *ILN*, 19 May 1962, pp. 801 ff.
[3] *Délos Primitive et Archaïque*.
[4] Op. cit. p. 109.

and had a finer threshold than was usual. These pointers were supplemented by the evidence of the precious objects of ivory and gold, of Mycenaean type, discovered in this area and which, it is claimed, could only have been deposited in a sanctuary (an argument which is perhaps not altogether cogent).

The exposition is said to be supported by the fact of the building of the archaic Artemision E immediately above Ac and on the same axis, an axis which differs from that of other contemporary archaic buildings, and also by the fact of the deposit under its foundations of the precious Mycenaean objects mentioned above, which thus establishes the continuity of this holy place. Gallet de Santerre stresses the excellent condition of these objects, and from this concludes that they had been carefully preserved, as being sacred. He asserts that the pre-Artemision Ac sanctuary only ceased to exist at the moment when the archaic Artemision E sanctuary took its place.[1] Continuous habitation is confirmed by the presence of Protogeometric sherds in this area.[2]

The case for building Γ being a sanctuary is based on its isolation from other buildings, its good construction (though not so good as that of the pre-Artemision Ac), and on the fact that it appears to have been surrounded by a *peribolos*. The objects found inside it have unfortunately disappeared in the course of time, but it is established that there were Mycenaean sherds.

The case for building H is less strong. No finds were recorded, but as Mycenaean pottery was associated with walls close to, and in the same level as, building H, the presumption is that this building as well is Mycenaean. The main argument for its being some sort of a shrine, however, seems to be the fact of its close proximity to the little Greek temple G: 'on comprendrait mal que le temple hellénique G lui eût directement succédé, s'il n'avait eu lui-même un caractère réligieux.'[3]

Weak though the argument may appear to be for building H, Gallet de Santerre is certain that he has traces of three Mycenaean sanctuaries on Delos. This, as he stresses, is most extraordinary, as in the whole of the rest of the Mycenaean and Minoan world there is only one sanctuary, that at Eleusis, which is in no way an appendage of a palace or a house, but stands as a shrine in its own right.[4]

The whole case is argued along two lines; first that these three buildings are sanctuaries, and second that there is continuity of religious practice into archaic times, especially with the pre-Artemision Ac and to a lesser degree with building H, continuity being confirmed in the former by the Protogeometric shreds. The continuity of settlement, as indeed the case for a prosperous settlement in Mycenaean times, is a subsidiary point and made dependent on the cult importance of Delos from Mycenaean times onwards.

The arguments are, taken as a whole, persuasive, and it is quite possible that Gallet de Santerre is right. I think, however, that there must remain some lingering doubt. For the existence of sanctuaries, the case for temple Γ may be the strongest—that for building H is certainly the weakest. But the critical case is that of the pre-Artemision Ac. Is it not just possible that this may have been simply a rich man's house, originally larger than we have evidence for, the precious objects in which had no special religious significance? May not

[1] Op. cit. p. 216.
[2] Op. cit. p. 213, n. 3.
[3] Op. cit. p. 93.
[4] Op. cit. pp. 96 ff. See, however, p. 43 above.

its owner, when he abandoned his property, have concealed these objects in the unrealized expectation that he would be able to retrieve them on his return, and may not this hoard, and the foundation of the house, have been discovered at a much later date by the builders of the archaic Artemision when they were digging for the foundations of their new temple, and may these builders not have believed that the preceding building was of a religious character, and in consequence built their own temple along the axis of the earlier house, and incorporated the hoard as their own foundation deposit? I do not put this forward as a probable alternative to Gallet de Santerre's reconstruction, but is it not a possible alternative? To my mind, the strongest argument for Delos' having had a religious significance in Mycenaean times is the simple fact of well-built edifices on the island coupled with objects of wealth. The island is so barren, and so relatively useless as affording a harbour, that the religious explanation does seem the only likely one.

As to continuity, this must partly depend on one's views on the persistence of a cult. There might still, naturally, have been continuity of settlement irrespective of religious survival. As things stand, continuity cannot be proved purely on the basis of pottery. There is evidence of LH. III C pottery, and one or two sherds might well belong to the later stages of LH. III C (p. 149); there are even a few Protogeometric sherds. But these are not plentiful enough, nor is the sequence clear enough, for continuity to be taken as assured.

I have discussed the Delian evidence at some length, as it provides the strongest case, except for the current excavations on Kea, for continuity of worship. The whole question of persistence of religious beliefs and cult is obviously of great importance in assessing the survival of Mycenaean elements into later times. Before suggesting any conclusions on the whole of the available evidence, it may be as well to stress the remarkable signs of reverence shown by the Greeks of Late Geometric and Early Orientalizing times (in other words at about the turn of the eighth to the seventh century) for the heroes of the Mycenaean civilization.[1] There seems little doubt that this was at least in part due to the popularity of, and the value attached to, the Homeric Epic. It may account for deposits of cult nature in Mycenaean tombs. May it not also account for the later worship at the shrine of Apollo Maleatas, at Delphi, and perhaps at Eleusis?

If this suggestion is acceptable, then there is no longer any need to suppose that there was continuous worship at any of the above places which were holy to the Mycenaeans. On the other hand, it does presuppose that the Greeks of the end of the eighth century had a clear knowledge, not only of where the tombs of their long dead heroes were, but also of the location of their places of worship. It presumes continuity of memory, even if not continuity of worship. The Greeks of this time were aware of a past with which they now consciously linked themselves.

The survival of memories, and presumably fairly accurate memories sometimes, seems fairly certain. But can one, on the evidence, go further than this, and claim continuity of worship? It must be admitted that we know virtually nothing of the places of worship of the Greeks in Protogeometric and early Geometric times. Negative evidence is notoriously

---

[1] Cf. J. M. Cook in Γέρας Ἀντ. Κεραμοπούλλου, pp. 112 ff. with particular reference to tombs. Also Marinatos, *AE*, 1933, p. 99.

misleading; may we not accept the possibility of some continuous worship? Such a possibility cannot be dismissed. But on the positive evidence so far available, on sites that have been thoroughly investigated, it is quite clear that, except on Delos, and probably at Ayia Irini, there was religious activity until LH. III B or LH. III C, and then a complete cessation and a long interval before worship was resumed. This is not the same sort of thing as the transfer of a settlement or of a cemetery to some other locality, for so far as religion is concerned it is normally the place itself that is sacred. A cessation of worship, as evidenced at the Apollo Maleatas shrine, in the cave of Pan, at Eleusis and at Delphi (presuming all these to have been cult places) must signify some fundamental change in the whole fabric of society, and very probably the admixture of new racial elements altogether.

B. ARTEFACTS

1. *Introduction and the Material from Hoards*

As well as the vases and terracotta figurines, there are a great variety of other Mycenaean artefacts which have survived in recognizable condition. The value of these objects in filling out the general picture of Mycenaean civilization is great, but in matters of chronological or geographical comparison it is much less, and varies according to the class of object.

It is not always possible to assign objects to a precise group, but the following general categories may be distinguished. First, there is a wide group that includes all objects of personal use or decoration, either to do with the dress (which will itself have perished) or comprising the purely individual ornaments, such as rings. Household utensils form a second category, and a third includes all artefacts connected with warfare. Finally, the tools used by craftsmen and farmers constitute two further categories, groups where the line of demarcation is not always exact.

In the case of pottery, a distinction was made between settlement and tomb material. Here, the difference is rather that almost all our material comes from tombs, and very little from settlements, so far as concerns the first three categories mentioned. But the implements which make up the last two categories are scarcely ever found in tombs, and it is on these that we may concentrate for the moment. If the tombs are unproductive, what is the situation with regard to settlements? Generally speaking, settlements yield little but pottery—and mostly coarse ware at that—but there are exceptions. For example, the House of Shields and House of Sphinxes at Mycenae contained remarkable deposits of ivories of many types,[1] providing an exciting record of the high achievement of this branch of Mycenaean art in LH. III B, and warning us, from the miniature replicas of columns and capitals, that we have still a great deal to learn about the skill of the Mycenaean architect. These, however, are unique finds, and are of no help in the study of agricultural and technical tools.

For knowledge of such implements we have to rely on one particular feature of some settlements, the hoard. Even here, not all types of hoard are relevant. For example, the

[1] *BSA*, xlix. 235 ff.

so-called Treasure of Tiryns contained relatively few such artefacts, as its owner was concerned with things of greater value; and in any case the very wide chronological range covered by the different objects diminishes their importance for comparative purposes.[1]

The relevant hoards are those which were probably assembled by some bronze founder. In these, the criteria are that the objects are almost exclusively of bronze, that they are very miscellaneous in type, and that many of them are of no value except for melting down. Five of these hoards have been discovered in the Mycenaean sphere, all on the Mainland.[2] Three of the hoards were found at Mycenae, one on the Acropolis at Athens, and one at Anthedon on the north-eastern coast of Boeotia. The variety of objects is great, and some of them can only be described as scrap metal, but the important point is that each hoard contains some implement which was used by craftsmen or for agricultural purposes. They are not very prominent in Tsountas' main Mycenae hoard—seven 'sickle-shaped' knives which may in fact be sickles, and five tools which could be adzes.[3] The hoard recorded by Stubbings contained, as well as sickles and a possible adze, a hammer head and three chisels.[4] These, except for the sickles, were no doubt craftsmen's tools, but the hoards of Athens and Anthedon produced implements which, whether they be called hoes or ploughshares, were certainly used for digging the soil.[5] Besides these, all five hoards had one or more double axes, but their popularity in other contexts indicates that they had purposes additional to their utility.

As a whole, then, these hoards give information on Mycenaean workers in metal which cannot be got from other sources. Can one say to which period of Late Helladic they belong? Unfortunately, this is a very difficult matter. There appears to have been no evidence, whether of stratification or associated pottery, to help in dating Tsountas' main hoard, though the swords suggest a date after 1250 (see p. 68). At Anthedon, a fragment of a tripod rim suggests the possibility of an LH. III C date.[6] Two sherds were recorded with the Athens Acropolis hoard, and Furumark is inclined to assign these to his LH. III A 2 b phase, though he stresses that it is not certain that the hoard should be dated by the sherds.[7] Stubbings, finally, puts his Mycenae hoard as not earlier than LH. III B, from its situation in the Prehistoric Cemetery, and gives it as his opinion that the Anthedon hoard is approximately contemporaneous.[8]

It has been pointed out that the internal evidence of the swords in Tsountas' hoard make a date earlier than 1250 most unlikely, but apart from that there is no internal dating criterion, by comparison with any Mycenaean objects. However, it seems that these tools and implements can almost all be paralleled in Cyprus among deposits of bronzes, found

---

[1] Karo, *AM*, lv. 119 ff.; cf. Catling, *PPS*, 1956, p. 111.

[2] A collection of bronze objects found at Polis in Ithaca (Benton, *BSA*, xxxv. 72 f. and Fig. 20; cf. *PPS*, 1956, p. 118) may also have been a hoard.

[3] *AE*, 1891, p. 25. Tsountas also found a second and smaller hoard (loc. cit.) and of this it need only be noted that it contained double axes, sickles, wedge-shaped tools, and part of a sword. (See Mylonas, *AJA*, lxvi. 406 ff. for a further hoard found at Mycenae in 1959, dated to LH. III B–C; it contained knives, short swords and double axes.)

[4] *BSA*, xlix. 292 ff.; cf. *BSA*, xlviii. Pl. 2.

[5] Montelius, *La Grèce Préclassique*, pp. 153 f., Figs. 481 ff. (Athens); Rolfe, *AJA*, vi (1st series). 99 f., 104 ff. (Anthedon).

[6] *AJA*, vi. 105 and Pl. 15, No. 8. Cf. Benson, *GRBS*, iii. 7 ff. and Pl. 2, No. 1; rod tripods do not seem to precede the twelfth century. I am indebted to Dr. Catling for pointing out to me the significance of this object from Anthedon.

[7] Montelius, op. cit. Figs. 500 and 501; cf. *Chronology*, p. 95, n. 1.

[8] *BSA*, xlix. 296.

principally at Enkomi, and dated to the twelfth century.¹ Furthermore, it may be that by a strange chance we have actual evidence of the transport of such objects from Cyprus to the Aegean, in the contents of the ship wrecked off Cape Gelidonya.² The considerable number of copper ingots that the ship was carrying indicate that she had taken on her cargo in Cyprus; it is also pointed out that 'out of 302 recognizable pieces of bronze, 232 have close parallels in Cypriot hoards'.³ The destination cannot be proved, as the ship may have been blown a long way off her course by the storm, but the location of the wreck agrees with an Aegean destination better than with any other; it is also possibly significant that some of the closest parallels to the tools found in the ship 'come from the Acropolis hoard in Athens'.⁴ Nor is it unreasonable to suppose that ingots were being despatched to the Aegean—several examples of them are known, including some from Stubbings's Mycenae hoard.⁵

The provisional date for the last journey of this ship is given as c. 1200, this being based on the pottery.⁶ Are we justified in drawing any conclusion from this date, or from the parallels in the tools, or from the Cypriot origin and probable Aegean destination, with respect to the Mycenaean hoards or to the situation in the Aegean? Connexion between the Aegean area and Cyprus does seem clear enough, and the fact that the Mycenaeans drew on the Cypriot copper mines; but this was known before the wreck was discovered. Does the similarity between the Mycenaean and the Cypriot tools lead to the inference that these tools were made in Cyprus and exported to the Aegean? This does not follow. It may be pointed out that there are no pre-twelfth-century hoards in Cyprus, and so no earlier evidence of such tools. Also, it is clear from the despatch of ingots to the Mycenaean world, from the few bronze vessels and many pottery vases imitating metal originals in the Aegean, and from the findings of the Linear B tablets, that the Mycenaeans were extremely expert metalworkers in bronze. It is more likely that, during the twelfth century, Mycenaean metal techniques were introduced to Cyprus. Finally, it would of course be helpful if one could use the Cypriot hoards to date the Mycenaean ones, on the grounds of similarity in the typology of the implements. This, however, cannot safely be done; there is nothing to show that these tools may not have retained their particular shape for some considerable time.⁷

The outcome of this discussion on the evidence for craftsmen's and farmers' tools is rather negative for the purposes of this work. In Cyprus, there is plenty of material in the Late Cypriot III period (roughly contemporary with LH. III C), but nothing prior to that. In Crete, the few bronze tools from the Dictaean Cave are of uncertain date,⁸ but the sickles, awls, saws, chisels and adze from Karphi are either contemporary with LH. III C or slightly later.⁹ Within the Mycenaean sphere the evidence is more or less confined to

---

¹ Cf. Schaeffer, *E–A*, pp. 31, 38 ff., 66 f.
² Bass, *AJA*, lxv. 267 ff.
³ Op. cit. p. 275, n. 55 (quoting Catling).
⁴ Op. cit. p. 275 f.
⁵ Pigorini, *BPI*, 1904, pp. 91 ff.; *BSA*, xlix. 295 ff. (Stubbings's Mycenae hoard); Svoronos, *JIAN*, ix. 153 ff. (= Seltman, *Athens, its History and Coinage*, pp. 4 f.)
⁶ *AJA*, lxv. 275 (cf. 271). Pieces of rod tripods were, however, also found in this wreck (op. cit. p. 274 and Pl. 89, Fig. 32). See p. 48, n. 6 for a probable twelfth-century date.
⁷ I am inclined to place the Aegean hoards shortly before 1200 B.C., in view of the disastrous events on the Mainland of Greece at about that time, but this is only an opinion.
⁸ Boardman, *Cretan Collection*, pp. 51 f.
⁹ Pendlebury, *BSA*, xxxviii. 115 f., 120 f.

the five hoards of the central Mainland, and in no case can it be proved that it is later than LH. III B. Consequently, the picture in LH. III C is unknown to us, though it is a reasonable hypothesis that, wherever the Mycenaean civilization persisted, the same tools and implements continued in use for agricultural purposes, if not for craftsmen, until such time as bronze gave way to iron, a stage about which, for objects of this type, we are completely ignorant.

2. *Objects of Personal Use or Decoration (Pl. 20)*

These are numerous and diverse, and yet remain remarkably homogeneous in type and distribution throughout the Mycenaean world during the course of Late Helladic III. It is therefore unnecessary to enter into any lengthy discussion. There has in fact been no detailed study of these objects, though extremely useful accounts will be found in Blegen's record of the prehistoric cemetery of the Argive Heraeum, in Wace's *Chamber Tombs at Mycenae*, in the discussion on the finds of the Ialysos cemeteries, and in Higgins's valuable general work on jewellery.[1] A brief but illuminating analysis has also been made by Furumark on the typology of the buttons.[2]

Generally speaking, it would seem that the Mycenaeans, especially the women, showed a tendency towards gaudiness in dress ornaments and accessories such as is lacking in later centuries. These objects, as stated above, are usually found in tombs, and the following summary picture is principally built up around the material from the major cemeteries of LH. III.

Necklaces were very popular indeed, and the beads or pendants that went to make them up were of many shapes and of a wide variety of material. Gold was favoured by the more prosperous, and one might consequently have expected to find silver in reasonably common use, but this was a metal either unpopular in, or unfamiliar to, the Mycenaean world. Several kinds of semi-precious stones were used, including agate, carnelian, onyx, amethyst and rock crystal. Beads of faience, steatite and glass were relatively common. The less prosperous, who could not afford gold, used glass-paste pendants, these often being made from a mould bearing a stereotyped Mycenaean motive.

The dresses themselves were, as Miss Lorimer has shown, shaped and sewed, and evidently required button fastenings.[3] These buttons (earlier called spindle-whorls) are commonly found in tombs, and they permit of chronological (but not geographical) typological distinction. Rings were also numerous—they were usually, I think, for the finger, and only rarely for the hair and ear. They may be just plain circles or be in the form of a spiral, or may have an oval bezel at right angles to the ring. The metal used is gold or bronze, rarely silver, exceptionally iron.[4]

Other objects which were rather less common, but still characteristically Mycenaean, include bronze bracelets and mirrors, and ivory combs. There were rather more pins than has been supposed; these are usually of bone, and short, and it may be doubted whether

---

[1] *Prosymna*, pp. 264 ff.; *C.T.* pp. 187 ff, *Ann.* vi–vii. 246 f.; *Greek and Roman Jewellery*, pp. 68 ff. See also Haevernick, *JRGZM*, vii. 36 ff.

[2] *Chronology*, pp. 89 ff.

[3] *Monuments*, pp. 358 ff.

[4] Op. cit. pp. 111 f.

they could have been used, as were the long bronze pins which will be discussed below, for fastening the dress.

These are the principal types of Mycenaean objects classifiable as ornaments or dress accessories. Except in the case of the buttons, little or no typological development is to be discerned, and there is no difference in type or distribution from one district to another of the Mycenaean world.[1] Furthermore, just the same types are found in LH. III C tombs as earlier, and this continuity, wherever it is found, may be taken as one of the criteria of the survival of Mycenaean culture—and so of Mycenaeans—in that particular district.

The fact that there is little or no difference in typology between, say, LH. III C and LH. III B does not exclude differences of other kinds. Whereas in LH. III B there seems to have been a fairly even spread, both in quantity and quality, the impression given is that that evenness was lost in LH. III C. One area does show, in LH. III C, the same richness and quantity as before, and that is the central Aegean, bounded by Rhodes to the east, and Perati to the west; the variety and quality of the small finds at Ialysos match those, for example, of the Argive Heraeum cemetery, and preliminary reports indicate a similar situation both at Perati and in the chamber tombs of Naxos. In the Argolid, however, it seems that the finds are fewer, and the quality lower, so far as one may judge from the tombs of Asine and Mycenae, and from the reports on the LH. III C graves of Argos. The contents of the cemeteries of both Achaea and Kephallenia also indicate relative poverty. This might simply be due to provincial separatism, but how are we, in LH. III C, to define provincialism?

So far, we have dealt with ornaments and dress accessories. There are also, however, objects of personal use that should no doubt be included in this section. Such are, for example, the engraved gems, which are found widely in Crete and throughout the Mycenaean world. But their popularity precedes the LH. III C period, and by the twelfth century there are scarcely any to be found, even in Crete, except for a few which can be classed as heirlooms.

If engraved gems are included, then surely important objects such as the cylinder seals from the East Mediterranean and the scarabs and other curiosities from Egypt have the same claim. They are better, however, placed in a class by themselves, with a different kind of importance from that of the other objects. They are in fact no more than curios and souvenirs, unless indeed their fortunate owners ascribed some mysterious or magical powers to them. As souvenirs they can give only a *terminus post quem*; this point emerges elsewhere, with regard to the scarabs (pp. 239 f.), and it is also clear for the cylinder seals, as is evident from the seal found in the Cape Gelidonya wreck, its date of manufacture being apparently not less than four hundred years before the time at which the ship sailed.[2] So these objects are in a sense chronologically valueless. On the other hand, their presence in a tomb indicates contact direct or indirect with countries in the eastern Mediterranean. Such a conclusion would obviously be of no particular value during the LH. III A and LH. III B periods, since contact with the Levant is already well-established during the centuries concerned. But it is of interest when such objects are found in LH. III C tombs, for at this time normal communication between the Aegean and the East Mediterranean seems to have been

---

[1] This applies also to Crete.　　　　　　[2] *AJA*, lxv. 274 and Pl. 90, Fig. 36.

somewhat precarious. Yet there were scarabs in two of the tombs at Ialysos,[1] and the Perati cemetery has already yielded two cartouches, several scarabs and a fine cylinder seal, as well as three Egyptian faience figurines, the duck-headed knife, and one or two other objects—a remarkable collection (see p. 116). It cannot of course be known just how these objects found their way to Rhodes and Attica in the twelfth century (they cannot all have been heirlooms, surely) but one must suppose it was either as a result of a personal visit to the East Mediterranean, or else they came in the course of trade—and indeed, it is clear from other evidence that some connexion was maintained between the Aegean and Cyprus at this time.

Just as there is connexion between the Aegean and the East Mediterranean in LH. III C, so there are links between Kephallenia and regions to the north, as exemplified by the continued import of amber and by the appearance of other objects (see pp. 104, 107). It is, however, a measure of the loss of cohesion in LH. III C that Kephallenia seems to have been the only area to have retained contacts with the north, and that neither in this island nor in Achaea is there much evidence of connexion even with the Aegean after the early stages of LH. III C.

Summarizing the situation in LH. III C as opposed to that in LH. III B, with regard to the objects of this category, we find the most important feature is the great similarity in the artefacts of local manufacture, the difference being on the whole confined to the relative poverty visible in certain areas, especially the Argolid and the districts where an increase of population is attested at the beginning of LH. III C. So far as concerns imported objects, the salient points are the exclusiveness of Kephallenia in retaining its northern contacts, and the surprisingly abundant evidence, in the Aegean area, of links with the countries of the Levant.

The end of LH. III C is marked by fundamental changes. No more objects of Syrian or Egyptian origin are to be found for quite a long time, even though links are known to have been maintained with Cyprus (pp. 200 f.). But that is of relatively minor importance beside the disappearance of nearly all the characteristic Mycenaean objects; this, taken in conjunction with the disuse of the chamber tomb, surely indicates a strong cultural break.[2]

The pottery of the succeeding period has, as will be seen (pp. 260 ff.), its origin in the latest Mycenaean pottery. Can the same be said of the objects of personal use or decoration that become the fashion? There are three types of object which characterize the immediately post-Mycenaean period; the ring, the fibula and long bronze pin. Plain rings are not susceptible of great change, and most of the post-Mycenaean examples are of this kind, but the dot rosette technique on the bezel of two rings from the Kerameikos is new,[3] and the rings 'terminating in a pair of spiral discs' from five of the Kerameikos tombs are of a Balkan type.[4]

---

[1] *Ann.* xiii–xiv. 261, Fig. 6 (tomb 61); 289, Figs. 32 and 33 (tomb 71).

[2] The break is not so sharp in Crete, where other evidence confirms greater continuity than elsewhere in the Aegean (pp. 193 f.).

[3] *Ker.* I, p. 86, Fig. 5; cf. also *Cretan Collection*, p. 37.

[4] Childe, *PPS*, 1948, p. 185 and Pl. 19 (= *Ker.* I, p. 85, Fig. 4).

As opposed to the rings, the fibulae and pins are dress attachments. The long bronze pins were not entirely unknown to the Mycenaeans, as they have been found in the very latest LH. III C chamber tombs of Argos (see below and p. 81), but on the whole they may be considered rather as an innovation of the succeeding period. On the other hand, fibulae had been sporadically used in the Mycenaean world throughout the LH. III C period, and possibly even earlier. Have we here a case of a characteristically Mycenaean object continuing in favour after LH. III C? A suggested answer to this will appear in the discussion on fibulae (pp. 56 ff.).

3. *Pins*

When Jacobsthal wrote his *Greek Pins*, in 1956, he gave as his earliest examples the pins from the sub-Mycenaean cemeteries of Salamis and the Kerameikos, and the pin from Mouliana tomb A. He concluded: 'These pins are bronze, shank and globe cast in one. The shank, above the globe, runs on, bearing engraved rings and ends with a projection "which is sometimes flat, sometimes semiglobular, sometimes shaped like a rivet-head" (Kraiker, *Ker.* I, 82)'.[1]

There is no doubt that the Athenian pins (Pl. 24*b*) are all of the same type, but perhaps the one from Mouliana is not. Evidence is now available that a second type was current at about this time, represented by three examples from Gypsades tomb VII (Pl. 24*c*) and by two examples from LH. III C tombs at Argos; and Miss Sandars, who has published an account of the Gypsades pins, considers that the Mouliana pin is related to them.[2] The characteristics of this second type are that they have 'an elongated globe-like swelling' (as opposed to the distinctive globe of the Athenian pins) 'in the upper part of the shank with zones of simple moulding above and below it', and a tapered-off moulded head with no enlargement.[3] A feature of both types of pin is the considerable length of some, between thirty and forty centimetres.[4]

All these pins are more or less contemporary, whether from Athens, Crete or Argos. Before the implications of the date are discussed, it may be pointed out that further pins may be added to the company. There are the long slender pins of Karphi in Crete which have the same elongated swelling as those of Gypsades but lack the shank moulding.[5] Not far from Gypsades, in a burial closely contemporary with that of tomb VII, two long pins were found, one on each side of the shoulder of the female interment, and one had an ivory head and so must be of a different type from those of Gypsades.[6]

There are also three sites where pins of uncertain shape are reported to have been found. In Crete, a bronze pin was found associated with the cremation in the tholos tomb at Photoula, in the Praesos district.[7] It is not described, but the tomb is dated to the beginning of LM. III C, which would be extremely early for a pin of the kind under

---

[1] *Greek Pins*, pp. 1 f.
[2] Sandars, *BSA*, liii–liv. 236 f. As at least four pins have been reported from the cemetery at Argos (*BCH*, lxxix. 312—tomb XIV; *BCH*, lxxx. 365—two from tomb XXIX; *BCH*, lxxxiii. 771—tomb XXXIII), it is possible that more than one type of pin is represented.
[3] *BSA*, liii–liv. 236.
[4] The Mouliana pin is the shortest (*c*. 0.10 metres) but part of it may be missing (cf. *BSA*, cit. p. 236).
[5] *BSA*, xxxviii, Pl. 28.
[6] *Archaeological Reports for 1959–1960*, p. 25.
[7] *Ergon* for 1960, p. 212; *BCH*, lxxxv. 864 ff.

discussion. No description, either, is given of the bronze pins found in the chamber tomb or tombs of Kamini on Naxos, which are probably datable to the concluding stages of LH. III C.[1] Finally, it is worth while mentioning the object found in 1960 at Perati, a globe of glass paste pierced with a fragment of iron. The excavator has suggested that this may be part of a pin, and if he is right then it may be put alongside an iron pin with an ivory head from Kerameikos sub-Mycenaean tomb 113.[2]

The total number of these pins is between thirty and forty, though it must be stressed that about half of them were found in Athens. They are, as has been said, roughly contemporary, and the important point is that though they belong to the time just before the final disappearance of the Mycenaean civilization, they are apparently not Mycenaean objects; their complete absence from the LH. III C cemeteries of Achaea, Kephallenia, Ialysos, Asine, Mycenae and even Perati (with the one possible exception noted above) seems to prove this.

But if they were not Mycenaean, what was their origin? One is tempted to suggest that they were introduced from some region to the north of Greece, as may have been the case with the fibula, and indeed Jacobsthal states that his sub-Mycenaean pins 'are related to pins from Proto-Villanovan South Italy and from Illyria of the Later Urnfield period, and are more or less contemporary with them'.[3] The relationship may be there, but the date of the Italian and Illyrian parallels does seem rather late, especially as some of these 'Greek' pins may even precede 1100. Miss Sandars suggests two alternatives for the origin of the Gypsades pins.[4] They may be 'a bronze version of the small ubiquitous pins of bone and ivory'—in which case they could be a Mycenaean or Minoan development, and one might cite the factor of change of climate as the occasioning cause. Or else they were adopted from outside the Aegean, rather from Asia than from Europe. The question therefore remains unanswered, though my own preference is for an origin from the north of Greece—even at Argos, where these pins are found in chamber tombs, there are objects which were of northern origin, as for example the votive wheel.[5]

4. *Fibulae*

The fibulae found in late Mycenaean contexts may be divided into two main types, the violin-bow and the arched fibulae. Of these, the violin-bow fibula had almost disappeared by the beginning of the Protogeometric period, while the arched fibula continued in use. The evidence taken as a whole makes it reasonably certain that the appearance of the arched fibula succeeded that of the violin-bow type.

The fullest and best account of fibulae in Greece is still that of Blinkenberg,[6] and the Italian fibulae have now been analysed by Sundwall.[7] The most recent typological

---

[1] *Ergon* for 1960, p. 191.

[2] Iakovidis, *Ergon* for 1960, p. 21, Fig. 28, d (Perati); Smithson, *Hesp.* xxx. 174 ff. (Kerameikos).

[3] *Greek Pins*, p. 181; reference is made to von Merhart, *BJ*, cxlvii. 40; 41, n. 1; 74; 80. Cf. Kraiker, *Ker.* I, p. 82, who also suggests a northern origin, at the time of transition from the Aunjetitz to the Lausitz culture.

[4] *BSA*, liii–liv. 237.

[5] *BCH*, lxxx. 361 (tomb XXII). It may be noted that two pins of the Gypsades type, found with Protogeometric pottery in a north Peloponnesian tomb (cf. p. 265), were also associated with objects of apparently northern origin.

[6] *Fibules grecques et orientales*.

[7] *Die älteren italischen Fibeln*.

discussion of these earliest fibulae is, however, that of Furumark,[1] and one point in his analysis must be dealt with immediately. He fully agrees with Blinkenberg that the violin-bow fibula is the earlier of the two typologically, but in the list given by him the earliest datable fibula is of the arched type. He realizes the difficulty here, but explains it away on the ground that a number of the earliest violin-bow fibulae are not datable, and so may well precede the arched fibula attributed to LH. III B. He claims that there is some confirmation of this from Italian and Central European parallels.

The arched fibula in question is in fact a gold object from chamber tomb 2 at Dendra.[2] It is 0·015 metres in length 'with one side and one end turned inward'. It is indeed described by the excavator as being the bow of an arched fibula, but neither the description nor the illustration leads to the conviction that this fragment was part of such a fibula. I shall disregard it, and assume that the latter half of LH. III C is the actual period when the arched fibula makes its début.

Reverting to the violin-bow fibula, it will be noted that there is one main typological development; the fibulae with simple bow of straight or twisted wire, with a catch-plate for the smaller fibulae and a spiral catch for the larger ones, precede those where the bow is leaf-shaped (often with incised decoration) or has two knobs, both strengthening features. This development, it must be stressed, does not necessarily imply any chronological differentiation.

The simpler types of violin-bow fibula are listed by Blinkenberg under his categories I, 1-4. Eleven of them are from Greece or the Aegean, eight from Mycenae, one from Korakou, one from Sparta and one from the Dictaean cave. To these may be added another from the Dictaean cave, one from Karphi, and perhaps one from Aetos in Ithaca (though it has a very large catch-plate compared with those of the others).[3] The dating of these fibulae is not satisfactory. The one from Korakou must presumably be either LH. III B or LH. III C—it cannot be later. The Karphi fibula must be sub-Minoan, the specimen from Aetos is not likely to be earlier than the latter part of LH. III C, and the fibula from the Orthia temple must surely be later than Mycenaean. No date can be assigned to the two examples from the Dictaean cave. Nor, most unfortunately, can any of the specimens from Mycenae be dated, even though five of them were found in tombs; this is all the more deplorable as they include some of the finest specimens known. They will not be later than LH. III C, and could well belong to LH. III B. Whatever their date, the quantity and quality of violin-bow fibulae, both of simple and advanced type, found at Mycenae are noteworthy—and there were no arched fibulae.

Three times as many of the advanced types of violin-bow fibula have been found as of the simpler types, and their distribution is far wider. Blinkenberg cites examples from Mycenae, Tiryns, Kephallenia, possibly Thermon in Aetolia, Delphi, Thebes, Therapnai in Laconia, Vrokastro, the Dictaean cave, and Enkomi in Cyprus. Since the time that his book was published further fibulae have become known from the Ionian islands (especially Kephallenia)[4] and the Dictaean cave,[5] and new find-spots have been added as follows:

[1] *Chronology*, pp. 91 ff.
[2] Persson, *Royal Tombs*, p. 102, No. 13, and Pl. 33, 6. This tomb is firmly dated to LH. III B.
[3] *Cretan Collection*, p. 37, No. 157 (Dictaean Cave); *BSA*, xxxviii. Pl. 29, 2 (Karphi); *BSA*, xlviii. 357, Fig. 36 (Aetos).
[4] Taylour, *MPI*, p. 186, n. 4.
[5] *Cretan Collection*, p. 37, Nos. 158–60.

Macedonia.	Vardino. Heurtley, *P.M.* pp. 101 and 231, Fig. 104, aa. Probably LH. III C.
Thessaly.	Iolkos. Theocharis, *Ergon* for 1960, p. 59. Protogeometric.
Attica.	Kerameikos. Two. *Ker.* I, Pl. 28. Sub-Mycenaean tomb 108 (Pl. 21).
	Perati. Two, unpublished, from chamber tomb 65. LH. III C.
Corinthia.	Derveni. Verdhelis, *AE*, 1956, suppl., p. 12. LH. III C?
Crete.	Mallia. *Maisons* II, Pls. 51 and 72. LM. III B-C.
	Karphi. Three. *BSA*, xxxviii. 114. Sub-Minoan.
	Moulina-Phaestos. Levi, *Ann.* xix-xx (N.S.), 359 and 357, Fig. 215. Protogeometric.
	Gortyn. Levi, *Ann.* xvii-xviii (N.S.), 215 and 238, Fig. 33. Sub-Minoan.

No doubt others could be added, but this list, together with Blinkenberg's, will suffice to show the extremely wide distribution, especially on the Mainland and in Crete.

The dates are more precisely known than for the simple types of violin-bow fibula. There are still a number to which no date can be assigned, such as those from the Dictaean cave and from Mycenae. Most of them, however, are fairly firmly anchored in the LH. III C period or its equivalent, with rare survivals into the Protogeometric period in Crete and Thessaly. Also, two of these fibulae bring the series up to the borders of LH. III B, if not entirely within it. Tomb 74 at Enkomi might be contemporary with the end of LH. III B, though it must be borne in mind that the tomb produced, as well as the fibula, a pin of iron.[1] The context of Metaxata (Kephallenia) tomb B is almost exclusively LH. III C, but it is a fact that the vases with which the violin-bow fibula were associated are LH. III B in character, and one would probably not be far wrong in assigning this piece to the time of transition from LH. III B to LH. III C.[2]

It may be inferred from this that the more advanced types of violin-bow fibula first appeared in the Mycenaean world not later than the end of LH. III B (and consequently the less advanced fibulae should be contemporary with or precede these), and that they were fashionable during LH. III C. Not that the Mycenaeans ever accepted fibulae as a characteristic dress accessory; this is a non-Mycenaean feature.

Before discussing the arched fibula, it will be best to consider briefly the use and origin of the violin-bow fibula. Miss Lorimer has suggested that these objects were used to fasten shawls, or if not shawls, at any rate a fairly loose and thick dress material, as opposed to the shaped and sewn dresses normally used by Mycenaean women.[3] Thus the fibula (and the long bronze pin) may well involve a change in dress fashion, and it has further been suggested that this change was made necessary by a worsening of climatic conditions; but it is reckoned that this worsening did not start much before 1100, by which time the fibula had already been known in the Mycenaean world for about a century.[4]

If then it is not considered likely that the fibula was invented in the Mycenaean world towards the end of LH. III B in order to fasten the thicker dress or shawl needed with the advent of colder weather, it may be suggested that this brooch was introduced from some area to the north of the Mycenaean world, where the climate would in any case be colder. No proof is forthcoming for this alternative suggestion, for although violin-bow fibulae are

---

[1] *Exc. in Cyprus*, pp. 16 and 53, Fig. 27, No. 1511.
[2] Marinatos, *AE*, 1933, pp. 92 and 93, Fig. 42.
[3] *Monuments*, p. 369.
[4] *MPI*, p. 79.

well known in Italy and in the Balkans, their context is never such as to show a clear chronological relationship with those found in Greece and the Aegean.[1] In spite of this, the following considerations may lead towards the conclusion that a northern origin is the more likely explanation. First, connexion between the Mycenaean world and Italy and Sicily is certain for the whole of LH. III,[2] from the amount of Mycenaean pottery found in the latter area—amounting, at least at Tarentum, to actual settlement. Second, the discovery in a LH. III B context at Mycenae of a winged-axe mould,[3] characteristic of the Terramara area and foreign to the Aegean, proves that objects from North Italy did reach the Mycenaean world at this time, travelling no doubt via sites such as Scoglio del Tonno. That this was not a solitary instance is confirmed by the metal objects that made their way to Kephallenia down the Adriatic (p. 104), in LH. III C times, and also to Crete from Italy and Central Europe in Late Minoan III.[4] There is consequently no good reason why fibulae could not have come originally from one of these areas. On a matter of detail, a fibula from one of the LH. III C tombs at Diakata in Kephallenia is worthy of note;[5] it has a multiple-loop bow, and there is only one other of its kind known in the Aegean area, from the Dictaean cave.[6] Bearing in mind that others of this type are found in Italy and the Balkans, it would seem certain that these fibulae at least came from the North.[7] Another point is that cut-and-thrust swords (Naue II) appeared in Greece and the Aegean at about the same time as the first fibulae, and it is thought that these swords came from the North to Greece rather than vice versa.[8] The same thing could have happened in the case of the fibulae. One must suppose either that fibulae originated in the Mycenaean area and spread thence northward, or that they originated in Italy or the Balkans and from there travelled to Greece. On the one hand, it would be more natural for fibulae to have developed in the North, inasmuch as they were attachments for dresses more suitable for cold climates; on the other hand, if they had spread from Mycenae, then one would have expected other types of Mycenaean objects as well to have been exported to North Italy and Central Europe, and such does not seem to have been the case. On the whole, then, an outside and northern origin for violin-bow fibulae seems the more likely, though that does not mean that most of the known examples may not have been made by Mycenaean craftsmen, or possibly by alien craftsmen working in Mycenaean territory. Although the fibula does not seem to be a truly Mycenaean object, it was used by Mycenaeans, and the finest specimens come from Mycenae itself.

If it is supposed that at least some of the violin-bow fibulae were made within Mycenaean territories, then it would seem a reasonable conclusion that the arched fibulae and their variations, which are an improvement on the violin-bow types, developed locally, and there would therefore be no need to seek an outside origin, even though arched fibulae were popular to the north of Greece.

---

[1] Sundwall, op. cit. in p. 54, n. 7; *Chronology*, pp. 92 f. For the chronological problems at Scoglio del Tonno see Hanfmann, *AJA*, xlv. 312 and Taylour, *MPI*, pp. 133 f.

[2] *MPI, passim*.

[3] Stubbings, *BSA*, xlix. 297 f.

[4] *Cretan Collection*, p. 18; Milojcic, *JRGZM*, ii. 153 ff.

[5] *AD*, v. 118, Fig. 33.

[6] *Cretan Collection*, p. 36, Fig. 16 A.

[7] Sundwall, op. cit. pp. 10 f., 50 f., 72 f. The two-piece fibula was introduced to Crete at a slightly later date; cf. *Cretan Collection*, p. 36.

[8] Cowen, *Ber. R.–G.K.* 1955, pp. 52 ff.; Catling, *Antiquity*, xxxv. 115 ff.

This may indeed be so, but the possibility of an outside origin cannot be altogether discarded, and the matter may be viewed in the light of the first appearance of the arched fibula. This type, with its variations—the D shape, the stilt, the swollen arch—is the characteristic fibula of the Protogeometric period. That is, however, not its first appearance, as it was already popular in the earlier sub-Mycenaean cemeteries of Salamis and the Kerameikos (Pl. 21); Blinkenberg lists six from Salamis,[1] while in Athens admittedly only fourteen of the hundred tombs contained examples, but these fourteen produced thirty-seven arched fibulae, of which seven were stilted.[2] This is the earliest context for the appearance of arched fibulae in bulk, but what evidence is there for earlier individual finds?

I have already stated that I do not consider the gold object from Dendra to be part of a fibula, so there is no need to go back into LH. III B. The evidence is then as follows:

Attica.   Perati. Two from tomb 19, *Pr.* 1954, p. 97, and tomb 36, *Pr.* 1955, p. 102. Two, unpublished, from tomb 74.[3] Late in LH. III C, in my opinion.

Argolid.   Argos. Chamber tomb XXIX. Fibula with twisted arch. *BCH*, lxxx. 365. End of LH. III C.

Thessaly.   Iolkos. *Ergon* for 1961, p. 58. Context not clear.

Crete.   Karphi. Nine. *BSA*, xxxviii. 114. Sub-Minoan.
Vrokastro. Three from tomb 4, one from tomb 5. *Vrokastro*, pp. 148, 151 and Fig. 87. Not earlier than sub-Minoan.
Phaestos. Two. From a tomb. *Boll. d'Arte*, 1955, p. 159. Sub-Minoan.
Gortyn. Two. From the settlement. *Ann.* xvii–xviii (N.S.), 216 f. and 238, Fig. 33. Not earlier than sub-Minoan.

Cyprus.   The earliest known to me are of the LC. III B period, and do not seem to be earlier than any of the Aegean or Mainland examples (cf. p. 204).

This is the sum of the evidence known to me. Certainly none of these arched fibulae is earlier than LH. III C. Where one can suggest a more precise date, the latter part of LH. III C is indicated, and none of the fibulae, whether on the Mainland or in Crete, need be earlier than this. It has already been argued that the Salamis and Kerameikos sub-Mycenaean cemeteries are partly if not wholly contemporary with the latter half of LH. III C (pp. 17 ff.) and consequently none of the above-mentioned arched fibulae can be proved to be earlier than those of western Attica. If, finally, the cist tomb cemeteries of this district belong to new arrivals, then it may remain possible that the arched fibula, as well as the violin-bow type, was introduced from the North.

5. *Household Utensils*

Apart from the pottery, only four classes of objects suggest themselves as falling under this category: metal vessels, tweezers, razors (or cleavers) and knives. Metal vessels may be

---

[1] Op. cit. II: 1, d–f; 2, a; 3, a; 19, f.

[2] *Ker.* I. The number is so large partly because of the ten in tomb 108 (Pl. 21).

[3] I am much indebted to Mr. Iakovidis for permission to mention these and for the information that the fibula from tomb 36 is of the arched type.

dismissed very briefly. There is no doubt that the Mycenaean metalworker was as expert in this as in other aspects of his work, at least during LH. III A and LH. III B. This we may conclude not only from the few vessels that have been found, but also from the fact that in many instances the potters were influenced by metal work, as is made clear in a valuable analysis by Stubbings.[1] What, however, was the position in LH. III C? Furumark says that, after a time when potters were not normally imitating metal prototypes, there was a revival of this practice in early LH. III C,[2] but one cannot infer anything from this as to the activities of the metalworkers themselves. The only vase known to me as being certainly attributable to LH. III C is the bronze beaker from Perati, and this is not exactly a work of art.[3] It would probably be reasonable to suggest that, consequent on the disasters of the Mainland at the end of LH. III B the conditions were not such as to encourage the craftsmen in metal, except perhaps in the Central and South Aegean, but such an argument must obviously be used with caution. So far, except possibly for tripod-lebetes and tripod stands (which probably came from Cyprus),[4] I know of no evidence of vessels of metal in the centuries immediately following the collapse of Mycenaean civilization.

Tweezers resist typological subdivision on the whole.[5] They are of uniform type, and appear (in no great quantity) throughout Greece and the Aegean (including Crete) in LH. III A and LH. III B. They continue into LH. III C; for example, two pairs have recently been found at Perati,[6] and another pair, of unusual size, in one of the latest chamber tombs at Argos.[7] Furthermore, tweezers of much the same type continued to be used in the Iron Age. This is natural enough: there was no need for the shape to change.

The razors or cleavers are divisible into three main types the earliest of which, leaf-shaped, is not found after LH. III A, and may in fact have been replaced by the other two varieties.[8] Both these latter have a single edge; the one has a very distinctive shape, 'a broad instrument, usually with a straight back, straight base, and only slightly curved cutting edge', and the other is more slender and more curved.[9] These two types were fairly well distributed in the Mycenaean area and in Crete in LH. III B and were certainly still in use in LH. III C.[10] They did not, however, survive the end of Mycenaean civilization —yet another item to be added to the list of losses.

The one-edged bronze knife,[11] as found in the Mycenaean world and in Crete, has been the subject of a recent article by Miss Sandars, who collected and classified all the known examples (over 170).[12] There are several types of knife, but the most common is that which has a 'straight back, slightly curved or parallel-edged blade, and a riveted haft, the rivets placed in a single line along it'.[13] This Class I is subdivided into *a* and *b* according to whether the haft has (*b*) or has not (*a*) flanges to it; the class accounts for about three-quarters of

---

[1] *BSA*, xlii. 60 ff.
[2] *Analysis*, pp. 86 f., 94.
[3] *Ergon* for 1960, p. 18, Fig. 20. I feel it better to disregard the bronze vessels found in Cypriot contexts, even though they may be of Mycenaean origin.
[4] Benson, *GRBS*, iii. 7 ff.
[5] *Cretan Collection*, p. 31, with references.
[6] *Ergon* for 1960, p. 20, Fig. 27; *Ergon* for 1961, p. 18, Fig. 16.
[7] *BCH*, lxxxiii. 771, Fig. 4 (tomb XXX).
[8] Sandars, *BSA*, liii–liv. 234 f.
[9] Op. cit. p. 235.
[10] e.g. Achaea: cf. Vermeule, *AJA*, lxiv. 16 and Pl. 5, Fig. 36.
[11] Two-edged knives are too rare to merit discussion.
[12] *PPS*, 1955, pp. 174 ff.; cf. also *BSA*, liii–liv. 232 ff.
[13] Op. cit. p. 175.

the knives listed. Class 2 is differentiated from I*b* in having no rivets; in Class 3 the flange continues round the top of the haft, whether the haft be riveted or unriveted. While in these classes the handle is of some perishable material, in Miss Sandars's Class 4 the handle itself is of metal. The distinctive mark of Class 5 is the considerable relative breadth of blade and haft. In Class 6, finally, there is no differentiation between haft and blade, and one subdivision of this class, found only in north-western Greece and Boeotia, has a curious small projection or snout at the back of the blade near the tip.

Although the total number of knives is impressive, valid conclusions are not easy to reach. For example, knives of Classes 3 and 5 have been found only in Crete and the Argolid, but as seventy per cent of all the knives come from these two areas it would be just as unsafe to infer that Classes 3 and 5 were confined to the Argolid and Crete as to infer that nearly three-quarters of the knives used found their way to these districts. In other words, the geographical picture is very uneven. No knife has been recorded from Thessaly; from the whole southern Peloponnese there are only the three from Malthi.

The only group where the find spots seem to lead to a reliable conclusion is Class 6*b*, where two came from Ithaca, and one each from Leucas, Elateia in Phocis, and Dodona. This sounds like a genuine area of distribution, and it is no accident, surely, that the only parallels to the distinctive projecting snout are north of this region.[1]

It would also be unsafe to venture any conclusion based on chronological evidence. Fewer knives are datable to LH. III C than either to LH. III A or to LH III B, but this need not reflect the true state of affairs. Nor is it possible to distinguish any chronological development within any particular class of knives.

Outside connexions are always an important matter, if they can be proved. Milojcic has suggested a link between the 'Urnenfeldermesser' from central Europe and certain Aegean knives, the line of influence going from north to south.[2] Counter-arguments have been put forward by Miss Sandars,[3] and at the very least it must be concluded that Milojcic's case has not been proved, so far as concerns the Mycenaean world. The Mycenaean world must not here be taken as including Crete, however, as there seems no doubt that northern knives did make their way to this island.[4] The knife found in the Dictaean Cave with a 'stop' at the end of the haft is a central European type, and is not paralleled elsewhere in the Aegean. It is claimed that the shapes of the blades of some knives, the instances of incised decoration, and the swallow-tail end to the haft, are also non-Aegean features. The last feature, the swallow-tail, is certainly of northern origin, as it is obviously connected with the same feature observable on the distinctive Peschiera daggers. As other bronze objects of northern origin are found in the Dictaean cave and elsewhere in Crete, it is reasonable to suppose that knives were also introduced, though it is important to realize that, judging from the context in which these objects were found, they were not the property of invaders, but came either through trade or by peaceful infiltration.[5] No exact information is available about the date of their arrival; it is presumably at some time within the Late Minoan III period, but such a conclusion is not very helpful.

---

[1] Op. cit. p. 184.
[2] *AA*, 1948–1950, pp. 12 ff.; cf. *JRGZM*, ii. 153 ff.
[3] *PPS*, 1955, pp. 183 ff.
[4] *JRGZM*, ii. 153 ff.; *Cretan Collection*, p. 18.
[5] *Cretan Collection*, p. 18.

Were Mycenaean knives, then, completely uninfluenced by any of outside origin? Generally, this may be so, though the curious 'north-western' group, mentioned above, does seem to have links with central Europe. There is, however, one small group of imported knives which, although it does not have any immediate effect on local products, is of the greatest interest. The knives are imports from the East Mediterranean, and though the shape may not exert any influence, the metal does. The shape of this class of knife is discussed by Miss Sandars in her account of the specimen (Pl. 24d) from Gypsades,[1] but the chief mark of distinction for my purpose is that these knives are all of iron, with the exception of bronze rivets on the haft. Furthermore, all the known examples of this class can be reasonably closely dated. The Gypsades knife comes from a sub-Minoan tomb; another was found in chamber tomb 5 at Vrokastro, a grave which was in use during the sub-Minoan period, though also later (cf. p. 186).[2] Part of a third was associated with one of the burials at Fortetsa, but in this case its date is not earlier than Late Protogeometric.[3] Two further knives have been found at Perati,[4] in tombs 28 and 38 (Pl. 24e), and are therefore in an LH. III C context, probably (though not certainly) late in the series, and so could be roughly contemporary with the first two Cretan knives. As they are of iron, an East Mediterranean origin is most likely, and it may be suggested that the knives came from or through Cyprus, where the metal was already becoming familiar (cf. p. 200). This suggestion is strengthened by the fact that the sixth of these knives was found by Dikaios in level I at Enkomi.[5] The group is completed by a knife found in a cremation burial at Hama in Syria; there is no reason why it should not be of the same date as the others, excepting, of course, the one from Fortetsa.[6]

It is not surprising that iron fairly soon became the normal metal used in manufacturing knives. It appears that, on the whole, the bronze Mycenaean shapes were continued into the Early Iron Age,[7] but not many knives are known within the Protogeometric period, and the evidence is not very satisfactory.[8]

6. *Armour and Weapons*

(A) ARMOUR

The most valuable general survey of defensive equipment, which includes all the material known up to 1949, is that by Miss Lorimer.[9] This survey, only in so far as it is concerned with the LH. III C period, and with the developments arising out of the fall of Mycenaean civilization, will form the basis of the following discussion, and account will also be taken of the discoveries made since 1949.

---

[1] *BSA*, liii–liv. 234.
[2] *Vrokastro*, p. 151 and Pl. 21, A.
[3] *Fortetsa*, p. 137, No. 1598.
[4] *Pr.* 1954, p. 98, Fig. 10 (tomb 28); *Pr.* 1955, p. 106, Pl. 31, *b* (tomb 38).
[5] I gratefully acknowledge permission from Dr. Dikaios to mention this knife, from an unpublished preliminary report.
[6] Riis, *Hama*, II, iii. 124 and 237: G. VIII 483 (= 5 E 347).
[7] *PPS*, 1955, p. 177.
[8] A selection is given in *PGP*, pp. 311 f.
[9] *Monuments*, pp. 132 ff.

(i) *LH. III C*

If one had to depend on the evidence of actual items of defensive equipment, or fragments of them, found in LH. III C settlements and tombs, one would be left with virtually a blank sheet. In fact, not a great deal more would emerge from the evidence of earlier periods. The Dendra panoply, dated LH. II B–III A I, provides us with knowledge of a boar's-tusk helmet with bronze cheek-pieces, a corslet with detachable collar, possibly a pair of greaves, and—with much uncertainty—the remains of a shield of wood and leather.[1] Apart from this, there is the LM. II helmet from Knossos,[2] the cheek-piece of a helmet from Ialysos, of uncertain date,[3] and various specimens of boar's-tusks which do not go below LH. III B.[4] Even the object from chamber tomb 8 at Dendra, at first identified as a helmet, is now considered more probably to be a neck attachment for a corslet.[5] If it is so, then it is welcome evidence for the continued use of metal corslets in LH. III, for there is no other trace of a corslet, nor any shields. Finally, there are the greaves from Kallithea in Achaea, on the borders of LH. III C, and probably contemporary with the greaves from British Museum tomb 15 and Swedish tomb 18 at Enkomi.[6]

This is the sum total of the recorded material, and the general conclusion must be that metal was only rarely used for defensive equipment; weapons are by no means uncommon, especially in tombs, and there would be no great advantage for the dead man to have his arms buried with him without his being able to defend himself. Whether metal was even more rare in LH. III C than in earlier periods one cannot decide from the material available—there is too little of it.

The second conclusion, arising from the first, is that most of the armour was made of some perishable material, leather or well-padded linen. For our knowledge of the various items and their shapes we are dependent on pictorial representations, whether on ivory, metal, stone, plaster or pottery. Such evidence is typologically important, but may be chronologically deceptive. The craftsman may represent some conventional, and perhaps obsolete, piece of equipment. So it is supposed to be in the case of the twelfth-century Cypriot ivories,[7] and so it may be in the renderings of the boar's-tusk helmets in the House of Shields at Mycenae—there is an ivory half-head, ivory inlays, and a sherd showing a curious petal-like arrangement of four such helmets.[8] Representations on vases are the most likely to be accurate chronologically (though not necessarily factually).

We are fortunate that there was a fashion for pictorial representation on vases at about the time of transition from LH. III B to LH. III C,[9] since we thus have additional information on the LH. III C period, for which the following comments may be made on the individual items of defensive equipment.

Throughout Late Helladic, the main shape of the helmet was conical,[10] but this general term embraced a considerable variety of subsidiary shapes. Except for the boar's-tusk

---

[1] *Archaeological Reports for 1960–1961*, pp. 9 f.
[2] Hood and de Jong, *BSA*, xlvii. 256 ff.
[3] *Monuments*, Pl. 13, 1: cf. p. 225, n. 3.
[4] Op. cit. pp. 212 ff.
[5] Persson, *New Tombs*, pp. 119 ff. and Pl. 1; cf. *Monuments*, pp. 225 f. *Archaeological Reports for 1960–1961*, p. 10.
[6] *BCH*, lxxviii. 125, Fig. 25; Catling, *Op. Ath.* ii. 21 ff.
[7] *Monuments*, pp. 151, 200; *PPS*, 1956, p. 123.
[8] *BSA*, xlix. 236 ff. and Pl. 35.
[9] See Benson's valuable survey in *AJA*, lxv. 337 ff.
[10] *Monuments*, p. 225; Hood, *BSA*, xlvii. 258.

helmet, for which there is no evidence so late as LH. III C, there is no such thing as a recognizable type of helmet used only at a certain period. Typological discussion is consequently eliminated for LH. III C. All that can be said is that there were several different sorts of helmet in use at the beginning of this period, and that most of them were probably made of perishable material.[1]

The corslets worn by the warriors on the Warrior Vase and stele are clearly of leather, or at least non-metallic,[2] and are different both from the scale corslets favoured in the Near East down to the tenth century, and from the ribbed corslets worn by the Philistine and Shardana warriors of the Land and Sea Raids, though they are closer to the latter than to the former.[3] They are also entirely different from the corslet of the Dendra panoply, a fact which would have no relevance for LH. III C if it were not that it has been suggested that the Dendra corslet resembles those depicted on Linear B tablets from Knossos and Pylos, the Pylos tablets being of course within measurable distance of LH. III C.[4] However, the ideogram was presumably conventional, and one cannot use this as evidence for the shape of corslets in the thirteenth century or later. The only justifiable conclusion that may be made is that non-metallic corslets were in use in the Argolid at the beginning of LH. III C. We can say nothing about the later stages of this period, nor is there any known trace of a metal corslet.[5]

As to shields, Miss Lorimer has demonstrated that the body shield, whether of the tower or the figure-of-eight type, went out of fashion during the first half of LH. III, giving way to a small, and generally round, shield.[6] The case is clear for the disappearance of the body shield, and it is also reasonable to suggest that the round shield was used in the late LH. III B and early LH. III C periods in the Argolid.[7] Since it was also used by the Philistines and Shardana,[8] this form of shield may have been generally popular at the beginning of the twelfth century. This shape, almost certainly non-metallic, may then be accepted for early LH. III C; but it must be borne in mind that there were other types of shield as well—for example, a sherd from Iolkos, probably LH. III C, shows the top of a shield that is far from round, and one of the two types of shield on the Warrior Vase is not altogether circular.[9]

Metal greaves must have been known and used in LH. III C, in view of the pair found at Kallithea, a tomb whose date is not much, if at all, earlier than this period. Whereas, however, the other items of defensive equipment do not involve any question of origin, from lack of evidence, this question does arise with the greaves, as well as that of the time when they were first used by the Mycenaeans. It has been suggested that their introduction was contemporary with that of the Naue II sword (see pp. 67 f., 70) as a defence against a new technique in attack,[10] and if these swords are of European origin, as seems very likely, then the greaves might also be of such origin, and indeed von Merhart

---

[1] *Monuments*, p. 230, Figs. 25 and 26, and Pl. 3. Note *Ergon* for 1960, p. 60, Fig. 73, *a*, from Iolkos.
[2] *Monuments*, pp. 200 ff. and Pls. 2, 3 and 12.
[3] Op. cit. p. 201.
[4] *Archaeological Reports for 1960–1961*, p. 10; cf. *Documents*, pp. 375 and 380.
[5] No inference can be made from the odd garment worn by the Iolkos archer (*Ergon* for 1960, p. 60, Fig. 73, *b*).
[6] *Monuments*, pp. 132 ff.
[7] Op. cit. p. 149, Fig. 9 (Tiryns); Pls. 2 and 3 (Mycenae).
[8] Op. cit. Pls. 4 and 5.
[9] *Ergon* for 1960, p. 60, Fig. 73, *a*; *Monuments*, Pl. 3.
[10] Catling, *Op. Ath.* ii. 35 f.

has argued at length that this is the case, even though he agrees that the Kallithea greaves are the earliest yet known.¹ On the other hand, if certain fragments connected with the Dendra panoply are correctly identified as greaves, then the case for an Aegean origin, unconnected with the Naue II swords, would be much strengthened.²

As well as the metal specimens, greaves of perishable material—as for the other items of armour—were also probably used, unless one supposes that all the leg coverings pictured on vases were of metal, which seems unlikely.³

No summary can be anything but brief, for there is so very little evidence. The information available belongs either to the very beginning of LH. III C or to the later stages of LH. III B, and from a restricted area only. The justifiable conclusions are minimal, that in the twelfth century the Mycenaeans had equipment with which to defend themselves, that with the possible exception of the greaves there is no reason to suppose that this equipment was radically different in LH. III C from what had previously been known, and that the use of metal for armour was almost certainly rare, and probably confined to the leaders in warfare.

(ii) *Later Developments*

Although it is so very far distant from the Mycenaean area, the late eighth-century suit of armour found in a tomb at Argos ⁴ stands out as a landmark in respect of post-Mycenaean developments, just as the Dendra panoply is a landmark in our knowledge of the armour of the Mycenaean age.

This Geometric armour consists of corslet and helmet, both of so advanced a design and technique that one must suppose the existence of earlier examples. On the other hand, there is no conclusive evidence either of shield or greaves; with regard to the latter, the excavator points out that one small piece of bronze might conceivably come from a greave,⁵ but that this is no more than a possibility. In fact, it must be less, in view of the perfect condition of helmet and corslet, and of the other finds. It must be considered very probable that both shield and greaves were normally made of perishable material, a conclusion which has its value for the preceding period.

Considering once more the individual items of equipment, both greaves and corslet may be briefly dismissed. There is no evidence relative to the use of greaves between LH. III C, when they are found at Kallithea, and the early seventh century when, apparently, they become part of the standard equipment of the hoplite phalanx.⁶ Also, apart from a rather doubtful exception mentioned by Miss Lorimer,⁷ we have no information about corslets until the appearance of the specimen mentioned above, though this piece must, as I said, have had predecessors.

There remain the helmet and the shield. With regard to the former, it is fortunately not necessary to wait until the eighth century before discovering the post-Mycenaean conception of a piece of armour. A recently excavated tomb at Tiryns, which may perhaps be

---

¹ *Ber. R.–G.K.* xxxvii–xxxviii. 91 ff.
² Catling, *Antiquity*, xxxv. 122.
³ *Monuments*, p. 251; Catling, op. cit. p. 36, n. 133.
⁴ Courbin, *BCH*, lxxxi. 340 ff.
⁵ Op. cit. p. 367.
⁶ *Monuments*, p. 252.
⁷ Op. cit. p. 202, n. 1.

dated still within the confines of LH. III C, but whose character is (in my opinion) non-Mycenaean, produced a fine bronze helmet (Pl. 24a), conical in shape, with embossed rosette decoration on the cheek-pieces as well as on the headpiece, and holes for the attachment of some inner covering of linen or other perishable material.[1] This is a helmet of very great interest, but it is unfortunately most difficult to assess its genealogy. In shape it could fit in to the Mycenaean series, but the embossing technique, found on one or two violin-bow fibulae and occasionally on shield-bosses, may suggest links with central Europe. It is an object which raises more problems than it solves.

It was established from vase-paintings that the early LH. III C shields of the Argolid were small and either circular or nearly so, but that these were not necessarily types current throughout the Mycenaean world—not, for example, in Thessaly. Subsequently, the evidence of pictorial representation is clear and helpful for the Geometric period, and has been thoroughly discussed by Miss Lorimer.[2] To bridge the gap, even partially, there is the horseman's curious basin-shield, slung on a telamon from his arm, on the Mouliana krater,[3] the date of which may on the latest evidence (cf. pp. 27, 177) be said to be contemporary with the end of LH. III C. It is, however, an isolated example, and the draughtsmanship of the painter does not inspire much confidence in the accuracy of the representation.

It is reasonable to presume that as a general rule the shield was made of perishable material, but an extremely interesting metal accessory to it appears to have been introduced at the time of the end of Mycenaean civilization. This is the shield-boss, and one such was found with the Tiryns helmet.[4] The known instances in the Aegean area were discussed by Miss Lorimer,[5] who made the point that, assuming that these objects were shield attachments, then the shields themselves must almost certainly have been round—though whether this is a survival of the LH. III C practice is not provable. A more comprehensive account has now been given by von Merhart.[6]

The shield-bosses now known in the Aegean and Cyprus are as follows:

Argolid. Tiryns. *AE*, 1956, suppl., p. 4; *BCH*, lxxxii. 707. Very late LH. III C-Protogeometric. In the same tomb as the helmet.

Sporades. Skyros. *AA*, 1936, pp. 229 f., Figs. 2 and 3. Cf. *Monuments*, Pl. VII, 1. Cist tomb. Probably Protogeometric (the iron spear-head).

Attica. Kerameikos. *Ker.* IV, pp. 27 ff., Pl. 37 (Pl. 23a, b).
Tomb 24. Sub-Mycenaean-Protogeometric.
Tomb 40. Protogeometric.
Tomb 43. Protogeometric.
Kynosarges. *BSA*, xii. 91 f., Fig. 12. Iron (the only example). Geometric.

Crete. Mouliana. *AE*, 1904, pp. 47 f., Fig. 11. Three. Tomb B. LM. III C = latter part of LH. III C. (Pl. 23c).
Vrokastro. *Vrokastro*, pp. 102 and 104, Fig. 58, H.

[1] Verdhelis, *AE*, 1956, suppl., p. 4; cf. *BCH*, lxxxii. 707 and 706, Fig. 26.
[2] *Monuments*, pp. 155 ff.
[3] *AE*, 1904, Pl. 3; cf. *Monuments*, p. 154, Fig. 10.
[4] See n. 1. As will be seen below, the identification of this type of object as a shield attachment is by no means certain. The original explanation that they were cymbals (Xanthoudidis, *AE*, 1904, 47 ff.) has not been disproved, though it seems unlikely.
[5] *Monuments*, p. 155.
[6] *JRGZM*, iii. 28 ff. The author comes to no definite conclusion as to the purpose of these objects.

Cyprus. Kavousi. Lorimer, *Monuments*, p. 155, n. 3. Not dated, apparently now disappeared.

Kaloriziki. *AJA*, lviii. 140 and Pl. 25. Three. Tomb 40. LC. III B = latter part of LH. III C.

The geographical range is fairly wide; the chronological range (except for the Kynosarges specimen) could be fairly narrow.

There is no doubt that this is not an object of Mycenaean type, and it is in my opinion not unlikely to have been a northern import. But does it appear in any specifically Mycenaean context? The Mouliana shield-bosses fall within the limits of LH. III C, but this is not a Mycenaean burial; even so, it is fairly certainly Minoan. It is very tempting to suggest that the Cypriot burial is that of an erstwhile Mycenaean prince, but the appearance of a non-Mycenaean object is not so surprising at this late date. For the rest, the context is certainly or probably not Mycenaean. The present evidence would suggest that the shield-boss was introduced into Crete before the end of the Mycenaean civilization, but at its end in the Mycenaean sphere itself. Its region of origin must still be considered problematic.

Then there is one further question one must ask—are these objects shield-bosses at all? Very similar, though rather smaller, objects have been found in quantity in the Vergina tumuli, and it has been established that these are not shield-bosses, but accessories for a woman's dress.[1] However, at least at Tiryns, if not at Mouliana, at Kaloriziki and on Skyros, the associations were with a male burial and with armour and weapons; therefore the objects cannot have had the same use as in Macedonia. On the whole, their identification as shield-bosses seems possible, and their similarity to the Macedonian objects, which are almost certainly of Danubian origin, tends to suggest that these, too, came from central Europe.

(B) WEAPONS

Just as with the armour, not much information can be obtained from weapons which might help towards a fuller understanding of the situation in LH. III C and thereafter. Of the kinds of weapon concerned, I intend to leave out of account the arrowheads, because it seems impossible to draw any useful conclusion from them.[2]

Spearheads can also be passed over very briefly, as the evidence is too slight for any typological classification such as would assist in chronological development. One group only needs further discussion, the spearheads called lanceolate, which are, it seems, of central European origin.[3] The following list includes, it is hoped, the known examples from the Mycenaean world and its fringes:

Epirus. Kalbaki. Dakaris, *AE*, 1956, p. 115, Fig. 1. LH. III B.

Gribiana (west of the Kalbaki tombs). Dakaris, *AE*, 1956, p. 131, Fig. 5. Undated.

---

[1] Andronikos, *Balkan Studies* ii, 93 f.
[2] Reference may be made to *Monuments*, pp. 277 f.; *C.T.*, pp. 59, n. 6, and 187; *Prosymna*, pp. 340 ff., 458 f.; *Asine*, p. 390; Valmin, *Malthi*, pp. 357 f.; *BSA*, xxxviii. 117; *PPS*, 1956, p. 111; *Cretan Collection*, pp. 29 ff.
[3] Cf. Childe, *PPS*, 1948, p. 185.

	Parga. Dakaris, *Ergon* for 1960, p. 110. 'Leaf-shaped' spearhead, Hallstatt A type. LH. III B.
Ithaca.	Polis. Benton, *BSA*, xxxv. 72. Undated.
Kephallenia.	Metaxata. Two. Marinatos, *AE*, 1933, p. 92, Fig. 41. LH. III C.
Achaea.	Patras district? Two possible instances. Cf. Vermeule, *AJA*, lxiv. 15 and Pl. 5, Fig. 36. Probably LH. III C.
Crete.	Mouliana. Xanthoudidis, *AE*, 1904, p. 48 and Fig. 11. LM. III C (Pl. 22c).
'Near Thebes.'	Ashmolean Museum. Cat. no. 1930.18 (Pl. 22d).

It will be seen that the distribution itself favours a northern origin, and indeed the earliest dated pieces are those from the area furthest to the north, barely on the fringe of the Mycenaean world. Whether this type of spearhead was introduced into Mycenaean territory just before, or during the course of, LH. III C cannot as yet be demonstrated, though its appearance in the tholos tomb of Parga suggests that the earlier date is the more likely. It will be noted that there is one exception to the distribution, the specimen (not a very clear one) from Mouliana. This, though surprising, must act as a warning that we have by no means the whole picture yet.

Swords and daggers are the most numerous of the weapons, the most susceptible to classification, and consequently the most productive of information. There have of course been general surveys of Bronze Age swords and daggers,[1] but here I am concerned only with these weapons as found in the Aegean area and the Eastern Mediterranean, according as to whether they are Minoan-Mycenaean in origin, or certainly or very probably of European origin. For the former, there are the earlier surveys of Evans and Montelius, the brief but valuable classification within LH. III by Furumark, and the recent and more detailed analysis of Dakaris.[2] The swords of European origin belong to the type known as Naue II, and are also called cut-and-thrust swords. The main recent general study on them is that of Cowen,[3] but the examples hitherto found specifically in the Mycenaean world, on its fringes and in the East Mediterranean, have been brought together, discussed and classified in two articles by Catling.[4] There are also a number of daggers of European origin which have been discovered in the Aegean, mainly in Crete. These are the Peschiera daggers.[5]

One further point may be noted before proceeding to a discussion, that it is not always easy to decide what should be called a sword, and what a dagger. In fact, any weapon longer than fifty centimetres should perhaps be called a sword, and anything under thirty centimetres a dagger. The weapons which come in between these two categories could be called short swords.[6] The distinction may not be of great importance typologically, but it is nevertheless worth making.

A start may be made with the swords or short swords of Naue II type (Pl. 22a1). These are, according to the evidence, the most commonly used swords in LH. III C,[7] and have a

---

[1] e.g. Naue, *Die Vorrömischer Schwerter*, and Peake, *The Bronze Age and the Celtic World*.

[2] *P.T.K.* pp. 105 ff; *La Grèce Préclassique*; *Chronology*, pp. 93 ff; *AE*, 1956, pp. 136 ff.

[3] *Ber. R.-G.K.* 1955, pp. 52 ff.

[4] *PPS*, 1956, pp. 102 ff.; *Antiquity*, xxxv. 115 ff.

[5] Peroni, *Badische Fundberichte*, 1956, pp. 69 ff; *Cretan Collection*, pp. 13 ff., with references.

[6] Or dirks, according to Catling, cf. *Antiquity*, xxxv. 121 f.

[7] Cf. *Antiquity*, xxxv. 117 ff. Most, though not all, in his list belong to this period.

sufficiently wide distribution to indicate that they were familiar to every part of the Mycenaean world, including Crete, and were also popular in Cyprus. Furthermore, it is this type which survives into the succeeding period, iron being substituted for bronze. Two questions naturally arise, particularly since this is almost certainly a European and not a Mycenaean type of sword: when were these swords first introduced to the Mycenaean world, and what is the situation in LH. III C concerning swords or daggers of Mycenaean or Minoan type?

It would naturally be impossible to give the exact date at which cut-and-thrust swords first appeared in Greece and the Aegean. Relatively numerous though they are, we can have a tiny fraction only of the total. Such evidence as there is, however, indicates an introduction not later than the end of LH. III B. That is to say, none of the swords which has a known date is within the LH. III B period, but the sword from Swedish tomb 18 at Enkomi probably belongs to the time of transition between LH. III B and LH. III C.[1] Taking into account the likelihood that we have not got the earliest specimen, and indeed that perhaps some of the undated swords are earlier, it may then be suggested that they were introduced towards the end of LH. III B.[2]

The problem of the time of introduction naturally involves the manner and route of introduction. These two subsidiary problems have been discussed by Catling, and I am inclined to agree on the suggested route 'overland south to the Adriatic, and thence by sea up the Gulf of Corinth';[3] if the evidence permits it, a route across from South Italy would also be possible, but a journey through the passes into Macedonia and thence south is, I believe, extremely unlikely. The further suggestion that they were brought by barbarian mercenaries rather than as objects of trade or introduced as a result of barbarian invasions is also likely to be correct, for although Catling underestimates the scope of barbarian invasions at this time, it is true that the swords of which we have knowledge were discovered in Mycenaean contexts. In fact, many of them were no doubt made in the Mycenaean area and used by Mycenaeans, since, as Catling says, these swords 'seem largely to have ousted Aegean types'.[4]

What swords and daggers of Mycenaean or Minoan type can be shown to have survived into LH. III C? The chief type in earlier Late Helladic was the cruciform sword or dagger.[5] As a sword, there is no certain example of it after LH. III A, but as a dagger it is still current in LH. III B[6]—to the Karpathos dagger may be added the one from Stubbings's Mycenaean hoard, which cannot be earlier than LH. III B.[7] If the Athens Acropolis hoard was deposited in LH. III C, then its dagger[8] may have to come down as well—but this hoard is very difficult to date. Apart from the cruciform weapon, there is a fairly popular class of short swords with rounded shoulders, defined by Catling as 'cast-hilted dirks', which seems to cover the whole LH. III period.[9] Furumark cites a specimen

---

[1] Catling, *Op. Ath.* ii. 26 ff. It might be argued that it was a little earlier.

[2] Note the importance of this for the date of Tsountas's main Mycenae hoard and for the Tiryns treasure. Cf. p. 48.

[3] *Antiquity*, xxxv. 121.

[4] loc. cit.

[5] *Chronology*, p. 94, type *a* 2.

[6] The specimen from Ialysos old tomb 4 could however belong to LH. III A; cf. op. cit. p. 95.

[7] *BSA*, xlviii. Pl. 2.

[8] Montelius, *La Grèce Préclassique*, Fig. 498.

[9] *Antiquity*, xxxv. 121: Furumark's types *b* 1 and *b* 3, which Catling thinks may be the same type of weapon, the shape of blade changing owing to constant use of the whetstone.

from Diakata in Kephallenia,[1] which must belong to the LH. III C period, and one came from the Mycenae Acropolis hoard.[2]

These are all either daggers or short swords, whereas the Naue II weapons are usually long swords—there are short swords among them, but they are mostly from Crete—and it is indeed hard to find any comparable contemporary swords of Aegean type. Catling mentions such swords, either of 'the rare type with cast-hilt and widening blade found in Crete and Cephallenia'[3] or of 'the almost equally rare cast-hilted weapons with cruciform, but down-turned handguards'.[4] These are indeed all in LH. III C (or LM. III C) contexts, but the latter class is not confined to this period, for there is a dagger of this shape from the Zapher Papoura cemetery which cannot, to judge from the date of the tombs with pottery in them, be later than LH. III B,[5] and there were two—a sword and a short sword—in the Mycenae Acropolis hoard.[6] Even so, these are both late forms of Aegean swords, and are attested in LH. III C alongside the Naue II weapons.

A mention may be made in passing of the Peschiera daggers which found their way to the Aegean. As was stated above, most of these were found in Crete. One was from Zapher Papoura tomb 86, and five have been discovered in the Dictaean Cave. Outside Crete, there is probably one from Phylakopi, and one from Naxos.[7] It must be presumed, I think, that these daggers came direct to Crete from Italy at a date which cannot be determined but was presumably at some time within LM. III (not later than LM. III B if the Dictaean Cave examples are contemporary with the one from the Zapher Papoura cemetery). Whether they also went directly from Italy to Melos and Naxos cannot be said, but it is reasonably certain that they never had the same vogue in the Aegean as the cut-and-thrust swords.

C. EXTERNAL INFLUENCES

The different artefacts have so far been discussed according to each individual type, but it may be instructive to bring together all types of object other than pottery that came into the Mycenaean world from outside it during or close to the LH. III C period. Only by looking at the whole can one hope to distinguish even the possibility of a pattern.

Some of the objects which were brought into the Aegean from other areas are not the concern of this section. Such are, for example, the winged-axe mould of Terramara type,[8] and the Levantine amphora,[9] both found at Mycenae in a LH. III B context. Nor am I concerned with the scarabs, cartouches and amulets of the LH. III C Perati cemetery (pp. 52, 116). These have their value, inasmuch as they establish contact, whether direct or indirect, with the countries of origin, but they had no influence on Mycenaean life, and

---

[1] *AD*, v. 118, Fig. 34.
[2] *PPS*, 1956, p. 110; *AE*, 1897, p. 110 and Pl. 8, No. 4.
[3] *Antiquity*, xxxv. 121. *AE*, 1904, pp. 29 f., Fig. 7 (Mouliana); *AE*, 1932, Pl. 16, left (Lakkithra). Pl. 22*a*2 shows the Mouliana sword.
[4] loc. cit. This is Furumark's type c 2 (*Chronology*, p. 94); one has recently been found at Perati (*Pr.* 1954, p. 96, Fig. 5), shown on Pl. 22*b*.
[5] *P.T.K.* p. 43 and Fig. 39, *a* and *b*. Tomb 14.
[6] Cf. *PPS*, 1956, p. 110.
[7] See p. 67, n. 5. *P.T.K.* p. 82, Fig. 90 (Zapher Papoura); *Cretan Collection*, Fig. 2, 56, and Fig. 3, *a–d* (Dictaean Cave); *BSA*, xvii, Pl. 14, 60 (Phylakopi); *Archaeologia*, lviii. 6, Fig. 7 (Naxos).
[8] *BSA*, xlix. 297 f.
[9] *BSA*, l. 179.

were not adopted or adapted for use by the Mycenaeans. Nor, finally, do I include amber, which found its way to the Aegean sporadically over a long period.

There seem to have been two main occasions when non-Mycenaean objects were introduced into the Mycenaean area; that of the transition from LH. III B to LH. III C, and the end of LH. III C.

For the earlier occasion, mention may first be made of the lanceolate spearhead (Pl. 22c, d), where the evidence strongly suggests that this type of object arrived through Epirus and was virtually confined to the north-western areas. Of much greater importance, however, was the introduction of the Naue II type of sword (Pl. 22a1), a symbol of the general unrest of the times, which made its appearance not later than the end of LH. III B. These swords came from the North, but it is unlikely that they were brought from Epirus, as swords and daggers of Mycenaean type were used in this district in LH. III B times. It has reasonably been suggested that they came down the Adriatic,[1] and were the possessions of mercenaries hired to fight for Mycenae. Access to Greece over the passes into Macedonia and thence south is also possible, but there is no evidence that this route was used.

A further route of access was by sea from South Italy, where the Mycenaeans had a settlement at Scoglio del Tonno, and although there is no indication that the swords took this route, it is likely that it was the channel of introduction for the next class of object, the violin-bow fibula (Pl. 21), which appeared on Mycenaean sites at much the same time as Naue II swords.

We have then three types of object, all of probable European origin, but each possibly entering the Mycenaean area by a different route. Mention may also be made of certain other objects of Italian or Sicilian origin—the two-piece fibulae, the multiple-loop fibulae, the Peschiera daggers and the knife with a stop-haft, most of which have been found in Crete and will have come direct from Italy or Sicily. The time of their introduction is, however, unknown, and they should perhaps be classed, like the winged-axe mould, as casual imports. Comparable objects om the frEast Mediterranean are not to be found, though it must be remembered that the Mycenaeans must have had to go to the Levant for their ivory, and to Cyprus for their copper.

The second main occasion for the arrival of external objects and customs was the end of LH. III C, in other words the time of final disintegration. One of the most important signs of outside influence does this time come from the Eastern Mediterranean, and that is iron. The knowledge how to work this metal was probably not introduced until the Protogeometric period,[2] but a number of imports are firmly located in LH. III C or sub-Minoan contexts. These include the iron knives with bronze rivets, from Perati (Pl. 24e), Gypsades (Pl. 24d) and Vrokastro, and the piece of iron enclosed in a glass-paste globe from Perati, mentioned above (p. 54). A bracelet from Ialysos [3] may be added to the list, and also a dagger from Kamini on Naxos.[4]

---

[1] e.g. the sword from Scutari, PPS, 1956, p. 117 and Pl. 9, D. Whether metal greaves were introduced at the same time as the swords is, as has been seen, a matter of doubt (pp. 63 f.).

[2] The iron pins from Kerameikos sub-Mycenaean tomb 113 (Hesp. xxx. 175 f.) are a possible exception.
[3] Ann. vi–vii. 127, No. 74 (tomb 17).
[4] Ergon for 1960, p. 191.

The list is a small one, but the objects all appear probably towards the end of LH. III C, and the knives and dagger are of particular interest as showing the more common use of iron in the East Mediterranean. So the Mycenaeans were just aware of the coming of the new metal, though it was their successors and not they themselves who were to enjoy the benefits.

In two of the tombs in which an iron object was found, Perati 38 and Ialysos 17, cremations were associated with the inhumations, and at Perati the knife apparently belonged to the cremated corpse.[1] One is tempted to seek a connexion here, but it does not seem possible to establish. It is true that the distribution of early cremations is concentrated in areas which look rather to the East—Perati, Kos and Rhodes (cf. pp. 115, 157), perhaps Assarlik in Caria,[2] and a number of Cretan sites (cf. pp. 187 ff.), most of which are in the eastern part of the island (Praesos, Mouliana, Vrokastro, Olous) as opposed to the central area (Liliana, Fortetsa tomb Π?)—but these cremations are not, I think, all of the same type, nor can it yet be proved that this custom was introduced to the Aegean from any outside region. Although it may be suggested that iron knives came from Cyprus, a similar origin for cremation is hardly possible, the only known instances of the custom in Cyprus being those of Kaloriziki tomb 40.[3] An alternative area of origin might be Syria, but this could not be accepted without strong corroborative evidence.[4] All that can be said is that if cremation was a practice introduced to the Aegean from outside, then the present known distribution would favour an eastern origin during the later phase of LH. III C.

The main features of possible northern origin appearing at this time are the cist tombs, the long bronze dress pins (Pl. 24b, c), the arched fibulae (Pl. 21) and the shield-bosses (Pl. 23). The degree of likelihood that they were introduced from the North varies, however, from case to case. It may, for example, be considered much more likely that the arched type of fibula developed within the Mycenaean area from the violin-bow type than that it was brought in as a new type from outside. On the other hand, the northern origin of cist tombs is, to my mind, reasonably certain. It is perhaps possible to attribute the appearance of this type of burial to local change of fashion, and to see in it the survival of an earlier type, but the evidence taken as a whole, including the fact of tombs of this type having been found north of Iannina (in other words, outside Mycenaean territory) in the LH. III B period, indicates strongly that a northern origin is to be preferred (cf. pp. 37 ff.).

It is equally likely that shield-bosses came from central Europe, though as far as I know there are no examples from that area which must antedate any found in Greece. The origin of the bronze pins, finally, must be considered to be open to doubt. From distribution and association a northern origin seems likely, but once again the northern parallels quoted by

---

[1] Tomb 5 at Vrokastro may provide another example, but it is not known whether the knife was associated with an inhumation or with a cremation.

[2] *JHS*, viii. 64 ff.; cf. *PGP*, pp. 218 f.

[3] *AJA*, lviii. 133 f.

[4] It is true that an iron knife with bronze rivets was found in a tomb of Period I of the cremation cemetery of Hama (cf. p. 61, n. 6) and that this period is dated within the twelfth and eleventh centuries (*Hama* II, iii. 202), but that is not sufficient to suggest that the custom of cremation came direct from Syria to the Aegean.

Jacobsthal do not appear to antedate the earliest of Greece and the Aegean, while Miss Sandars has tentatively suggested an eastern origin (p. 54).

In spite of these doubts, it must be borne in mind that there are undeniable instances of central European artefacts making their appearance in Greece during this period. There are the rings found in five tombs of the sub-Mycenaean cemetery of the Kerameikos,[1] and the votive wheel from a very late chamber tomb of Argos;[2] and if the embossing technique originated in central Europe, then one should include the objects on which this technique was used: the Tiryns helmet,[3] the Mouliana shield-bosses,[4] and two rings of sub-Mycenaean date from the Kerameikos.[5] It may also be remembered that both in the Argolid and in Athens the burials of this time provide evidence for an increased proportion of northern types of skull.[6]

All the objects or features mentioned above appear within a short space of time during or immediately following the final stages of LH. III C, and it is to be noted that they accompany or succeed the disappearance of many characteristically Mycenaean features, as will be evident from this chapter generally. It seems clearly indicated, taking this factor into consideration together with all the instances of new features of fairly certain or possible northern origin, that we have evidence of the gradual infiltration into Mycenaean lands, and settlement there, of intruders coming from the North. In this matter, the innovations of the end of LH. III C involve different conditions from those of the transition from LH. III B to LH. III C.

For the earlier period, three routes were suggested: from South Italy, down the Adriatic (both by sea), and overland through Epirus. For the end of LH. III C a passage through central Greece, the earlier stages being Epirus or West Thessaly, is the likeliest, though at a later stage, during the Protogeometric period, intruders may rather have come down from north-west Greece and across the Corinthian gulf into western Peloponnese, if one may base any sort of conclusion on the cist tombs of Achaea, Elis and Messenia (p. 39).

---

[1] *Ker.* I, p. 85 and Fig. 4.
[2] *BCH*, lxxx. 361.
[3] *BCH*, lxxxii. p. 706, Fig. 26.
[4] *AE*, 1904, pp. 47 ff., Fig. 11.
[5] *Ker.* I, p. 86 and Fig. 5.
[6] See p. 40, n. 1.

CHAPTER III

THE PELOPONNESE

1. *The Argolid and Corinthia*

(A) THE ARGOLID

ANY discussion of this area must start from the site of Mycenae,[1] the centre of the civilization to which it gives its name. Besides this, it is the site which has been the most extensively and frequently explored, though this very fact has made its evidence difficult to interpret. The first full-scale excavation was undertaken by Schliemann[2] in the years 1874 and 1876; the scope of his investigations covered the acropolis and a tholos tomb outside the citadel. There followed excavations by Tsountas,[3] from 1886 onwards, concerned both with tombs outside the citadel and with the citadel itself. As yet, the importance of stratification, and of pottery within such stratification, had not been fully realized, and the publications that ensued were not so helpful as they might have been.

By the time that Wace recommenced excavations, in 1920, a good advance both in knowledge and in method had been made, and it is possible to discuss the results in so far as they concern the period dealt with by this book. Wace's excavations continued until 1923, and were still confined, on the whole, to the acropolis and to the burial areas outside it.[4] The main fact of importance established was the destruction of the Granary by fire, with which building was associated a useful stratified area between it and the Lion Gate. Wace showed that the material from the Lion Gate stratification belonged entirely to Late Helladic III (the pottery had by now been to this extent divided, but further subdivision into A, B and C was as yet not used), that the destruction came towards the end of Mycenae's history as a capital, and that with it was associated a rather simplified kind of pottery which he christened the Granary Class, and showed to be at least in part contemporary with the Close Style—both of which are indeed characteristic products of LH. III C.

Wace's final assessment of this evidence, of the relative and absolute chronology provided, and of the relationship of this excavated area to the Lion Gate and the surrounding fortification, appear in his contribution to the volume dedicated to Professor Goldman.[5] He set the building of the Granary as posterior to the Lion Gate and to 'the adjoining parts of the Cyclopean wall'.[6] The Lion Gate deposit apparently started at a time when alterations took place to the Granary, and Wace put levels I to V in LH. III B, levels VI

---

[1] For a more detailed account of work undertaken up to 1955, cf. Mylonas, *Ancient Mycenae*, pp. 8 ff., with full references.

[2] *Mycenae*.

[3] *Pr.* 1886–9 except 1894 and 1898. *AE* 1887, 1888, 1891, 1896, 1897, 1902.

[4] *BSA*, xxv, *passim*; Chamber Tombs at Mycenae (*Archaeologia*, vol. lxxxii).

[5] *The Aegean and the Near East*, pp. 126 ff.

[6] Op. cit. p. 128.

to IX (the destruction level) in LH. III C, and called levels X and XI post- or sub-Mycenaean,[1] corresponding to part of Furumark's LH. III C 1 b and to his LH. III C 1 c. To this final period Wace also assigned [2] the latest groups in his tombs 502 and 515, the unenclosed burial in the Cyclopean terrace building, and tomb XXXIX of the Prehistoric Cemetery; on the other hand, he equated [3] sherds of Level I with finds outside Mycenae in the Houses of the Oil Merchant and Wine Merchant.

This leads on to a further development (leaving the story of the citadel for the moment), the discovery of a group of important houses outside the acropolis,[4] with evidence that they were destroyed while LH. III B was still current, long before the destruction of the Granary—in fact, the difference (for Wace) between levels I and IX of the Lion Gate deposit. This meant that, at least so far as the settlement was concerned, the only pottery to close the gap between the two destructions was that of the Lion Gate strata, and this had become irretrievably mixed during the war, so that one had only the brief published account as a record.

Since these discoveries, a modest amount of intervening evidence has been accumulating, first in connexion with the Poros Wall, where the sherds accompanying its destruction were assigned 'to the latter part of III B' and some to early LH. III C.[5] There was also the significant fragmentary bowl [6] found in a burnt deposit suggesting strongly the time of the destruction of the Palace itself. This piece is called LH. III C, but it is in any case nothing like so late as the Granary Class with which Wace wished to connect it, and should be classed as LH. III B rather than LH. III C. Finally, there is the deposit of pottery in the Prehistoric Cemetery,[7] which was said to belong mainly to the later part of LH. III B, though certain pieces cannot be far from LH. III C. It will be noticed that in two of the instances given there is evidence of a third destruction, coming between the two already mentioned and which, if its effects reached the Palace, must have been rather violent. Latest reports now confirm such a third destruction, as found in the investigation of the hitherto unexplored Citadel House. The excavators have assigned this to the end of LH. III B, before the emergence of LH. III C.[8]

Excavation has taken place in many other parts of Mycenae at differing times, but it is only necessary to mention here the important work of Mylonas [9] in the area round the Lion Gate, the results of which would mean that the Gate, the road to and through it, and Wace's level I of the Lion Gate stratification all belong to the same period, namely mid-LH. III B. This would presumably also imply a strengthening of the fortifications at this time.

Three occasions of destruction, it would seem, are now to be accepted. The first of these belongs to mature LH. III B, and affects only the outer settlement, so far as is known, but may have had as its result the strengthening of the fortifications and the building of the Granary. The second penetrated within the citadel, in spite of the strong walls, and in

---

[1] Op. cit. p. 130.
[2] Op. cit. p. 131.
[3] Op. cit. pp. 128 f.
[4] Petsas, *Pr.* 1950, pp. 203 ff.; *BSA* xlviii–li.
[5] *BSA*, l. 221 f.
[6] *BSA*, li. 105 and Fig. 2.
[7] *BSA*, lii. 207 ff.
[8] Papademetriou and Taylour, *ILN*, 23 September 1961, pp. 490 ff.; *Archaeological Reports for 1960–61*, 30 ff.
[9] *Ergon* for 1959, pp. 93 ff.; *AE*, 1958, pp. 153 ff.

this it may well be that the Palace was burnt; there was also further destruction outside the citadel, though no attempt had been made to rebuild as a result of the previous disaster. This second destruction is placed at the end of LH. III B. The result may have been that only a small part of the acropolis was still held—traces of LH. III C are few—and continued to be held until the third and final disaster, in which the Granary was burnt, the time of this being well on in LH. III C, after the Close Style had come to maturity and the Granary Class had already become popular. Thereafter, occupation continued for a while, and there could have been a subsequent gap in occupation, or else a settlement by people with no strong Mycenaean traditions, as from Protogeometric times there was no hesitation in burying the dead within the ruins of the outer houses.

The tomb evidence supplements that of the settlement, chiefly on the question of the situation at Mycenae after the final disaster. Many tombs have of course been excavated, but most of them belong to a much earlier period than that which concerns this work, and some of the rest have not been adequately reported, and consequently cannot be fitted into the picture. The only tombs of the latest Mycenaean and subsequent periods which may be used for comparative purposes are those excavated by Wace, or at least under his auspices.[1] Most of them are chamber tombs, from two cemeteries at a little distance from the acropolis, and in no case was any of these originally built in LH. III C; they are all re-used, which suggests that at least some of the original population were still occupying the site until after the destruction of the Granary, to which period two of these burials are assigned.[2] On the other hand, there is nothing in them that cannot be called Mycenaean in character. For the rest, there are two burials,[3] one in a pithos, the other unenclosed, found associated with the Cyclopean Terrace building; the vases were in each case LH. III C. Inside the citadel,[4] in level XI of the Lion Gate deposit, an unusual bath larnax burial was found, and this, from its very position, belonged to the period after the destruction of the Granary. It is perhaps significant that by now there seems to have been no hesitation in burying inside the walls. The burial may be regarded as transitional, as may the contemporary child burial in the Prehistoric Cemetery—again an unusual type, as it is a true cist—a small stone box.[5] Thereafter a series of Protogeometric and Geometric cist tombs continues the sequence, set mostly in the ruins of the LH. III B houses of outer Mycenae.[6] These tombs do not provide an uninterrupted sequence; there may very easily be a gap between the latest Mycenaean and the earliest Protogeometric.

These are then the salient points with regard to the site of Mycenae during the century or so before its final downfall, and it is essential that they should be given as fully as reasonably possible as, to my mind, the coherence of the whole Mycenaean political fabric depended on the continued strength of this town, and any signs of disintegration would not only be reflected in the remainder of the Argolid, but would also have repercussions much further away. There is a tendency to think of other sites and areas in relation to Mycenae.

The fact, however, that it has never been possible to excavate Mycenae as a planned whole, the relative inadequacy of earlier excavations which must have led to confusion

---

[1] *C.T.*; *BSA*, xlviii ff.
[2] Tombs 502 and 515. Cf. p. 74, n. 2.
[3] *BSA*, xxv. 406 f.
[4] Op. cit. p. 36.
[5] *BSA*, xlix. 258 f.
[6] *BSA*, xlix–li.

and difficulty of interpretation, and the amount of important material which, as having only recently appeared, still awaits full recording, mean that there are problems which are not yet solved. It may seem on the surface that the story as given so far is simple and straightforward, but that impression is somewhat deceptive. This is particularly evident in the relative dates based on the pottery. First, it is said that the earliest disaster took place well before the end of LH. III B; the style is not yet sufficiently known in detail, however, for one to be able to determine at what point during its course the destruction took place —indeed, it may never be practicable to be precise, as judgments on style alone do not invariably reflect the true state of affairs. Furthermore, in this instance not much of the pottery concerned has been illustrated or analysed; one cannot yet attempt to judge for oneself.

The evidence for the second disaster is, as has been stated, still very recent, and in consequence it is not possible critically to assess the conclusions arrived at, namely, that this event occurred at the end of LH. III B, and before the appearance of any LH. III C ceramic elements. Some pieces have been illustrated, and there is discussion, but the impression left is one of uncertainty. This is of particular relevance when it is a matter of transition from LH. III B to LH. III C. It is clear that LH. III B and LH. III C are different styles. At Mycenae, in the settlement, there is one point, that of the destruction of the Granary, where we are confronted with a reasonable body of ceramic evidence which can be claimed to be representative of LH. III C at this time; and we find that two differing strains, entirely foreign to LH. III B conventions, have by now matured—the Close Style and the Granary Class. This is at one point only, and takes us back no further; we cannot tell from it when and how LH. III C first broke away from LH. III B. The evidence is not yet there in sufficient quantity. Also, there is much more to LH. III C than the two stylistic variations mentioned, both of which are fairly individual, especially so the Close Style, whose perfection of elaboration (Pl. 4) is an entirely fresh idea, and very possibly involved the products of one workshop only. LH. III C also consists of elements which are rather more indeterminate, and develop almost imperceptibly out of LH. III B, to such an extent that it is impossible to say when the one starts and the other finishes, and thus at times impossible to point to any one motive or shape as being characteristic of LH. III C.

This may be exemplified in Wace's own treatment of the material which should help the most, the sherds from the Lion Gate deposit. His final judgment [1] was that the sherds of levels I to V were LH. III B but that LH. III C began in level VI, and that a very gradual process of change then took place, the previous style not having really given way altogether to the new one much, if at all, before the destruction of the Granary. In the original publication,[2] he stated that the pottery of level VI was characterized by a slight change, that in the main the patterns were as those of earlier layers, but that for the first time there were sherds typical of levels IX to XI. Such sherds seem to be from jugs of hydria type, according to the more detailed analysis, but in the case of the deep bowls, which provide the majority of our settlement pottery, it was simply noted [3] that 'patterns

[1] *The Aegean and the Near East*, pp. 129 f.
[2] *BSA*, xxv. 27 f.
[3] Op. cit. p. 28.

resemble those of preceding strata, but are generally simpler'. This is presumably the tendency that is to lead to the Granary Class (Pl. 12), but it does not make the distinction between LH. III B and LH. III C at all an easy matter. Evidently, also, the question becomes all the more difficult with the greater amount of material available, as can be seen in the discussion [1] of a group of LH. III pottery from the Prehistoric Cemetery, where the main criterion for stating that the material is LH. III B rather than LH. III C is the lack of any sherds in the Close Style. It may be that here we have a criterion which would be unacceptable to Furumark, who clearly envisages that early LH. III C may be in part defined as a deterioration—and no great one—of LH. III B. It is consequently most desirable to be able to point to as many motives and shapes as possible as peculiar to LH. III C, and use has to be made both of other material than that of Mycenae, and of tomb material, where the distribution of vases is rather different, the stirrup jar replacing the deep bowl in popularity. I have indeed endeavoured to isolate one or two such elements and to attempt some analysis of transition (pp. 4 ff.), but I am well aware of the deficiencies. It is unfortunate that the initial change over to LH. III C, both in the sense of flight from LH. III B canons and in the sense of introducing new ideas, is much more clearly observable on stirrup jars than on deep bowls, as in this case it is the settlement evidence, with its preponderance of deep bowls, that is of the greater importance, and the tombs are rather subsidiary.

These then are the difficulties that have to be borne in mind when one is endeavouring to paint the general archaeological picture, and to relate the evidence of Mycenae to that of other sites.

A good example of such difficulties appears as soon as we consider the history of a number of important sites in the Argolid and Corinthia, which seem to have been deserted before the end of LH. III B. Writing recently,[2] Blegen has cited the settlements of Berbati (on the information of Åkerström), Prosymna and Zygouries 'and other smaller places', as having been completely abandoned during the period that LH. III B was changing to LH. III C. Midea, on the other hand, seems to continue into LH. III C.[3] The question that arises is whether LH. III C had emerged before these sites were abandoned, and if not, whether it is possible to be precise about the time of desertion in LH. III B. There was presumably some connexion with one of the first two disasters at Mycenae: but with which?

The tombs at Midea have produced a solitary LH. III C amphoriskos;[4] but none of the vases from the tombs of Berbati, nor any of the published material from the settlement here, is in the LH. III C style;[5] evidently, in fact, nothing can be later than the transition to LH. III C, according to Åkerström, and the same conclusions are to be reached from Zygouries in Corinthia (cf. p. 84). At Prosymna, finally, Blegen stresses [6] that his chamber tombs (over fifty of them) contained no LH. III C; but there is the settlement as well, where excavations have been conducted by Waldstein,[7] and Caskey and Amandry.[8]

[1] *BSA*, lii. 217 f.
[2] *AJA*, lxiv. 159 f.
[3] Persson, *New Tombs*, p. 15.
[4] Persson, *Royal Tombs*, pp. 31 and 67, Fig. 47.
[5] Åkerström, *AF*, pp. 32 ff. and 34 f., Figs. 3–6; *Bericht VI. Int. Kongress*, p. 297.
[6] *AJA*, lxiv. 159 f.
[7] *Argive Heraeum*, II, pp. 71 ff. and Pls. 53–55.
[8] *Hesp.* xxi. 165 ff. and Pl. 44.

Generally speaking, the sherds and vases are not later than LH. III B, but there are one or two cases where one might suppose a period of transition to LH. III C. Caskey and Amandry assigned two of this handful of sherds to LH. III B-C;[1] the amphora illustrated by Waldstein is of a type more commonly known in LH. III C,[2] though there are LH. III B examples—presumably belonging rather to the end of this style; and two or three of the fragments of bowls, also from Waldstein's publication, do not look far in date from the goblet at Iria (see below), which Furumark classifies as early LH. III C.[3] My impression is that the end of this settlement—not reoccupied till late Geometric—may more suitably be connected with the second disaster at Mycenae, and a similar conclusion is likely, on Blegen's statement, for Berbati and Zygouries (where a violent fire destroyed the potter's house); but he is evidently visualizing only one destruction at Mycenae prior to the Granary fire. One is thus left in a state of doubt.

The circumstances of the house dug at Iria, a coastal site not far to the south-east of Asine, and well away from the Argive plain, are not easy to interpret, either.[4] There were two levels concerned, and Furumark assigned the nine vases of the upper level to his LH. III C 1 a phase.[5] The solitary krater illustrated from the lower level[6] should presumably, then, be late LH. III B. In fact, the flavour of LH. III B is very strong in the higher level, though it is interesting to find two vase shapes, the jug with strainer spout and perhaps also the goblet, which are more familiar to Dodecanesian LH. III C. Is there here an indication of a settlement which came in between the first two disasters at Mycenae (assuming that Furumark's 'sub-III B' would be classed by the excavators at Mycenae rather as LH. III B), or was there a brief occupation, perhaps of a refugee kind, immediately after the second disaster? It is to be hoped that these questions will eventually be answered. In the meanwhile, it may be suggested that we have in any case insufficient evidence at Iria, as one would thus be arguing from the evidence of one house to that of the whole settlement.

A brief mention may be made at this point of the site of the sanctuary of Apollo Maleatas,[7] near Epidaurus, as this place of worship, which can be traced back to the seventh century B.C., also yielded impressive evidence of being used for worship in Mycenaean times, from the number of figurines (both human and animal) and other objects found. It was further established that the area where these earlier finds were made was carefully preserved as a cult spot. Unfortunately, it is not possible to prove that any of the material was later than LH. III B—in fact, the sherds mainly precede LH. III—but the excavator claimed[8] that there must have been continuity of worship here. This seems somewhat doubtful; there must have been the memory that the site was used for religious purposes, but there are no objects suggesting continued worship between the thirteenth century and the seventh.

So far, it has been a matter of clearing away the sites whose survival was connected with one or other of the two destructions at Mycenae in LH. III B, and which were

[1] Op. cit. p. 173, Nos. 52 and 53.
[2] *Argive Heraeum*, II, p. 83, Fig. 13; cf. *Analysis*, type 69.
[3] *Argive Heraeum*, II, Pl. 54; cf. *OA*, iii. 197.
[4] Gebauer, *AA*, 1939, coll. 294 and 287 ff., Figs. 15–19.
[5] *OA*, iii. 197.
[6] *AA*, 1939, coll. 287 f., Fig. 15.
[7] Papademetriou, *Pr.* 1948, pp. 90 ff.; 1949, pp. 91 ff.; 1950, pp. 194 ff. See pp. 42 f.
[8] *Pr.* 1949, p. 97.

certainly or probably abandoned not later than the beginning of LH. III C. One very important site remains—that of Tiryns; and here the evidence may be divided into that of the period up to and including the destruction, and that of the subsequent history of the site.

Until recently, no evidence had been published to indicate precisely when the destruction of Tiryns took place.[1] This difficulty has now been in part remedied by recent excavation,[2] the preliminary report on which disclosed that of four clearly distinguished layers the upper ones indicate that there was violent destruction. Verdhelis assigned the pottery of the top levels to LH. III B, and that seems well confirmed by the pieces illustrated. He also placed the date roughly at the end of the thirteenth century, which would mean the end of LH. III B. He considered that the burnt nature of the uppermost level, in conjunction with the evidently hasty burial of two men just beneath this level, represented a hostile onslaught in which the citadel was destroyed. The third level also showed signs of some burning, but of a more localized and lighter nature; and apparently the pottery of these three levels was more or less contemporary. That is the evidence of the citadel, and it is implemented by a similar catastrophe and similar pottery in the excavated area outside the citadel, above which the next sign of activity is a cemetery which the excavator says stretches from sub-Mycenaean to late Geometric. This will be discussed below; the major point is that of the destruction, and the question again arises—with which (if with either) of the first two destructions at Mycenae was it connected? And the provisional answer, accepting the conclusion of Verdhelis, must be that it was connected with the second one, at the end of LH. III B.

This is the last evidence of destruction at the end of LH. III B, and we can now turn to such further sites as are known to have been occupied in LH. III C or immediately afterwards. The situation in Mycenae having already been discussed, it will be best first to conclude what needs to be said about Tiryns.

It seems clear that the citadel was virtually deserted after the disaster, and that so also was some of the outer city—one cannot perhaps speak for all of it. The next sign of occupation is that of the very late LH. III C (or sub-Mycenaean) graves, which with their successors were built within the ruined houses, as at Mycenae.[3] This could be a considerable gap, and it does look as though the feeling of continuity was lost. However, it does not necessarily mean a complete flight from the neighbourhood; there are vases in the museum at Nauplia, from some tomb or tombs at or near Tiryns, which are LH. III C. An LH. III C stirrup jar from this site has in fact recently been illustrated.[4]

Such burials will presumably, as at Argos, have been made in chamber tombs; whether so or not, these had been superseded by the time of the cemetery which partly overlies the LH. III B houses. Here there are pithos and shaft burials, but the most numerous and earliest were the cist tombs lined and covered with slabs, and the first of these contained vases which may be considered as stylistically sub-Mycenaean. Two or three of the vases in the cemetery excavated by the Germans look earlier than Protogeometric, but only one,

---

[1] Müller, *Tiryns*, III, pp. 207 ff. But cf. Blegen, *Korakou*, pp. 130 ff.
[2] Verdhelis, *AE*, 1956, suppl., pp. 5 ff.
[3] Müller, *Tiryns*, I, pp. 127 ff.
[4] Biesantz, in *Illustrierte Welt Kunst-Geschichte* (ed. Rimli and Fischer), p. 408.

an amphoriskos,[1] was found in what may be a genuine and uncontaminated context, in a cist tomb. Most recently, however, attention has been focussed on the contents of a remarkable tomb,[2] the earliest of the cemetery then uncovered, and the only one to be dated earlier than the first introduction of Protogeometric elements. It was a pit grave, not lined with slabs, and contained two skeletons, the grave goods being associated with the one skeleton only, and consisting of a helmet of previously unknown type (Pl. 24a), a shield-boss and a spearhead, all of bronze, and a dagger of iron. One vase was also found—a stirrup jar of the latest type. The excavator dates the burial to the end of the twelfth or the beginning of the eleventh century, but it is not an easy group to date either relatively or absolutely.

From this time, the burials continued into Protogeometric and Geometric, and there one may leave this site. It is of obvious interest that the Mycenaean ceramic tradition had survived, in spite of discontinuity in other ways.

Three sites remain to be described, and one of them, Nauplia, may be dealt with fairly briefly. Here there was a sizeable Mycenaean cemetery; thirty-one chamber tombs were dug by Stais in 1892,[3] but hardly any of the contents have been recorded, except for a LH. III B tankard and a fragmentary three-handled amphora [4] with incised potmarks on the handles, and animals in between—a vase which could have originated from Cyprus in LH. III B times. As well as this, however, a selection of the vases is now exhibited in the National Museum, and at least three of the vases (two stirrup jars and a cup) are well down in LH. III C, and so the cemetery was still in use then. Since the war, Charitonidis has excavated four more chamber tombs, but the only datable evidence is from LH. III A. He also investigated the post-Mycenaean settlement and cemetery, which seems to have been fairly close to the Mycenaean tombs. The cemetery was in use from early Geometric to Hellenistic times, but the settlement was mainly Geometric, with a few sporadic Protogeometric sherds.[5]

We may go on from here to Argos, a site almost as close to Tiryns as Nauplia. The French School have done much work here, and interesting evidence has been forthcoming both from settlement and tombs. The material from the settlement is not so interesting as that of the tombs, but a useful picture emerges from excavations and soundings made in several different areas. The first area to be tested was on the Aspis, by Vollgraff,[6] but the publication is not adequate. The only illustrated sherd is assigned by Furumark to LH. III C.[7] Apart from this, the conclusions from later excavations seem to be that in no case was an LH. III B. or LH. III C level found in connexion with a Protogeometric (including sub-Mycenaean [8]) layer. On the one hand, levels containing LH. III B, and perhaps also LH. III C, pottery, underlay Geometric or even later material.[9] On the other hand, sub-Mycenaean sherds were associated with Protogeometric ware in levels immediately above virgin soil.[10] The sub-Mycenaean sherds are from deep bowls painted

---

[1] *Tiryns* I, p. 128 and Pl. XVI, No. 8. Grave 3.
[2] Verdhelis, *AE*, 1956, suppl., p. 4; *BCH* lxxxii. 706, Fig. 26, and 707.
[3] *Pr.* 1892, pp. 52 ff.
[4] *FLMV*, Pl. 21, 150; *AE*, 1895, p. 261 and Pl. 11, 4.
[5] *Pr.* 1953, pp. 191 ff.; *Ergon* for 1954, pp. 33 ff.; *Ergon* for 1955, pp. 75 f.
[6] *BCH*, xxx. 43, Fig. 71.
[7] *Analysis*, p. 302, motive 20, No. 11.
[8] Charitonides, *Pr.* 1952, p. 425, Figs. 16 and 17.
[9] Courbin, *BCH*, lxxx. 207 ff. and 370.
[10] *BCH*, lxxxi. 677 and 680 f., Figs. 30 and 32; *BCH*, lxxxiii. 762 ff.

all over except for a panel between the handle which has a wavy line; originally deriving from the Granary Class, they persist into Protogeometric.[1] The answer is that there was probably discontinuity of a sort, in the sense that the settlement and (as will be seen) the site for burials were moved, but there was perhaps only a small gap, if any (see below, p. 82).

The tombs tend to confirm the picture given by the traces of settlement, and supplement it in so far as the question of continuity from LH. III B to LH. III C is concerned. A Mycenaean cemetery was discovered on the Deiras, and excavated by Vollgraff.[2] The nine tombs he recorded were later reported in greater detail and with many illustrations by Deshayes,[3] and the latter discovered and excavated further tombs in the same area or near it, until a total (including Vollgraff's tombs) of thirty-six chamber tombs and twenty-seven pit graves had been reached.[4]

Of most of the pottery and other objects accounts have not yet been published, but certain preliminary conclusions appear to be justifiable. The cemetery itself was in use at least from LH. II, and both chamber tombs and pit graves seem to cover the whole period, which continues at least into LH. III C. Most of the chamber tombs, such as can be dated, belong to LH. III B, but there is no doubt that some go on being used in LH. III C; one tomb (XXXV)[5] is said to contain vases of LH. III B-C type; others contain only LH. III C vases, and were therefore originally constructed in this period—the only known instances in the Argolid.[6] The pit graves are not so useful for dating evidence, as they tend to be lacking in material, but from their siting, and association with the chamber tombs, look as though they also were used in LH. III C.

A problem that is of great interest, but which is not yet entirely resolved, is how long this cemetery remained in use, relatively speaking. In three cases, the contents of a chamber tomb are said to be sub-Mycenaean, in four the pottery continues from LH. III C to sub-Mycenaean, and in two tombs there is a secondary deposit of a sub-Mycenaean nature.[7]

The problem of terminology arises, inasmuch as I have tended to restrict the term sub-Mycenaean to the users of cist tombs as opposed to chamber tombs in western Attica (cf. pp. 17 ff.), though suggesting that this material may be substantially contemporary with the latest Mycenaean in the Argolid. That these latest Argive tombs may be contemporary with the Salamis and Kerameikos sub-Mycenaean is suggested by the small finds other than pottery, where the pattern of pins and rings, and the fibula with twisted arch, is very similar to that of the cist tombs.[8] Furthermore, a neck amphora from a secondary deposit[9] in tomb XXIV is of a shape which in Athens would not be considered earlier than transitional from sub-Mycenaean to Protogeometric. The deposit may be secondary, but it is only 20 cm. above the original floor.

---

[1] e.g. *BCH*, lxxvii. 262, Fig. 55.
[2] *BCH*, xxviii. 364 ff.
[3] *BCH*, lxxvii. 59 ff.
[4] *BCH*, lxxix. 310 ff. (tombs I–XV); lxxx. 361 ff. (tombs XVI–XXIX); lxxxiii. 769 ff. (tombs XXX–XXXVI).
[5] *BCH*, lxxxiii. 773.
[6] *BCH*, lxxx. 361.

[7] Sub-Mycenaean: tombs XXIX, XXX and one above XXIII; LH. III C to sub-Mycenaean: tombs XVI–XVIII, XXII; secondary deposit: tombs XXIV, XXXIII.
[8] Pins: tombs XIV (*BCH*, lxxix. 312), XXIX (2) (*BCH*, lxxx. 365), XXXIII (*BCH*, lxxxiii. 771). Fibula: tomb XXIX.
[9] *BCH*, lxxx. 362.

Finally, there is fresh evidence now available on the later history of Argos.[1] It has been noted that the latest Mycenaean settlement area is different from that of the sub-Mycenaean and Protogeometric inhabitants (here sub-Mycenaean is taken as the continuance of the Mycenaean tradition, probably contemporary with, or only very slightly earlier than, the beginning of Protogeometric in Attica). The same picture is presented by the tombs; the cist tomb was now introduced, and the vases contained were, at the beginning, sub-Mycenaean or Protogeometric—and it is, I think, the case that almost every one of these tombs shows the influence of Protogeometric from the very beginning; one must return to Tiryns for a cist tomb with material which need not be contemporary with Protogeometric. Furthermore, as far as one can tell, the contrast in the distribution of vase types, and indeed in the style, is much more sharply marked between these tombs and the preceding chamber tombs than it is between the sub-Mycenaean cist tombs of west Attica and their predecessors or contemporaries in east Attica or the Argolid. So it would appear that there was discontinuity; but my strong impression is that there is little or no gap in time. The bowls with wavy line, or monochrome with the lower part unpainted, found in settlement deposits or in tombs of the earliest Protogeometric times, must be closely connected with those from the latest Mycenaean deposits and tombs. Argos is therefore a very instructive site, giving much information not available elsewhere.

Finally, there is the site of Asine, which provides not only settlement and tomb material, but a sanctuary as well.[2] The conclusions to be drawn from the houses are not entirely clear. Various building periods are identified, and of these Period 5 is equated, apparently, with LH. III A, Period 6 with LH. III B, and Period 7 with LH. III C.[3] Now the houses attributed to Period 6,[4] lettered G, I, K and L, all on the same level, must from the evidence of G, and one piece from I, have been built already well down in LH. III C. House G is the centre one of three superimposed houses; House H lies above it, with material belonging to the very end of LH. III C, and House F below it, 'at a much lower level',[5] comprising the only evidence for Period 5. No object is mentioned or illustrated as having come from House F; indeed, the only evidence for habitation in LH. III B is the statement of Furumark[6] that 'In the walls and below the upper floor of House G characteristic III B ware was found, *i. a.* fragments of types 253, mot. 23 (kylix, murex decoration) and 284, mot. 53: 27 (bowl, panel decoration)'. It is realized that not all the sherds from this site were recorded (Furumark himself illustrates additional sherds from Houses G and H),[7] but even so it certainly looks as though habitation of Asine in LH. III B was meagre in the extreme. Furthermore, as will be seen below, this situation is reflected in the tombs.

Indeed, it would appear that this site was in any case not one of great size or importance, unless much that might once have existed has been washed away. The LH. III C houses probably give only a part of the picture of the occupation of this period, as the vases and sherds from Houses G and H belong to the latter half, and from the illustrated material could well postdate the destruction of the Granary at Mycenae. There is nothing which gives any further information about the early stages of LH. III C.

---

[1] *BCH*, lxxx. 376; lxxxi. 662 f.; lxxxiii. 766 ff.
[2] *Asine, passim.*
[3] Op. cit. p. 90.
[4] Op. cit. p. 89.
[5] Op. cit. p. 63 (walls 47–51).
[6] *Chronology*, p. 76.
[7] *OA*, iii. 209, Fig. 3 (House G); 211, Fig. 4 (House H).

House G is of unusual interest, as it included a small shrine,[1] a feature elsewhere in the Mycenaean world mainly confined to the palaces. It could be then that this house was that of the ruler of Asine, but the large terracotta head of a deity shows connexions with Crete, where there is a tradition of domestic, as opposed to palatial, shrines.[2] On the other hand, the little terracotta 'goddess' (or worshipper?) figurines that accompany the head are in the Mycenaean tradition.

Above this house another, House H, was built, and the sherds from here are still of LH. III C character.[3] With this, the Mycenaean occupation fades out—there is no sign of violent destruction—and there is certainly some gap before the miserable walls which were the only remains of the Protogeometric and Geometric periods.[4]

In the cemetery, the most productive burials were those of the chamber tombs, but it is to be noted that, as at Argos, a number of pit graves were also identified, nine of them unconnected with a chamber tomb, two in dromoi, and almost all child burials.[5] Beyond this, one cannot say much about them, as there were practically no associated objects. There were also three cist tombs.[6] Of these, LH. 12 is probably Protogeometric,[7] the context of LH. 13 is obscure and its contents (a steatite button and a vase) not illustrated,[8] but the third, although very close to a Middle Helladic cist, has vases which are surely LH. III B. Of the eight chamber tombs excavated,[9] one produced only two LH. III A vases, and two others were unused but contained a burial in a niche of the dromos, one of these having three LH. III A vases, the other just one early LH. III C stirrup jar. The bulk of the material comes from the five remaining tombs, all in use prior to LH. III C, but the LH. III B period is represented by five vases only,[10] and these closer perhaps to LH. III A than to LH. III C, a fact which may support the settlement evidence, to the effect that Asine was very sparsely inhabited in LH. III B. The similar picture provided by the settlement material of slight occupation in early LH. III C is, however, not reflected in the tombs, as their eighty LH. III C vases cover the whole of this period, and afford the bulk of the published evidence from the whole Argolid for early LH. III C. As to the small finds other than pottery, it is probable that the picture observed elsewhere in the Argolid, of a notable diminution both in quantity and quality, is likewise to be found here.

The graves of the succeeding period are, with one exception, in a different part of the site, and are all cist or pit graves, the chamber tomb having been discarded.[11] The one exception is that of the cist tomb found in the north dromos of chamber tomb 1,[12] presuming that the skyphos (No. 35) with high flaring foot does belong to this tomb. For the rest, there are thirty-eight cist tombs and five pit graves, and the associated pottery is a mixture of the earlier Mycenaean tradition, of Protogeometric innovations, and of hand-made pottery of a type unknown in Mycenaean times. A new racial strain seems not unlikely, but

---

[1] *Asine*, pp. 298 ff.
[2] Alexiou, *KX*, 1958, p. 216, n. 127.
[3] Cf. p. 82, n. 7.
[4] *Asine*, p. 81, Fig. 61 (above House I).
[5] Except No. 2: *Asine*, p. 128.
[6] *Asine*, p. 354 f.; cf. also p. 129.
[7] *OA*, iii. 210. The vase may be *Asine*, p. 366, Fig. 237, No. 35.
[8] I can find no mention of this tomb elsewhere in the publication.
[9] *Asine*, pp. 356 ff.
[10] *Chronology*, p. 70. All from tomb 7.
[11] *Asine*, pp. 422 ff.
[12] Cf. n. 7.

it would be difficult from this alone to say how close in time these tombs were to the preceding Mycenaean.

The above discussion has revolved almost entirely around the pottery. No more than a postscript is needed on such other objects as may be dated to LH. III C. Personal ornaments of the conventional Mycenaean type have been found in the chamber tombs of Mycenae, Asine and Argos, but in no great quantity, and of no high quality, thus possibly reflecting a lowering of standards; a contrast may indeed be made between these and the finds from Perati, Naxos and the Dodecanese, to the detriment of the former, though one must always bear in mind the relatively small number of LH. III C tombs in the Argolid, and the devastating consequences of looting.

There were also ornaments of non-Mycenaean type in LH. III C contexts. It is unfortunate that the fine violin-bow fibulae from Mycenae have no datable context, but they were either surface finds or from tombs the nature of whose pottery is not known.[1] It is certain, nevertheless, that they did come from Mycenae, and are not likely to have been later than LH. III C. Evidence for this period is available only in the chamber tombs of Argos where an arched fibula and several long dress pins have been found, as well as a bronze wheel, claimed to be of northern origin.[2]

No weapons or armour have been found in clear LH. III C contexts (again, those from Mycenae and Tiryns are not precisely datable), but it may be significant that the earliest known iron weapon, the dagger at Tiryns, associated with bronze spearhead, shield-boss and helmet, comes from a pit grave which is the earliest of a cemetery in which a break had been made with the chamber tombs of LH. III C.

(B) CORINTHIA

There is no good natural boundary between the Argolid and Corinthia, and indeed the Catalogue of Ships gives Agamemnon for his own territory the whole of the area from Mycenae to Aegion, thus including all of Corinthia, even though excluding most of the Argolid.[3] It is not unreasonable to deal with Corinthia in the same section in which Mycenae is discussed.

On the way to Corinth from Mycenae the nearest site by one road is that of Zygouries, excavated by Blegen.[4] It was never a great city, and it does not seem to have been fortified, but it was prosperous enough in LH. III, and Blegen considers the large building on the hill to have been the dwelling of some local governor or noble.[5] This building, which on account of its very considerable number of vases was called the Potter's Shop, was destroyed, and here the one important fact is that the destruction can be dated to the end of LH. III B and no later.[6]

The next site is that of Gonia, three miles to the east of Old Corinth. It needs no more than a mention, for although the excavator states that the material from the LH. III

---

[1] Blinkenberg, *Fibules*, pp. 46 ff.
[2] Cf. p. 81, n. 8. Bronze wheel, *BCH*, lxxx. 361 (tomb XXII).
[3] *Iliad* ii. 569 ff.
[4] Blegen, *Zygouries*.
[5] Op. cit. p. 221.
[6] *Chronology*, p. 65; *AJA*, lxiv. 159 f.

settlement is 'identical with the corresponding stage at Korakou' (see below), and should presumably include LH. III C, it is neither described nor illustrated.[1]

Before discussing Old Corinth, it may be advisable first to deal with the situation at Isthmia. Here, in the sanctuary area, only a few odd Mycenaean sherds have been found; two may be LH. III C,[2] and one should rather be called sub-Mycenaean, though it may be contemporary with the earliest Attic Protogeometric (cf. p. 20), and Broneer rightly compares it with sherds from Old Corinth.[3] As well as this evidence, however, we have that of the Mycenaean fortification wall which runs from the south-east end of the Isthmus roughly in a south-westerly direction.[4] Its precise extent is as yet uncertain, but it is a strong wall, provided on its northern side with towers; the position of these, Broneer says,[5] 'and the fact that wherever possible the builders took advantage of the terrain to make the approach from the north over steeply rising ground, indicate that the wall was built to ward off invasions from the north into the Peloponnesus'. The date of its construction is therefore of some importance, and it has been established from the pottery that it must be placed in LH. III B, during the second half of the thirteenth century. It may thus well come into line with the fortifications, or strengthening of such, elsewhere.

At Old Corinth nothing, unfortunately, is yet known of the Mycenaean settlement, though a deposit of LH. III B pottery does at least prove that there was a settlement here.[6] What happened after LH. III B is uncertain, for the next evidence belongs to a period which, although its pottery retains to some extent the latest Mycenaean tradition, looks forward to Protogeometric.[7] Weinberg considers that the vases and fragments found in a poor hut belong to the resettlement of the site. The bowls display the latest stage of the Granary Class, and in this retain the Mycenaean tradition, but the two remaining feet are high, and in general this is the period of transition to Protogeometric. Similar bowl sherds were found more recently, and were associated with sherds with compass-drawn concentric semicircle and circle decoration, as well as with a sherd of a fine krater which again reflects the Mycenaean tradition.[8] If these are contemporaneous, then one may suggest that the resettlement occurred only just, if at all, before the appearance of Protogeometric in Athens. Comparison may be made with rather similar material from the Argolid (cf. pp. 80 ff.).

In many ways, the most interesting of the Corinthian sites is that of Korakou,[9] on the Gulf immediately north of Old Corinth. It was only a small settlement, but its evidence was thoroughly investigated and published, and it is indeed the only site in Corinthia where continuity from LH. III B to LH. III C is clearly visible. The LH. III C pottery includes a deep bowl of the best Close Style,[10] and it is clear from the report that a fair number of monochrome bowls were found;[11] one or two of the kylikes are probably LH. III C, and the collar-necked four-handled jar seems certainly to belong to this period.[12] No evidence was available of any houses being built later than LH. III B, but the site provides much

---

[1] *Metropolitan Museum Studies*, vol. iii, pt. i, p. 78.
[2] *Hesp.* xxvii. 29 and Pl. 12 c: *a*, *b*.
[3] Op. cit. p. 29 and Pl. 12 c: *f*.
[4] *Hesp.* xxviii. 299; *Antiquity*, xxxii. 81, Fig. 1, and 82.
[5] *Antiquity*, xxxii. 82.
[6] *Hesp.* xviii. 156 f. and Pls. 22–24.
[7] *Corinth* VII, pt. i, 3 ff. and Pl. 1.
[8] *Hesp.* xx. 293 and Pl. 89 *a* and *b*.
[9] Blegen, *Korakou*.
[10] Op. cit. p. 62, Fig. 86.
[11] Op. cit. p. 72 and Fig. 103, p. 71.
[12] Op. cit. p. 68, Fig. 98.

information on domestic non-palatial LH. III architecture, and the characteristic structure is a *megaron*, 'a long quadrilateral building'.[1] The small finds included a number of human and animal terracotta figurines,[2] a bronze pin with an enlarged head decorated in herring-bone pattern,[3] and a bronze violin-bow fibula of twisted wire.[4] The two last objects probably belong to the LH. III C period, though it is not possible to prove this. It should be stressed that there is no destruction or abandonment of the site in or at the end of LH. III B, as is the case with so many sites in the region to the south. Nor indeed was the site destroyed later; it may, however, have been abandoned rather hurriedly at some point in LH. III C.[5]

A few sherds came to light at Perachora,[6] and these would indicate occupation both in LH. III B and LH. III C—there is even part of a Close Style bowl.[7] The excavator is no doubt right in suggesting the existence here of nothing more important than a small fishing community.[8]

Along the coast beyond Korakou there is as yet a blank, though no doubt this is accidental. The final site to be mentioned is at Derveni,[9] in hilly country on the borders of Corinthia and Achaea, where a most interesting chamber tomb was discovered recently, the point of particular significance being the presence in it of fourteen oblong pits,[10] clearly recalling the unique tombs of Kephallenia (cf. p. 104). The tomb had been used for earlier burials swept aside when the pits were dug, and these as a rule held one skeleton, though there were instances of two, and one of five; unfortunately, the tomb had been plundered and the finds were few, though the vases and the cheap ornaments indicate the latest period of LH. III (no detailed description is available). Whether in course of time any link will be found between this tomb and those of Kephallenia remains a matter of speculation.

A few yards from this tomb another one was discovered,[11] a rectangular rock-cut chamber without dromos, in which were three pits of the type in the big tomb. One vase 'of alabastron type of the latest Mycenaean times' was found in each of two of the pits, while the third had the upper part of a bronze fibula 'of a type with sharp-pointed leaf with incised decoration', presumably a violin-bow fibula of the kind found in Thebes and the Kerameikos. It could then well be that these burials are late in LH. III C.

The following points emerge from the above survey of Corinthia. The realization of some imminent threat from north of the Peloponnese during the LH. III B period is probably indicated by the fortification wall at Isthmia; and the destruction of Zygouries at the end of LH. III B, especially when taken with the contemporary evidence of the Argolid and other districts, shows that the attack materialized, and that the defensive measures were fruitless. It is not clear how extensive was the effect of the attack on Corinthia, but early LH. III C pottery has been identified only at Korakou and Perachora. Korakou was abandoned at some time in LH. III C, and subsequently there are

---

[1] Op. cit. p. 98.
[2] Op. cit. pp. 106 f., Figs. 131 f.
[3] Op. cit. pp. 109 and 108, Fig. 133, 4.
[4] Op. cit. pp. 109 and 108, Fig. 133, 6.
[5] Op. cit. p. 126.
[6] Payne, *Perachora*, i, pp. 9, 20, 51 f. and Pl. 10.
[7] Op. cit. p. 52 (Nos. 19 and 20) and Pl. 10.
[8] Op. cit. p. 20.
[9] Verdhelis, *AE*, 1956, suppl., pp. 11 f.
[10] Op. cit. p. 12, Fig. 24.
[11] Op. cit. p. 12.

indications of occupation at Old Corinth and Isthmia, possibly contemporary with that visible at Argos (cf. pp. 80 f.), following on the disuse of the chamber tomb cemetery, not far from the time when the Protogeometric style emerged in Athens. Finally, the tombs discovered at Derveni seem to indicate connexions rather with regions further to the southwest than with Corinthia, and the provisional record of their contents suggests burials in LH. III C.

2. *Arcadia*

In comparison with most of the rest of the Peloponnese, Arcadia has not been extensively investigated, nor have the results of survey [1] or excavation thrown much light on LH. III C or on subsequent periods.

One site in this area, that of Palaiokastro, will be discussed in the section devoted to South-western Peloponnese, as it belongs more naturally with that area (cf. p. 92). Apart from this, Fimmen [2] recorded Mycenaean sherds at Orchomenos and tholos tombs at Tegea, where a later excavation of the sanctuary of Alea Athena uncovered at least two sherds from stirrup jars.[3]

Excavation has also taken place at Vourvoura,[4] but nowhere except at Palaiokastro does it appear to have been established that any of the finds can be assigned to the LH. III C period, even though settlement during this time is exceedingly probable.

Evidence is also almost non-existent for the Protogeometric period. There was a reasonable amount of late Geometric pottery at the sanctuary of Alea Athena; of earlier material, only one sherd [5] can be claimed definitely to be Protogeometric, though one or two other pieces may belong to this style,[6] and one sherd is similar in type to the Protogeometric pottery of Amyklai.[7]

3. *Laconia*

To judge from Homer, this region must have constituted one of the most important kingdoms of the Mycenaean world. Furthermore, we know that Laconia became the stronghold of the Dorians. It is therefore all the more disappointing to have to record that the archaeological evidence for this period is at present extremely scanty; even though important sites have been identified, they still await excavation.

Our knowledge of prehistoric Laconia, whether through excavation, survey or casual find, was briefly summarized by Mrs. Waterhouse for the period up to 1956,[8] since when she and Hope Simpson have been engaged in preparing a more detailed survey (embodying further investigation up to 1959), which has now been published.[9] Full references to earlier work are contained in these articles.

---

[1] Charneux and Ginouvès, *Reconnaissances en Arcadie* (*BCH*, lxxx. 522 ff.).

[2] *Die kretisch-mykenische Kultur*, p. 10.

[3] Dugas, *BCH*, xlv. 403 and Figs. 59 (No. 247) and 61 (No. 248).

[4] *Ergon* for 1956, pp. 81 f. *JHS*, lxxv. suppl., p. 10; *Archaeological Reports for 1956*, p. 12; *BSA*, lvi. 130.

[5] *BCH*, xlv, Fig. 57 (No. 312).

[6] Op. cit. Fig. 54 (No. 256), and the pyxis on Fig. 59 (No. 304).

[7] Op. cit. Fig. 56 (No. 261).

[8] *BSA*, li. 168 ff.

[9] *BSA*, lv. 67 ff; lvi. 114 ff.

Only a small number of Mycenaean settlements have yet been excavated in Laconia. Sparta needs only a passing mention; over the whole site, no more than a handful of Mycenaean sherds was found, and these not associated with any habitation; LH. III B was identified, but nothing later.[1] Two miles south-east of Sparta, however, on naturally defensible hills, the traces were recognized of what was evidently a sizeable Mycenaean city. This city was so thoroughly destroyed by fire that there remained only one house at all well preserved, and no further use was made of the area till Geometric and later times, when a shrine of Menelaos and Helen was erected.[2] It would clearly be of great importance to be able to tell at what point this site suffered catastrophe. The illustrated sherds[3] are unfortunately not very great in quantity; nevertheless, from the excavator's reference to Furtwängler and Löschcke's 'Third' style, as well as from the sherds themselves, it is certain that LH. III B is represented, and some are perhaps late in it, but there is no sherd that can with certainty be assigned to LH. III C. It is reasonable to assume that the destruction occurred during or at the end of LH. III B (not earlier, anyway). One should perhaps not entirely rule out the possibility of destruction in early LH. III C, though it must be presumed that any Close Style sherds found would almost certainly have been illustrated.

A similar picture seems to be emerging from the excavations in progress at Ayios Stefanos, in the Helos Plain; the one vase illustrated is LH. III C, but its prominence is due to the fact that 'hardly any other pottery later than Myc. III B was recovered during the excavations'.[4] In fact, the settlement seems to stretch from Early Helladic to LH. III B, the extremely rare later material being very possibly from tombs. The other excavated site in this area, Asteri, was 'much denuded', but LH. III pottery was plentiful, the majority belonging to LH. III B, with just a few sherds tentatively assigned to early LH. III C.[5]

The general impression, as will be seen, is one of destruction and desertion at the end of LH. III B or the transition to LH. III C. However, a notable exception is Amyklai;[6] the Late Helladic material from this site makes it clear that it was used as a sanctuary, and it was also so used from Archaic times onwards. Protogeometric and Geometric pottery were found, connected rather with the Mycenaean sanctuary than with the Archaic,[7] but whether this can be interpreted as proving continuity from Mycenaean into the succeeding period, and whether the place was used as a sanctuary in Protogeometric and Geometric times, is most doubtful (see p. 42). It is certain enough, however, that there was a Mycenaean sanctuary, from the quantity of votive figurines, both human and animal.[8] Sherds were evidently rare, but of the few illustrated the ribbed kylix stem (presuming that such identification is correct) must be LH. III C, and the other four sherds could all be of the same period. Most of the figurines illustrated are not precisely datable, but there are two of animal type which are; one of them is decorated in the elegant Close Style, and the other, from its concentric loops and triangles, either plain or

---

[1] *BSA*, xxviii. 38 f., 79 and Pl. 5; *BSA*, xlv. 298, Fig. 19; *Archaeological Reports 1957*, p. 10.

[2] Tsountas, *AE*, 1889, pp. 130 f. *BSA*, xv. 108 ff.; *BSA*, xvi. 4 ff. and Pls. I–III; *BSA*, lv. 72.

[3] *BSA*, xvi. 8 f., Figs. 3 and 4.

[4] *Archaeological Reports for 1959–1960*, pp. 9 f. and Fig. 10.

[5] Loc. cit. and *BSA*, lv. 91.

[6] *AE*, 1892, pp. 1 ff.; *AM*, lii. 1 ff.; *JdI*, xxxiii. 107 ff.; *BSA*, lv. 74 ff.

[7] *AM*, lii. 32 f. Cf. *PGP*, pp. 284 ff.

[8] Op. cit. Beil. vi.

with a fringe of dots, is equally to be placed within LH. III C.[1] It may be that the whole of this material belongs to LH. III C; that is not provable, but at least the existence of a cult site in LH. III C is certain, and this runs counter to the impression gained from the previously discussed sites, and does not make the problems of interpretation any easier, nor can one say what stage of LH. III C is reached, relative to other areas.

Such is the record of settlements excavated or in course of excavation. The tomb material, except in one area, does not increase in any way our knowledge of Laconia at this time. The published pottery from the chamber tombs at Pellanes, north of Sparta, has been dated by Furumark to LH. III A.[2] A chamber tomb was dug near Tsasi in the Helos plain, by Karachalios, but only two vases have been illustrated, and these are assigned to LH. III A 2–B.[3] A slab-covered shaft tomb at Krokeai,[4] north of Gythion, excavated by Christou, contains pottery of even earlier date. The tholos tombs at Palaiochori, in Kynouria, were perhaps not used later than LH. III B.[5]

The one exception is the district round Monemvasia, where chamber tombs have been found on three sites.[6] A fair number of the vases from these burials are reported to belong to LH. III B and LH. III C. A few are illustrated, and one of these is a stirrup jar of the octopus type, while another stirrup jar is in a similarly flamboyant style, but most probably of local design. Fuller publication is awaited, but it may be noted that the vases (some of which are LH. III C) reported as coming from Epidaurus Limera, now in the Sparta Museum, are presumably from these sites, as the recent excavations are only a continuation of past unrecorded digging.[7] The interest of these tombs and their contents lies as much in their geographical location as in the evidence they produce of continuity into LH. III C (though not beyond this, so far as we know). This district is part of the south-east coast of the Peloponnese, and not only is its outlook naturally towards the Aegean, but it is also remote and somewhat difficult of access from the central Spartan plain—rather in the same way as Perati is cut off from the Athenian plain. The LH. III C pottery so far illustrated confirms the Aegean rather than the Mainland character of the area; indeed, Monemvasia would be a very useful harbour along a coastline which has few such facilities. In view of the fact that the Central and South Aegean were not affected by the Mainland disasters at the end of LH. III B, it is not surprising to find LH. III C flourishing here.

Apart from the relatively remote area round Monemvasia, the evidence so far discussed has suggested destruction or desertion at the end of LH. III B or at the time of transition from LH. III B to LH. III C, exception being made of the site of Amyklai. The survey undertaken by Mrs. Waterhouse and Mr. Hope Simpson has added considerable detail to the picture, and generally confirms the conclusions based on the material from the few excavated sites. A large number of new sites are identified, and some of these are of great potential interest.

---

[1] Op. cit. Beil. vi. 13–15.
[2] Karachalios, *AD*, x. suppl., pp. 41 ff. *Chronology*, p. 63. *BSA*, lvi. 125 ff. (a full discussion, in which it is concluded that early LH. III B pottery may also be represented).
[3] *AJA*, xlii. Pl. 21, 8; *BSA*, lv. 94, Fig. 12.
[4] *BSA*, lv. 103 ff., with references.
[5] *BSA*, lvi. 132 ff. Cf. *AD*, ix. suppl., 18 f.
[6] *Ergon* for 1956, pp. 96 ff.; *Archaeological Reports 1956*, p. 13 and Fig. 14; *BCH*, lxxxi. 552 f.; *BSA*, lvi. 136 f.
[7] *AJA*, lviii. 235; *AJA*, lix. 226.

The main new site is south of Amyklai, that of Palaiopyryi,[1] with which the Vaphio tomb is associated; the sherds collected suggest a Late Helladic settlement about 200,000 square metres in extent—much the largest site in all Laconia—with a time of greatest prosperity in LH. III B. No LH. III C sherds or objects are mentioned as having been found here, and a similar situation holds for the possibly fortified settlement of Ayios Vasilios,[2] two or three miles south of Palaiopyryi, stated to be second only in importance to it in the central Spartan plain, and equally flourishing in LH. III B. The same picture also emerges from the settlements at Goritsa, east of Amyklai, Lekas (probably walled) in the Helos plain, and Apidia to the east of Lekas.[3] There are reported to be major sites at Daimonia and Neapolis,[4] on the western side of the Malea peninsula, from both of which LH. III B sherds have been recovered, but none indicating LH. III C occupation. Finally, there is the important settlement at Mavrovouni,[5] south-west of Gythion, the material from which includes sherds tentatively assigned to early LH. III C.

Altogether, over fifty sites in Laconia are now known to have been occupied in the Late Helladic III period. For most of them, allowance has to be made for the fact that investigation has not yet penetrated below the surface, but there seems no doubt that the greatest expansion came during LH. III B.[6] As opposed to this, the evidence for LH. III C occupation is very slight indeed, only four sites (Amyklai, Ayios Stephanos, Asteri, Mavrovouni), apart from those in the neighbourhood of Monemvasia, having produced pottery of this period. The situation suggested by the bulk of the evidence (Amyklai still seems to occupy an exceptional position) is that of desertion of sites—the Menelaion settlement providing evidence also of destruction—before or at the end of LH. III B, or at latest at the time of transition to LH. III C, and therefore parallel to the situation in the south-west Peloponnese (cf. p. 97).

4. *South-West Peloponnese*

This area includes the regions treated by McDonald and Hope Simpson in their valuable recent survey,[7] which summarizes previous work and adds a great deal of new information. It may be divided, roughly, into the districts of Elis and Messenia.

(A) ELIS

The first district that may be considered is that of the lower Alpheios valley. McDonald and Hope Simpson conclude rightly that it was 'heavily populated in the late Bronze Age',[8] and it is therefore of importance to assess the information available for occupation in LH. III C and immediately thereafter. At the mouth of the river stands the site of Ayios Andreas,[9] the Pheia of classical times, providing the only natural harbour along the whole

---

[1] *BSA*, lv. 76 ff.
[2] Op. cit. pp. 79 ff.
[3] Op. cit. pp. 83, 95 ff., 86 f.
[4] *BSA*, lvi. 141 ff.
[5] Op. cit. pp. 114 ff. It may be noted that two fragmentary Protogeometric vases and part of an iron weapon have been found close to this site (op. cit. p. 115, Fig. 2; cf. *JHS*, lxxvii. suppl., 12).
[6] Op. cit. pp. 170 ff.
[7] 'Prehistoric Habitation in Southwestern Peloponnese', in *AJA*, lxv. 221 ff.
[8] Op. cit. p. 226.
[9] Op. cit. p. 224; and Yalouris, *AE*, 1957, pp. 31 ff.

coast of Elis. There is no doubt as to its occupation from very early times, and it appears to have flourished in LH. III A and B. Surface investigation [1] seems to indicate almost continuous habitation after these periods as well, as there is mention of 'sub-Mycenaean', Protogeometric and Geometric sherds, though there is nothing specifically called LH. III C. In the tests made by Yalouris there is no report of LH. III C or of Protogeometric, but the sporadic find of two 'sub-Mycenaean' vases is of particular interest. The vase illustrated [2] is a small two-handled (?) jar; the belly decoration of concentric fringed loops is a characteristic LH. III C motive, particularly prominent in Achaea, but the whole shape,[3] and also such features as the sharply angled belly and the high foot, reflect later developments. I would not like to hazard a guess at the date of this vase, but it may afford a link between Mycenaean and post-Mycenaean. Another item of interest from Yalouris's[4] report is that in four trenches dug down to virgin soil the lower level contained a few Mycenaean sherds and some Geometric pieces, which would indicate a gap in occupation on this part of the site.

As we move up the river, a brief mention may be made of the sites of Etia and Ayios Georgios,[5] both clearly occupied in LH. III B but not later, although a sherd from Ayios Georgios is probably close to LH. III C. The main district is, however, that of Olympia and its neighbourhood. Earlier excavators naturally concentrated on the overriding importance of the sanctuary, and little deliberate investigation of the period preceding the establishment of the sanctuary took place until recently. It has now been established that the main Mycenaean site was at and above the junction of the Kladeos and Alpheios rivers.[6] McDonald and Hope Simpson speak of 'masses of undecorated LH. III B pottery', and Yalouris has reported [7] finds suggesting uninterrupted habitation from Middle Helladic to Byzantine times, as well as a number of chamber tombs, one of which was excavated and found to contain three vases. In the area of the sanctuary itself not much has emerged. Most recently, tests in the stadium area produced a few late Mycenaean sherds underlying an archaic level.[8] From the earlier excavations we have one sherd,[9] with fringed concentric loops, which is certainly LH. III C,[10] perhaps of Achaean type; and a hydria from beneath the Heraeum might possibly, according to Furtwängler,[11] be Mycenaean. Note may also be made of a ribbed kylix stem,[12] which is very late in LH. III C, if not contemporary with Protogeometric, and of Willemsen's claim that the earliest tripod cauldrons go back to Protogeometric times.[13] There are then traces of LH. III C occupation, though it may be stressed that both this period and the ensuing Protogeometric are very poorly represented, and that it looks as though there was at least considerable depopulation, if not a break in occupation at some point. In any case, there are no grounds as yet for supposing that Olympia was a sanctuary area of the Mycenaean period.

[1] *AJA*, lxv. 224.
[2] *AE*, 1957, p. 38, Fig. 4.
[3] Cf. Vermeule, *AJA*, lxiv. Pl. 5, No. 57. Late Protogeometric from Derveni in northern Achaea.
[4] *AE*, 1957, pp. 40 f.
[5] *AJA*, lxv. 226 f. (Nos. 6 and 12).
[6] Op. cit. p. 226 (No. 7). Cf. *BCH*, lxxxiii. 655.
[7] *BCH*, lxxxiv. 720; *BCH*, lxxxv. 722.
[8] *BCH*, lxxxiv. 714.
[9] *AM*, xxxvi. 177 and 176, Fig. 20a.
[10] Cf. however, the remarks on the vase from Pheia, above.
[11] *Olympia* iv. 199 and Pl. 69: 1287.
[12] Benton, *BSA*, xliv. 311 and 309, Fig. 1, 2.
[13] *Olympische Forschungen* III, pp. 166 ff.

With this evidence from Olympia may be taken that of three sites, west and north of the sanctuary. A settlement not far to the west, at Ayios Elias,[1] produced nothing certainly later than LH. III B. This site may be connected with the major settlement close to Olympia. To the west of this, two chamber tombs were excavated at Kania, near Makrysia, the vases from which are LH. III B and show Rhodian influence.[2] To the north, at Kafkania, Yalouris has found a group of cist tombs, of which he has so far explored only one half-open one, which contained glass paste beads.[3] These finds might suggest a Mycenaean date for the tombs, which would be a matter of much interest, in view of the great rarity of this type of tomb in LH. III, but it is best to await further excavation.

As well as these sites, there are two others, further up the course of the Alpheios, which merit attention. The one is near Diasela,[4] some seven miles east of Olympia, and south of the river. Here, a group of three chamber tombs was excavated. Two of them contained no pottery later than LH. III B, but tomb B, of four burials, produced several vases which may cover the transition from LH. III B to LH. III C and early LH. III C. Glass paste ornaments of the conventional type were also recovered. Trial trenches on the high ground above the tombs have revealed a small fortified Mycenaean settlement[5] and pottery which extends from LH. III B to LH. III C, and may perhaps continue into 'sub-Mycenaean'. The other site, Palaiokastro,[6] is some fifteen miles further up the Alpheios, well into the interior, and in fact in Arcadia. The importance of this site lies in its strategic position, and in its extensive chamber tomb cemetery; it has not as yet been scientifically investigated, but the one vase illustrated is an LH. III C stirrup vase in the Achaean manner. There is no reason why both these sites should not have escaped the invasion of the end of LH. III B and perhaps have provided centres of refuge.

The three remaining sites[7] lie south of Olympia. They are the coastal settlements of Klidhi and Kakovatos, and Lepreon slightly inland.[8] In all there is evidence of occupation into LH. III B, but nothing later.

Apart from the above sites, which have produced evidence for Mycenaean occupation, two of slightly later date deserve mention. The first is Palaiopyrgo,[9] north of the Alpheios, some seven miles west of Olympia. Here a pithos burial was found, containing Protogeometric vases. No description is yet available of the pottery, but the manner of burial, in a pithos, is of much interest, as it is paralleled in Protogeometric times at Derveni in North Achaea (p. 101) and at Nichoria in Messenia (p. 96), but virtually unknown elsewhere during this period, though there are instances among the earliest burials at Vergina in West Macedonia, where the dead seem to have been of Balkan origin (pp. 144 f.).

The second site is that of the ancient Elis, some twenty miles north of any of the Mycenaean sites of this region. Excavations had originally been undertaken by the Austrian School,[10] and have now been resumed by Yalouris and others.[11] For the most part, the finds

---

[1] *AJA*, lxv. 229 (No. 14).
[2] Yalouris, *Pr.* 1954, pp. 295 ff.; Taylour, *MPI*, pp. 178 ff. and Pl. 16.
[3] *BCH*, lxxxv. 722.
[4] *BCH*, lxxxi. 574 ff. (Yalouris).
[5] Op. cit. pp. 578 f.; *AJA* lxv. 229 f. (No. 17).
[6] *BCH*, lxxx. 522 ff. and Fig. 18; *AJA*, lxv. 227 (No. 11).
[7] Note may also be made of the report of an LH. III C alabastron from Goumeron, *BCH*, lxxxiii. 658.
[8] *AJA*, lxv. 230 ff. (Nos. 19–21).
[9] Op. cit. p. 226 (No. 5).
[10] Tritsch, *ÖJh*, xxvii. 64 ff.
[11] *Ergon* for 1960, pp. 129 ff.; *Ergon* for 1961, pp. 177 ff.

belong to the Classical and later periods, but nine tombs discovered beneath the theatre are considerably earlier.[1] These are simple pits, enclosing one skeleton only, and covered by unworked slabs of stone; they thus appear to be a variation of the cist tombs found elsewhere in the Southwest Peloponnese and Achaea (cf. p. 39). The associated vases are said to be stylistically transitional from sub-Mycenaean to Protogeometric, and are thus of the greatest importance. Amphorae and jugs were represented, and of these, two jugs, one neck-amphora (with rope handles) and one belly-amphora are illustrated;[2] no necessarily sub-Mycenaean features are visible, but Protogeometric characteristics are clear. As well as the vases, the usual Protogeometric small finds came to light—pins, fibulae and rings, all of bronze—and an amber bead. Whatever the precise date of these burials, they are certainly not later than Protogeometric, and thus add greatly to our knowledge of this period in the West Peloponnese; in particular, the break with the preceding Mycenaean culture seems complete. New racial elements may be involved (cf. pp. 37 ff.).

(B) MESSENIA

There is a slight topographical gap in our knowledge between the southernmost settlement of the preceding area, Lepreon, and the sites which run eastwards from Kyparissia in Messenia. This may be accidental, but it is also convenient. The material from Messenia may be divided roughly into three groups;[3] that mentioned above, the very thickly populated area round Ano Englianos (Nestor's Palace), and the sites which are thinly strung out round the Messenian Gulf.

Of the dozen or so sites[4] which comprise the first group, most are either completely unrewarding or show no evidence, from surface exploration, of having been inhabited beyond early LH. III B, though it is presumed from their situation that Kyparissia was a major Late Bronze Age centre, and that Krebeni was an important site during this time. Only Mouriatadha and Malthi need further comment, both having been excavated.

Preliminary reports only are available for Mouriatadha, still in process of excavation by Marinatos.[5] This site has produced several interesting features. First, there is a very fine fortification wall, which the excavator has related to that at Gla in Boeotia. Second, there is an impressive *megaron*, which is identified as the ruler's palace. Third, a building of *megaron* type was uncovered, with remains of three columns, and this has provisionally been called a temple. Finally, a tholos tomb was dug, though only a few sherds were discovered.[6] The obvious question to which an answer is needed is that of the date of this settlement. Marinatos has stated[7] that the 'temple' belongs to the late thirteenth century, and it is reported by Mrs. Vermeule[8] that 'the town was destroyed by fire near the end of the thirteenth century B.C.'. According to the conventional system,[9] this should mean that the settlement was destroyed at the end of LH. III B, which would make its fall contemporary with that of the palace at Pylos, but it is clear that Marinatos believes the

---

[1] *Ergon* for 1961, pp. 186 ff.
[2] Op. cit. Fig. 188 (neck-amphora); Fig. 191 (belly-amphora); Figs. 189, 192 (jugs).
[3] Cf. *AJA*, lxv. Pls. 74 and 75.
[4] Op. cit. pp. 232 ff.

[5] *Ergon* for 1960, pp. 149 ff.
[6] A general lack of pottery is characteristic of this site.
[7] Op. cit. p. 157.
[8] *AJA*, lxv. 193.
[9] Cf. *AJA*, lx. 101.

catastrophe here to have come perhaps two generations later than that at Ano Englianos.[1] The relative, as well as the absolute date of the end of Mouriatadha must therefore be considered still to be obscure.

The settlement of Malthi,[2] a few miles east of Mouriatadha, is in a good strategic position, and from the full excavation one might have hoped for valuable information, but unfortunately the harvest of pottery was small and undistinguished. The site was occupied over a long period, and it is very likely that the occupation continued into LH. III C, from the sherd of a deep bowl,[3] and from the ribbed and swollen kylix stems[4] which suggest a possible link with Kephallenia and Ithaca. The stems also suggest an advanced stage of LH. III C, and a late date is confirmed by the discovery of an iron dagger and knife, and of other fragments of this metal.[5] It may be that we have here a survival into the Protogeometric period. The town was finally destroyed, and not again occupied.[6]

The central region of Messenia is dominated by the Palace of Nestor at Ano Englianos. There is no doubt that the palace was violently destroyed; the bulk of the pottery awaits full recording, but it has been very carefully studied, and Blegen has recently stated[7] that 'we can date the fire to a time when the style of Mycenaean III B was nearing its end, but had not yet been superseded by that of Mycenaean III C'; in his view, no more than a dozen out of eight thousand vases have LH. III C characteristics.[8] It so happens that two of this dozen have been illustrated:[9] an amphora with handles from shoulder to neck (apparently a feature of LH. III C), and a krater-bowl in dark ground technique[10] with a narrow band between the handles.

After the destruction of the palace and its dependencies (and it may be noted that no serious attempt was made to fortify the site) there was no reoccupation. Of the tombs close to the palace, only one tholos tomb (E6) is mentioned as having been in continuous use from LH. III A to LH. III C.[11] None of the later pottery from this tomb has been illustrated, but there is other evidence of slight occupation of the immediate area of the palace after its destruction.[12] A chamber tomb about two miles to the south produced pottery that was mainly LH. III B in character, but the kalathos could well be considered early LH. III C.[13] Furthermore, it is in this area that a small tholos tomb was excavated and found to contain Protogeometric vases.[14] There was no indication that this was simply a re-used Mycenaean tomb, and it seems therefore that this type of tomb was still being constructed in later times.

Apart from Ano Englianos, over thirty prehistoric sites have been identified in this small region, owing to the researches and excavations of Marinatos and Blegen, or newly recorded by McDonald and Hope Simpson.[15] Both cemeteries and settlements are well represented, and the general impression is that, where one can date the pottery within

---

[1] *Ergon* for 1960, p. 158.
[2] Valmin, *Swedish Messenia Expedition*.
[3] Op. cit. p. 325, Fig. 69 and Pl. XXIV, E4.
[4] Op. cit. p. 328.
[5] Op. cit. pp. 371 ff.
[6] Op. cit. p. 406.
[7] *AJA*, lxiv. 159.
[8] This statement must be taken to override any prior ones, e.g. *AJA*, lxi. 133.
[9] *AJA*, lxi, Pl. 43, Fig. 13.
[10] For the difficulties concerning the dating of bowls, cf. pp. 5 f., 11.
[11] *AJA*, lxii. 179.
[12] Cf. *AJA*, lxv. 238.
[13] *AJA*, lxiv. 158 and Pl. 48, Fig. 28.
[14] *AJA*, lxiii. 127 and Pl. 34, Fig. 17.
[15] *Pr.* 1953 ff.; *Ergon* for 1954 ff.; *AJA*, xliii and lvii ff.; *AJA*, lxv. 237 ff. and Pl. 75.

reasonably precise limits—as is possible in many cases—most of the sites were occupied into LH. III B but no later. A possible exception may be provided by the stag rhyton from Volimidhia tomb A6; It might belong to the LH. III C period, but I do not think there is any certainty of this.[1]

The only clear case of LH. III C occupation is provided by the tholos tomb at Tragana,[2] a couple of miles to the south-west of the palace. The first burial or burials in this belong to LH. I/II A and LH. III A 1; there was then a gap, and the tomb was not used again until LH. III C.[3] The evidence for this later use comes from two graves, both rectangular pits in the floor of the tomb (possibly made to house the earlier corpses?).[4] The first of these contained a krater and a belly-handled amphora, both in fragmentary condition and quite clearly LH. III C, though they may be early in the style, while the second had five vases—three one-handled jugs, a lekythos and a one-handled bowl with a surprisingly high foot, for which vase there are comparable parallels in Athens and at Emborio on Chios (see pp. 117, 159). From internal evidence, this second burial is the later,[5] and stylistically as well the dark-ground system on the jugs indicates a very late stage in LH. III C. Finally, the disturbed fill above the floor of the tomb produced further vases and sherds. Two of the vases are jugs, of much the same type as those of the later burial, but the remainder, bowl or amphoriskos sherds, are in a local Protogeometric style.[6] There is a temptation to suggest continuity, but I think one should resist this until further evidence is available. The tomb was re-examined in 1955 by Marinatos,[7] but no further information was gained about the LH. III C and Protogeometric use, nor were there any such traces in another tholos dug nearby—a tomb remarkable for perhaps the earliest instance of cremation in Mycenaean times.

The third group of sites is only nominally a group, for the settlements are spread out round the Messenian Gulf, including the rich plain of Kalamata.[8] The occupation picture is precisely the same as in the Pylos area. The two most important sites are those of Kaphirio and Nichoria on the west side of the gulf, at which trial excavations have taken place. At Kaphirio,[9] hardly any traces of the Mycenaean city were found, but LH. III and sub-Mycenaean sherds have been reported, and occupation in the Protogeometric period has been established.

Nichoria is in any case strategically important, since it controlled 'the pass on the main land route between eastern and western Messenia'.[10] The preliminary investigations have been exceptionally rewarding.[11] The acropolis contained the Mycenaean city, which was occupied from Middle Helladic down to LH. III B, and then destroyed probably at the same time as the Palace of Nestor. Cemeteries connected with this settlement have also been located, including at least four tholos tombs. Of almost greater interest, however, is the fact of later occupation, not on the acropolis itself, but in the surrounding area. This

---

[1] *Pr.* 1953, p. 242, Fig. 3; cf. *Archaeology*, xiii. 74, Fig. 14. It may be noted that Volimidhia provides an example of a later hero-cult.
[2] Kourouniotis, *AE*, 1914, pp. 99 ff.
[3] *Chronology*, pp. 55, 73, 76, 78.
[4] Cf. *PGP*, p. 282.
[5] *Chronology*, p. 73.
[6] *PGP*, p. 282.
[7] *Pr.* 1955, pp. 247 ff.; *Ergon* for 1955, pp. 88 f.
[8] Hope Simpson, *BSA*, lii. 231 ff.; *AJA*, lxv. 247 ff.
[9] *BCH*, lxxxiv. 700; *AJA*, lxv. 248 (No. 75) and 258, n. 16.
[10] *AJA*, lxv. 249 (No. 76).
[11] *ILN*, for 30 April 1960, pp. 740 f.

occupation stretched at least from Protogeometric onwards, and may have been earlier as well, for one report[1] claims that there was no discontinuity, and that there were tombs not only of the Protogeometric period but of the sub-Mycenaean as well. This report awaits confirmation so far as sub-Mycenaean is concerned, and presumably LH. III C also, but further investigation[2] of tombs has clearly established the fact of Protogeometric occupation. The burials took place in cist tombs and pithoi; there are no details available concerning the pithoi, except that they contained Protogeometric vases, but six cist tombs were excavated, and these were constructed in the dry-stone technique, and were apsidal.[3] It is said that a large number of Protogeometric vases were found, including oinochoai and amphorae, and also bronze pins. The only object to be illustrated is a small belly-handled amphora, ovoid in shape, in dark-ground technique, and with cross-hatched decoration between the handles; it certainly looks Protogeometric, though there is little trace of any Attic influence. It is also worthy of note that evidence of a hero cult has been found in a nearby chamber tomb. There is obviously no need further to stress the importance of this site for the whole early history of Messenia, though it should be remembered that the earliest Protogeometric burial is not likely to have taken place less than a hundred and fifty years after the destruction of the Mycenaean city.

As well as the Protogeometric pottery from Kaphirio and Nichoria, similar pottery has been recorded on other sites in this region, at the major site of Thouria,[4] and possibly at Kokkinochomata.[5] There is also a significant report of a remote site at Volimnos,[6] near Artemisia, close to the top of the Langadha pass connecting Kalamata and Sparta, on the Kalamata side. No Mycenaean pottery has been found, but occupation in the Protogeometric and Geometric periods is certain, the Protogeometric pieces including 'a jug neck and a krater piece, both with concentric compass-drawn semicircles and lattice pattern; high conical feet of skyphoi'. It would seem, then, that Attic Protogeometric technique had penetrated to this site, which is considered likely to have been a place of refuge (and it would be very interesting to know why).

(c) SUMMARY

Reference may most conveniently be made to McDonald and Hope Simpson for the conclusions justifiable on the present evidence. They are correct in stating that 'the time is not yet ripe for a comprehensive synthesis with far-reaching general conclusions',[7] but such observations as they make are of significance for this period.

Even allowing for the superficial nature of surface finds, the very considerable number of sites now identified presents a remarkable picture. There are thirteen certain, and seven probable, Late Helladic sites in Elis, while in Messenia nearly fifty sites are known to have been inhabited during this time. With reference to Mycenaean occupation, it is worth repeating the statement of McDonald and Hope Simpson that 'it is our definite impression

---

[1] *BCH*, lxxxiv. 700.

[2] Yalouris, *BCH*, lxxxv. 697 and 696, Fig. 7. Cf. p. 92 for a pithos burial in Elis.

[3] Cf. *BCH*, lxxxv. 682 for similar tombs of Geometric date near Chalandritsa in Achaea.

[4] *BSA*, lii. 245 (Laconian Protogeometric).

[5] *AJA*, lxv. 251 (No. 80).

[6] Op. cit. p. 255.

[7] Op. cit. p. 255.

... that a good number of the LH. sites were newly founded or much enlarged in LH. III, and particularly in the subdivision labelled B'.[1]

The flourishing state of affairs in LH. III B is in direct and startling contrast to the situation in LH. III C. The two writers mentioned above consider that only two sites, Diasela in Elis and Ano Englianos, have produced pottery of this period;[2] this may be so, though it is probable that Olympia, and Palaiokastro in Arcadia, should be added, and perhaps also Malthi. They also speak of sub-Mycenaean at Ayios Andreas in Elis and at Nichoria, and perhaps at Ayios Elias near Makrisia in Elis and at Kokkinochomata in Messenia. The basis for this subdivision is not entirely clear, as the material is not yet published, except for the one vase at Ayios Andreas, which does admittedly seem to contain elements both of the LH. III C style and of succeeding developments. In any case, the conclusion[3] of McDonald and Hope Simpson that the whole area was thoroughly depopulated in LH. III C, and indeed until Protogeometric, is clearly a valid one. It may also be added that throughout this period, probably not less than a century and a half, there is no evidence whatsoever of intrusive elements such as might be expected from the occupation of the land by invaders from outside Mycenaean territory.

It will be claimed that the Protogeometric period is not at all well represented, either, but there is more evidence for it than for the preceding period. Two sites in Elis are mentioned, and there are eight certain or probable ones in Messenia.[4] Furthermore, the pottery and tombs, except for the small tholos tomb south of Ano Englianos, are of an entirely different type from those characteristic of the Mycenaean age. This would appear to be the likely occasion for the arrival of new settlers. Also, as has been argued (pp. 37 ff., 72), the cist tombs at least were probably of northern origin.

5. *Achaea*

This area, which comprises the Panachaic mountain and its immediate surroundings, has produced a fairly regular output of Mycenaean sites since 1920,[5] the war years excepted. Preliminary reports have appeared from time to time, and a reasonable number of objects, considering the limitations, have been illustrated. Recently, Mrs. Vermeule has published a valuable general article on these sites and their contents, in which some vases are now illustrated for the first time, and others pictured with greater clarity.[6] The majority of the vases still await full publication, though at least the distribution of shapes is usually available.

The evidence is almost exclusively from tombs; only two settlements have been identified,[7] one of which, near Leontion, is known from surface finds, while the other, in the district of Pharai, near the village of Katarraktis, has on excavation produced various stone-built constructions, and a quantity of pottery, including shapes as yet noticeably absent from the tombs, such as kraters (one is illustrated), kylikes and hydriai. This dearth

---

[1] Op. cit. pp. 257 f.
[2] Op. cit. p. 258, n. 16.
[3] Op. cit. p. 258.
[4] Op. cit. p. 258, n. 16. The site of Volimnos should be added.
[5] The excavations were mainly undertaken by Kyparissis, cf. *AD*, ix and *Pr.* 1925 ff.
[6] *AJA*, lxiv. 1 ff. The map on p. 2 shows the sites.
[7] *BCH*, lxxxiii. 619 f.; *Ergon* for 1958, pp. 139 f.

of settlements may be due to ill-fortune or, as Professor Wace once suggested to me, it may be due to natural conditions, the buildings having been washed away in course of time. Or, of course, the building material may simply have been re-used, as was indeed confirmed in the case of the tombs from a considerable Mycenaean cemetery of over a hundred tombs at Prostovitsa.[1]

In view of the almost complete lack of published information with regard to settlements, one is bound to concentrate on the tombs, which are known from at least twenty sites. The startling fact which emerges from these is that all but a very few belong solely to the LH. III C period. Vrachneika,[2] the only coastal site not protected by the hills, was used down to LH. III B, but not later; Kato Goumenitsa,[3] the most remote site of all, has LH. III A pottery; the few sherds from the tholos tombs near Katarraktis[4] are said to be LH. III B (and may thus provide the date of the nearby settlement). Apart from this, the material is uniformly LH. III C with occasional LH. III B survivals, and indicates, as Mrs. Vermeule says,[5] 'an extensive Mycenaean penetration' at the beginning of LH. III C; this material deserves rather more detailed discussion, though it may first be noted that all the LH. III C burials were inhumations in relatively small chamber tombs, thus typically Mycenaean.

As to the finds other than pottery, little need be said. The two cut-and-thrust swords and the greaves from Kallithea[6] probably belong to the early LH. III C period; the cut-and-thrust sword from the Klauss cemetery[7] could also be early in LH. III C, though the tombs go down some way into the period. Apart from one or two spearheads, there are hardly any other weapons. The ornaments are predominantly Mycenaean in character, the majority necklace beads, mostly of glass paste; precious metals are noticeably absent, in contrast to LH. III C sites in the Aegean, and one may reasonably conclude that the inhabitants were either unable to afford such luxury, or were cut off from the source. Amber is found, but in very small quantities; contact with the North directly or, more likely, indirectly, is thus established, but no fibulae or long pins were found at all, suggesting that these innovations may never have been accepted in this district (their absence may nevertheless simply be accidental).

As to the vases, it is not always quite clear from the description what type of shape is in question, but a fair amount of probability can be arrived at by comparison with the illustrations given. The stirrup jars (Pl. 10d, e) are the most popular shape, and would seem to comprise a good half of the total; they may be divided into two categories, large and small. For the rest, the amphoriskoi (one of which has a curious high openwork base)[8] are fairly popular, and so are the alabastra and pyxides; there are several one-handled jugs, though in nothing like such quantities as have been found in the Kephallenian cemeteries. A few three-handled piriform jars carry on the LH. III B tradition, but there was only one kylix, and no mention at all of any deep bowls. Two kalathoi, one of which is spouted, are illustrated from the rich Klauss cemetery not far from Patras, and these

[1] *Pr.* 1928, p. 115.
[2] *BCH*, lxxviii. 124; *BCH*, lxxx. 291.
[3] *Pr.* 1925–6, pp. 43 ff., 130 f.; *Pr.* 1927, p. 52.
[4] *BCH*, lxxxi. 579.
[5] *AJA*, lxiv. 18.
[6] *BCH*, lxxviii. 124 f. Cf. pp. 63 f.
[7] *Pr.* 1938, pp. 118 f.
[8] *AJA*, lxiv. Pl. 3. Cf. a vase from Volimidhia in Messenia (*Pr.* 1953, p. 242, Fig. 3).

also produced four bird-vases (Pl. 10 *f*) of an astonishingly developed type, the closest parallels to which come from the early Geometric tombs of Cyprus and from Protogeometric tombs at Fortetsa near Knossos (the Cypriot tombs are in fact earlier than the Cretan)—one is bound to wonder whether any connexion is possible.[1] Then there are five ring vases, of the kind found sporadically throughout the Mycenaean world at this time.

The two most distinctive shapes, however, are the large four-handled amphora or storage jar (Pl. 10*a-c*), and the large belly-handled amphora with warts on the shoulder, rather less common in Achaea than the former, but certainly uncommon elsewhere. These, with the bird vases, may be said to be peculiar to Achaea, and the general distribution of shapes is individual (cf. p. 10). There is no sense of dependency on any central region. Also, it is worth stressing that this is by no means a decadent type of LH. III C pottery. The technique and draughtsmanship of the vases are excellent.

To return to the stirrup jars. These are usually globular, with sloping shoulders—though there are still some whose shoulders are angular. The LH. III B system of bands disappears, as in other regions; only a few retain the alternation of thick and thin bands, which may be a survival from the earlier practice. Much more commonly, a succession of equally-spaced thin bands covers a large area of the body below the shoulder, even at times carried on right down to the foot; and there are a number of stirrup jars with the whole, or most, of the body painted over. Just occasionally there are subsidiary zones of decoration below the shoulder, but in the main decoration is restricted to the shoulder itself, the motives having much in common with those found elsewhere in Greece and the Aegean. Concentric semicircles are particularly popular, the outermost semicircle often being fringed or dotted; the fringe, indeed, is something of a local peculiarity,[2] though by no means unknown in other areas. There is even one case (on a four-handled jar) where the imagination of the painter has led him to transform the semicircles into birds.[3]

The other chief decorative motive is the cross-hatched triangle, as the excavator makes clear;[4] there are other motives as well (e.g. chevrons), but it is not always easy to make them out from the original illustrations.[5]

The concentric semicircle motive, dotted or fringed, is also the motive most frequently encountered on the big four-handled jars and the belly-amphorae, but the decoration of these vases may be more elaborate, and there are definite reminiscences of the Argive Close Style.[6] The belly zone of the four-handled jars may be decorated; a single wavy line may be noted in one instance.[7] In general, a closely banded or dark-ground system is used, as on the stirrup jars.

Other shapes have a fairly limited range of mainly rectilinear and curvilinear motives—chevrons, semicircles, vertical and diagonal lines, cross-hatched and hatched triangles, spirals. Some are simply banded. Mention may finally be made of the shallow saucer with high handle, displaying three rather fierce fish inside, not unlike those of the Dodecanese, and showing that the Achaean potter could produce a naturalistic design.[8]

---

[1] Cf. *SCE*, IV, 2, Fig. VII: 7 and 13 (CG.IA), and *Fortetsa*, especially Pl. 106, No. 1518.
[2] *AJA*, lxiv. 17.
[3] Op. cit. Pl. 1, Fig. 2. See Pl. 10*b*.
[4] *Pr.* 1939, pp. 103 ff.
[5] Presumably motives L–R, in *AJA*, lxiv. Pl. 6, belong in part to stirrup jars.
[6] *AJA*, lxiv. 17 and Pls. 1 and 2.
[7] Op. cit. Pl. 2, Fig. 9. Pl. 10*a*.
[8] Op. cit. Pl. 4.

There remains the problem of relative chronology. At the earlier end this is not too difficult, as the occasional vase of LH. III B type in otherwise LH. III C groups shows a time of transition; also, there do seem to be connexions with the Argive Close Style, and these suggest the earlier part of III C. On the other hand, no conclusions can be reached from the semicircles and cross-hatched triangles, as the former motive certainly became a popular feature of LH. III C from the beginning, and the latter need not have been far behind it.

Two vases of probably Achaean type have been found outside this district. One of them, a belly-handled amphora with warts, was discovered in a tomb at Pteleon in South Thessaly,[1] associated with a hydria which is not unlike the Achaean four-handled jar, and a three-handled piriform jar which indicates an early date in LH. III C (cf. p. 130). The other, a four-handled jar, was found in Phocis [2]; it looks rather late, but unfortunately has no datable context (cf. p. 126).

It is then reasonable to suppose that an influx of Mycenaeans took place when LH. III C had started to take over from LH. III B—not far from the time of the establishment of the Perati settlement in Attica. Contact was maintained with some other areas in early LH. III C, but what happened after this? Mrs. Vermeule sees the influence of the Granary Class in the wavy line on the belly of a four-handled jar and in the transformation of the semicircles into a dark blob, and connexion with Protogeometric in the dark-ground style, the rope and double loop handles, and in certain shapes—the duck vases, a pyxis and a four-handled jar.[3] As to the Granary Class, the instances given do not seem to be altogether convincing, and it is a great pity that we have no similar shapes for comparison, especially deep bowls—but cups, lekythoi and trefoil-lipped oinochoai are also lacking. On the other hand, the links with Attic Protogeometric are very tempting, but even here I do not think we can be sure. The development of the dark-ground system could well come early in the Achaean LH. III C series, and be peculiar to it. The twisted rope handle is to be found in Athens at the transition of LH. III B to C.[4] But the double loop handles on the pyxis look very late, and the pyxis, also strutted, from a transitional sub-Mycenaean-Protogeometric tomb in the Kerameikos,[5] could suggest a link, though for the decoration and the double loop handle one might find something even closer in Crete. The remarkably late and developed appearance of the duck vases has already been commented on.

On the whole, I am inclined to think that the influence of the Granary Class is not demonstrable, but at the same time it does seem quite possible that the Mycenaeans maintained themselves in Achaea for some long time. In the latter part of LH. III C there may have been a relative isolation (it is noticeable that the ceramic developments centred in the Aegean do not seem to have reached this district), though it may be that some of the stirrup jars in the late LH. III C Temenos tomb at Delphi reflect continued contact with Achaea.[6] Nor is there any reason why the Achaean tombs should not still have been in use when Athenian sub-Mycenaean was giving way to Protogeometric, especially if one supposes that this sub-Mycenaean was mostly contemporary with the latest LH. III C (see

---

[1] Verdhelis, *Pr.* 1953, pp. 122 f.
[2] Lerat, *Les Locriens de l'Ouest*, Pl. 52.
[3] *AJA*, lxiv. 17 f.
[4] Broneer, *Hesp.* viii. 393 f., Figs. 74, 75.
[5] *Ker.* I, Pl. 61, No. 533.
[6] *FD*, v. 9 ff.

pp. 17 ff.). But I do not think we are yet quite in a position to prove it. What we can at least be sure of, however, is that the inhabitants of Achaea in LH. III C times preserved the pure Mycenaean tradition (there is no hand-made pottery, as in Kephallenia, and fibulae and long bronze pins do not find their way here). It could well be that most of them were fugitives from disaster in the Argolid, and Mycenaean civilization may have survived untainted for longer here than in most parts of Greece.

After the abandonment of the Mycenaean cemeteries there was apparently a complete break. Only a few traces have so far been found of the eventual successors to the Mycenaeans, but such as there are show an entirely different type of culture. The earliest post-Mycenaean evidence is that of a late Protogeometric burial at Derveni near Aigion.[1] The pottery shows connexions with that of Ithaca,[2] and the manner of burial, inhumation in a pithos, has interesting contemporaneous parallels in Elis and Messenia (cf. pp. 92, 96). Apart from this, three sites have produced burials of the Geometric period, on one of which, near Pharai, cist tombs were presumably connected with a nearby settlement.[3] The second is the site of Troumbe,[4] close to Chalandritsa, and from both of these sites Geometric pottery, which needs no further comment, has been recorded. The third site has only recently been discovered, and this also was near Chalandritsa.[5] The Geometric pottery from the burials has not yet been published, but the manner of burial is again worthy of comment. Cist tombs were used, as at Pharai—a type of tomb widely known in Greece and the Aegean during this period; it is reported, however, that they were built in the dry-stone technique, and that the ends of one were apsidal, features which are also known in the Protogeometric tombs of Nichoria in Messenia (cf. p. 96). A further feature is that the tombs were covered by two tumuli. To what extent this is significant I do not know, but it is clear that it was a practice common to Central Europe,[6] and not familiar to Greece.

[1] *BCH*, lxxvi. 222; *AJA*, lxiv. 16 f. and Pl. 5.
[2] Cf. e.g. *AJA*, lxiv, Pl. 5, No. 51 with *BSA*, xxxiii. 49, Fig. 26, No. 75 (Aetos).
[3] Zapheiropoulos, *Pr.* 1952, pp. 400 ff.
[4] *Pr.* 1930, pp. 85 f.
[5] *BCH*, lxxxv. 682.
[6] Cf. Dakaris, *AE*, 1956, p. 149. A similar practice is found at Vergina in Macedonia.

CHAPTER IV

NORTH-WEST GREECE AND THE IONIAN ISLANDS

With the exception of Kephallenia and Ithaca, our knowledge either of Mycenaean occupation of or contact with the Mycenaean world in these areas is extremely slender. So far as North-west Greece is concerned, the report of Miss Benton [1] some thirty years ago indicated that such contact or occupation in LH. III B or LH. III C was restricted to inland Thermon and to coastal Kryoneri, Koronta and Astakos. Later cross-references to the material from Polis in Ithaca added slightly to our knowledge of Astakos,[2] but the excavation of the Ayios Nikolaos site near Astakos produced one Mycenaean sherd only, and that a poor one.[3]

In view of this dearth of material, the recent investigation of a tholos tomb south-east of Parga is of great value.[4] The contents, apart from the corpses, consisted of sherds of LH. III B and of native pottery, and a bronze lanceolate spearhead. The excavator connects this evidence with material from the Acheron district, in all giving a clear indication of Mycenaean settlement in western Epirus.[5]

While admitting that there were probably Mycenaean outposts on the coast of North-west Greece (an important fact by itself), one must realize that the area was principally peopled by non-Mycenaeans, and that it cannot be considered part of the Mycenaean empire. These contacts were chiefly, and naturally, to be found on the coast, and their strength diminished as one went inland, as is shown in the extremely interesting cist tombs discovered at Kalbaki, near Iannina.[6] Here, the pottery was entirely non-Mycenaean, but the other finds suggested Mycenaean contacts, and included a short sword which is of Mycenaean character, and which Dakaris placed, on typological grounds, late in LH. III B.[7] The possible significance of the cist manner of burial is discussed in chapter II, but the main point to be made here is that culturally this was a different world from that of the Mycenaeans. Such a difference in cultures does not of course rule out the possibility of racial affinity, but Mycenaean political control is most unlikely. Future exploration may naturally modify this picture, but it is at present reasonable to conclude that the Achaeans, so far as North-west Greece is concerned, had only a precarious hold on the coast and on areas easily accessible from the coast—perhaps even 'hold' is too strong a word.

---

[1] *BSA*, xxxii. 239 f. and 237, Fig. 18 for a useful map showing the sites.
[2] Benton, *BSA*, xxxix. 9, n. 3; 10, n. 7; 13, n. 6.
[3] Benton, *BSA*, xlii. 173 and Pl. 28, 1.
[4] Dakaris, *Ergon* for 1960, pp. 110 f.
[5] Op. cit. p. 111. Cf. *AE*, 1956, pp. 120 ff., 152 f.; *Pr.* 1951, p. 182, Fig. 7; *Pr.* 1952, p. 365, Fig. 3 (Kastritsa).
[6] Dakaris, *AE*, 1956, pp. 114 ff.
[7] Op. cit. pp. 143 f.

In the Ionian islands, there is no certain LH. III C pottery from Leucas,[1] while a site on Zakynthos, which included a tholos tomb, seems to have presented much the same picture as Astakos.[2] The dearth of material is probably to some extent due to lack of systematic exploration and excavation. Certainly a very different situation applies in Kephallenia and Ithaca, islands that lie in between Leucas and Zakynthos, and to which the remainder of this chapter is devoted.

1. *Kephallenia*

Excavations have taken place on this island over a long period, and hence the quality of publication is somewhat uneven. Kephallenia is unfortunately one of the districts known to us almost exclusively through cemeteries; the only settlement which has received any attention is that of Krania,[3] where a Mycenaean house was identified, as well as traces of others—but no useful chronological indication could be obtained either from the architectural remains or from the few sherds.

For the rest, it is a matter of tombs, and almost invariably these can be assigned to the LH. III C period, although at times there are clear vestiges of LH. III B survival. The one cemetery which was probably earlier than LH. III C is that of Kokkolata.[4] Four cist tombs were found, the contents of which are not easy to date—they could be Middle Helladic. Two tholoi were also discovered, and a number of shaft burials, perhaps similar to those found commonly on other sites. One vase only was illustrated, a triple cluster of miniature piriform jugs, which could be either LH. III B or LH. III C, but which is more likely to be the former.[5] A surprisingly large number of sealstones was found in the tholoi and shafts;[6] taking into account the scarcity of such objects in the tombs which are known to be LH. III C, one is tempted to suggest a date for these not later than LH. III B.

Apart from this, the vases from Livatho,[7] now in the Museum at Neuchâtel in Switzerland, are mainly LH. III C, and so are those (such as are illustrated) from the extensive cemetery of Mazarakata,[8] in the Livatho district. This latter cemetery consisted of sixteen rock-cut tombs, with shaft burials to a total of eighty-three in all. The persistence of LH. III B pottery types is observable in the small three-handled piriform jar, but otherwise this seems to be a predominantly III C series. There is a strong element of local ware, possibly representing a native, non-Mycenaean, population—a factor which recurs, as will be seen, in the more fully recorded cemeteries. Furthermore, two violin-bow fibulae were found (presumably both of the same type—only the one is illustrated[8]), as well as conventional Mycenaean jewellery, bronze spearheads and knives, and bronze pins, one at least of which has a double spiral head.[9]

---

[1] Benton, *BSA*, xxxix. 9, nn. 2 and 3; 10, n. 7.

[2] Taylour, *MPI*, pp. 186 f. (Miss Benton's information). Cf. op. cit. p. 186: 'Excavations at Zante seem to show that all periods were represented.'

[3] Marinatos, *AE*, 1932, pp. 14 ff.

[4] Cavvadias, *Pr*. 1912, pp. 250 ff.

[5] Cavvadias, Προϊστορική Ἀρχαιολογία, p. 371, Fig. 471.

[6] *Pr*. 1912, pp. 264 ff. and 256 f., Figs. 10–27.

[7] Cavvadias, *CRAI*, 1909, pp. 382 ff.

[8] Προϊστορική Ἀρχαιολογία, pp. 355 ff.

[9] Cavvadias, *CRAI*, 1911, pp. 6 ff.

The three most important cemeteries, from the point of view both of finds and publication, are Metaxata,[1] where the influence of LH. III B is still apparent at the beginning, but where the bulk of the material belongs to LH. III C, and Lakkithra[2] and Diakata,[3] where the pottery is almost without exception LH. III C in style.

The cave-like chambers, hollowed out of the soft rock, each contained a number of pits for the corpses. Whereas there is no particular evidence of a dromos at Diakata and Lakkithra, a stepped dromos was provided at Metaxata, parallels to which can be found in Crete and occasionally at Mycenae and Ialysos.[4] At Metaxata, also, the top two-thirds of the chambers were built up in stone in the fashion of a tholos, a phenomenon perhaps paralleled at Volimidhia in Triphylia.[5] While there were few burials at Diakata, the tombs of Metaxata and Lakkithra contained from ten to twelve burial pits each, in which the inhumated bodies were placed (there is no trace of cremation in any tomb). In two of the tombs at Lakkithra the pits were laid out in two parallel lines of five, but in the rest there was no particularly systematic arrangement.

The small finds, that is to say the personal ornaments and weapons, are of great interest. It is clear that most of them reflect the continuance of Mycenaean civilization; there were numerous necklaces, of beads of differing kinds of stone; there were many little bronze plaques with Mycenaean patterns, such as rosettes and ivy-leaves; there were gold rosettes and other golden objects of Mycenaean character—almost all found at Lakkithra, which may then have been the richest of the three cemeteries; there were many buttons of steatite, and bronze knives.[6]

The fact that no object of iron has yet appeared may be to some extent a chronological pointer, though it may equally mean only that iron took rather longer to reach this area than the Aegean—in any case, it is a matter of negative evidence. On the positive side, there were non-Mycenaean objects, among which I would number the few fibulae: three or four were found at Metaxata, one of which came from the earliest burial of all, B2, datable to LH. III B rather than to LH. III C.[7] Diakata had the curious double spiral fibula,[8] but no fibulae at all were found in the Lakkithra cemetery. The long bronze pins of Diakata[9] are not Mycenaean and could perhaps have come from the north, though there is no proof of this. More certain evidence of objects of northern origin is provided by the amber beads, found in some quantity;[10] and a similar northern origin has been suggested for the two lanceolate spearheads.[11]

It is very likely that the population of this island included a native element, distinct from the Mycenaean. The numerous hand-made vases found in the tombs suggest this conclusion; it was only very exceptionally the Mycenaean practice to introduce hand-made vases in a burial deposit, and it was never done to the extent that it is in Kephallenia. The Lakkithra and Metaxata cemeteries combined produced rather over four hundred

---

[1] Marinatos, *AE*, 1933, pp. 73 ff.
[2] Marinatos, *AE*, 1932, pp. 17 ff.
[3] Kyparisses, *AD*, v. pp. 92 ff.
[4] *AE*, 1933, pp. 74 ff., 95, Figs. 13, 17 and 19.
[5] Op. cit. p. 77 f., Figs. 17 and 19; cf. *Pr.* 1952, p. 494.
[6] *AE*, 1932, pp. 38 ff., Pls. 14–18; *AE*, 1933, pp. 90 ff., Figs. 39 ff. and Pl. 3.
[7] *AE*, 1933, pp. 92 and 93, Fig. 42.
[8] *AD*, v. 118, Fig. 33.
[9] Op. cit. p. 117, Fig. 32.
[10] *AE*, 1932, p. 42; *AE*, 1933, pp. 92 f. and 94, Fig. 43.
[11] *AE*, 1933, p. 92, Fig. 41; cf. *PPS*, 1948, p. 184, Fig. 2.

vases, of which about fifty were of the local hand-made variety—quite a fair proportion of the whole.

The remainder of the pottery is in the Mycenaean tradition, though there are a number of peculiarities distinguishing it from that of other areas. The distribution list of shapes differs from that found elsewhere (p. 10). Stirrup jars are indeed as popular as in other districts, but they are equalled in popularity by the little one-handled jugs, one variety of which, with a rather large handle placed vertically on the body, seems peculiar to Kephallenia. The kylix (Pl. 9b) is found more commonly in these tombs than in any others of LH. III C date; there are nearly forty of them as compared, for example, with the solitary one recorded from the Achaean cemeteries. They have almost invariably a funnel-shaped body, the stem often being swollen, and in one or two cases sharply ribbed (a similar feature is found in Ithaca, p. 109). Amphoriskoi and pyxides are reasonably common, the latter having the slightly curved base which is characteristic of LH. III B. High-handled dippers are on the whole more numerous in Kephallenia than elsewhere, but one of the most popular shapes of this district is the krater (Pl. 8). Nearly forty of these were found, almost all from Lakkithra, and seventeen of them have vertical side-handles—another peculiarity of this part of the Mycenaean world. It is in any case rare to find kraters of any sort in tombs of this period. Three-handled piriform jars of LH. III B type are known, but are not common—so it is with the deep bowls, on one of which a trace of the Granary Class may be detected.[1] Two double vases, a four-handled amphora, a belly-handled amphora (rather of the amphoriskos type, as found at Asine), a three-handled amphoriskos, a ring-vase, a cup, two straight-sided 'bottles' or jugs, and a few oddments, more or less make up the tally.

This vase distribution shows the independence of the Kephallenian series, but not its isolation. Certain decorative elements common to the early phase of LH. III C elsewhere are found here as well.

The stirrup jars form, as usual, the best point of comparison with stylistic tendencies observed in other districts. One only is of the LH. III B period,[2] and is almost certainly an import; it is noticeable that only the top half of it remains, whereas all the rest are complete. It is a survivor in an otherwise LH. III C congregation. In shape, Kephallenian stirrup jars are generally globular, with sloping shoulders (as in the Rhodian series), just a few having a flattened shoulder, and the maximum diameter coming above the belly. The disc of the stirrup is either level, or has a shallow indentation, or may have a slightly protruding knob. An airhole was found on only one vase, from Metaxata.[3] The foot is as a rule of the ring-base variety, but it may on occasions be slightly conical.

The LH. III B system of band decoration is entirely discarded, only a few retaining even the alternation of thick and thin bands. For the most part, after three or four thin bands below the shoulder, the rest of the body is either left clear or else completely painted over; a few have bands all the way down or, as on one of those from Diakata,[4] bands to below the belly, and then paint.

Apart from this, decoration is almost entirely confined to the shoulder, a narrow

---

[1] *AE*, 1932, Pl. 12, No. 185.
[2] Op. cit. Pl. 11, No. 180.
[3] *AE*, 1933, p. 88.
[4] *AD*, v. 108, Fig. 24, 3.

subsidiary zone of zigzags, wavy line, or vertical lines being found on a handful of vases only. Knowledge of the Argive Close Style is suggested by the shoulder decoration of two stirrup jars, one of which has a triangle motive with angle-filling multiple arcs, and the other an antithetic spiral.[1] Rather poor evidence; either the connexion itself was very tenuous and not at first-hand, or the potters of this area did not feel themselves competent to undertake anything elaborate. Indeed, there are no birds, fish, octopods or anything of this nature, such as are found on the Argive, Dodecanesian, Cretan, or even occasionally the Achaean vases. Much more common are the simpler motives evolved at or near the beginning of LH. III C, the concentric semicircles and the hatched or cross-hatched triangles (not outlined); these are the motives found on about one half of the stirrup jars. Apart from these, lozenges and spirals are occasionally used, and in one case a double arc connected with vertical lines,[2] a motive much more popular in the Dodecanese. Although the decoration of many of the stirrup jars cannot be discerned, the popularity of semicircles and triangles, motives equally popular in most other Mycenaean districts at this time, indicate the persistence of some intercommunication at least for a while.

Most of the stirrup jars are small; of the larger type, one may show connexion with Achaea.[3] It has a double strip handle, a rather conical foot, has dotted sets of concentric semicircles round the shoulder, supported by three bands, and is entirely painted over below these.

Turning to the kraters, it is noteworthy that they usually have a high foot, conical, flaring, pedestal or ribbed.[4] As to the manner of decoration below the handles, there are various systems of bands, or else the surface is wholly painted over. The main motives come between the handles, and in most cases consist of a succession of spirals, occasionally interrupted by cross-hatched lozenges or hatched triangles.[5] The larger of these vases sometimes have panelled motives, as opposed to the spiraliform, and the panelling consists of vertical lines in conjunction with collateral semicircles, cross-hatched lozenges, zigzags and loops. One of the two kraters from Diakata is painted with special care, and probably reflects the influence of the Argive Close Style.[6]

The most important feature about the kylikes, apart from their quantity and shape, is the decoration of some of them, which is highly individual. This decoration is applied between the handles, and is linear—cross-hatched triangles, triangles placed sideways, collateral semicircles flanking vertical lines, one instance of a wavy line.[7] The general effect is not too happy, and the painter evidently no longer had a satisfactory model to go by.

The pyxides, as stated above, usually have a curved base, but the flat base also is found.[8] Their handle decoration varies between chevrons, semicircles, spirals, cross-hatching,

[1] *AE*, 1932, Pl. 6, Nos. 39 and 41.
[2] *AE*, 1933, p. 86, Pl. 1, B 10.
[3] *AE*, 1932, Pl. 10, No. 148.
[4] They sometimes have a spout on the lip; cf. *AE*, 1932, Pl. 4. A similar practice is found at Athens.
[5] The close similarity between one of the Kephallenian kraters (*AE*, 1932, Pl. 4, No. 8) and a krater from Philistine Gezer (Macalister, *Gezer*, iii. Pl. 163, 2) might indicate some link between the two areas, but this is not confirmed by other evidence and it may only signify that we have an as yet unfilled lacuna for kraters in other districts. Even so, the vertical-handled kraters seem to be peculiar to Kephallenia.
[6] *AD*, v. 102 f., Figs. 17 and 18.
[7] *AE*, 1932, Pl. 6; *AE*, 1933, p. 80, Fig. 23.
[8] The two straight-sided bottles may have developed from this shape.

zig-zags and a wavy line; similar motives are to be found on the amphoriskoi, though here the hatched triangle also appears, and the vase may be monochrome.

There are three instances of a single wavy line in a panel on a vase which is otherwise painted over—on one of the amphoriskoi, on the four-handled vase and on the collar-neck amphora.[1] This system of decoration is strongly evocative of the Granary Class, and indeed the collar-neck amphora is itself a very late shape in other areas. If Granary Class influence is to be supposed, then it may be that the monochrome application of paint to certain vases may also be taken into consideration, though not with the one-handled jugs, which are almost all monochrome.

There is good reason confidently to assign these three sets of tombs, at Diakata, Lakkithra and Metaxata, to the LH. III C period. Such few vases then as still show the characteristics of LH. III B will belong to the end of that period when LH. III C elements had already started to appear. An analysis of the pottery shows an individual local style, with one or two shapes apparently peculiar to the district, and a different distribution of vase types from that which is found elsewhere; in addition to the wheel-made Mycenaean, a quantity of hand-made vases suggests the possibility of a native non-Mycenaean population. Individuality did not mean isolation, as is quite clear from the adoption of LH. III C shapes and decorations known in other areas. Contact was maintained, probably with the Mainland rather than with the Aegean, as none of the factors peculiar to the Dodecanese and its sphere of influence is to be identified in Kephallenia. These contacts can be claimed to exist during the earlier part of LH. III C (though there is no attempt to reproduce the elaboration of the Argive Close Style); with such motives as triangles, semicircles and lozenges it is not necessary to imagine that contact persisted after the initial adoption. Continuation of contact is best shown through links with the Granary Class, and there does indeed appear to be some evidence of this, slight but possibly sufficient to suggest that these cemeteries were still in use towards the end of LH. III C, after the destruction of the Granary.

The small finds, for the most part, indicate the existence of a Mycenaean community of mediocre prosperity. Taking into account the surprising absence of cemeteries of earlier than LH. III C date, the users of the necklaces and other ornaments of Mycenaean type could have arrived in Kephallenia as refugees from the Mainland as a result of disasters at the end of the LH. III B period. The parallel in detail of tomb construction noted above shows that the Messenia-Triphylia district could have been the fountainhead of flight. The destruction of Pylos and the geographical propinquity are in favour of such a hypothesis.

Some of the small finds, however, reflect contact with regions to the north, outside the Mycenaean world. This is not surprising, although the fibulae, with one exception, need not be evidence of such contact.

The general impression this series gives is, I think, one of progressive isolation, even though it may still be possible to observe a link with the Mainland in the latter part of LH. III C. There is no evidence, in terms of the other areas of the Aegean world, to show when these cemeteries ceased to be used. Nor can any useful information be obtained from

[1] *AE*, 1932, Pl. 7, Nos. 80 and 85; Pl. 10, No. 150.

Kephallenia itself, as there is a subsequent lacuna of many centuries. What happened, or may have happened, to the people who buried on these sites? That is a question which admits of no answer yet, but at least the evidence of the adjacent island of Ithaca provides valuable proof of continuity of occupation here into later times.

2. *Ithaca*

Evidence for the Mycenaean and immediately subsequent periods has been found at one site, Aetos, on the narrow neck which connects the northern and southern parts of the island, and in one area in the northern half. The sites of this latter area lie inside a narrow strip of land, about two miles in length, running north from the Bay of Polis. They consist of the cave of Polis on the bay, Tris Langadas 'just above Polis Bay', Stavros perhaps half a mile north of the bay, Asprosykia close to it, Pelikata Hill, to the north of Stavros, and Ayios Athanasios, furthest to the north.[1]

A brief investigation only has been made at Asprosykia and Ayios Athanasios, the material from Tris Langadas is as yet unpublished, and the Mycenaean and Protogeometric sherds from Stavros,[2] few in number, do not add anything to what is known from the three main sites, Pelikata, Polis and Aetos.

These last three may be grouped chronologically in the order given. At Pelikata, the main settlement belonged to the Early Helladic period. Middle Helladic was poorly represented, and only sixty sherds, all from one area, were identified as Late Helladic III, though a building and a fortification wall have been assigned to this period.[3] These Mycenaean sherds—kylix stems, fragments of krateriskoi and handles from vases of undetermined shape—are assigned to LH. III B, and it is true enough that the kylix stems are stylistically earlier than those found on the other two sites. So the attribution of this material to LH. III B is likely to be correct, though some extension into LH. III C would seem quite possible. The site was not subsequently occupied until the fifth century B.C., and is in any case of minor importance when compared with the nearby cave on Polis Bay.

It is clear that the Polis cave was used as a sanctuary, a place of cult offerings, at some periods in its history;[4] whether such was its use in Mycenaean times and soon afterwards is not provable, though it is certainly possible. It was in any case not a place of burial, and consequently the pottery (constituting the only manufactured objects down to the Geometric period) is of a different type from that deposited in tombs.

A very small number of sherds could be described as LH. III B. The greater part of the material, however, has strong links with the LH. III C series of Kephallenia. The shapes are fewer—jugs with cut-away necks, small jugs, kraters, a three-handled jar, bowls with high as well as low feet, kantharoi (mainly with high feet), cups, mugs, a spouted cup, kylikes, stirrup jars and dippers. The distribution is different, many more bowls and hardly any stirrup jars, but that is due simply to the difference between funerary vases and those used in settlements or shrines. Even so, almost all the shapes found at Polis can be

---

[1] Heurtley, *BSA*, xxxv. 1 ff. (Pelikata); xl. 9 f. (general summary). Benton, *BSA*, xliv. 307, n. 6 (position of Tris Langadas). Waterhouse, *BSA*, xlvii. 227 ff. (Stavros).

[2] *BSA*, xlvii. 238 ff. and 239, Fig. 9.
[3] *BSA*, xxxv. 31 ff.; xl. 9 f.
[4] Benton, *BSA*, xxxv. 45 ff.

paralleled at Lakkithra or Metaxata, and a particularly close connexion is to be seen in the kylikes, the stirrup jars, the spouted cup, and the dipper. Of the shapes which are the more favoured at Polis, the kantharos is the only one not represented in Kephallenia, but it could be considered a miniature edition of the vertical-handed kraters found on the larger island.[1]

At Polis, there is no great variety in the decorative motives: spirals, triangles and diamonds (hatched and cross-hatched), and concentric loops are the chief stocks-in-trade. Similar motives appear on the Kephallenian vases—and, for that matter, in other LH. III C styles. Some of the vases of Polis, however, display elements both in construction and design that may indicate a later stage than that reached in Kephallenia. At first, the excavator (Miss Benton) assigned certain pieces to a transitional period, and some to Protogeometric;[2] later, she revised these views, and classified as Protogeometric all that had earlier been labelled 'transitional' and some as well that had been called Mycenaean.[3] In consequence, the transitional period was eliminated. The criteria of the post-Mycenaean material were in part details of construction of the vases—the conical feet of bowls, kraters, kantharoi and cups, the sharp ridges of some of the kylix stems—and in part the decorative motives, the rigidly geometric designs.[4] These factors were accounted for by analogies with other parts of Greece, but not entirely convincingly. It is true, for example, that in Attica the conical foot did not establish itself before the end of sub-Mycenaean, but there is no need to seek a link here between the Attic and Ithacan styles; the conical foot is clearly apparent in the Kephallenian series, and there is no reason to suggest other than a local development either for this feature or for the sharp ridges on the kylikes. Similarly, the geometric nature of motives appears widely as certain LH. III C styles progress—and Kephallenia is one of these. A concentration on motives of this sort, and the expertness displayed in their drawing, do nevertheless seem a later development from that visible in Kephallenia, as also may the stronger accentuation of the feet and of the kylix-ridges. It looks then as though we have here pottery in part stylistically later than that of the Kephallenian tombs, without there being any need to look further than Kephallenia for the causes of the development.

On this evidence, it would be possible to argue that settlement in Ithaca probably extended beyond the chronological limits of Mycenaean in other parts of Greece, but there would be no proof, and indeed the record of this site allows for the possibility of a break in occupation after the Mycenaean period.[5] The only sherd that may show the influence of the Attic Protogeometric style is from a cup with wavy lines round the rim.[6]

Fortunately, continuity into later times is established by the material from the settlement at Aetos,[7] principally from that section of the excavation whose characteristic was blackened earth in conjunction with accumulations of stones; known as the 'Cairns', the area was probably used rather for occupation than for burial.[8] It has been considered

---

[1] For a detailed account of the Mycenaean vase shapes and decorations, see Benton, *BSA*, xxxix. 8 ff.
[2] Op. cit. pp. 16 f.
[3] *BSA*, xliv. pp. 307 ff.
[4] Cf. *BSA*, xxxix. Pls. 6, 8 and 9.
[5] *BSA*, xxxv. 52.
[6] *BSA*, xxxix. Pl. 6, No. 49.
[7] Heurtley and Lorimer, *BSA*, xxxiii. 22 ff.; Benton, *BSA*, xlviii. 255 ff.
[8] *BSA*, xlviii. 255.

doubtful whether any of the sherds from this section, even those from stirrup jars, are contemporary with the latest Mycenaean period,[1] but it is certain that much of the pottery overlaps that found in the Polis cave, and continues it into a later stage; it is also certain, from sherds with compass-drawn circles and semicircles, that part of the material is contemporary at least with developed Protogeometric as found elsewhere in Greece, if not also with early Geometric. As it is in any case clear from the evidence of the rest of this site that occupation was continuous from Protogeometric onwards, the link between Mycenaean and historical times is thus proved for the island of Ithaca.

On matters of detail, the principal types of the local ware from the 'Cairns' are similar to those of the Polis site—bowls, cups, kantharoi, kraters and kylikes—though a certain development of shape is to be recognized, as in the bowls. The decorative motives are also similar, but the spirals have been discarded and an advance has been made in the schematic application of the geometric motives, and zigzags have become more prominent.[2] Otherwise, there is nothing new in these motives—even the fringed triangle is to be found on a stirrup jar from Polis,[3] and is presumably a legacy of the latest Mycenaean in this area. As to the Protogeometric style, this manifests itself, as mentioned above, in the circles and semicircles, and probably also in the profile of the jugs; pottery exhibiting the influence of Protogeometric was made locally, but at least one piece, the shoulder of an oinochoe, was an import.[4]

A small number of objects other than pottery deserve a passing mention, as being probably assignable to the early occupation. A much mutilated terracotta figurine from the 'Cairns' retains the Mycenaean tradition, and might still be contemporary with LH. III C.[5] The upper part of a large bronze pin, with disk and bulb, was found close to the 'Cairns'.[6] Fragments of four violin-bow fibulae of twisted bronze wire, one of which was almost complete and had a relatively large catch-plate, can probably be assigned to the earliest settlement.[7]

3. *Summary*

In general, from the combined evidence of the Kephallenian cemeteries and the Ithacan settlements of Polis and Aetos, uninterrupted occupation from LH. III C into historical times can be demonstrated; there may not have been many descendants of the Mycenaeans, but there were some. The local features of the pottery are strongly marked, and the evidence suggests that the potters, while using shapes and decorations in common use in the early stages of LH. III C, whether as a legacy from LH. III B or developed in LH. III C, were relatively unaffected by the latest manifestations of LH. III C elsewhere in Greece, and thereafter progressed independently until the Protogeometric period, when the new ideas gave rise to some slight measure of innovation and modification.

There seems no doubt that Kephallenia and Ithaca should be considered together for this continuity, owing to their very close proximity, and a similar continuity in the other

---

[1] *BSA*, xliv. 308; cf. xlviii. 267.
[2] For a detailed analysis, cf. *BSA*, xxxiii. 37 ff.
[3] *BSA*, xxxix. 16, No. 70.
[4] *BSA*, xxxiii, Pl. 6, No. 84; cf. *BSA*, xlviii. 267.
[5] Op. cit. p. 61, Fig. 43.
[6] Op. cit. p. 61, Fig. 44.
[7] *BSA*, xlviii. 350, and 357, Fig. 36, No. E219.

Ionian islands is likely, though there is as yet no evidence for it. On the other hand, no such conclusion can be suggested for North-west Greece; one cannot argue here from the islands to the mainland.

One minor problem emerges. So far as I know, no trace of the hand-made pottery, as found in the Kephallenian cemeteries, has appeared on the Ithacan sites. What is the significance of this? The absence of the non-Mycenaean strain in Ithaca, a later fusion of culture, or simply lack of sufficient evidence?

CHAPTER V

CENTRAL AND NORTHERN GREECE

1. *Attica*

THIS area gives us, after the Argolid, probably the fullest archaeological picture of the end of Mycenaean civilization and of what succeeded it.

So far as the Mycenaean material is concerned, Attica has already admirably been dealt with by Stubbings for all sites and pottery up to 1946.[1] Much has, however, been discovered since then. Here I shall give first a general conclusion permissible from Stubbings's analysis of what may be termed minor sites, and then deal separately with the evidence from Voula and Aghios Kosmas, as well as with that from the major sites of Athens, Eleusis, Perati, and the island of Salamis.

There are altogether some twenty minor sites, and the pottery they produce is all from burials in chamber tombs. LH. III A and LH. III B are both fairly well represented, especially the latter, but LH. III C is less common. The richest site is that of Vourvatsi, which covers most of Late Helladic, though tailing off at the beginning of LH. III C. The main conclusion, which must be borne in mind for confirmation or otherwise on the other, mostly major, sites, is that the cemeteries on the west coast of Attica were not used after LH. III B, while the LH. III C material is concentrated on or near the east coast.

The recent excavations of the cemetery at Voula, on the west coast south of Athens, suggest a slight modification of the above conclusion. A dozen chamber tombs, all with unusually long dromoi, and side-niches, and containing an average of six burials apiece, were dug here by Papadimitriou and Theocharis, and there were in addition burials in pit graves. The few vases illustrated do not go lower than LH. III B, but the reports indicate that some belong to the transition from III B to C.[2]

A similar situation is probably to be recognized in the settlement of Aghios Kosmas, quite close to the Voula cemetery.[3] The main occupation of this site belonged to the Early Bronze Age, but there was a later settlement which the excavator, on the basis of the pottery found, assigned to the end of LH. III C.[4] Nevertheless, with two exceptions the vases are not later than the transition from LH. III B to C, and indeed reflect LH. III B more strongly than they do the succeeding period (see below, p. 118). The exceptions are two deep bowls,[5] which do indeed look late in LH. III C, but I do not think they can take the rest of the vases with them; one of them was found immediately below the surface.[6]

[1] *BSA*, xlii. 1 ff.
[2] *Pr.* 1954, pp. 72 ff.; *Pr.* 1955, pp. 78 ff.; *Pr.* 1957, pp. 29 ff.
[3] Mylonas, *Aghios Kosmas*.
[4] Op. cit. pp. 59 f.
[5] Op. cit. Fig. 139, Nos. 9 and 68.
[6] Op. cit. p. 59 (No. 68).

We may now pass straight on to the evidence from Athens, which produces material both from tombs and settlement. The references for burials have been collected by Mrs. Vermeule[1] in her account of one of the most interesting of the tombs, and a good idea of the area covered may be obtained from Mrs. Hill's *The Ancient City of Athens*, on a map which includes not only the Mycenaean burials but also those of sub-Mycenaean and Protogeometric times.[2] It is clear that, although no large-scale cemetery was identified, burials took place over a wide area to the north and west of the Acropolis, either in chamber tombs or in pit graves, nearly forty such (or traces of such) having been found. The vases cover a range from LH. II to LH. III C, but the majority of them belong to LH. III A and B, and in fact in one burial only, the last one in the chamber tomb under the temple of Ares, was the associated vase clearly of LH. III C date—a kalathos with a rudimentary fish adorning the interior.[3] This scarcity of LH. III C material is in direct contrast to the considerable number of sub-Mycenaean and Protogeometric tombs around the Acropolis and in the nearby Kerameikos.

It may seem in consequence a complete negation of the evidence that a high proportion of the settlement pottery discovered should be LH. III C—and there is no possible doubt that there was a settlement in this period—but the site and circumstances of this settlement help to give a more balanced picture. Instead of being concerned with the area surrounding the Acropolis, we now have to deal with the Acropolis itself.

Much Mycenaean pottery was found here in the earlier excavations, and this, as Stubbings says, includes 'representative pieces of all the LH. III periods. But the latter half of the period is much more fully represented than the earlier'.[4]

A more important body of material has been uncovered more recently. This consists of the finds in and near the Mycenaean dwellings on the North Slope, and also in the underground fountain.[5] The North Slope houses are more or less contemporary with the digging of the fountain, and the period seems clearly to be that of transition from LH. III B to C; furthermore, Broneer has argued that the defences of the Acropolis were strengthened at this time. The houses on the North Slope were then abandoned, and it is obvious that at least a portion of the population retired to the Acropolis itself.

The underground fountain did not remain long in use as such, but became a sort of refuse pit. The bulk of the sherds found belong to the early LH. III C period, with frequent LH. III B survivals, but the later stages of LH. III C were very scarce.[6] From this one may conclude that, although the fountain had only a short duration of use, people continued to live for a while on the Acropolis. The building of the fountain, and the strengthening of the defences, indicate the possibility of danger; the fact of continued occupation suggests that, although the immediate danger was past, there was not much feeling of security in the years that followed.[7] The possibility of some movement of population is thus strengthened by this evidence; when the people who held the only easily fortifiable point of the western plain of Attica felt insecure, it is very likely, as is shown by the evidence

---

[1] *Hesp.* xxiv. 188, nn. 3 and 4.
[2] p. 9, Fig. 3. See also Travlos, Πολεοδομικὴ Ἐξέλιξις τῶν Ἀθηνῶν, p. 23, Fig. 7.
[3] *Hesp.* xxiv. 200, Pl. 75, No. 24.
[4] *BSA*, xlii. 5.
[5] Broneer, *Hesp.* ii. 351 ff.; Hansen, *Hesp.* vi. 539 ff.; Broneer, *Hesp.* viii. 317 ff.
[6] *Hesp.* viii. 422.
[7] Cf. op. cit. pp. 423 ff. for Broneer's general historical conclusions.

of the cemeteries and settlement along the west coast, that the rest of the population would feel doubly insecure, and seek other places of habitation. Once again it may be stressed, in contrast, that those who buried in the sub-Mycenaean cist tombs here, as on nearby Salamis, had every confidence in their security.

At Eleusis, almost the westernmost point of Attica, there is also settlement and cemetery evidence. This is of course primarily a great sanctuary site of historic times, and has been extensively excavated on several occasions during the last seventy years.[1] The earlier results were brought together by Mylonas in 1932,[2] and since this there has been further work, by Mylonas[3] and Kourouniotis[4] before 1939, and by Mylonas and Travlos after 1945.[5]

A large number of prehistoric tombs were found, principally of the Middle Helladic period but extending into LH. III; and it may be noted that there was a particularly strong continuity from the earliest times, as visible in the tomb construction, where the MH. cist tomb principle was retained, though with modifications, down into LH. III, and thus much more strongly than anywhere else in the Mycenaean world. Chamber tombs were, it would seem, the exception rather than the rule in this latter period. The question of immediate interest is of course how far down into LH. III the cemeteries were used, and the answer is that so far only the two chamber tombs are said to have contained LH. III C vases.[6] One of these was a child burial with an LH. III C oinochoe, and the other contained three skeletons with vases ranging from LH. III B to C. None of these vases has yet been illustrated. Subsequent to this, the earliest tombs belong to the Early Geometric period. Late Protogeometric cremations have indeed been found elsewhere on the site, but there is no trace, to my knowledge, of any burials which could fill the gap.[7]

Evidence has also been produced for settlement from Middle Helladic into LH. III times, but once again the traces of LH. III C are extremely scanty, and appear to be limited to the area under the Lesser Propylaea, where nine of the sherds associated with the inscribed stirrup jar are said to belong to the Granary Class. In default of illustrations, and bearing in mind that the stirrup jar is earlier than LH. III C, and that none of the sherds pictured from other parts of the sanctuary is later than LH. III B, it is a little difficult to suggest any precise conclusion, but it does seem doubtful that there was any sizeable or long occupation of the site in LH. III C. Furthermore, it is stated that the Late Helladic remains, here and elsewhere in the Sanctuary area 'are immediately followed by those belonging to the Geometric period', so a considerable gap is probable.[8]

There remains one piece of evidence which may suggest a continuity hitherto undisclosed, that of the Mycenaean building excavated below the Peisistratid Telesterion. This was a *megaron* with a forecourt, surrounded by a *peribolos* separating it from nearby houses; from the pottery, it was probably built in LH. II, and various dependencies were added during LH. III, though no LH. III C sherds are illustrated. It is possible that this

---

[1] See generally, Mylonas, *Eleusis and the Eleusinian Mysteries*.
[2] Προϊστορικὴ Ἐλευσίς.
[3] *AJA*, xl. 415 ff.
[4] *AD*, xv. suppl., 1 ff.
[5] *Pr*. 1952 ff.; *Ergon* for 1956, pp. 17 ff.
[6] *Ergon* for 1956, p. 19; *BCH*, lxxxi. 512.
[7] Skias, *AE*, 1898, pp. 76 ff. and Pl. 3, 4; *Ker*. I, Pls. 42, 48.
[8] *AJA*, xl. 426 f.

was a sacred area in Mycenaean times, and the presence of the Telesterion above it is in that case of interest. Nevertheless, there is a long period of disuse after LH. III B, and the continuity cannot have been one of worship, but must be attributed either to memory or to rediscovery.[1]

The evidence, then, from Eleusis, though not entirely clear, seems to fall in line with that of the western part of Attica: at least a serious diminution of occupation by the beginning of LH. III C, and thereafter a break.

It was stated earlier that the material from the 'minor' sites indicated that LH. III C flourished on or near the east coast. There is now one major site on this coast, that of Perati, and it provides valuable support for the hypothesis of a possible internal shift of population during the transition LH. III B/C. Excavations, by Iakovidis, have now been in progress for several years, and an extremely interesting picture is already emerging from the preliminary reports.[2] Over two hundred tombs have been excavated, and more than eight hundred vases found; an excellent general idea has thus been gained of the scope of the cemetery. There was undoubtedly a large settlement associated with the tombs, but this awaits discovery and investigation.

The vast majority of the burials were in chamber tombs, but just a very few were in slab-covered pits, and may perhaps be related to the cist tombs of Salamis and the Kerameikos.[3] A third, and otherwise unknown type, was a narrow pit covered with slabs, to which a shallow dromos led; only two of this type have so far been found.[4]

The primary interest of this site is that its material lies almost entirely within LH. III C. At the upper end, a very few vases illustrate the end of the transition from LH. III B to C, and it is significant that only two kylikes have been reported; at the lower end, some of the vases could perhaps be called sub-Mycenaean on stylistic grounds, and in any case some of the tombs could well be contemporary with the sub-Mycenaean cist tombs, from the nature of the small finds.

The material from this cemetery shows that the community had its main contacts with the Aegean rather than with the Mainland, was Mycenaean in character, and was prosperous. The Aegean contacts are most readily visible in the comparative material from Naxos and the Dodecanese. There is the same relative distribution of the main vase shapes, so far as one can tell, and certain types of vase, particularly the stirrup jar with octopus decoration (Pl. 6c-d) and one or two types used for cult purposes, are most popular in, and characteristic of, this general area; a type of terracotta figurine, with arms joining on the head (Pl. 7b), is peculiar to Perati and Naxos; and there are several cases of cremation associated with inhumations in the Perati chamber tombs, which have exact counterparts in Rhodes and Kos, but nowhere else (cf. p. 157). The link was no doubt strongest between Perati and Naxos, but it certainly also existed between these two and the Dodecanese. It may be added that the pottery also indicates contact with the Argolid in early LH. III C, as is evident from the appearance of the Close Style vases (Pl. 6d), but it is not so strong.

[1] Mylonas, *AJA*, xxxvii. 274 ff.; *AJA*, xl. 417 ff.; *AE*, 1950, p. 11. Cf. Gallet de Santerre, *Délos Primitive*, pp. 96 ff.
[2] *Pr.* 1953 ff.; *Ergon* for 1954 ff.
[3] *Ergon* for 1958, 1959 and 1960.
[4] *Ergon* for 1958 and 1959.

The Mycenaean character of the inhabitants is clear from the pottery, from the fact of continued burial in chamber tombs, and also from the nature of the bulk of the small finds. The small finds are also the main evidence for the prosperity of the settlement; gold and semi-precious stones and ivory were by no means rare. As well as this, however, they provide, in their exceptions from the standard Mycenaean ornaments, useful information on two other points. There are quite a number of objects which have their origin in the East Mediterranean and particularly Egypt (the scarabs, cartouches, and little figurines);[1] these may have been regarded simply as souvenirs or amulets, but they prove contact east of the Aegean during at least some of the period. Equally important are the occasional objects of iron (the two iron knives with bronze rivets (Pl. 24e) and the glass-paste bead with iron adhering to it),[2] which not only show contact with the East Mediterranean directly or indirectly, but show it at a very late date, which can hardly be earlier than that of the sub-Mycenaean cemetery of the Kerameikos. There are also simple arched fibulae, a type not elsewhere antedating the sub-Mycenaean series.[3]

It seems extremely likely that the Perati tombs were still in use during much of the time that cist tombs had replaced chamber tombs in the west of Attica, but they did not, I think, survive into Protogeometric times—at least there is no evidence for it. The cemetery was no longer used; what happened to the inhabitants we do not know. But the Attic story must now be continued in its western districts.

We have seen that the existing evidence suggests some depopulation in West Attica at the time of transition from LH. III B/C, but that the Acropolis of Athens continued to be occupied into LH. III C. The fill in the fountain indicates that the earlier half of this period was well represented, but that there was a subsequent falling off—the Granary Class is not at all prominent. The next stage is surely that of the inauguration of the cist tomb cemeteries, both in Athens and on Salamis,[4] and I have argued elsewhere (pp. 17 ff.) that this took place during the second half of LH. III C. The principal characteristics of these cemeteries are: the abandonment of the chamber tomb, the continuance of Mycenaean pottery in a debased style (Pls. 14, 15) with a restricted range of shapes, the replacement of the usual small Mycenaean objects by objects of a different type, of possible northern origin, a higher proportion of Alpine types of skull, and at the end the first use of iron for weapons and a gradual change to cremation and to a pottery which foreshadows Protogeometric. The possibility that a new racial element may be recognizable in these conditions is a matter which I have also discussed elsewhere (pp. 37 ff.). At least there seems to have been a return to security. Following on this, in Athens but not on Salamis, there comes the Protogeometric period which leads straight through to historical times.

---

[1] Cartouches: tombs 1 and 104. Scarabs: tombs 13 (4), 75 (2), 90. Faience amulets: tomb 30. Bronze duck-headed knife: tomb 12.

[2] Knives: *Pr.* 1954, p. 98, Fig. 10 (tomb 28); *Pr.* 1955, p. 106, Pl. 31b (tomb 38). See p. 61 for other examples. Pin fragment?: *Ergon* for 1960, p. 21, Fig. 28 (tomb 108).

[3] *Pr.* 1954, p. 97 (tomb 19). The fibula from tomb 36 (*Pr.* 1955, p. 108) is arched, and there are two from tomb 74, for permission to mention which I acknowledge most grateful thanks to the excavator, Mr. Iakovidis.

[4] Wide, *AM*, xxxv. 17 ff.; Kraiker and Kübler, *Kerameikos* I. Smithson, *Hesp.* xxx. 174 ff. In the Kerameikos cemetery, all the earliest tombs, and sixty-nine altogether, were slab-built. There were also twenty-seven burials in pit graves, all of which are late in the series. Cf. op. cit. pp. 9 f.

Again in Athens, the tomb material is supplemented by that from the disused wells of the Agora, which appears to give a reasonable sequence from sub-Mycenaean onwards, and provides the small but valuable evidence of settlement pottery.[1]

This more or less completes the brief survey of the material from Attica down to Protogeometric, and of the conclusions that may be drawn from it. The section may be concluded with a short discussion on the pottery, especially as found in Athens, and a brief mention of the other objects.

The settlement material from the Acropolis is of particular importance, as it provides virtually our only recorded evidence for the transition from LH. III B to LH. III C and for early LH. III C, and it also exemplifies the difficulties that arise in assessing the stylistic development of the deep bowl and krater, the typical settlement shapes.

Before discussing these two shapes, the evidence of the stirrup jars may be considered. Here there were clear indications of LH. III B, both from the North Slope houses and from the Fountain.[2] There were also early LH. III C pieces, recognizable by the semi-circles on the shoulder and below the shoulder, and there were a few Close Style sherds.[3] The general impression gained from the stirrup jars is that they represent only the transition and the earliest stages of LH. III C—there is just one sherd with an air-hole,[4] and later types of shoulder decoration are absent. A similar conclusion may be reached from the alabastron and pyxis shapes, and the majority of the closed vases seem to be early.[5]

When we turn to the open vases, one shape, rare elsewhere, deserves notice, as it is known at Tarsus and in the LH. III C settlement of Emborio on Chios. This is a rather funnel-shaped bowl, with a single horizontal handle and decorated with bands on a light ground.[6]

As to the familiar deep bowls and kraters, the following points can be made. Only two bowls of the Granary Class are illustrated, but it is clear from the account that a fair number of dark-ground bowl sherds were recovered, and that many of these had the lower body and the foot unpainted; they came mostly from the upper levels, but some were found in the lower ones, and it is indeed probable that monochrome deep bowls were made from the beginning of LH. III C, if not earlier (cf. p. 11).[7] On the other hand, there were no examples of bowls with a reserved panel between the handles, with or without wavy line decoration. It would seem that Granary Class bowls are represented in this deposit, but not the later type of them.

The above point bears mainly on the end of the series. At the beginning, there are pieces of bowls and kraters which should be classified as LH. III B. In between the two extremes, there is one sherd of the Close Style,[8] and a great mass of sherds, of considerable variety of decoration, the motives of which are always traceable back to LH. III B, but whose treatment, especially in the filling ornaments and in the tendency towards closeness,

---

[1] See the forthcoming study by Mrs. Smithson.
[2] *Hesp*. ii. 370, Fig. 43, *b*; *Hesp*. viii. 388 ff., Figs. 69, *a*; 70; 71, *q, r, u, v*.
[3] e.g. *Hesp*. viii. 390, Fig. 71, *e*.
[4] Op. cit. p. 389, Fig. 70, *n*.
[5] Op. cit. p. 386, Fig. 67; p. 389, Fig. 70.
[6] Op. cit. pp. 377 ff., with Figs. 59, *a* and 60. Cf. pp. 206, 159 for Tarsus and Emborio; a vase of this type has also been found at Tragana in Messenia (p. 95).
[7] Op. cit. pp. 366 f. and 370, Fig. 49, *b, c*.
[8] Op. cit. p. 368, Fig. 46, *n*.

may indicate LH. III C developments. With a large number of these one might reasonably hesitate, if they appeared out of context, whether to call them LH. III B or LH. III C, especially in view of the recent analysis of a group of mainly LH. III B pottery from Mycenae, where it is stated that 'various Panel schemes which might otherwise be assigned to early LH. III C or to a III B-C period can be shown here to have existed earlier'.[1]

The difficulty of interpretation is thus evident, especially as there is no doubt that many of the bowls and kraters of the Acropolis must be placed in LH. III C, on the basis of the Close Style sherds and even more from the fact that early Granary Class sherds are found. The main conclusions are two: that generally a far greater amount of comparative material is needed before one can analyse the stylistic development of deep bowls and kraters from LH. III B to early LH. III C; and that the bulk of the Acropolis material does not go beyond the early stages of LH. III C. The further point may be provisionally made, bearing on the interconnexion of local styles in early LH. III C, that it is extremely difficult to point to any particular area of contact for the bowls and kraters, because parallels in decoration can be adduced, from the relatively small evidence available, from most parts of the Mycenaean world. This may be due to no more than the survival of LH. III B motives; or else it may be taken to show that the lack of security did not lead to isolation.

The other site which contained settlement pottery is that of Aghios Kosmas, and here the excavator has assigned the final stage of occupation to the end of LH. III C.[2] I think it is possible that it may be somewhat earlier; the vases comprise four short-stemmed kylikes, three ladles, a bridge-spouted cup, four jugs of which two have the handle from shoulder to neck, two deep bowls, a feeding bottle, a fragmentary krater, three stirrup jars, and a curiously shaped bowl with high flaring foot (a surface find).[3] Most of these vases were complete, an unusual state of affairs for a settlement. No mention is made of destruction, but there may have been a hasty desertion. The distribution and types are not what one would expect at the end of LH. III C, and would accord better with a time of transition from LH. III B-C. The decoration of the stirrup jars would lead to a similar conclusion; two of them appear rather to be LH. III B in style.[4] Only the dark-ground deep bowl with rudimentary alternating sets of lines in a panel certainly belongs to the Granary Class, though the other deep bowl may also belong to it (cf. p. 112). Mylonas has dated the whole in accordance with the latest vase, but I do not feel entirely convinced of this, as I find it difficult to believe that some of the vases can come down so far. The problem is not an easy one. In my opinion, it is likely that the site was deserted in the LH. III B-C period.

LH. III C tomb pottery is most fully represented at Perati, and I have already mentioned the salient points. The whole course of this style is represented, with only rare survivals from LH. III B—a very different picture from that of the settlements on the Acropolis and at Aghios Kosmas. Particular stress has been laid on the connexions with Naxos and the Dodecanese, but this should not obscure the fact that Perati possessed an individual style of its own.

[1] *BSA*, lii. 218.
[2] Mylonas, *Aghios Kosmas*, pp. 59 f.
[3] Op. cit. Figs. 136–9.
[4] Op. cit. Fig. 137 (No. 20) and 139 (No. 61).

In the Salamis and Athenian cist tombs, the repertory of shapes is limited, and the following list gives an idea of types and distribution: 18 deep bowls, 31 lekythoi, 34 stirrup jars, 40 amphoriskoi, 12 trefoil oinochoai, 3 cups, 5 amphorae, one one-handled jug, one hydria, and two or three oddments. Perhaps the greatest difference is to be noted in the poverty of decoration; for the lekythoi and stirrup jars, vertical wiggly lines, semicircles, and occasionally triangles; for bowls and amphoriskoi, one or more wavy lines; for the oinochoai, languettes. There are exceptions, but not many. A dark-ground system was adopted for the lekythoi and stirrup jars and deep bowls (which may have the lower body and foot unpainted); the oinochoai are clay-ground, and so is the cup; the amphoriskoi may be either the one or the other.[1]

So far as concerns the other objects, the only tomb evidence worth considering is that of the cemeteries of Perati, Salamis and the Kerameikos. At Perati, as has been noted, the ornaments, implements and weapons were of the conventional Mycenaean type, exception being made of the objects of East Mediterranean origin, of the iron knives, of a ring of probably northern provenience, and of the fibulae of both violin-bow and simple arch type. As opposed to this, the cist tombs of Salamis and the Kerameikos betray a total absence of Mycenaean dress ornaments (rings need not be taken into account, as they were not peculiar to the Mycenaean world, though even here there were several of northern origin),[2] and there are no further examples of terracotta figurines. The stress is rather on the fibulae (Pl. 21), and on the long bronze dress pins which now make their first appearance; the grave contents indicate a somewhat simple, if not almost poverty-stricken, way of life.

2. *Aegina*

There are only two sites on this island which have yielded Mycenaean material, and both were later occupied by sanctuaries. A few Mycenaean sherds were found in the precincts of the Aphaia temple, but none is later than LH. III B.[3] It is perhaps worth noting, however, that Mycenaean terracotta 'goddess' figurines and animals were recovered;[4] it seems very possible that this spot was considered sacred in Mycenaean times. The other site is that of Kolonna, where the temple of Aphrodite was situated, on the coast near a harbour, and eminently suitable for a settlement. No LH. III pottery has been published from the temple area itself, though sherds are to be found by the casual visitor. In the vicinity, three tombs were excavated by Keramopoullos,[5] but again nothing was later than LH. III B. Nor has anything of relevance to this work emerged from Welter's investigations.[6]

There is just one LH. III C vase from this island, and that is a stirrup jar of Close Style type in the British Museum.[7] It is a large vase, over 25 centimetres high, and has a pronounced ring base, a high knob and an air-hole; on the basis of the two latter features

---

[1] A representative selection is shown on Pls. 14 and 15.
[2] *Ker.* I, pp. 85 ff.
[3] Furtwängler, *Aegina, das Heiligtum der Aphaia*, pp. 370 ff., 432, 434 f., Pl. 122, 7 and 11, Pl. 127, 2 and 3.
[4] Op. cit. Pl. 109.
[5] *AE*, 1910, pp. 182 ff.
[6] *AA*, 1938, pp. 511 f., Fig. 25; *Aigina*, pp. 21 ff., 54 f.
[7] *CVA*, GB 7 (BM5), IIIA, 12 and Pl. 11, No. 9 (= *B.M. Cat.* I, 1, A 1092).

it may be supposed that this stirrup jar should probably be assigned to the latter part of LH. III C.

It may be concluded that the relative absence of Mycenaean finds on this island is accidental, and that further investigation is desirable.

3. *Boeotia*

According to the Catalogue of Ships, this district was thickly inhabited at the time of the Trojan War, though there is mention only of a 'Ὑποθῆβαι;[1] our present state of archaeological knowledge does not reveal such riches. This does not mean that the Catalogue was incorrect, as even a survey of a small area by Heurtley produced a fair number of sites.[2] Valid conclusions must, however, be based on excavations, and only five sites in Boeotia have been dug: Haliartos, Orchomenos, Eutresis, Gla and Thebes.

Haliartos[3] sounds a promising settlement, as Mycenaean fortification walls were identified, but very few sherds seem to have been found, and none is illustrated. For one sherd only is a date suggested, and that is *c*. 1400; from the fact that there were kylix fragments, it is likely that there was occupation in LH. III A or B. But without anything more definite, this evidence is of no value, and the same conclusion must unfortunately be reached for the clearly important site of Orchomenos. Stirrup jars and kylikes are mentioned in one report,[4] and the frescoes are stylistically similar to those of the later palace at Tiryns, so we should be into LH. III B.[5] The next possibly identifiable pottery is the trefoil oinochoe mentioned by Wide,[6] who suggests that it is sub-Mycenaean; and after that there are Protogeometric and Geometric tombs.[7] It is obviously better, as so often, to await the full record.

The evidence from Eutresis is much clearer than that of the two preceding sites. The settlement was fortified during the LH. III period,[8] but before LH. III C, as the latest material (that from House V), after which the site was abandoned until the sixth century, is placed by Furumark[9] as very early in LH. III C, though LH. III B elements are very strong. There were apparently no signs of the site having been destroyed, but it is interesting to note that the fortification wall enclosed a very much greater area than that covered by the houses. It does not look as though it would have provided a serious obstacle to any invader.

Though Eutresis may not have been destroyed, Gla certainly was, as is made clear in the reports of the early excavations as well as in those of the recent ones.[10] This site consists of an acropolis on the north-eastern side of the Lake of Copais, and it was fortified very strongly indeed, and one complex of buildings inside is so impressive that it is rightly called a palace. The general situation was made clear in the original excavation, but

---

[1] *Iliad*, ii. 505.
[2] *BSA*, xxvi. 38 ff.
[3] Austin, *BSA*, xxvii. 81 ff; *BSA*, xxviii. 129. Cf. *JHS*, xlvi. 234 ff.
[4] De Ridder, *BCH*, xix. 179.
[5] Bulle, *Orchomenos*, I, pp. 71 ff., Pls. 28–30.
[6] *AM*, xxxv. 35.
[7] *P.T.* p. 247; *PGP*, p. 198.
[8] Goldman, *Eutresis*, p. 68.
[9] *OA*, iii. 197.
[10] De Ridder, *BCH*, xviii. 284 f.; Threpsiades, *Ergon* for 1957, p. 29.

little or no definite indication was given of its date.¹ Since 1955, the Greek Archaeological Service has renewed excavations, and these have greatly increased our knowledge both of the circuit wall and of the constructions it protected.² It has been established that the wall was built in LH. III times, though evidently no more precise dating has been possible. Sherds are remarkably scarce, and consequently the selection recently illustrated is extremely valuable, especially as the excavator states that the sherds found in other parts of the excavation were similar to these.³ It would seem that both LH. III A and B are represented, and there is no trace of LH. III C; furthermore, one of the sherds from a bowl, with confronted semicircles, belongs rather to the latter part of LH. III B—and a similar motive continues elsewhere into early LH. III C.⁴ It is certainly a possibility that the destruction of this fortress is to be linked up with the catastrophe in the Argolid at the end of LH. III B.

Finally there is the material from Thebes, from which a different picture is obtained, though not one that contradicts the hypothesis of troubles at the transition from LH. III B–C. Here we have evidence both for a settlement and for tombs, as a result of excavations by Keramopoullos.⁵ The most impressive part of the settlement was the building identified as a palace, and it is clear that this was destroyed in LH. III A,⁶ after which the major importance of the town must have ceased, though a complete desertion did not ensue, as a few sherds from the settlement attest a continuance of occupation in LH. III B.⁷

The tomb evidence confirms that there was no break in occupation after the destruction of the palace, and as well as this provides proof of continued inhabitation into LH. III C. The main necropolis uncovered was that on the hill of Kolonaki,⁸ where twenty chamber tombs were dug, and a rather smaller one was excavated to the south-west of this hill.⁹ The LH. III C tombs were confined to the main area, and it is unfortunately rather difficult to say how far down within this period they reach, though the two one-handled cups from tomb 16 seem to belong to the later phase.¹⁰ The small finds were almost invariably of the standard Mycenaean type, but it is of some importance that three of the LH. III C tombs (14, 15 and 16)¹¹ contained a fibula with a leaf-shaped bow and incised decoration, objects which are probably non-Mycenaean in origin (see pp. 56 f.). It may also be noted that tomb 16 produced evidence of a cremation.¹²

This does not entirely conclude the story of this site, for mention must be made of a further set of graves, in the area of the Electran Gates, some distance from Kolonaki. These are slab-built cist tombs, as appears from the description and from the plan, and they lay within and close to the ruins of a Mycenaean building.¹³

All the burials were inhumations, but unfortunately five of the tombs contained hardly anything else but the skeleton. Of the remaining four one contained vases which could be called late LH. III C or sub-Mycenaean, one had a Protogeometric vase, the third

---

[1] De Ridder, *BCH*, xviii. 271 ff. and Pls. 10 and 11.
[2] Threpsiades, *Ergon* for 1955 ff.
[3] *Ergon* for 1960, p. 38, Fig. 52.
[4] Cf. *Hesp.* viii. 359, Fig. 35 (Athens).
[5] *AE*, 1909, pp. 57 ff.; *AE*, 1910, pp. 209 ff; *AD*, iii. 80 ff., 123 ff.
[6] *Chronology*, p. 52.
[7] *AE*, 1909, p. 100 and Pl. 3, 6–9.
[8] *AD*, iii. 123 ff.
[9] Op. cit. pp. 187 ff.
[10] Op. cit. pp. 167 and 163, Fig. 121, 1.
[11] Op. cit. pp. 151, 159 ff., 162.
[12] Op. cit. pp. 163 f.
[13] Op. cit. pp. 25 ff. and p. 6, Fig. 3.

produced a jug which is hardly later than LH. III B (a survival?) and the fourth two vases, one of which is sub-Mycenaean, the other Protogeometric.[1] It is not easy to assess the comparative value of this material, especially as one of the vases appears to be late in the Protogeometric series. It does seem that Thebes provides evidence of the use of cist tombs before the end of LH. III C, and it may be that there was continued use of a sub-Mycenaean type of pottery after the start of Attic Protogeometric. In any case, inhumation in cist tombs was still the custom here after cremation had become universal in Attica.

Furthermore, the change from chamber to cist tomb may well denote a break, as in Athens and Salamis, at some time while LH. III C was still current in the Argolid and elsewhere; but this point is discussed earlier (cf. pp. 37 ff.). From the rather slender evidence for Boeotia one may provisionally suggest a disaster at Thebes in LH. III A, a more extensive catastrophe which could belong to the end of LH. III B, a survival of a few of the original inhabitants into LH. III C, and finally the arrival of some new people before the inception of Protogeometric in Attica.

4. *Euboea*

The finds from this island do not, up to the present time, contribute anything towards the problems of this book. So far as the Mycenaean period is concerned, one need do little more than refer to two accounts: the work of Papavasileiou, Περὶ τῶν ἐν Εὐβοίᾳ ἀρχαίων τά ων, and the article by Mrs. Hankey,[2] recording in full the excavations of Papavasileiou at the site of Trypa-Vromousa near Chalkis.

This site is the only one both excavated and published. Twenty chamber tombs were investigated, and the material from them covers the whole Late Helladic period, the majority of the two hundred vases being attributable to LH. III, but of which only four or five seem to belong to LH. III C, and just one perhaps to the latter part of this style.[3]

Apart from this site, tombs (chiefly tholoi) were found in other parts of the island by Papavasileiou, but the contents of these have not been published.[4]

Surface sherding has shown that many other sites were in fact occupied in Mycenaean times, but until such sites are excavated, no sort of picture can be gained of the situation in Euboea either in LH. III C or in the immediately succeeding period.

5. *Phocis and Locris*

The principal excavated site of this district is Delphi, and the situation with regard to Mycenaean finds is by now as full and clear as possible. It was already stated in the main report[5] that the only traces of Mycenaean, apart from some tombs at Pylaea, occurred in the two sanctuaries of Apollo and Athena,[6] the most prolific area being that to the northeast of the temple of Apollo. Subsequent excavation has in general confirmed this

---

[1] Cf. *PGP*, pp. 195 f.
[2] *BSA*, xlvii. 49 ff.
[3] Op. cit. Pl. 25, 554, and p. 81, Fig. 5, pattern 45.
[4] Op. cit. p. 49, n. 1.
[5] Perdrizet, *FD*, v. pp. ii f.
[6] Cf. Demangel, *FD*, ii: 5, 6 ff.

conclusion, while sharply differentiating between the character of the deposit in the two areas.[1]

The area of settlement seems to have been confined to the east and north-east of the temple of Apollo, and it was not very extensive. The remains of walls were for the most part rectangular, two only being apsidal, these belonging to the earliest period of occupation.[2] It is argued that the settlement belonged exclusively to LH. III, and in this period the evidence of the pottery would suggest that the LH. III B phase was the most important and that there was some extension into LH. III C. The end of the settlement most probably came about through a catastrophic fall of rocks, and there are but few traces of later occupation on this spot until the beginning of Late Geometric.[3]

The pottery has been well recorded and illustrated,[4] although stratification was impossible to establish in most cases. Lerat mentioned only one vase [5] which he specifically assigned to a relatively late building, though it is likely that the vases from the house reported in his second article belong to LH. III C, and so to the latest period of occupation.[6] Apart from this, conclusions have to be drawn on the basis of style, and it is unfortunate that this is one of the very few sites where a rather degenerate local pottery was in existence, as a consequence of which it is not always easy to decide whether a sherd is a poor local version of LH. III B, or a reflection of the debasement of LH. III B which characterizes early LH. III C. Furthermore, most of the pottery came from deep bowls and kraters, where the division between LH. III B and C is difficult enough to establish in the central areas. There is no doubt that many of the deep bowls, both from their shape and decoration, can safely be placed within LH. III B; there are others whose motives can be paralleled both in LH. III B and in LH. III C, but there are hardly any whose decoration certainly implies an LH. III C date. On the other hand, it is mentioned that a number of sherds came from monochrome bowls, and it is reasonable to assume that most of these must belong to LH. III C, though not necessarily particularly late in this period.[7] No example has been found of the Argive Close Style—on this or on any other shape—nor of the Granary Class, in the sense of flaring lip, highish foot, panelled wavy line or unpainted lower body.

A similar picture is presented by the kraters, though the one assigned to the later level should be LH. III C.[8] The arrow-like designs on the shoulders of the closed vases are also probably III C,[9] while on the other hand the few fragments of stirrup jars look back to III B.[10]

It is thus exceedingly difficult to make a proper assessment of this body of pottery; the most likely conclusion is that the settlement did continue into LH. III C, but not far into it.

As well as the pottery, a certain number of terracotta figurines, both human and animal, were found in this area, though not in sufficient quantity for one to be able to

---

[1] *BCH*, vols. lix, lxxiv, lxxxi. The latest excavations (Lerat, *BCH*, lxxxv. 357 ff.) make it clear that the inhabited area was greater than originally thought.
[2] Lerat, *RA*, 1938, pp. 194 ff.
[3] Op. cit. pp. 188 ff.; *BCH*, lxxxv. 352 ff.
[4] Lerat, *BCH*, lix. 329 ff.; *RA*, 1938, pp. 194 ff.; *BCH*, lxxxv. 357 ff.
[5] *BCH*, lix. 343 and Pl. 21, 5.
[6] *RA*, 1938, pp. 197 ff.
[7] *BCH*, lix. 341. Cf. *RA*, 1938, p. 199, Fig. 7.
[8] See n. 5.
[9] *BCH*, lix. 348, Fig. 7, and 361, Fig. 17.
[10] Op. cit. p. 347, Fig. 6.

infer that the spot was used for cult purposes.¹ Nevertheless, their appearance is suggestive, and with them may be taken the considerable number found in the deposit in the area of the sanctuary of Athena Pronaia.

The main point is that this deposit does not belong to a settlement; no walls were found in association with Mycenaean objects, and there was no reliable stratification.² A fair quantity of pottery was retrieved (of much the same type as in the settlement), and a few small objects of stone, metal or glass paste.³ The most remarkable find, however, was that of some 175 complete or fragmentary terracotta 'goddess' figurines.⁴ Lerat, who undertook the later supplementary excavation, is obviously right both in stating that there was no Mycenaean settlement on this spot, and also in his conclusion that the builders of the archaic sanctuary assembled these objects (sherds, as well, evidently) for use as a special religious deposit.⁵ There seems no doubt that these figurines and other objects were transferred from another spot within the site, and it would appear most likely that they came from the one area known to contain Mycenaean buildings, north-east of the temple of Apollo. Furthermore, the place, wherever it was, from which they came must have been a cult spot. Such a place could have been that of the great Altar of Apollo—thick with Mycenaean sherds—and there would then be a very striking instance of the tradition of a sacred spot. Such an inference is in any case valid, even if the area of the Altar was not the cult centre; so we have continuity of memory, though no evidence of continuing worship (cf. pp. 43 f.).

Mycenaean chamber tombs have also been found at Delphi, but only a very few yielded significant objects. The earliest is the Museum tomb,⁶ the vases of which are certainly LH. III B—and of reasonable quality, from the illustrations. Another tomb, much plundered, was investigated in the area between the Museum and the Stadium, Pylaea;⁷ the two fragmentary kraters are assigned by Furumark⁸ to LH. III C, but it is possible, in view of the kylix sherds reported, that an LH. III B or LH. III B/C date would be more appropriate.

There is no such doubt about the rich tomb to the west of the Temenos.⁹ It was in fact one of five, but the remainder had been thoroughly robbed (though identifiable as Mycenaean). There is no mention of any bones, and one cannot even guess at the number of burials, though at least one warrior can be inferred from the dagger, spearhead, razor and knife. Other objects include ten buttons, part of a pair of tweezers, an amulet and a fragmentary violin-bow fibula. The main tomb deposit was, however, that of the pottery. Fifty-two vases were found, of which twenty-five were stirrup jars, and eighteen were one-handled jugs. Three lekythoi, two amphoriskoi, two askoi, a ring-vase and a coarse jug make up the remainder. One of the stirrup jars is LH. III B, but it must be a stray or a survival; all the rest, and the other shapes as well, belong to LH. III C, and some indeed belong to its end. Many of the stirrup jars have an air-hole, and the favourite shoulder decoration is concentric semicircles, which may be dotted or fringed; one jar is most

¹ Op. cit. pp. 329 ff.; *FD*, v. 14 f.
² *FD*, ii: 5, 13 ff.; Lerat, *BCH*, lxxxi. 708 ff.
³ *FD*, ii: 5, 28 ff.
⁴ Op. cit. p. 15, n. 2.
⁵ *BCH*, lxxxi. 708 ff.
⁶ *FD*, v. 12 ff.
⁷ Op. cit. pp. 10 ff.
⁸ *Chronology*, p. 74.
⁹ *FD*, v. 6 ff.

elegant, and combines the Argive Close Style with the Dodecanesian octopus—a feature also found at Perati.[1] Two of the lekythoi look extremely late, and some of the pottery might be contemporary with Athenian sub-Mycenaean.

This third tomb suggests that occupation continued at Delphi until the end of Mycenaean times, and so it may well be. There may always have been at least a handful of inhabitants, though whether they were of the same stock is another matter. The occasional pieces of settlement or tomb pottery which help to bridge the gap between the Temenos tomb and the middle of the eighth century show a rather different character from that of the earlier pottery.[2]

The history of this site is of interest because of the evidence it affords of a cult in Mycenaean times, and also because it survived into LH. III C, in which it contrasts sharply with the much more important fortified settlement of Krisa,[3] in the plain below, for this suffered a violent destruction at or before the end of LH. III B, and was not subsequently reoccupied till Byzantine times.[4]

This settlement had a long though chequered life, as the earliest buildings go back to Middle Helladic; its fortification, however, dates from LH. III only,[5] and enclosed, as at Eutresis, a wide area, probably intended to serve as a place of refuge for the inhabitants of the surrounding district in case of danger. The Late Helladic houses are rectangular, and a room of *megaron* type is assigned to LH. I.[6] As to the pottery, only the latest concerns us, and this need not go beyond the limits of LH. III B, though some pieces must be very late in the series.[7] It is of interest that the decorated sherds appear to be of a more conventional LH. III B type than many of those at Delphi, and it is a factor which may affect one's view of the date of the latter material.

The final destruction by fire may then reasonably be placed at the end of LH. III B. This, and the consequent complete desertion of the site, are of obvious importance for the overall pattern of destruction at this time, and are discussed elsewhere (pp. 221 ff.).

These two sites of Delphi and Krisa contribute the most important material. The remainder of the sites, whether in Phocis or in Locris, can be dealt with very briefly, as there has been no proper excavation. East Locris seems to be quite unknown for this period except inasmuch as it impinges on the Spercheios valley (cf. pp. 126 f.). West Locris has been studied by Lerat,[8] and he has assembled the known evidence for Mycenaean sites: a chamber tomb with stirrup jars at Gouva,[9] a possible Mycenaean wall near Vitrinitsa,[10] and two vases from Galaxidi,[11] reported to be sub-Mycenaean, though the amphoriskos sounds rather LH. III C (it cannot be earlier), and the stirrup jar could be so as well. In a recent survey, Mastrokostas has identified a further site as having been inhabited in Late Helladic times.[12]

[1] Op. cit. p. 9, Fig. 26. Cf. *Ergon* for 1954, p. 11, Fig. 10 (Perati), shown on Pl. 6*d*.
[2] Lerat, *BCH*, lxi. 44 ff., and Pls. V and VI (tomb). Protogeometric sherds: *FD*, v. 17, Fig. 74; 136, Fig. 516. Cf. *PGP*, pp. 199 ff.
[3] Lerat, *RA*, 1936, pp. 129 ff.; *BCH*, lxi. 299 ff.
[4] *BCH*, lxi. 326.
[5] Op. cit. p. 323.
[6] Op. cit. pp. 318 f.
[7] *BCH*, lxii. 135 ff.; cf. p. 140, Fig. 21 and Pl. 25, 1? (it looks more Geometric than Mycenaean).
[8] *Les Locriens de l'Ouest*.
[9] Sotiriadis, *Pr.* 1906, p. 134; *AM*, xxxi. 394 ff.
[10] *Locriens*, p. 112.
[11] Op. cit. p. 157.
[12] *AE*, 1956, suppl., p. 22 (Palaeopanayia).

Back in Phocis, Lerat illustrates a few vases from tombs in the neighbourhood of Itea.[1] Of these, certainly three, and possibly all five, of the vases shown on his Pl. 51 are LH. III B, while of the other four illustrated the deep bowl and the jug presumably belong to LH. III C, the third is a four-handled vase probably reflecting the influence of Achaean LH. III C, (cf. pp. 99 f.), and the fourth is a trefoil oinochoe which should possibly be given a late Protogeometric date. A stirrup jar is also mentioned in the text, but not illustrated; from the description—concentric triangles outlined with dots—it should be LH. III C. It is thus a very mixed bag, but at least it indicates occupation both in LH. III B and in LH. III C. Mastrokostas has now added a Mycenaean settlement on the rocky hill of Gla, close to Itea, and the sherds illustrated may suggest occupation in LH. III C as well as earlier.[2] Besides this, Mastrokostas shows sherds of LH. III B, and possibly C, type from a small hill at Stenos,[3] near Antikyra, and identifies a Mycenaean acropolis, of LH. III B date, at Teithronion[4] near Amphikleia.

6. *The Spercheios Valley*

This region lies between Thessaly and central Greece, and has been singularly unproductive of Mycenaean remains of any sort. The early survey conducted by Wace and Thompson[5] revealed no trace of Mycenaeans whatsoever—remarkable inasmuch as they were primarily concerned with prehistoric times, and undertook excavations at Lianokladhi. Subsequently, the survey of Béquignon,[6] embracing a much wider period of time, produced equally negative results.

More recently, however, Marinatos[7] reported the discovery of a cist or shaft tomb of unique type, containing Mycenaean pottery, at Vardhates, close to Heraclea Trachis. The tomb was a rectangular shaft, with upright slabs set down the middle, thus making it easy to roof the tomb over with large and small slabs. Several skeletons were found, and the funeral gifts were heaped together, consisting of a bronze lance and about a dozen vases. The lance was not described, but the vases were stated all to belong to the latest phase of Mycenaean culture, to be of strongly provincial character, and to be similar to those of Kephallenia and Salamis. From this account, it would certainly appear that the pottery is LH. III C, but the only vases illustrated[8] are rather to be assigned to late LH. III B than to LH. III C. There is then little information of value that one can obtain from the pottery, except for the significant fact that it was Mycenaean of late type. The tomb itself has no parallels that I know of.

Finally, Hope Simpson and Lazenby[9] have made a further survey of the whole district, and on this occasion identified three or four sites from which Mycenaean sherds of a rather indeterminate type were recovered. It is therefore probable that there was at least some measure of Mycenaean ceramic influence, though one cannot gauge either its nature or its extent.

---

[1] *Locriens*, pp. 164 ff. and Pls. 51 and 52.
[2] *AE*, 1956, suppl., pp. 23 f. and 24, Fig. 5.
[3] Op. cit. p. 25, Fig. 6.
[4] Op. cit. pp. 25 f. and 26, Fig. 8.
[5] *P.T.* pp. 11, 171 ff., 247.
[6] *Recherches dans la vallée du Spercheios*.
[7] *Bericht VI. Int. Kongress 1939*, p. 334. Cf. *BCH*, lxiii. 311 f.
[8] *BCH*, lxiii. 310, Fig. 21.
[9] *Antiquity* xxxiii. 102 ff.

If any conclusion on this meagre evidence is legitimate, it is that the region was rather marginal so far as the Mycenaeans were concerned. Geographical considerations tend to confirm the likelihood of this. It is not only that the river Spercheios travels deep into the mountainous north-western areas; as well as this, access to this district from Phocis is to be made only through rugged and difficult country. Nor is it easy to get from this valley to the great central plain of Thessaly. It may also be argued that, although we do not know a great deal about the inland defences and frontiers of the Mycenaean power, if the Mycenaeans had intended to assure for themselves the land route through central Greece to Thessaly, there would surely have been some well-fortified town or towns in the Spercheios valley.

Finally, it may be noted that there is as yet no evidence for occupation in this area during the Protogeometric period.

7. *Thessaly*[1]

The identification of Mycenaean influence in Thessaly has been a lengthy and laborious business, beset with many vicissitudes.

The admirable work of Wace and Thompson, *Prehistoric Thessaly*, published in 1911, brought together the material then known. From this one would deduce that the impact of Mycenaean civilization on Thessaly was long-lived—originating in LH. II and continuing into LH. III—but superficial.[2] The report clearly suffers from the relative lack of knowledge of the course of this civilization.[3]

Between this time and 1940, a few further discoveries were made, but except in the case of Béquignon's unstratified material from Ktouri, these finds were not adequately recorded.[4]

Hence, when Furumark came to publish his comprehensive work on Mycenaean pottery in 1941, only six Thessalian sites are recorded in his Index of Sites, and of these only that of Ktouri represents any advance on Wace and Thompson's information.[5] Since 1940, the ravages of war have intervened, and severe earthquakes resulted in the temporary destruction of the central museum of the area, at Volos. Nevertheless, the recent activities of the ephors Verdhelis and Theocharis have enormously increased our knowledge of the Mycenaean period in Thessaly, and have given hope that we may obtain something like a complete picture in the near future.

One fact that had already become certain by the time Wace and Thompson were collating their material was that the indigenous culture of Thessaly was not Mycenaean. Mycenaean is intrusive, and the first point to establish, therefore, is where the Mycenaeans first arrived.

From what has been said in the section on the Spercheios valley it will be clear that the route of approach was not overland; the mountainous nature of the country, and the

---

[1] This is an area on which, for the Mycenaean period, not a great deal has been written, and I have therefore widened the scope of my discussion in the interests of clarity.

[2] *P.T.* pp. 206 ff.

[3] e.g. vases claimed as LH. II by Wace and Thompson are now said by Verdhelis to be sub-Mycenaean. *P.T.* p. 207, referring to *AM*, xiv, Pl. XI. Verdhelis, p. 52.

[4] *BCH*, lvi. 147 ff. Cf. Skeat, *Dorians*, p. 10.

[5] *Analysis*, pp. 644 ff.

archaeological evidence so far available, make this extremely unlikely. By far the easier means of communication is by sea, and the seaboard of Thessaly is virtually restricted to the Pagasaean Gulf. The nearest point for anyone arriving from the south is the district close to Pteleon, but the best harbour, and the best area for any further expansion into Thessaly, is the Homeric Iolkos, the Volos of today. From here there are two main passages of penetration—north-west through Pherae up to Larisa and the plain of North Thessaly, and more or less due west to Pharsala and the great central plain. At the same time one must assume that the Krokian plain and the Magnesian peninsula, rounding off the Pagasaean Gulf, would come naturally within the Mycenaean orbit.

The importance of Iolkos is clearly stressed in the literary tradition, and it was already known by the beginning of the century that LH. II pottery had been found nearby.[1] The discoveries of Theocharis in Volos itself of a palace which must be that of Iolkos, and of the closely adjacent harbour site which is most likely the ancient Neleia, have now proved beyond question that this was the centre of Mycenaean influence for the whole of Thessaly.

So far as Iolkos is concerned, it is now known from Theocharis' preliminary report[2] that contact with the South had been made in LH. I, and that a considerable building, probably a palace, had been established here in LH. II. The importance of the place was, however, at its greatest in LH. III, and a large quantity of Mycenaean pottery of first-rate quality, not only imported but also made locally, has been found. The 'palace' built in LH. II continued in use until LH. III A, and was rebuilt in LH. III B.

Evidence of a similar nature has also come to light in a trial excavation at Neleia.[3] The excavator stressed that the quality of the Late Helladic material, stretching from LH. I to LH. III, is no lower than that of the Argolid. This being the harbour site, it seems likely that it was the main port for Mycenaean ships coming from the South. The material from it—a provisional statement, obviously—continues no later than LH. III B. If this evidence is confirmed by further excavation, one will be strongly tempted to conclude that the abandonment of the site was connected with the disasters that overtook the central part of the Mycenaean world—the Argolid and the South Peloponnese—towards or at the end of LH. III B.

Though Neleia may have been abandoned, the palace and adjacent settlement of Iolkos continued to be occupied. In his latest reports[4] Theocharis has shown that both palace and settlement remained intact and inhabited at least into the early part of LH. III C. Therefore the wave of disaster that overcame important sites further south at the end of LH. III B did not directly affect this part of Thessaly. There was, however, an LH. III C destruction of the palace of Iolkos—but only of the palace; the surrounding settlement was not harmed. Even though the settlement did not suffer, it appears from the excavations so far undertaken that there was a break in occupation at about the same time as the destruction of the palace, as the pottery in each had reached the same stylistic stage. Above the palace there was a Protogeometric stratum, but no evidence of any important buildings. But above the settlement, as opposed to the palace, good stone-

---

[1] *AE*, 1906, Pl. 12.
[2] *Ergon* for 1956, pp. 43 ff.; *Archaeology*, xi. 13 ff.
[3] *Ergon* for 1957, pp. 32 ff.
[4] *Ergon* for 1960, p. 57; *Ergon* for 1961, pp. 51 ff.

built constructions of the Protogeometric period were found, and these represented four stages of building, and should thus cover a considerable period of time. There is evidently a distinct break between the end of the Mycenaean settlement and the beginning of the Protogeometric one, but the excavator considers that the time involved was no more than a generation, because of the essential continuity both in the architecture and in the pottery, and that thus a certain proportion of the previous Mycenaean population must be involved, though no doubt mingled with new arrivals.[1] The whole matter is of considerable interest for the time of the effective end of Mycenaean civilization at Iolkos, and for the course of events thereafter, involving both the arrival of intruders and the relative chronology of the Protogeometric period throughout Greece. The problems involved are more suitably discussed later (pp. 135 ff.), as there is further evidence of Mycenaeans elsewhere in Thessaly which needs attention, but for the moment it may be noted that the fact that no pottery later than early LH. III C was found need not mean more than that this area remained uninfluenced by subsequent developments further south, and one is not forced to conclude that the pottery of the Mycenaean settlement of Iolkos cannot have been later in date than, for example, the early LH. III C pottery of the Argolid.

Before moving outwards from Volos it may be noted that there is further evidence from this area. At Pagasae or Demetrias, which is in fact the Neleia site, a rectangular stone-built tomb was discovered, containing LH. II B vases.[2] Similarly, a tholos tomb close to Volos, at Kapakli, though obviously extensively plundered, produced three vases of LH. II type.[3]

Kapakli has, however, produced another tholos tomb, the contents of which were very different—at least seventy burials, over three hundred vases, and some small finds which have now disappeared;[4] its contents are exclusively post-Mycenaean, though one or two vases certainly recall Mycenaean,[5] and it continued in use down into the sixth century. Protogeometric and Geometric wares are particularly prominent, and there is also a certain amount of pottery which shows the native Thessalian influence, though at what point in the sequence this appears it is not easy to say. The evidence of this tomb must surely be taken in conjunction with that of the post-destruction settlement at Iolkos. In any case, it is clear evidence of the continuance of this type of Mycenaean tomb—and there are further examples of it in Thessaly. The tholos cannot have been reintroduced into Thessaly after the destruction of Iolkos, as by that time it is most unlikely that it was still used in the South, except in one or two remote districts.

Still fairly close to Volos, the site of Dimini produced four tombs in which Mycenaean objects were found. Two of these were tholoi, one of which contained only 'small beads and ornaments of gold and paste'—presumably Mycenaean; the other, besides small finds, produced numerous fragments of kylikes, which have been assigned to LH. III.[6] The other two tombs were cist tombs, from which came LH. III B vases and figurines, the one containing also a vase of native ware.[7] Not far from Volos, Theocharis has found

[1] Op. cit. pp. 58 ff.
[2] *AM*, xiv. 263 and Pls. IX and X. Cf. *Chronology*, p. 50.
[3] See p. 128, n. 1.
[4] *AE*, 1914, p. 141; *PGP*, p. 132; *Verdhelis, passim*.
[5] *Verdhelis*, Fl. I.
[6] *P.T.* p. 82.
[7] *Δ-Σ*, pp. 150 ff. For the rarity of the cist tomb in LH. III, see p. 33.

evidence of Mycenaean occupation on the coast at Nea Anchialos, which he identifies with the Homeric Pyrasos.[1]

Elsewhere, in the Krokian plain, sherds are mentioned from Zerelia[2] and Phthiotic Thebes,[3] but at Phthiotic Thebes the stratification was far from satisfactory, while at Zerelia the evidence is even more curious, as the cist tombs found on top of the remains of the eighth settlement—in which the Mycenaean sherds were discovered—are quite likely to be dated to Minyan times.[4]

Next may be considered the tombs close to Pteleon (well south of the Krokian plain) investigated by Verdhelis. There are two sites here. On the one site,[5] a tholos tomb was excavated. It had a tankard, a stirrup jar and two three-handled jars, all belonging to the LH. III A2 period, and as well as this a typical set of small finds, including a sword, a knife blade, buttons, beads and sealstones.

The other site[6] had a long history, being already occupied in Middle Helladic times. Besides MH. cist tombs, four Mycenaean tholos tombs were excavated. The first produced pottery ranging from LH. III A 2 to LH. III C, as well as small finds. The second contained a figurine of Ψ type, and five vases which Verdhelis assigned to LH. III C—a judgment which is probably correct.

The vases from the third tomb are also most probably III C, and include a globular stirrup jar; there were a few Mycenaean beads and buttons, but also the iron blade of a lance, and an iron dagger, which must have been later intrusions. It may be noted that this tomb had already been almost completely destroyed before excavation.

The fourth tomb had a long period of use; immediately below its floor were three shallow MH. cist tombs, while at the present preserved height of the tholos two rectangular tombs of stone slabs were found, with one of which were possibly associated the fragments of an iron sword and two bronze coins of Roman date. In the debris in between appeared, beside scattered bones and some conical buttons, six vases. Three of these vases are clearly Mycenaean—a three-handled jar, an amphora with belly-handles and a wart on the shoulder, and a hydria with two handles on the belly, one on the shoulder, and a distinctively III C decoration.[7] The interesting point is that these two latter vases strongly recall, to my mind, the typical III C ware from Achaea, which is practically exclusive to that area (cf. p. 99). There could be a connexion, especially as a vase of Achaean type has been found in Phocis.[8] The journey is a possible one.

The other three vases[9] are very different and must surely belong to a later burial. Of these the two trefoil-lipped oinochoai are Protogeometric, but Verdhelis claimed that the jug is sub-Mycenaean, on the basis of the quality of the varnish.[10] I must admit that this does not immediately convince me, but I have not handled the vase.

Thus the evidence from Pteleon is interesting, but unfortunately it raises more problems than it solves; it should indeed perhaps be considered, from its position, as quite separate

---

[1] *Thessalika*, ii. 60, Fig. 26, 63 f., 68.
[2] *P.T.* p. 159.
[3] Op. cit. pp. 166 f.
[4] Op. cit. p. 161.
[5] *Pr.* 1951, pp. 150 f.; 1952, pp. 181 ff.
[6] *Pr.* 1951, pp. 141 ff.; 1952, pp. 164 ff.; 1953, pp. 120 ff.
[7] *Pr.* 1953, p. 122, Fig. 2.
[8] Lerat, *Locriens*, Pl. 52.
[9] *Verdhelis*, p. 16, Nos. 25–27.
[10] Op. cit. pp. 52 and 54.

from the rest of Thessaly, as it may depend directly on the South and not on Iolkos. At least there is clear evidence here of LH. III C.

It is a good deal more certain that the plains of Central and North Thessaly depended on the harbour at Iolkos, at any rate for the Mycenaean features found there. So far as Central Thessaly is concerned, Wace and Thompson could report one sherd only, from Tsangli,[1] in the valley which runs from Pherae to Pharsala. Fortunately, much more information is now available.

First comes the district round Pharsala itself. Close by the town, Verdhelis uncovered[2] a remarkable construction, a tholos tomb with a dromos and a circular enclosure surrounding both tomb and dromos; this he has assigned to the end of the Archaic period, though it continued in use till Hellenistic times. More important, its purpose seems to have been to preserve a Mycenaean burial—though that did not prevent its being robbed. Within a few feet of this monument one rectangular and one square tomb were found; no vases emerged, but from the small finds it is clear that these burials went back to Mycenaean times. The main tomb, however, lay partly beneath the later Archaic tholos; it is of the chamber tomb type, rectangular, with a dromos issuing from one corner. Except for one skeleton, the burials had been disturbed, but at least ten dead had been deposited. The assorted objects were purely Mycenaean, and the small finds, including fragments of gold, silver, bronze, rock crystal, faience and amber, indicate the prosperity of the deceased. Eight vases were also found, of which seven are undoubtedly LH. III B, while the eighth is a monochrome clay bowl, which at first sight would seem to indicate a date well down in LH. III C. However, the discovery of a not unsimilar vase at Mycenae[3] in a context which is late LH. III B or transitional to LH. III C at the latest, suggests that this bowl is more satisfactorily associated with the other seven.

As well as burial evidence, there is also that of a settlement, at Ktouri,[4] eight miles north-west of Pharsala. There was no stratification, but the excavator came on a large body of sherds showing, in his opinion, occupation from LH. III B to Byzantine, with possibly a gap for the Geometric period, but the bulk of the pottery covering 'sub-Mycenaean' and Protogeometric.[5] The finds came from a mound and its surrounding area.

With regard to the earlier material[6] (the designation of sub-Mycenaean would now be considered incorrect), which is fully and admirably illustrated, the facts appear to be as follows. There is one undeniable LH. III B kylix.[7] Apart from this, the sherds are almost all from deep bowls and kraters in a clay-ground style for the outside, and over half were monochrome inside. Where decoration appeared, it was mostly that of spirals; other motives include the U pattern, the murex, netted semicircles, and one or two panel divisions. There are two examples of very thick wavy lines, and one sherd[8] (from a krater) had two parallel wavy lines. The encircling bands are generally fairly thick. Certain bowls or kraters display banded decoration only.

[1] *P.T.* p. 207.
[2] *Pr.* 1953, pp. 127 ff.
[3] *BSA*, lii. Pl. 43, *b*.
[4] Béquignon, *BCH*, lvi. 147 ff.
[5] Cf. *PGP*, p. 313 for the difficulties in assessing the 'Protogeometric' sherds.
[6] *BCH*, lvi. Figs. 42–46.
[7] Op. cit. Fig. 43.
[8] Op. cit. Fig. 45, No. 480.

These are the salient points and it seems fairly evident that we have to do here neither with sub-Mycenaean nor with the Granary Class—the only possible evidence of the latter is the krater sherd with two wavy lines, and that does not appear to be sufficient proof. Otherwise, the universally clay-ground system as well as the decorative motives suggest a time earlier than that of the Granary Class. There is LH. III B, as we have seen; can all or most of it belong to this style? Here I think we must take into account the thick bands and the preference for coating the inside of the bowl with paint. These are symptoms found in LH. III C but, it should be noted, already apparent towards the end of LH. III B.[1] It does seem possible that the inspiration for the material from Ktouri is to be dated not later than the transition to LH. III C. As, however, early LH. III C pottery has been identified at Iolkos, it is simplest to assume that this area remained in touch with the coastal district.[2] It should be noted that neither in this settlement nor in the tombs discussed above does any native Thessalian ware appear.

Mycenaean penetration did not stop at Pharsala, but continued westwards over the plain—or alternatively southwards from the Larisa district. Earlier researches had been remarkably unproductive,[3] and the Mycenaean tholos tomb excavated at Karditsa by Arvanitopoullos in 1917 was not published.[4] A tholos tomb of early LH. times investigated near Karditsa, however, and LH. II vases from Palamas (north-east of Karditsa), show the spread of Mycenaeans before LH. III, in which period Mycenaean sherds of local manufacture have been found at Kierion and elsewhere.[5] The extent of eventual penetration is best shown by the pottery found recently at Trikkala; this would not seem to be earlier than LH. III, and indeed the decorated sherds are LH. III B or C.[6] A few sherds were imports from the South, but the rest were made either locally, or at least in Thessaly. The most interesting piece is a jug with a rather unusual shoulder decoration, but there is also a sizeable fragment of a deep bowl, with one wavy line between the handles.[7] Mrs. Theocharis, to whom is due the most detailed account, considers that this pottery does not post-date 1200.[8] Again, there is apparently no trace of native Thessalian influence on this site, but a different picture emerges from the cist tombs at Agrilia, on the foothills of Mt. Chasios, east of Karditsa.[9] These are reported to contain mainly native hand-made vases, and just a few Mycenaean. The pottery has not yet been published and so comment must be deferred (cf. pp. 37 ff. on the distribution of cist tombs).

Finally to the northern plain of Thessaly, with Iolkos as the starting point. The first site of importance, on the road to Larisa, is Pherae, the modern Velestino. No Mycenaean settlement or tombs have as yet been found here, but it is worth noting that one vase from the post-Mycenaean cist tombs excavated by Béquignon looks very late Mycenaean[10] (cf. p. 151).

---

[1] Cf. *BSA*, lii. 207 ff. and Pls. 42 and 43 (late LH. III B).

[2] Mr. and Mrs. French picked up a sherd from a stirrup jar with octopus decoration in the Pharsala district, clear evidence of LH. III C.

[3] *P.T.* p. 145: one LH. III sherd from Tsani Magula.

[4] Cf. *BCH*, xliv. 395.

[5] *Thessalika*, ii. 69.

[6] Op. cit. pp. 72 ff.; *Ergon* for 1958, pp. 68 f.

[7] Op. cit. p. 75, Pl. I, and p. 76, Fig. 6.

[8] Op. cit., p. 79.

[9] *Verdhelis*, p. 61.

[10] *Recherches à Phères en Thessalie*, p. 73, No. 7 and Pl. 22. Cf. *PGP*, p. 133; *Verdhelis*, p. 52. The relation of the handle to the spout of this jug is, however, not Mycenaean.

In the northern plain itself, the finds have been rather sparse until recently. Wace and Thompson mention four LH. II vases from Maghula near Elassona.[1] For LH. III, there are III B (or C) vases from Gonnos,[2] a Mycenaean tholos tomb from Marmariani,[3] and another tomb, perhaps a tholos, at Rakhmani,[4] which contained an LH. III vase of unusual shape, a piece of glass paste, typically Mycenaean, and other small finds of Mycenaean type. Rakhmani also produced a 'fair quantity' of LH. III sherds on the top of the mound, the main shape being the kylix—so probably LH. III B.[5] The few sherds from near Metiseli have not been described.[6]

Of these sites, Marmariani and Rakhmani are the most interesting. The former is east of Larisa, on the foothills of Ossa, the latter north of Larisa, not far from Tempe. Marmariani is best known for its series of tholos tombs,[7] the pottery of which proves the arrival of migrants, or invaders, from Macedonia, and the gradual fusion of native with Protogeometric pottery. These tombs were built on the mound which constituted the previous settlements, the last of which produced, according to report, LH. III, this ware being also found in the fields round about.[8] Skeat noted that 'the Mycenaean town was suddenly deserted'.[9]

At Rakhmani the evidence appears to be somewhat different. I have mentioned earlier the Mycenaean pottery found at the top of the mound; the excavators note that it was, however, found 'especially at the bottom of the east slope with $\Delta_1\alpha$ (Iron Age) ware. It is all of the latest style (LM. III), and many pieces might even be called Sub-Mycenaean.'[10] There were no sherds of stirrup jars.[11] As to the $\Delta_1\alpha$ ware, the further statement is made: 'They were mixed up with the Mycenean sherds and so seem to be contemporary. They do not differ from the usual style of this ware, as shown in the finds from Marmariani and Theotoku.'[10] Unfortunately none of these sherds is illustrated, but one must assume that the excavators are right in the matter: $\Delta_1\alpha$ is the native Iron Age pottery. But are the excavators equally correct in their suggestion that $\Delta_1\alpha$ is contemporary with some of the Mycenaean? If this is so, then there should be continuity, and this runs counter to the evidence from Marmariani. The lack of stratification makes it difficult to speak with any certainty.

With this evidence may be taken that of Retziouni.[12] Here, on the southern foothills of Olympus, Verdhelis made a trial excavation and dug two cist tombs, each of which contained two hand-made vases of Marmariani type, while outside one was found an amphoriskos which Verdhelis considers to be sub-Mycenaean, both in shape and decoration, though locally made. If it is sub-Mycenaean then we may have once again an instance of continuity. It is also of interest that the burials were made in cist tombs, in view of the popularity of the tholos type of tomb in the Iron Age.

These three sites will be further discussed below, within the general picture.

Finally, we come to the work of the German School within the last few years. Of particular interest was the excavation of a fine mound at Gremnos,[13] some three miles west of

---

[1] *P.T.* p. 207.
[2] Op. cit. p. 207, Fig. 143.
[3] Op. cit. p. 54.
[4] Op. cit. pp. 40, 47, Fig. 23, *e*; p. 50, Fig. 26, *h*.
[5] Op. cit. p. 35.
[6] Op. cit. p. 207.
[7] Heurtley and Skeat, *BSA*, xxxi. 1 ff.
[8] Op. cit. p. 3.
[9] *Dorians*, p. 11.
[10] *P.T.* p. 35.
[11] Stirrup jars are exceedingly scarce over the whole of Thessaly, so far as is known.
[12] *Verdhelis*, pp. 52 f. and Pl. 3, 9.
[13] Milojcic, *AA*, 1955, pp. 192 ff.

Larisa on a bend of the river Peneios, and apparently important in antiquity as a crossroads. Although the greater interest attaches to the material from the lower layers, it is only the top ones which concern us here. In the topsoil itself sporadic sherds of many periods were found, but immediately beneath it a few foundation remains are reported of a miserable dwelling of the sub-Mycenaean to Protogeometric period, while near this, but reaching down rather deeper, were the remains of a better built edifice, surrounded by LH. III B/C sherds. Below this again came imposing layers where no Mycenaean sherds were found, the dominant ware being monochrome, the shapes of which betrayed strong Middle Helladic influence.

In a trial pit dug at the north edge of the mound, the stratification descended from Hellenistic to Middle Geometric, while under the latter came a deep layer, one metre thick, with post-Mycenaean pottery of Marmariani type. The Mycenaean level had not been reached here when the excavation was terminated.

In the general conclusions, it was noted that the Mycenaean population lived mainly in the area surrounding the mound rather than on it—a statement presumably based on surface finds. The report is a preliminary and provisional one, and there are no Mycenaean, sub-Mycenaean, or Protogeometric sherds illustrated. But it is noteworthy that no other ware is mentioned alongside the LH. III B-C material, and there is as yet no clear evidence of continuity after this period. On the other hand, sub-Mycenaean and Protogeometric are closely linked. I feel that until the material is more fully recorded there is no purpose in further speculation on this matter.

Besides this excavation, the Germans did some extremely useful survey work on two other sites. At Tatar Magula,[1] in the plain about five miles north of Larisa, LH. III B pottery is reported to be plentiful, and it was concluded that this was probably the site of Homeric Orthe, as previously suggested by Stählin. Secondly, the site of Petra,[2] on the edge of Lake Boebeis, was investigated. This consists of three large hilltops, and although no Mycenaean pottery is mentioned as having been found, there was a circumferent wall over two miles long which, Milojcic argues must, from the nature of its construction, have been built in Mycenaean times; and he further concludes that if it is a Mycenaean wall, it marks out the circumference of the largest Mycenaean town yet found on Greek soil.

Furthermore, he connects this wall with others, one being the lower perimeter wall of the Ktouri acropolis (close to the mound), and the other at Arne (Kierion), not far from Ktouri. He concludes that at these sites we are probably concerned with large Mycenaean towns and settlements, and he suggests that on the whole the evidence for Mycenaean settlements is to be found rather in the actual plain than on the mounds.[3]

At this point an attempt may be made to assess the general picture of Mycenaean influence and its successor or successors in Thessaly.

The first question which needs discussion is the nature and extent of Mycenaean influence in Thessaly. Wace and Thompson came to the following conclusion:[4] 'Thus it was only at the end of the prehistoric age that Mycenean civilization really reached Northern Greece, but before it could supplant the older cultures, and gain a firm hold on

[1] Op. cit. p. 221.
[2] Op. cit. pp. 221 ff.
[3] Op. cit. pp. 229 ff.
[4] *P.T.* p. 247.

Thessaly, it was itself swept away by the northern invasions that mark the dawn of historic Greece.' Fifty years ago, this was a reasonable conclusion on the known evidence. Today, the statement needs profound modification. It will be clear from the preceding analysis that at least by LH. III B Mycenaean culture had spread over most of Thessaly.

As to the survival of a native population following on the arrival of the Mycenaeans, the position earlier than LH. III B is, in fact, uncertain,[1] but the sites and tombs in which LH. III B pottery has been found are remarkable for their absence of anything that can be called native Thessalian, with the exception of a single vase at Dimini (p. 129),[2] and there is no evidence that Iolkos was other than purely Mycenaean from the very beginning of Late Helladic. Either then, by LH. III B times, the native population was entirely superseded, or else their culture was submerged by the dominant and superior Mycenaean culture. The latter is likely to be the true answer, as it seems most improbable that the native element should have been completely obliterated. In this case we have a single culture representing both a dominant and a no doubt subject population. One may note the difference here from the state of affairs in Kephallenia in LH. III C times, where a native element was definitely not submerged (pp. 104 f.).

So then, at least before the end of LH. III B, the Mycenaeans controlled most of Thessaly. This is shown by the evidence of sherds from settlements, and by the evidence of vases and other typically Mycenaean objects from the burials. The principal site was that of Iolkos and, although close contact was maintained with the South, a great deal of the pottery was locally made and of first-rate quality. The Mycenaeans had a firm hold in Thessaly and were clearly capable of maintaining their culture.

Next, what happened in Thessaly at the time of the disasters at the end of LH. III B in southern Greece? The district round Pteleon may be set aside, as its situation kept it separate from the main area of Thessaly to which access was made, so far as concerned the Mycenaeans, from Iolkos; contacts were maintained between this district and Achaea (cf. p. 130). For the rest of Thessaly, it is certain that the Mycenaeans retained a temporarily undisturbed hold at Iolkos, and probably over much of the inland area, as for example in the region round Pharsala. It is strange that the port of Neleia does not seem, on present evidence, to have been occupied after LH. III B, but it would be unsafe to speculate on the significance of this until further excavation confirms the results of the preliminary investigation.

The effective end of Mycenaean power in Thessaly can be put at the time of the destruction of the palace of Iolkos, for it must have been the chief town, and although the houses close to the palace were not destroyed there appears to have been a break in occupation at about the time of the destruction. This break, and destruction, involve more than one problem.

A major problem is that of the time, in relation to the course of events in Southern Greece and the Central Aegean. As only brief preliminary reports are available, and as hardly any of the material has been illustrated, the problem cannot yet be solved, but the

---

[1] How much earlier than LH. III B the Mycenaeans gained dominance over Thessaly is a question that is not the concern of this work.

[2] The tombs at Agrilia (*Verdhelis*, p. 61) may provide another exception, but the vases have not yet been published.

peculiar nature of the difficulties arising should be recognized. The information given (see p. 128 and n. 4) is that the stage in the pottery style reached at the time of destruction and break in occupation is that of early LH. III C, while the re-occupation is described as being characterized by Protogeometric pottery. There would be no inherent difficulty here, but we have the further information that the Protogeometric buildings come immediately above the Mycenaean houses, and the architectural and ceramic continuity is such that some of the preceding Mycenaean population must be involved, and the gap between the end of the Mycenaean and the beginning of the Protogeometric period can hardly be more than a generation.

If one assumes that the destruction of the palace is in fact contemporary with some time in early LH. III C in the south of Greece, and also that the Protogeometric style arises first in Athens at about the end of the LH. III C period, a gap of only one generation is clearly impossible. But if one presumes, as one must, that the excavator is reasonably correct in suggesting so short an interval, then one of the above assumptions must be incorrect. As to the former assumption, I have already stated (p. 129) that it could have happened that the inhabitants of Iolkos continued to produce an early type of LH. III C pottery; as the later stage of this style is more of a degeneration than anything else, there is no reason why this should not have happened. On the other hand, it is perhaps unsafe as yet to assume that no traces of late LH. III C appeared in Thessaly. At one point of his report, Theocharis states[1] that there was a small amount of this pottery at Iolkos. Also, there are two other indications that it may not have been unknown. The first is the existence of a very deep bowl,[2] of unknown provenience but certainly from Thessaly, which is rather like Granary Class vases. The second is the technique, on a few of the Protogeometric vases,[3] of leaving the lower part of the body unpainted, a Granary Class feature not taken over by Athenian Protogeometric; if this is one of the features of Thessalian LH. III C pottery persisting into the Protogeometric period, then it also suggests contact with the South in late LH. III C.

However this may be, it is evidently the view of the excavator that it is incorrect to suppose that the Protogeometric style arose first in Athens, and that it is very likely that such a style arose quite independently in Thessaly, based on the preceding Mycenaean, and thus quite possibly earlier than Athenian Protogeometric. He considers, in fact, that certain characteristics of the Thessalian Protogeometric style are already to be found in the local LH. III B ware of this region.[4]

This theory of the independent rise of Thessalian Protogeometric pottery is based on that of Verdhelis, but Theocharis has a great deal more material available. It is a theory which I discuss rather more fully later (pp. 261 ff.), and will deal with only briefly here. One of the crucial factors is that of the technical innovation of the compass-drawn circles and semicircles, an innovation which I am convinced cannot have been made in two areas independently. If the innovation was made in Thessaly, then it travelled from there to Athens. It must, of course, be admitted that this is not in itself impossible, but account

---

[1] *Ergon* for 1961, p. 57: 'examples of late III C are fewer.'
[2] *Verdhelis*, Pl. 8, No. 51.
[3] e.g. *Ergon* for 1960, p. 59, Fig. 71 (the cup).
[4] *Ergon* for 1961, p. 59.

has also to be taken of other innovations and of the whole understanding of the style, factors which seem to go together and to be best realized in Athens. The creation of the style does involve a relation of decoration to shape, and this seems not to have been too happily achieved in Thessaly; the Protogeometric cup with circles round the body, recently illustrated by Theocharis, may be instanced as an example.[1]

Such an aesthetic consideration may not be altogether convincing, and it may be that I am wrong, but I would continue for the present to maintain that certain features involving technical innovation, ascribed by Verdhelis to local Thessalian development (cf. pp. 261 f.), are much more likely to have come from Athens.

One is also at a disadvantage in not knowing precisely what are the characteristics of the pottery of the earliest Protogeometric level at Iolkos, though it must be assumed that there is a clear difference between this and the preceding Mycenaean. That then is the situation; if the earliest pottery of Protogeometric Iolkos includes the use of compass-drawn circles or semicircles, I am inclined to think that the early LH. III C pottery of the end of the Mycenaean settlement is contemporary with late LH. III C further south; if on the other hand this early Protogeometric has no features traceable to the Athenian style, then it may well be a local development, inasmuch as it is probable that many of the characteristics of this style are to be derived from the preceding local Mycenaean style, and in that case the time of the destruction of the palace could be contemporary with early LH. III C in, for example, the Argolid.

This regrettably long discussion has been concerned with one problem only (though involving others), that of the time of the destruction. The second problem is whether anything can be said of the cause of destruction, and that involves the situation in the rest of Thessaly.

It is, of course, possible that the destruction of Iolkos was the result of internal unrest, but the culture of the succeeding re-occupation is evidently sufficiently distinct from its predecessor for an admixture of intruders to be considered likely, and there are in any case signs of two separate groups of newcomers into Thessaly at about this time. Both may have had a hand in determining the end of Mycenaean civilization in this area, and one or other may have been involved in the end of the palace at Iolkos.

The first group is that which is best known from the contents of the tholos tombs of Marmariani (p. 133), who at first used hand-made pottery which shows links with Macedonia, but continued the system of multiple burial in a Mycenaean type of tomb. Marmariani had previously been inhabited by people who used Mycenaean pottery, but there is no trace of such influence among the burials of the new arrivals. This suggests that the Mycenaeans had abandoned the site before this group arrived; it seems unlikely that the newcomers would have continued to make hand-made pottery if the knowledge of the wheel was available—and indeed in due course of time they did adopt the wheel to fashion their own characteristic ware, and it is possible that the knowledge came from Protogeometric Iolkos. Consequently this particular group is unlikely to have been concerned with the destruction of the palace at Iolkos (unless they retreated after destroying) and

---

[1] Op. cit. p. 57, Fig. 57, a.

will have arrived from Macedonia perhaps not long afterwards.[1] One must not forget, however, the evidence of Rakhmani (p. 133) where pottery of Marmariani type was found with Mycenaean sherds; it is true that there was no stratification available here, but a slight doubt must remain as to whether the conclusion above is an accurate one.

The second group is recognizable not by its pottery but by its use of the cist tomb. Several sites are involved: Agrilia, Retziouni, Palaiokastro, Dimini, Iolkos, Theotokou and Halos.[2] The situation with regard to them is by no means clear. The earliest are the two cist tombs containing LH. III B vases at Dimini, and they are so early that one must doubt whether they are in any way connected with the later ones. The cist tombs of Palaiokastro and Halos contained nothing earlier than the Protogeometric period nor, so far as is known, did those of Iolkos (which are all child burials). On the other hand, a sub-Mycenaean lekythos was found in the earliest of the Theotokou tombs and, whether this vase was imported or local, it precedes the rise of Protogeometric pottery. The picture is further complicated by the Retziouni finds, where the vases are reported to be mostly of the Marmariani type, with just one amphoriskos which is either very late Mycenaean or, more likely, Protogeometric. And finally, the vases of the Agrilia tombs are also mainly local, with only a few which are said to be Mycenaean.

There is thus much obscurity, but if these tombs with the exception of the two at Dimini belong to a second group of new arrivals (and this is also open to question), then it is tempting to suppose that these were the intruders who effectively disturbed the Mycenaean hold over Thessaly, and may have been involved in the calamity at Iolkos—at any rate, the child burials in cist tombs are a characteristic here of the subsequent Protogeometric occupation.[3] And they may have been gradually pushing their way across Thessaly (from the North-west?) for some time, and may be connected with other similar groups infiltrating into the Mycenaean world (pp. 37 ff., 72). The absence of any distinctive pottery need not be a stumbling-block, as they may have adopted the technically superior wares they no doubt encountered.

It is unnecessary to stress the hypothetical nature of this reconstruction. There is much yet to be discovered, and much of what has been found is not yet fully recorded; the eventual picture will probably be very different from what I have imagined it to be. But above all, it is of the greatest importance that so much archaeological work is taking place in a region too long neglected.

8. *The Sporades*

Skyros alone of these islands has been archaeologically productive, and its material was admirably recorded by the late Professor Hansen.[4] Surface sherds, the remains of a cemetery at the foot of the acropolis of the town of Skyros and a few vases in the

---

[1] Cf. *PGP*, pp. 176 and 314, for the later diffusion of their pottery over other parts of Thessaly. (The argument based on tomb types no longer holds.)

[2] The references are given, except for Dimini (*Δ-Σ*, pp. 150 ff.) on p. 38.

[3] Yet the adults at nearly Kapakli continued to bury their dead in a tholos tomb (p. 129).

[4] Prehistoric Skyros, in *Studies Presented to David M. Robinson*, vol. i, pp. 54 ff.

museum all testify to habitation in Mycenaean times, as also do the rosettes in gold leaf and numerous beads of blue glass found in a cist tomb the contents of which are otherwise of Protogeometric date.[1]

9. *Macedonia*

In view of the particular problems set by this district, and its generally marginal character in relation to the Aegean world, it will be clearest to discuss both the Late Bronze Age and Early Iron Age in this section.

Geographically, this area may be divided into three parts, Eastern, Central and Western Macedonia, and in each case there is a passage through to the North. Eastern Macedonia, where the connecting link with the North is the river Strymon, falls entirely outside the scope of these investigations, there being no material recorded. Western Macedonia is predominantly mountainous, and here the river Haliakmon, closely linked with the river Tserna in Jugoslavia, takes a circuitous course from Florina southwards through Kastoria to Grevena, then turning north-east until it emerges into the plain of Central Macedonia. Central Macedonia, finally, comprises the great plain which stretches from Thessalonica to the west, and for present purposes may be taken also to include a small area to the east of Thessalonica, and the western part of Chalcidice. The plain is dominated by the river Axios, which leads directly to the Balkans.

Our archaeological knowledge, then, both for the Bronze Age and for the succeeding Early Iron Age, is confined to Central and Western Macedonia. The results of discoveries recorded until 1937 have been most admirably brought together by W. A. Heurtley in his *Prehistoric Macedonia*, published in 1939. In spite of the considerable time which has since elapsed (though naturally one must take into account the wartime conditions, which may be said to have continued here until 1947), there has been no further record of any Bronze Age site, though there have been a few casual finds. For the Early Iron Age, there is an account of work undertaken at Karabournaki,[2] a suburb of Thessalonica, the record of pottery found in the later campaigns at Olynthus,[3] and the exceedingly important series of tombs from a cemetery at Vergina,[4] at a point south of where the Haliakmon comes out into the central plain. Generally speaking, our knowledge of this area is not so full as it might be.[5]

So far as concerns the Late Bronze Age, the material comes from settlements only, such settlements being (as commonly in North Thessaly) on mounds, only a small section of which has as a rule been excavated.

It is not necessary to describe in any detail the Matt-painted and Incised hand-made native ware which characterized these areas. Western Macedonia should still apparently

---

[1] Papademetriou, *AA*, 1936, pp. 228 ff., Figs. 1–4; cf. *Ker.* IV, p. 26, n. 26, and for the armbands *CVA*, Mainz I, pp. 12 ff.
[2] Rhomaios, 'Ἐπιτύμβιον, pp. 358 ff.
[3] *Olynthus*, xiii. 45 ff., Pls. 1–11.
[4] *Pr.* 1952 ff.; *Ergon* for 1957 to 1961; Andronikos, *Balkan Studies* ii. 85 ff., *BCH*, lxxxv. 789 ff. (Petsas).

[5] The most recent finds are recorded in *BCH*, lxxxv. 773 (Tsiotili, Axiocastron), 773 and 775 (Aetos), 777 (Kozani) and 782 (Aeani). There is a fuller record of Kallipolitis' investigations at Kozani in *Ergon* for 1960, 99 ff.; the slab-built cist tomb XXIII and its contents are of particular interest.

be considered as isolated from the central plain, and the whole displays a culture that is essentially different from that of the Mycenaeans. In view of this, it is unlikely that Mycenaean objects would penetrate in any great quantity overland. On the other hand, Mycenaean pottery could, and did, travel up through the Aegean, and its superior technique certainly influenced local potters, even though the hand-made tradition remained.

It is to be expected, then, that Mycenaean vases would make their appearance in or near the coastal districts. In Chalcidice, one site only has such pottery, and that is Ayios Mamas,[1] on the north shore of the Gulf of Cassandra. According to the report, Mycenaean was predominant at the end of the Bronze Age settlement, after which the mound was deserted. Little enough has been recorded, but it is notable that this is one of the four sites where imports were found, though it is also evident that the bulk of the Mycenaean material was made locally. As far as one can tell, this pottery is LH. III B, with a few pieces that might be later.[2]

At Gona and Sedes, just to the east of Thessalonica, Mycenaean pottery is also said to be the characteristic ware of the Late Bronze Age, and the few illustrations show good LH. IIIB but nothing later.[3] Both sites continued to be occupied in the Early Iron Age.

A similar preponderance of Mycenaean ware is noted at Saratse,[4] to the north-east of Thessalonica. Imports reached this settlement from the South, and the illustrated pieces, which include examples of local imitations as well, suggest LH. III B and perhaps the beginning of LH. III C.

Other sites were occupied in these districts during the Late Bronze Age, and some continued into the Early Iron Age, but our knowledge of the pottery associated with these is either very slight or non-existent, and mostly based on surface finds.[5] On the whole, it seems a likely hypothesis that pottery of LH. III B type did have a considerable influence over this coastal area, to judge from the reported evidence of the four sites discussed individually. There is no indication that any site suffered violent destruction; some were deserted at the end of the Bronze Age, but others continued into the Iron Age; in other words, the position is far from clear.

Important additional information is however available from four sites on or close to the river Axios, the southernmost of which is some thirty-five miles north-west of Thessalonica. From north to south, they are Kilindir, Chauchitsa, Vardino and Vardaroftsa. These sites, and apparently only these, have yielded traces of invaders coming from the North towards the end of the Bronze Age.

All four have also produced Mycenaean pottery, though in small quantities only at Kilindir,[6] and no more than a single sherd at Chauchitsa.[7] Vardino[8] and Vardaroftsa, situated close to each other, did however have a fair quantity of Mycenaean; as the evidence from these two sites is closely similar, it will be best to discuss that site which was the more extensively excavated, and produced the fuller results—Vardaroftsa.[9]

---

[1] Radford, *BSA*, xxix. 118 ff.; *P.M.* pp. 1 ff.
[2] *P.M.* p. 226.
[3] *BCH*, xli–xliii. 248, Fig. 46 and Pls. 47 and 48.
[4] Heurtley, *BSA*, xxx. 131 f.; *P.M.* pp. 222 f.
[5] *P.M.* pp. xxii f. Surface Mycenaean from Tsair and Giatsilar. Also a sherd from Kalamaria in the B.S.A. collection.
[6] Casson, *AJ*, vi. 59 ff. Cf. *P.M.* p. 31.
[7] Casson, *Archaeologia*, lxxiv. Pl. 27, 1, 1.
[8] Casson, *LAAA*, xii. 15 ff. Cf. *P.M.* p. 35.
[9] *BSA*, xxvii. 1 ff.

The evidence from this site is indeed remarkable. It gives the clearest indication of the length and type of Mycenaean influence, of the invasion at the end of the Bronze Age, and of the subsequent Iron Age settlement. The relative depths of the deposits must be mentioned, though it will be obvious from the analysis how dangerous it can be to make any chronological deductions based only on such evidence. The top half metre yielded mostly Hellenistic sherds, and the next three half metres covered the fourth and fifth centuries. Beneath this, a similar depth of deposit extended probably over half a millennium. Then, beneath this, Mycenaean pottery was found from the eighth to the twentieth half metre, and within this the invasion strata covered the ninth and tenth half metres. What length of time is then to be allocated to the period of Mycenaean influence?

As is generally the case elsewhere in Macedonia, the earliest Mycenaean material is not earlier than LH. III B. In fact, from the illustration of a reconstructed bowl [1] from the lowest layer, it could be advanced LH. III B; and the thick wavy line on the sherd of a bowl [2] from the eighteenth half metre suggests that we are already not far from LH. III C. The sixteenth half metre produced sherds of two kylikes, so here we may still be in LH. III B, though the shape does persist into LH. III C. Other evidence [3] of LH. III B is to be seen in the three-handled piriform jug, the alabastron and the straight-sided pyxis (nineteenth half metre); on the other hand, the fifteenth half metre contained a stirrup jar with concentric semicircle motive on the shoulder, [4] and this, if correct, should belong to LH. III C (cf. pp. 6 f.). Then it is stated that the fourteenth to the ninth half metres produced 'the usual sub-Mycenaean deep bowl', and that 'in the upper part of the deposit, i.e. the burnt layer, and 25 centimetres above it, no shapes except the sub-Mycenaean bowl were found'.[5]

With regard to the terminology used, it must be remembered that the definition of the term 'sub-Mycenaean' has narrowed since the appearance of this report. The characteristics of these bowls, in so far as one can make them out, are bands below the handles, often one or more wavy lines between the handles, and no other decoration. The majority of them must have been unpainted inside, as it is stated that 'nine pieces are completely glazed on the inside',[6] and that must represent a small fraction only of the whole.

The correct interpretation of this material is not easy, though I think one should speak of LH. III C instead of sub-Mycenaean, and one may perhaps recognize LH. III C as already appearing in the fifteenth half metre, in other words well below the burnt 'invasion' layers.

It is of importance that the excavators state [7] that of one hundred and fifty fragments only twelve were imported, though it is not specified at which levels these occurred. At any rate, the imitation of LH. III B and LH. III C may well have continued over a long period, conceivably after Mycenaean had ceased to be manufactured further south. It is also of great importance to realize that the manufacture of the Mycenaean bowls continued both during, and for a brief period after, the invasion from the North. It indicates

---

[1] Op. cit. p. 21, Fig. 10, 4.
[2] Op. cit. Pl. 16, *a*, 16.
[3] Op. cit. pp. 21 f.
[4] Op. cit. pp. 22 and 21, Fig. 10, 8 (shape restored); cf. Pl. 15, *a*, 14.
[5] Op. cit. p. 22 and Pl. 16, *b*.
[6] Op. cit. p. 21.
[7] Loc. cit.

that the destruction had only a limited effect, the characteristic fluted ware of the invaders appearing alongside the local Mycenaean, and very possibly giving way to it.

From the above considerations it will be seen that the relative chronology for the persistence of Mycenaean shapes, and hence also for the time of the invasion, is extremely difficult to assess, as is also the precise relationship to material from further south. The excavators could even be right in assigning the invasion to about the middle of the eleventh century.[1]

One further small point of interest may be noted, from the nearby site of Vardino. Here, in the layer immediately below the burnt strata, the excavators found a violin-bow fibula[2] with flattened arch, of a type which may have its origin outside Greece (possibly introduced from Italy? cf. pp. 56 f.), not certainly to be assigned to any context earlier than the time of transition LH. III B/C, and mostly well down in LH. III C (pp. 55 f.). This fibula should at least confirm the LH. III C nature of some of the local Mycenaean pottery on these sites.

The likelihood that Mycenaean pottery continued to be made in this area for a long time is suggested by the very close contiguity, at Vardaroftsa, of the last Mycenaean sherds and the earliest pottery of Protogeometric or Geometric type. The former continues into the eighth half metre, while the first sherd with a concentric circle motive (not of an early kind) appears in the seventh half metre.[3] One must of course be extremely cautious in assessing the value of this evidence, as it is clear that the upper layers of this mound cover a vast period of time. Even so, the close association may be borne in mind.

The Early Iron Age may most conveniently be distinguished from the Late Bronze Age by the appearance of the Axios invaders, their pottery, and the evidence of burning. The distinction is by no means, however, a sharp one, and it has already been noted that there is no evidence of destruction in the coastal area. Of thirteen Late Bronze settlements investigated, eight continued to be occupied, among them three of the sites affected by invasion. Only two or three sites (e.g. Karabournaki, Sare Omer) were unoccupied before the Iron Age.

Whereas the Bronze Age sites provide settlement material only, certain cemeteries, widely separated, supplement the settlement evidence of the Early Iron Age: these are the tombs of Chauchitsa, of nearby Bohemica, of the rather remote Patele in the valley of the Tserna river, and of Vergina, south of the Haliakmon at the point where it emerges into the central plain.[4]

The continuity established by settlement stratification is in general confirmed by the pottery. The majority of the local vases are hand-made and, as Skeat notes: 'The various unpainted wares, whether plain, incised, or scraped, are all of native origin, and many of their characteristic features can be traced back continuously to the beginning of the Bronze Age.'[5]

The most popular shape is the jug with cut-away neck, and here a feature seems to

---

[1] Op. cit. p. 63.
[2] *P.M.* pp. 101 and 231, Fig. 104, *aa*.
[3] *BSA*, xxvii. 28 and Pl. 21, *a*4.
[4] Casson, *BSA*, xxvi. 1 ff. (Chauchitsa); Rey, *Albania*, iv. 40 ff. (Bohemica); *P.M.*, pp. 104 f. (Patele); see p. 139, n. 4 for Vergina.
[5] *Dorians*, p. 2.

have been taken over from the invaders, the application of two or three twists to the handle, to give a firmer grip; this feature is widely found in Central Macedonia, and in conjunction with the vase shape provides important evidence for a move from Macedonia south at least as far as Marmariani in North Thessaly (cf. p. 133), but it is not clear whether it is to be found at Patele.[1] As well as this, the fluted technique of the invaders is still used later, but only very rarely—otherwise, their pottery appears to have left no trace.

There are a few regional innovations, as is natural, and these may for the most part be left undiscussed. One shape, however, deserves mention—a bowl with two vertical handles each surmounted by a flat disk. At Vergina, these appear in quantity[2] from the earliest tombs onwards, and are second in popularity to the jugs with cut-away necks; and the cups occasionally have a similar handle. It is the handle which is the distinctive feature, and it cannot be exactly paralleled elsewhere in Macedonia. It does not appear at all at Patele or Chauchitsa—or in the Marmariani tombs—which may suggest that the influence from Macedonia precedes the introduction of this shape. On the other hand, an approximation to it is found on a cup at Saratse,[3] and an elongated variation on the bowls is reasonably common at Olynthus.[4] There is also one example from Karabournaki.[5]

One other distinctive feature of the Vergina vases is worthy of notice—the warts on the hand-made amphorae and hydriae.[6] These do not appear elsewhere in Macedonia, to my knowledge, and one would like, as in the case of the 'disk' handle, to know something of the origin.

So far, the stress has been on continuity either with the previous Bronze Age inhabitants or with the invaders, and it will be remembered that the local wheel-made Mycenaean survived the invasion period. At some time during the Early Iron Age, however, contacts were resumed with areas further south, and these are principally recognizable in the appearance of wheel-made vases, many of which were decorated with concentric semicircles or circles. This material I have discussed briefly in my earlier book,[7] and concluded that there was influence from the Thessalo-Cycladic area, assignable rather to the ninth century than to the tenth. The finds at Vergina have now added considerably to the number of vases known; about twenty-five have been found in the tombs so far excavated. The most popular shape remains the skyphos with low base and pendent semicircles, but there are also skyphoi with high flaring foot, with or without semicircles, a high-handled bowl with standing semicircles, cups on flat base or high foot with zigzag decoration round the rim, low-based skyphoi with no semicircle decoration, and one or two other shapes. On the whole, the previous impression of influence from Thessalo-Cycladic Protogeometric is confirmed. There is no doubt that many of the Vergina vases were made locally, but some are imports, in particular a remarkably fine skyphos[8] with a low base and two sets of full circles between the handles, on each side; the clay and the excellence of technique and of paint are very reminiscent of Attic Protogeometric, but neither the shape nor the

---

[1] *P.M.* p. 252, Pl. 23.
[2] *Pr.* 1952, pp. 242 f.
[3] *P.M.* p. 236, No. 486.
[4] *Olynthus*, v. Pls. 23, 24; xiii. Pl. 11.
[5] Ἐπιτύμβιον, p. 367, Fig. 3, 1.
[6] e.g. *Pr.* 1952, p. 246, Fig. 27 (E 24 and A 14).
[7] *PGP*, p. 180.
[8] *Pr.* 1952, pp. 252 and 250, Fig. 29, E26.

two sets of circles can be paralleled there. Comparison may perhaps be made with a stray find from Phthiotic Thebes in Thessaly.[1]

Two problems arise from this evidence from Vergina. The first concerns the relative date of the appearance of the vases of Protogeometric type, as it has been pointed out by Andronikos that in two of the tombs (admittedly covering a certain length of time), besides Protogeometric vases, a pyxis of Mycenaean type was found, the one wheel-made, the other probably hand-made.[2] Does this mean that the Protogeometric vases should be given an earlier dating, so as to form the link with the vases of LH. III C type?[3] I think this might be difficult to maintain in view of the evidence further south, and I would prefer to believe that the Mycenaean tradition may have been retained longer than previously thought, though there are two factors which might affect or ease the situation: the closer approximation of Attic Protogeometric to LH. III C through the equation of Attic sub-Mycenaean with LH. III C (suggested pp. 17 ff.), and the possibility that the skyphoi with pendent semicircles may go back rather earlier than I previously supposed, a matter which further excavation at Iolkos may decide.[4]

The second problem is that of the latest date of the Protogeometric vases. What extent of time is to be attributed to them? Apart from this ware, there is an extraordinary absence of datable pieces in Macedonia before 600 B.C. One may suppose that the Thessalo-Cycladic Protogeometric persisted into the eighth century, but not later, unless Macedonia was once more completely isolated, a supposition which the tradition of early colonies from the South would hardly permit.

In the preceding discussion no signs have appeared of influence or movements from the North in the Early Iron Age. That does not mean that they did not exist; there is strong evidence for such influence, and probably movement, but it is to be recognized in objects other than pottery, and principally in the bronzes.

For this evidence cemeteries are more important than settlements, as scarcely anything of note has been recovered from the latter. An excellent review of the finds other than pottery has been given by Rey,[5] and he gives a list of other sites, covering much of Macedonia and even reaching over into Thrace, from which bronze objects of this period have been recovered. The overwhelmingly northern origin is plainly demonstrated, to such an extent that one may wonder whether the iron weapons and bronze arched fibulae may not also have come from this direction. Rey concludes, however, that this material belongs to the end rather than to the beginning of the Early Iron Age, that is to say, closer to the sixth century than to the tenth. This hypothesis is valuable inasmuch as it lays stress on the considerable length of occupation of cemeteries, but it is insufficiently founded on the associated pottery (which, indeed, had almost entirely perished on his site at Bohemica). There seems no reason to suppose that some of these objects were not contemporary with the Protogeometric vases, and recent excavation at Vergina has

---

[1] *PGP*, p. 153. Cf. also Athens, National Museum, No. 17480: unknown provenience.

[2] *Pr.* 1952, p. 242, Fig. 23, *Δ* 5; *Ergon* for 1958, p. 82 f. (tomb N).

[3] Implied by Andronikos, *Ergon* for 1958, pp. 83 f.

[4] The length of use of some of these tombs must also be borne in mind; centuries may have divided the first and last burials.

[5] *Albania*, iv. 40 ff.

produced evidence which makes it most probable that the introduction of bronzes of northern type preceded the first appearance of Protogeometric.

The earliest tomb here is C, and all the objects are from four or five burials.[1] The salient points are as follows. All the vases are hand-made, and there is evidence neither of Mycenaean survival nor of Protogeometric wheel-made innovation. The 'disk' handles and warts are already in evidence. There are two arched fibulae of very early type, the bow being rectangular in section and with no bulb strengthening such as appears later. There are no spectacle fibulae. There are bronze rings and string-spirals. And finally, one grave contained a sword of Naue II type not, as the other swords of the Vergina cemetery, of iron, but of bronze. This sword may be late in the series of the known bronze examples, but one would hesitate to put it lower than the tenth century at the latest, and it might even belong to the eleventh. Furthermore, no iron objects of any sort were found in this tomb.

It is very likely, then, that this group, as well as indicating the introduction of influences from the North at an earlier date than the resumption of communications with the South, also helps in establishing what bronze objects were introduced first. The simple arched fibula preceded the later arched type and the spectacle type, even as it succeeded the violin-bow type in the pre-invasion context at Vardino.[2] The bronze sword will probably have come from the North, though whether the iron weapons found in later contexts must have a similar origin is not necessarily the case. The curious bronze string-spirals are already in evidence, and other spiraliform bronze ornaments may be equally early, as similar ornaments are found in earlier northern contexts;[3] but for many of the bronzes, including the bracelets with incised decoration, the *tutuli*, and the long pins, and also the amber beads, one cannot yet claim an equally early time of origin, though they also will have come from the North.

The fact of a northern origin also involves the question of the route taken. On this, my impression is that one route followed the course of the Haliakmon, and it may be added that bronzes of northern type have been found in cist tombs south-east of Kozani;[4] on the other hand, it is quite possible that the passage of the Axios may have been taken as well, but it does seem to be possible, on the basis of the pottery, to distinguish between Central Macedonia and the western district. From the evidence of Vergina tomb C, this distinction may be made at an early date, perhaps as early as the eleventh century, and this would in its turn mean that the probably overland move of Macedonians to Marmariani and no doubt to other inland sites of North Thessaly, should precede the movement down the Haliakmon (or be caused by it?), as those pottery features peculiar to the Vergina tombs are not to be found at Marmariani.

Subsequently, objects of northern type also find their way to Thessaly and further south, and, also subsequently, the appearance of Thessalo-Cycladic Protogeometric in Macedonia, at Vergina just as much as in the central plain generally, is an indication of

---

[1] Cf. *BCH*, lxxxv. 792 and 794. I am most grateful to the excavator, Mr. Petsas, for permitting me to mention unpublished objects.

[2] See p. 142, n. 2.

[3] Dakaris, *AE*, 1956, pp. 114 ff.

[4] Μακεδονικά, ii. 638 f.; *BCH*, lxxxv. 777; *Ergon* for 1960, pp. 96 ff.

the restoration of communication between these two areas, most likely by sea, perhaps as early as the end of the tenth century, and certainly continuing into the ninth. After this the situation is obscure, and I do not feel justified in putting forward any further hypotheses; it may be felt that what has already been suggested is altogether too sanguine. In any case, the proposals made above still leave certain problems unsolved: it is not clear yet whether the Protogeometric influence came from the Cyclades or from Thessaly; and, more important, the appearance of at least one wheel-made vase of Mycenaean type in conjunction with local vases which are invariably hand-made does require explanation, for if the knowledge of the use of the wheel had been retained in Vergina, one would expect that it would have been applied to other vases as well.

CHAPTER VI

THE CENTRAL AND EAST AEGEAN

1. *The Cyclades*

THE relative poverty of our knowledge of the Cyclades during the last stages of Mycenaean civilization is evident from a recent article by Miss Scholes, entitled *The Cyclades in the Later Bronze Age*, which brings together all the material known until 1953.[1] For the LH. III A and B periods, Miss Scholes lists material from twelve islands, only five of which reappear in her account of the succeeding LH. III C period—Amorgos, Delos, Melos, Naxos and Paros.

It might seem from this that settlements in the Cyclades were much restricted after LH. III B, but that is not necessarily the case. On six of the islands where up till then LH. III C had not been identified—Andros, Tenos, Kimolos, Kythnos, Seriphos and Siphnos—the LH. III finds were the result of accidental or surface discovery. On the only excavated site which produced prehistoric pottery, that of the Kastro on Siphnos, there was 'no trace of any habitation between the Middle Cycladic and Geometric periods'.[2] There is no reason to suppose, especially in the case of the large and fertile islands of Andros and Tenos, that systematic survey and excavation would not reveal the presence of LH. III C, and perhaps later material as well. This may be illustrated by the seventh island, Kea, which has produced the site of Ayia Irini, for which we have a preliminary report by Welter,[3] and is now in process of further excavation by Caskey, the most important discovery so far being a sanctuary of the LH. III C period, with possible continuity into later times.[4] Details of this find are given in the section on sanctuaries (p. 44).

Of the five islands listed by Miss Scholes as producing LH. III C pottery, only Amorgos has never been systematically excavated. Sherds from this island, now in the British Museum, are from deep bowls and a krater;[5] the deep bowl sherds are not illustrated, but their decorative motives include simple and antithetic spirals; the krater sherd, on the other hand, with its netted curved triangles, is certainly to be connected with the Argive Close Style—it is one of the few pieces of this style to have been found in the eastern half of the Aegean. Other casual finds comprise a side-spouted jug,[6] which could perhaps be LH. III C, and a trefoil-lipped oinochoe, with languettes pendent from the neck and warts on the shoulder, which is very late in the LH. III C series.[7]

[1] *BSA*, li. 9 ff.
[2] Brock and Mackworth-Young, *BSA*, xliv. 31.
[3] *AA*, lxix. 48 ff.
[4] Caskey, *Hesp*. xxxi. 278 ff.
[5] *B.M. Cat.* I, i, A 1028 and A 1029 (Fig. 289).
[6] Op. cit. A 1027.
[7] *CVA*, Belgique I, IIIA, 2 and Pl. 2, 9 (provenience apparently not certain).

The evidence from the excavated site at Paroikia on Paros is just sufficient to demonstrate continuity of occupation into LH. III C, in the shape of a deep bowl with antithetic spirals.[1] Whether the site continued to be occupied thereafter must remain an open question.

Melos is represented by the well fortified coastal site of Phylakopi, an important prehistoric settlement from which, most unfortunately, only a small fraction of the finds was recorded in any detail.[2] The site was inhabited from early times, and the latest period (III) included LH. III pottery as well as some earlier material. During this time the settlement was of considerable extent, and was dominated by a building of palatial character with a *megaron*.[3] It was reckoned that 'nine-tenths of the pottery' [excluding the coarse ware] 'from the highest stratum is imported Mycenaean',[4] and the bulk was great; the excavator noted that in trench J2 'in the first half-metre, out of a total of 3,500 fragments, 2,000 were imported Mycenaean, 1,300 were of coarse local ware . . . and 200 or so belonged to painted local pottery of the later style'.[5] The subsequent excavations produced similar results, and gave valuable additional information.[6] The excavators speak of the discovery of 'a mass of very late and much debased Mycenaean pottery, which formed everywhere the uppermost stratum'.[7] This find 'formed a stratum above a thick deposit of pottery of the usual Ialysos style',[8] the latter, from the illustrated sherds, being clearly LH. III A 2-B. Thus the material from the uppermost stratum is LH. III B or later—only a few sherds and vases are illustrated, and the sherds are classed by Furumark as early LH. III C;[9] so, very likely, are the few vases—a one-handled goblet, a monochrome kylix with rather funnel-shaped body and slightly swollen stem, a monochrome deep bowl, painted inside as well as out, and a curious little alabastron-pyxis,[10] in shape somewhat recalling the Cretan type of pyxis. On the other hand, the prevalence of kylikes may perhaps indicate that some of the material from this level is still contemporary with LH. III B. Sherds of stirrup jars were infrequent, but that is not unusual in a settlement.[11]

It is evident then that the settlement continued to be occupied in LH. III C, a conclusion which is confirmed by the illustrated material from the earlier excavations.[12] In fact, Furumark assigns a deep bowl with rudimentary antithetic spirals to the later phase of LH. III C.[13] There is no evidence that the settlement continued to exist after LH. III C, and it must have been abandoned at some time, not ascertainable, at or before the end of this period.

The excavations on Delos were naturally concerned mainly with the remains of historic times. Some evidence of prehistoric settlement was found, but much even of the small amount of Mycenaean pottery was never recorded; the existing material has recently been collected by Gallet de Santerre,[14] and from this it is established that the island was still

---

[1] Rubensohn, *AM*, xlii. 72, Fig. 80.
[2] Hogarth and others, *Excavations at Phylakopi*; *BSA*, xvii. 1 ff.
[3] *Phylakopi*, p. 56, Fig. 49 and Pl. 2.
[4] Op. cit. p. 160.
[5] Op. cit. p. 162.
[6] *BSA*, xvii. 1 ff.
[7] Op. cit. p. 18.
[8] Op. cit. p. 19.
[9] Op. cit. Pls. 12 and 14, Nos. 39–44; *Chronology*, p. 77.
[10] Cf. *BSA*, xlii. 43 f.
[11] *BSA*, xvii. 18 f.
[12] *Phylakopi*, p. 147, Figs. 124 and 125, and Pl. 32.
[13] *Chronology*, p. 77; cf. *BCH*, lxxx. 250, Fig. 13 (Perati).
[14] *Délos Primitive et Archaïque*.

inhabited in the LH. III C period. One of the bowl fragments from *Trésor* 5¹ and its vicinity appears to be LH. III C; certainly so are two sherds from the Artemision,² the one from a monochrome deep bowl, the other from a stirrup jar, which is said to have had a shoulder decoration of concentric semicircles and of dots arranged in a semicircle.³ There are also a few sherds with the wavy line motive, which Gallet de Santerre thinks could be sub-Mycenaean.⁴

Habitation in LH. III C can then be deduced from a handful of sherds, as on Paros; a few Protogeometric sherds were also found, but by themselves they are no guarantee of continuity after LH. III C. However, the evidence does not depend solely on the pottery; there were prehistoric buildings as well, and, basing himself on these, on the superimposition of the archaic Artemision over one of these, on the foundation deposit of Mycenaean character below the same archaic Artemision, and on the fact that the island could have had little importance except as a cult centre, Gallet de Santerre has argued that there was indeed a continuity of worship here from pre-Mycenaean times into the archaic and later periods. This possibility—or probability—I discuss elsewhere (pp. 44 ff.), but it may be noted here that such persistence of worship presupposes continuity of habitation.

So far, then, except for the matter of continuing worship on Delos, it has only been possible to establish that a few of the islands of the Cyclades were inhabited in LH. III C, and that Phylakopi on Melos was abandoned at or before the end of this period. Fortunately, the recent excavations on Naxos have greatly added to our knowledge.

These excavations have been centred round the modern town of Naxia, and have produced evidence of both settlement and tombs. As far back as 1930 Welter reported⁵ the discovery of a prehistoric site slightly to the north of Naxia, and soon after the war Condoleon excavated an important settlement here, at Grotta, which was occupied in all periods from Mycenaean times to Geometric.⁶ The encroachment of the sea made excavation extremely difficult, but important results were nevertheless obtained. The excavator was able to recognize three constructional levels,⁷ the earliest being Mycenaean, the second (an extension of the first) sub-Mycenaean, and the third, which included an edifice of *megaron* type, belonging to Protogeometric and Geometric times. He stressed that the walls of the third period completely ignored the earlier foundations;⁸ they are set on a different axis, and this suggests, though it by no means proves, that there was some interval between these final constructions and the preceding ones.

The site produced both LH. III A and LH. III B pottery, and LH. III C pottery was equally prominent.⁹ Miss Scholes assigns to this latter period part of a kylix¹⁰ with a narrow wavy line as the only decoration of the handle zone, numerous deep bowls or fragments of such, including one¹¹ with antithetic spiral patterns, one with paint all over except for a

---

¹ Op. cit. Pl. 14, No. 28.
² Op. cit. Pl. 28, No. 64.
³ Op. cit. pp. 213 f.
⁴ Op. cit. p. 214; cf. *Délos*, xv. 9, No. 8 (Pl. I, D, No. 8).
⁵ *AA*, xlv. 132 ff.
⁶ *Pr.* 1949, pp. 112 ff.; 1950, pp. 269 ff.; 1951, pp. 214 ff.
⁷ *Pr.* 1951, pp. 214 ff. and 215, Fig. 1.
⁸ Op. cit. p. 222.
⁹ *BSA*, li. 32 f. with references to *Praktika*.
¹⁰ Op. cit. p. 34.
¹¹ *Pr.* 1950, p. 278, Fig. 11.

wavy line between the handles, two stirrup jar sherds,[1] the one with 'lozenges or triangles with dotted borders', the other [2] with vertical wavy lines flanking vertical straight lines and a zigzag, two krater fragments, the one panelled, with angle-filling fringed arcs and a bird of Dodecanesian type, the other with antithetic tongue pattern,[3] and sherds from neck amphorae of presumably late date. These vases and sherds, with others, constitute excellent evidence of occupation throughout LH. III C, and may well cover that part of sub-Mycenaean which in West Attica is contemporary with the latest Argive LH. III C (see pp. 17 ff.). These finds belong to the first two building periods, and a seal was also identified as coming from the second period, though the argument for its attribution to sub-Mycenaean does not seem very cogent.[4]

The material of the third period of settlement remains as yet unrecorded, except for two little Protogeometric one-handled jugs,[5] whose position in the series is not altogether clear, though it is noteworthy that at least in one case the lower part of the body, and the foot, are left free of paint, thus continuing a fashion observable in the latter stage of LH. III C (cf. p. 11). Condoleon is confident that there was continuity from Mycenaean to Geometric, and this conclusion of the excavator must be accepted, although the preliminary reports are not sufficiently detailed to prove his assertion. The full account must be awaited, and further excavation may assist, as it has now been established[6] that the settlement extends inland and presents much the same picture as that part of it on the coast; and in any case the material from the tombs helps considerably in filling in the picture, and towards a solution of the problem of continuity.

Several tombs have been excavated, and the first two of these were chamber tombs, on a coastal ridge called Aplomata,[7] and had been partly destroyed by the action of the sea. Tomb A had been plundered, but not tomb B. Both had evidently been in use over a long period, but the final burials were made in LH. III C, and to this time the majority of the vases belonged. Two main points are to be observed with regard to the pottery. First, it is clear that certain shapes and decorative motives were closely connected with those typical of the Dodecanese and of Perati in East Attica; stirrup jars with octopus decoration (Pl. 6b) were reported to be very numerous,[8] and a hydria was found with excrescent cup and fictile snakes (Pl. 7d); a triple amphoriskos may provide a further link.[9] The second point bears on the date of the last burials, as shown by two of the vases published from tomb A.[10] One of these is a stirrup jar of rather globular shape, with a shoulder decoration of concentric semicircles and solid half-moon filling such as is found on some of the sub-Mycenaean vases from the Kerameikos; the other is a lekythos, monochrome except for the lower part of the body and the foot, both shape and decoration being characteristic of the latest phase of LH. III C. Thus it appears that burials continued until the end of LH. III C—but there is no trace of anything later. The finds other than pottery may for

---

[1] BSA, li. 34.
[2] Said to be early LH. III C, but it has an airhole.
[3] Cf. p. 149, n. 11.
[4] Pr. 1951, p. 217.
[5] Verdhelis, Pl. 15, Nos. 7 and 8.
[6] Ergon for 1960, p. 189; Ergon for 1961, pp. 196 ff.
[7] Condoleon, Ergon for 1958, pp. 165 ff.; Ergon for 1959, pp. 125 ff.
[8] Ergon for 1959, p. 128, cf. Fig. 139.
[9] Op. cit. Figs. 136 and 137.
[10] Ergon for 1958, p. 168, Fig. 176.

the most part have belonged to earlier burials, but a bronze sword of Naue II type is associated with the LH. III C material.[1]

Further tombs have been excavated by Zafeiropoulos at Kamini, close to Aplomata.[2] These comprise three chamber tombs, a child burial in a pit, and a cremation. A total of one hundred and fifty vases was found, and these are said to be mostly LH. III C with simple decoration, though the Octopus Style stirrup jars were again common, and two hydriae with excrescent cups, one of them with a frieze of 'dancers', are illustrated.[3] A further close link, at least with Perati, is to be seen in the two terracotta figurines with arms folded over the head.[4]

Only one kylix was found, and it would seem that the use of these tombs was confined to LH. III C, and consequently the objects other than pottery[5] belong to this time—an important fact, since the tombs were particularly rich in gold objects, and thus give the same impression of a prosperous community as is found at Ialysos and Perati. Furthermore, the discovery of an iron dagger in Kamini tomb A is of exceptional interest, as confirming the evidence of Perati that iron was introduced to the Aegean—in this case for a weapon— before the end of LH. III C. The mention of pins is also most notable, for these are only paralleled in an LH. III C context by the examples from the latest chamber tombs of Argos, thus forming a further argument for the contemporaneity of the latest LH. III C chamber tombs with the cist tombs of Salamis and the Kerameikos. Finally, there are the two burials not in chamber tombs; the child pit burial can be paralleled elsewhere in LH. III C, but the cremation, if on its own, and not associated with inhumations, is most important. Details are not yet, however, available.

There is no trace of any Protogeometric pottery in these tombs, and so there is still no sign of what happened after LH. III C. But some indication of this emerges from a final group of tombs, situated on the lower part of the Aplomata hill. Condoleon undertook excavations here, and found many tombs not only of the Protogeometric period but of succeeding times down to Archaic.[6] These tombs were either rock-cut pits or cremations, but unfortunately all had been disturbed by later constructions, to the extent that it was neither possible to ascertain whether the rock-cut pits were ever slab-lined and covered, nor to assign more than one vase to a tomb (and then only rarely). The excavator illustrated three of the Protogeometric vases:[7] one is a feeding bottle, with the handle at right angles to the spout (a non-Mycenaean feature), dark-ground except for two wiggly lines round the belly; the second is a cup with somewhat flaring foot, and full compass-drawn concentric circles on the body; and the third is a lekythos with a shoulder decoration of hand-drawn concentric semicircles with half-moon filling (Pl. 15c). It is this last vase which is the most revealing, as it is in the earlier tradition, and to be compared not only with the sub-Mycenaean lekythoi of the Kerameikos but also with the stirrup jar, mentioned above, from chamber tomb A of Aplomata. The interval of time between the last chamber tomb burials and the earliest succeeding ones at the foot of the hill can only have been very

---

[1] Catling, *Antiquity*, xxxv. 117.
[2] *Ergon* for 1960, pp. 189 ff.
[3] Op. cit. p. 191, Fig. 219.
[4] Op. cit. pp. 191, and 190, Figs. 216 and 217; cf. *Ergon* for 1961, p. 15, Fig. 11.
[5] Op. cit. p. 191.
[6] Op. cit. pp. 185 ff.; *Ergon* for 1961, pp. 199 f.
[7] *Ergon* for 1960, p. 187, Fig. 209.

brief indeed. Furthermore, in spite of the ceramic continuity, the system of multiple burial has now been discarded, and we appear to be faced with the same phenomenon as in West Attica, the Argolid, and perhaps Boeotia.

Taking the evidence from Naxos as a whole, it seems fair to say that there was very little, if any, interruption of habitation at the end of LH. III C; on the other hand, it seems equally clear, both from the different axis of the Protogeometric and later buildings at Grotta, and from the abandonment of the chamber tombs, that there was some dislocation. A new element of population is very probable, though there may well, from the evidence of some continuity in the ceramic tradition, have been a fusion with the existing inhabitants.

The material from Naxos is thus vital to the understanding of the course of events in the Cyclades during LH. III C, though one must naturally beware of generalization, as these islands cover a considerable area, and each island may have suffered a different fate. The link between Naxos and both the Dodecanese and East Attica must surely involve other islands as well, and the evidence of Miletus does suggest that the first movement of the Ionian migration passed through the Cyclades at the time of transition to Protogeometric, but no really clear picture of the situation at the end of LH. III C is yet available—for example, the Protogeometric pottery of Naxos, from the little that is known about it, seems to be related not so much to that of Attica, but rather to that of the area to the North, including Thessaly. Much remains to be learnt.

2. *The Dodecanese*

The area of the Dodecanese, and especially its main island of Rhodes, was one of the great centres of Mycenaean civilization during the Late Helladic III period.

So far as this period is concerned the bulk of our evidence is from Rhodes and, with the exception of the settlement at Trianda, which was no longer occupied after LH. III A 1, comes exclusively from tombs found on the island. The major site is that of Ialysos, where excavations have taken place intermittently over the course of nearly a hundred years on the two small hills east of the acropolis, Makri Vunara and Moschou Vunara, which comprise the cemetery area. The first excavations were undertaken by Biliotti on behalf of the British Museum, and the material was reported rather piecemeal—nor does there appear to be a record of all the finds from each separate tomb.[1] A further group of tombs was dug by the Italian Archaeological Mission in 1914, and the material from these and from a third group were recorded in the Italian School's Annual.[2] Altogether, somewhere near a hundred and fifty tombs were investigated, all of them chamber tombs, dug into the side of the hill, as was most convenient and as usually happened in other parts of the Mycenaean world. Many of the tombs were unproductive, as having been too thoroughly plundered, but some were used over a long continuous period, and at least seventeen were apparently constructed and used only in LH. III C—a number which may seem rather small, but not when compared with the number of tombs at Ialysos which can be assigned

---

[1] *CVA*, GB 7, IIIA, 1 ff. Pls. 1–8(= *B.M. Cat.* I, i. pp. 139 ff.); *FLMV*, pp. 1–18, Pls. A–E and I–XI.

[2] Maiuri, *Ann.* vi–vii. 83 ff.; Jacopi, *Ann.* xiii–xiv. 253 ff.

to any single phase of Mycenaean pottery. Some also were used for burial in LH. III C after interrupted or uninterrupted use in earlier times. In so far as tomb evidence allows of such conclusions, it is reasonably clear that no disturbance marked the transition from LH. III B to LH. III C, and that there was no lessening of prosperity in LH. III C.

Ialysos is the main coastal site; a second one is Kameiros, where only five chamber tombs have so far been discovered. All contained LH. III C vases, and three were used only in this period. This cemetery, just as those of Ialysos, is in no way connected with the burial areas of later times. Finally, there are very slight traces of a Mycenaean settlement at Lindos.[1]

Apart from these coastal sites, there are a few inland ones as well, covering the central and southern parts of the island. It has been reckoned that the burials would have been attached to perhaps seven settlements. The material has not come from systematic excavation, and by no means all of it has been recorded. So far as is known all the burials were in chamber tombs, and the vases tend to show a strong local conservatism; it is also clear that some of the material comes down into LH. III C. Finally, there are many vases of unknown provenience.[2]

Rhodes is thus a rich source of Mycenaean material, though the lack of any settlement is a serious drawback. On the other hand, a settlement has been excavated, but not yet recorded in detail, on the island of Kos,[3] in the modern town which overlies the ancient Meropis.[4] This site was dug by Morricone, and it seems that the three levels of occupation identified by him cover most, or the whole, of the Late Bronze Age.[5] No precise indication could be obtained of the date or circumstances of the end of the settlement; there must in any case be a gap before the use of the site as a cemetery, the earliest tombs of which are Late Protogeometric, but Morricone mentions a quantity of sherds, both Protogeometric and Geometric, in the upper level of the settlement, which he doubts to have come from tombs.[6] It can in any case be said that no signs of disaster were observed and that presumably LH. III B continued into LH. III C without a break. Morricone noted that the houses were all rectangular, and seemingly inhabited by people of no great prosperity. Excavation in this area has now been resumed by the Greek Archaeological Society, and evidence has appeared of an apsidal construction.[7]

As well as the settlement there were two cemetery sites, a few miles inland, at Langada and Eleones, and more than eighty chamber tombs have been dug.[8] The full account is awaited here also, but the groups illustrated show that there were burials in LH. III C as well as in LH. III B, and it is particularly noteworthy that there was a case in one of the tombs of cremation alongside inhumation,[9] similar to LH. III C instances at Ialysos and Perati (cf. pp. 115, 157). No doubt evidence of occupation will be found elsewhere on this island, but apart from traces of settlement near the Asclepieion[10] little else seems to be known.

---

[1] Jacopi, *CR*, vi–vii. 133 ff. (Kameiros); Maiuri, *Ann.* vi–vii. 252 f. (Lindos).

[2] Stubbings, *Levant*, map on p. 6; *Analysis*, Site Index; *Ann.* vi–vii. 248 ff.; *Ann.* xiii–xiv. 335 ff.; *CR*, vi–vii. 44; *CVA*, Denmark 1 and 2; *Rhodes Museum*, Akari collection (from Vatoi and Siana).

[3] *Boll. d'Arte*, 1950, pp. 320 ff.

[4] Bean and Cook, *BSA*, lii. 121.

[5] *JHS*, lxv. 102.

[6] *Boll. d'Arte*, 1950, p. 322.

[7] *Ergon* for 1959, pp. 133 f.

[8] *Boll. d'Arte*, 1950, pp. 323 f.

[9] Op. cit. p. 324.

[10] Op. cit. p. 327.

Remains of Mycenaean inhabitation were also found on Kalymnos. No systematic excavation has taken place, but the vases now in the British Museum are reported to have been found together, and to have come from a group of tombs near Pothia. The vases are either LH. III B or LH. III C (in one or two cases very late in the style), but there is no record of the type of tomb.[1]

Finally, there is evidence from the island of Karpathos, which lies in between Rhodes and Crete. First, there are seven vases in the British Museum,[2] and these, as Stubbings says 'are apparently of Myc. III B date'.[3] There seem to be both Cretan and Mycenaean elements, but no sign of LH. III C (or LM. III C). Second, there is a group of vases known at present from one reference only, where it is reported that at Pigadhia, the main harbour on the south-east corner of the island, either one or two tombs produced some ninety vases said to belong to the twelfth century (a statement to be treated with great caution) and to show close connexions between Karpathos and Crete.[4] This is clearly an important group, but failing even a partial record no use can be made of it, and the subsequent discussion will take no account of the material from this island, inasmuch as there is no certain evidence of LH. III C.

The chief point of interest that emerges from the two islands, Rhodes and Kos, where proper excavation has taken place, is surely that there are no signs of destruction either during the course of, or at the end of, LH. III B such as occurred in the Argolid and elsewhere on the Mainland. To my mind, one may indeed go further than this, and say that there are positive signs that there was no destruction: the continuity of the settlement on Kos, the continued use of tombs and the construction of new tombs in LH. III C, and the apparent maintenance of prosperity at least at Ialysos.

Various problems remain. There is no doubt that the Dodecanese evolved its own brand of LH. III C to take the place of LH. III B—what is the nature of this, what was its origin, and when did it appear in relation to LH. III C found elsewhere in Mycenaean Greece (and primarily the Argolid)? How did this pottery style develop, internally and in relation to other regional styles? And what was the occasion, and when, for the abandonment at least of the Rhodian cemeteries of Ialysos and Kameiros?

A fundamental and detailed discussion of most of these problems has already been provided by Furumark,[5] though it must be realized that certain factors prevent a complete understanding, principally the fact that comparisons have to be made on the basis of tombs only, and that in this case the volume of material for comparative purposes in the Argolid is rather small.

The first appearance of LH. III C in the Dodecanese, the development of a local style, and the relationship of this to other local styles, especially that of the Argolid, are matters which have been discussed in the general chapter on pottery (pp. 5 ff., 12 f.). It would seem possible that LH. III C developed later, but only slightly later, than it did in the Argolid. It is also clear that the type of LH. III C stirrup jar with octopus decoration,

---

[1] Paton, *JHS*, viii. 446 ff.; *CVA*, GB 7, III A, 9 f., Pl. 8, Nos. 22–28, and Pl. 9 (= *B.M. Cat.* I, i. pp. 189 ff.).

[2] Paton, *JHS*, viii. 446; *CVA*, GB 7, III A, 10 f.; Pl. 10, Nos. 8–14 (= *B.M. Cat.* I, i, A 971–7).

[3] *Levant*, p. 21.

[4] *BCH*, lxxiv. 312 f.

[5] *OA*, iii. 194 ff.

so great a favourite in this area (and so widely distributed outside), was copied from Cretan originals which may be dated to LM. III B.

There is no reason to doubt Furumark's contention that there is a clear distinction between the Dodecanese and the Argolid during the early development of LH. III C. There may be two solitary attempts to copy the Argive Close Style,[1] but generally speaking closeness in decoration is seen only in the octopus stirrup jars (Frontispiece), where a breakaway from Crete appears in the insertion of birds and fish between the tentacles of the octopus. Otherwise, the style is an open one and tends to make use of LH. III B motives. The new shape of the amphoriskos (Pl. 5) becomes popular from the beginning, and the three-handled variety of this seems peculiar to the Dodecanese (cf. p. 8), as also is a type of small belly-handled amphora. Other noteworthy LH. III C developments in this area are the stemmed goblet, the jug with strainer spout, the jug with excrescent cup from which fictile or painted snakes are drinking (Pl. 7c), and the kalathos with figurines on the rim (Pl. 7a); of these shapes, there are just one or two examples of the first two in the Argolid at the transition from LH. III B to C, but all except the first are also found in the tombs of Naxos and Perati—and indeed connexions are so close between the Dodecanese and these sites (not only in the pottery) that a strong community of interests is to be inferred (cf. pp. 115 f., 150 f.).

The subsequent development of Dodecanesian (in effect, Rhodian) LH. III C is not such as to require lengthy discussion, as the style proceeds, apart from the disappearance of LH. III B ideas, along the lines already set down; it diverges, according to Furumark,[2] ever more sharply from Argive LH. III C, though the links were maintained to the end with Naxos and East Attica.

During the latest stage of the style, however—visible in only a very few tombs—Furumark demonstrates a renewal of presumably direct ceramic contact between this area and the Argolid, the movement coming from the Argolid.[3] His arguments are drawn from shape as well as from decoration: for shape, the profile of certain stirrup jars and the introduction of the storage jar with collar neck, and for decoration the appearance of the wavy line as being characteristic of the later Granary Class, and pendent curves attached to handle bases, also a Granary Class element. As well as this, instances of the debased Close Style are noted in Rhodes, though it is not clear that there is any necessary connexion here with the Argolid.

So far as concerns the influence of the Granary Class, this may presumably be accepted —the instances given from Rhodes are from amphoriskoi from Ialysos tomb 87,[4] which also in other ways looks late (the cup and the monochrome bowl could both belong to the final stages of LH. III C). For the rest, except for Ialysos tomb 20 and Kameiros tomb 50,[5] the evidence is mainly from Kalymnos, from among the vases now harboured by the British Museum.[6] This is evidently not a single group, but some are as late as, or later than, anything in Rhodes (by Argive standards), notably the belly amphora, the neck amphora,

---

[1] *Ann.* xiii–xiv. 296, Fig. 40 (tomb 73); *CR*, vi–vii. 143, Fig. 167 (tomb 47).
[2] *OA*, iii. 206.
[3] Op. cit. pp. 218 ff. (in his LH. III C 1 c, i.e. after the destruction of the Granary at Mycenae).
[4] *Ann.* xiii–xiv. 330, Fig. 79.
[5] *Ann.* vi–vii. 133 ff.; *CR*, vi–vii. 150.
[6] *B.M. Cat.* I, i. pp. 189 ff. (Nos. A 1001–1024).

the storage jar with collar neck, possibly the cup, and certainly the bowl A 1021,[1] with its very pronounced foot, its general profile, and its handle area decoration of a wavy line between two bands—a clear example (and apparently locally produced) of the later post-destruction stage of the Granary Class.

At the same time, it must be stressed that this Dodecanesian LH. III C retains its individuality of character, as opposed to the Argolid. The distribution of shapes is different, and certain shapes persist which are more or less peculiar to the Dodecanese.

The tombs of Rhodes and Kalymnos were still then in use after the fall of Mycenae, but apparently not for much longer; the material which can be adduced for this late period is very scanty, and thereafter the cemeteries were abandoned. There seems to be no means of determining the time of desertion in relation to the Argive series, and it is more likely that some definition may be arrived at by comparison with the material from Naxos and Perati, when the full results are available; the account of the settlement on Kos should also be of great assistance. Furumark, it may be noted, mentions the possibility that 'a number of vases representing the last, entirely geometricized stage of the provincial style' are parallel in time to his LH. III C 2 (sub-Mycenaean), and he quotes examples, of which the only cases of a known provenience are from Apollakia, inland in the southern half of the island.[2] This is possible, but not I think probable, and need not in any case mean that these vases are chronologically later than Furumark's LH. III C 1 (LH. III C as opposed to sub-Mycenaean).

Leaving for the moment the problem of the end of this period and of its successor, we may turn to the other evidence available from the Dodecanese during LH. III C. So far, there has seemed no reason to suppose that this was not a time of reasonable peace and prosperity, with no trace of disasters such as occurred in the Argolid. On the whole, this state of affairs is confirmed by the small finds other than the pottery. Vases only were found at Kameiros, though this could be due to looting. At Ialysos—where there was also some plundering—the situation is different; there are numerous gold and silver rings, but only two of bronze. There are other gold ornaments as well, and large numbers of beads and buttons of various materials—particularly glass paste, but also terracotta, steatite, agate, amethyst, cornelian and sardonyx. Ivory and faience are present, but not at all common. Five cylinders were found (two of which are engraved) and two scarabs. Bronze is the material for three mirrors, three knives, an axehead and various indeterminate fragments; iron, fragments of a bracelet, was found in one tomb only.[3] There is no particular change as compared with the finds in LH. III B, and it sounds as though a reasonably high standard of living was maintained—as opposed to the Argolid, where the small finds of ascertainable LH. III C date are much fewer than in earlier times (a comparison which demands caution, in view of the usual record of plunder and of the generally smaller body of evidence, but which seems to be justifiable)—but in complete agreement with Naxos and Perati.

Weapons were only rarely deposited in Rhodian tombs at this time,[4] and the tomb on

---

[1] Op. cit. p. 196 and Pl. 15.
[2] OA, iii. 222.
[3] Ann. vi–vii. 127 (tomb 17, No. 74).
[4] Ann. vi–vii. 175 and 174, Fig. 101 (tomb 15); 181, Fig. 106 (tomb 32); FLMV, Pl. D.

Kos which produced a sword of Naue II type has not yet been published in detail, and so its date is unknown.[1]

Burial was in all known cases in chamber tombs, but a slight and not insignificant variation is to be observed in the manner of burial. In five tombs of the Ialysos cemetery, and in one tomb of the Langada cemetery on Kos, cremations were introduced among the inhumations.[2] The only parallel to this, in manner and context, is at Perati (cf. p. 115). It is a remarkable innovation, but there is no need to suppose that a new racial strain has been introduced, as in all other ways the material remains are wholly Mycenaean in nature.

As to contact with other areas, it is clear that there was communication over a very wide sphere, on the basis of the distribution of the Octopus Style stirrup jars, but that the South and West Peloponnese, and the islands adjoining it, seem to have been excluded from this sphere. Whether such communication was maintained throughout the period is not so clear; contact with Crete, for example, exists during the earlier stages, but then lapses, possibly due to disturbed conditions on that island (cf. pp. 191 ff.); and it is by no means certain that the earlier links with Cyprus were maintained after the destruction of Enkomi level V and other sites.

Apart from these contacts, which are no doubt no more than commercial, there is the evidence of the very strong ties across the Aegean with Naxos and with East Attica; as has been seen, this is demonstrated by the pottery (including vases of cult significance), by the quality and type of the small finds, and by the appearance of cremation. Whether these ties indicate any political cohesion is not susceptible of proof, but it does seem that the centre of Mycenaean culture may have moved from the Argolid to this general area.

A point of possible significance arises from the fact that no fibulae were found either at Ialysos or at Kameiros, and only one object of iron (a bracelet) at Ialysos. With regard to the fibulae, several of which were discovered at Perati, their absence from Rhodes may only mean that these objects were circulated primarily on the Mainland, being northern in origin. Iron, on the other hand, was introduced from the East Mediterranean, and here the picture in the Dodecanese must be contrasted with that of Naxos, which produced an iron dagger, and that of Perati, where two iron knives were found, as well as one or two other objects of this metal. It is quite possible to suppose that the almost total absence of iron in the Dodecanese is accidental; but if it is not, then it may indicate that the cemeteries of this district were deserted rather earlier than were those further west in the Aegean.

Very little, unfortunately, can be said on the problem of survival and continuity. It has already been seen that the chamber tomb cemeteries continued in use until some time during the final phase of LH. III C in the Argolid, on Naxos and at Perati, but that they may have been abandoned before the end of this phase—the great majority of their material, in any case, belongs to the earlier phases.

There is no clue as to the cause of the final desertion; there must have been some serious disaster, but no destruction is visible in the only settlement yet investigated, on

---

[1] Catling, *PPS*, 1956, p. 114.
[2] *Ann.* vi–vii. 240 (tombs 15, 17 and 32); *Ann.* xiii–xiv. 254, 285 (tomb 71); 329 (tomb 87); *Boll. d'Arte*, 1950, p. 324.

Kos. It can hardly be supposed that there was a complete depopulation, and yet there is no clear evidence of continuity into the Protogeometric period. On Rhodes, the next available material is Late Protogeometric;[1] this does not prove discontinuity, but it does suggest it, and the evidence from the tombs on Kos is precisely similar.[2] As to any conclusions from the material from the settlement on Kos, the full account must be awaited; it is a fact that the tombs of Late Protogeometric to Middle Geometric date were sunk within a preceding settlement, and there is therefore a clear case of interruption, but at what point the interruption occurs one cannot say. Perhaps the recently renewed excavations on this site will provide the answer.

3. *The Aegean Islands and the West Coast of Asia Minor*

In considering the western coastline of Asia Minor and the islands which adjoin it, I have preferred to deal separately with the islands of the Dodecanese and the settlement of Troy. They represent, roughly, the northern and southern extremities of this area, and from their evidence it is reasonable to conclude that some district in between the two formed the frontier of the Mycenaean empire, beyond which there may be occasional commercial or cultural contact, but no settlement on a large scale.

The intervening region may be subdivided into the island and Mainland districts. A brief review of the evidence, mainly according to this subdivision, has already been made by Stubbings.[3] With certain exceptions, there is little to add to his information.

The available material is, on the whole, unsatisfactory, a fact which emerges particularly clearly from the important island of Samos, the southernmost of the island group. Here, excavation has been concentrated on the site of the temple of Hera, and little has been undertaken elsewhere. The main interest of the Heraeum site naturally lies in its archaic and classical buildings, and there was no particular reason to suppose that a Mycenaean sanctuary or settlement underlay the archaic *temenos*. In fact, some Mycenaean was found, but the only specifically LH. III material recorded is the contents of a chamber tomb, which included stirrup jars and a pyxis.[4]

Apart from the Heraeum site, surface investigation has revealed LH. III A and LH. III B sherds at Tigani,[5] but that is all. It is fairly clear that, on such evidence, no arguments can be developed either for or against the island coming within the confines of the Mycenaean world. From its geographical position, however, at the end of one of the island bridges across the Aegean, and from its proximity to Miletus, where a Mycenaean settlement is a certainty, it does seem more than likely that Samos came within the Mycenaean *koine*. It is only necessary to consider the case of Naxos to realize how stubbornly hidden Mycenaean material can remain.

Some distance to the north-west lies Chios, and this, judging from the evidence of the adjacent Asiatic coast, could be outside the Mycenaean orbit. Recent excavations at Emborio, however, on the south coast of the island, have revealed an extremely interesting

---

[1] *PGP*, pp. 232 f.
[2] *Boll. d'Arte*, 1950, p. 322.
[3] *Levant*, pp. 21 ff.
[4] *Gnomon*, iii. 189.
[5] Technau, *AM*, liv. 7; Huxley, *Achaeans and Hittites*, p. 21.

situation.[1] There is hardly any Mycenaean pottery earlier than LH. III B—one or two sherds only. Nor indeed is there much LH. III B: a few sherds of stirrup jars, kylikes and deep bowls indicate some contact, and this is confirmed by the only tomb which produced pottery, as its four vases belong to this period.[2] This tomb, furthermore, is most unusual, being a cist, with pebble floor and slab-lined sides; roofing slabs were not found, but it is not unlikely that there were such. From this evidence it would not be possible to determine whether there had been a Mycenaean settlement here, as opposed to simple contact in the sense in which, for example, the evidence from Troy should be interpreted.

In contrast to this, there is no doubt that there was a Mycenaean settlement here in LH. III C. There is no great variety of pottery shapes but, apart from two or three that appear to be of local inspiration, all are typical of LH. III C, and mainly of a stage of this style well after its beginning. The deep bowls are mostly either entirely monochrome or monochrome with two or three narrow reserved bands below the belly, or light-ground with a wavy line between the handles; there is also one with paint all over except for the lower body and foot. On the other hand, there are no bowls that recall the later Granary Class as found in the Argolid after the final destruction of Mycenae. A type of light-ground bowl with one horizontal handle is popular, and paralleled in the Fountain deposit in Athens. Kylikes are not so common, and there are no examples of swollen or ribbed stems. Stirrup jars are very rare, but the discs have high knobs, and there is one sherd with an airhole. There is one amphora with handles to the rim, but quite a few with handles to the neck, and decoration which Furumark considers to be typical of the Granary Class; similar decoration is found on the hydriae. An almost complete kalathos has its best parallels in the Dodecanese, as also do the small undecorated handleless kalathoi, where however the original connexion may have been with Crete. Generally speaking, decoration is rare and motives of the simplest. This is particularly noticeable on the deep bowls, and would seem to indicate that that stage of LH. III C which still looked back to LH. III B was well past. On the other hand, there is little to indicate the latest phase of LH. III C as found on the Mainland, though that need not mean that some of the Emborio pottery may not be contemporary with it.

There is no means of determining when this settlement came to an end, which it did as a result of destruction—there is no trace of any Protogeometric, nor indeed of any further settlement before the eighth century. It is nevertheless of great interest that a group of people from the Mycenaean world should have decided to settle here after the beginning of LH. III C.

Travelling northwards again, one reaches the great island of Lesbos. The two main sites are those of Thermi and Antissa, both excavated by Miss Lamb, and both producing Mycenaean pottery or imitations thereof. In both cases, also, it is certain, from the great preponderance of Red and Grey wares, that the Mycenaean pottery was intrusive, however popular it may have been; the picture is in fact much as we have it at Troy.

---

[1] I acknowledge grateful indebtedness to the Managing Committee of the British School of Archaeology at Athens and to Mr. Hood for permission to mention unrecorded material.

[2] Cf. *JHS*, lxxv. suppl., 20. Traces of a second cist tomb were found.

Thermi [1] is the earlier of the two sites, and there is nothing to indicate that it survived the fourteenth century, either from the Mycenaean sherds and imitations, or from the connexions with Troy.

Antissa [2] is in part contemporary with the later phase (3) at Thermi, but is mainly subsequent to it, and continues to be occupied into historical times. The characteristic Red Ware of later Thermi is gradually replaced at Antissa by the equally characteristic Grey Ware, a certain variety of which is paralleled in Troy VIII.[3] Mycenaean sherds are reported but they were evidently not well stratified, nor of sufficient quality for the particular phase of style to be established (though Miss Lamb thinks it likely that the early rather than the late stage of LH. III is represented).[4] The only piece illustrated is a fine imitation of a kylix in Red Ware,[5] but it is noted that there was a fragmentary stirrup jar in the later Grey Ware.[6] The only other information [7] is of a small stirrup jar, decorated with bands only, from Antissa, and of some sherds from Mitylene. From this evidence it is obviously difficult, if not impossible, to determine the importance or extent of Mycenaean influence. Lesbos is not far south of Troy, and it is then likely enough that contact was maintained with the Mycenaean world into LH. III C; but this cannot yet be proved.

This concludes the review of the islands, there being no evidence from Lemnos or Imbros. The results to some extent match the range of excavation. The probable inferences are that in LH. III C Lesbos lay, as before, outside the Mycenaean sphere, but Chios and Samos within it. It may be added that the succeeding Protogeometric style is barely represented at all in the three islands discussed, though this could be accidental in the case of Samos.

The power of Mycenae was based on the Greek Mainland and extended over the South Aegean; consequently, a further extension to the Mainland of Asia Minor is not necessarily to be expected, the more so as Asia Minor was, until the twelfth century, in the main under the control of the Hittites, and this people would be reluctant to admit settlement or infiltration by any power not subject to them. Contact between Mycenaean centres and the west coast of Asia Minor would be reasonable and likely, but a settlement is only to be expected on a maritime site, easily provisioned from the sea and easily defensible against land attack.

Inland from the coast, casual contact (but apparently no more) is now established between Mycenaean lands and the site of Sardis.[8]

Along the coastline, surface exploration has not been very successful in uncovering traces of Mycenaean objects, although much of the southern area has been carefully investigated.[9] We are dependent either on organized excavation or on the stray vase, which very likely comes from a burial.

Chance accounts for the stirrup jar reported to have come from the southernmost site, Telmessus on the Lycian coast; [10] but neither this nor the piriform jar from Mylasa,[11] not far

---

[1] *Excavations at Thermi*.
[2] *BSA*, xxxi. 166 ff.
[3] This ware is evidently characteristic of western Anatolia: cf. Hanfmann, *AJA*, lii. 153.
[4] *BSA*, xxxi. 161.
[5] Op. cit. p. 170, Pl. 28, 2.
[6] Op. cit. p. 169.
[7] *FLMV*, pp. 33 and 83.
[8] *ILN* for April 1, 1961, p. 537, Fig. 6.
[9] Bean and Cook, *BSA*, xlvii. 171 ff.; *BSA*, l. 85 ff.; *BSA*, lii. 58 ff.
[10] *B.M. Cat.* I, i, A 1030.
[11] *AM*, xii. 230.

south-east of Miletus, is later than LH. III B. On the other hand, the stirrup jar from the northernmost site (excluding the Troad), Pitane [1] on the Elaitic Gulf south-west of Pergamon, is LH. III C of Dodecanesian origin. It is one of the class with octopus decoration, close in style to a vase from Kalymnos.[2] Dodecanesian contact with the northern coastline is then extremely likely.

As to excavation, most of the major sites of classical antiquity have been at least partially explored, and the profusion of post-Mycenaean remains has proved a serious drawback, though it is very possible that in most cases there was no Mycenaean site beneath the archaic or classical one.

Moving southwards from Pitane, a group of four excavated sites surrounds the Gulf of Smyrna, of which Phocaea, Old Smyrna and Clazomenae are coastal, and Larisa (on the river Hermos) slightly inland. At Phocaea, excavations are still in progress; Protogeometric has been reported, but no trace of Mycenaean, although Early Bronze Age pottery has been identified.[3] Earlier reports of Mycenaean sherds seem to have been incorrect.[4] The completed excavations at Old Smyrna revealed only a handful of Mycenaean sherds,[5] which indicates with fair certainty that there was neither Mycenaean settlement nor much contact along this stretch of coast (a picture very different from that of Protogeometric times), evidence confirmed by that of Larisa, where one sherd only can be identified as Mycenaean.[6] Clazomenae, finally, on the southern shore of the gulf, was excavated—under some difficulties—by Oikonomos. No Mycenaean pottery is mentioned in his preliminary report, but Kallipolitis, now charged with the recording of previously unrecorded material, has established that a number of Mycenaean sherds were associated with this site—an association which he interprets as one of commercial contact rather than as a settlement.[7]

The conclusion from these four sites is that the area was outside the Mycenaean world, but just occasionally in contact with it.

South of this area lies the region of the Cayster and Meander rivers, the most important town of which was Ephesus, whence in classical times proceeded two of the chief roads leading to the interior. No Mycenaean finds have yet been made here, but the site is so considerable that the absence of Mycenaean—or indeed of anything earlier than Geometric—may be quite accidental. Indeed, a few miles to the north of Ephesus, at Colophon, a tholos tomb was discovered, containing at least some Mycenaean pottery as yet unrecorded.[8] This could obviously be a site of some importance, but one cannot say more.

Miletus, the one certain Mycenaean settlement along the coastline—a stronghold, in fact, from the size of its fortification wall—occupies the promontory opposite the mouths of the Meander. Before discussing its material, however, it may be best to consider whether there is any case for Mycenaean control not only over the promontory on which Miletus stands, but also over the whole Halicarnassus peninsula which partly overlaps the island of Kos. The site of Mylasa may be used to link these two areas since, as well as

[1] *Perrot-Chipiez*, vi. pp. 929, and 931, Figs. 489 and 491.
[2] *B.M. Cat.* I, i, A 1015.
[3] *Archaeological Reports for 1959–1960*, p. 41.
[4] *CRAI*, 1921, p. 122.
[5] *JHS*, lxxii. 105, Fig. 10.
[6] *Larisa*, iii, Pl. 57, upper left.
[7] Sakellariou, *La Migration Grecque en Ionie*, p. 506.
[8] Goldman, *AJA*, xxvii. 67 f.; Holland, *Hesp.* xiii. 91 and 94.

the stray piriform jar, recent excavations by the Swedes have uncovered LH. III pottery on this spot—but of what phase is yet unknown.¹ Furthermore, there have been finds of Mycenaean and sub-Mycenaean sherds at Iasos, on the south side of the Milesian promontory.² However, until more information is available, no conclusions are justifiable, nor are they for the Halicarnassus peninsula, where the only site of interest is that of Assarlik, and there the earliest material from the cremation burials can hardly be placed much before the end of sub-Mycenaean (of the Athenian type).³ Assarlik, as will be seen, falls into line with the reoccupation material at Miletus after the destruction of the LH. III C settlement, but provides nothing contemporary with that settlement. Even so, this peninsula is so close to the Mycenaean island of Kos, the main known settlement of which faces directly towards Halicarnassus, that it is surprising that no LH. III pottery has yet been found.⁴

The exploration of Miletus has been pursued by misfortune, but the recent excavations have at last given us a reasonably clear picture of the early history of this site.⁵ It is now established that the original settlers came from Crete, but that at a later date the place came under Mycenaean influence. The main interest here centres on the very impressive fortification wall and its accompanying bastion. The latest analysis⁶ provides evidence that the settlement (II *b*), destroyed by fire, which immediately preceded the construction of the wall, and in part underlay it, was still occupied in LH. III B; consequently the wall must have been built not before the beginning of LH. III B. This is of importance with regard to the activities of the Hittites, and means that the wall almost certainly belongs to a later period than that of the Tavagalavas and Milavata letters (see p. 220), though its architecture would seem to have connexions with that of the Hittites.⁷

Its building then lies in LH. III B, and cannot yet be more closely dated; its destruction came at some time during LH. III C.⁸ This is evident from the material associated with it and with the contemporary houses (period III). There is no evidence of any violent interruption at the end of LH. III B; after the LH. III C destruction, however, there is a definite gap in occupation, according to the excavators.⁹ Can one determine at all closely at what stage of LH. III C the settlement was destroyed? It is clear enough from the published material that early LH. III C was well represented,¹⁰ including connexions with the Dodecanese, but the identification of later material, which usually has to be judged in relation to the Granary Class (cf. pp. 11 ff.), is exceedingly difficult. One cup¹¹ (dark-ground, with wavy line) can hardly be earlier than the Granary Class, but it could be later, and it is unfortunate that it is in a disturbed context 'dem obersten Abhub'.¹² Apart from this, the sherds and vase specifically associated with the layer of destruction do not seem necessarily to be late in the III C series.¹³

---

¹ Hanfmann, *AJA*, lii. 145.
² I am most grateful to Dr. Levi, Director of the Italian School of Archaeology in Athens, for allowing me to give this information (see now Addenda, p. 279).
³ Paton, *JHS*, viii. 64 ff.; cf. *PGP*, pp. 218 f.
⁴ For recent discoveries at Halicarnassus see Addenda, p. 279.
⁵ Weickert, *Ist. Mitt.* vii. 102 ff.; ix–x. 1 ff.
⁶ *Ist. Mitt.* ix–x. 5 and 36.
⁷ Op. cit. pp. 73 ff.
⁸ Op. cit. pp. 37 f.; cf. *Archaeological Reports for 1959–1960*, p. 48.
⁹ *Ist. Mitt.* vii. 132.
¹⁰ *Ist. Mitt.* ix–x, Pls. 16 and 17.
¹¹ *Ist. Mitt.* vii, Pl. 32, 4.
¹² Op. cit. p. 119.
¹³ *Ist. Mitt.* ix–x. 23 and Pl. 14, probably Nos. 1 and 2, Pl. 52, and Pl. 49, 2.

The great fortification wall and the settlement were then destroyed at some unspecified time in LH. III C. Traces of burning were found with this destruction,[1] but apparently not throughout, though evidently there was a clear interruption. The interval between this and the re-occupation cannot be gauged accurately, mainly I think in view of insufficient evidence as to the time of destruction. The earliest re-occupation pottery (not connected with any buildings) is sub-Mycenaean and Protogeometric,[2] with evidently a sizeable proportion of Protogeometric, much of which is still unrecorded.[3] The sherds and vases illustrated[4] are extremely illuminating, and in my opinion the period represented is contemporary with what at Athens would be transitional from sub-Mycenaean to Protogeometric, early Protogeometric and onwards. The ware is local, but there do appear to be connexions with Athens, and this is of course of some significance (cf. p. 254). And if, as is argued elsewhere, sub-Mycenaean in Athens was mostly contemporary with the later phase of LH. III C, the interval before re-occupation need not have been great. Nevertheless, the fact of an interruption must not be disregarded.

No finds apart from the pottery have been published, and it only remains to note that the chamber tombs excavated on the nearby Degirmentepe site produced pottery of the LH. III B and LH. III C styles.[5]

So the general conclusion as to the western coastline of Asia Minor must, I think, be that we cannot yet argue with confidence that the Mycenaeans controlled any other territory in Asia Minor except that of Miletus, and just possibly that of Colophon. Further excavation may well change this picture radically, but I doubt whether it will do so for any of the region from the gulf of Smyrna northwards. In contrast to this, the succeeding period, the Protogeometric, saw a considerable extension of settlement, reaching from Assarlik to Phocaea.[6]

4. *Troy*

The evidence and conclusions with regard to this site will be taken almost exclusively from the detailed account of the excavations undertaken by the Americans. This should not be considered as derogatory to the original excavations of Schliemann and Dörpfeld, but it is a fact that the problems of stratification within this city are so considerable that only the modern and more scientific methods of excavation could be expected to unravel them. The earlier excavators did indeed recognize several successive settlements, but their work was not sufficiently exact, and their record lacked completeness.[7]

The very fact that considerable excavation had already taken place in the nineteenth century was a grave disadvantage to the excavators of the 1930s—it is clear that there remained only a few areas where the stratification was undisturbed. Nevertheless the combination of expert knowledge and exemplary caution ensured that the conclusions reached were as near to being the whole truth as it was possible to get.

---

[1] Op. cit. pp. 23 and 37 f.
[2] Op. cit. pp. 37 f.
[3] Op. cit. p. 52, n. 1.
[4] Op. cit. Pls. 51–53 and 55.
[5] *Levant*, p. 23.
[6] *Archaeological Reports for 1959–1960*, p. 40.
[7] Schliemann, *Ilios*; Dörpfeld, *Troja und Ilion*.

Three stages in the history of Troy are relevant to the period with which this book is concerned. First of all, there is the settlement known as Troy VII *a*. It is this city which, according to the excavators, underwent siege and destruction as narrated in the Iliad: 'we believe that Troy VII *a* has yielded actual evidence showing that the town was subjected to siege, capture, and destruction by hostile forces at some time in the general period assigned by Greek tradition to the Trojan War, and that it may safely be identified as the Troy of Priam and of Homer.'[1]

In view of this, it is obviously essential to be able to demonstrate the connexions with the Mycenaean world and to establish a relative chronology. These connexions are, as usual, to be found in the pottery, for Mycenaean vases were exported to Troy, and were locally imitated.[2] The main account states[3] that while there was still a certain amount of LH. III A in this settlement, the bulk of the pottery could be attributed to LH. III B, no single sherd being able to be assigned with certainty to LH. III C. This statement leaves the terminal date of Troy VII *a* rather vague, but Blegen, the director of the excavations, has recently said that, while many of the Mycenaean sherds belonged to LH. III A, the majority could be dated to early LH. III B, thus suggesting a time of destruction in the first half of LH. III B, or within the first half of the thirteenth century.[4]

In view of the evidence of the subsequent settlement, Troy VII *b* 1, this suggestion appears rather tendentious. It is stated that VII *b* 1 represents 'an immediate re-occupation of the site'[5] by the survivors of the disaster, and that its duration, though relatively short, was of at least one generation. Not much Mycenaean pottery was found in this settlement, either imported or imitated; it is however implied that it was wholly of LH. III C type.[6] The only complete vase was a straight-sided pyxis, with a decoration characteristic of LH. III C.[7] The stems of several kylix fragments,[8] of local Grey Minyan ware, were ridged or swollen—a feature that in the Mycenaean series would belong to the later part of LH. III C. Some sherds of locally made bowls and cups[9] are considered to be similar to the Granary Class material, and in general the excavators were no doubt correct in claiming that Troy VII *b* 1 'is at least in part synchronous with the period when the Granary Class . . . was in use'.[10]

In the face of this evidence, that is to say the immediate re-occupation, the relatively short duration of the settlement (the wording suggests that it was not longer than two generations), and the presence of imitations of the Granary Class of LH. III C pottery, it seems impossible to suppose that the destruction of the previous settlement VII *a* can have occurred long before the end of LH. III B. And as the material indicates that VII *a* fell not later than LH. III B, it seems that we have a useful relative date for the Trojan War, a date which from other evidence (cf. pp. 220 f.) may be given in absolute terms as between 1250 and 1230.

Troy VII *a* was then Priam's city, and VII *b* 1 was built on its ruins by those who

---

[1] Blegen, Boulter, Caskey and Rawson, *Troy*, iv. p. 13.
[2] Op. cit. p. 23.
[3] Op. cit. pp. 8 f.
[4] *AJA*, lxiv. 159. Blegen suggests *c*. 1250, in *CAH*, vols. i and ii (rev. edn.) fasc. i (Troy), p. 14.
[5] *Troy*, iv, pp. 142 f.
[6] Op. cit. p. 145. Blegen now says (*CAH*, loc. cit.) that some LH. III B sherds were found in this settlement.
[7] Op. cit. Fig. 276.
[8] Op. cit. Fig. 268, 13 and 14.
[9] Op. cit. Fig. 277, 18 and 27; Fig. 278, 12 and 18.
[10] Op. cit. p. 146.

survived. Following on this comes Troy VII *b* 2, and the difference between it and VII *b* 1 is much greater than between VII *b* 1 and VII *a*, or even than between VII *a* and VI *h*. Houses were remodelled, and there was a fair amount of rebuilding. This settlement was also characterized by a new type of pottery, the Knobbed ware, attesting the apparently unresisted arrival of a new group of people who used this pottery and continued to make it on the spot, where in fact it became the dominant ware.[1]

The arrival of the newcomers did not mean the cessation of contacts with the Mycenaean world. The excavators speak of imported and local Mycenaean of exactly the same style as that current in VII *b* 1, and they conclude that 'the change from VII *b* 1 to 2 must be attributed to a time when the Granary Class was still flourishing'.[2] Sherds were found of a small jug with dotted decoration on the shoulder,[3] of a large jug which was compared with one found in stratum XI of the Lion Gate at Mycenae,[4] of a vase with lozenge decoration paralleled only in LH. III C,[5] and of a bowl with thick wavy line which may perhaps be equated with the later stage of the Granary Class.[6]

Troy VII *b* 2, whose duration is given as at least two to three generations, was then still in part contemporary with LH. III C, though there is no indication when contacts ceased. One may suppose that the links were rather with that part of the Mycenaean world which lay in the East Aegean, the northern outpost being probably the island of Chios—so not very far from Troy. In that case, the contacts presumably ceased at the time when disaster struck this area (perhaps a little before the end of LH. III C, cf. pp. 158 f.), though quite possibly the Mycenaean style continued to be imitated after the links had been broken, as may also have happened in Macedonia (p. 141).

We are no longer concerned with Troy after the end of VII *b* 2, for the site was abandoned and probably not re-occupied for some three centuries. Its history during the thirteenth and twelfth centuries is, however, certainly of great interest. In one sense purely marginal to the Mycenaean world, it was yet for a while the centre of that world, and was to become the keystone of later Greek tradition.

[1] Op. cit. pp. 143 f.
[2] Op. cit. p. 146.
[3] Op. cit. Fig. 279, 4*a* and *b*.
[4] Op. cit. Fig. 279, 13; cf. *BSA*, xxv. Pl. 6*b*.
[5] Op. cit. Fig. 279, 14 *a-c*.
[6] Op. cit. Fig. 279, 12.

CHAPTER VII

CRETE

This great island, with a civilization more ancient than that of the Mycenaean, presents circumstances and problems different from those to be found elsewhere in the Aegean area.

Only the latest stage of Minoan archaeology and history will be discussed; thus no account will be given of the time at which the palaces of Crete ceased to be inhabited as palaces, nor of the causes of this catastrophe. It is realized that controversy still surrounds the date of the Linear B tablets found at Knossos, but no attempt will be made to discuss this matter.

Mycenaean influence over Knossos, in the political sense, has been proposed for the period after the destruction of the palace. This is not borne out, either in Knossos or generally over Crete, by the archaeological evidence. In the Mycenaean world, as opposed to Crete, the culture of the fourteenth and thirteenth centuries is extraordinarily homogeneous, and probably indicative of a central political domination (see p. 219). But in Crete at this time (Late Minoan III A and B), the differences are far more striking than the similarities, in relation to the Mycenaean world.[1] The pottery remains quite distinctive; there is still some connexion with Mycenaean—as well as certain shapes and decorations inherited by both sides—though it is reckoned that, if anything, influence proceeds from Crete and not to it at the outset (a process to some extent reversed later). There is no serious break in the burial customs; the now very popular method of burial in the coffin or bath-shaped larnax is peculiarly Cretan, with virtually no parallel on the Mainland or elsewhere in the Aegean.

There is no general change in the style of architecture, which differs from that of the Mycenaeans. The little sanctuaries of Crete, with their goddesses and other objects, find no parallel in the Mycenaean world in LH. III B. Only in late LH. III C is there a comparable sanctuary, at Asine (p. 42). On the other hand, the religious terracotta figurines so popular in LH. III B and LH. III C are most rare in Crete, and belong almost exclusively to post-LM. III B contexts. There is a general similarity in the jewellery and ornaments, but nothing can be deduced from this. Altogether, Crete retained its own distinctive culture, civilization and customs.

The Minoans had however suffered a serious diminution of strength, and had lost their overseas power and contacts to Mycenae. It is therefore possible that the Cretans may at this time have acknowledged the overall supremacy of the ruler at Mycenae, though the cultural and religious differences enumerated above imply that his authority may not have

---

[1] *Contra* Dessenne (*Mallia, Maisons*, II, p. 133) who considers the ceramic connexions to have been close.

been very strong—or they may simply mean that Crete was on the whole far more resistant, on account of her previous civilization, to Mycenaean cultural influence.

Life in Crete goes on tranquilly enough, to judge from the position of the settlements, so at least there was no cause for fear. It must be remembered that the fourteenth century and at least the early part of the thirteenth were times of relative peace generally; the Achaeans had not yet shown the signs of aggression that they did from the mid-thirteenth century onwards. My impression is that life in Crete was one of peace, but of a lower standard of prosperity, perhaps under the protection of the Mycenaean power.

At some time subsequent to the mid-thirteenth century there is a partial abandonment of sites in Crete and, probably after an interval, sites of a rather different nature are occupied. This period and these movements have been equated with what is called the sub-Minoan or Intermediate period, and lead straight on to Protogeometric and later developments. These are the circumstances that need closer discussion.

A definition of terms is necessary at this point. These terms refer primarily to differing pottery styles, and an equation will be made with the corresponding terms for the Mainland. First comes Late Minoan III A (LM. III A), which is said to correspond to Late Helladic III A (LH. III A), and to end about 1300. After this comes Late Minoan III B (LM. III B); here there is a divergence. Certain archaeologists subdivide into B 1 and B 2; for others, the B 2 division is called Late Minoan III C. Pendlebury, finally makes no subdivision at all.[1] It seems fairly generally agreed that LM. III B, or LM. III B 1, corresponds to Late Helladic III B (LH. III B). The approximate absolute date for its end varies between 1230 and 1200. LM. III B 2 (= LM. III C) is rather more complicated; those who speak of LM. III C would, I think, make this period correspond roughly with Late Helladic III C (LH. III C), and date it between 1200 and 1100. Pendlebury would place his latest LM. III B well within the twelfth century—in other words, his sub-Minoan (or Intermediate) starts c. 1150. Furumark, finally, who has made the most detailed study of the pottery,[2] writes of LM. III B 2 as corresponding to his LH. III C 1, and further subdivides in the same manner as this latter style, with precisely similar dates, thus:

$$\text{LM. III B 2 } a = \text{LH. III C 1 } a = 1230 - 1200.$$
$$\text{LM. III B 2 } b = \text{LH. III C 1 } b = 1200 - 1130.$$
$$\text{LM. III B 2 } c = \text{LH. III C 1 } c = 1130 - 1075.$$

Sub-Minoan then emerges from the latest Minoan, and progresses into other styles, the date of its emergence varying between 1150 and 1075. The critical period is, I think, LM. III C, and I shall use this term rather than LM. III B 2.

To return then to the main discussion. LM. III A—the fourteenth century, one may say—needs no lengthy description. The chief interest lies in the effect of the disasters of the preceding century. According to Pendlebury, the effect was surprisingly light: 'This disaster, however, seems to have had little effect on the density of population, its result being rather to break up the large communities into smaller ones.'[3] Other general points are

---

[1] *The Archaeology of Crete.*
[2] *OA*, iii. 262.
[3] *AC*, p. 235.

that the 'old low-lying sites are still favoured' in the central and eastern parts of the island,[1] the evidence showing that life was still reasonably peaceful and that some attempt was made to open up the western part of the island.[2]

These are the main points made by Pendlebury, and they are of importance in virtue of his very extensive knowledge, although much of his evidence may be from surface finds only. Excavation since 1945 has tended, on the whole, to confirm his general picture, though not all his points of detail.

With LM. III B it will be best to deal only with sites from which material has been recorded, and to leave surface finds out of account. In view of the intensive excavation that has taken place, and of the size of the island, the amount of recorded LM. III B material is rather disappointing.

To the west of the island, there are chamber tombs at Kydonia, but no corresponding settlement has been identified.[3]

In the great southern plain of the Mesara, the picture with regard to Phaestos and Agia Triadha is not as full or clear as could be desired. These sites are said to have been re-occupied after the disasters of the palatial period; no precise division into LM. III A or B, or even C, has apparently been possible, but the evidence suggests continuous habitation. At Phaestos, no actual constructions succeeding the destruction of the palace are known until those, recently found, which cannot have been built until after the beginning of LM. III C, and which thereafter lead on to Protogeometric and Geometric times (pp. 182 ff.); consequently it is unlikely that the intervening settlement was one of much significance. The few published sherds which may be attributed to LM. III B, either from the settlement or from the Liliana cemetery, will be discussed below, p. 183. At Agia Triadha, on the other hand, a number of edifices are assigned to LM. III: a portico, a building of *megaron* type, a village and a shrine.[4] In default of any associated pottery, this must be accepted, and in fact many of the little terracottas from the *Piazzale dei Sacelli* may justifiably be assigned to LM. III, and some with more likelihood to the end of the period.[5] Three snake-tubes were found, and these also probably belong to either LM. III B or C (but see below on Mitropolis).[6]

On the acropolis at Gortyn, the settlement belongs to the sub-Minoan period (p. 183), but at nearby Mitropolis a Minoan villa was excavated, and within it a shrine, with a snake tube and statuettes which have been compared with those of Gazi and Karphi. It has been contended, from an associated stirrup jar, that this shrine and the religious objects are of LM. III B date, but all other objects can be assigned to LM. II, and it might be unsafe to state categorically that the shrine was built in LM. III.[7]

To the east of the Mesara, substantial buildings of a settlement at Kefala have been excavated. This settlement is assigned to the period LM. III A 1–B, its life is given as one hundred to one hundred and twenty years, and destruction by fire provided its end.

---

[1] Op. cit. p. 239.
[2] Op. cit. p. 239.
[3] Matz, *Forschungen auf Kreta*, pp. 72 ff., Pls. 48–63 (Jantzen).
[4] Pernier-Banti, *Guida degli scavi italiani in Creta*, p. 7.
[5] *Ann.* iii–v (N.S.), 1 ff.
[6] Op. cit. p. 34.
[7] *Ann.* xix–xx (N.S.), 392 f.; Alexiou, *KX*, 1958, pp. 198 f.

Reports are only in the preliminary stage, but none of the illustrated material is later than LM. III B.¹

Passing from the south to the north coast, the palace of Knossos was still in part occupied in LM. III B, and presumably may have continued later, though no later material is known. The important Shrine of the Double Axes belongs to LM. III B, and the Royal Villa and Little Palace also provide evidence of occupation at this time, evidence confirmed by that of some of the tombs.²

Recent excavation has made good progress at the port of Knossos, Katsamba, a settlement occupied well before LM. III B, with one room continuing, according to the excavator, into LM. III C. Preliminary reports only are so far available, as also at Arkhanes, where the settlement was destroyed in LM. III, and then not re-occupied till Geometric times.³

Extremely detailed and important information has now been published as to the history of Mallia subsequent to the destruction of its palace. It has been established that there was a re-occupation, but one confined to a very small area only of the original site. This very constricted settlement certainly persisted through LM. III A and B, and may have gone on into LM. III C (the violin-bow fibula and one or two sherds might suggest this), and there was then a destruction.⁴ A number of tombs in the neighbourhood also belong to this general period of LM. III, and thus confirm the settlement evidence.⁵ After this time, there seems to have been no further use made of the site till the Geometric period.⁶

There are four other sites in this area which are represented by cemeteries rather than settlement—Karteros (Amnisos), Tylissos, Gournais and Milatos.⁷ The evidence from Amnisos indicates continuous occupation more or less throughout Crete's history, but as to the other three, only one vase, from Milatos, is clearly later than LM. III B, though it is noteworthy that two of the stirrup jars from another tomb on this site have a semicircle motive characteristic of LH. III C (p. 7).

Moving across to the East, mention should be made of the cemetery at Olous, on the west side of the Gulf of Mirabello; most of the vases seem to be LM. III B in style, and find parallels at nearby Gournia.⁸ These are associated with the larnax burials; the material connected with the cremations will be discussed later (pp. 188 f.).

The re-occupation period of Gournia itself, and that of one site in the extreme East, Palaikastro, belong rather to LM. III A, and are not very extensive; even less so are the traces of LM. III B habitation of these sites, and they cannot be shown to continue into LM. III C.⁹

One sherd from the precipitous site of Vrokastro may belong to LM. III B, but the re-occupation here is perhaps rather to be ascribed to the LM. III C period (cf. pp. 185 ff.).

---

¹ See most recently *Ergon* for 1959, pp. 134 ff. and *Ergon* for 1960, pp. 202 ff.

² Evans, *BSA*, ix. 142; Hartley, *BSA*, xxxi. 89 f. and Pl. 19, 3; *AC*, pp. 239 f.; *Chronology*, p. 105.

³ *KX*, 1957, pp. 329 f.; *Ergon* for 1957, pp. 82 ff.; *Archaeological Reports 1957*, p. 17.

⁴ *Mallia, Maisons*, II, pp. 153 f.

⁵ Gallet de Santerre in *KX*, 1949, p. 319, n. 125.

⁶ Op. cit. p. 390.

⁷ Marinatos, *Pr.* 1929, pp. 95 ff.; *AC*, p. 305 (Amnisos). Hazzidakis, *Tylissos, Villas Minoennes*, pp. 92 f. (Tylissos). Hazzidakis, *AD*, iv. 62 ff. (Gournais.) *P.T.K.* pp. 93 ff.; Xanthoudides, *AD*, vi. suppl., 154 ff. (Milatos).

⁸ van Effenterre, *Nécropoles du Mirabello*, pp. 7 ff., 50 ff.

⁹ *Chronology*, pp. 105 ff. (See, however, p. 279.)

Four further cemetery sites may be mentioned: a larnax burial at Praesos could just belong to LM. III B; a tomb from Pachyammos has produced vases and other objects datable to early LM. III B; a group of tombs from Episkopi in the Ierapetra district falls entirely, from the published material, within this period; and very recently twelve chamber tombs have been investigated near Myrsini in the Seteia region, the contents of which are LM. III, and do in fact give a range from LM. III A down into LM. III C.[1]

Thus we have a score of sites—though there are of course many more, either unexcavated or unrecorded—and they may be said to confirm Pendlebury's general picture of continuance of occupation of low-lying sites. It is reasonably clear that there was some depopulation, and the situation may even have degenerated in LM. III B as opposed to LM. III A. What is not at all easy to assess is the amount of desertion of sites that may have taken place towards or at the end of LM. III B. New local stylistic elements do, as will be seen, seem to characterize the emergence of LM. III C, but they do not by any means imply a new distribution of sites. The settlement evidence and, to a much lesser extent, that of the tombs where the attached settlement is as yet unidentified, show occasional persistence into the beginning of LM III C, so far as can be seen. In other cases, there is a desertion, sometimes accompanied by destruction, but the whole process may be gradual—some sites abandoned at the end of LM. III B, some before or even long before. This probably gradual state of affairs does not, however, detract from the significance of sites being deserted; the causes are not clear, though it may be said that there is no evidence to suggest hostile pressure from outside the island.

The pottery of this period may be analysed on the basis of both settlement and tomb material, though in fact were it not for the recent account of the vases and sherds from Mallia, a discussion of settlement pottery could not have been justified, and I shall do little more than summarize Dessenne's remarks.[2]

On the basis of the Mallia evidence, the two most common shapes found in settlements are the stirrup jar and the stemmed cup, and it is stressed that a similar state of affairs exists at Knossos and Gournia.[3] Most of the decorated sherds illustrated from Mallia are said to belong to these two shapes, and the motives are of varying types, spirals, triangular and semicircular motives, chevrons and quirks, the tricurved arch, besides variations of the stylized flower, shell and palm decoration, argonauts and octopods. On the whole, the system for the cups seems a horizontal continuum, and attempts at panelling are comparatively rare; the shoulders of stirrup jars do not, on the other hand, have any one system, and one sherd, with a dotted tentacle motive, is almost in the Fringed Style.[4]

Other shapes are not so common; note is made of the alabastron, the tripod (both LM. III A), and the pyxis with vertical rim handle. Besides this, there are little jugs, kylikes, a kalathos with handles below the rim, a bowl with two ribbon handles, one with one horizontal handle, and one (and one only) with two horizontal handles (of a very different system of decoration from that found in Mycenaean contexts).

[1] *BSA*, viii. 245 (Praesos). *AD*, vi. suppl., 157 ff. (Episkopi). *KX*, 1959, 372 f. *BCH*, lxxxiv. 819 ff. (Myrsini).
[2] *Mallia, Maisons*, II, pp. 122 ff.
[3] Op. cit. p. 124, n. 1.
[4] Op. cit. Pl. 71, a.

Two vases, from their context, are assigned to the very end of the occupation, the one being a pilgrim flask and the other best described as a miniature amphoriskos; both were burnt, and the pilgrim flask was found with a violin-bow fibula.[1] (These and the possible Fringed Style sherd suggest that occupation may have gone on into LM. III C.)

The most popular shape in LH. III B settlements is the deep bowl with two horizontal handles. The evidence for this type of vase in Crete, irrespective of its decoration, has so far been rather scanty, though the material from Phaestos and Agia Triadha certainly includes examples, some of which are to be assigned to LM. III C, as they are in the Fringed Style, but others, with a decoration of spirals and whorl-shells, should belong to LM. III B, by analogy with the decorative motives found at Mallia and elsewhere.[2] Are these to be considered as more or less a solitary phenomenon, and thus perhaps even reflecting some ceramic influence from outside Crete? Recent examination of unrecorded sherds from the re-occupation period in the Little Palace and Royal Villa at Knossos suggests that bowls with horizontal or vertical handles may in fact be the characteristic settlement shape,[3] their decoration being similar to that of the sherds in House E at Mallia.[4] It would in any case seem that this shape is not in fact so rare in Crete, though its system of decoration, and also probably its profile, are quite different from those current in LH. III B.

So much for settlement pottery. In the tombs, the larnax type of burial is by now very common, and so there are a fair number of these receptacles, usually fully decorated, the style showing a certain conventionalization as opposed to LM. III A, and the most favoured motive being an octopus with very stylized loop tentacles. This motive is also occasionally found on stirrup jars—as in settlements—and one form of it provides the origin of that type of octopus-covered stirrup jar which is one of the characteristic elements both of LM. III C and Dodecanesian LH. III C. It is also to be found on pithoi. Little more need be added on stirrup jars, though their remarkable range of profile comes out much more clearly in the tomb material than in that of the settlements. Their decoration is rather unimaginative, and the few one-handled jars have similar decorative motives.

Pyxides are either handleless or have two horizontal handles, and still reflect the LM. III A style; there are not many of them, but tankards are fairly popular. Stemmed cups are common, and kylikes are still current. Amphoroid kraters are a feature of this period; hemispherical cups are rather rare, while shallow spouted bowls, with rim handle, are relatively common. There is a single example of a bowl with horizontal handles, similar to the one from Mallia. Kalathoi are occasionally found, either handleless or with a vertical handle on the rim associated with an excrescent cup.

There are other shapes as well—for example, the spouted feeding bottle and the rhyton, but those mentioned above seem to be the main ones. Continuity from LM. III A is evident, though the style has become more sober; the fabric is usually excellent.

Connexions with LH. III B are, as has been seen, possibly observable in the introduction of the deep bowl. And indeed, Furumark considers that such motives as the

---

[1] Op. cit. pp. 132 f. [2] Op. cit. Pls. 64 and 67.
[3] Cf. Hartley, BSA, xxxi, 89 f. I am much indebted for this observation to Mr. M. Popham, who has been making a study of the unpublished material.
[4] It may be noted that at Mallia the intact cups are either undecorated or monochrome.

symmetrical double whorl-shell, the stylized flower and a palm type, owe their origin to the Mainland.¹ Dessenne remarks that on the whole there is no great difference between the Cretan style and that of LH. III B,² and there may indeed have been some borrowing. Even so, LM. III B appears to remain an individual style, and in many ways unaffected by Late Helladic. Certain shapes popular in LH. III B (for example, the alabastron and the straight-sided pyxis) are relatively unknown in Crete, especially with their characteristic decoration; one or two Cretan shapes (particularly the larnax) are not found outside the island.

The independence of Minoan pottery is reflected in the relative chronology. It is usually assumed that LM. III A and LH. III A end at the same time; so far as I can see, there is no proof of this. On the other hand, there is the correspondence made by Furumark between LH. III C 1 and LM. III C;³ this is worked out in the most admirable detail, but to my mind the evidence strongly implies that LM. III B continued in Crete after the development of LH. III C on the Mainland and elsewhere. This is indicated for the Mainland by two stirrup jars from Milatos (p. 7), and for the Dodecanese by the analysis of the development of the Octopus Style stirrup jar (pp. 7 f.).

Before embarking on the intricacies of the period immediately succeeding LM. III B it will be best first to consider the evidence from Karphi,⁴ which is in a sense the type site of the following period, even though its foundation may not go right back to the beginning. An analysis of this material may, however, facilitate the discussion of the time intervening between the settlement's foundation and the end of LM. III B.

The site of Karphi, high and inaccessible, contains material from settlement, sanctuary and tombs, and the culture of its inhabitants is strongly rooted in past Cretan history. These roots are particularly recognizable in the objects of religious significance—the sanctuary itself, with its goddesses with raised arms and bell-shaped skirts, the ritual objects—the rhyta and the snake tubes—and the vases, some of which (the kalathoi and pyxides) probably have a religious connexion. All these are Minoan in character and can be paralleled in LM. III B, if not earlier as well. Furthermore, there were hardly any objects connected with the cult which can be shown to have had an origin outside Crete. The terracotta altar is an exception, as it is Cypriot in inspiration.⁵

The religious cult, then, is predominantly Minoan in character. The architecture of the city, however, provides some evidence for the introduction of elements from outside Crete. Even some of those buildings considered to be the earliest have a non-Minoan feature, in that the entrance to the rectangular rooms was on the short side instead of on the long one. More important, however, two of the main buildings, the group 138–140 and the 'Great House' are of the *megaron* type, and this is surely a Mycenaean feature, even though it is by no means in universal use on the Mainland and in the Aegean. At the same time, the excavators noted that 'many other houses conform to the rambling style of Gournia and other Minoan sites'; they suggest that the appearance of the *megaron* type of construction is to be attributed here to the arrival of a small ruling caste of Achaeans,

---

¹ *Analysis*, p. 178.
² *Mallia, Maisons*, II, p. 133.
³ *OA*, iii. 262.

⁴ Pendlebury and others, *BSA*, xxxviii. 57 ff. Seiradaki, *BSA*, lv. 1 ff.
⁵ Boardman, *The Cretan Collection in Oxford*, p. 133.

who occupied existing settlements and palaces on their coming, but who built according to their own traditional plan when such cities of refuge as Karphi were founded.[1] This view will be discussed further in relation to other sites.

The evidence from tomb architecture is more difficult to interpret. The excavators considered that the tholoi were the burial places of the nobles,[2] and the inference is that the remainder of the community used pithos burials. As to the tholoi themselves, it is pointed out that in general the Cretans preferred the rectangular keel-vaulted tombs, and that the circular vaulted tholos only appeared at the end of LM. III, becoming common in the Intermediate (sub-Minoan) period, and that even then the foundations were frequently rectangular or polygonal.[3] This theory should be modified in view of the true circular tholos at Kephala near Knossos,[4] whose construction can hardly be later than the fifteenth century, and certain other evidence; even so, the preference for a rectangular keel-vaulted tomb is a fact. The Karphi tholoi have the local peculiarity of being wholly or partially free-standing, and apart from that are circular with either circular or rectangular foundations.

The manner of burial is inhumation, but that is of little consequence, as in the Aegean area and on the Mainland this remains the normal custom until the change-over to cremation in Attica, at a time roughly contemporary with the development of the Protogeometric style.

The pottery to some extent confirms the evidence of the settlement architecture. There are numerous shapes which have a Minoan ancestry. Such are the vessels mentioned above, certainly or probably used in religious connexions; other shapes include the pithos, the tripod, the feeding bottle, the tankard and certain types of jars or jugs. An alien origin, on the other hand, seems probable for the kraters and kylikes, and for the rare amphoriskoi and kantharoi (Pl. 17a and b).

The manner of decoration shows a similar blend of Minoan and non-Minoan, and it is of interest that, as has rightly been observed by Mrs. Seiradaki, Minoan decorative motives were sometimes applied to non-Minoan shapes.[5] There is no doubt that the Fringed Close Style was a local Cretan development, arising out of the LM. III B style, though in certain ways different from it (p. 176). This style is found chiefly on pyxides (Pl. 11), tankards and kraters, though also occasionally seen on stirrup jars and kylikes. The so-called Open Style seems to derive from earlier Crete, but not so the occasional habit of covering most of the vase with paint, and the use of the wavy line; this dark-ground system, with its simplicity or lack of decoration, is found in the later stages of LH. III C. The elaborate triangles on stirrup jars may owe their origin to external influences. On the other hand, the 'blob' technique originated in Crete itself.[6]

It seems likely, then, that some of the elements of shape and decoration derive from LH. III C, and perhaps from its later stage. On the other hand the Octopus Style (an element of the Fringed Style) as applied to stirrup jars, common to Crete and the

[1] *BSA*, xxxviii. 137.
[2] Op. cit. p. 65 and n. 2.
[3] Op. cit. p. 138.
[4] Hutchinson, *BSA*, li. 74 ff.
[5] *BSA*, lv. 31.
[6] Op. cit. pp. 20 f. Cf. *BSA*, Supplementary Volume I, p. 111, Fig. 96, *b* and *c* (Palaikastro).

Dodecanese from shortly after the beginning of LH. III C, is still current. There are also traces of survivals from LM. III B. If, however, as seems likely, the intrusive ceramic elements cover the whole term of existence of the city, then the city itself may not have been founded until the latter part of LH. III C.

Before discussing this matter further, another body of material should be taken into account—the small finds, and in particular the ornaments of dress.

A very wide selection of objects other than pottery was found in the city and in the tombs, and the site was especially rich in bronze implements and tools. These, the excavators say, show little difference from those of earlier times in Crete.[1]

Weapons were not very common; there are three daggers, part of a sword, a leaf-shaped spearhead and three arrowheads—all of bronze and all from the city. Knives were more popular, eighteen altogether of bronze, ten of which are single-edged, five curved, and three with twisted handles. These also were all found in the city. In addition to this material, however, part of a knife blade in iron was found in one of the tombs, and the same tomb produced a piece of an arched iron fibula.

So we come to two new features—iron and the fibula. Iron was indeed very scarce at Karphi; only three other fragments of this metal were found, and it would seem extremely likely that its introduction took place well after the city's foundation. By the end of the city's history there may indeed have been much more iron in use, but it is likely that objects of iron would have been removed when the site was abandoned.

The fibulae may be considered together with other personal ornaments, such as formed the main categories of small objects found in the tombs, and here comparison is easier, as much of the earlier material comes from burials.

Apart from the single fragmentary iron fibula, there were thirteen of bronze, six of which came from tombs. All were of the violin-bow or simple arched type, and there seems no doubt that these originated from outside Crete.[2] As has been argued elsewhere (pp. 56 f.), the violin-bow type may be of northern origin, and probably did not appear in Greece until the end of LH. III B, while the arched type, which did develop in the Mycenaean world, cannot yet be traced back beyond the end of LH. III C. The fibulae also, therefore, have a chronological value.

Another feature is to be recognized in the fourteen straight bronze pins that were found, eight associated with burials; they are of a size not known earlier in Minoan times, nor have they any exact counterparts on the Mainland where, however, bronze pins generally cannot be dated earlier than the end of LH. III C, and are probably intrusive.

Of eight bronze finger rings five came from tombs, and all four of the bronze spiral ear-rings had a similar context. Rings are indeed known earlier in Crete, but not, so far as I know, this type of spiral ear-ring, to which the nearest examples are those of the sub-Mycenaean cist tombs of Attica.

Some negative evidence deserves cautious mention, that of the absolute or relative absence of objects common down to LM. III B. Necklaces are frequently to be found in Minoan, as indeed in Mycenaean, burials, and comprise beads of a variety of different

[1] *BSA*, xxxviii. 112 ff.
[2] There was also the swivel pin of a two-piece fibula, which may have come direct from Italy or Sicily. Milojcic, *JRGZM*, ii. 163, and Boardman, *Cretan Collection*, p. 36.

stones, or pendants of gold or glass paste. At Karphi, only eight beads were found, and of these only two (one of clay, one of bone) in the tombs; the remainder, from the city, are of steatite, with the exception of one of glass and one of faience.

Sealstones were popular in the preceding period, but only two were discovered at Karphi (one from the sanctuary), and these were thought likely to have been heirlooms. Gold and silver had they none—at least, none was found; but no argument can be based on this.

Such then is the evidence from Karphi. The mixture of two traditions, the one Minoan, the other intrusive, is evident. Some of the outside connexions are with the Aegean or the Mainland; others, rather less strong, are with Cyprus (p. 27). The pottery suggests that the city's foundation dates, in terms of the Mycenaean series, rather to the middle or latter part of LH. III C. The time of the abandonment is more difficult to establish. The excavators speak of the appearance of 'only one or two sherds of the true Proto-Geometric style',[1] so it may well be that the site remained inhabited after this style made its way to Crete, probably from Attica. The site is given a possible two hundred years of existence, from 1100 to 900—rather too long, perhaps. It was apparently not possible to subdivide houses into earlier and later periods, and it is unlikely that Karphiotes continued to inhabit this bleak site, four thousand feet up, longer than was necessary. A hundred years might be nearer the truth, and the date of the Protogeometric sherds is perhaps not entirely incompatible with this (see pp. 28, 241).

However, it is the foundation of the town rather than its desertion that is of greater immediate interest, and with it the problem of what happened in Crete between this time and the earlier abandonment of such sites as Gournia and Palaikastro. There are indeed some indications that the potters of Karphi were at the beginning within striking distance of the end of LM. III B. Two instances may be quoted: the main one is the fragment of a rhyton from K 123, for which Mrs. Seiradaki cites a reasonably close parallel from Palaikastro;[2] and the second is the stirrup jar from K 26,[3] the decoration of which is a later development of that found on a stirrup jar from Milatos, in a group which is predominantly LM. III B.[4] In fact, the distribution of vases with this decorative motive is interesting; other published examples are known from Mouliana, Vrokastro, Dreros (the latest), and Ialysos in Rhodes. Except at Dreros, they seem to mark the transition from LM. III B to LM. III C, and early LM. III C.[5]

As well as this, there are stirrup jars at Karphi with octopus decoration, a style which originates in LM. III B and is most popular at the beginning of LM. III C, but is somewhat decadent by the time the simple style (sub-Minoan or Intermediate) has been adopted. Though it is not altogether safe to suggest a chronological range, it is generally true that elaborate decoration is more susceptible to change than simple motives. I feel doubtful whether a life of more than two generations, or three at the most, could be given to the 'octopus' stirrup jars.

---

[1] *BSA*, xxxviii. 134. Cf. *BSA*, lv. 30.
[2] *BSA*, lv. 28 and n. 62, and Fig. 20 (p. 27).
[3] Op. cit. Pl. 6, *a* (right).
[4] *P.T.K.* p. 96, Fig. 105, F.
[5] *AE*, 1904, p. 28, Fig. 6 (Mouliana—note the high foot); *Vrokastro*, Pl. 27 (Khavga pithos burial); *Nécropoles*, Pl., 11*a* (Dreros); *FLMV*, Pl. 11, No. 69 (Ialysos).

Finally, it may be noted that although the simple pottery style appears to be co-extensive with the settlement of Karphi, the fibulae and pins, whose probable date may not be earlier than the end of LH. III C, need not belong to the earliest occupation of the city.

It is then by no means easy to suppose that the settlement of Karphi followed immediately on the LM. III B sites already mentioned, and yet the Minoan character of the finds is still so strong that a link may be assumed. The direct evidence for this is somethat meagre and elusive, and may best be demonstrated by comparison with Mycenaean pottery; the situation is most clearly and fully set out by Furumark in an article in *Opuscula Archaeologica* iii, and his analysis forms the basis of the following discussion.

The likelihood that LM. III B still continued in use after the introduction of LH. III C on the Mainland and in the Dodecanese is suggested, as has been mentioned, by the two stirrup jars, with a motive of dotted semicircles of early LH. III C type, found in a tomb from Milatos which is clearly assignable to LM. III B.[1] The alternating standing and pendent semicircles on a stirrup jar from Palaikastro, a site which apparently did not survive LM. III B, probably come into the same category.[2]

This link with LH. III C pottery could originate in the Dodecanese—connexion with Karpathos in LM. III B is quite clear [3]—and contact between the two areas continued into LM. III C, on the evidence of the series of stirrup jars with octopus decoration (cf. pp. 7 f., 157).

Even, however, if LM. III B overlaps the beginning of LH. III C there is still a gap to be filled before the time when Karphi was founded. Is there any pottery which fills this gap? Such pottery is known, and its manifestation is the earliest stage of the Cretan Fringed Style. This is a style quite different in spirit from LM. III B; the rather sober conventionalism of the preceding style is now replaced, on certain shapes, by an elaborate and colourful close style (though very different from the Argive Close Style); the motives may be derived from LM. III B, but they are displayed in an almost flamboyant manner. The shapes affected are kraters and bowls, pyxides (Pl. 11) and tankards, and the style is strongly recognizable in the development of the octopus decoration on stirrup jars (Pl. 6), where the creature gradually spreads over most or all of the vase, and its tentacles come to enclose a large variety of filling decorations.

It is this variety of stirrup jar which forms the most important feature of Furumark's analysis [4] of the material which he assigns to his LM. III B 2 *a* and beginning of LM. III B 2 *b* (= early LM. III C), both with regard to continuity from his LM. III B 1 (= LM. III B) and with regard to the similar stirrup jars in early Rhodian LH. III C. Of the sites which he lists, Milatos has already been mentioned, being predominantly LM. III B (cf. p. 169), the two stirrup jars from Knossos have no datable context, and the Fringed Style tankard from the Dictaean cave is rather to be linked with the Karphi material, both stylistically and geographically. Three further sites are mentioned or discussed, and these need rather more detailed treatment. Vasilike,[5] first, is a low-lying site,

---

[1] *AD*, vi. suppl., p. 156, Fig. 3. *Chronology*, p. 105.
[2] *BSA*, x. 225, Fig. 8*b*.
[3] *B.M. Cat.* I, i. pp. 177 ff.
[4] *OA*, iii. 222 ff.
[5] Seager, *Transactions of the Department of Archaeology, University of Pennsylvania*, ii. 129 ff., Pl. 30, *c*, *d*.

not far from the LM. III B settlements of Gournia and Episkopi. All the material comes from one tholos tomb, the vases, apart from the stirrup jar, consisting of the burial larnax, which has traces of 'conventionalized octopus design' and is thus in the LM. III B tradition, two kalathoi with concave sides and handles on the rim, one of which is certainly decorated in the Fringed Style, and a flask, unillustrated, presumably similar to one from Mouliana tomb A (see below). The evidence is not very plentiful, though similar kalathoi are not unknown in LM. III B.[1] The few small finds—bronze dagger, a gold pendant and three beads of carnelian—imply a period earlier than that of Karphi.

The site of Mouliana [2] is well to the east of Vasilike, on high but fertile ground, with easy access to the sea. It has an advantage over Vasilike; there are two tombs. Unfortunately, tomb A provides a chronological problem, as there were two periods in which burials were made, and two kinds of burial, inhumation and cremation, discussion of which may be deferred for the time being (p. 188). The stirrup jars with octopus design (Pl. 6a) came from tomb B, and apart from these there were two other stirrup jars with triangular decoration on the shoulder and a single octopus tentacle encircling the belly. There was only one other vase, the burial larnax, and this has the tentacle motive flanking a chequerboard pattern; the strong continuing influence of LM. III B is shown by comparison with a larnax from Episkopi.[3] The two decorated stirrup jars from tomb A (the third may once have been decorated, but nothing remains) are possibly even closer to LM. III B; there is a very near parallel in Evans's Milatos tomb, whose vases otherwise belong to the end of LM. III B.[4] These three stirrup jars were reported to have been associated with the inhumations, the other vases with the cremations. The relative chronology of the latter vases is not clear; there is a large flask, presumably of the same type as found at Vasilike, there is a fine pyxis in the Fringed Style, there is the splendid krater which I have previously—and perhaps incorrectly—assigned to the Geometric period,[5] and there is a deep bowl with horizontal handles and the lower part of its body and raised foot unpainted, perhaps a precursor of the later ubiquitous bell-kraters, and strongly reminiscent of a bowl from the Granary at Mycenae.[6] A puzzling group, indeed, and in view of the difficulties raised by the cremations—the krater is certainly, and the pyxis probably, connected with them—and by certain of the other objects, these vases cannot be related to the emergence of LM. III C.

The third site is that of Erganos, in the mountainous area south-west of the Lasithi plain.[7] As at Vasilike, there was just one productive tomb, but containing six burials; the finds consisted of a large pyxis, used as an ossuary, a very small handleless kalathos, and three stirrup jars, one of which from its shape looks very close to LM. III B, while the other two betray the influence of the Octopus Style.

Finally, a brief mention may be made of a rectangular tholos found near Praesos.[8] This contained two inhumations, one of which is in a bath larnax; but the larnax also contained a pyxis-shaped vase with the burnt bones of a youth; so this provides an instance

---

[1] *AD*, iv. 83, Fig. 28 (Gournais). *Mallia, Maisons*, II, Pl. 48, 2.
[2] Xanthoudides, *AE*, 1904, pp. 21 ff.
[3] *AD*, vi, suppl., p. 159, Fig. 7.
[4] *P.T.K.* p. 96, Fig. 105, F.
[5] *AE*, 1904, Pl. 3; cf. *PGP*, pp. 269 f. See p. 27.
[6] *AE*, 1904, p. 28, Fig. 6, extreme right; cf. *BSA*, xxv. Pl. XI, m.
[7] *AJA*, v. 262 ff. and Pl. VI.
[8] Platon, *Ergon* for 1960, pp. 212 f.

of the mixture of burial customs. Except for a small jug, the vases were stirrup jars, one of which had an extraordinary bronze 'belt' encompassing it. The other finds include an extremely fine gold ring, a spearhead and a bronze pin. The whole is dated by the excavator to the beginning of LM. III C.

This completes the evidence, and it will be clear how meagre it is, how exclusively confined to tomb material, and how closely related to LM. III B. The Fringed Style is indeed a new stylistic conception, but it does not entail any serious ceramic break, nor does the evidence necessarily mean any change in site occupation; nor can one prove that the sites discussed above were not occupied at an earlier date.

The close connexion between LM. III B and early LM. III C is confirmed by those sites, mentioned above, whose material indicates a continuation into the latter period. It may be that the final stage of Mallia's occupation did not end before the beginning of LM. III C; there is LM. III C occupation at Katsamba, though so far it is limited to one room only; recorded sherds from Knossos, Phaestos and Agia Triadha, though they have no clear stratified context, would allow for the possibility of continuity. So much for the settlements; for the cemeteries there is the Fringed Style stirrup jar (not of the octopus type) of Milatos, deposited in a tomb whose contents are otherwise LM. III B. There are finally the recently-discovered tombs at Myrsini,[1] where two of the tombs contained LM. III C vases. Tomb A had an octopus stirrup jar of relatively advanced type, and tomb B has two of these, one early, the other more advanced. The two advanced types should be considered LM. III C, though in neither case does the octopus cover the whole body of the vase, as happens in the later stage. Many of the other vases from these tombs are clearly LM. III B, but there are also stirrup jars and a monochrome deep bowl which could be contemporary with LH. III C—though of course this need not mean that they are later than LM. III B. Note should also be made of the Naue II sword in tomb A, a type more commonly found in LH. III C than earlier.[2]

From the limited material available, therefore, it is possible to say that on several Cretan sites there was continuity of occupation from LM. III B into early LM. III C, and in terms of the Mycenaean pottery, well into the early phase of LH. III C.

The question now arises whether at some point in early LM. III C there was a period of disturbance in the island such as resulted in the foundation of Karphi and is indicated not only by its foundation but also by the objects of non-Cretan origin.

Such disturbance should suppose some evidence of disaster, caused possibly by newcomers and resulting in depopulation, flight of the existing inhabitants, and new settlements, either (on the part of the natives) in places difficult of access, or elsewhere on the part of the intruders.

For disaster and desertion, the evidence discussed above is not more than suggestive—certainly not persuasive. Mallia was finally destroyed, but there must remain a doubt as to the time of its destruction; there may have been abandonment of sites, but the material is too incomplete to prove it—and there is some evidence for destruction and desertion

---

[1] Platon, *KX*, 1959, pp. 372 f. *BCH*, lxxxiv. 819 ff. I am much indebted to Dr. Platon for permission to mention these unpublished vases.

[2] *KX*, 1959, pp. 372 f. Catling, *Antiquity*, xxxv. 117 (his group I).

earlier on. It is suggestive that there does seem to have been a break of ceramic contact with the Dodecanese in the early stage of LM. III C, but it would be unsafe to base any conclusions on this. No convincing reason, then, has yet presented itself for believing in any serious disturbance in early LM. III C.

This is only half of the picture, however, and the other half belongs to those sites whose material belongs to the latter stage of LM. III C (whether called sub-Minoan or Intermediate) until such time as it gives way to Protogeometric or Geometric influences. One of these sites, Karphi, has already been examined; much of the rest of this section will be devoted to the others, the general picture which emerges providing evidence not only for the possibility of disturbance mentioned above but also for the whole nature of the period.

It will be best to concentrate first on Central Crete, both on account of the greater amount of recorded material and because of the two extremes of the island, the West is virtually unknown, and the East is, at the end of LM. III C, rather isolated both from the central area and from the outside world.

The principal site of the north central plain is, as before, Knossos. It is extremely unlikely that it was ever deserted, but the evidence from it for this period is less than one would expect, in view of the intensive excavation. This is particularly noticeable, unfortunately, in the settlement material, where the published record consists only of those sherds illustrated by Miss Hartley, from the Palace area and from the Little Palace.[1] None of the sherds need belong to a time later than the beginning of LM. III C, though the appearance of three sherds in the Fringed Style, one of which has an octopus motive, is welcome in showing that the style was known to this part of Crete.

The tombs are much more productive. Of the vases from them, the earliest succeeding LM. III B are two Octopus Style stirrup jars, the one from the Mavrospelio cemetery,[2] the other a secondary deposit in the Royal Tomb at Isopata.[3] The tholos tomb on the Kephala ridge (not far from Isopata) provides further evidence from a secondary deposit, two stirrup jars and two bowls which clearly belong to LM. III C.[4] Little can be made of the decorations on the stirrup jars, though one has fringed semicircles on the shoulder. Of the bowls, one has sets of loops pendent from the rim,[5] the other is in the Fringed Style; a third bowl from this tomb has a rather debased fringed motive. All three are painted inside, and one has a semi-conical foot. There is in fact a fourth bowl, not mentioned in the account, which is monochrome except for a reserved panel between the handles enclosing a thick wavy line. It is painted inside, and has a semi-conical foot. In shape and decoration, there is no doubt that there is a connexion with the Argive Granary Class of the time after the destruction of the Granary, but yet it appears to be locally made.[6] If these vases were deposited at the same time, they must be appreciably later than the stirrup jars of Mavrospelio and Isopata; the evidence of influence from outside Crete is clear.

[1] *BSA*, xxxi. Pls. 18 and 19.
[2] *BSA*, xxviii. 258, Fig. 12.
[3] *P.T.K.* p. 141, Fig. 122.
[4] Hutchinson, *BSA*, li. 78, and Pl. 10, *c* and *d*.

[5] For the type see perhaps *Hesp.* viii. 359, Fig. 35 (from Athens).
[6] e.g. *BSA*, xxv. 33, Fig. 9. I am most grateful to Mr. R. W. Hutchinson for permission to mention and describe this vase.

Apart from the above material, the tombs of Knossos exemplify particularly well the sub-Minoan (or Intermediate) stage. There are two groups from the Gypsades cemetery, one from the Agios Ioannis area, and tomb *II* of the Fortetsa cemetery.[1] As to the pottery, the most popular shape is still the stirrup jar, with a shoulder decoration usually of the elaborate triangle type, including a variant in which a triangle encloses an arc (Pl. 18*d*)— a motive undoubtedly indicating a link with similar vases from Cyprus at the transition from LC. III B to CG. IA (see pp. 26 ff.). Knobs on top of the discs are common, and so are airholes, the latter in particular indicating a late stage, contemporary with the concluding phase of LH. III C. The Minoan tradition is preserved in the one larnax, in a shallow spouted bowl and in the pyxides, and in the late persistence of Fringed Style motives, but the three belly-handled amphorae and the neck-handled amphora show signs of LH. III C influence in shape and decoration. Similar influence is to be observed in the trefoil oinochoe with wavy line on the shoulder, and in the cups and bowls of tomb *II*, especially with regard to the system of decoration on two of these, the upper vase being painted over but the lower part being left free (the typical decoration of the bell-kraters so popular in the succeeding period, but found first in sub-Minoan, and taking over a Granary Class idea, cf. Mouliana, p. 177). The kalathoi also indicate the Mycenaean, as opposed to the Minoan, tradition. For the finds other than pottery, the beads could belong to the previous Minoan tradition, and the two sealstones are apparently heirlooms. The long bronze dress pins (cf. p. 53) are not Minoan, however. Those from Gypsades tomb VII (Pl. 24*c*) find their best parallels in the pins of the latest chamber tombs at Argos (cf. p. 81), which are considered to be not of Mycenaean but of Northern character. The custom of wearing one pin on each shoulder, as visible in the Agios Ioannis tomb, only appears on the Greek Mainland at the time of transition from LH. III C to Protogeometric. The iron knife with bronze rivets also finds its closest parallels in Greece, in the LH. III C tombs of Perati (cf. p. 61), but in this case the originating area will have been the East Mediterranean, probably Cyprus. The appearance of iron is, of course, a further proof of lateness, and it may be noted that tomb *II* had fragments of a pin of this metal.

One further body of material belongs to this period, the votive objects from the shrine of the underground Spring Chamber.[2] The pottery was contemporary with that of the tombs, but included shapes not found in these, a bell-krater, a krater, an amphoriskos and an askos, all of Mycenaean rather than Minoan origin. However, in spite of the generally non-Minoan character of the vases, it seems clear, from the hut urn with the figure of a Minoan goddess inside, that the worshippers were of Minoan stock.

The whole of this material contains evidence of value for relative chronology. On the one hand, there are links with the latest phase of LH. III C on the Greek Mainland, and on the other, connexions with Cyprus at the time of transition from LC. III B to CG. I A (cf. pp. 25 ff.). These chronological indications are confirmed for the Aegean area by the fact that the subsequent burials show the influence of Attic Protogeometric pottery.

---

[1] *BSA*, liii–liv. 205 ff. (Gypsades). *Archaeological Reports for 1959–1960*, p. 25 (Agios Ioannis). Brock, *Fortetsa*, pp. 8 ff.

[2] *P. of M.* ii. 128 ff. *PGP*, pp. 236 f.

What is not quite so clear, unfortunately, is the link at Knossos itself between the material from these tombs and the shrine, and the earlier material.

In fact, a remarkable variety of influences is to be observed. The latest Mycenaean pottery has undoubtedly stamped its mark on the native style, and there is not much left of the preceding ceramic tradition. There are clear links with Cyprus in the pottery and in the introduction of iron—links which are confirmed in other parts of Crete at this time, and continuing into Protogeometric times, as shown by the bronze tripods from Vrokastro and Knossos,[1] and the iron pikes from the early Fortetsa tombs.[2] Influence from the Balkans or the Adriatic (coming through Greece?) may be visible in the pins—and further evidence of this influence will be found elsewhere (pp. 69 ff.). There is then good evidence for contact with, and influence from, areas outside Crete, but it is not at all easy to interpret it. Furthermore, it must be stressed that the inhabitants of Knossos who display these alien characteristics were most probably of Minoan descent. This is not simply a matter of preservation of the preceding Minoan ceramic tradition. The religious observances, as at Karphi, are Minoan—only one 'goddess' figurine of Mycenaean type is known from Knossos.[3] Also, the Minoan burial customs still persist, as may be inferred from the larnax of Gypsades Tomb VII, and also probably from the fact that this tomb is connected with others going back in time, though not with complete continuity, to the beginning of LM. III—unless this is an instance of the re-use of an earlier tomb.[4]

The interpretation of this evidence is thus clearly not an easy matter, and it is best to leave it until the material from the rest of Crete has been discussed. Furthermore, the evidence of the succeeding Protogeometric period must be borne in mind, and it may here be stated briefly that so far as the tombs of Knossos are concerned[5] (there is no excavated settlement), the salient features are the clear influence of Protogeometric pottery alongside the shapes and decorations that survived from the preceding period, the regular use of iron for weapons, the introduction of cremation as a popular method of burial, the disappearance of the larnax not only in tombs where cremation is found but also in the tombs where inhumation was still practised, and the continuance in use (or re-use?) of the Minoan chamber tomb.

The remainder of the north central plain does not add much to our knowledge. The harbour town of Knossos, Katsamba, has indeed revealed evidence of continued occupation, in one small sector, from LM. III B to LM. III C, but the vases so far illustrated serve only to indicate the continuance of the Minoan tradition, and there is as yet no evidence to show what happened after early LM. III C (cf. p. 169). Another harbour site, that of Amnisos, a few miles to the east of Katsamba, is said to have been inhabited continuously, but no material from this period has been adequately recorded.[6] Ayia Pelagia, another coastal site, not far north-west of Heraklion, produced a solitary stirrup jar which may be dated rather to the Protogeometric period than to the sub-Minoan.[7]

---

[1] *Vrokastro*, pp. 132, 133, Fig. 80 and Pl. 34, 1; *BSA*, vi. 83. Cf. Benson, *GRBS*, iii. 7 ff.

[2] *Fortetsa*, p. 202.

[3] *Tylissos, Villas Minoennes*, Pl. 29.

[4] *BSA*, liii–liv. 195 ff. Cf. *BSA*, lv. 143, n. 10.

[5] *BSA*, xxix. 224 ff.; *Fortetsa*; *BSA*, lv. 128 ff.

[6] *AC*, p. 305.

[7] *Cretan Collection*, p. 97 and Pl. 31.

Finally, there is Tylissos, inland and to the west of Knossos. A single burial from this site contained a solitary stirrup jar which Furumark assigned to his LM. III B 2 *c* phase—in other words, earlier than sub-Minoan. However, I hold to my former opinion in assigning this vase to the Protogeometric period. The other objects, and the fact of cremation, could perhaps belong to an earlier context, but they fit more comfortably within the Protogeometric period, and the stirrup jar has the ovoid shape so popular with the Protogeometric potter. I would regard this vase as an example of conservative survival.[1]

The main route from the north to the southern central plain of the Mesara did not follow the modern highway, but passed through Arkhanes, Kanli Kastelli, Pyrgos and Panasos.[2] Although it had to traverse mountainous country, there seems to have been no interruption of communication during this period or later. Two upland sites which lay not far off its course may be mentioned briefly, those of Prinias and Kourtes. Prinias is better known from the Geometric period onwards, but a shrine had already been set up here in LM. III C times, as one of the characteristic Karphiot goddesses was found, as well as fragments of others, and snake tubes. No such objects have yet been found in a Protogeometric context, and an earlier date is confirmed by a few Minoan sherds, two of which are in the Fringed Style.[3] At Kourtes, the tholos tombs contained no vases certainly earlier than Protogeometric, but the persistence of sub-Minoan characteristics might perhaps suggest that there was an original settlement contemporary with that of Karphi.[4]

The principal earlier site of the Mesara plain is Phaestos, and it provides us with the best material for this period as well. It has already been observed (p. 168) that the situation after the destruction of the palace is obscure. No buildings belonging to LM. III A or B have been identified, but from the evidence of sherds it can be said that at least part of the site continued to be occupied until the beginning of LM. III C. In recent years the Italian excavators have uncovered buildings of a later date than the palace, over it and abutting on to it.[5] There was in fact a new settlement, which Levi calls Proto-Hellenic, the earliest pottery of which he considers to be LM. III B 2 (Furumark's classification) and sub-Mycenaean, the settlement being subsequently enlarged and occupied into the Protogeometric and Geometric periods. Not a great amount of pottery has yet been illustrated, but what has been is valuable and instructive.[6] Most of the sherds come from bowls or kraters (though there are one or two kylix stems), and these are in Mrs. Seiradaki's Open Style.[7] The chief decorative motive is the spiral, and that may imply the continuation of the Minoan tradition as found in LM. III B. Two sherds belong to the Fringed Style, but as well as this there are five where the sole decoration is one or more wavy lines, a motive not previously found on Minoan bowls, but familiar to the later stage of LH. III C. It appears to be possible to conclude that the building of

---

[1] Marinatos, *AM*, lvi. 112 ff. Cf. *OA*, iii. 227 and 229; *PGP*, p. 255 (note the inexcusable error—there is, of course, only *one* stirrup jar); *Fortetsa*, p. 153 (on the concave disc being a late feature) and Pl. 134.

[2] *AC*, pp. 11 f.

[3] *AM*, xxvi. 247 ff. and Pl. XII. *Boll. d'Arte*, 1908, p. 15 and Fig. 11. *Ann.* i. 71, Fig. 40. Cf. *KX*, 1958, pp. 81 ff.

[4] Halbherr and others, *AJA*, v. 292 f., 306 ff., Pl. 8.

[5] Levi, *Ann.* xix–xx (N.S.). 255 ff. (esp. Fig. 86*a* and *b*).

[6] Op. cit. pp. 286 f. (Fig. 125) and 292 f. (Fig. 135).

[7] Cf. *BSA*, lv. 30 f.

this settlement is contemporary with that of Karphi, and that some of the pottery shows the influence of the later phase of LH. III C.

Phaestos is then an example of a settlement built in the plain after the beginning of LM. III C. A second one has been found at nearby Gortyn, and from the few sherds illustrated it may be deduced that it must have been built at very much the same time, because precisely the same trends are observable—the spirals, the Fringed Style, and the wavy line. As well as these sherds, fibulae of violin-bow and arched types came from this site, but they need not have been contemporary with the original foundation.[1]

For the evidence from tombs we must return to Phaestos, as all the material of this district is from here. First of all, there is the group of eight tombs from Liliana which, as Furumark implied, deserved a fuller and better account than they received.[2] Most of the tombs were roughly circular, with a dromos, but there was one without a dromos (C), and one (E) which consisted of three larnakes in a simple trench. There was apparently nothing of interest in tombs F, G and H, but of the other five all had larnakes, B and E had a feeding bottle each, and A and D contained a number of vases and other objects.

The pottery is assigned by Furumark mainly to the sub-Minoan period, with a few pieces attributed either to LM. III B (notably two stirrup jars from A, because of their flat shape) or to the period in between LM. III B and sub-Minoan. The Minoan tradition is continued in the spouted jugs and in one or two other shapes, but an outside origin may be suggested for a four-handled jar, a deep cup, and a deep bowl, these last two being monochrome. The four-handled jar, both in its shape and in its decoration (cross-hatched triangles on the shoulder, wavy lines on the belly) is reminiscent of a belly-handled amphora from Gypsades Tomb VII.[3] The most popular shape is once again the stirrup jar, and the shoulder decoration is a combination of triangles and arcs—here the lines tend to be curved, less straight than at Gypsades, and the bodies are generally squatter, though the feet are equally high.[4]

This group of tombs provides valuable supplementary information to that of the two settlements discussed above, presuming some of the burials to have been contemporary with the earliest stage of these settlements. The dark-ground system of decoration on some of the vases is of particular interest, as none of the illustrated settlement sherds shows this system—though that does not mean that none was found.

Another tomb, found recently on the slopes of the hill of Phaestos, contained thirteen vases of the sub-Minoan period.[5] Several of these were in the dark-ground system, notably a remarkable four-handled vase with elaborate decoration on shoulder and belly, three monochrome deep bowls, and a small askos, monochrome except for the foot. These vases are not in the Minoan tradition, nor are the two kalathoi with wavy-line decoration. Four stirrup jars and two amphorae make up the total of vases, but the small objects are also of interest, as they include, besides a hair-ring and a steatite button, two arched fibulae. The presence of these fibulae, themselves foreign to the Minoan tradition, shows that the date of the tomb cannot be earlier than the final stage of LH. III C on the Greek

---

[1] Levi, *Ann.* xvii–xviii (N.S.). 215 ff.
[2] *MA*, xiv. 627 ff. Borda, *Arte cretese-micenea*, Pls. 33 and 34. Cf. *OA*, iii. 230.
[3] *BSA*, liii–liv. Pl. 56c and e.
[4] Cf. Borda, op. cit. Pl. 34.
[5] *Boll. d'Arte*, 1955, p. 159 and Fig. 28.

Mainland. On the other hand, the tomb may be slightly later in date than the foundation of the settlements discussed above.

This concludes the evidence from Phaestos for the latter part of LM. III C, though, as with Knossos, a brief note may be made of the salient features of the succeeding Protogeometric period, now known through the burials recently uncovered at Moulino and Petrokephali.[1] Here, as at Knossos, the same ceramic fusion of Protogeometric and persisting sub-Minoan is discernible, and the same indication of the regular use of iron for weapons. Furthermore, cremation (the bones were evidently partially burnt only, not completely calcified, as for example at Athens) takes the place of inhumation in these burials, and the chamber tomb has been discontinued.

Apart from Phaestos and Gortyn, little is known of the Mesara during this period, but two further sites (as Kourtes and Prinias, marginal) may be mentioned. The one is Atsipadhais, which lies in an upland valley west of the Mesara plain. Pendlebury reports the discovery of Mycenaean 'goddess' figurines on this site, but their present whereabouts is unknown, and they do not seem to have come from the curious child cemetery excavated here, the contents of which could belong to this period.[2] The other site is Panagia, situated in the hilly area between the eastern end of the Mesara and the Pedhiadha plain. A number of rectangular vaulted tombs were found and investigated, and the pottery is on the whole very similar to that of the sub-Minoan tombs of Phaestos. A date subsequent to these is, however, suggested by indications of Protogeometric influence in one or two of the shapes and decorations, and by the iron weapons.[3]

In East Crete we are faced with a rather different situation from that of Central Crete, in that there is hardly any trace in this part of the island of the influence of Protogeometric pottery.[4] Consequently, sub-Minoan pottery probably survived much longer than it did in the central region, and this affects the relative chronology. The division between the two areas would appear to be the mountainous region which encircles the plain of Lasithi. In fact, the passage from the north central plain to eastern Crete is not an arduous one, crossing the upland plain in which Neapolis lies, and continuing down to the bay of Mirabello. Even so, this passage may not have been much used during the Protogeometric period.

Possible evidence for this relative isolation may already be provided by the material from Dreros, not far from Neapolis. This site is well known from Archaic times, but a cemetery belonging to an earlier period was found at the foot of the acropolis. With one exception the burials were cremations in pithoi or in rectangular trenches, and the few vases were of Geometric type, to which period also belonged the small finds. It is the exception that is of greater interest, for this was a rectangular tomb, lying at a lower level than the rest, containing three inhumations and a dozen vases which are thoroughly sub-Minoan in character. It may be accidental that this tomb lay in the same small area as the others, but a connexion is more likely, and in that case it will not have been so

[1] *Ann.* xix–xx (N.S.). 355 ff.
[2] *AE*, 1915, pp. 48 ff. Cf. *AC*, p. 255 and n. 3.
[3] *AJA*, v. 283 ff. *Ann.* x–xii. 389 ff. *PGP*, pp. 253 f.
[4] *PGP*, pp. 270 f. I should like to make it clear that my definition of Protogeometric covers only Brock's Early and Middle Protogeometric (*Fortetsa*, pp. 142 f.). This is simply a matter of terminology and I would not wish it to be inferred that I disagree in any way with his admirable classification.

very much earlier, and should represent a survival of sub-Minoan into Protogeometric times.¹

Another site, that of Olous, lies in an isolated position on the coast to the east of Dreros, close to Spinalonga, but it raises problems that are better discussed at a later point (pp. 188 f.).

Of much greater interest, anyway, is the naturally fortified settlement of Vrokastro, overlooking the bay of Mirabello. This is a site of equal importance to, if not greater than, that of Karphi, though not of equal value, as the account of the finds is neither so full nor so systematic.²

Vrokastro was first occupied in Middle Minoan times, but there is a definite gap between this and the next occupation which continued into the Geometric period. This second occupation is the immediately relevant and interesting one. It was almost impossible to distinguish any stratification, but it is clear that the site was re-occupied in LM. III, as the excavator says: 'From its output of sherds a series might be arranged which would show the gradual transition from the Late Minoan III, or, more properly, the late Mycenaean style to the geometric style.'³ In her conclusions the excavator distinguished three periods, the first of which, her late Mycenaean, was represented by 'the pottery from below floor levels in the town '.⁴ But from her detailed account of what evidence was available from stratification it looks as though there was no clear chronological dividing line between this and the subsequent pottery.⁵ Continuous occupation seems more than probable.

The illustrated sherds such as may be assigned to LM. III C or before are few in number.⁶ The earliest is very likely the kylix fragment shown in *Vrokastro*, Fig. 49, I; it shows part of what could be an octopod, and also a netted semicircle pattern hanging from the rim. This piece could be contemporary with LM. III B,⁷ though it is noticeable that the stem already has a slight bulge, a feature far more characteristic of later times. Other pieces shown in the main report could all postdate LM. III B, and are so interpreted by Furumark.⁸ A similar interpretation can reasonably be placed on the sherds illustrated by Levi, though it is remarkable that two of these sherds again show the pendent netted semicircles, a motive not known to me elsewhere in Crete, and reminiscent of LH. III B/C pieces from the Mainland of Greece and elsewhere.⁹ Apart from these sherds, a few indicate influence from outside Crete, that is from the LH. III C style; Furumark would assign them to his LH. III C 1 b phase.¹⁰ The remainder belong to the native Fringed Style.

Without the full details, however, it is very difficult to assess this material; for example, a violin-bow fibula was found in Room 27, associated with what are termed (there is no

---

¹ *Nécropoles*, pp. 17 f.; *PGP*, pp. 260 ff. The excavator thinks (op. cit. p. 17) that this may have been a small tholos with rectangular plan, but neither door nor dromos was found.
² Hall, *Vrokastro*.
³ Op. cit. p. 93.
⁴ Op. cit. p. 179.
⁵ Op. cit. pp. 89 ff.

⁶ Op. cit. Figs. 49, 50 and perhaps 51, *k*. A further small selection is published by Levi in *Ann*. x–xii. 553, Fig. 614.
⁷ Cf. *Analysis*, p. 178.
⁸ *OA*, iii. 227, n. 5.
⁹ *Analysis*, Motive 42, 22, p. 343, Fig. 57.
¹⁰ *OA*, iii. 227.

detailed description nor illustration) Late Minoan III B sherds[1]—are these sherds in fact LM. III B, in accordance with today's terminology? The presence of the fibula suggests a later context.

No sanctuary was found at Vrokastro, and there remains the evidence of the burials. The tombs are not so useful as the settlement for the beginning of the re-occupation, as the vases they contain belong either to the sub-Minoan or to later periods.

One of the burials, the pithos interment from Chavga, may be earlier than the others, from its stirrup jar, but it should be noted that the excavator speaks of the 'usual air-hole' of this vase, and that is a characteristic of lateness.[2] The style of the jar can be traced back to Milatos, and a similar one to this has been found at Karphi (cf. p. 175).

Besides the Chavga burial, seven chamber tombs were investigated.[3] Three of them, numbered 5, 6 and 7, were found in the same spot; tombs 2 and 3 were found together; the other two were on their own. Each tomb contained several burials—an interesting point, as this was not the usual Minoan custom—and tomb 2 produced a total of twenty-four. A long period of use may then be inferred. Also, a mixture of inhumation and cremation can be observed, which I shall discuss below (pp. 188 f.). The chief value of these tombs, however, emerges from the evidence they produced of the existence of sub-Minoan pottery in this part of Crete, and of its persistence into the Geometric period with little or no trace of Protogeometric influence.

Tombs 4 to 7 were probably the earliest, and the vases included stirrup jars (some with elaborate triangle decoration), kylikes, kalathoi of Mycenaean type, bird vases, and small bell-kraters with the lower body and foot unpainted. On the whole, good parallels can be found for the pottery in the sub-Minoan material from Knossos, and it is worth noting that tomb 5 contained an iron knife with bronze rivets, similar to the technique found on knives from Gypsades and Perati (cf. pp. 61, 116, 180). The other small finds indicate, however, that the period of use of these tombs may have continued into the Protogeometric period, as there were other objects of iron, including a spearhead. Two bronze fibulae of advanced type may also belong to this period, though earlier types occur as well.

Tomb 2, presumably the longest in use, had unfortunately been extensively looted, but it is at least clear that it was still in use in the Geometric period. Tomb 3 is difficult to assess, as most of the vases were not illustrated, though the imprint of sub-Minoan is less visible than in tombs 4 to 7, and one vase may, from its description, show Protogeometric influence, while others are Geometric in type.

Tomb 1 produced the largest amount of pottery, and it is possible that the evidence from here is nearly complete. The sub-Minoan tradition is still strongly represented, but at a later stage than that of tombs 4 to 7 (there is only one stirrup jar, no kylikes, and the curvilinear technique has almost entirely disappeared). Other vases are to be classed as Geometric; and finally, one vase, a neck amphora, is in the Protogeometric style, though it is of a type not found at Knossos. The bronze tripod is proof of a link at some point with Cyprus, and the popularity of iron confirms the date suggested by the pottery, namely contemporary with Protogeometric and slightly later.

[1] *Vrokastro*, p. 113 and Pl. XIX, A.
[2] Op. cit. p. 173 and Pl. XXVII, 1.
[3] Op. cit. pp. 123 ff. Cf. *PGP*, pp. 262 ff.

Such is the evidence from Vrokastro. It is unfortunate that the date of its re-occupation after Middle Minoan times is not capable of clear definition, as in its natural strength the site is comparable to Karphi, although it does not have the mountainous character of the latter. Its re-occupation could be contemporary with the foundation of Karphi, but one cannot state this with any assurance from the few illustrated sherds.

Kavousi lies to the east of Vrokastro, very much a mountain site, though it cannot be considered as remote, since it commands the road leading to the extreme eastern part of Crete. Little need be said of this site; the settlement on the acropolis did not produce material earlier than Geometric, but the tholos tombs contained vases of sub-Minoan type as well as Geometric, and once again there is no certain example of a vase of Protogeometric type.[1]

Apart from this, there are several sites of which summary reports only have been given, in Κρητικὰ Χρονικά and in the *BCH* Chronique des Fouilles.[2] The evidence is that of tombs, not of settlements, and these tombs, except for the two cave burial places near Piskokephalo, are square tholoi, of survival interest inasmuch as the associated pottery is said to be Protogeometric and Geometric. The identification of Protogeometric vases on these sites would seem to nullify the assumption made earlier, that such ceramic influence was hardly felt at all in Eastern Crete, but it is better to await the full publication before passing judgment on this matter.[3]

As so much of the material comes from tombs, a brief discussion on burial customs is desirable. The tendency in LM. III C, as in LM. III B, is to bury in earth-cut or stone-built chambers, round or (more often) rectangular in plan, with a dromos, and in the case of the stone-built tombs with a circular vault above. Furthermore, these types of tombs continued to be used in succeeding periods. Whether or not any Mycenaean influence is to be observed in the construction of the tombs, there is one fundamental difference, in that the Minoans did not practise multiple burial; very few interments were made in any one tomb.[4] Another fundamental difference lies in the use of the larnax—there are only one or two isolated instances on the Mycenaean Mainland. In Crete, larnakes continued to be popular throughout LM. III C, and provide excellent evidence of the continuance of the old Minoan tradition. There are also just a few pithos burials, but their significance is somewhat unclear.[5]

The manner of burial remains, as a rule, inhumation, but there are instances of cremation which are worth noting. The western region of Crete produces no cremations assignable to LM. III. In central Crete, tomb D from Liliana, in the south, contained a vase in which lay the partially cremated remains of a child;[6] in the north, it seems very possible that tomb Π from the Fortetsa cemetery enclosed a cremation, since no bones were found in the tomb.[7] In both cases the cremation must belong to LM. III C or sub-Minoan, at Fortetsa to the very end of sub-Minoan. These are the only cremations in this

---

[1] *AJA*, v. 125 ff.
[2] e.g. Berati-Piskokephalo: *KX*, 1952, p. 476; *BCH*, lxxvii. 239. Patela Sphakia: *KX*, 1955, p. 563; *BCH*, lxxx. 359. Seteia: *BCH*, lxxxii. 778.
[3] It may be assumed that Brock's classification is being used. See my remarks on p. 184, n. 4.

[4] Cf. Hood, *BSA*, liii–liv. 196.
[5] *AC*, p. 242 (LM. III, Gournia); 316 (Vrokastro); *AE*, 1915, pp. 48 ff. (Atsipades); *Nécropoles*, pp. 11 f. (Olous).
[6] *MA*, xiv. 641 f. Cf. *AM*, lvi. 118.
[7] *Fortetsa*, p. 8.

part of Crete, of LM. III date.¹ It is consequently a matter of considerable interest that, contemporary with the arrival of Protogeometric ceramic influence cremation replaced inhumation, so far exclusively at Phaestos, and with only a few exceptions at Knossos.²

The situation is very different in Eastern Crete, though one must always bear in mind the probable persistence of sub-Minoan pottery into the Protogeometric period. There is nothing that antedates LM. III C, but the cremation, associated with inhumation, in the recently discovered tholos tomb near Praesos, in the Seteia district, has been dated to early LM. III C, and may thus be the earliest example that we have (in late Minoan times).³

Returning westwards, there is the well-known instance of tomb A at Mouliana, where both cremation and inhumation were found. The cremation or cremations are later than the inhumations (which belong to early LM. III C), but it is not certain how much later they are. This is a group which needs more profound investigation, every object being taken into account, including the pin, the pieces of iron, and the bronze handles with bull protome. I am inclined to think that the krater which held the cremation is sub-Minoan in style, but Protogeometric in date.

At Vrokastro, cremation and inhumation seem to have been practised quite arbitrarily. In the earliest chamber tombs, some of the pottery from which must surely be placed within the sub-Minoan period, inhumations took place in 6 and 7, partial cremation in 4 and 5. Tombs 2 and 3, contemporary with Protogeometric and Geometric, contained only inhumations. But tomb 1, which may well be of the same date as tombs 2 and 3, showed unmistakable signs that the dead, with the exception of one child, were burnt either partially or completely.

Finally, there is the evidence of Olous, a remotely-situated coastal site, close to Spinalonga.⁴ The cemetery excavated here consisted of twenty-six larnax burials and twenty-five pithos burials. Fifteen of the pithos burials contained completely calcified bones, and three had child inhumations. Most of the larnakes contained inhumations, but in three there were cases of partial cremation. The problem is that of the date. One factor, stressed by the excavator, would suggest that the cremations may be contemporary with the Protogeometric period, and that is the shape of the pithoi themselves: with one exception, pithos O 38 from burial 27, they are of a non-Minoan type, usually with an ovoid body and two handles from shoulder to neck or on the shoulder; even the pithos from larnax burial 25 (O 49) is of this type. Apart from this, the smaller vases, particularly the spouted vases and the 'pelike', reflect LM. III B; there is no recorded instance among them of the Fringed Style, nor of any shape or decoration that might suggest the introduction of outside elements. Similar conclusions may be obtained from the few small finds; so far as I can see, there is nothing that is not Minoan, while, on the other hand, no iron was found, nor any fibulae or pins. As larnakes become extremely rare by the Protogeometric period, this is a point which might indicate that the cremations cannot be much, if at all, later than sub-Minoan. But there are also larnakes with inhumations;

---

¹ The cremation at Tylissos is to be assigned to the Protogeometric period, cf. p. 182.
² For the exceptions at Knossos, cf. *BSA*, lv. 143 f.
³ Platon, *Ergon* for 1960, pp. 212 f.
⁴ *Nécropoles*, pp. 7 ff.

the associated objects do not appear to be later than LM. III B. What is the situation elsewhere in Crete with regard to pithos burial—whether with cremation or inhumation? Pendlebury knows of hardly any of this period.[1] How can one reconcile the apparently late date of the non-Minoan pithoi with the entire lack of any pottery element which is elsewhere characteristic of LM. III C, and the appearance of pottery elements rather of LM. III B type—all associated with cremation? I cannot see a clear answer to this, nor consequently to other questions about the originating area of the system of cremation.

The main conclusion suggested by the above instances of cremation is surely that their appearance is not connected with the arrival of Protogeometric pottery. A possible case might have been made for such a connexion in Central Crete, but even here isolated cremations precede Protogeometric, while the situation in Eastern Crete proves that there can be no connexion. On the other hand, it seems equally clear that there is no link between the cremations of Crete and the few instances that occur in the Aegean or in Attica before the development of the Protogeometric style in Athens (cf. pp. 115, 157).

So much for the evidence from tombs and burial customs. The types of tomb, and the tendency towards individual burials, indicate a persistence of purely Minoan habits. Similarly, there is no sign of interruption in religious beliefs, on the basis of the evidence provided by the sanctuaries and the objects found in them. The shrines are usually fairly small and rectangular; the most distinctive objects associated with them are the goddesses with bell-bottomed skirts, and the curious tubular vases, often with 'snake' handle attachments. The goddesses have recently been the subject of an important article by Alexiou,[2] and I will do little more than summarize his chronological attributions. The Shrine of the Double Axes at Knossos[3] is certainly LM. III B, from its stirrup jar with early octopus decoration; the equally interesting sanctuary at Gazi, a few miles west of Heraklion, could also be LM. III B, on the basis of the associated kylix, though Marinatos, who published the material, would prefer to put it into LM. III C.[4] The Gournia shrine[5] should be LM. III B, as the settlement was abandoned before the end of this period, and it contained a plastic vase of a child-bearing woman to which there is a close parallel in a shrine at Kefala,[6] where the settlement was destroyed before the end of LM. III B.

Alexiou places the date of the shrine at Mitropolis as within LM. III B,[7] on the evidence of a stirrup jar, and compares the goddesses to those both of Gazi and of Karphi. He is also inclined to assign to LM. III B the isolated goddess statuette from Pankalochori,[8] in West Crete, not far south of Rethymnon; such analogies as are possible are with the Knossos goddesses.

On the other hand, there is no doubt of the date of the sanctuary at Karphi, a shrine presumably in continued use until the desertion of the site, which may postdate the introduction of Protogeometric. This shrine has both goddesses and snake-tubes. Snake-tubes are also found in a shrine at Katsamba,[9] which Alexiou dates to LM. III C; and he

---

[1] *AC*, p. 242 (LM. III, Gournia); p. 316 (Vrokastro).
[2] *KX*, 1958, pp. 179–299.
[3] *P. of M.* ii. 335 ff.
[4] *AE*, 1937, pp. 278 ff. Alexiou hesitates between the two periods (*KX*, 1958, pp. 191 f.).
[5] *Gournia*, pp. 47 f., Pl. 11.
[6] *Ergon* for 1957, pp. 88 ff. and Figs. 86 and 88.
[7] *Contra* Levi, *Ann.* xix–xx (N.S.), 392 f.
[8] *AD*, xv. suppl., 55 f., Fig. 12; *AA*, 1933, pp. 297 f., Figs. 6–8.
[9] *BCH*, lxxx. 351, Fig. 22.

considers that the snake-tubes and statuettes from Prinias (cf. p. 182) can best be paralleled at Karphi, and so would belong to the sub-Minoan period. Agia Triadha also has a sanctuary with a snake-tube, but I do not know its period—the remainder of the evidence would suggest LM. III C (cf. p. 168).

So the continuity and persistence of Minoan religious practices from LM. III B at least down to the end of the sub-Minoan period, with no great change, is undisputed. Furthermore, a cross-reference is most likely available with the late LH. III C shrine at Asine in the Argolid.[1] The shrine itself has analogies with Cretan ones, and the terracotta head is stylistically very close to one from Kalochorio in the Pedhiadha plain[2]—an isolated find, but the date of the site, according to preliminary investigation, is mainly Protogeometric and early Geometric.[3] No precise indications as to relative chronology can be suggested, but the fact of the link is obviously of great interest.

As to the objects other than pottery, I have already commented that at Karphi the usual Minoan—and Mycenaean—ornaments of dress, in the sense of necklaces of glass paste or precious or semi-precious stones, or of other material, whether clay or metal, were but rarely found, and that sealstones and gems were extremely scarce. Other sites of this period do not give quite such an extreme picture—Vrokastro had necklaces, tomb A at Liliana had glass paste ornaments, Gypsades Tomb VII had sealstones and beads (probably re-used as amulets)—but even so these ornaments were not popular.[4] As against this, there is the introduction of long straight pins and fibulae. The latter are found on most of the sites of the sub-Minoan period (the earliest violin-bow fibula, that from Mallia, being indeed close to LM. III B), but the distribution of the former is more restricted—chiefly at Karphi and Knossos (very late), but also at Vrokastro and Mouliana. Such a distribution may be accidental, for the arched fibulae which on the Mainland appear at about the same time as straight pins, at the end of LH. III C, are found in the south of Crete rather than in the north—in fact, no fibulae at all are known from Knossos at this time. On Mycenaean chronology, violin-bow fibulae may be found at any time during LH. III C, but arched fibulae and straight pins belong very much to the end of this period. This does not run counter to what is known of the contexts of these objects in Crete.

With regard to weapons and knives, it is unfortunate that the votive deposits in the Dictaean cave are not more closely datable than within LM. III, for they provide the main bulk of the material, and are of great interest in that some of the daggers and knives appear to have their origin in Italy.[5] The circumstances of these and other finds show, as Boardman points out, that they were in use by Minoans, and there is therefore no need to envisage their introduction by invasion.[6] Apart from this material, it is certainly of interest that no fewer than nine bronze Naue II type swords have been found in Crete (Pl. 22*a*1), all except two from the eastern part of the island, with the earliest datable specimen (from Myrsini) belonging to the time of transition from LM. III B–C, and classified by

---

[1] *Asine*, pp. 298 ff.
[2] *KX*, 1958, p. 216, n. 127; cf. Pl. 10, Fig. 3.
[3] Platon, *KX*, 1951, pp. 98 ff.
[4] *Vrokastro*, pp. 136 f., Pl. 35; 143; 147 f. (chamber tombs 1, 3 and 4); *MA*, xiv. 633 f., Fig. 103 (Liliana, tomb A); *BSA*, liii–liv. 208 and 209 (Gypsades tomb VII—some heirlooms, all perhaps of amuletic value?).
[5] Boardman, *Cretan Collection*, pp. 1 ff. and especially pp. 13 ff.
[6] Op. cit. p. 18.

Catling in his Group I.¹ These swords were as popular in Crete as they were in the rest of the Aegean and on the Mainland.

The general change from bronze to iron weapons probably took place at about the time when Protogeometric pottery began to have its influence over the central part of the island. There are no iron weapons which can be said to be certainly dated to LM. III C, although in Eastern Crete they are at times associated with sub-Minoan pottery. Furthermore, iron weapons which are probably contemporary with the Protogeometric period are relatively numerous. There are hardly any from Knossos, but they were found with the Moulino cremations at Phaestos, at Panagia, Vrokastro and Kavousi, as well as in the possibly later tombs of Modi in Western Crete.² It may be suggested that the period was still a troubled one, at least in Eastern and Western Crete. And there seems no reason to suppose that by now these weapons were not made in the island, although the metal, and the knowledge of its working, will originally have been introduced from the East Mediterranean—this may have been the area of origin of the two iron knives with bronze rivets, the knife from Vrokastro, as well as the one from Gypsades, still belonging to a sub-Minoan context.

A return may now be made to one of the central problems of this period, namely the circumstances which resulted in the foundation of so remote and inaccessible a site as Karphi. The cause must have been some disturbance within the island; but was this internal, or the result of intrusion from some area outside Crete? The evidence must be considered as a whole, and in doing so it will become apparent how serious the gaps in our knowledge are.

For one to be able to judge the course of events, a reasonably adequate settlement and cemetery pattern should be available, and this is notably lacking. For settlements, it can safely be said that after the destruction of the palaces there was some depopulation, in that only some part of the previously inhabited area continued to be occupied. Inferences have, however, to be made from a mere handful of sites, and in certain cases from pottery quite unassociated with any buildings. By the end of LM. III B, Gournia and Palaikastro had been abandoned and Kefala destroyed. At the beginning of LM. III C, it is reasonably clear that Knossos and Phaestos were still inhabited, though at Phaestos the evidence is from stray sherds only, and at Knossos there is no evidence as to what happened after early LM. III C—to prove desertion of the site one should have stratigraphic evidence allied to buildings, and this is not to be found. At Agia Triadha the position remains obscure; at Katsamba one room only has provided evidence for LM. III C, and that surely of a very early character. Amnisos is said to have been occupied throughout, but the material on which this statement is based is not recorded. The small area of Mallia that was reoccupied may have continued to be inhabited into early LM. III C. As against this, there is the fact that Karphi was founded after the beginning of LM. III C, and that the rebuilding at Phaestos, the new settlement at Gortyn, and the re-occupation of Vrokastro may all be contemporary with the foundation of Karphi. And that is all.

---

¹ Catling, *Antiquity*, xxxv. 117.
² Platon, *KX*, 1953, 485 f.

There is no reason why one should not use the evidence of cemeteries to illuminate the picture given by settlements, even where the settlement corresponding to the cemetery has not been identified. But one must have a sufficient number of tombs to be able to speak of a cemetery in the first place. In this sense cemeteries are extremely rare. There is the Zafer Papoura cemetery at Knossos,[1] which does not postdate LM. III B, and also the Gypsades cemetery, still in use in the sub-Minoan (late LM. III C) period, but not showing a completely uninterrupted series of burials, as early LM. III C does not seem to be represented. The six tombs at Gournais may just qualify as a cemetery, and the contents are not later than LM. III B. On the other hand, the twelve tombs of Myrsini, in the Seteia region, were still in use in early LM. III C, but not subsequently. Several tombs were found at Episkopi, in the Ierapetra region, and these seem to finish at the very end of LM. III B. On the other hand, one would like to be able to make inferences from the tombs of Milatos, where the pottery just oversteps the bounds of LM. III B, but there are only three tombs. In the same way, no deductions as to continuity can be made from the two tombs at Mouliana, the single tomb at Vasilike, or the single productive tomb at Erganos.

As a result of this situation, it is exceedingly difficult to recover a clear continuing series in the all-important pottery, whether through stratification or from tombs. Reference to the earlier part of this section will underline the uncertainties involved, especially in the early stage of LM. III C. Also, it is obvious that caution must be used in passing judgments based on metal objects. The reasonable, but unfortunately not precisely datable, number of such objects from the Dictaean Cave, as opposed to their extreme scarcity almost everywhere else in Crete, is a warning of how much must have been lost to us. Argument must therefore be based largely on insufficient evidence, and conclusions can be no more than provisional.

The case for some disturbance in Crete, simply as based on the existence of a settlement such as Karphi, is a reasonable one. But why should it not be localized, and be the result of no more than internal dissension? The geographical extent of the unrest is indeed not demonstrable. For one thing, we have no knowledge of what was happening in Western Crete. On the other hand, the occupation of Vrokastro, not far from the bay of Mirabello, may indicate similar unrest in this area, and if the date of the final destruction of Mallia is as has been suggested, then the north central plain could have been involved—a hypothesis that receives some confirmation from the geographical situation.

The remainder of the case depends mainly on inferences based on the appearance in Crete, at this time, of pottery of a non-Minoan type. New shapes are now found—a particular kind of krater and cup and kalathos, the belly-handled amphora, the bird vase, and one or two others, and new and very simple decorative ideas are adopted—for example, the wavy line, the system of covering the upper half of a bowl with paint and leaving the lower half and foot unpainted, and probably certain varieties of elaborate triangle decoration as found on stirrup jars. These innovations gradually transform the existing Minoan style into the simple sub-Minoan style in which they dominate. They are not very strongly marked at Karphi, but are known from the later tombs of Knossos,

[1] *P.T.K.* pp. 1 ff.

and appear in the Spring Chamber sanctuary. Furthermore, they make their appearance in two newly-built sites of this time in the Mesara, that above and alongside the palace of Phaestos, and that at Gortyn. They are also prominent in tombs at Phaestos.

This evidence may then suggest that the origin of the unrest in Crete came from outside the island, and that the southern central area was affected as well as the North. Finally, it might be suggested that the appearance of fibulae and long dress-pins (non-Minoan objects) on certain of these sites may be a further mark of intruders. It may in any case be argued that the conjunction of ceramic innovations from outside the island with the fact of disturbance suggests that the origin of the disturbance was at least in part due to external factors.

Just how strong is such a case? It will naturally be objected that it is based on incomplete evidence. There are, however, other possible objections. It may be pointed out that when the influence of the Protogeometric style makes itself clearly felt in the centre of the island, this is not taken to indicate the presence of any large number of intruders, hostile or not. This objection may be met on the grounds that the Protogeometric style was technically superior to the sub-Minoan pottery, and it was therefore natural that it should make an appeal to Cretan potters, whereas no such claims can be made for the pottery which affected the island during the course of LM. III C. A second objection is that the substitution of iron for bronze, a major change, did not involve, so far as is known, any particular disturbance. Again, a similar counter-argument may be used, in that iron was clearly superior to bronze, at least for tools and weapons, and came naturally into use once it was known to be available.

A third objection is rather more compelling. If the supposed intruders forced some of the local inhabitants to seek places of refuge, and succeeded in imposing to some extent their pottery on the existing style, one should find other instances of their presence especially in the plains, for example in the type of architecture, or in burial or religious customs. So far as concerns house construction, the rectangular plans of the buildings at Phaestos and Gortyn do not yet seem to permit of conclusions one way or the other. The tombs, however, whether at Liliana near Phaestos or at Gypsades near Knossos, preserve the same features as had long been characteristic of Minoan burials: inhumation, individual and not multiple burial, and the larnax in which the body was deposited. Also, such evidence as we have shows that Minoan cult-practices still persisted; the hut-urn of the Spring Chamber at Knossos is an example of this. This continuity may be set against the evidence of the Greek Mainland, where the intrusion of new people is especially visible in the discontinuance of the Mycenaean chamber tomb with its multiple burial, and the apparent disuse of Mycenaean shrines. It may also be pointed out that the appearance of the chamber tomb in Cyprus is one of the marks of new arrivals from the Aegean world, though in this case other forms of tomb were in use as well.

The argument, it will be seen, concentrates chiefly on the plains of Central Crete, where intruders might be supposed to have settled, and there is no doubt that it implies the survival of a strong element of the original population in these areas—not all took to the mountains, whatever the nature of the disturbance. The points made may also imply that, if there were intruders, they exerted no great influence. Again, it may be argued that, the picture being so incomplete, we may not yet have chanced upon any of the tombs of the intruders, nor have recognized their religious practices—but such an argument can carry no conviction.

The conclusion must be that it is not provable that the unrest of this period was principally due to the arrival of new people from outside Crete, but that at the same time some explanation seems demanded for the coincidence of the flight to Karphi, and new settlements at Phaestos and Gortyn, with the arrival of new ceramic ideas which were not acceptable to the local potters purely on account of their excellence. Even with regard to this, a further objection can be advanced. Can one prove either that the new ceramic ideas arrived all at the same time, or that there is this link with the new settlements? One cannot say that there is certainty, though in my opinion there is a strong likelihood.

A further question arises. Assuming there to have been some newcomers, whatever their intentions, where did they come from? Cypriot features are undeniable, both at Knossos and elsewhere, and are sufficient to suggest the possibility that some people made their way from Cyprus to Crete. These people probably came during the sub-Minoan period, and in peace, but one cannot say how many arrived, nor over what period. From the West, there is the evidence of certain types of knife and dagger and fibula of Italian and Sicilian origin, and their virtual absence from the rest of the Aegean indicates that they came to Crete direct from these areas. It has been shown that there are no grounds for thinking that they were brought by invaders, and also that such imports appeared at least as early as LM. III B. These objects are probably to be left out of account as indicating any single intrusion.

On the other hand, there are the new ceramic elements mentioned above. On existing evidence, the likelihood is that they came from the Greek Mainland during the later phase of LH. III C, after the Granary Class had become established. One might suppose that those who introduced this pottery were refugees from the Argolid after the final destruction of Mycenae; but if so, they would hardly have been in a position to create much disturbance. If it were possible to establish that the invaders of the end of LH. III B had settled in Laconia and Messenia, then one might suggest that they were the intruders, and we could call them Dorians. But this cannot be established, and it is much more likely that no settlement took place in South Peloponnese (cf. pp. 90, 97). If, as is possible, the appearance of the fibula and the long bronze pin, neither of which is a Mycenaean object, is to be assigned to this period, this is another factor which must be taken into consideration. It is on the whole wiser to conclude that there is as yet insufficient evidence to show the origin of the intruders who appear to have been responsible for the disturbances in Crete at some point in the course of LM. III C.

One other possible occasion of disturbance may be considered. It has been suggested that during the Protogeometric period there was some measure of cultural isolation between the eastern and central parts of Crete. Also, at about the same time as Protogeometric pottery began to make its mark, cremation began to be practised more frequently in Central Crete. May this not indicate a period of disturbance due to intrusion from outside? It may do so, though the fact that the ceramic influence is Attic seems to rule out the Dorians. The significance of cremation is in any case rather obscure, and its appearance is not confined to Central Crete. On the other hand, there is, so far as is known, no break in occupation at this time, either in East or Central Crete. Even so, this curious cultural isolation of East Crete is a matter which needs some explanation.

Altogether, it must be admitted that there are many problems that remain unresolved, and it is to be hoped that further research will shed light on them.

CHAPTER VIII

THE EAST MEDITERRANEAN

1. *Cyprus*

A FAIRLY detailed analysis of the ceramic links between Cyprus and the Mycenaean world has already been provided in the section dealing with Late Helladic III C pottery (pp. 22 ff.). This chapter aims simply at providing the general picture which forms the background to those links. The main emphasis will be on the period covered by LH. III C, but some account must be taken of the earlier period in Cyprus, culturally defined as Late Cypriot II C, when LH. III B was current.

The island has indeed produced a considerable number of LH. III B vases—as it also has of LH. III A and even earlier Mycenaean pottery[1]—and most of these vases have come from tombs. It is clear from the quantity of this pottery that there were close links with the Aegean, and from the fact that LH. III B ware in Cyprus can be in certain respects differentiated from that of the Argolid and Rhodes it has been concluded that there were numerous Mycenaean settlers, if not settlements, in the island during this time.

Whether the latter conclusion is correct or not, and whatever view may be taken of the origin of the 'pictorial' vases which were so popular in Cyprus, it must be stressed that Mycenaeans can have formed an insignificant fraction only of the population.[2] The influence of Mycenaean culture is confined to the pottery. In other respects, the differences are far more marked than the similarities. The material, as mentioned above, comes mainly from tombs, and the tombs themselves are of a different type from any found in Greece and in the Aegean. The small finds, the ornaments, are on the whole of a different type from those familiar to the Mycenaean sphere, even though their decorative motives often echo those of the Aegean. There are, with one exception, no weapons or knives of Mycenaean type. The exception is the Naue II type of sword—and this is of northern rather than of Mycenaean origin, see pp. 67 f.—of which five are known in Cyprus; the only well dated example is the one found in Swedish tomb 18 at Enkomi, and it is significant that the burial with which this sword is associated, and also the burial coupled with a bronze greave which may be paralleled on the Mainland of Greece, are among the very latest attributed to LC. II C.[3] Finally, this tomb is the only one in which the majority of the vases were Mycenaean; in other tombs, LH. III B vases are normally heavily outnumbered by the native LC. II C wares.

Thus, however friendly its relations may have been with the Mycenaean world, Cyprus lay outside that world. During the course of the thirteenth century it seems to

---

[1] Stubbings, *Levant*, pp. 25 ff.
[2] Sjöqvist, *Problems*, pp. 198 ff. Cf. Catling, *PPS*, 1956, 124 and n. 3.
[3] Catling, *Op. Ath.* ii. 29; cf. *PPS*, 1956, p. 115 and *Antiquity*, xxxv. 115 ff.

have been thickly populated, and pursued a reasonably peaceful existence, though a presage of the trouble to come may be found in the decision by the inhabitants of Enkomi to strengthen their fortifications at some time during this period.[1]

On the basis of a change in the style of pottery, the following period is known as Late Cypriot III (LC. III = Schaeffer's Chypriote Fer I), and is further divided into LC. III A and LC. III B, and I shall use these terms, although features of the LC. II C pottery style are still found in the early phases of LC. III A, and although the division between the latest LC. III B pottery and the earliest Cypro-Geometric is unclear, remaining a matter for individual interpretation.[2] General studies of this period have been made by Sjöqvist in his *Problems of the Cypriote Bronze Age*[3] and by Miss du Plat Taylor, in her *Late Cypriot III*.[4] Besides these, specialized studies of the pottery have been undertaken by Gjerstad and Furumark.[5] Most recently, the survey carried out by Catling has greatly added to our knowledge of the Bronze Age in Cyprus, and his conclusions are of much value in establishing the character of this period and its relationship to other periods.[6]

The period covers the transition from the Bronze to the Iron Age and, as Miss Taylor points out, is not well known.[7] Our ignorance of it is based in part on objective grounds; in other words, many of the sites previously occupied were abandoned at or before the beginning of LC. III, and the number of sites continuing to be occupied into this period, or first occupied during it, are extremely few. There are also, however, subjective grounds for our lack of knowledge. Where excavation of an LC. III site has taken place, it has for the most part either been incompletely recorded, or is still in progress. The position with regard to individual sites will become clear in the course of this chapter, and it will be evident that the greatest caution must be exercised with regard to the drawing of conclusions.

The reasons for separating this period from its predecessor are as follows. The preceding period seems to have ended in some catastrophe, which is indicated not only by possible desertion of sites but also, and principally, by evidence of destruction at Sinda[8] and at Enkomi.[9] There is a marked difference in the local pottery style, and the LH. III B ware is now replaced by LH. III C, no period of transition being visible between the two. At the major site of Enkomi, two further changes are found. The beginning of LC. III is characterized by extremely impressive ashlar constructions; and although there is some re-use of the earlier type of tomb, burials mostly took place in a new type, the shaft grave.[10] To what extent similar changes were made on other sites in the island is not known. The masonry at Maa[11] and Sinda resembles that of Enkomi, but that of other sites

---

[1] *JHS*, lxxv. suppl., p. 29.

[2] The question will be fully dealt with by Benson when he records the Bamboula material, and I adopt his provisional classification (which he has with great kindness communicated to me), which places Kaloriziki tombs 25, 26 A and 40 in LC. III B, and Lapithos tombs 406 and 420 as transitional to CG. IA. Cf. Benson, *GRBS*, iii. 14, where tomb 40 is dated between 1100 and 1050; CG. IA should then run from c. 1050 onwards.

[3] Stockholm, 1940.

[4] In *PEQ*, 1956, pp. 22 ff.

[5] *OA*, iii. 73 ff. (Gjerstad); 231 ff. (Furumark).

[6] *Cypriot Bronzework and the Mycenaean World*.

[7] *PEQ*, 1956, p. 22.

[8] *AJA*, lii. 531; *Arkeologiska Forskningar och Fynd*, p. 59.

[9] *E–A*; Dikaios, Κυπριακὰ Γράμματα, 1956, pp. 25 ff., and *AA*, 1962, pp. 1 ff.

[10] Op. cit. and Sjöqvist, *Problems*, p. 25.

[11] *JHS*, lxxv. suppl., p. 30.

does not, so far as I know. A shaft grave similar to the Enkomi ones has been found at Kition,[1] but the Kouklia cemeteries retain the earlier shape of tomb.[2]

The sites occupied during the whole or the earlier part of LC. III are as follows. On the south coast, running from west to east, Kouklia, Kourion (Bamboula), Kition and Enkomi; Sinda, not far inland from Enkomi; Idalion and Nicosia in the central plain; Lapithos on the north coast; Ayia Irini and Pigadhes, in the north-west corner of Cyprus; Apliki, in the Troodos foothills; and Maa, on a peninsula at the extreme western part of the island. Many of these sites had been occupied earlier, but not so the fort at Maa, nor the sanctuary of Ayia Irini, nor the fortified acropolis of Idalion, the two latter apparently commencing later than the beginning of LC. III. At Nicosia and Lapithos the evidence is insufficient for one to be able to say whether there was, or was not, immediately earlier occupation. Not all the sites were continuously occupied throughout LC. III; a further disaster took place during the phase known as LC. III A. At Enkomi and Sinda destruction was followed by partial re-occupation, but the contemporary destruction of Apliki, Ayia Irini and Pigadhes led to the complete desertion of these sites. If the destruction of Maa belongs, as is likely, to this time, then we have a further instance of desertion. So three, and possibly four, sites were abandoned in LC. III A. Of the remainder, only Lapithos, Kouklia, Kition and Kourion are known still to have been occupied in Cypro-Geometric I, though Pigadhes was re-occupied at this time. Sinda was deserted soon after the second disaster; Enkomi and Idalion were abandoned at or before the end of LC. III B; and at Nicosia, again, the evidence is insufficient.[3]

Although the number of sites occupied in LC. III A is appreciably lower than in the preceding period, the level of the material culture seems to have been higher. It was during this time that an extremely flourishing bronze industry established itself. The workers in ivory showed a similarly high degree of craftsmanship, and the achievements of the stone-masons are clearly visible in the massive constructions at Enkomi.

To what extent did the Mycenaeans contribute to the character of this period? Their presence, probably as new arrivals settling in the island, is mainly attested by the early LH. III C pottery which now appeared. This pottery has been found on most of the sites of this period, though not on all—for example, not at Bamboula. It is extremely difficult to assess its importance, as very few pieces have been illustrated, and as no full record is yet available for the majority of the sites. A true and full picture should give the quantitative and stylistic relationship between the Mycenaean pottery and the local Cypriot ware. Stylistically, such evidence as we have indicates no close link between the two; only the shallow bowls of Decorated Late Cypriot III seem to show the influence of LH. III C motives. On the other hand, the proportion of Mycenaean pottery to the local ware cannot yet be gauged with any great accuracy. It was evidently rare at Pigadhes and Apliki (perhaps because these sites were outside the main area of diffusion), but it was found 'in large quantities' at Sinda.[4] We know almost nothing of the position at Enkomi,

---

[1] *BCH*, lxxxiv. 515 (Karageorghis).
[2] *JHS*, lxxiv. 172 f.
[3] For most of these sites see *PEQ*, 1956, pp. 22 ff., with references. Kouklia, see n. 2, and *ILN*, 2 May, 1953.

Kition, *Problems*, p. 133; *BSA*, xli. 94; *BCH*, lxxxiv. 504 ff. Lapithos, *SCE*, I. Nicosia, *BCH*, lxxxiii. 354 f.
[4] *AJA*, lii. 531.

the most important site of all, though it may reasonably be supposed that the conditions here were nearer those of Sinda than those of the north-western sites.

It is also important to be able accurately to assess the relationship of LH. III C pottery in Cyprus with that current in the Mycenaean world, both with respect to relative chronology and to area or areas of origin. Here we are at least fortunate in having the high authority of Furumark for the material from Sinda. He reports that the earliest Mycenaean pottery in period 2 of this settlement was LH. III C 1 *a*, imported from Rhodes, but that the bulk of the material belonged to his LH. III C 1 *b* phase, was mainly locally made, and showed close connexions with Argive LH. III C of this period.[1] The illustrated vases and sherds from this settlement as well as from others[2] (no LH. III C vases have yet been reported from tombs) generally confirm his conclusions, although it is not possible to decide whether the material from other sites belongs to LH. III C 1 *a*[3] or LH. III C 1 *b*, and although the decoration of the spouted jug from Enkomi[4] is not paralleled anywhere in the Mycenaean world. Provisionally, it may be concluded that the earliest stages of LH. III C are represented in Cyprus at this time, and that connexions with the Aegean continued during the course of this early phase.

The evidence for the arrival of Mycenaeans is not confined to their pottery. The fine constructions of this period at Enkomi, Schaeffer's *Bâtiment 18* and Dikaios' sanctuary, display a skill in monumental architecture not previously known in Cyprus, but familiar to the Mycenaean world of the thirteenth century. It would seem that these buildings are also reminiscent, in certain details, of Hittite architecture, but if this is so it is unlikely that there was a direct link with the Hittites, there being no other evidence of their presence. These constructions may be dated to the beginning of LC. III A and are contemporary with the sudden appearance of early LH. III C pottery. To this period also belongs the finest ivory and metal work known in Cyprus, the objects coming chiefly from Enkomi and Kouklia. The influence of Mycenaean craftsmen is certain for the ivories, and is very probable for the metal work as well.[5]

These are then the main contributions of the Mycenaeans to the culture of Cyprus in LC. III A. They are significant in that the brilliance of this short period is in some measure due to them. They are also significant, however, in that they reflect a Mycenaean brilliance which, especially in the Argolid, from which Furumark derives much of the LH. III C pottery at Sinda, no longer exists on the Mainland of Greece at this time. The skills in architecture, in metal and ivory work belong to the departed age of LH. III B. It may not be unreasonable to conclude that many of the foremost craftsmen of the Mycenaean world took flight to Cyprus, most probably consequent on the disasters that overcame the Greek Mainland (cf. pp. 221 f.).

Is it possible to go further, and suggest that Mycenaeans came in such strength as to obtain some political control over part of the island? It is an attractive hypothesis, but it fails to take certain other factors into account. If Mycenaean political control is to be

---

[1] *AF*, pp. 64 f.
[2] Cf. Coche de la Ferté, *Essai*, Pl. IV, 4 and 6, Pl. IX, 1–8 (Enkomi); *BCH*, lxxxiii. 354, Fig. 19 (Nicosia); *AJ*, xxxii, Pl. 28A: 4 (Apliki).
[3] A bowl from Enkomi (*Arch. Reports for 1958*, p. 26, Fig. 2) may be LH. III C 1 *a*.
[4] *E–A*, p. 271, Fig. 91.
[5] Catling, *PPS*, 1956, p. 123; Karageorghis, Κυπριακαὶ Σπουδαί, 1961, p. 16; Dikaios, *AA*, 1962, pp. 1 ff.

found anywhere, it should surely be centred on Enkomi and Sinda. The situation at Sinda is not yet well enough known, but at Enkomi it is clear that, in the first place, LH. III C pottery did not oust, or even seriously influence, the local LC. III A ware. *Bâtiment 18* may have been the work of Mycenaean masons, but there is no clear trace of a *megaron*. Dikaios' temple, also a massive ashlar construction, is not the type of building familiar to the Mycenaean world. No trace has been found, during this period, of any tomb of the conventional Mycenaean type, whether tholos or chamber tomb with dromos. Either the previous type of tomb continued to be used, or, as at Enkomi and Kition, a new type appears, 'a shaft grave lined with rubble and usually containing not more than two burials',[1] in other words, quite different from the usual Mycenaean practice of multiple burials, though one must not forget the pit graves that have been found on many LH. III sites (cf. pp. 33 f., 36). Taken together, these factors counsel caution against putting forward the theory that the Mycenaeans actually ruled any part of the island at this time.

The early stage of LC. III A, a period of prosperity for those districts of Cyprus still inhabited, was interrupted by catastrophe. As already mentioned, three of the twelve sites, Ayia Irini, Pigadhes and Apliki, were permanently or temporarily deserted as a result; thus the sites in the north-west were affected. Maa may also have been abandoned, and there is no record of any later occupation at Nicosia, though it must be remembered that no systematic excavation was possible here.

It would thus seem possible that only seven sites survived the catastrophe, and of these there is no published settlement evidence from Kouklia or Lapithos, or until later from Kition, and so one cannot tell to what extent they were affected. For the rest, there is no sign of destruction either at Bamboula or at Idalion, but the towns of Sinda and Enkomi underwent serious damage, and the subsequent occupants used only a part of the earlier inhabited area—at Enkomi, in fact, we have little more than a squatters' settlement. In general, though one or two sites may have escaped, the calamity[2] must have been widespread, and the later stage of LC. III A saw the fortunes of the Cypriotes at a very low ebb.

Not a great deal more can be said about this later stage, which is chiefly represented by level IV at Enkomi and period 3 of Sinda (the Bamboula excavation has not yet been fully recorded, and the Idalion material does not seem very rewarding). Four points, however, merit brief mention. First, the amount of pottery of early LH. III C type shrinks considerably—indeed, Schaeffer goes so far as to say that it is completely absent from Enkomi IV;[3] this could mean some interruption of relations with the Mycenaean world, where in any case there was trouble on the Mainland. Second, the bronze industry continued to operate at Enkomi, which shows that the disaster did not succeed in stifling all craftsmanship. Third, it has been reckoned that iron was introduced to Cyprus after the disaster,[4] and this may have been an added encouragement to the metalworkers. Finally, the connexions with Egypt attested for the earlier period[5] may have been maintained,

---

[1] *PEQ*, 1956, p. 25.
[2] It is unlikely that the Land and Sea Raiders were responsible for this. Cf. pp. 237 ff.
[3] *E–A*, pp. 309 ff., 417.
[4] Op. cit. p. 418.
[5] *BCH*, lxxxiv. 538 ff.

from the fact that scarabs of Ramses III, and possibly of his immediate successors, were found in tombs at Enkomi assigned to this time—a point which also, of course, has a bearing on absolute chronology.[1]

The period known as Late Cypriot III B is based on a stylistic distinction in the pottery. In his general study of the Late Bronze Age in Cyprus, Sjœqvist defined the division purely in terms of the local ware; however, it seems undeniable that a new ware, christened Proto-White-Painted by Gjerstad,[2] appeared at the same time as the local style underwent a change. That this ware had its roots in the Aegean at a time not earlier than that of the destruction of the Granary at Mycenae has been ably demonstrated by Gjerstad and Furumark, who wrote before the vital excavations at Enkomi, which have now established the moment of its first appearance. As this is the ware which subsequently dominated Cypriot pottery, it seems more satisfactory to consider it as the main ceramic criterion for this period. Its appearance involves the arrival of new settlers and is the first sign of a revival in Cyprus's fortunes; in this sense, the emergence of Late Cypriot III B has a much greater importance than that of a mere change in the ceramic fashions.

The period does not start auspiciously, for of the seven sites previously inhabited we find that Sinda has now been deserted. We are left with just six settlements in Cyprus known to have been occupied, and of these only Idalion lies inland; and yet it is from this nucleus that, from Cypro-Geometric onwards, the main resettlement of the island took place.

Late Cypriot III B, the extent of which I have defined earlier,[3] is not an easy period to study. At Enkomi, a considerable area of the town has been excavated, and it is clear that it was deserted before the end of the period; the settlement produced a considerable amount of pottery of the latest Mycenaean type, but the few tombs contained only the local ware.[4] The well deposit at Kition,[5] contemporary with Enkomi I, is indeed most valuable, as it is published in detail, and the settlement on the acropolis is contemporary in its earliest stage with the well deposit, but unfortunately the pottery of the subsequent stage has not been fully recorded.[6] The only relevant tomb, probably to be assigned to LC. III B, is that whose contents (apart from two intrusive objects) were published by Myres.[7] Full excavation has taken place at Bamboula, yielding both settlement and tomb evidence, and also at the nearby Kaloriziki cemetery, but the full report, except for three of the Kaloriziki tombs, is still in preparation.[8] The Bamboula settlement came to an end before Cypro-Geometric, but the Kaloriziki cemetery continued in use. At Idalion[9] the settlement also came to an end before the start of Cypro-Geometric, and there is certainly a considerable gap in the tomb evidence after LC. III B. On the other hand, a sanctuary was erected on the site at the beginning of Cypro-Geometric. The LC. III B settlement at Kouklia has not yet been investigated, but the tombs found in various parts of the site

---

[1] *E–A*, p. 318 and n. 3. Certainty of attribution to later Ramessids does not, unfortunately, seem to be forthcoming.
[2] *OA*, iii. 75.
[3] Cf. p. 197, n. 2.
[4] *Problems*, p. 135; *E–A*, pp. 156 ff., 230 ff.
[5] *BCH*, lxxxiv. 570 ff. See Pl. 13.
[6] *BSA*, xli. 85 ff.; *SCE*, III, 18, 68 ff.; *Problems*, p. 133; *BCH*, lxxxiv. 507, n. 6. Further important excavations are in progress. See Addenda.
[7] *LAAA*, iii. 107 ff. Cf. *SCE*, IV: 2, 216.
[8] Daniel, *AJA*, xli. 56 ff. and xlii. 261 ff.
[9] *SCE*, II, 460 ff.

show that it must have been continuously inhabited.[1] Unfortunately, very little is known of the contents of these tombs. The material from Lapithos also comes exclusively from tombs, but in this case a reasonably full publication is available.[2]

There is thus an unevenness both in excavation and in publication. If the following Cypro-Geometric period was fully documented, it might be possible to argue backwards, in some matters, into LC. III B; but even this is denied us. The record of tombs is reasonable, but apart from this there are only two small sanctuaries known to have been erected at the beginning of Cypro-Geometric, those of Ayia Irini and Idalion, and settlement material is almost entirely lacking—as Gjerstad has said '. . . the domestic architecture of the epoch is still almost unknown to us. Only fragmentary remains of a house have been discovered on the acropolis of Kition.'[3]

Problems also arise concerning the pottery, that evidence on which relative chronology is chiefly based. There are two types of pottery current during LC. III B, the local Cypriot ware, and the 'wavy line' style which was introduced from the Aegean. The two fuse to form a new style, as is visible in the tombs of the later phase of LC. III B and of Cypro-Geometric, but it is extremely likely that the intrusive Mycenaean pottery was at first confined to two or three sites only. The spread, and consequent fusion, may have been a matter of some time. The early stage of the arrival of the 'wavy line' ware is only visible at Enkomi and Kition, in settlement contexts, and it is unfortunate that no contemporary tombs containing this pottery have been found on these sites, nor indeed on any of the other sites, though the unpublished group from Idalion and Ohnefalsch-Richter's Lapithos group may not be appreciably later than the material found in Enkomi I and the Kition deposit (cf. pp. 24, 26). With the exception of the Idalion group, the vases from the tombs belong to the stage when the potter in Cyprus was already developing his own style. A further point is that not only are the earliest tombs missing, but that after this the settlement evidence fails us, and therefore we cannot yet study the tomb and settlement material side by side.

Yet another difficulty is that although studies have been made of the local ware and of the intrusive Mycenaean-type pottery separately, there is no good analysis of both as considered together. It would be a useful work, for the relationship between the two is not entirely clear. The position is that there are two sites where the settlement material indicates an increasing extension of the wavy line pottery (at Enkomi) or its predominance (at Kition) and it may be noted that, if the Mycenaean sherds from Enkomi have received only scanty illustration, the sherds of local ware of levels III to I have not been illustrated at all. As opposed to this, there are two sites whose settlements seem to produce almost exclusively the local Cypriot pottery, Bamboula and Idalion. There would be no necessary objection to this, as it might simply mean that the newcomers from the Aegean had not settled in these towns. At Idalion, it is in fact just possible to suppose that the settlement was abandoned for another site at some time before the end of LC. III B, and that the belly amphora and stirrup jar of Mycenaean type,[4] as well as the vases from the unpublished tomb, were deposited later than the end of the settlement. But at Bamboula, where

[1] *JHS*, lxxiv. 172 f.
[2] *SCE*, I. 162 ff.
[3] *SCE*, IV: 2, 433.
[4] *FLMV*, Pl. 22, 160 and Pl. 14, 91.

periods 2 to 4 represented the LC. III B occupation, Daniel found, in a context belonging to period 2 (the earliest of the three), a neck amphora similar to one from Kaloriziki tomb 26A.[1] Tomb 26A should definitely be assigned to the later phase of LC. III B, and its contents showed the clear fusion of the Cypriot and Mycenaean styles. It might then be that the amphora found in the settlement was of an earlier date, representing a type which had not changed much, but even so one would suppose that periods 3 and 4 must be contemporary with the Kaloriziki tombs,[2] and in this case there would still be a radical difference between the pottery of the settlement and that of the cemetery of Kaloriziki. The answer may be, as Daniel suggested,[3] that at the beginning of period 3, when the inhabited area was greatly reduced, the population moved to another site (not yet identified). Perhaps they may have joined an already existing community which contained a nucleus of Mycenaean settlers.

It will thus be seen that there are certain obscurities in LC. III B, but the detailed reports of the excavations will no doubt remove them.

An account has already been given of the pottery current in Cyprus during LC. III B, from the point of view of relations with the Aegean (pp. 23 ff.). It was concluded that a stream of migrants from the Mycenaean world arrived in Cyprus soon after the destruction of the Granary at Mycenae, and that further groups from this area continued to make their way here for a while, bringing with them Mycenaean pottery and introducing the chamber tomb (found at Lapithos and, notably, at Kaloriziki).[4] It was also concluded that there was a reverse movement from Cyprus to certain parts of the Aegean, probably of objects only and not of people, at the very end of LH. III C and at the beginning of Protogeometric in Attica, and during the sub-Minoan period in Crete, and that this was the occasion when iron was introduced to the Aegean.

There is no need to repeat the arguments on which these conclusions were based, but it may be of interest to assess the degree of prosperity achieved in Cyprus at this time on the basis of objects other than pottery.

It does in fact seem that this time was one of artistic achievement, and probably of prosperity, for Cyprus. Speaking of the Cypro-Geometric I period, Gjerstad has said: 'We feel the fresh and inspired artistic spirit and the energetic power of creation produced by the tension of the Cypriote and Mycenaean components. It is an artistically young and dynamic period.'[5] The same judgment is valid for Late Cypriot III B, of which Cypro-Geometric is the the natural extension. The 'tension' of the Cypriot and Mycenaean components had indeed contributed to the brilliance of early LC. III A; the disaster at the end of this period may have had a serious effect on those inhabitants who survived, but the infusion of further Mycenaean stock from the Aegean made a revival possible, and the continuance of peaceful conditions ensured it. The earlier craftsmanship did not disappear. Schaeffer states how even in level I Enkomi's 'metal industry was still very active',[6] and this is confirmed by the contents of Kaloriziki tomb 40.[7]

---

[1] Daniel, *AJA*, xlii. 267, citing *AJA*, xli, Pl. III, 12. He produces other parallels as well.
[2] So Sjöqvist thought; cf. *Problems*, pp. 132 f., n. 4.
[3] *AJA*, xlii. 265.
[4] *AJA*, xli. 57; *SCE*, IV: 2, 30.
[5] *SCE*, IV: 2, 435.
[6] *E–A*, p. 418.
[7] *AJA*, lviii. 131 ff. (McFadden).

The bronze workers had not lost their art. Furthermore, one by-product of the destruction during LC. III A was that iron became generally accessible to the island, and no doubt the craftsmen benefited by it. To what extent contacts were maintained with countries bordering on the Eastern Mediterranean at this time is not fully known, but links existed at least with Egypt and the Palestine coast. Ivory was still commonly used, and gold was certainly accessible. The worth and artistic standard of the deposits in Kaloriziki tomb 40 denote wealth, even allowing for the fact that this was a royal tomb. Describing one of the burials in Lapithos tomb 420 (transitional to Cypro-Geometric) the excavator says that the body was 'richly adorned with gold ornaments'.[1]

It is not therefore surprising that Cypriot artefacts, both of pottery and metal, found their way to the Aegean. But to what extent did this period in Cyprus depend for its achievements on Mycenaean craftsmanship, and on Mycenaeans themselves? Mycenaean influence in LC. III A is clear enough, but the renewal of that influence in LC. III B, through the arrival of further settlers, may have gone deeper. This is the time when the characteristic Mycenaean chamber tomb was introduced to the island. The pottery which these settlers brought with them eventually succeeded in dominating the local style. And may not the sceptre found in Kaloriziki tomb 40 have belonged to a Mycenaean ruler? The fusion of Mycenaean and Cypriote was probably more complete on this occasion, and the dominating influence culturally, and possibly even politically in certain areas, was the Mycenaean.

Further evidence of influence from the Aegean is to be seen in the adoption of fibulae and, less commonly, dress pins.[2] It is said that a major climatic change led to the use of these objects,[3] which imply a warmer type of dress, but their origin may be traced to the Aegean, even though (not surprisingly) the Cypriotes soon developed their own individual types.

This last point may lead to a certain doubt concerning the validity of a previous conclusion, that those who migrated to Cyprus were all of Mycenaean stock. Fibulae were sporadically worn in the Mycenaean world at least from the beginning of LH. III C, but the dress pin, in a true Mycenaean context, is an object of the utmost rarity, and its use confined to the very end of LH. III C. As opposed to this, both fibulae and dress pins are distinguishing features of those whom I have identified as intruders into the Mycenaean world, the people who buried their dead in the cist tombs of Salamis and the Kerameikos (pp. 116, 119).

However this may be, dress pins are known in the latest LC. III B tombs only, and so are perhaps contemporary with the beginning of Protogeometric, by which time they could have been in fairly general use in the Aegean. Thus the conception of earlier and purely Mycenaean groups making their way to Cyprus needs no reconsideration. Nor are there any other factors which might disturb such a conclusion—even the unparalleled case of cremation in Kaloriziki tomb 40 may be linked more naturally, from the associated

---

[1] *SCE*, I. 236.

[2] e.g. Kaloriziki, T. 25: two bronze fibulae, one bronze pin with conical ivory head; T. 26A: four bronze fibulae, *AJA*, xli. 79 f. T. 40: nine bronze fibulae, one gold pin, *AJA*, lviii, 139 and Pl. 24. Lapithos, T. 406: four bronze fibulae, three bronze pins, *SCE*, I. 197 ff. and Pl. XLVI.

[3] Taylour, *MPI*, p. 79.

objects, with the occasional cremations of the Dodecanese and Perati (cf. pp. 115, 157) than with the emergence of this rite as the custom for adults in Protogeometric Athens or Crete. In general, it would not be incorrect to say that in Cyprus we encounter the last stronghold of Mycenaean culture and civilization.

2. *The Southern Coast of Asia Minor*

Prehistoric finds in this part of the world have in the main been confined to Cilicia, as is made clear in Mellaart's survey of the area (which incorporated the results of more limited research by Hood).[1] In fact, no prehistoric settlement has been identified west of Silifke (Seleuceia),[2] and there is consequently no evidence that the Mycenaeans penetrated, or wished to penetrate, this area of Asia Minor. A few early settlements are noted between Silifke and Mersin, but there is no report of any Mycenaean. It may therefore be concluded, until positive evidence to the contrary is produced, that no Mycenaeans visited, far less settled in, any part of the coast west of Cilicia.

Cilicia itself has been the subject of two surveys, by Gjerstad[3] and Miss Seton-Williams,[4] and a brief analysis of the Mycenaean pottery has been made by Stubbings.[5] Besides this, Burton-Brown illustrates two surface sherds of Mycenaean type.[6] From these surface finds it would appear that only Kazanli produced LH. III A or B sherds, but Stubbings[7] is of the opinion that Gjerstad's Hellado-Cilician may be imitative of LH. III B, and if this is so a further nine sites will have had contact with Mycenaeans at this time.[8] Miss Seton-Williams also lists eight sites on which LH. III C sherds have been found, and concludes that Mycenaean occupation was fairly widespread.[9]

Without further details of these sherds it is difficult to make any useful assessment, and in any case evidence from the surface is not very satisfactory.

It might have been hoped that the excavations at Mersin would give a fuller picture, but unfortunately the Mycenaean finds were almost negligible; the three sherds recorded are possibly LH. III B or earlier, and the intervening centuries down to the eighth are virtually unrepresented.[10]

There is only one excavated site in the area that is of value to this study—that of Tarsus.[11] The town had a long history and eventually came under Hittite domination; then, at some time in the thirteenth century, not earlier than the reign of Hattusil III but very possibly later, there was a severe destruction, and another settlement was built above the levelled debris.[12] The houses of this settlement were at the beginning reasonably well constructed but, as the excavator says 'they became increasingly more flimsy and temporary so that the area soon took on the character of a squatter's settlement'.[13] The

---

[1] *AS*, iv. 175 ff.
[2] Op. cit. p. 177.
[3] *RA*, 1934, pp. 155 ff.
[4] *AS*, iv. 121 ff.
[5] *Levant*, pp. 88 f.
[6] *LAAA*, xxi. 51 ff., Pl. 8, 1 and 2.
[7] *Levant*, p. 89.

[8] These include Miss Seton-Williams's sub-Mycenaean sites, as she equates sub-Mycenaean with Hellado-Cilician (*AS*, iv. 134 f.).
[9] *AS*, iv. 134 f.
[10] Garstang, *Prehistoric Mersin*, p. 256, Nos. 1–3.
[11] Goldman, *Tarsus* II.
[12] Op. cit. pp. 50, 58 and 63.
[13] Op. cit. p. 58.

important fact here is that the characteristic pottery of the re-occupation was Mycenaean, of the transition from LH. III B to C, with the accent rather on LH. III B.[1]

Of the shapes represented the deep bowls are naturally in the majority,[2] but the bowls with carinated shoulder were almost as numerous, and there were a fair number of one-handled bowls (shape 8 of the Acropolis Fountain);[3] no certain identification was made of any kylikes, but small stirrup jars were fairly numerous, and there were also a few sherds of amphoriskoi, and one kalathos. Sherds of larger vases probably came from kraters, and it is remarkable that no pieces of jars, amphorae or hydriae were recognized. On the whole, it looks as though a valid comparison can be made with the pottery from the houses on the north slope of the Acropolis, and from the earliest stages of the Fountain. It is particularly noticeable that only two sherds of monochrome bowls were found 'among hundreds of sherds'.[4] The division between LH. III B and early LH. III C is extraordinarily difficult to make for bowls (cf. pp. 5 f., 11), and it would seem that many of the sherds of this shape were not painted all over inside;[5] at the same time, a few of the sherds should belong to LH. III C, as also a few of the stirrup jars (particularly the one with the octopus decoration), and the amphoriskoi.[6]

The proportion of local ware to imported is not at all easy to judge, though it is the opinion of the excavator that much of the imported pottery came from the Argolid.[7] As only the end of LH. III B and the earliest stage of LH. III C can be recognized, it is difficult to assess the length of the period of occupation—ceramic contact with the Aegean may have been very slight. The final stage of this settlement, however, is characterized by a very rudimentary ware,[8] in which elements of the final phase of LH. III C are possibly to be recognized, as well as links with Cyprus, Syria and Palestine. The conclusion that the end of the twelfth century saw the 'extinction of the Mycenaean tradition'[9] is probably correct, providing that it is realized that this Mycenaean tradition was not continuous from LH. III B–C onwards.

It is assumed, finally, that the destruction of the Hittite town was the work of those, the users of LH. III B–C pottery, who built the succeeding settlement; but I am not sure whether this is a provable matter. In any case, after the settlement faded out, there seems to have been some interval before the introduction of pottery of the Iron Age.[10]

In conclusion, then, there is no known contact between the Aegean world (or Cyprus) and the south coast of Asia Minor west of Cilicia, while in Cilicia there is evidence of probably not more than casual contact during LH. III, with the one exception of the settlement of a group of Mycenaeans at Tarsus, commencing at the period of transition from LH. III B to C, and probably continuing through the twelfth century, but progressively impoverished and not visibly in touch with the Mycenaean world.

---

[1] Op. cit. pp. 205 ff., Figs. 330 ff.
[2] Op. cit. pp. 207 f.
[3] *Hesp.* viii. 377.
[4] *Tarsus*, II, p. 206.
[5] e.g. op. cit. Nos. 1262, 1295(?), 3111–12(?).
[6] e.g. op. cit. Nos. 1278, 1282, 1284, 1286, 1338.
[7] Op. cit. p. 206.
[8] Op. cit. pp. 208 f.
[9] Op. cit. p. 209.
[10] Op. cit. p. 205.

3. Syria

Writing in 1951, Stubbings said that after LH. III B there were no further Mycenaean imports to Syria.[1] Further discoveries since that date have only confirmed this conclusion. There has indeed been no great addition to our knowledge. The finds of Atchana have now been recorded in detail,[2] and so have the LH. III B vases from the tomb at Sarafend, already briefly mentioned in Stubbings's work.[3] Further excavation has been carried out at Ras Shamra,[4] and one important new discovery (relating to Mycenaean affairs) has been made. The relevant conclusions from this, as well as from the recent Danish excavations at Tell Sukas[5] (a coastal site a few miles south of Ras Shamra), will be discussed below.

The absence in this area of any Mycenaean pottery later than LH. III B might lead to the conclusion that there was no further need for discussion. As, however, the destruction of three of the Syrian sites, Ras Shamra, Atchana and Tell Sukas, has been attributed by their excavators to the activities of the Land and Sea Raiders who attacked Egypt in c. 1191, and as these activities may perhaps be placed in the earliest stages of LH. III C, the Mycenaean material from the three sites concerned is of great importance. Their evidence also has a special bearing on the circumstances of the development of Philistine pottery (cf. pp. 212 f.).

Schaeffer has long been convinced that the destruction of Ras Shamra was due to the Land and Sea Raiders.[6] This view has recently had a twofold confirmation. First, there was the discovery, in a level immediately preceding the destruction, of a sword bearing the cartouche of Merneptah (1236–23); as Schaeffer says, this gives the latest Egyptian date yet known.[7] Second, and even more convincing, chronological researches on the kings of Ras Shamra (Ugarit)[8] have shown that Ammistamru II of Ugarit was a contemporary of the Hittite king Tudhaliyas IV (c. 1250–30), and that three kings followed Ammistamru, covering at least two further generations; from this one must conclude that 1191 is about the earliest date assignable to the destruction of Ras Shamra— and it is unthinkable that the Land and Sea Raiders should have left this city unharmed.

The virtual certainty as to the date of the destruction is unfortunately not echoed by a similar certainty as to the date of the latest Mycenaean pottery. It can reasonably be assumed, from Stubbings's book,[9] that there was much L.H. III B ware, and that nothing later had been found up till 1951, but one cannot yet take this for granted in regard to the Mycenaean pottery found associated with the sword mentioned above. Schaeffer says that it was 'de facture tardive',[10] and one cannot then go further than Professor Wace's comment, 'If the Mycenaean pottery in this context is of the style usually found at Ras Shamra it would mean that about the time of Merneptah LH. III B pottery was still in

---

[1] *Levant*, p. 109.
[2] Woolley, *Alalakh*.
[3] Baramki, *Berytus*, xii. 129 ff.,; cf. *Levant*, pp. 77 f.
[4] Schaeffer, *Syria*, xxxi. 14 ff., and other publications.
[5] Riis, *AAS*, viii–ix. 107 ff.; x. 111 ff.; xi–xii. 133 ff.
[6] e.g. *Ugaritica*, i (1939), p. 105.
[7] *Syria*, xxxi. 65 ff.; cf. *Antiquity*, xiii. 356 ff.
[8] Nougayrol, *Le Palais Royal d'Ugarit*, iv. 6 ff.
[9] *Levant*, pp. 70 ff.
[10] *Syria*, xxxi. 65.

use. We cannot, however, rely on this completely until Professor Schaeffer has finished the excavation of that house.'[1]

The evidence from Atchana presents the opposite picture to that from Ras Shamra. Here it is quite certain that the Mycenaean pottery in the destruction level was LH. III B and no later—there is no trace whatever of LH. III C.[2] On the other hand, there is no literary evidence to show that the town cannot have been destroyed before 1191.

The third site, Tell Sukas, was also destroyed, and Riis is of the opinion that this, too, was the work of the Land and Sea Raiders.[3] All one can say here is that, so far as is known, no Mycenaean pottery later than LH. III B was found.

One might perhaps include a fourth site, just within the borders of Palestine, Tell Abu Hawam.[4] The settlement here suffered destruction on two separate occasions, but unfortunately there is no agreement on the specific dates concerned. The excavator dates stratum V to c. 1400–1230 and suggests that its partial destruction may have been due to a campaign by Merneptah.[5] He subdivides his next stratum into IVa and IVb, and considers that the violent destruction of IVa was due to the Land and Sea Raiders.[6] Against this, Maisler (Mazar) has argued that stratum V lasted from c. 1300 to c. 1180, that there was then a considerable gap in the occupation, and that stratum IV cannot be dated earlier than c. 1050.[7] As the situation with regard to the pottery does not seem to be entirely clear, it is better to leave this site out of account.

Taking the evidence from the three Syrian sites as a whole, however, the probability that they were all destroyed shortly before 1191 is very great, and it is also extremely likely that the Mycenaean pottery in the destruction levels was in no case later than LH. III B. The importance of these conclusions for the absolute dating of Mycenaean pottery needs no stressing, and Stubbings has recorded it as his opinion that LH. III C cannot have started to develop before the 1180s.[8] It must be admitted that the idea that the Philistines, a major group of the Land and Sea Raiders, brought their 'Philistine' pottery with them is no longer tenable, as the stylistic connexions of this ware are rather with Furumark's LH. III C 1 b than with his LH. III C 1 a;[9] and the hypothesis that Philistine pottery was introduced into the region eventually occupied by the Philistines at a slightly later date than the original foundations is much strengthened. On the other hand, it must also be borne in mind that LH. III B pottery probably continued to be current in the East Mediterranean after LH. III C had started to develop in the Aegean area, for LH. III B pottery in the Levant mainly originated from Cyprus,[10] and in Cyprus itself, at Enkomi and Sinda, the results of excavation seem clearly to show that, after a destruction, a type of very early LH. III C pottery was introduced from the Aegean, replacing—and unconnected with—the LH. III B pottery which immediately preceded the destruction (cf. pp. 23, 197). It would consequently still be possible for LH. III C to have started to develop in the central Mycenaean regions c. 1200 (cf. pp. 237 ff.).

[1] *The Aegean and the Near East*, p. 134.
[2] *Alalakh*, p. 374.
[3] *AAS*, viii–ix. 131.
[4] Hamilton, *QDAP*, iv. 1 ff.
[5] Op. cit. pp. 66 and 68.
[6] Op. cit. p. 69.
[7] *BASOR*, No. 124 (1951), pp. 21 ff.
[8] *CAH* (rev. edn.), I, chap. vi, p. 75 (separate fascicle).
[9] *OA*, iii. 260 and 262.
[10] *Levant*, p. 108.

4. *The Philistines and Philistine Pottery*

It is a fact that the Peleset, an important group of the raiders who were defeated by Ramesses III on the borders of Egypt in the eighth year of his reign (*c.* 1191), are the Philistines of the Bible, and it is also true that they settled in the southern part of Palestine after their defeat. Whether the settlement took place at the order of Ramesses III is not certain. A passage in the Papyrus Harris[1] suggests that it could have happened this way, but on the other hand Ramesses' control over this district does not at any time appear to have been strong. Perhaps the original settlement was due to this Pharaoh, but his control over the Philistines may have subsequently lapsed. It is in any case reasonable so suppose that the Philistines settled in South Palestine very shortly after their defeat; from then on their power increased and flourished until their eventual eclipse by the Israelites in the latter part of the eleventh century and thereafter.

Now at about the time of the Philistine foundations, in this part of Palestine, there appeared a type of pottery the chief elements of which, both in shape and decoration, are traceable to some Mycenaean area.[2] Geographically, this pottery is found in greatest abundance within and near the area of Philistine setttlement.[3] It is found further afield as well, for example at Megiddo and Hazor,[4] but when so found the quantities are relatively smaller. So, territorially, it is a pottery associated with the Philistines. There is also a chronological correspondence, as it can be established that the pottery is current only during the time when the Philistines were powerful; it flourishes in the twelfth century, and there is then a decadence, especially noticeable in the latter part of the eleventh century.

That Philistine pottery is mostly of Mycenaean type and decoration is not to be doubted. It is, however, locally made, and often displays a bichrome technique unfamiliar to the Mycenaeans but known on earlier Syro-Palestinian wares, and also found on Cypriot Proto-White-Painted and Cypro-Geometric pottery.[5] It is indeed almost always so crude, even in the earliest contexts, as at Tell Fara, that one hesitates to assign its manufacture to any reputable Mycenaean potter. Just a very few pieces are close to Mycenaean originals. A deep bowl found at Askalon has a carefully designed antithetic tongue pattern[6] —the sole instance of the use of this pattern, which stylistically could be LH. III C 1 *a* or *b*: a not unsimilar piece at Sinda is dated by Furumark to LH. III C 1 *b*.[7] As well as this bowl, there is a sherd from Tell Fara,[8] which has a fish (again, the only instance of this motive in Philistine ware) and a bird, both of which are close to Mycenaean early LH. III C examples.

---

[1] Breasted, *Ancient Records of Egypt*, iv. 201, para. 403.
[2] *Chronology*, pp. 118 ff.; *OA*, iii. 260; Dothan, *Antiquity and Survival*, ii. 151 ff. (referred to below as *Dothan*).
[3] Albright, *The Archaeology of Palestine*, p. 114.
[4] Maisler, *BASOR*, No. 124 (1951), p. 23, mentions unpublished Philistine sherds from these two sites.
[5] Benson, *JNES*, xx. 81.

[6] Phythian-Adams, *PEFQ*, 1923, p. 71 and Pl. 2, 12. Unfortunately, it is not absolutely clear from the excavation report whether this vase belonged to the Philistine level or to that which preceded it.
[7] *AJA*, lii, Pl. 58A.
[8] Petrie, *Beth-Pelet*, ii, Pl. 63, No. 46; cf. Ohnefalsch-Richter, *Kypros, the Bible and Homer*, Pl. 98, 4 for two very similar fish from Cyprus.

The main shapes of Philistine pottery are four in number:[1] the deep bowl, the krater, the stirrup jar and the one-handled jug with strainer spout. Of these, the jug with strainer spout is more at home in the East Mediterranean, popular in Cyprus, occasionally found in LH. III C tombs of the Dodecanese, rare on the Greek Mainland. Its earliest appearance does not so far, in the Mycenaean sphere, antedate the end of LH. III B. The other three shapes are fully and characteristically Mycenaean, and may indeed be said to be the most commonly used vases of LH. III C, the deep bowls and kraters being characteristic of settlements, the stirrup jar the most favoured offering in tombs.

Of these four shapes, the deep bowls (Pl. 19c, d) and kraters may be treated together; there is a considerable variation in size, to the point where one is not sure whether to call a vase a large bowl or a small krater. In shape they are similar to their Mycenaean prototypes, though the sides of the bowls tend to come down more vertically, and there is a sharper bend inwards to the foot. This feature recalls certain deep bowls in Crete,[2] though the similarity may be only accidental. The inside of these vases is, from what I have seen, left free of paint, and the general effect is that of a clay-ground style.

The chief element of decoration is the spiral, a motive far more commonly found than any other. There are usually two spirals between the handles, at times placed antithetically with a wiggly line or a hatched or cross-hatched lozenge dividing them, but as often as not they are simply placed side by side, with little attempt at symmetry; occasionally the centres of the spiral have a filling ornament, the Maltese cross being a favourite. Spirals are also found in panel arrangements, the dividing element here often being a set of vertical lines fringed by collateral semicircles, plain or with a dot inside (see Pl. 19a, b). Similar metopes flank a variant to the spiral, the bird, usually pluming its wings (see Pl. 19b). Other—and much rarer—motives include chequers (on the larger vases), concentric semicircles and cross-hatched rectangles. The decoration is generally applied in rather a careless manner.

The style apparent on these bowls and kraters contains motives common both to LH. III B and LH. III C. The birds have no connexion with Mainland fowls, and not a great deal with those of the Dodecanese (Cyprus is rather an unknown quantity). Their posture seems peculiar to the Philistines.[3] The dotted semicircle motive is extremely rare in the Aegean area,[4] but there is a useful parallel (see below, p. 212) on a LH. III C sherd from Nicosia in Cyprus. The spirals can be paralleled almost anywhere in the Aegean. It is in any case clear that there is no trace of the characteristic elements of the later phase of LH. III C. The wavy-line technique is entirely absent, and so is its often accompanying dark-ground system of decoration. These bowls and kraters form an overwhelming majority of the Philistine decorated material from the settlements, though deep bowls are also to be found in tombs, especially those of Tell Fara.

The stirrup jars (Pl. 19a) are by no means so common, but that is to be expected, as they are associated rather with tombs, and the Philistine material comes mainly from

---

[1] There are indeed shapes and decorations of non-Mycenaean origin (e.g. Egyptian and Cypriot, cf. *Dothan*, pp. 152 f.), but they are relatively uncommon. There is also plenty of plain Palestinian ware in addition to the Philistine pottery.

[2] Cf. Seiradaki, *BSA*, lv. 21, Fig. 14, bowl 1.

[3] Cf. Benson, *JNES*, xx. 73 ff.

[4] Cf. *Hesp.* viii. 368, Fig. 46, *o* (Athens); *BSA*, lv. 33, Fig. 23 (Karphi).

settlements. They vary somewhat in shape, but there is none of the rather squat or piriform types which are so familiar to LH. III B. Occasionally the disc of the stirrup has a knob on it (a feature of LH. III C), but there is no evidence of the airhole in the shoulder such as may be found in the latest phase of LH. III C.

Decoration is applied to the belly as well as to the shoulder, an innovation subsequent, on the whole, to LH. III B. On the belly are found birds in the pluming position, and vertical lines with flanking semicircles, as on the open vases. Other motives include multiple concentric semicircles, both standing and pendent, lines slanting simply or in alternate directions, and one example of the dog-tooth pattern and chevrons placed horizontally. On the shoulder, the characteristic motives are multiple concentric loops or semicircles (see Pl. 19a), the latter in one case dotted. These motives seem typical of the LH. III C series in the Aegean, and bring the whole of this pottery down within LH. III C; but it may be noted that there is no example of the elaborate triangles which are a feature of the end of this style.

The jugs with strainer spout (Pl. 19b) are not quite so common as the stirrup jars, though the decorative motives used are very much the same, to the extent that it is not always easy, from a sherd, to determine which type of vase is represented. If anything, decoration is more varied on the jugs.

These then are the main shapes and motives of Philistine pottery. It will be evident how uniform the style is in its decorative motives and its application of them. For the bowls, spirals, antithetic or adjacent, or (both for bowls and kraters) a panelled system with a limited repertory of motives which tends to reappear on the bellies of stirrup jars and the strainer-spouted jugs; for the shoulder decoration of the latter two shapes, concentric loops or semicircles. The pottery is also, furthermore, uniform from site to site, both in shape and in decoration.

From the available information it should be possible to suggest some area of origin, as LH. III C is so diverse. That it is not yet possible to do so with confidence is a sign of our continued relative ignorance of many areas. The Mainland of Greece does not, on the whole, seem a likely source. There are parallels both in contemporary Cretan and Dodecanesian pottery, but there is no trace in the Philistine style of the Cretan Fringed ware, for instance, nor of the octopus-type stirrup jar. As between the two areas mentioned, the Dodecanese is a more likely source than Crete, where the dissimilarities are far more marked; and one must not forget that there is as yet no published settlement material from the Dodecanese.

Perhaps the strongest case can be made for a Cypriot origin,[1] during the earlier period of LH. III C influence, before the arrival of the 'wavy-line' style, even on the scanty material so far illustrated. An attempt has indeed already been made to link Philistine pottery with that from Enkomi, mainly on the basis of the fragments of jugs with strainer spouts found on the latter site.[2] Coche de la Ferté placed these sherds in his 'Submycénien Inférieur' level, which is perhaps equivalent to Schaeffer's floor III or II. However, in the later definitive publication, Schaeffer explains that the stratification at this point was

---

[1] Cf. *Dothan*, p. 154.   [2] Coche de la Ferté, *Essai*, pp. 30 f.

not 'intacte'.¹ It is in any case clear now that the shape concerned is already known in Cyprus at the end of LC. II, and Schaeffer publishes a fine specimen from Floor V in Building 18.²

The best parallels with Philistine ware, however, are to be found on the only two sherds yet to be published from recent excavations in Nicosia.³ One of these sherds has dotted collateral semicircles, the rarity of which motive outside the Philistine area I have mentioned, and the other, from the shoulder of a closed vase (quite possibly a jug with strainer spout), is decorated in very much the same way as the jug from Tell Fara tomb 542 (one of the earliest of the tombs).⁴ One must not, of course, overstress this, but the coincidence is remarkable. As well as this, it is clear from illustrations of the Enkomi sherds that the antithetic spiral motive, sometimes with cross-hatched lozenges, was well known in Cyprus in early LH. III C. And finally, one of the closest parallels to the solitary example of a fish on Philistine pottery is on a bowl or krater from Cyprus (cf. p. 209, n. 8).

To summarize the conclusions so far available, it has been seen that the pottery discussed above was both geographically and chronologically characteristic of the Philistines as settled in South Palestine. The analysis of the salient features of this ware have made it clear that its chief inspiration derived from one of the local variations of early LH. III C pottery, that current in Cyprus providing, so far as is yet known, the closest parallels. To this it may be added that Furumark, who has made the most thorough analysis of Philistine pottery,⁵ has placed its earliest appearance some ten years after the beginning of his Myc. III C 1 *b* phase.⁶

A further characteristic of this ware is its remarkable and continuing uniformity. From this two deductions may be made. First, it is very probable that the influence of LH. III C pottery was felt at one point of time only, that of the creation of the ware; Philistine pottery was in no way affected by any of the later developments of LH. III C. The second deduction is the very attractive one of Benson,⁷ who has suggested that, excluding the time of decadence during the second half of the eleventh century, the style owed its being to one man, or to one workshop dominated by one man, with his sons carrying on the tradition.

There remains one final, and vital, problem. In view of the fact that the activities of the Philistines are firmly fixed within absolute chronological limits, can one demonstrate precisely or approximately when the Philistines started to use this pottery that became their characteristic ware? Did they adopt it before they settled in South Palestine, or was its appearance exactly contemporaneous with their foundations in this area, or was it taken over at some later date than that of the original settlement?

Reference to the section on Syria (pp. 207 f.) will show that it is impossible to suppose that the Philistines had taken over this type of pottery before their defeat by Ramesses III, and almost impossible that its adoption should be contemporary with their original foundations in South Palestine, some years after this defeat, even allowing for

---

¹ *E–A*, p. 307.
² Op. cit. p. 271, Fig. 91.
³ Karageorghis, *BCH*, lxxxiii. 354, Fig. 19.
⁴ *Beth-Pelet*, i. Pl. 23, 3.
⁵ *Chronology*, pp. 118 ff.
⁶ *OA*, iii. 260, and the table on p. 262.
⁷ *JNES*, xx. 82.

the survival of LH. III B pottery on Syrian sites after the LH. III C style had started to develop in the Aegean area.

The deductions from the pottery found on Syrian sites also lead to the conclusion that the Philistine ware cannot have been current in South Palestine before the settlement there of the Philistines. This conclusion is fully confirmed by the evidence from sites occupied by the Philistines. In no case does their characteristic pottery appear, in this area, in conjunction with LH. III B and Cypriot wares such as were current during the thirteenth century. This is particularly noticeable at Askalon,[1] where a destruction level separated the above wares from the Philistine material, and where, although it is conceivable that the destruction of the town was not the work of the Philistines and their fellow-raiders, the subsequent settlement must surely be that of the Philistines. Also, a useful *terminus* emerges from the situation at Tell Fara, where the earliest Philistine pottery, found on the floor of the cobbled courtyard of the 'Residency', is associated with a sherd bearing a cartouche with the figure of Set, most probably to be assigned to the reign of Seti II (1216–10),[2] and thus indicating that the Philistine ware was in any case hardly earlier than the reign of this Pharaoh, and more probably later than it.

It is also possible to make use of the internal evidence to show the likelihood that Philistine pottery was introduced at a date later than that of the original foundations. The arguments for this have been set out in Mrs. Dothan's article,[3] the evidence being based on the material from Beth Shan, a site to the north of the main Philistine area. Here, anthropoid clay coffins and other objects (pottery, scarabs, amulets, a forked spear butt) displaying Egyptian associations were found with objects of Aegean origin, including only a small quantity of Philistine pottery. Mrs. Dothan's conclusions are, first that the burials belonged 'to Philistine high-ranking mercenaries', and second that the 'almost complete absence' of Philistine pottery means that the Philistines were settled here as garrison troops immediately after their defeat and capture, before the appearance of their characteristic pottery.[4]

The argument is no doubt valid for Beth Shan, but not necessarily so for all other Philistine settlements, as what presumably happened was that Philistine pottery first appeared in one town only, and spread from there. Even so, as it is clear that the Philistines did not bring their pottery with them, there is no reason for supposing that the fact of their settling in South Palestine should lead to the immediate adoption of a Mycenaean type of pottery. Although they probably did pass through Mycenaean territory during the course of their travels, there is no proof that they were of Mycenaean stock.

It is then a reasonable conclusion, from both the external and the internal evidence, that Philistine pottery was introduced into South Palestine at a later date than that when the Philistines first settled there. But although this is an acceptable conclusion, it must be stressed that the interval between the original settlement and the introduction of Philistine pottery can have been only a very short one. All the evidence shows that Philistine pottery is so closely and fully connected with the life of the Philistine foundations that

---

[1] Garstang, *BBSA*, iii. 20 ff.; cf. Albright, *AASOR*, xii. 54.
[2] *Beth-Pelet*, ii. p. 30.
[3] *Dothan*, 154 ff.
[4] Op. cit. p. 157.

it must have been adopted, and spread over the whole area, in the very early years of occupation.

The chronological and historical implications of this matter will be discussed elsewhere (pp. 237 ff.). In my opinion, what may have happened is that a potter made his way to Philistine territory from Cyprus, perhaps as a result of the second period of destruction in that island (p. 200), not more than fifteen years after the Philistines established themselves, and that it was he who introduced a type of Mycenaean pottery which immediately became fashionable throughout Philistia.

CHAPTER IX

ITALY AND SICILY

I HAVE purposely omitted any detailed discussion of Mycenaean finds in these lands, both because they are of marginal value only to this work, and because they have been adequately and admirably published by Lord William Taylour.[1] The quantity of Late Helladic III pottery found is indeed remarkable. So far as LH. III C is concerned, no pottery of this style has yet been identified in Sicily, but it is considered possible that the local ware was influenced by LH. III C shapes.[2] There is, on the other hand, a little LH. III C pottery on the island of Lipari,[3] to the north of Sicily. On the whole, however, pottery of this style was concentrated in South Italy, on the coast of the Gulf of Taranto, and especially at Scoglio del Tonno,[4] where the large number of sherds found suggests the existence of a sizeable group of Mycenaeans on the site during the whole of LH. III. Further along the coast, to the south-east, the sites of Leporano[5] and Torre Castelluccia[6] have also produced LH. III C pottery, and it is certainly of interest that on these two sites only one vase (datable to LH. III B) earlier than LH. III C has been found.[7] Indeed, the majority of the sherds are assigned to the later phase of LH. III C.[8]

Generally speaking, Taylour provides evidence for contact between South Italy and Sicily and the Mycenaean Mainland and, more strongly, Rhodes and Cyprus, with the Rhodian links continuing into LH. III C, during which period there were also links with Kephallenia.[9]

The evidence proves that there is no difficulty in presuming normal traffic between Italy and Sicily and the Mycenaean world at least down to the end of LH. III B. Taylour suggests[10] that there may initially have been a murex industry at Taranto which attracted the Mycenaeans, and he continues:[11] 'A further possibility is that this ideally situated township served as an outlet for trade from the north of Italy. That it became so seems to be attested by the appearance of certain Terramara products in the Aegean, and the finding of a mould for making a winged axe of Terramara type at Mycenae is of particular importance. Relations between Taranto and the Terremare were certainly close. The land route along the coast from the Po valley is not too difficult but an alternative means of communication may have been via the Adriatic with stopping-points along the seaboard as far as Brindisi, the last lap of the journey being made overland. The finding of Mycenaean

---

[1] *Mycenaean Pottery in Italy and Adjacent Areas* (*MPI*). Cf. also Biancofiore, *Studi Salentini*, ii. 32 ff. and *Rivista dell' Istituto Nazionale di Archeologia e Storia dell' Arte*, vii. 5 ff.
[2] *MPI*, p. 74.
[3] Op. cit. pp. 41 ff.
[4] Op. cit. pp. 105 ff.
[5] Op. cit. pp. 139 f.
[6] Op. cit. pp. 144 ff.
[7] Op. cit. p. 144 and Pl. 15, 1.
[8] Op. cit. p. 185.
[9] Op. cit. pp. 184 f. Cf. pp. 128 ff. for Scoglio del Tonno.
[10] Op. cit. pp. 135, 185.
[11] Op. cit. pp. 185 f.

vases at San Cosimo, which lies roughly midway between Taranto and Brindisi, lends some weight to this theory. One of the stations on the sea-route may have been on the Gargano where a violin-bow fibula and another of the arched type were found.'

Further discussion of the objects of Italian and Sicilian origin which may have been introduced into the Mycenaean world will be found in another chapter (pp. 56 f., 69 f.), and this section will serve simply to show the familiarity of the Mycenaeans with the Central Mediterranean area.

CHAPTER X

SUMMARY AND HISTORICAL INFERENCES[1]

Introduction

IN this chapter I shall endeavour to give some idea of what may have happened during the concluding stages of the history of the Mycenaean world. The chapter will be divided into several sections. The first will indicate the general situation in LH. III B and the course of events leading up to and including the serious invasion or invasions on the Mainland which came at the end of LH. III B. The second, covering at least one generation and perhaps two, will explain the situation existing immediately after invasion. The third, of some two or three generations in length, will endeavour to analyse the circumstances of the final disappearance of the Mycenaean way of life in the respective areas of its world. The activities of the Land and Sea Raiders (defeated by Ramesses III in *c.* 1191), and the relevance of these activities to events in the Mycenaean world will form part of the fourth section, which will also contain a discussion on absolute chronology. A fifth section will be devoted to an analysis of what Mycenaean characteristics, whether of political system, of arts and crafts, of religious belief or of burial custom, were lost or survived, and of the general significance of these losses and survivals. The chapter will then end with some consideration of the consequences of setting alongside one another the picture given by the archaeological material and the contemporary written records, the picture provided by the distribution of dialects in later times, and the picture revealed by the oral tradition.

The conclusions suggested are based mainly on archaeological data, and a note of warning is advisable. Considering the Mycenaean world as a whole, there are many serious gaps in our knowledge; even in those areas which have been extensively excavated the full picture is not available, and only very rarely on a single site—as the work since 1950 at Mycenae has clearly shown. It follows that any attempt to interpret the whole archaeological material in a historical sense is liable to error. Error, furthermore, is not only possible in forming conclusions from incomplete evidence and in making inferences from what is known to what is not; it is equally possible in the interpretation of the material as such. So my conclusions are at best tentative, and some, as will appear, a good deal more tentative than others.

1. *c.1300 - c.1200*

Before dealing with the events which lead up to the end of Mycenaean civilization it is essential that a general picture should be gained of the Mycenaean world during the thirteenth century, or rather, during the early stages of LH. III B.

[1] This chapter is not fully annotated, as references for most of the statements will be found elsewhere in the book.

Geographically, this world covered the Peloponnese and the islands adjoining it to the west, Central Greece as far as the mountainous area to the north of Phocis, coastal Thessaly and at least some part of its central plain, the islands of the Central and South Aegean, and at least one settlement on the West coast of Asia Minor, at Miletus. There were some areas where occupation was apparently only slight, such as North-west Peloponnese and the islands to the west of the Peloponnese, but others were densely populated.

Politically, there is little doubt that the whole was divided into a number of kingdoms of varying size. The Homeric epic provides evidence of this, and it is likely that the tradition is correct here, as the tablets afford confirmatory evidence and the palaces—for such they must be—uncovered by excavation point to the same conclusion.

Were these kingdoms entirely independent? Were they united in some sort of loose federation, or did they simply form parts of one larger political unit, with their rulers owing allegiance to an overlord? I am firmly convinced that there was one ruler over the whole Mycenaean territory, with his capital at Mycenae, although the tablets are of no assistance one way or the other in this matter, and although the overlordship of Agamemnon clearly envisaged by Homer can perhaps be explained simply as a military leadership for the purpose of waging war against Troy. The burden of proof must therefore depend on other evidence, the archaeological material taken in conjunction with the fairly frequent mention by the Hittites, in the fourteenth and much of the thirteenth centuries, of the king of a land called Ahhiyawa, which I believe to represent the entire Mycenaean orbit.

This identification was first expounded in detail over twenty years ago by Schachermeyr,[1] but since then it has been the custom to locate the kingdom of Ahhiyawa either outside Mycenaean territory altogether, or in one part of it only. In recent years research has succeeded in placing this land either to the west or to the south of the centre of Hittite power, and has also shown that it did not lie in Asia Minor, as access to it lay, at least in part, by sea. It seems hardly possible to identify this kingdom with the island of Cyprus, as that was most probably the land known to the Hittites as Alasia, and the inference is inescapable that Ahhiyawa must be either the whole or some part of Mycenaean territory.[2]

For the latter solution two candidates have been suggested, Crete and Rhodes.[3] Everything we know of Crete during this time argues against the possibility of its being identified as Ahhiyawa. After the destruction of its great palaces Crete lapsed into relative obscurity, and was indeed probably dominated politically by Mycenae. In particular, for Crete to qualify as Ahhiyawa would entail her control over the area which lay between her and the coast of Asia Minor, especially the Dodecanese; and while she may well have controlled this district before the fourteenth century, her hold had been irrevocably broken by the beginning of the century. Crete may therefore be set aside.

---

[1] *Hethiter und Achäer.*

[2] See generally Gurney, *The Hittites*, pp. 52 ff.; Page, *History and the Homeric Iliad*, chap. 1; Garstang and Gurney, *The Geography of the Hittite Empire.*

[3] Crete: Gurney, op. cit. pp. 55 f.; Rhodes; Page, op. cit. pp. 8 ff., 15 ff.

A much stronger case can be made for Rhodes, and has indeed recently been so made by Page. His discussion is of great value, and his argument showing that a linguistic equation may be made between Ahhiyawa and the Homeric 'Αχαίοι is convincing. He uses the Tavagalavas Letter as his basic text, and here again the identification of Millawanda (or Milawata) with Miletus is entirely acceptable. However, he considers that this text proves that the land of Ahhiyawa must lie close to the coast of Asia Minor and especially to Miletus. The Mainland of Greece is too remote, and therefore we are left with Rhodes. This is the main point of his argument (though not the whole of it) and Huxley has subsequently shown that it is not firmly based, in fact that the wording of the Tavagalavas Letter does not necessarily require the king of Ahhiyawa normally to reside so close to Asia Minor.[1]

So far, the argument has confined itself mainly to geographical considerations, but Huxley also introduces, and very rightly, the factor of the cultural uniformity of the whole Mycenaean world.[2] There is no doubt that the introduction of such a factor is historically valid; it need not perhaps have such validity when taken by itself, but even so it is remarkable enough. This uniformity (in which Crete alone is excluded) has many facets, and may be said to cover almost every type of object or custom revealed by archaeology. Weapons, ornaments of dress, cult objects, manner of burial and type of tomb—all are much the same throughout; nor does settlement architecture vary greatly, so far as can be seen. In all these elements a general uniformity may be observed, but on the other hand there is no indication that any one district took the lead, though it is worth mentioning that the citadel and town of Mycenae present the most impressive remains so far brought to light.

There remains one further factor, however, and that is the most important one of pottery. This is not a matter of coarse ware, or of a number of uninspired, undecorated and unvarying domestic shapes, but of an elaborate and sophisticated style, capable of a great deal of variation, in which both potter and painter were artists as well as technicians. And here, excepting only for minor regional variations, the same uniformity is visible throughout the Mycenaean world. Furthermore, the LH. III B style, as well as its predecessor, LH. III A, was created in the Argolid, and diffused from there (cf. p. 4). In other words, in this matter the rest of the Mycenaean world followed the lead of the Argolid.

In view of this general uniformity of culture and custom I find it difficult to believe that the Mycenaean world was not united by extremely close ties; and the evidence of the pottery suggests that Mycenae was the acknowledged leader of this world. And from this it appears to me that the powerful kingdom of Ahhiyawa—and it was sufficiently powerful for the name of its king to be inserted alongside those of the kings of other great powers, even though the insertion was subsequently erased—is with much greater probability to be identified with the whole Mycenaean world, ruled by the one king at Mycenae, than with the island of Rhodes. It may be that the smaller kingdoms had much independence of action, but in foreign relations the king at Mycenae spoke for the whole.

I shall therefore assume in the discussion which follows that the kings of the smaller kingdoms were in some sense subject to the king who had his capital at Mycenae, and I shall speak of a Mycenaean empire.

[1] Huxley, *Achaeans and Hittites*, pp. 15 ff.   [2] Op. cit. pp. 25 ff.

It is clear that this Mycenaean empire was a flourishing one, and also that it had many connexions with areas outside it. Its pottery, for example, was widely distributed, especially over areas accessible by sea, such as Cyprus, Syria, and South Italy; on the other hand, its influence in the North Aegean was much less, and it hardly penetrated at all to territories held by the Hittite king. Prosperity then depended on the sea, not only for exports but for imports as well, for metals seem not yet to have been mined at all extensively in Greece and the Aegean. It is also clear, from what can be recovered from the tablets, that the social and economic structure of at least one kingdom was elaborate.[1]

The survival of such a structure in the Mycenaean world, as well as the continuance of prosperity, would depend in any case on the maintenance of internal peace and on the ability of the Mycenaeans to defend themselves against outside attack.

Internally, the only evidence of disturbance during the fourteenth and early thirteenth centuries is that which may be suggested from the destruction of the palace at Thebes, probably late in the fourteenth century;[2] apart from this, there is no hint of internal disruption.

Externally, the Mycenaean empire lay open to attack from the sea at almost every point, and by land either from peoples beyond its frontiers in North and North-west Greece, or from Asia Minor in the case of its possession or possessions on the western coast of that area.

Attack from the sea seems never to have been a peril of any consequence. No details are known of the existence of a Mycenaean fleet, or fleets, but on the other hand there was no other naval power at that time in the Mediterranean, so far as we can tell. The only kingdom capable of creating serious trouble was that of the Hittites, and this was not a sea power. But there was an eventual clash of interests between the Hittites and Mycenaeans on the West coast of Asia Minor. For most of the fourteenth century relations between these two powers were amicable, but signs of a change are visible in the Tavagalavas and Milawata letters—not precisely datable, but to be placed near the end of the fourteenth century or the beginning of the thirteenth.[3] It is very probable that the Hittite king gained control of Miletus for a while, but this he subsequently lost, as the fortification of the city, after the beginning of LH. III B and presumably within the thirteenth century, is very likely the work of the Mycenaeans, since the pottery continues to be purely Mycenaean.

Furthermore, after the middle of the thirteenth century there are signs of aggression on the part of the Mycenaeans, as the only known record of a king of Ahhiyawa present in person in Asia Minor belongs to this time.[4] The tablet is mutilated, but some sort of military operation is probably to be inferred, and the district of this operation is that of the river Seha, which recent research has placed in North-west Asia Minor.[5] Also, I believe that the war against Troy should be placed at about this time, because the destruction of Troy VII A occurs when LH. III B pottery is still current, and because such a war must have taken place some time before the destruction of Pylos (which I shall assume to be Nestor's

---

[1] Ventris and Chadwick, *Documents in Mycenaean Greek*, and many other publications.
[2] *AE*, 1909, pp. 57 ff.; *Chronology*, p. 52.
[3] Gurney, *The Hittites*, p. 51.
[4] Huxley, *Achaeans and Hittites*, pp. 7 f. (with references).
[5] Garstang and Gurney, *The Geography of the Hittite Empire*, pp. 96 f., 120 ff.

capital), at the end of LH. III B (cf. p. 94). The effects of this policy of aggression may have resulted in a serious weakening of the military power of the Mycenaean empire. The position soon after 1250 is that the Mycenaeans, though still in no apparent danger from the sea, nor consequently in danger of invasion from a Hittite empire which was itself soon to be swept away, were probably less capable than before of repelling any land attack on the main part of their empire, in Greece.

On the Mainland, the inhabitants were by no means unaware of the danger of attack, whether by land or sea. The important towns were often built in naturally defensible positions, and in certain areas, notably the Argolid, Attica, Boeotia, Phocis and Thessaly, were provided with fortifications. There was in fact no natural land frontier. The Peloponnese was the easiest area to defend, providing the isthmus was strongly held, but north of this, and especially north of Boeotia, the mountainous nature of the country made it impossible to prevent either a marauding attack or a major invasion. The Spercheios valley may have been but very sparsely occupied, and it seems to have been only in LH. III B that any significant advance was made inland in Thessaly. The liability to attack may indeed account for the nature of some of the fortifications north of the Peloponnese. At Eutresis in Boeotia and Krisa in Phocis the extent of the fortifying walls is disproportionately large for the size of the settlements. A similar phenomenon is perhaps observable in the defence walls of Petra, by Lake Boebeis, of Ktouri and of Arne, all in Thessaly (cf. p. 134). These fortifications may have constituted centres of refuge, both for man and beast, in case of attack from the mountains.

In the event, these precautions were quite inadequate, and the history of the latter part and the end of the LH. III B period—roughly the last quarter of the thirteenth century (see pp. 237 ff.)—can possibly be reconstructed as follows. The first sign of trouble is visible in an attack on Mycenae itself; it does not seem that the attackers penetrated within the citadel, but considerable damage was done to imposing buildings immediately adjoining the citadel. There is no proof that other sites suffered destruction at this time, nor do we know the cause of the attack. Steps were consequently taken at Mycenae to strengthen the fortifications, though no attempt was made to restore the buildings which had already been destroyed. At the isthmus of Corinth a wall of a defensive nature was built, though it is not known whether it was completed. The fortifications of the Acropolis at Athens were also strengthened. The shock must have been considerable, but was not catastrophic.

Fairly soon afterwards, however, at the end of LH. III B, a really serious invasion took place, the effects of which are visible in destruction of sites, in their desertion, and in a movement of population. Krisa in Phocis, Gla in Boeotia, Zygouries in Corinthia, Mycenae and Tiryns in the Argolid, the Menelaion site in Laconia, Pylos and Nichoria in Messenia, all suffered very serious damage, and of these sites only Mycenae seems subsequently to have been occupied in any strength. Besides this, many sites were abandoned without our knowing whether there was destruction as well—such were Eutresis in Boeotia, possibly some minor sites in West Attica, two important sites in the Argolid (Berbati and Prosymna) as well as some minor settlements, and probably a considerable number of sites in Laconia and the South-west Peloponnese, to judge from the provisional results of the surveys undertaken in those regions. As a result of this destruction and desertion there was a movement of population to less dangerous and, in some cases, originally less populous areas. Achaea in the North-west Peloponnese and the island of Kephallenia are examples of areas where a considerable increase in the Mycenaean population is to be observed. But the east coast of Attica now becomes more fashionable than previously, and it is fairly clear that a sizeable body of refugees made their way to Cyprus and to Tarsus in Cilicia. Of these movements we can speak with some confidence; other groups may have gone elsewhere.

The route followed by the invaders and their geographical origin obviously need careful attention, as well as the further effects of their destructiveness on the Mycenaean world, but it is necessary first to emphasize that the reconstruction given above is only a possible one (though I think it is the most likely). It must be realized that archaeology has not yet provided us with anything like the full picture, and that certain areas, for example Boeotia and Thessaly, need much fuller investigation. Also, we cannot even be sure of the relative course of events in the case of some of the disasters and desertions already mentioned. It cannot yet be proved that the destructions north of the Argolid were contemporary with the second and major disaster at Mycenae rather than with the first, which apparently affected its outer town only. Nor can we be sure that the abandonment of sites may not have followed the first attack rather than the full-scale invasion. What we can, I think, be reasonably sure of is that the destruction at Tiryns and Pylos was contemporaneous with the second disaster at Mycenae, and that the general dispersal followed on these, and did not take place earlier. This latter fact suggests strongly that other destructions and desertions also belong to this time, but there is no proof that they do. These reservations should then be borne in mind in what follows, though I shall work on the assumption that the reconstruction given is correct.

The direction and route of this major invasion may be considered in the light of the areas which were affected, and in the light of the direction taken by refugees from the regions which suffered disaster. Destruction and desertion of settlements are known in Phocis, Boeotia, Corinthia, the Argolid, Laconia and Messenia, along a line running roughly from north to south, with Attica apparently untouched, though the dispositions taken in Athens show that there was cause for serious alarm. Groups of refugees moved both westwards and eastwards from this line, into areas already within the Mycenaean sphere or strongly influenced by Mycenaean civilization. As to other areas, we can be fairly certain that at least the islands of the South Aegean remained secure, and there is no evidence of any catastrophe at Miletus. This is the general picture, and from it an attempt may be made to decide the probable or possible direction and origin of the attack.

First, is it possible that this was an attack organized from within Mycenaean territory? Was this an internal revolt on the part of one or more of the lesser kings against the ruler at Mycenae? All the areas affected by disaster would have to be excluded, and also Athens, whose inhabitants feared rather than originated the attack. This does not leave many regions with sufficient power to create such havoc. Crete is one such region, but the evidence shows that at this time the island was far from strong, and that it had indeed become progressively weaker since the end of the palaces; and it is likely that there had been an appreciable fall in population. Or else an attack might have originated in the Dodecanese, perhaps in conjunction with the larger islands of the Cyclades. In this case it is not easy to understand the extent of the devastation, nor why there is no subsequent trace of Dodecanesian domination over parts of the Mainland, nor how refugees from the Argolid could have dared to make their way to Cyprus and Tarsus, as they would almost inevitably have had to travel through an area hostile to them. Could the attack have come from Thessaly? This is a district which is still relatively unknown, though most important excavations are now in progress, but from what one can tell it seems likely that the Mycenaeans here may have been more concerned with keeping at bay threats to their own territory. It is then extremely unlikely that the attack can be explained as a rising of lesser kings against the central authority.

A further possibility is that the disasters were the result of a number of local revolts within the separate kingdoms, arising from a prolonged absence of Mycenaean leaders in Asia Minor and their misfortunes there. This would be supported by the remarks of Thucydides[1] on the state of affairs following on the Trojan War, combined with the account of the *Nostoi*. Such revolts would, however, mainly be centred on the royal residences, and it is hard to see why so many other sites were abandoned, and why there was so much depopulation.

It may therefore more reasonably be supposed that the attack was launched from some area outside the Mycenaean world. If the invasion was seaborne, it could have come from one of several quarters, but of these it does not seem possible that it came from the East Mediterranean, as it would have had to pass through the South Aegean, which remained unharmed. Also, it is hardly likely that it came from north-west of the Peloponnese, down the Adriatic or from South Italy or Sicily, since there would not then have been a movement of refugees to Kephallenia, in the precise direction from which the invaders had come.[2] We cannot exclude the possibility of a sea attack starting from somewhere south or south-west of the Peloponnese, but in this case, as in the case of any attack by sea, the invading fleet must have contained a force of fighting men sufficient to penetrate through the Peloponnese and into Boeotia and Phocis. And any attack from this direction must take into account the extent of open sea which had to be crossed. Finally, there is the possibility of an attack from the North-east Aegean. This does not at first sight seem a likely place of origin, but it must be remembered that there may have been considerable disturbance around this part of the world at about this time, and account must also be taken of the area from which the maritime section of the Land and Sea Raiders started, as the details given by the Egyptian scribe suggest some sort of activity in the Aegean area close in time to that of the invasion of the Mycenaean centres. I shall discuss the activities of these raiders separately (pp. 237 ff.), and simply stress two points here: once again, the fact that any seaborne attack must have been made in very great strength to do the damage it did, and the difficulty of explaining why the islands of the South Aegean, and

---

[1] Th. i. 12.

[2] It may be objected that the Pylos tablets are witness to the expectation of an attack by sea, and to measures taken to counter this attack (*Documents*, p. 138; Palmer, *Minos*, iv. 122). I believe, however, that Page is rightly sceptical of such an interpretation being able to be placed on the tablets concerned (*History and the Homeric Iliad*, pp. 193 ff.).

especially the Dodecanese, remained unharmed. On the whole, an invasion involving a long sea journey is not easily to be accepted.

It is more natural to suppose that the invaders came overland, and in this case the logical route is one which would bring them down through Phocis and Boeotia, across the isthmus of Corinth, into the Argolid, and then on to Laconia and Messenia. The question of their ultimate origin remains archaeologically unanswered; they could well have come from somewhere in North-west Greece or from north of there—though a Macedonian origin is not very likely. Another question to which no certain answer can yet be given is whether a group of these invaders penetrated into Thessaly; on the whole, it seems that they did not, or at least they did not reach the main Mycenaean strongholds at this time.

The hypothesis of a land invasion has two merits. The route followed would be more suitable to an invasion of this type, and it would explain why the islands were left untouched. It also, however, raises the problem of the invaders' eventual settlement, a problem not so necessary of solution in the case of invasion by sea. They might of course have occupied all the areas through which they passed, but there are good reasons for rejecting this idea, as will be seen later. May they not however have settled in the terminal area of the route they took, namely in Laconia and Messenia? The answer to this may be dealt with in two parts. First, it must be stressed that there is no single object or custom which can be associated with the invaders in any region passed through by them. Objects of non-Mycenaean origin do make their appearance at about this time (cf. pp. 69 f.) but they are invariably found in Mycenaean contexts. One cannot, however, safely rely on a negative argument of this type. Against it, it could be argued that the culture of the invaders was probably primitive, and anyway far inferior to that of the Mycenaeans; their artefacts may for the most part have been of perishable materials, such as wood and leather, and thus no trace would be left of them.

The second part of the answer is based on the picture of settlement now available for Laconia and Messenia (cf. pp. 90, 96 f.). In both areas there is evidence of considerable depopulation. In Laconia there is one notable exception, the sanctuary of Amyklai which clearly continued in existence, retained its Mycenaean characteristics and kept in touch at least with the Argolid. This matter itself would need explanation if we were to suppose that the invaders settled in Laconia. More important, however, is the fact that in the great majority of cases archaeological excavation or survey shows that the abandonment of sites both in Laconia and in Messenia was an absolute one. That is to say, there was no further occupation of the sites by anyone—at least not till considerably later. This is not a matter of a few sites only; the number that has now been identified is very considerable. It may be argued that this is also negative evidence, but it is of a very different type from that mentioned above. Not only have we no evidence of any alien objects, we have no evidence of any settlement at all. The natural and logical answer is that the invaders did not settle in any of the areas which they overran, but departed. Ancient history provides similar cases.

Such then is the picture which may be developed purely from the archaeological evidence at present available, for the magnitude of the invasion, for its origin and course, for the destruction it wrought, for the dispersal of the Mycenaeans from the areas that had suffered, and for the probable eventual departure of the invaders. But more than one interpretation is possible; the invasion may not have been a matter of a single great sweep from north to south; more than one group of invaders may have been involved at different times and in different places, and in any case the events may have covered a number of years. For the moment, however, we may leave these archaeologically rather elusive invaders, and consider the further history of the surviving Mycenaeans.

2. *c.1200 - c.1150 or Later*

We have seen one major effect on the areas overrun by invasion, in the depopulation and in the removal of many of the survivors to other areas. Apart from this, the effect on the political cohesion of the Mycenaean world was disastrous. Assuming that there was a central government for the whole empire, and that this was located at Mycenae, such a government must have been shattered. Even if we do not assume this, it is clear that the strength of the Mycenaeans was concentrated on the Mainland, rather than in the islands, precisely in those areas where there had been devastation. Even if, as is probable, the invaders did not occupy Laconia and Messenia, these previously flourishing districts were now almost denuded of their inhabitants. The blow was equally serious, whether one thinks in terms of a single state or of a number of independent yet interconnected kingdoms. On the Mainland south of Phocis there was indeed to be no real recovery, and hence the situation of the islands in the Central and South Aegean and of Thessaly would be correspondingly weakened.

In some respects, we can still speak of objects and customs as characteristic of the whole surviving Mycenaean world. The gaudy dress ornaments remained the same. The little terracotta 'goddess' and animal figurines are still found everywhere, and the uniformity in burial customs was unchanged. These features and customs were, however, common to the whole area, and not liable to stylistic change or variation in the same way as the pottery. And it is precisely from the pottery that we get clear confirmation of the effect of the invasion on the unity of the Mycenaean world. The Argive-inspired and diffused LH. III B ware degenerated and gradually disappeared, not only in the Argolid itself but in other districts, and was replaced by that multiplicity of regional ceramic variations which together comprise what is known as the LH. III C style. Ceramic dependence on one area was a thing of the past.

It is not possible clearly to understand the situation immediately following the invasion except by considering separately each of the main areas which constituted the Mycenaean world. So far as concerns the lands that had lain in the path of destruction, it will already be clear that not much more information is to be expected from Laconia and Messenia. A complete lack of evidence prevents us from saying anything about the district of Arcadia. With regard to the Argolid, however, the first point to be made is that this district was not occupied by the invaders; there is no doubt that the Mycenaean forces were defeated, but the victors did not stay to reap the fruits of their victory. The proof of this is that on such sites as still survived—including Mycenae—there is no change from the Mycenaean way of life, and that clear links were maintained with other parts of the Mycenaean world which had not been affected by disaster. Next, it is evident that only a shadow of the former greatness remained. There was little or no attempt to re-occupy or rebuild the sites that had been destroyed or abandoned, nor do we know of any occupation of new sites, though it may be that the port of Asine became relatively more important than it had been in LH. III B—this itself is significant, as the site lies well away from the passage of a land invader, and affords an easy means of escape, in case of further trouble, to the secure islands of the Aegean. The capital of the district was still Mycenae, however, and from the existence of the Granary it must have been considered worth defending—it is of course a site of great natural strength. Whatever may have happened to the previous ruling dynasty, there is extremely interesting evidence showing that attempts were made to keep up the external appearance of power, as there seems little doubt that the most brilliant manifestation of LH. III C pottery, the elaborate and delicate Close Style, originated in this city—or, if not, at least somewhere in the Argolid—and found its way thence to other parts of the Mycenaean world and even to Laconia. It may be that the rulers who survived, or those who took over, still had dreams of greatness—for which they were later to suffer. In fact, in spite of the flight from the district, there was some attempt at recovery, and it may be that the population felt that those who had fled to Achaea would support them in case of renewed danger.

There is not much evidence available from the other districts which had been overrun, but it is nevertheless sufficient to suggest that they also were inhabited by Mycenaeans and not by invaders. Korakou in Corinthia had in any case escaped destruction, and survived into LH. III C, and a few LH. III C sherds were found at Perachora. The contents of the chamber tombs of Thebes in Boeotia indicate survival, and so does the material from Delphi and perhaps one or two other sites in Phocis.

Even so, there is as yet no indication, in Central Greece north of the Peloponnese, of the signs of attempted recovery visible in the Argolid, and the general apprehension in this part of the Mainland is well reflected in the situation in Attica, in whose western plain there seems to have been a desertion of sites, only leaving the inhabitants of Athens who, though access to the fountain from the top of the Acropolis was no longer felt necessary, apparently decided it was wiser still to occupy the Acropolis, while on the other hand the settlements on the eastern coast flourished, secure in their links with the Aegean.

As stated above, the invasion resulted in certain group movements from the affected areas. There were two such movements westwards, to Kephallenia (and probably Ithaca), and to Achaea, of which Achaea was within the Mycenaean sphere, but the islands perhaps only on the fringe. It is reasonable to suppose that the South-west Peloponnese was the homeland of those who went to the islands, though some may also have gone to Achaea, to which region many may have fled from the Argolid. Both regions were obviously chosen as affording security, and it is clear that in this the refugees were not deceived, as the cemeteries indicate undisturbed habitation probably for at least two or three generations. On Kephallenia, however, the presence of a fair amount of hand-made pottery in the tombs suggests that the Mycenaeans joined forces with local inhabitants of non-Mycenaean origin; even so, the Mycenaean culture was that which dominated. There are indications, not unnaturally, of links with areas to the north, along and up the Adriatic. Communication seems also to have been maintained for some time with other Mycenaean lands, but it may not have been frequent, and there is no evidence of contact with the Aegean.

In Achaea there is no such fusion with a non-Mycenaean population as in Kephallenia, and there is no evidence of contacts with areas outside the Mycenaean world to the north and west. The Mycenaean character of the culture was preserved untainted, and contacts were certainly maintained for a while with the Argolid, though there is again no sign of any communication with the Aegean. The known sites are clustered on and around the Panachaic mountain, with a bias towards the coastal area to the west of this mountain, and nothing yet found in the coastal area to the north. This would suggest the absence of any contact with Mycenaean areas north of the Corinthian Gulf, but such was evidently not the case, as LH. III C pottery of the characteristic Achaean type has been found at Itea, is probably to be recognized in a tomb at Delphi and, significantly, has appeared in a tomb at Pteleon in the southernmost coastal area of Thessaly, associated with a vase which is probably a late survivor of LH. III B. This evidence is of great interest, as it seems to show that at a time not long after the invasion free movement was possible from Achaea across the northern part of Central Greece to South Thessaly. For the time being, there was probably peace in this part of the world, even though it may have been an uneasy peace.

The mention of South Thessaly leads on naturally to a discussion of the situation of the Mycenaeans in Thessaly generally; unfortunately, it is by no means clear what was happening here. We know that during LH. III B Mycenaean civilization had gained a firm hold over the central plain, and there is no doubt that it spread from the coast, and especially from Iolkos. For Iolkos itself, we must depend on the provisional conclusions of the excavator, namely that the destruction of the palace occurred during LH. III C; this would mean that in any case Iolkos fell later than the great centres further south. The course of events inland, however, is not yet ascertainable, though while Iolkos stood, Mycenaean control over this district was perhaps maintained (see below, pp. 234 f.).

The regions bordering the north Aegean lay outside the Mycenaean world, and as such may be left aside. It is, however, of importance to note that the two districts of which we have some knowledge, Macedonia and Troy, remained in touch with the Mycenaeans during at least the early part of LH. III C. The area with which contact was maintained was probably chiefly that of the Central Aegean which, as will be seen below, was not affected by the disasters on the Mainland.

This area comprised the islands of the Central and South Aegean, including the settlement of Miletus on the coast of Asia Minor, but excluding Crete. The whole of this region was left untouched by the invasion which had such disastrous effects on central and south Mainland Greece. We have nothing like the whole picture, and some of the islands are still virtually archaeologically unknown in Mycenaean times, but the evidence we have is sufficient, in my opinion, to prove the above point. First, there are four excavated settlements, widely separated, in this area—Phylakopi on Melos, Grotta on Naxos, Serraglio on Kos, and the town of Miletus. In all of these, habitation continues without any sign of violent interruption from LH. III B well down into LH. III C. And second, although the island of Rhodes has as yet produced no settlement of this period (or of LH. III B), the great cemeteries of Ialysos show burials equally continuing from LH. III B into LH. III C.

Escape from disaster is then reasonably clear. The evidence also suggests, however, that parts of this area (Melos is now excluded) maintained sufficiently close interconnexions for it to be considered in some sense a unity. This conclusion is based mainly on the pottery. As I have shown above, the LH. III C ceramic period is sharply distinguished from the preceding LH. III B by its regional diversity. Now, in the Central and South Aegean, there is a clear relationship between LH. III C vases as found in the Dodecanese and at Miletus, and those found in the settlement and tombs of Naxos; and furthermore, the pottery of Perati, on the East coast of Attica, is also closely related to that of the islands, though here connexions are also to be found with the Argolid. The evidence is not, however, entirely confined to the pottery, for a curious innovation in burial customs is now found, that of a single cremation associated with inhumations in a chamber tomb, and so far it is known on three sites only, Ialysos on Rhodes, Langada on Kos, and Perati.[1]

So we can envisage close connexions as existing from East Attica across to the Dodecanese, and including Miletus. Whether this is to be interpreted as a political unity is another matter, but at least there was a community of interests.

The objects other than pottery deposited in the tombs of Rhodes, Kos, Naxos and Perati supply further information. They include a fair amount of gold, and semi-precious stones are commonly used for beads, and it is possible to conclude that the standard of living was fairly high, similar to the state of affairs in LH. III B, but in apparent contrast to that of other areas during this time, the early part of LH. III C. It meant also that the Central and South Aegean remained in contact with outside areas which produced gold and semi-precious stones, and one such area was certainly the East Mediterranean, as objects of Egyptian origin were found—little figurines, scarabs, faience—and also cylinder seals, which probably derive from Syria or its neighbourhood. In general, the sea remained a free highway to those who lived on the shores of the Central and South Aegean, as may be seen from the very wide distribution of the characteristic stirrup jars with octopus decoration; these travel northwards as far as Pitane in Aeolis, eastwards as far as Tarsus in Cilicia (but there are no others yet known in the East Mediterranean), and westwards to Scoglio del Tonno in South Italy. On the Mainland of Greece, however, they are less conspicuous, and are more or less confined to such sites which have easy access to the Aegean. Through them, also, close connexions with Crete are established, as they originate from this island (see p. 7).

Finally, it may be noted that this miniature Mycenaean *koine* was, at some time during LH. III C (though possibly not during the earliest stages), territorially enlarged, to judge from the appearance of a settlement at Emborio on the south coast of Chios, an island which so far has produced no evidence of being inhabited by Mycenaeans earlier than this. Furthermore, this settlement justifies us in assuming that the island of Samos, to the south of Chios, must have lain within the Mycenaean orbit, even though scarcely any Mycenaean pottery has yet been found there.

---

[1] The separate cremation reported from Kamini on Naxos might constitute an intermediate link (*Ergon* for 1960, p. 189).

Taking all the evidence together, it is clear that the situation in the Central and South Aegean contrasts markedly with that in the kingdoms of the Mainland. The inhabitants of the islands, of Miletus in Asia Minor, and indeed of coastal sites on the Greek Mainland remote from the route of invasion, such as Perati, felt no apprehension for the future. The sea protected them, and they pursued their way in security and prosperity; closely united, they probably constituted one of the last strongholds of the Mycenaean way of life.

The island of Crete, though an integral unit of the South Aegean, presents a different picture, owing to the fact that, although it had for some time perhaps formed part of the Mycenaean empire, it was never of it in the same way as the other districts. It had seen the birth and rise of the Minoan civilization which dominated the Aegean scene, overshadowing Mycenae. At the beginning of the fourteenth century some disaster had overwhelmed its palaces, and its maritime power (and possessions?) were lost to Mycenae. The population of the main centres was severely reduced in numbers, and the island lapsed into mediocrity. Even so, the Minoan culture and way of life remained firmly implanted in the survivors, and if the Mycenaeans did try to impose their own culture on the island (and we do not know that they did so to any serious extent) they were unsuccessful. The fourteenth and thirteenth centuries were a period of stagnation for Crete. It appears to have been an island without a history, in the sense either of recovery or of further disaster. Contact was maintained with other areas of the Aegean, and links were probably closer with Melos and the Dodecanese than elsewhere, but no greatness remained.

Crete seems no more to have been affected than the other islands at the time of the invasion on the Mainland; one settlement in southern Crete, that of Kefala, was destroyed perhaps at about this time, but this is presumably coincidental, nor can any reason be given for the destruction. There is very little that we yet know of what happened on the island in the years following on the Mainland invasion. It is clear that links were maintained with the Dodecanese, as the Octopus Style stirrup jar was adopted by the Dodecanesians from Crete, and the two series ran parallel for a while. It is also of interest that the Argive Close Style contained elements traceable to Crete. The artistic life of the Minoans was by no means defunct, as indeed appears in the introduction of the Fringed Style, the characteristic ware of early Late Minoan III C, but this does not tell us much about the general situation. It is a period which has not received the full attention of archaeologists, and further investigation may amplify the picture considerably.

One further area deserves brief discussion, and that is Cyprus. The island had already come very strongly under Mycenaean ceramic influence during LH. III A and LH. III B, and some Mycenaeans must have taken up their residence there, though it does not appear that there was any sort of colonization of the island. Then, at or near the end of LH. III B, certain of the towns of Cyprus suffered destruction, notably Enkomi, which may have been the capital, and Sinda; and when these towns were rebuilt, the pottery was a mixture of local Cypriot and early LH. III C of Argive type. This LH. III C ware is found in sufficient quantities to suggest the arrival of a body of migrants, and it is reasonable to suppose that they were refugees from the disastrous attack on the Argolid. Whether they were in fact responsible for the destruction in Cyprus is not provable (see p. 238 for a discussion of such a possibility), but they may have organized the rebuilding at

Enkomi, as the fine ashlar construction is reminiscent of earlier work at Mycenae. Since much of the fine metal and ivory work of this period in Cyprus is probably of Mycenaean craftsmanship, it appears that the migrants were remarkable for their quality—to the detriment of their area of origin.

This seems on the whole to have been a time of prosperity for Cyprus, but it was short-lived, as a second and even more violent wave of destruction engulfed the island, resulting in serious depopulation; a number of settlements were not subsequently re-occupied, and Enkomi itself was partially deserted. The subsequent events, which involve a further group of immigrants from the Aegean, I will discuss below (p. 236), but two possible results of the disaster may be stressed. First, there may have been a temporary cessation of communication with the Aegean, and second, the Mycenaean community which settled, at the time of transition from LH. III B to C, in the ruins of Tarsus in Cilicia, may have been affected by this disaster, as the site lapses into obscurity.

To sum up, the salient point is the profound disruption which the invasion caused in the Mainland kingdoms of the Mycenaean world. It is visible not only in the destruction of great centres such as Mycenae and Tiryns and Pylos, but even more in the flight in considerable numbers from the affected areas, and even from those which were only threatened. It takes a very great catastrophe for such a flight to occur. Even though the invaders probably did not occupy the devastated territories, and even though there are signs of some recovery in the Argolid, the central power of Mycenae was broken, and the lesser kingdoms of the Mainland were so weakened that they were in no condition to resist any further attack. On the other hand, the Mycenaeans retained their command over the sea in the Central and South Aegean, a fact confirmed by the continued prosperity and security of those who inhabited this area.

3. *c.1150 or Later - c.1075/1050*

The period of recovery which I have discussed may be taken as reaching to the time of the final destruction at Mycenae, after which Mycenaean civilization enters on its final stage. This is an arbitrary date, but I have chosen it both because this final disaster at the centre of the Mycenaean world symbolizes the end of any hope of real recovery, and also because the course of events in the Argolid is clearer than in most other districts.

In this disaster the Granary at Mycenae was destroyed by fire, and no attempt was made to rebuild it. We do not know what other parts of the citadel suffered, but then we do not know much about what other parts were still occupied. We do know, however, that the town was not entirely deserted, the survivors using that type of LH. III C pottery, with very simple decoration, known as the Granary Class, which had in fact already appeared before the destruction.

There is no known trace of destruction elsewhere in the Argolid at this time, and the evidence of such sites as Argos and Asine shows that the inhabitants continued the Mycenaean way of life for a while. There is no sign of any intrusive element, and indeed the cause of the disaster at Mycenae has not been established.

It is clear enough that there could be no recovery in the Argolid after this, and there may have been a further flight from this district, as pottery of the Granary Class, closely resembling that of the Argolid at this time, appeared in Cyprus at some time after the violent second disaster there, and profoundly affected the subsequent ceramic development of that island (see pp. 23 f., 202 ff.).

The apparently undisturbed survival of the Mycenaeans in the Argolid perhaps lasted nearly three generations, according to evidence discussed below (p. 241), and the visible signs of the end of their civilization are the abandonment of the system of family burial in chamber tombs, this being replaced by single or double burial in cist tombs, whose pottery almost invariably shows the influence of the Attic Protogeometric style, the disappearance of typically Mycenaean ornaments of dress and of the equally typical 'goddess' figurine, and perhaps the removal to new sites (though closely adjacent to the previous ones). We seem here to be faced with the arrival of people of non-Mycenaean origin, though there is no need to suppose that the existing population was annihilated; it is more likely that the newcomers simply moved peacefully into a depressed and depopulated area. They became the dominant element, but did not expel the existing inhabitants, whose presence is still probably to be seen in the continuation of the local ceramic tradition alongside the Protogeometric.

If, as I believe, newcomers were responsible for the disappearance of Mycenaean culture in the Argolid, the question of their geographical origin needs discussion. In fact, an earlier movement of a similar kind is attested in West Attica, where two large cist tomb cemeteries have been found, the one on Salamis, the other in the Athenian Kerameikos. It has been reckoned that these cemeteries represent a period of use of somewhere under two generations, until the time when the Protogeometric style was developed, and cremation replaced inhumation as the universal custom for adults. As Protogeometric pottery developed in this area from the pottery which preceded it, and from here influenced the Argolid (and not the other way round), the cist tombs of West Attica must be earlier than those of the Argolid. The pottery associated with these earlier cist tombs is in fact Mycenaean in character and, as in the Argolid, presumably represents the surviving population; it is a debased version of the Granary Class of LH. III C, and as such has been called sub-Mycenaean and considered to be chronologically later than any Mycenaean material in the Argolid. This inference is, however, not a necessary one, as I have shown (pp. 17 ff.), and it is very probable that newcomers arrived in West Attica soon after the final destruction at Mycenae (hardly earlier, as then there might well be difficulty in explaining the pottery, since the Granary Class itself seems to be an Argive creation of a time not long before the Granary's destruction). So we have an earlier stage in the movement of the newcomers, and they will no doubt have found West Attica to be in the same depopulated condition as the Argolid, as earlier evidence suggests (pp. 112 ff.).

The path of the newcomers before their arrival in West Attica is not yet to be traced with any certainty, though I think it is likely that they came down overland from the North-west. There are indications, for example (though based on rather poor evidence), that one or two cist tombs of Thebes in Boeotia belonged to the same period as the Salamis and Kerameikos cemeteries. On the other hand, the discovery of cist tombs at Kalbaki, near Iannina in North-west Greece, is of great interest, as although the grave goods show that those buried were not Mycenaeans, one of the objects, a short sword, has been identified as of Mycenaean origin, datable to late LH. III B. This area could be the original home of the newcomers, but additional evidence is strongly to be desired.

If we assume that these people moved slowly down overland from North-west Greece, through Phocis and Boeotia—and it will be clear that the existing inhabitants of these districts were in no condition to resist their infiltration or passage—then we should conclude that Mycenaean culture disappeared in these areas even before it did in West Attica, though perhaps not long before. On the other hand, if the assumption is wrong, then I can suggest no answer to the problem, as the evidence available from Phocis and Boeotia (and Locris, for that matter), is quite insufficient to sustain any other explanation.

A possible explanation has then been given of what happened in Central Greece and in the Argolid. In Corinthia, though again there is very little material on which to work, the situation appears to be the same as in the Argolid, and these two areas should very likely be treated together.

It will be noted that I have so far spoken only of West Attica—deliberately so, for circumstances were different on the East coast, whose inhabitants belonged to the restricted but prosperous Mycenaean region of the Central and South Aegean. The evidence for East Attica comes almost solely from the cemetery of Perati, but the tombs are numerous enough for the site to be regarded as typical of the area. Here, although there are a few tombs of unusual type, it seems clear that the chamber tomb predominated until the time when the cemetery fell into disuse; but it is also clear, from a comparison between the objects found in these tombs and those found in the sub-Mycenaean cemeteries of Salamis and the Kerameikos, that at least the later tombs of Perati were contemporary with some of those of the newcomers to West Attica. Hence the newcomers did not spread to the East coast, and Mycenaeans may have continued their way of life at Perati as long as they did in the Argolid. On the other hand, the date of the desertion of the site cannot be later than that of the changes in the Argolid, as there is no trace of Protogeometric pottery, which was diffused fairly widely from Athens—notably overseas to Asia Minor (cf. pp. 162 f., 269)—and therefore unlikely not to have influenced a district so close to Athens itself.

The situation in Naxos was probably very similar to that of Perati. It is again likely, from certain of their contents, that the chamber tombs, Mycenaean both in type and in funeral gifts, were still used after the inauguration of the cist tomb series in West Attica. We have also, however, slight evidence of what happened after the chamber tombs were abandoned. The subsequent cemetery, the earliest burials of which may have been in cist tombs (see p. 151) has produced a vase which is sub-Mycenaean in style (Pl. 15c), and not Protogeometric, and so the change probably took place at the time of transition between these two styles. The finds from the adjacent settlement are not yet fully published, but it does seem likely that the constructions built over, but on a different axis from, the Mycenaean town began their life at this same time of transition. The interval in time is, I think, extremely small, and there are no signs of destruction, and it is probable that we have here the same picture, as in the Argolid, of relatively peaceful penetration. It is reasonable to suppose that Mycenaean civilization persisted in East Attica and in Naxos (and no doubt in the intervening island area) as long as it did in the Argolid.

In fact, to judge from the previous immunity of the Central and South Aegean, there seems no reason why the Mycenaean way of life should not have survived much longer than on the Mainland. A change in East Attica is understandable, because it is part of the Mainland, but a change in Naxos is a different matter, and may be related to events in that part of the Aegean to the east of it, for this latter area was overtaken by a catastrophe which seems in no way connected with events on the Mainland.

The area affected comprises the eastern islands, from Chios to the Dodecanese, and the settlement of Miletus. Our evidence is based on incomplete knowledge, but nevertheless permits possible conclusions. Two settlements are known to have been destroyed, Emborio on Chios at a very late stage of LH. III C, and Miletus. At Emborio there was no re-occupation for centuries, but at Miletus the pottery of the subsequent settlers is very similar to that of Athens at the time of transition from sub-Mycenaean to Protogeometric, thereby establishing a *terminus* for the destruction, though not allowing us to conclude that this destruction was the work of the new settlers.

There is only one other settlement known in this area, that of Serraglio on Kos, and here there is no evidence of destruction, and it is not certain when the site was abandoned, though desertion must have occurred before it was used as a cist tomb cemetery of advanced Protogeometric and early to middle Geometric times. There were, however, two Mycenaean cemeteries nearby, and in them there is no trace of other than chamber tomb burial or Mycenaean objects. Their abandonment must have marked the end of Mycenaean civilization on this island, but there is no means yet of judging when this occurred, in relation say to Naxos or the Argolid, as the pottery has not yet been fully recorded.

Fuller information is available from the cemeteries of Rhodes, and there is a similar desertion, to be dated well within the second half of LH. III C. Even with this information it is not possible to suggest more precisely when, in relation to areas to the west, the desertion took place, though it could have come slightly before the cemeteries of Naxos and Perati fell into disuse, since only one iron object (a bracelet) was found in the Rhodian tombs, while this metal, introduced from the East Mediterranean, was already being used for knives and daggers at the former sites. This evidence is of course suggestive only, and by no means conclusive.

Whatever the precise dates of these destructions and desertions in the islands (and they may not all be contemporaneous), it is most likely that they occurred before the arrival of the new settlers at Miletus. So in this part of the Aegean Mycenaean civilization collapsed no later than it did in the Argolid or on Naxos or at Perati, and the circumstances of its collapse may have been more violent than in those areas. There is unfortunately no explanation available to account for these happenings, though one need not rule out the possibility that those who came, most probably from Attica, to settle at Miletus, were in part responsible.

Back on the Mainland, the situation in the Peloponnese elsewhere than in the Argolid and Corinthia is either unknown or obscure. There is virtually no material from Arcadia, and this area must be left out of account. In Laconia and Messenia it is certain that invasion had been followed by wholesale depopulation (Mycenaean survivors being recognizable only at Amyklai and on one or two other sites), and probable that the invaders did not stay to occupy these territories. The land will have lain fallow for a considerable time. Elis as well seems to have been virtually deserted. It is only in Achaea that we find a Mycenaean, probably refugee, nucleus persisting during LH. III C, but then disappearing, without archaeological trace, probably towards the end of this period —in spite of certain interesting details of similarity between their vases and those of the Attic Protogeometric style, no more precise date can be given.

It appears, then, that by the end of LH. III C the whole of Western Peloponnese and Laconia was only extremely thinly populated. What happened subsequently must remain a matter of hypothesis, but recent discoveries may point the way. In the north of Achaea, at Derveni, a pithos burial was found with pottery of the transitional period from Protogeometric to Geometric, in part closely related to that of Ithaca; near Chalandritsa, in South Achaea, cist tombs, covered by a tumulus, and one of which had apsidal ends, were found, containing Geometric pottery; slab-covered single graves containing Protogeometric pottery have been discovered at Ancient Elis; at Nichoria in East Messenia, cist tombs with apsidal ends, and pithoi, were associated with Protogeometric pottery; at Amyklai in Laconia the earliest post-Mycenaean pottery, called Protogeometric but apparently unrelated to the Attic style, shows certain similarities with that of Ithaca. The one Protogeometric vase illustrated from Nichoria is unrevealing—though not Attic.

It is too early to be definite, but it may be that we have here, presumably in the Protogeometric period, evidence for the earliest re-occupation of Laconia, Messenia and Elis after the disaster at the end of LH. III B, and the successors to the LH. III C inhabitants of Achaea. The cist tombs suggest intrusion from the north. As to the pottery, there might conceivably be a connexion with the LH. III C material of Kephallenia and Ithaca, for although the cemeteries of Kephallenia, which contained a mixture of Mycenaeans and native inhabitants, were abandoned before the Protogeometric period, the pottery shows that there was continuity in Ithaca. The slenderness of this argument must be stressed, but it has seemed worth while setting out the evidence as now available.

It has already been stated in the preceding section that the situation in Thessaly is somewhat obscure. The main evidence is that of Iolkos. Here, the palace was destroyed in LH. III C, but not the adjoining settlement, though it is not unlikely that it came to an end at about the time of the destruction of the palace. Above the Mycenaean settlement there arose a new one, whose architecture and pottery show strong links with its predecessor, and it is therefore considered that the interval between the two settlements cannot have been much more than a generation. The new settlement is, however, called Protogeometric. The problems which this raises have been discussed elsewhere (pp. 135 ff.) and will only be resolved in the light of fuller knowledge. One thing is certain, that on this site Mycenaean features survived strongly into later times.

Whether or not the destruction of the palace is to be attributed to some internal disturbance, there are clear signs of the intrusion of new people into Thessaly generally, at about this time. A group made its way down into North Thessaly from Macedonia, people who followed, or took over, the Mycenaean practice of multiple burial in tholos tombs, but who used hand-made pottery until the influence of the Protogeometric style made itself felt. It seems unlikely that these people were concerned in the disaster of Iolkos, their time of arrival being probably after rather than before it. A further group of newcomers (unless it be the same as that mentioned above, which is improbable) is to be recognized in the appearance of burial in cist tombs on certain Thessalian sites. Neither the progress of this infiltration, nor the place and date of its origin, is yet recoverable, but the general process of diffusion of cist tombs suggests an origin in the North-west of Greece, and such evidence as we have from Thessaly may indicate a time, in the inland area, when Mycenaean culture was still extant. It is in any case probable that Mycenaean control over Thessaly was proportionately less in relation to the distance from the coast and the stronghold of Iolkos, so inasmuch as cist tombs were associated with Mycenaean pottery, as they appear to have been at Agrilia (cf. p. 132), well in the interior, and were not so associated in the eastern coastal area, it is possible that the arrival of these newcomers preceded the destruction of the palace at Iolkos, and that they could have been responsible for it. Even so, the cist tombs of Protogeometric date on this site were those of children only, while the adults, from the evidence of nearby Kapakli, continued to use tholos tombs. The Mycenaean population of Thessaly, though no doubt evicted from the central inland region, may have remained dominant at Iolkos.

There are also difficulties in interpreting the available material from Crete, where it is a matter of the Minoan, and not the Mycenaean, way of life. During the preceding period, roughly the generation after the Mainland invasion, peaceful conditions seem to have prevailed on the island, the potter's art had expressed itself in a rather florid new style, and communications had been maintained at least with the Dodecanese. In this period the situation changes, and there is some disturbance on the island, quite possibly to be placed at about the same time as the destruction of the Granary at Mycenae. Evidence of such a disturbance appears in the foundation of new settlements in inhospitable and remote areas, suggesting the aftermath of some disaster. There should also be some complementary evidence of actual destruction, but the only instance is the annihilation of the small settlement which had replaced the once great city of Mallia—and even in this instance it is by no means certain that the destruction took place at this time. There is, however, evidence that pottery of non-Minoan origin found its way to Crete in this period, and it is of that very simply decorated type associated with the Granary Class—though that does not necessarily mean that it originated in the Argolid. It is found at Knossos (of which we know too little in this phase of its history), in small quantities only at the remote site of Karphi, and also in two new settlements in the plain of the Mesara, at Phaestos and Gortyn, with Phaestos providing similar evidence from tombs. Gradually, the simple style of pottery, to which Minoan shapes were adapted, seems to have permeated the Central and Eastern parts of Crete (of the West nothing is known), and the elaborate Fringed Style gave way to it.

It does seem likely that the arrival of a group of newcomers disrupted conditions on the island, and the appearance of fibulae and long dress-pins may confirm this arrival (unless they belong to some later intrusion). There is as yet no solution to the question of the origin of the newcomers (cf. above, pp. 192 ff.)—presumably they came from the

Aegean area or from the Mainland of Greece. It is interesting to note that there were links with Cyprus during this period, to be dated to the last stages of Late Cypriot III.

The effect of the disturbances in Crete was to drive some of the population (which is unlikely to have been numerous) to the hills, and so they must have been of a violent nature, and are very probably to be explained by the arrival of newcomers, according to the available evidence. The Minoan way of life was not however destroyed, and it survived in the plains as well as in the mountainous area. It is likely that the newcomers settled down among the existing Minoan inhabitants, but one cannot go further than this. From this time onward, the Central area of Crete has to be separated from the Eastern region, as those who lived in the East probably became isolated from the outer world, only renewing their contacts in the Geometric (or late Protogeometric) period, while the inhabitants of the central districts remained in touch with the Aegean, and adopted certain features of the Protogeometric style (see pp. 181, 184).

Events in Cyprus, finally, need only a brief discussion. The serious disaster of the preceding period led to the desertion of many sites, and probably to a wholesale depopulation. At some time after this (during the course of Enkomi level III, the destruction having taken place at the end of level V, and level IV being of brief duration only) intrusive pottery appeared, closely resembling the Granary Class of the Argolid, and a likely deduction from this is that it was introduced by further refugees from the Argolid, after the final disaster at Mycenae. They also probably introduced the chamber tomb system of burial which is found at a slightly later period in Cyprus, but whose introduction could belong to this time, as there is a gap in tomb evidence at this point. It is not necessary to suppose that they came as invaders. They may simply have amalgamated with the few inhabitants left. They may however have come in fairly large numbers, as their pottery had a considerable influence on later ceramic developments. It should also be noted that these migrants were Mycenaeans, and thus we can speak of a Mycenaean survival here as well as in certain districts of Greece and the Aegean. The persistence of Mycenaean culture could even have been stronger here than in most other areas, and it is tempting to identify the sceptre in a tomb at Kourion as that of some erstwhile Mycenaean ruler.

Generally speaking, in the one area, the Central and South Aegean, where the Mycenaeans had remained solidly and securely entrenched, their way of life was rudely terminated by disaster or imminent threat of disaster. Destruction at Mycenae also further weakened the Mycenaean system in the Argolid (an area which had previously suffered extensive damage), and subsequently newcomers were able to occupy this district unresisted; these newcomers probably arrived from the North overland, and similarly occupied much of Central Greece before reaching the Argolid. In Thessaly, the inland area was probably overrun by groups from North-west Greece and Macedonia, thus implying that the Mycenaeans lost their hold over this district; on the other hand, in spite of the destruction of the palace at Iolkos, Mycenaean elements persisted strongly here into later times.

No satisfactory explanation can be given for any of the destructions on Mycenaean sites during this final period. As a result of that at Mycenae there was probably a further exodus to Cyprus, where the migrants were able to settle peaceably among the remaining inhabitants. Conditions in Crete, finally, were of a disturbed nature, and some hostile attack on the island, with subsequent settlement of the invaders, is likely, though this did not result in the disappearance of Minoan culture.

4. *The Land and Sea Raiders, and Absolute Chronology*

Some sort of historical picture of the final stages of Mycenaean civilization has thus emerged. It is far from full, and the events recorded in this section may help to amplify it and go some way to justifying the absolute dates that have been used.

In *c.* 1191, a serious invasion, in which both land and sea forces were involved, was defeated by Ramesses III on the borders of Egypt. The invaders were composed of a number of different peoples, whose names have not led to undisputed identification, but among whom were the Peleset, who soon after their defeat settled in South Palestine, and are in fact the Philistines of the Bible. They had united their forces in Syria before making their way south to Egypt, and were responsible for much devastation in this region as well as in other districts at earlier stages of their invasion. Mention is made of these districts, and the appearance of Kode, Carchemish and Hittite territory proves that some groups were operating in Asia before making their way to Syria. On the other hand, the districts of *irtw* and *irs* are said to have been devastated, and these have been interpreted respectively as the kingdom of Arzawa, located in the west of Asia Minor, and Alasia, identified as the island of Cyprus. At least those raiders who attacked Cyprus must have come by sea, and the location of Arzawa indicates that they may have been operating in the Aegean. Furthermore, the fact of a maritime origin for an important section of the invaders is attested by the phraseology of the Egyptian scribe who records the invasion, for he stresses that the whole affair started because 'the Northerners were disturbed in their isles'. Unless these sea invaders came from the Adriatic or from Italy and Sicily—in which case the devastation of Arzawa would need explanation—the Aegean is almost inevitably involved and the activities of these raiders must find some place in the picture given above.[1]

An examination of the activities of the Sea Peoples, in particular with regard to the contacts observable between them and the Mycenaeans or Mycenaean culture, is important not only for a fuller understanding of events in the Aegean but also for the establishment of an absolute chronology for these events, through the medium of the ceramic links.

The raiders' activities, whether on the move or as settled subsequent to their defeat by Ramesses III, have already been discussed in the sections on Syria and the Philistines (pp. 207 ff.). The relevant points, for the present purpose, are as follows.

The pottery characteristic of the Philistines after their settlement in South Palestine was strongly Mycenaean in style, reflecting a period in early LH. III C but well after its

---

[1] On the activities of the Land and Sea Raiders see Breasted, *Ancient Records of Egypt*, iv. 33 ff., and Edgerton and Wilson, *Historical Records of Ramses III*, pp. 49 ff. On the identification of Arzawa and Alasia see Gardiner, *Ancient Egyptian Onomastica*, i. 129* ff., and Garstang and Gurney, *The Geography of the Hittite Empire*, map 1 and pp. 83 ff.

beginning—Furumark's LH. III C 1 b. This 'Philistine' pottery cannot have been introduced at any great length of time after the original foundations, as the archaeological evidence shows that it was present in all stages of the occupation; if one supposes the settlement in South Palestine to have taken place not later than c. 1180, the introduction of 'Philistine' pottery can hardly be put later than c. 1165. There is some internal evidence to show that this pottery was neither brought with them by the Philistines nor exactly contemporaneous with the original date of the foundations, but the proof of this is afforded by the evidence from Syria, where it is reasonably certain that the three towns of Ras Shamra, Atchana and Tell Sukas were destroyed by the Land and Sea Raiders shortly before the descent on Egypt, at a time when LH. III B pottery was still in use by their inhabitants.

If it could be demonstrated that the presence of LH. III B pottery on these sites meant that LH. III C had not yet started to develop in the Mycenaean world, then one would probably have to deny any introduction of 'Philistine' pottery before c. 1150. This cannot however be demonstrated, and it can, on the contrary, reasonably be shown that LH. III B pottery persisted in Syria after LH. III C had started to develop in the Aegean. The proof of this comes from the situation in Cyprus, from which island it is thought that most or all LH. III B pottery was exported to the Levant. In Cyprus there was destruction at least at Enkomi and Sinda, comparable to that in Syria inasmuch as LH. III B pottery was current at the time of the disaster; but in the apparently immediate resettlement at Enkomi and Sinda one of the main ceramic features is the disappearance of LH. III B, and its replacement by very early LH. III C pottery unconnected with the preceding local LH. III B and evidently originating in the central Mycenaean area (cf. pp. 23, 197).

It is reasonable to suppose that the disasters in Cyprus were the work of the Land and Sea Raiders, as they are specifically stated by the Egyptian scribe to have devastated Alasia. And if this was so, then it is a probable conclusion that at this point of their journey the Land and Sea Raiders were accompanied by a fairly powerful group of Mycenaeans—there is other evidence of the influence of Mycenaeans in Cyprus in the period immediately after the destruction (cf. pp. 199 f.). And so a new factor is introduced, which leads us back to the situation in the Aegean itself.

It is in any case likely enough that the Sea Peoples were operating in the Aegean, since they are reported to have devastated Arzawa, located on the west coast of Asia Minor. This being so, it is important to bear in mind the fact that there is no evidence of destruction in the islands of the Central and South Aegean, especially the Dodecanese, either at this time or anywhere near it. What is the explanation of this?

There is one possible explanation, and that is to suppose that the various ethnic groups which went to form the Sea Peoples had been joined in the Aegean by a powerful group of Mycenaeans. May it not be that this group consisted of the main body of the refugees who fled after the catastrophic invasion of the Mainland at the end of LH. III B? It will be remembered that some of the areas affected by this invasion were densely populated before being attacked, and subsequently severely depopulated. Some refugees went to Achaea and Kephallenia, but the largest, and probably best organized, force took to their ships and sailed eastwards, making common cause with other disturbed groups. Whether the Mycenaean group had any hand in the devastation of Arzawa is unknown, but at least it will have been able to ensure the immunity of such Mycenaean territory as was traversed (some Mycenaean islanders may have joined in), and will have been responsible, together with the non-Mycenaean ethnic groups, for the first of the two destructions in Cyprus. At this stage, either the whole Mycenaean group or part of it decided to establish itself in Cyprus, perhaps to be followed shortly after by other Mycenaean groups. Also, it could have been a small offshoot of the main Mycenaean group which settled at Tarsus in Cilicia. The rest of the raiders then moved on to Syria (where it was quite natural for LH. III B pottery still to be current) and joined forces with other groups coming overland from Asia, thus creating the formidable body which went southwards, by land and sea, towards Egypt.

This explanation would appear to take into account all the known facts, and the consequence would be that we could date the invasion of the Mainland of Greece reasonably accurately to *c.* 1200, and could give a similar approximate date for the emergence of LH. III C pottery in the Aegean.

Before accepting this date (even if the theory is correct) it is desirable to consider what other criteria for absolute datings exist, and whether they would permit the date suggested.

For the most part, absolute dates depend on cross-references between Mycenaean and Egyptian objects, inasmuch as the latter can be assigned to the reign of any one Pharaoh.

So far as concerns the appearance of Mycenaean objects (inevitably, vases) in some Egyptian context, it is well known that LH. III B vases have been found in Egypt during the reign of Ramesses II, but that no LH. III B—or LH. III C—pottery is known from subsequent reigns.[1] This is useful, but does not take us very far, in view of the great length of the reign concerned (1304–1237).

Besides Mycenaean pottery being found in an Egyptian context, however, datable Egyptian objects, mainly scarabs, are found outside Egypt in Mycenaean contexts. It would seem that this type of evidence must be treated with the greatest caution. At the time when Pendlebury published his *Aegyptiaca*, not one of the six scarabs of the Nineteenth Dynasty had been found in a contemporary context, and four of them were associated with Geometric pottery. Also, seven of the eleven Eighteenth Dynasty scarabs were similarly misplaced.[2] One must bear in mind the reason for the object having found its way to the Aegean area. It is most unlikely that the owner would be able to decipher it, and he must therefore have acquired it as a charm or just out of curiosity. All one can say, therefore, is that the date of the pottery with which a scarab or other object with cartouche is associated cannot be earlier than that of the dynasty or reign indicated.

Three sites may be considered in the light of this conclusion. At Perati in Attica, two cartouches of Ramesses II were found.[3] The associated pottery, as all that from this site, was LH. III C, and consequently it can be said that these cartouches are of no value in dating the beginning of this style, in view of the great probability that LH. III B was still current in the time of Ramesses II's successor.

In a house near the Palace at Ras Shamra (Ugarit) in Syria, a sword was found

[1] *Chronology*, pp. 114 ff.
[2] *Aegyptiaca*, pp. 114–15 (cf. the two tables).
[3] In tomb 1 (*Pr.* 1953, p. 95, Fig. 7) and 104 (*Ergon* for 1960, pp. 19, and 18, Fig. 21).

bearing the cartouche of Merneptah, and this was associated with Mycenaean vases 'de facture tardive'.[1] It is also reported that this pottery was of the ordinary Mycenaean type found on the site. As until now no certainly identifiable LH. III C vase or sherd has been published from Ras Shamra, it is reasonable to suppose that the vases in question are LH. III A or LH. III B. They cannot be LH. III A, since LH. III B is attested in the reign of the preceding Pharaoh, and so they should be LH. III B, and this style must still then have been current by the beginning of Merneptah's reign, and LH. III C can hardly have started to emerge before c. 1230. This would then be the highest possible date for this style, and is that in fact accepted by Furumark.[2] It may be added that in this instance the Egyptian object concerned—the sword—is in a different category from a scarab or cartouche, and is far more likely to be contemporary. But no knowledge is yet available of the stage in LH. III B reached by the vases. If it can be shown that the style was already in existence before 1300 then one might well be near its end; but that is an unsafe argument, and the sword itself may have been deposited much nearer 1200 than 1230.

Enkomi, finally, produces interesting evidence. Here, a number of tombs have been established as contemporary with levels IV to II,[3] in other words, subsequent to the destruction of level V, where the pottery was early LH. III C in type, and at least in part prior to the settlements (levels III to I) in which some of the pottery can reasonably be considered contemporary with that of the Argolid shortly after the destruction of the Granary (see pp. 23 f.). It is reported that scarabs of Ramesses III or of his immediate successors were found in certain of these tombs. If any scarab could be proved to belong to one of Ramesses III's successors rather than to his own reign, it would be very important, but such proof is not forthcoming, and therefore one can say no more than that the settlements and tombs represented by levels IV and III (and perhaps II) cannot be earlier than c. 1200. The recent discoveries at Kition suggest strongly that the 'wavy-line' pottery of the well is later than the vases of the tombs, which are contemporary with the Enkomi ones, and so the second stage of the Granary Class cannot easily be put higher than c. 1180. This may, however, appear too high a date to allow for the original evolution of LH. III C as not earlier than 1230.

And so far, of course, there is no evidence to show that LH. III B may not have persisted for some long time after 1230—a hundred years, for all one could tell. Here, however, a brief return may be made to the Philistine evidence. 'Philistine' pottery was not introduced until after the Philistines occupied South Palestine, but all the evidence suggests that it can only have been slightly after. Presuming the occupation to have been not later than c. 1180, I do not think that 'Philistine' pottery can have been introduced later than c. 1165. Since it is mainly a stylistic offshoot of early LH. III C, the first appearance of LH. III C in the Aegean can hardly be less than twenty years earlier.

Consequently, the situation is that LH. III B is still current in 1230, while LH. III C cannot have started later than 1185. Therefore a date of c. 1200 for the end of LH. III B and the transition to LH. III C is perfectly admissible.

[1] *Syria*, xxxi. 65; cf. *The Aegean and the Near East*, p. 134.
[2] *Chronology*, p. 115.
[3] *E–A*, pp. 38 and 318.

A reasonably satisfactory date is thus assignable to the beginning of LH. III C. The date of its end (in the Argolid) is much more difficult to determine, and there would be no good purpose served by going into any detailed analysis. The main lines of approach seem to run as follows. In the Aegean, the Protogeometric style of West Attica probably started to emerge at about the same as Argive LH. III C ended (cf. pp. 17 ff.). Cross-references between Athens, Crete and Cyprus lead to the likely conclusion that the latter part of Late Cypriot III B and the beginning of Cypro-Geometric I were roughly contemporary with the transition in West Attica from sub-Mycenaean to Protogeometric. Cypro-Geometric I pottery is thought, according to the most recent research (cf. p. 197, n. 2), to have started *c*. 1050, and so that date may provisionally be assigned to the end of LH. III C in the Argolid and the rise of Athenian Protogeometric. But it must always be realized that the Cypriot dates, dependent as they are themselves on cross-references with Palestinian material, are liable to revision.

If the dates of *c*. 1200 for the beginning, and of *c*. 1050 for the end, of LH. III C are accepted, then we are assigning a period of a hundred and fifty years to this style—a long time indeed, though no less long than that assigned to it by Furumark.[1] To suggest absolute dates for events occurring within its limits would be sheer guesswork, though in my opinion the time of the destruction of the Granary at Mycenae (almost certainly later than the second period of destruction in Cyprus) can hardly be earlier than *c*. 1150, and could be as much as twenty years later. It is difficult to envisage a long time of survival after its destruction.

5. *Mycenaean Civilization and the Implications of its Collapse*

Mycenaean civilization, Mycenaean culture, the Mycenaean way of life: these are words and phrases that have constantly appeared throughout this work, but have so far not been adequately analysed. What would be the archaeologist's definition of this civilization? A whole consisting of a number of parts. For him, it is the houses in which the Mycenaeans lived, and the palaces of the kings who ruled them; the fortification walls in which they sought refuge, and the armour and weapons they used in war; their writing; the way the men and women dressed, their ornaments and jewellery and their personal possessions; their pottery in all its many uses; the objects that were of cult value to them; and, at the end, the tombs in which they buried their dead, the manner of burial, and the objects reverently deposited (though admittedly not so reverently treated when further burials took place in the same tomb).

All these are indeed the material aspects of any civilization, but certain features were prominent in the Mycenaean world; such were the *megaron* plan of many of the houses, the massive and sophisticated architecture in stone, as found particularly in the palaces, the fortifications and the tholos tombs, the great delicacy and skill of the metalworker in gold as well as in bronze, and the similar ability of his companion worker in ivory, the remarkably high standard reached by the potter, and the very individual style he

---

[1] *OA*, iii. 262.

produced, the language as set down on the tablets, the very distinctive terracotta human and animal figurines used as votive offerings, and the custom of multiple burial.

All these features, and others with them, constitute the archaeologist's picture of Mycenaean civilization. This civilization had another, and very remarkable, feature: its almost complete uniformity, even in the pottery, throughout the whole Mycenaean world, during the fourteenth and thirteenth centuries. Such uniformity in a sophisticated culture has not been known before or since in Greek lands.

Some of the features of this way of life may be said to be characteristic of all the inhabitants in the Mycenaean sphere. Such are the *megaron* type of house, the system of multiple burials in chamber tombs, the clay votive offerings and in general the pottery. Other features, such as the palaces, the tholos tombs, the objects of precious metal or ivory, and the knowledge of writing, were the preserves of the ruling class, or of the wealthy.

Such a division leads to further considerations. First, are the elements common to the whole population sufficient to indicate a single people racially? This, I feel, is by no means the case, though they are the elements that would be the most tenaciously retained. If, however, we need not suppose that the Mycenaeans were a racial unity, how are we to account for the uniformity? This I believe to be due to the existence of a single closely united ruling caste, probably acknowledging one overlord, whose seat was at Mycenae.

This conception emerges from other evidence as well as that of archaeology, and it introduces a further and most important feature of Mycenaean civilization, the system of rule and administration. The Homeric epic sees the Mycenaean world as a number of districts of varying size, each ruled by a king, and the archaeological data, as well as the tablets, confirm this. Furthermore, it is clear that Homer's kings wielded very great power; they had divine ancestry, and should thus have been supreme in religious matters and in the law that issued from the gods; and they were the leaders in war. On their side, the tablets reveal that beneath the king came a complex social and administrative organization (though details are much disputed), which apparently depended ultimately on the king; the king also appears to have had the virtual monopoly of the import of bronze in quantity from outside the Mycenaean world. Taking this evidence in conjunction with the homogeneity of culture, it seems certain that we have here a monarchical system as the basis of government, quite powerful enough to impose its commands on all its subjects. Furthermore, it seems likely to me, as I have suggested above (pp. 218 f.), that there was one supreme king who held all the kingdoms together.

It was, to my mind, the existence of these all-powerful kings that was responsible for many of the characteristic material features of Mycenaean civilization, above all those which reflected the prosperity of this world. There were obviously many beside the kings who were exceedingly wealthy, and no doubt there was a flourishing commercial class, but their prosperity depended on the kings and existed within the system as a whole. Among these features, it must be stressed, was the knowledge of writing.

If these arguments are valid, then one conclusion of major importance follows. If for any reason the system of rule collapses, then many of the other features of Mycenaean civilization will disappear with it, in so far as they are the outward manifestation and creations of this system. It should be stressed, however, that the system depends on other things as well as on the existence of a ruling house. It probably needed a fairly considerable subject population to maintain it, and an assured supply of certain materials, especially bronze, from elsewhere. What I have in mind is the situation on the Mainland immediately after the disasters at the end of LH. III B. The population had seriously diminished, and it is my impression that those mainly concerned in promoting the material prosperity of the kingdoms had fled. The skilled class had gone, and the labour available, as for example in big architectural works, was no longer adequate. Furthermore, difficulty may have been experienced in getting copper from Cyprus, or wherever else it may have come from. Even supposing no difficulty from the source of origin, had those on the Mainland a suitable return to make?

It may be that a king remained, especially in the Argolid, but in some aspects the system of administration had broken down. In consequence, architecture seriously deteriorated, and the craftsman's art in metal and ivory—and in fact I think it very possible that written records may no longer have been used in those areas overcome by disaster. The system of rule had also depended on peace and prosperity, and these had gone or were seriously threatened, and with them went those features of the Mycenaean way of life which were either dependent on the system of rule or aimed at enhancing the brilliance of court life.

As we have seen, certain areas were untouched by disaster at the end of LH. III B, and stability and prosperity no doubt ensured the continuance of the *status quo*. In the end, however, whether as a result of the arrival of new people, or of destruction which led to disruption and depopulation, all areas of the Mycenaean world were profoundly affected. Three stages can be recognized: first, the disruption of the central authority which had bound the kingdoms into a whole and had ensured the uniformity; second, and consequent on the first, the severe weakening (to say the least) of Mycenaean rule in several of the important kingdoms of the Mainland; and third, the eventual disruption in every kingdom.

Inasmuch as Mycenaean civilization depended on the system of monarchical rule for the whole and the parts of its world, which I think it did to a great extent, it was now finished with. Furthermore, many districts had received a greater or lesser influx of new people. One question now remains: what features of the Mycenaean way of life were likely to have persisted among the survivors? We have to take into account the fact that the material culture of the new arrivals was lower than that of the Mycenaeans, and might quite well be influenced by contact with the Mycenaeans.

So far as can be seen, only one element of the previous civilization had such an influence, and that was the potter's craft.[1] This itself had been a product of Mycenaean rule, but it was not dependent for its existence on its survival. Wheel-made vases were evidently a novelty to the newcomers, but a very useful one, and so we can say that at the outset Mycenaean styles had a great influence. Even so, it was not long before something entirely new arose, and there was a complete breakaway.

---

[1] A localized exception is probable at Iolkos, where the Protogeometric structures seem to show the continuance of the Mycenaean stonemason's craft. The settlement of Grotta on Naxos may provide another exception.

It might perhaps have been expected that the Mycenaean manner of dress would have prevailed, but its elegance was a symbol of the more leisurely times that had vanished, and so it also gave way to something new. Yet another feature which one might have thought would survive at least among the remaining Mycenaeans was that of multiple burial in chamber tombs; but there is no trace of it in most areas. The only clear instance is in Thessaly, with the continued use of the stone-built tholos tombs. This may have been due in part to the strong persistence of people of Mycenaean origin, as at Iolkos, but it could also be the case that some of the newcomers were themselves accustomed to multiple burial, as perhaps at Marmariani.

Finally, there are the religious beliefs and practices of the Mycenaeans. There was of course some form of state religion, in which the king and his priests played the leading part; that presumably either disappeared or was transformed. But there should also have been a hard core of local popular cults. Unfortunately, archaeology has produced no evidence of such, or of any clear continuity of worship in any one spot, except probably Delos and perhaps Kea. Otherwise, such sanctuaries as we know of suffered at least an interruption extending over a considerable period, and the small 'goddess' and animal votive figurines do not survive. On the other hand, the tablets provide evidence of deities worshipped alike in Mycenaean and later times.

To sum up, the Mycenaean system of rule and administration was eradicated, and with it most of the material manifestations of the civilization, including architecture (except at Iolkos), the knowledge of writing, and even the burial customs. This does not mean that much may not have survived on the religious side, and even in the realms of thought; above all, the memories of past glory were retained, and the surviving Mycenaeans may have contributed much, of which archaeology can tell us nothing, to the civilization which succeeded their own.

6. *The Evidence of Dialect and the Oral Tradition*

If no archaeological evidence was available, to what extent would it be possible to acquire any knowledge of what happened in the centuries preceding the eighth, the century when the alphabet was first introduced into Greece and the Aegean? There are two categories of testimony, the picture as deducible from the distribution of Greek dialects, and the stories handed down by word of mouth.

The evidence from dialect, which barely goes higher than 700 B.C. in one or two cases, and not even above 600 B.C. in others, is as follows.[1] The fundamental division is into East Greek and West Greek. The East Greek dialects are divisible into Arcado-Cyprian, Aeolic and Ionic. Of these, the Arcado-Cyprian is, as its name implies, confined almost exclusively to Arcadia and to Cyprus. The Ionic dialect comprised the Attic variation, spoken in Attica, and three further subdivisions, Eastern Ionic, spoken in Ionia, that is to say the central part of the coast of Western Asia Minor and the adjacent islands, Central Ionic as spoken in the Cyclades, and the Western Ionic of Euboea. The Aeolic

---

[1] Cf. Buck, *Greek Dialects* (ed. 1955), pp. 3 ff., whose analysis I follow in the main.

dialect was spoken in Aeolis, in other words the northern part of the coast of Western Asia Minor and the adjacent islands, in Thessaly and in Boeotia. This last dialect was diversely influenced, slightly by Ionic in Aeolis, greatly by North-western Greek in Boeotia, to some extent by North-west Greek in West Thessaly, but only slightly in East Thessaly.[1] The West Greek dialect is also divided, into North-west Greek and Doric. Of these, the North-west Greek was spoken in Phocis, Locris and Aetolia; it also exercised influence over the Aeolic dialect in the areas, and to the extent, mentioned above. It was also spoken in Elis. Doric was the dialect of Acarnania and Corcyra, of Laconia, Messenia, the Argolid, Corinthia and the Megarid, of the southern Cycladic islands of Thera and Melos, of Crete, of the Dodecanese and of some districts of the southern coast of Western Asia Minor. For certain areas, the evidence is not clear; it is generally believed, for example, that North-west Greek was spoken in Achaea, while in the Ionian islands it is not known whether the North-west or the Doric dialect prevailed.

It would not be possible to make many deductions from the dialect evidence without the support of the oral tradition. The eventual picture might conceal much complication and interchange of movement in the earlier centuries. Indeed, in two areas the situation was due to relatively recent events. The establishment of the Doric dialect in Acarnania and Corcyra was evidently due to the late eighth and seventh century colonizing activity of the Corinthians, and the Doric tongue of Messenia could reflect the Spartan conquest of that district, also in the eighth and seventh centuries. But the broad lines of the oral tradition take us further back; they show that the movement on the Mainland went from North and North-west southwards and eastwards, with the 'West Greek' speakers pushing out the 'East Greeks', there then ensuing a triple thrust across the Aegean by both West and East Greeks. Those who spoke the East Greek language would then be the earlier inhabitants, and one might surmise on the dialect evidence that there were three original divisions, the Arcado-Cyprian covering the Peloponnese, the Aeolic in Boeotia and Thessaly and the Ionic in Attica. One cannot tell either from the dialect evidence or from the oral tradition what lay behind this tripartite division, but it is of interest that in one matter the linguistic evidence may run slightly counter to that of the tradition. The tradition claimed that the inhabitants of Attica had always maintained their purity of race, but there appear to be linguistic grounds for thinking that certain Doric features were introduced into Ionic at a time before the division of this dialect into Attic and Ionic,[2] and this would then indicate an early, though only temporary, influence of the Doric tongue in Attica.

The oral tradition in turn may be said to be supported by the dialect evidence; to the story of the movements across the Aegean, for example, the dialects add that the inhabitants of Lesbos spoke much the same language as those of East Thessaly, and that there were similar links between the Ionians and the Athenians, and between the Rhodians and the Dorians of the Peloponnese.

Such confirmation is valuable, but the traditional stories give far more information

---

[1] Chadwick, *Greece and Rome*, 1956, pp. 38 ff.; cf. Risch, *Museum Helveticum*, 1955, pp. 61 ff., and Porzig, *Indogermanische Forschungen*, 1954, pp. 147 ff.

[2] Chadwick, op. cit. pp. 42 ff.

than anything that the dialects can produce. They give, with almost incredible complexity, the time, the place and the actors. It is not proposed to discuss the oral tradition in any detail, but there are certain phases and trends that stand out.

Whatever may have been the extent and trustworthiness of the information available to the Greeks of historical times concerning their past, there appears to be no doubt that by far the most important and influential was that contained in the Homeric epic, which may be said to have become firmly established by 700 B.C.[1] This epic, and its subsidiaries, told of an age of heroes, and its focal point was the Trojan War. It spoke of a Greek world divided into numerous small kingdoms of which the leading one was that of Mycenae, and it covered in considerable personal detail a period from about two generations before the Trojan War until two generations after. Its effect on the Greek world at and after the time of its appearance can hardly be overestimated. The cult of Homeric heroes, and the depicting of Homeric scenes on vases may be instanced as two of its manifestations. One feature of the epic must however be made clear. Homer and his followers made no attempt to link the age of heroes with that in which Homer himself spoke or wrote. The collapse of this age was foreshadowed; there are warning notes of the disaster to come, but the nature of the end was left in darkness.

It is not surprising that other Greeks should feel the need to forge the link that Homer had failed to provide. And indeed there seems to have been in existence a considerable body of information, albeit diverse and unco-ordinated. First, the Greeks knew that there had been a movement of tribes from the North-west and North of Greece; the main group concerned was that of the Dorians, who occupied the Peloponnese, but there were other groups as well, as for example the Thessalians and Aetolians. Secondly, it was known that certain subsequent movements took place from the Mainland across the Aegean, in three roughly parallel lines, the Dorians across the south Aegean, the Ionians through the central chain of islands, and the Aeolians to the north.

The question then arises, was the remaining material sufficient to make three connexions, that between the movements of the Dorians and others on the Mainland and the end of Mycenaean civilization, that between the Mainland invasions and the subsequent trans-Aegean migrations, and finally that between these movements generally and historical times? Evidently it was considered to be, for by the fifth century a reasonably clear and correlated account had emerged.

The link between the invaders and the Heroic Age was of a twofold nature. It was not sufficient for the invaders simply to make contact with the last of the heroes; they were Greeks, sharers in the glorious past, and therefore they too must have a heroic connexion. This connexion was made not with any of the heroes of the Trojan War itself, but with one who preceded them and was in many ways the greatest hero of all, Heracles. He and his descendants provided the lineage of the Dorian kings—there is no doubt that such was the later belief; and he was also connected with the Thessalians by the early fifth century.[2] A further link was also made with the Aetolians, but this does not appear earlier than the fourth century.[3]

[1] Lorimer, *Monuments*, pp. 462 ff.
[2] Pindar, *Pythians*, x. 1–3.
[3] Paus. v, 3, 5.

SUMMARY AND HISTORICAL INFERENCES

So we have the invaders firmly established in the Heroic Age. The main invaders were of course the Dorians, especially as they conquered the central part of the Homeric region. It is consequently natural enough to find the Dorian leaders, descendants of Heracles, engaging in a final struggle with the grandson of Agamemnon, Teisamenos.[1] Teisamenos was defeated, and the invaders divided the spoils, Temenos taking the Argolid (or rather leaving it to his son, as he died), Cresphontes Messenia, and the sons of Aristodemos Laconia. Arcadia was left unconquered, Elis was soon after to be overrun by the Aetolians, pressing on behind the Dorians. What happened to Achaea? Here we get a further link in the story.[2] Teisamenos' forces took the territory over from its existing inhabitants, the Ionians; the Ionians made their way to Attica, and from there, in the course of time, took ship across the Aegean in company with many other non-Attic groups. A connexion of a similar type appears in the story of Codros, of Neleid descent, whose father had fled from Pylos to Athens, and whose sons were evidently numerous enough to found many of the cities of Ionia in Asia Minor.[3]

So the Dorians were linked with Heracles and their invasion was the final blow to the Achaean power in the Peloponnese. They spread yet further over the Mainland, and secured the Megarid; indeed, they attempted an invasion of Attica, but this was unsuccessful.[4] Their major subsequent expansion, however, was across the Aegean, to Melos[5] and Thera,[6] to Crete and the Dodecanese and the adjacent coast of Asia Minor.[7] The principal figure in the foundations in Crete and the Dodecanese seems to have been Althaemenes, and the date within a generation or two of the main Dorian invasion, but this character cannot be traced higher than the fourth century.

The movements involving the Thessalians are not so well documented, though the actual thrust of the Thessalians is mentioned by both Thucydides and Herodotus;[8] Herodotus states that they came from Thesprotian territory to occupy Aeolian land, and Thucydides makes their move precede that of the descent of the Dorians on the Peloponnese, and adds that they displaced Boeotians, who thus went from Central Thessaly into Boeotia. These Boeotians were very likely themselves intruders from North-west Greece, forced southwards by the Thessalians.[9] This being so, it would be natural to suppose that the Aeolian migration across the Aegean was the effect of intrusion both into Thessaly and into Boeotia (events in any case clearly reflected in the dialect evidence). It is indeed recognized by Thucydides that some went from Boeotia to Aeolis,[10] but the account found in Strabo[11] takes the process back to Orestes, this giving it priority over the Ionian migration, and speaks of a double movement: the main body taking some four generations to make its way overland through Thrace and thence across to Asia Minor and turning south, while another group, under two descendants of Agamemnon, stayed for some time in Locris, and only later crossed over to found Kyme. It is altogether a strange

---

[1] Paus. ii. 18, 6 f.
[2] Hdt. i. 145 f.
[3] *F Gr H* 4 F 125 (Hellanicus); 3 F 155 (Pherecydes). Cf. J. M. Cook, *CAH* (rev. edn.), II, chap. xxxviii (separate fascicle), pp. 10 ff.
[4] Hdt. v. 76.
[5] Th. v. 84 and 112.
[6] Hdt. iv. 147.
[7] Strabo 653.
[8] Th. i. 12; Hdt. vii. 176.
[9] Cf. Buck, *Dialects*, p. 5.
[10] Th. iii. 2, 3; viii. 5, 2.
[11] Strabo 582.

story, and it is perhaps significant that Herodotus, who goes into detail on the origins of the Ionians, remains silent about the Aeolian foundations.

One further subsidiary tribal movement may be mentioned, that of the Dryopes, a group perhaps situated in the Spercheios valley, probably evicted by the Dorians before they reached the Peloponnese, and eventually settling in south Euboea and on the South-west coast of the Argolid.[1]

We have then a number of major themes or complexes of events all related, the Trojan War, the subsequent internal troubles of the Homeric heroes, the end of their age brought about by tribes from North-west Greece, of whom the Dorians and Thessalians were connected with Heracles, and the subsequent movements of Dorians, Ionians and Aeolians across the Aegean, the migrations of the latter two being occasioned by the invasions on the mainland. The movements are regarded as definitive and occupying a brief time only, except in the case of the Aeolian migration, and it is particularly to be noted that the Dorians, having eventually reached the Peloponnese after the Trojan War, stayed there and occupied Messenia, Laconia and the Argolid.[2]

What information had the Greeks of the dates when all this took place, and of the extent of time covered? Once again, the Trojan War may be taken as the focal point. It is true enough that, not surprisingly, there were divergent views on the year in which Troy fell, but even so, disregarding Douris' millennium calculation at one end of the scale, and Ephoros' date of 1135 at the other, the dates cover a fairly short span, between 1250 (Herodotus) and 1171 (Sosibios).[3] Herodotus' date thus goes back into the thirteenth century, and it has been argued that Thucydides also considered the capture of Troy to have taken place *c.* 1250.[4]

Thucydides also provided the extremely important statement that the displaced Boeotians reached Boeotia sixty years after the Trojan War, and that the Dorians, in company with the Heraclids, occupied the Peloponnese eighty years after this war.[5] For the most part, however, calculation was made by generations; Teisamenos was the grandson of Agamemnon, the Aeolian migration was finally completed by the great-grandson of Orestes, the grandsons of Melanthos, who had been driven out of Pylos by the Dorians, founded many cities in Ionia, Althaemenes was active in Crete and the Dodecanese after the death of Codros. It may be supposed that not more than a hundred and fifty years elapsed from the fall of Troy to the end of the trans-Aegean migrations, and by this final date we are still in the eleventh century—and at its very beginning if the calculation of Herodotus (and perhaps Thucydides) is accepted. In other words, there was still a gap of some three hundred years before the introduction of the alphabet.

It will naturally be asked on what basis these dates were calculated, and the probable answer provides the link with historical times. It would appear, in fact, that the intervening gap was covered by certain royal genealogies, and above all those of Sparta. The genealogy of the Spartan kings did not cover this gap only, however, as it went directly

---

[1] Cf. Skeat, *Dorians*, pp. 56 ff.
[2] This is the clear inference from Thucydides' words (i. 12, 3): Πελοπόννησον ἔσχον.
[3] Cf. Forsdyke, *Greece before Homer*, pp. 62 ff. Herodotus gives his date in ii. 145.
[4] Huxley, *La Parola del Passato*, 1957, pp. 209 ff.
[5] i. 12.

back to Heracles. The divergencies in the names of the Eurypontid line may be disregarded; the important point is that the calculation of the reigns was based on a forty-year tenure, and that this fits in roughly with the date of the Trojan War.[1] Whatever the likelihood of such a calculation being accurate, it is a fact that it was used, and also that the only means of reaching from historical times to that of the Homeric world and the subsequent movements of people seems to have been through these royal pedigrees, slender branches supporting a truly exotic mass of foliage.

The oral tradition, in so far as it gives a picture of the concluding stages of the Heroic Age, of the invasions which accelerated the end of this Age, and of the immediately ensuing movements of peoples related to these invasions, is in its general lines consistent, and may be said to be supported by the evidence from the distribution of dialects. What then happens when it is set alongside the archaeological evidence? And here the main questions that arise are: are the traditional stories correct, are they correctly dated, and are they correctly interrelated?

A start may be made with the Trojan War. The contemporary evidence is unable to tell us that the Achaeans laid siege to Troy, but it gives us the following information. We learn from the Hittite records (admittedly incomplete) that the only known occasion of the presence of the King of Ahhiyawa in Asia Minor can be dated between 1250 and 1230, and he is found operating in the area of the Seha river, which recent research has located not far south of Troy (cf. p. 220). The archaeological evidence has shown that Troy VII *a* was destroyed by human agency at just about this time, in the latter part of the LH. III B period (cf. p. 164). There were indeed earlier and later destructions of the town, but the end of the preceding settlement VI was probably due to natural causes. On the other hand, the eventual destruction of Troy VII *b*, by which time the imported or imitated Mycenaean pottery had reached an advanced stage of LH. III C, is too late for our purposes, as it is inconceivable that the Achaeans could have mounted any sort of combined attack after the catastrophic disaster that overcame many of the Mainland centres at the end of LH. III B, *c*. 1200. A final piece of evidence, though inconclusive in itself, is the mention in the annals of the Hittite King Arnuwandas III, the successor of Tuthalijas IV, of an individual named Muksas, possibly connected with Attarrsijas 'the man of Ahhia', who has been considered to be identifiable with the seer, Mopsos, active before the Trojan War, and even more after it, when he led a band of Achaeans to the southern coast of Asia Minor.[2]

In conclusion, then, the contemporary evidence would permit an Achaean war against Troy between 1250 and 1230, but at no other time. We can therefore claim that we have a remarkable confirmation of the accuracy of the date ascribed by the Greeks (and particularly by Herodotus) to the Trojan War, and of the fact of the event itself. Furthermore, it can be claimed that the Homeric picture of the geographical extent of the Achaean world, and of its division into numerous small kingdoms of which the most important was that of Mycenae, is reasonably faithfully mirrored in the findings of archaeology.

---

[1] Wade-Gery, *The Poet of the Iliad*, pp. 27 ff. with references. Note Burn, *The Lyric Age of Greece*, pp. 405 ff. for the alternative suggestion of a thirty-nine year tenure.

[2] Cf. Huxley, *Achaeans and Hittites*, p. 25.

As to the situation after the Trojan War, neither Homer nor his school says anything of an invasion from outside the Achaean territories, but it is clear from these accounts that a number of the royal heroes encountered trouble on their return from Troy;[1] and Thucydides speaks of civil strife in most of the cities, and the foundation of new cities by those exiled.[2] Archaeology is unable to verify this situation, unless the destruction of outer Mycenae before the end of LH. III B (cf. p. 74) is one of its manifestations—but the evidence is not precise enough to indicate whether this event took place before or after the destruction of Troy. One thing, however, is clear. It cannot have been internal strife which was responsible for the disasters at the end of LH. III B. The wide area over which the disasters took place is an argument against the cause being internal unrest, especially as most of the leaders of the Trojan War did reach home safely, even though with some delay and with probably much reduced forces. The widespread desertion of settlements is, however, more convincing. This seems entirely contrary to the natural course of internal unrest. Many would no doubt be expelled, but the essence of such strife is that one party would get the upper hand and remain in control of the town. Also, rebuilding is to be expected in the towns where destruction had taken place, and this does not happen. Nor would there be any wholesale depopulation such as is observable in the Argolid, and even more in the South-west Peloponnese. It is far more likely that the damage was caused by intruders from outside. So we may leave the Achaeans, and turn to the stories of invasion.

As has been seen, the oral tradition speaks of several movements to within Mycenaean territory from North or North-west Greece shortly after the fall of Troy. The Thessalians pushed into Central Thessaly, displaced Boeotians, themselves perhaps intruders of an earlier date, and forced them south into Boeotia, twenty years before the Dorians accomplished the final stage of their wanderings, by invading and occupying much of the Peloponnese. The invasion of the Peloponnese took place eighty years after the capture of Troy, and during the course of the invasion the Dorians fought against the grandson of Agamemnon, defeated him, and settled in Messenia, Laconia and the Argolid. At some unspecified later date the Aetolians occupied Elis, leaving only Arcadia in the hands of the original inhabitants, and Achaea, at the expense of the expulsion of the Ionians.

Are these movements and settlements reflected in the archaeological picture? To start with, it must be admitted that the evidence is insufficient to confirm or deny that the Thessalians occupied Central Thessaly.[3] It is true that the palace of Iolkos was destroyed at some time during the first half of the twelfth century, but the cause of this disaster is not known, and this is in any case not an area which the Thessalians are reputed to have reached, though they might have reached it and then retired. Thus we get no assistance so far as the Thessalian thrust is concerned, although it may be added that the archaeological evidence indicates one invasion, or rather intrusion, which is quite unknown to the tradition, that of a Macedonian group which moved into North Thessaly at a time probably not less than a hundred years after the Trojan War.[4]

[1] *Od.* i. 11 f.
[2] i. 12.
[3] Here, as in Southern Greece, however, there is evidence of the substitution of burial in cist tombs for that in tholos tombs, though only partial (p. 138). If this indicates the arrivals of Thessalians, then they will probably have started to infiltrate during the twelfth century.
[4] Skeat, *Dorians*, p. 48.

Leaving Thessaly, we come to the central and southern Mainland. This is the area of the great invasions of *c.* 1200 according to archaeology. The time is rather too close to the Trojan War for the traditional story, but that perhaps need not matter. Do these invasions not reflect the traditional movements into Boeotia and into the Peloponnese?

So far as concerns Boeotia, excavation might be said to confirm the actual course of invasion. The destruction of Krisa in Phocis, and the desertion of Gla and Eutresis in Boeotia would be reasonable effects. Unfortunately, there is no subsequent evidence for the settlement of any new group in Boeotia at this time, such material as there is indicating only the continued existence, at a rather low level, of a Mycenaean community at Thebes —and also, incidentally, at Delphi. The presence of violin-bow fibulae in Theban LH. III C chamber tombs might possibly suggest the presence of intruders, but it is a weak argument. On the whole, one must again admit that archaeological survey has not been thorough enough to provide any reliable answer; the only criterion which can be used is a comparative one, the situation in the Peloponnese.

The course of events in the Peloponnese is in any case the most important, for this is the area on which the tradition concentrated, and claimed to know most about. So special attention must be paid to the districts of the Argolid, Laconia and Messenia, where the invaders are said to have settled. In these areas, the following archaeological picture emerges. In the Argolid, in spite of destruction at Mycenae and Tiryns, and the abandonment of certain other sites, there is no evidence of settlement by newcomers. The survivors have all the usual Mycenaean characteristics. There is even some attempted recovery, and later, perhaps about the middle of the twelfth century, in spite of a further and final destruction at Mycenae, there is still no trace of settlement by intruders, evidence for this not appearing until a date which cannot be earlier than 1100, and is probably much later. Laconia is the least well known of the three areas, but recent survey and excavation have suggested on the one hand a serious depopulation, and on the other the continuance of the Mycenaean sanctuary at Amyklai. Once again, there is no evidence for invaders settling in this area, the earliest evidence of an obviously new culture being the later pottery of Amyklai, which can hardly precede the beginning of Attic Protogeometric and should therefore come down into the eleventh century. Our relative archaeological ignorance of this district may be considered to affect the strength of the evidence, but it is remarkable that precisely the same picture has emerged from Messenia, an area also subjected to a very intensive survey. Messenia was closely populated in LH. III B, but traces of habitation are almost non-existent for a long period after the destruction at the end of LH. III B (cf. pp. 93 ff.).

Such is the evidence from these three regions, and it is worth adding that a similar picture of depopulation is to be found in Elis, although the material is much more slight. The overall picture is remarkable. Invasion caused widespread destruction, and led to partial or almost complete depopulation. In the areas of partial depopulation, the survivors continued to retain Mycenaean characteristics. Nowhere is there any evidence of settlement by new peoples. Is this a reliable and accurate picture? May it not be said that in the regions where Mycenaean features survived these features were simply taken over by the invaders, using a subjected Mycenaean remnant? Where there seems to have been almost complete depopulation, may not the culture of the invaders have been so primitive that all trace of their settlements has been lost? This may be just possible, though it is not exactly easy to believe in both of the above hypotheses. But it is much more likely that in fact the invaders, having wreaked their destruction, went elsewhere or returned whence they had come.

Nevertheless, it still remains undeniable, from the evidence of the dialect if from nothing else, that all four areas mentioned above were overrun and occupied by North-western peoples. If the occupation did not take place at the time of the invasion, when did it occur? To this also archaeology has a possible answer. New features appear in the Argolid probably in the first half of the eleventh century (the cist tombs, new settlement), replacing the characteristic Mycenaean objects and customs (cf. pp. 79 ff.). In Laconia, there is the evidence of Amyklai, mentioned above (p. 251). And now, cist tombs and pithos burials have been found in Achaea, Elis and Messenia, associated in each area with pottery of Protogeometric type (cf. pp. 39 f.). In every case something entirely different from the Mycenaean is introduced, and must be dated, very probably, to some time during the second half of the eleventh century.

It need hardly be stressed that this picture, if it is correct, has very serious consequences for the traditional conception of the Dorian invasion, and for the related Aetolian thrust. It is still possible to claim that the actual invasion of *c.* 1200 was the work of Dorians, but the occupation of the territory concerned is as important to the tradition as the invasion, and it may now be suggested that this was connected with a much later series of movements than the original invasion, settlement in the Argolid probably not occurring until *c.* 1075, and in the South and West Peloponnese not till appreciably later, perhaps not till *c.* 1000. Such a conclusion affects the whole cohesion of the Dorian part of the oral tradition, especially in regard to its relationship to the Heroic Age. It means that Aristodemos' sons Eurysthenes and Procles cannot have become kings of Sparta until at least two hundred years after the Trojan War, as a consequence of which the line of descent from Heracles must be open to grave doubt, and indeed any links with the Achaeans, as for example with Teisamenos. Similar doubts must also be expressed with regard to Temenos, although the occupation of the Argolid probably preceded that of Laconia—a factor which should also be noted, as it implies a denial of the inner cohesion of the traditional story.

Before continuing with the analysis of the oral tradition in the light of the archaeological evidence, it is worth asking whether excavation or survey provides any further indication of movement into the Mycenaean world from beyond its boundaries, such as the Macedonian thrust into North Thessaly (mentioned above), of which the tradition had no knowledge. There does appear to be one such movement, accompanied by settlement, that reflected by the sub-Mycenaean cemeteries of Athens and Salamis (see pp. 37, 231 f.), attested both by the appearance of new features and by the disappearance of some Mycenaean characteristics. This intrusion is not only unknown to the traditional account, it is opposed to it. In this instance it is to be noted that the dialect evidence generally supports the tradition, though it is also significant that traces of the Doric speech have been identified in the Ionic dialect, before its division into Attic and Ionic (p. 245). For a possible explanation, it must be borne in mind that this is about the earliest of the recognizable movements from the North, that it took place possibly two generations before newcomers arrived in the Argolid, and that the eastern part of Attica was still occupied by the original inhabitants. May it not be that there was a fusion between the new arrivals and surviving Mycenaeans (a flourishing element, part of the Central Aegean LH. III C nucleus), and that as a result the indigenous speech prevailed, as well as the local ceramic style, although it was soon to be transformed and revitalized by the potters who created the Protogeometric style?

To return to the tradition, to what extent does the doubt cast on the date and inner cohesion of the Dorian invasion affect the account of the movements across the Aegean? *A priori*, it should affect the expansion eastwards of the Dorians, whether from Laconia or the Argolid, but it need not necessarily affect the migration of the Ionians and Aeolians, since these movements may have been the result of invasion unconnected with any immediate occupation by the invaders.

So far as concerns the Dorians, a brief mention may be made of Homer's knowledge of them in Crete before the Trojan War,[1] and of the interpretation of the Rhodian entry in the Catalogue of Ships,[2] to the effect that the threefold division under Tlepolemos indicates the presence of Dorians. Archaeology has no comment on this evidence, except only to say that if there were Dorians either in Crete or Rhodes before the Trojan War they are indistinguishable from the Minoan and Mycenaean inhabitants. It may be added that the presence of Dorians on Rhodes cannot be regarded as proved on the internal evidence of the Catalogue.[3]

With regard to expansion after the occupation of the Peloponnese, the islands of Melos and Thera were colonized from Laconia (see above, p. 247); here the archaeological material is insufficient for an answer to be suggested, though it may be noted that if the preceding criticism of the time of occupation of Laconia is correct then Thucydides' date for the Dorian settlement of Melos can no longer stand.[4] The main areas of expansion, as confirmed by the dialect evidence, were Crete, and the Dodecanese with the adjacent coastline of Asia Minor. The district of origin seems in this case to have been the Argolid, where it has been suggested, on the basis of excavation, that a break in culture came after 1100. The course of events in Crete is not, as has been seen (cf. pp. 191 ff.), easy to interpret from the archaeological information available, but there do seem to be signs of intrusion during the latter half of LH. III C, and this might be too early a date for a Dorian invasion or infiltration from the Argolid. It is very difficult to find at any later date a cultural break of a sort consonant with Dorian intrusion, and yet it cannot be doubted that the intrusion took place; this is the type of case which exposes the limitation not of the traditional, but of the archaeological, evidence. In the Dodecanese, it is clear that Mycenaean cemeteries were abandoned, very probably before the end of LH. III C, but evidence is almost totally lacking which might indicate what kind of culture replaced that of the Mycenaeans, though it is tempting to see in the cist tombs of Serraglio on Kos,

---

[1] *Od.* xix. 177.
[2] *Iliad*, ii. 653 ff.
[3] Page, *History and the Homeric Iliad*, p. 148; Andrewes, *Hermes*, 1961, p. 133, n. 1.
[4] Th. v. 112.

situated over the ruins of the preceding Mycenaean settlement, and containing pottery of a relatively advanced Protogeometric style of non-Attic type, the burials of the first Dorian settlers. It is also worth noting that the earliest Greek pottery at Assarlik on the Halicarnassus peninsula, an area later taken over by the Dorians but where an Ionic substratum remained,[1] is possibly related to that current in Attica at the time of transition from sub-Mycenaean to Protogeometric; so the Dorians probably came here later than this. It may be concluded that, if the cist tomb cemetery on Kos represents the colonization of Dorians, then once again the traditional account has given too high a date, but the matter is better left until the fuller record, or further discovery, of archaeological material.

The mention of Assarlik, with its very early possible link with Attica, may serve to introduce the situation with regard to the Ionian migration. It may be claimed that on this occasion we have a movement for which the traditional date given is reasonably accurate, but a brief discussion is first desirable on the preliminaries to this migration, the arrivals in Attica of many refugees who helped to swell the numbers who subsequently colonized the islands of the Central Aegean and Ionian coast of Asia Minor. I will omit any comment on the various Boeotians, Phocians, Pelasgoi, Molossians, Dryopes, and even Dorians, mentioned by Herodotus,[2] but two other groups were directly or indirectly affected by the Dorian invasion of the Peloponnese, the Pylians under Codros, and the Ionians who had been ejected from Achaea after Teisamenos' people, defeated by the Dorians, seized that territory.[3] Might this reflect the situation brought about by the invasion of c. 1200? There is no doubt that the inhabitants of Pylos fled at this time and presumably at this time only, for there were afterwards probably not many left to flee (assuming the palace at Ano Englianos to be correctly identified as Nestor's capital), and there is also no doubt that Achaea received at this time a large number of new Mycenaean settlers (cf. pp. 98, 226 f.). But that is as far as we can go; there is no indication that any went from Pylos to Athens—indeed, it is unlikely, from the situation in that city; and there is no indication even that the new settlements in Achaea involved the expulsion of any existing inhabitants, far less that these unidentifiable refugees made their way to Attica for some time after this—probably not for a hundred years.

It had long been supposed that the archaeological evidence did not warrant an early date for the Ionian migration,[4] but the recent excavations at Miletus (cf. p. 162 f.) have shown that this belief must be revised, for the earliest re-occupation pottery is, as at Assarlik, similar to that of Athens of the transitional period between sub-Mycenaean and Protogeometric, and must belong within the first half of the eleventh century. It seems to me doubtful whether this move can be related to the traditional story of the Dorian invasion and occupation, but it is possible that the excavated material may reflect the relative accuracy of an Ionian tradition as unconnected with any other body of tradition.

Finally, there is the Aeolian migration. There is no doubt that this is a historical fact; though the schematic story of Strabo is open to serious doubt, both Herodotus and

---

[1] Bean and Cook, *BSA*, l. 95 ff.
[2] i. 146.
[3] Hdt. i. 145 and 147.
[4] Cf. e.g. Wade-Gery, *The Poet of the Iliad*, p. 5.

Thucydides are witness to the thrust of Thessalians into Thessaly, and Thucydides states not only that this resulted in the Boeotians (themselves perhaps of North-western stock) being pushed southwards into the district they inhabited in later times, but also that some displaced Aeolians eventually made their way across the Aegean to Aeolis. The tradition is confirmed by the distribution of dialects, on both sides of the Aegean; the North-west dialect penetrated both into Boeotia and into Western Thessaly, while the Aeolic dialect was strongest in East Thessaly and in Aeolis, but was also to be found in Boeotia.

The archaeological material, if I am correct in assuming that the spread of cist tomb burial was a mark of intrusion from North or North-west of Mycenaean territory, agrees reasonably well with the traditional account of what happened on the Mainland of Greece. The evidence is only slight for Boeotia, but there is an increasing amount of material showing the early establishment of the practice of burying in cist tombs in Thessaly, although at Iolkos, where the signs of Mycenaean survival are so strong, the tholos tomb multiple burial system survived for adults. There is also the evidence of the intrusion of some Macedonians who also, at least at Marmariani, buried their dead in tholos tombs. One may indeed wonder whether these Macedonians may not themselves have been responsible for the introduction of cist tombs, but there is no proof of this, and it would run counter to the evidence of tradition and dialect. In any case the circumstances were certainly suitable for a migration, the survival of the presumably Mycenaean Aeolic strain being confirmed by the evidence of Iolkos.

In consequence, we should expect some clear signs in Aeolis of movement over to this region on the part of Aeolians (Mycenaeans?) from the Mainland. All that can be said, however, in our present state of knowledge, is that no trace has been found of these migrants. No great amount of excavation has taken place but where there has—notably at Antissa and Pyrrha on Lesbos—the usual pottery in strata of this period, and indeed down to the eighth century, is a monochrome grey bucchero related to that of Troy VIII, but in no way characteristic either of Thessaly or Boeotia.[1] It may be that the right sites have not yet been found—Mitylene should be one such, but the modern town must directly overlie all earlier settlements—but as things stand archaeology knows of no Mycenaean settlers, nor of any Greek pottery earlier than the eighth century B.C. However, Miletus must serve as a warning against undue archaeological dogmatism.

Thus it appears that at many stages the traditional account is not supported by the archaeological evidence. The dates may be questioned, the interrelation of the stories is open to doubt, even the facts may not stand up to examination. To what extent are we justified in setting aside the oral tradition?

In certain respects, the nature itself of oral tradition is a bar to accuracy. There is a tendency to a lack of proportion in assessing the importance of events and of those who participated in them, and an accurate and coherent chronological scheme is not to be expected.

In Greece, it must above all be borne in mind that a period of almost five hundred years of illiteracy had intervened between the last stages of Mycenaean civilization and

---

[1] Lamb, *JHS*, lii. 1 ff. For the characteristic grey ware and its geographical distribution, see Hanfmann, *AJA*, xlix. 580 f. and *AJA*, lii. 146 and 153; Dunbabin, *The Greeks and their Eastern Neighbours*, pp. 65 f.

the introduction of the alphabet, and the effect of this is undoubtedly reflected in the extreme poverty of information available for the two or three centuries preceding the eighth. Then there are peculiar circumstances which characterize the Greek oral tradition. It so happened that a remarkably healthy body of tradition concerning the events of some five hundred years earlier had survived, to be embodied in the Homeric epic. This epic, belonging to so remote a period, was bound to suffer from the usual disadvantages affecting the transmission of oral tradition, and it is only too likely that the accuracy of the account would be further vitiated by the fact that Homer wrote as a creative artist, not as a mere editor of the stories which had survived. On the other hand, there is no reason to suppose that the general picture of the civilization was seriously inaccurate, nor to doubt the existence of the Trojan War, though its relative importance may have been exaggerated.

As has been explained, the publication and diffusion of the epic had a very strong effect on the Greek world of c. 700, and the age of Mycenae became for the Greeks the authentic picture of their heroic past, in which the activities of the Olympian deities in no way detracted from the belief in the existence of the mortal heroes. Unfortunately, the epic stood on its own, entirely unrelated to the world in which Homer lived. Consequently it became obligatory, almost a matter of national prestige, that the gap should be bridged.

In bridging the gap the Greeks were confronted with serious difficulties. The whole civilization of which Homer wrote had been swept away, and there can have been hardly a single district which was unaffected by the invasions which ended that civilization. The Greeks knew of the existence of the invasions, and that the invaders were of their own race, and they also knew of the later migrations across the Aegean. How much did they know? It will be borne in mind that information concerning the centuries immediately preceding the eighth appears to have been confined to lists of kings, certain foundations of settlements, and the occasional isolated event. It may also be that each city had tended to have its own local traditions, but it is certainly unlikely that any attempt was made to integrate these.

On the other hand, there is no reason why the oral tradition, as separately preserved, may not have been fairly explicit on the invasions and subsequent migrations; but was it possible to link these together, and to connect the whole with the circumstances during and after the Trojan War? The crux of the difficulty surely appears in the need to postulate a far too long average reign for the Spartan kings. It may be suggested that there was sufficient information available to tell approximately when the Trojan War took place[1]—and we have seen how close the Greeks got to it—and that in consequence the Spartan chronology, as representing most reliably the tradition of the Dorian invaders, had to be fitted in. If one adds to this the desire of the Dorian element to show its kinship with the Homeric heroes, one realizes the strong possibility of fabrication and distortion over and above that which might naturally be found in any oral tradition. The factor of Spartan expansion in the centuries following the eighth must also be taken into account; by the sixth century, this city had become the most powerful in Greece.

[1] This point raises a question of obvious importance, to which I can offer no answer.

It seems therefore justifiable to doubt the accuracy of the oral tradition, in particular that part which involved the Dorians, on internal grounds, quite irrespective of the evidence provided by archaeology.

Much use has indeed been made of the archaeological material, and it is equally important to inquire to what extent this type of evidence, also, may be considered reliable. It must naturally be recognized that archaeology has very strict limits; there are so many things of which it can tell us nothing or next to nothing—it can, for example, tell us nothing of the processes of thought of the people concerned, nor can it say much about matters such as political organization. Even within its own limits, great caution must be observed. The less complete the picture is, the more hesitant the conclusions must be; this is an obvious fact, but there is no harm in stressing it. And by completeness must be understood both geographical and cultural completeness. By cultural completeness I mean simply that conclusions should not be made simply on the basis of the pottery, but on every other type of evidence available. Geographical completeness needs no elaboration; if an area has been only partially explored, inferences cannot be more than hypothetical. The recent excavations at Miletus are a case in point, but while one may use these as a warning against too great haste in reaching conclusions in certain other areas, one may not do so in the case of districts which have been thoroughly investigated, such as the Argolid, and now Messenia and Laconia.[1]

It will be clear, then, that the archaeological evidence must be interpreted with the greatest care. The reader himself must judge whether I have interpreted with sufficient caution. The totality of the evidence does however, to my mind, lead to the conclusions that I have drawn. On the basis of these, it should be possible to probe the subsequent history of the Greek world with a better understanding of its origins. This lies beyond the scope of my book, but I have felt it worth while to devote a brief concluding chapter to the early stages of the Protogeometric period.

[1] Even here, of course, one must be careful not to exaggerate the importance of survey work, the conclusions of which are based on surface finds.

CHAPTER XI

EPILOGUE: THE EARLY STAGES OF THE PROTOGEOMETRIC PERIOD

When, some years ago, I published the results of my researches on Protogeometric pottery, I stressed certain general features and arrived at certain main conclusions,[1] of which the following are of relevance to the present work. I was unable to point to any evidence for clear continuity of settlement after the end of LH. III C except in Athens, North Central Crete, and Ithaca. For most of the other areas there seemed to be a gap of some hundred and twenty-five years which I was unable to bridge. On the assumption that LH. III C came to an end *c*. 1075, I concluded that the rise of the Protogeometric style in Athens took place *c*. 1025.[2] I considered that this style developed on its own, with no outward diffusion until the middle of the tenth century, and that until this time the various districts of Greece and the Aegean remained, with certain minor exceptions, in relative isolation. Then I visualized that *c*. 950 there was a resumption of communications especially throughout the Aegean, at which time the Athenian style, which I regarded as the original and basic manifestation of Protogeometric, influenced to a greater or lesser extent the ceramic styles of most other regions, with the exception of Ithaca and Laconia.

The general picture available, and the conclusions reached, must now be modified radically. The reasons for this are threefold: the recent finds and publications of LH. III C pottery and the conclusions to be drawn therefrom, as recorded elsewhere in this book, the newly-discovered material of the Protogeometric period, which I list at the end of this chapter, and a fresh hypothesis (cf. pp. 261 ff.) which argues for the development of a Protogeometric style in Thessaly independent from that in Athens. It is thus desirable that the present situation should be clarified, particularly as it is closely related to some of the views and conclusions embodied in this work.

The first point that may be made is that, through interconnexions between Attica, Crete and Cyprus, it seems extremely likely that the rise of the Protogeometric style in Athens should be placed *c*. 1050 rather than at any time later (cf. pp. 25 ff., 241). The date given depends on the relative and absolute chronology of the Cypriot ceramic series, as most recently formulated (cf. p. 197, n. 2).

Secondly, there is the probability that the sub-Mycenaean period in Athens and Salamis was not entirely subsequent to the end of LH. III C, but in the main contemporary with its later stages (cf. pp. 17 ff.). This hypothesis involves the deletion of the time during which sub-Mycenaean was in fashion at Athens (some fifty years or more) as a separate chronological entity. As a result, and taking into consideration further discoveries of LH. III C and Protogeometric material, it can be stated that there was virtual

[1] *PGP*, pp. 296 ff.   [2] Op. cit. p. 294.

EPILOGUE: THE EARLY STAGES OF THE PROTOGEOMETRIC PERIOD

continuity of settlement not only in Athens, North Central Crete, and Ithaca, but also in the Argolid, at Iolkos in Thessaly, on Naxos, and in Southern Crete. Also, although there is some gap, the recent excavations at Miletus have shown that the re-occupation of the site was contemporary with the transition from sub-Mycenaean to Protogeometric in Athens. A much more complete and accurate picture has then emerged for the Aegean, and the theory of relative isolation must be abandoned, as clear links seem to be able to be established between Athens and the areas concerned almost from the beginning of Protogeometric if not before.

The history of the Greek and Aegean area during the eleventh century cannot, however, be understood without reference to the arrival of new people in what had been the Mycenaean area. I have argued (pp. 37 ff.) that the chief manifestation of the intrusive elements is the appearance of a new type of tomb, the cist tomb—and to a lesser extent the pithos burial. If the argument is valid, several different intrusions may have taken place. First there are the cist tombs of Athens and Salamis, with which certain burials at Thebes are probably to be connected, representing a group of new arrivals during the latter half of LH. III C. Then there are the cist tombs of the Argolid, signifying the establishment of further newcomers at the end of LH. III C, barely if at all before the development of the Protogeometric style in Athens. Third, there is the recent discovery of cist tombs and pithos burials of Protogeometric and Geometric date in Achaea, Elis and Messenia, both types of burial being confirmed for the Protogeometric period at Nichoria in Messenia. These, together with certain ceramic features which suggest links between Laconia, Messenia, Ithaca and Achaea,[1] indicate yet a further group, though it must be stressed that the ceramic links are rather tenuous, and that until there are detailed reports and fuller knowledge from further excavation the conclusions must remain extremely tentative. A fourth group (or groups) may have made its way into Thessaly, certainly not later than the Protogeometric period and probably before, from the evidence of cist tombs at Palaiokastro, Halos, Retziouni, Iolkos and Theotokou (cf. pp. 38 f., 138).[2] To the North again, the cist tombs of Kozani, as well as the cemetery of Vergina in Western Macedonia (cf. pp. 38, 144 ff.) with its pit graves, cist tombs and pithos burials, and its distinctive bronze objects, indicate a fifth group, coming from the Danube area possibly before the rise of Protogeometric in the South. And finally, mention should be made of that group of intruders who came down from Macedonia into North Thessaly, either in consequence of the above movement or before it; this group is recognizable not by its tombs, for the newcomers adopted the tholos tomb, but by its pottery.[3]

Besides this, there were also certain subsidiary movements, again recognizable by the cist tombs, into and across the Aegean, in Protogeometric (and possibly in Geometric) times. Such may be observed on Skyros, presumably from Thessaly, on Andros and Tenos, either from Thessaly or Attica, on Naxos, from Attica probably just before the rise of Protogeometric, and in Late Protogeometric on Kos, perhaps from the Argolid.[4]

---

[1] Cf. p. 234 and *PGP*, pp. 280 f. and 288.

[2] The unpublished cist tombs excavated by Verdhelis at Agrilia should perhaps be added (*Verdhelis*, p. 61); these are reported to contain hand-made pottery and a few Mycenaean vases.

[3] Heurtley and Skeat, *BSA*, xxxi. 44.

[4] Cf. *PGP*, pp. 306 f.

In this account, I have assumed movement either from north to south, or from west to east. This is not provable, but the relative chronology seems to support it. Also, it can by no means be shown that the movements on the Mainland of Greece all belonged to separate groups and may not have been offshoots in certain cases of groups already established. Much yet remains to be made clear.

It is unfortunate that there are hardly any criteria by which to judge these newcomers apart from their manner of burial, except in the case of those who settled at Vergina and the displaced Macedonians. The long dress pins of bronze may be one of their characteristic objects, and it is noteworthy that there are two distinct types of these (cf. pp. 53 f.), though even so they are not clearly traceable to areas north of Greece. They might have brought the arched fibulae, but this seems doubtful (cf. pp. 57 f.). And there are a few isolated bronze objects for which a northern origin can be suggested (cf. pp. 71 f.). Certainly the disappearance of Mycenaean types of ornament (cf. pp. 50 ff.) is significant, but one would like much more than this.

In particular, we know virtually nothing of the original pottery of the intruders. It may be hazarded that the hand-made vases found in some Protogeometric tombs of the Argolid reflect a previous tradition,[1] and that so also do the curious figurines found in Protogeometric Athens,[2] but that is all. Not that this need be a matter for great surprise, for as in many cases the intruders probably merged with a surviving Mycenaean population whose pottery, however degenerate, was almost bound to be superior to their own (if they did use pottery at all), it was natural that they should adopt the superior type of article.

That then is the rather hypothetical general picture of intrusions into Greece and the Aegean which the evidence seems to allow. That there were intruders is not really, I think, a matter of doubt, nor the fact that they came into Greece at varying times during the second half of the twelfth century and during the eleventh century.

It is also extremely probable that there was in many cases a merging of population, and thus a merging of cultures, the Mycenaean of superior but decadent culture blending with the relatively uncultured but more dynamic northerner. Even if the two elements did not mix, the intruders were very liable to be influenced by a culture that they would be much more closely aware of than in their country of origin.

From this point we may proceed to an analysis of the development of pottery styles. Two factors must be stressed. In the latter part of LH. III C the homogeneity of LH. III B had been lost, and there were several regional styles going their own way, in varying degree connected with one another. That is one factor; the other is that which has been mentioned above, the arrival of new racial elements. And from the combination of these two factors there are two likely results: one, that new styles will probably arise, and second that these styles will by no means necessarily develop in the same way—even though based generically on LH. III C, one must take into account both the variation of LH. III C and the particular quality of the new racial infusion.

These considerations, taken together with the conception of an early diffusion of the Attic Protogeometric style, lead on to a reappraisal of what is meant by the Protogeometric

---

[1] *Asine*, p. 436; *BSA*, xlix. 264 f.; *BCH*, lxxvii. 260.   [2] *Ker.* iv, Pl. 31; Smithson, *Hesp.* xxx, Pl. 30 (Nea Ionia).

EPILOGUE: THE EARLY STAGES OF THE PROTOGEOMETRIC PERIOD

style as such. Is it something relatively uniform, depending mainly on influences from one region only, or is it a multiple style, as LH. III C is (see Chap. 1)?

In my *Protogeometric Pottery* I made it clear that there were two slightly related local styles, those of Laconia and Ithaca, whose development owed little or nothing to the Attic series.[1] Apart from this, the general conclusion was that in other areas the varying styles could only be called Protogeometric in virtue of their having come under the influence, direct or indirect, of the Attic style. Was this a correct conclusion?

In a recent work by Verdhelis,[2] it has been argued that in Thessaly a Protogeometric style was developed long before the influence of the Attic style was felt, being based on a combination of preceding Mycenaean and native styles. This view has been strongly upheld by Theocharis,[3] on the evidence of a considerable body of further material. As the bulk of this material is as yet unrecorded, no use can be made of it, but the theory of Verdhelis deserves close attention.

So far as concerns the shapes and decorative motives attributed to a native origin, there is no need for argument; their part in the development of the style may be accepted. Verdhelis argues,[4] however, for the derivation of certain shapes and decorative motives from a previously existing local Mycenaean ceramic tradition—and it is admitted, especially taking into account Theocharis's discoveries, that the existence of this, at a very late stage, is certain. The shapes that are said to be so derivable are the hydria, the amphoriskos with vertical handles on the shoulder, the trefoil-lipped oinochoe, the lekythos, the one-handled jug, the skyphoi with high and low feet, and the cups with high and low feet. The decorative motives are the wavy lines, the groups of lines slanting in alternate directions, the compass-drawn circles and semicircles, and the handle decoration. As opposed to this, Verdhelis will allow, as inspired by the Attic style, the dark-ground scheme of decoration, the system of flanking a central motive by sets of semicircles, the system of decoration in panels, occasionally the ovoid shape of a vase, and minor motives such as the central fillings of the circles.[5] This is not very much, and as well as this he points out that these features are late, in particular the use of the dark-ground scheme, and consequently he concludes that a Protogeometric style arose in Thessaly quite independently of that in Attica—though not necessarily earlier in time.

In this conclusion, he presumably accepted my view that the diffusion of the Attic style did not take place until the beginning of the late phase, at some time during the tenth century. As I have explained, this is no longer a tenable view.

With regard to his derivation of certain shapes from the local Mycenaean tradition, it is perfectly possible that he is right for the hydria, the lekythos, the one-handled jug, and the low-footed or flat-based skyphos and cup. The amphoriskos with vertical handles on the shoulder may be so derived, but its Mycenaean ancestry is not very clear. The trefoil-lipped oinochoe is known in very late LH. III C contexts further south, but evidence of its existence in Thessaly is desirable, and it may be noted that all the examples given are in the dark-ground system of decoration. Finally, there is the question of the high feet;

[1] *PGP*, pp. 280 f. and 288.
[2] 'Ο Πρωτογεωμετρικὸς 'Ρυθμὸς τῆς Θεσσαλίας, pp. 49 ff.
[3] *Ergon* for 1960, p. 59; *Ergon* for 1961, p. 59.
[4] *Verdhelis*, pp. 53 ff.
[5] Op. cit. pp. 75 ff.

although there is a tendency for the feet of bowls and cups to become more pronounced in the latter part of LH. III C, this stage has yet to be established in Thessaly, and in any case the true high conical foot seems to appear first in Attic Protogeometric, possibly (cf. p. 25) as a result of Cypriot influence.

Much of what Verdhelis says concerning the derivation of shapes is therefore reasonable. He does not appear, though, to mention the neck-handled amphora, the earliest examples of which have a clay-ground system of decoration.[1] In Athens, this characteristic shape certainly derives from an LH. III C prototype, but such a prototype has not yet been identified in Thessaly.

With regard to the decorative motives, the wavy lines and the handle decoration may quite well originate from the local Mycenaean style, and so possibly may the groups of alternating lines, though it is again noticeable that they are to be found only on dark-ground vases, and so could be a motive taken over from Attic Protogeometric.

The crucial point, however, is to be found in Verdhelis's derivation of the compass-drawn circles and semicircles from the local Mycenaean motives. He does not suggest that this new technical innovation travelled from Thessaly to Athens and elsewhere, but he claims that the innovation was made independently (this indeed he must do, as the clay-ground amphorae have compass-drawn circles on the shoulder), and in consequence one would be able to claim that other regions may have made a similar independent technical advance.

There is no doubt, I think, that the inspiration for compass-drawn circles and semicircles is to be found in LH. III C motives, in particular the hand-drawn semicircles, but it must be stressed that this is a different matter from the mere survival of a motive. The change is a technical one—a very simple one, admittedly, but one that no Mycenaean potter ever thought of. The point is not susceptible of proof, but in my opinion it is in the highest degree unlikely that this change was originally effected in more than one district. Can it be accepted that some Athenian potter was responsible for this technical innovation? From the evidence available, it would seem so; and there are other considerations as well. The use of a faster wheel is another technical advance of the Protogeometric style: did this originate in Athens? Again, one cannot prove that it did, but it should be borne in mind that the style also involved a new conception of design, and in this case there can be no doubt that it was best understood and carried out in Athens, and this means that the introduction of the faster wheel, as well as the use of compasses and the multiple brush, are more likely to have come about in Athens than anywhere else.

It is realized that arguments based on technique and on aesthetic factors are not wholly satisfying, and that there is no concrete proof, but I believe that they are valid, and to a certain extent they are supported by the appearance of vases of Attic manufacture elsewhere—though not in Thessaly. On the supposition that my explanation is correct, and bearing in mind the probability of an early contact between Attic Protogeometric and other contemporary styles, it follows that when the signs of technical or stylistic improvement worked out in Athens appear in other styles, they are due to contact with that city.

[1] Op. cit. Pl. I.

So far as concerns Thessaly, I therefore believe that the initial debt to the Athenian Protogeometric style is earlier and greater than Verdhelis supposes, though on the other hand it is probably much less than I originally thought.

Other areas, for the most part, received a similar impulse from the Athenian style. In Central Crete, the transformation of sub-Minoan into Protogeometric is due to new features from Athens—the fact that there was no independent development seems clear from what is known of the pottery of East Crete, which indicates stagnation until the Geometric (or Late Protogeometric) period (cf. pp. 184, 187). The Argive Protogeometric style was similarly influenced by the Attic, though still affected by the preceding Mycenaean, and here with a new racial element probably present. The Protogeometric pottery of the Kos tombs appears fully fledged, and so one cannot assess the manner of its origin. The earliest reoccupation pottery of Miletus is linked with the transition from sub-Mycenaean to Protogeometric as observable in Athens (cf. p. 163). Only the ceramic development of South and West Peloponnese, with that of Ithaca, remains relatively uninfluenced by the Attic style, and even here the compass-drawn circles and semicircles, and certain other features, prove that there was some contact.

In general, it can be said that each district had its own individual Protogeometric style, based in part on the previously existing pottery, and in certain areas affected to an extent which cannot be gauged by the arrival of newcomers. But for the most part the fact that we can call these styles Protogeometric is due to the acceptance of technical and stylistic innovations originating in Athens.

It is not my intention to pursue the later development of the Protogeometric style. The revised picture of the early stages, however, when taken with other evidence, permits certain conclusions as to the general state of affairs in Greece and the Aegean. From the beginning of the Protogeometric period, there was peaceful intercommunication more or less throughout the central and southern Aegean area, though parts of Crete probably remained culturally isolated, and one does not yet know the situation in the Dodecanese. The North Aegean does not seem to have been much visited; the evidence for this is reasonably clear in Macedonia, and for the rest one has to rely on the admittedly dubious factor of negative evidence. On the Mainland of Greece, from Thessaly southwards, there were periodical arrivals of newcomers from the North and West, and in course of time these were extended across the Aegean. These thrusts do not, however, seem to have been of a particularly destructive nature; for the most part the intruders settled down with the surviving local population. On the other hand, there may have been an occasional disturbance of the native inhabitants (it could have happened in Achaea), as there has to be some explanation for trans-Aegean movements such as that of the Ionian Migration—the spirit of adventure and overpopulation are probably insufficient causes at this period.

If there was a major area where contacts with the rest of Greece were only slight, it was probably the South and West Peloponnese, areas previously almost entirely abandoned and now (the second half of the eleventh century?) populated afresh perhaps almost exclusively by new racial elements. On the other hand, the link between the Aegean and Cyprus remained firm, especially visible in the connexions between this island and Crete and Athens. With the beginning of the Protogeometric period, a new age is introduced.

APPENDIX A

PROTOGEOMETRIC FINDS SINCE 1951

Attica

ATHENS

Smithson, E. L. *The Protogeometric Cemetery at Nea Ionia, 1949*, in *Hesp.* xxx. 147 ff. This is the one major report for the Athenian Protogeometric period since 1950. The pottery and other objects belong to the late phase of the period. Note also the publication of Kerameikos sub-Mycenaean tomb 113.

Dontas, G. S. *AE*, 1953–4, pt. iii, pp. 89 ff. Protogeometric vases and an iron sword and spearhead from a burial beneath the Metropolis Cathedral of Athens.

Charitonides, S. *AE*, 1958, pp. 2 ff. A few scraps of pottery found near Constitution Square in Athens.

Meliadis, J. *Ergon* for 1955, p. 13. Report of a Protogeometric cremation and cinerary urns in the area south of the Acropolis. A fuller report in *Pr.* 1955, pp. 43 f. gives details of the contents of the cremation, but makes it clear that the cinerary urns belong to the Geometric period.

Meliadis, J. *Ergon* for 1957, p. 7. Mention of five Protogeometric tombs in the area south of the Acropolis.

Stavropoullos, Ph. *Ergon* for 1958, p. 9. A collection of some two hundred Protogeometric vases, used as sacrificial offerings, from close to Plato's Academy.

The Argolid

1. ARGOS

Courbin, P. *BCH*, lxxvii. 260 and 262, Fig. 55.; lxxviii. 177; lxxix. 312 and 314; lxxx. 376; lxxxi. 647, 655 f., 662 f., 677 and 680 f.; lxxxiii. 762 ff.

Charitonides, S. *Pr.* 1952, p. 425; *BCH*, lxxviii. 412, 421 and 419, Figs. 19 and 20.

Alexandris, O. *BCH*, lxxxv. 675, cf. 678, Fig. 11.

Protogeometric material from tombs and settlement. Extremely important for the whole of this period in the Argolid. It is evident that the potters evolved an individual style while maintaining close links with Athens.

2. MYCENAE

Desborough, V. R. d'A. *BSA*, xlix. 259 f.; l. 240 f.; li. 129 f. The contents of three tombs.

3. TIRYNS

Verdhelis, N. M. *AE*, 1956, suppl., p. 4. Brief mention of Protogeometric tombs.

4. NAUPLIA

Charitonides, S. *Pr.* 1953, pp. 191 ff. Tomb material, mostly Geometric, but a few Protogeometric sherds as well.

Messenia, Elis and Achaea

McDonald and Hope Simpson, *AJA*, lxv. 221 ff., have brought together the evidence for the Protogeometric sites now known in Messenia and Elis. Since their article appeared in 1961, further details of Nichoria in Messenia have been published by Yalouris, *BCH*, lxxxv. 697, and Yalouris has found Protogeometric tombs at Ancient Elis, *Ergon* for 1961, pp. 186 ff.

In Achaea, Mrs. Vermeule has recorded and illustrated some of the vases from the pithos burial at Derveni, in the northern part of this district, *AJA*, lxiv. 16 f.

It will be apparent from the sections of the book dealing with these districts (pp. 90 ff., 97 ff.) that there has been a great advance in our knowledge since the appearance of my *Protogeometric Pottery*. No conclusions can be drawn (except on the types of tomb, see pp. 37 ff.) until the full report of the pottery and other finds, but the ceramic link between Derveni and Ithaca may be noted, and also the fact that in Messenia at least there was some knowledge of the Protogeometric style as found in the Aegean. The links with the Aegean were probably not very strong, but it does seem possible that there were interconnexions between the three districts mentioned, and also between them and Ithaca, and perhaps Laconia (cf. *PGP*, pp. 280 f.).

Laconia

Apart from two fragmentary Protogeometric vases found near Mavrovouni, southwest of Gythion (Waterhouse and Hope Simpson, *BSA*, lvi. 115, Fig. 2), a sherd from Apidia (*BSA*, lv. 87) and a sherd from Amyklai (*CVA*, Mainz I, Pl. 2, 2), nothing new has been recorded from this district.

North Peloponnese

CVA Mainz I, 12 ff., Pl. 3 and Figs. 1–10. The contents of a grave, said to come from somewhere in this rather wide area. The pottery consisted of four vases, a small amphora with handles from lip to shoulder (cf. op, cit. Pl. 1, 1 and 2, considered to be Attic Protogeometric), a small neck amphora, a shallow bowl and a ring vase.

The small finds included several bracelets (perhaps of northern origin?), three fibulae with swollen arch and strengthening collars, and two very long pins, of the type found at Gypsades and Argos (see p. 53). This is altogether a very interesting group, and it is unfortunate that precise knowledge of its provenience is not available.

Phocis

DELPHI

Lerat, L. *BCH*, lxxxv. 352 ff. A few Protogeometric sherds from the area east of the Sanctuary of Apollo. Connexions mainly with Thessaly, and date perhaps not earlier than the ninth century.

Thessaly

1. PTELEON

Verdhelis, N. M. *Pr.* 1951, pp. 141 ff. At least two vases from a tomb near this site appear to be Protogeometric.

2. KAPAKLI (close to Iolkos)

Verdhelis, N. M. ʽΟ Πρωτογεωμετρικὸς ʽΡυθμὸς τῆς Θεσσαλίας. The Protogeometric vases from this extremely important tholos tomb are fully reported in this work, and add greatly to our knowledge of the style in Thessaly. Even more important, however, is Verdhelis's detailed analysis of the Thessalian Protogeometric style; much other material is discussed as well as that of Kapakli. The value of this book will be clear from my use of it elsewhere.

3. IOLKOS

Theocharis, D. *Archaeology*, xi. 18; *Ergon* for 1960, pp. 55 ff.; *Ergon* for 1961, pp. 51 ff. First reports of the very important Protogeometric settlement, and of the child burials in cist tombs. Referred to elsewhere in this book, pp. 128 f., 136 ff.

Macedonia

VERGINA

Andronikos, M. *Balkan Studies*, ii. 96 and Pl. 8, 16; *Pr.* 1952 ff.; *Ergon* for 1957 to 1961.

A substantial number of Protogeometric vases were found in this large cemetery, alongside the native hand-made ware. The most popular type was the skyphos with pendent semicircles, but other shapes as well were represented. One skyphos in particular (*Balkan Studies*, ii. Pl. 8, 16, *top left*), with full circles, is extremely fine, and presumably an import. The date of these vases is not certain, but my impression is that they belong in the main to the early ninth century and later.

Cyclades

1. MELOS

Kunze, E. *ÖJh*, xxxix. 53 ff. Record of an amphora. This vase is locally made, and Kunze suggests that a separate Cycladic style developed in this period.

2. NAXOS

Condoleon, N. M. *Pr.* 1949, pp. 112 ff.; 1950, pp. 269 ff.; 1951, pp. 214 ff. Preliminary reports on the settlement at Grotta, which was occupied in the Protogeometric period; the only vases yet illustrated are two jugs, Verdhelis, 'Ο Πρωτογεωμετρικὸς 'Ρυθμὸς τῆς Θεσσαλίας, Pl. 15, Nos. 7 and 8.

Condoleon, N. M. *Ergon* for 1960, pp. 185 ff.; *Ergon* for 1961, pp. 199 f. Protogeometric material from tombs not far from the settlement at Grotta.

This material has already been discussed (pp. 149 ff.); there are links both with sub-Mycenaean in Attica and probably with Thessalian Protogeometric.

3. KEA

Caskey, J. L. *Hesp.* xxxi. 281. Mention of Protogeometric sherds from Ayia Irini.

Crete

1. KNOSSOS area

Brock, J. K. *Fortetsa: Early Greek Tombs near Knossos*. A comprehensive account of tombs and their contents, including some Protogeometric material. Contains also a valuable analysis of the development of the pottery style.

Boardman, J. *Protogeometric Graves at Agios Ioannis near Knossos*, in *BSA*, lv. 128 ff. An important addition to *Fortetsa*, and particularly interesting for the appearance of both cremations and inhumations.

Coldstream, J. N. *A Geometric Well at Knossos*, in *BSA*, lv. 159 ff. Settlement pottery, the earliest being of Middle Protogeometric date.

2. PHAESTOS area

Levi, D. *Ann.* xix–xx (N.S.), 255 ff., 283 ff. (settlement adjacent to the Palace), 355 ff. (tombs at Mulino and Petrokephali near Phaestos). For recent finds, see the Addenda.

Extremely important finds, establishing a link between North and South Central Crete in the Protogeometric period, and providing a connexion with the preceding sub-Minoan.

3. GORTYN

Levi, D. *Ann.* xvii–xviii (N.S.), 215 ff. The account makes it clear that there was a settlement here both in sub-Minoan and Protogeometric times.

4. MODI (West of Canea)

KX, 1953, pp. 485 f. Tombs excavated by Dr. N. Platon; some were rock-cut, some pithos burials. The finds included a large number of iron weapons, among which were swords; iron tools and bronze fibulae (one of which is arched) were also uncovered. There were over fifty vases, and I am much indebted to Dr. Platon for permission to give a brief account of these. The principal shape represented was the bell-krater with conical foot and the upper part only of the vase painted over; the profile of the body has a pronounced curve, however, as opposed to the almost vertical walls of the examples found elsewhere in Crete. A similar shape is also popular, with handles from lip to belly instead of on the belly, and with either a conical foot or, more often, a flat base. Of other shapes, there are several globular pyxides with ribbon handles, impressive four-handled jars, two small one-handled jugs with ovoid body and the same system of decoration as that of the bell-kraters, one or two squat trefoil-lipped oinochoai, cups, a shallow dish with vertical handles, a belly amphora with conical foot, a large jug and two squat pithoi. The larger vases were usually decorated in panels, the motives including combinations of triangles and diamonds, usually cross-hatched, and a pattern of opposed curves set vertically, similar to those on a krater from Diakata in Kephallenia (*AD*, v. 103, Fig. 18). There was only one example of concentric circles. Whether these vases can properly be called Protogeometric I do not know, but it seems likely that they were contemporary at least with the later Protogeometric vases of Knossos. The importance of these finds from an area previously unknown needs no stressing.

As well as the material from the above sites, brief reports have been made by Dr. Platon of excavations on other sites, as follows:

5. THE SETEIA DISTRICT

a. Berati-Piskokephalo. *KX*, 1952, p. 476; *Pr.* 1953, pp. 292 ff.; *BCH*, lxxvii. 239 f.; *BCH*, lxxviii. 154 f.

b. Sykia.
c. Aghios Stephanos. } *KX*, 1954, pp. 511 f.; *BCH*, lxxix. 307; *Pr.* 1954, pp. 365 ff.

d. Patela Sfakia. *KX*, 1955, p. 563; *BCH*, lxxx. 359.

This is all cemetery material, the burials being either in caves or in tholos tombs with square foundations. A considerable amount of pottery and other objects was recovered, apparently ranging from sub-Minoan to Geometric. It is clear that burials took place during the Protogeometric period, but such vases as have been illustrated (mainly from Berati) are in my opinion stylistically Geometric (see p. 184, n. 4). Until the full report it must remain uncertain whether the Protogeometric period was represented by vases in the Protogeometric style, or whether sub-Minoan persisted.

Other Cretan Sites

1. STOUS LAKKOUS KRITSA

KX, 1953, p. 485; *BCH*, lxxviii. 155. South-west of Aghios Nikolaos. Two Protogeometric tholos tombs.

2. ROTASI MONOPHATSIOU

KX, 1954, p. 516; *BCH*, lxxix. 304; *BCH*, lxxx. 343. In the Mesara area. One Protogeometric tholos tomb containing, as well as vases, idols with raised arms, these presumably continuing the Late Minoan tradition.

3. KALOCHORIO PEDHIADOS

KX, 1951, pp. 98 ff. Dr. Platon reports a settlement here, occupied in the Protogeometric and Early Geometric periods. A clay head found on this site (Levi, *Ann.* x–xii, Fig. 650a; Alexiou, *KX*, 1958, p. 214) is a survival of a Late Minoan type.

4. VASILIKA ANOGEIA

Alexiou, *KX*, 1958, p. 277, Pl. 13, Fig. 1, *left*. A clay figurine with Minoan antecedents, but considered to be stylistically Protogeometric.

5. ARKHANES

Alexiou, *KX*, 1950, pp. 441 ff.; *KX*, 1958, p. 278. It is now established that the terracotta hut-urn of Protogeometric B date in the Giamalakis collection came from this site.

6. AYIA PELAGIA

Boardman, *Cretan Collection*, p. 97, No. 433 (Pl. 31). A stirrup jar.

Western Asia Minor

1. MILETUS

Weickert, C. *Istanbuler Mitteilungen*, vii. 121 f., 132 and Pls. 36 and 37; ix–x. 37 f., 52 f., and Pls. 51–53 and 55. This comprises the most important body of new material from Western Asia Minor. The earliest post-Mycenaean settlement, which is said to have been established at no long interval after the end of the Mycenaean occupation (op. cit. vii. 132), starts with a small quantity of sub-Mycenaean pottery and continues on into Protogeometric. Connexion with Athens at the outset is probable, but one cannot yet say for how long the links remained close; much of the Protogeometric material is still unrecorded. The succeeding Geometric settlement was evidently more prosperous.

2. OTHER SITES

The finds of Protogeometric pottery at Old Smyrna have already been noted in my *Protogeometric Pottery*, p. 314. The material is not yet fully recorded, but a general account of the early history of the Greek settlement appeared in *BSA*, Vol. liii–liv. The joint leader of the Smyrna excavations, Professor J. M. Cook, has also undertaken, with Professor Bean, an intensive survey of the west coast of Asia Minor, the results of which were summarized in *Archaeological Reports for 1959–1960*, pp. 27 ff. Protogeometric sherds are reported, op. cit. p. 40, from Kuşadasi (probably Pygela) and Mordoğan (perhaps Boutheia). It is also noted in this review, op, cit. p. 41, that Professor Akurgal has discovered Protogeometric pottery at Phocaea.

Cyprus

1. AMATHUS

Desborough, V. R. d'A. *JHS*, lxxvii. 212 ff. Publication of a group which included two imported Protogeometric vases, probably of tenth-century date.

2. SOLI

Karageorghis, V. *BCH*, lxxxv. 277 ff. Two skyphoi with pendent semicircles, dated to the end of the eighth century.

3. KOUKLIA

Karageorghis, V. *BCH*, lxxxvi. 388 and 387, Fig. 83. Skyphos with pendent semicircles.

4. UNKNOWN PROVENIENCE

Hanfmann, G. M. A. *The Aegean and the Near East*, pp. 173 f. and 179, Fig. 16. A skyphos with pendent semicircles, bought in Nicosia, now in the Fogg Museum.

Syria

TELL SUKAS

Riis, P. J. *Annales Archéologiques de Syrie*, x. 123 f. and Fig. 13. Two sherds of skyphoi with pendent semicircles.

Cilicia

TARSUS

Hanfmann, G. M. A. *The Aegean and the Near East*, pp. 173 ff. Mention of skyphoi with pendent semicircles and a general discussion of the dating of this type of vase.

Summary

Reference to the Site Index of *Protogeometric Pottery* will indicate the advance of our knowledge. Certain areas are outstanding: the West Peloponnese, South Crete, West Asia Minor, Thessaly and, to a lesser extent, Macedonia and the Argolid. The main sites are those of Argos, Nichoria, Iolkos, Vergina, Knossos, Phaestos, Modi, Grotta and Miletus. Some areas still remain relatively unknown, such as the Megarid, Boeotia and Euboea, Corinthia, Arcadia and Laconia, many of the Cyclades, and Rhodes. Much of the new material is known only from brief preliminary reports. Even so, the general picture is becoming much clearer, and there is every hope that the next years will clarify the situation further. The main gap which still remains is that which needs to be filled by settlement and sanctuary material.

APPENDIX B

OCTOPUS STIRRUP JARS (FRONTISPIECE AND Pl. 6)

A list of the known examples was given by Skeat (*Dorians*, p. 25) and additions were made by Stubbings (*BSA*, xlii. 23). Since then, many more vases of this type have been found, and the list below may therefore be of use. It will be noted that I do not include the stirrup jar from Troy; the catalogue entry in the National Museum at Athens does not justify this attribution.

I have not discussed the stylistic development of these vases, as many of those found on Naxos and at Perati have not been illustrated; an analysis has, however, been made by Furumark (*OA*, iii. 212 f., 224, 226 f.).

The conception of covering the greater part of, if not all, the stirrup jar originated in Crete in LM. III B (p. 7). Vases of this type have been found on the following sites on the island.

Kydonia	Matz, *Forschungen auf Kreta*, Pls. 56, 3 and 60, 3 (= Mackeprang, *AJA*, xlii. Pl. 28, 5).
Knossos area	Palace. *BSA*, xxxi. Pl. 19. Sherds.
	Isopata. *P.T.K.* p. 141, Fig. 122.
	Mavrospelio. *BSA*, xxviii. 259 and 258, Fig. 12.
Phaestos	Borda, *Arte cretese-micenea*, Pl. 37. Sherds.
Karphi	*BSA*, lv. 17 f. and Pl. 6*b*. Several.
Gournia	*Gournia*, p. 45, Fig. 25 (assuming this sherd to have been from a stirrup jar).
Vasilike	Seager, *Transactions of the Department of Archaeology, University of Pennsylvania*, ii, Pl. 30.
Episkopi Ierapetras	*AD*, vi. suppl., 160, Fig. 9.
Mouliana	*AE*, 1904, pp. 42 ff., Fig. 10 and Pl. 1. Two from tomb B.
Myrsini	See p. 178. Two.

It will be noted that the distribution covers most of Crete.

'Octopus' stirrup jars were also made in the Dodecanese, on Naxos and at Perati; it is unnecessary to give full details.

Rhodes	Examples found in eleven of the tombs excavated by the Italians (15, 17, 21, 32, 35, 38, 71, 73, 84, 85, 87); over twenty altogether. There was also one from old tomb 10 (*B.M. Cat.* I, 1, A 932).
Kos	One of the finest of these vases is illustrated in Morricone's preliminary report (*Boll. d'Arte*, 1950, p. 324, Fig. 99).

Kalymnos	To the one in the British Museum (A 1015) may be added another in the Ashmolean Museum (1953. 535).
Naxos	It is only necessary to refer to the statement (*Ergon* for 1959, p. 128) that they were very numerous; this is significant in view of the small number of tombs excavated.
Perati	Also numerous, as will be clear from Iakovidis's reports in *Praktika* and in successive numbers of the *Ergon*.

Apart from the main centres of manufacture in Crete and the Central Aegean the distribution is as follows.

Attica	Athens. *Ker.* i, Pl. 5 (sub-Mycenaean tomb).
	Keratea. Welter, *Bausteine zur Archäologie* I, Pl. I, 1.
	Porto Raphti road. *BSA*, xlii. 23, Fig. 8 and Pl. 2, 3.
Asine	Asine, p. 401, Fig. 263, 2 (tomb 6, No. 4).
Monemvasia	*Archaeological Reports 1956*, p. 13, Fig. 14.
Delphi	*FD*, v. 8 f., Fig. 26 (Temenos tomb).
Thessaly	One sherd found near Pharsala by Mr. and Mrs. David French; I am very grateful to them for allowing me to mention this.
Pitane (in Aeolis)	Perrot-Chipiez, vi. 929 ff., Figs. 489 and 491.
Scoglio del Tonno	*MPI*, Pl. 14, Nos. 12–14. Three sherds.
Tarsus	*Tarsus*, ii, p. 226, Fig. 333, No. 1338.

It may be noted in conclusion that not one of these stirrup jars has been found in the extensive cemeteries of Achaea and Kephallenia. Their rarity in the Argolid is also remarkable.

BIBLIOGRAPHY

W. F. ALBRIGHT *The Archaeology of Palestine*, London, 1954.
P. ÅLIN *Das Ende der mykenischen Fundstätten auf dem griechischen Festland*, Studies in Mediterranean Archaeology, vol. i, Lund, 1962.
Y. BÉQUIGNON *La Vallée du Spercheios des Origines au IVe Siècle*, Paris, 1937.
—— *Recherches archéologiques à Phères en Thessalie*, Paris, 1937.
C. W. BLEGEN *Korakou; a Prehistoric Settlement near Corinth*, Concord, New Haven, 1921.
—— *Zygouries; a Prehistoric Settlement in the Valley of Cleonae*, Cambridge, Mass., 1928.
—— *Prosymna; the Helladic Settlement*, Cambridge, 1937.
—— C. G. BOULTER, J. L. CASKEY, MARION RAWSON and J. SPERLING *Troy*, Princeton, 1953 onwards.
C. BLINKENBERG *Fibules grecques et orientales (Lindiaka, vol. v)*, Copenhagen, 1926.
J. BOARDMAN *The Cretan Collection in Oxford*, Oxford, 1961.
J. BOEHLAU and K. SCHEFOLD *Larisa am Hermos; Ergebnisse der Ausgrabungen*, vol. iii, Berlin, 1942.
M. BORDA *Arte cretese-micenea nel Museo Pigorini di Roma*, Rome, 1946.
R. C. BOSANQUET and R. M. DAWKINS *The Unpublished Objects from the Palaikastro Excavations 1902–1906. BSA*, Supplementary Paper I.
HARRIET BOYD-HAWES *Gournia, Vasiliki and Other Prehistoric Sites on the Isthmus of Hierapetra, Crete*, Philadelphia, 1908.
J. H. BREASTED *Ancient Records of Egypt*, vol. iv, Chicago, 1906.
J. K. BROCK *Fortetsa*, Cambridge, 1957.
C. D. BUCK *The Greek Dialects*, Chicago, 1955.
H. BULLE *Orchomenos*, vol. i, Munich, 1907.
A. R. BURN *The Lyric Age of Greece*, London, 1960.
J. L. CASKEY See under C. W. Blegen, *Troy*.
H. W. CATLING *Cypriot Bronzework in the Mycenaean World*, Oxford, 1963.
E. COCHE DE LA FERTÉ *Essai de Classification de la céramique mycénienne d'Enkomi*, Paris, 1951.
R. DEMANGEL *Fouilles de Delphes*, II, 5, Paris, 1926.
V. R.D'A. DESBOROUGH *Protogeometric Pottery*, Oxford, 1952.
A. DESSENNE and J. DESHAYES *Fouilles exécutées à Mallia*, fasc. 2 (*Etudes crétoises* xi), Paris, 1959.
W. DÖRPFELD *Troja und Ilion; Ergebnisse der Ausgrabungen*, Athens, 1902.
T. J. DUNBABIN *The Greeks and Their Eastern Neighbours*, London, 1957.
W. F. EDGERTON and J. A. WILSON *Historical Records of Ramses III: the Texts in 'Medinet Habu'*, vols. i and ii, Chicago, 1936.
H. VAN EFFENTERRE *Nécropoles du Mirabello (Etudes crétoises*, viii), Paris, 1948.

Sir Arthur Evans *The Palace of Minos*, London, 1921–36.
—— *Prehistoric Tombs at Knossos* (*Archaeologia*, vol. lix), London, 1906.
D. Fimmen *Die kretisch-mykenische Kultur*, Leipzig and Berlin, 1924.
Sir John Forsdyke *Greece before Homer*, London, 1956.
O. Frödin and A. W. Persson *Asine; Results of the Swedish Excavations*, Stockholm, 1938.
A. Furtwängler *Aegina, das Heiligtum der Aphaia*, Munich, 1906.
—— and G. Löschcke, *Mykenische Vasen*, Berlin, 1886.
A. Furumark *The Chronology of Mycenaean pottery*, Stockholm, 1941.
—— *The Mycenaean Pottery; Analysis and Classification*, Stockholm, 1941.
H. Gallet de Santerre *Délos primitive et archaïque*, Paris, 1958.
Sir Alan Gardiner *Ancient Egyptian Onomastica*, vols. i-iii, Oxford, 1947.
J. Garstang *Prehistoric Mersin*, Oxford, 1953.
—— and O. R. Gurney *The Geography of the Hittite Empire*, London, 1959.
E. Gjerstad *The Swedish Cyprus Expedition*, vol. iv. 2, Stockholm, 1948.
Hetty Goldman *Excavations at Eutresis in Boeotia*, Cambridge, Mass., 1931.
—— *Excavations at Gözlü Kule, Tarsus*, vol. ii, Princeton, 1956.
B. Graef *Die antiken Vasen von der Akropolis zu Athen*, vol. i, Berlin, 1909.
O. R. Gurney *The Hittites*, London, 1954.
Edith H. Hall *Excavations in Eastern Crete, Vrokastro. University of Pennsylvania, the University Anthropological Publications*, iii. 3, Philadelphia, 1914.
J. Hazzidakis *Tylissos, Villas Minoennes* (*Etudes crétoises* iii), Paris, 1934.
W. A. Heurtley *Prehistoric Macedonia*, Cambridge, 1939.
R. A. Higgins *Greek and Roman Jewellery*, London, 1961.
Ida T. Hill *The Ancient City of Athens*, London, 1953.
D. G. Hogarth and others. *Excavations at Phylakopi in Melos*, London, 1904.
R. W. Hutchinson *Prehistoric Crete*, London, 1962.
G. L. Huxley *Achaeans and Hittites*, Oxford, 1960.
G. Jacobsthal *Greek Pins and Their Connexions with Europe and Asia*, Oxford, 1956.
P. Kavvadias Προϊστορικὴ Ἀρχαιολογία, Athens, 1914.
W. Kraiker and K. Kübler *Kerameikos: Ergebnisse der Ausgrabungen*, Bd. 1, Berlin, 1939.
K. Kübler *Kerameikos: Ergebnisse der Ausgrabungen*, Bd. iv, Berlin, 1943.
Winifred Lamb *Excavations at Thermi in Lesbos*, Cambridge, 1936.
L. Lerat *Les Locriens de l'Ouest*, Paris, 1952.
H. Lorimer *Homer and the Monuments*, London, 1950.
J. A. S. Macalister *Excavations at Gezer*, vol. iii, London, 1912.
F. Matz *Forschungen auf Kreta, 1942*, Berlin, 1951.
O. Montelius *La Grèce Préclassique*, Stockholm, 1928.
K. Müller *Tiryns; die Ergebnisse der Ausgrabungen*. . . . vol. i (with others), Athens, 1912; vol. iii, Augsburg, 1930.
A. S. Murray, A. H. Smith and H. B. Walters *British Museum Excavations in Cyprus*, London, 1900.
G. E. Mylonas *Aghios Kosmas; an Early Bronze Age Settlement and Cemetery in Attica*, Princeton, 1959.

G. E. Mylonas *Ancient Mycenae, the Capital City of Agamemnon*, London, 1957.
—— Προϊστορικὴ 'Ελευσίς, Athens, 1932.
—— *Eleusis and the Eleusinian Mysteries*, Princeton, 1961.
J. Naue *Die vorrömischer Schwerter aus Kupfer, Bronze und Eisen*, Munich, 1903.
M. Ohnefalsch-Richter *Kypros, the Bible and Homer*, London, 1893.
D. Page *History and the Homeric Iliad*, Berkeley and Los Angeles, 1959.
G. Papavasileiou Πέρι τῶν ἐν Εὐβοίᾳ ἀρχαίων τάφων, Athens, 1910.
H. Payne and others. *Perachora; the Sanctuaries of Hera Akraia and Limenia*, vol. i, Oxford, 1940.
H. Peake *The Bronze Age and the Celtic World*, London, 1922.
J. D. S. Pendlebury *Aegyptiaca*, Cambridge, 1930.
—— *The Archaeology of Crete*, London, 1939.
P. Perdrizet *Fouilles de Delphes*, vol. v, Paris, 1908.
L. Pernier and L. Banti *Guida degli scavi italiani in Creta*, Rome, 1947.
G. Perrot and C. Chipiez *Histoire de l'Art dans l'Antiquité*, vol. vi, Paris, 1894.
A. W. Persson *The Royal Tombs at Dendra, near Midea*, Lund, 1931.
—— *New Tombs at Dendra, near Midea*, Lund, 1942.
Sir William Flinders Petrie *Beth-Pelet (Tell Fara)*, vols. i and ii, London, 1930 and 1932.
P. J. Riis *Hama: fouilles et recherches 1931–1938*, vol. ii, 3; *les cimetières à crémation*, Copenhagen, 1948.
M. B. Sakellariou *La Migration grecque en Ionie*, Athens, 1958.
F. Schachermeyr *Hethiter und Achäer*, Leipzig, 1935.
C. F. A. Schaeffer *Enkomi-Alasia*, Paris, 1952.
—— *Ugaritica*, vol. i (1939); vol. iii (1956), Paris.
H. Schliemann *Ilios*, London, 1880.
—— *Mycenae: a narrative of researches and discoveries at Mycenae and Tiryns*, London, 1878.
R. B. Seager *Excavations at Vasiliki. Transactions of the Department of Archaeology, University of Pennsylvania*, vol. ii, 2, Philadelphia, 1907.
E. Sjöqvist *Problems of the Late Cypriote Bronze Age*, Stockholm, 1940.
T. C. Skeat *The Dorians in Archaeology*, London, 1934.
C. G. Starr *The Origins of Greek Civilisation*, London, 1962.
F. H. Stubbings *Mycenaean Pottery from the Levant*, Cambridge, 1951.
J. Sundwall *Die älteren italischen Fibeln*, Berlin, 1943.
Lord William Taylour *Mycenaean Pottery in Italy and Adjacent Areas*, Cambridge, 1958.
J. Travlos Πολεοδομικὴ ἐξέλιξις τῶν Ἀθηνῶν, Athens, 1960.
C. Tsountas Αἱ Προϊστορικαὶ ἀκροπόλεις Διμηνίου καὶ Σέσκλου, Athens, 1908.
N. Valmin *The Swedish Messenia Expedition*, Lund, 1938.
M. Ventris and J. Chadwick *Documents in Mycenaean Greek*, Cambridge, 1956.
N. M. Verdhelis Ὁ Πρωτογεωμετρικὸς Ῥυθμὸς τῆς Θεσσαλίας, Athens, 1958.
A. J. B. Wace *Chamber Tombs at Mycenae (Archaeologia*, vol. lxxxii), Oxford, 1932.
—— *Mycenae*, Princeton, 1949.
—— and M. S. Thompson *Prehistoric Thessaly*, Cambridge, 1912.

H. T. WADE-GERY *The Poet of the Iliad*, Cambridge, 1952.
C. WALDSTEIN *The Argive Heraeum*, vol. ii, Cambridge, Mass., 1905.
S. WEINBERG *Corinth*, vol. vii, part i, Cambridge, Mass., 1943.
F. WILLEMSEN *Dreifusskessel von Olympia: alte und neue Funde* (*Olympische Forschungen*, vol. iii), Berlin, 1957.
SIR LEONARD WOOLLEY, *Alalakh*, Oxford, 1955.

ADDENDA

General

P. ÅLIN. *Das Ende der mykenischen Fundstätten auf dem griechischen Festland.* (Studies in Mediterranean Archaeology, vol. i). Lund, 1962.

Mention of this work will be found in the Introduction and in the Bibliography, but it appeared too late for me to be able to make use of it. It is a book of great value for all Mycenaean sites on the Mainland of Greece from Thessaly southwards, and has been compiled with exemplary thoroughness. All known sites are listed, and particular attention is paid to the evidence for destruction and for continuity into the Protogeometric period. The detailed exposition of the archaeological evidence for the two major sites of Mycenae and Tiryns is specially noteworthy. The reader who wishes to have a more complete view of the distribution of Mycenaean sites on the mainland, and what these have produced, is strongly advised to consult this book.

C. W. BLEGEN. *The Mycenaean Age.* The University of Cincinnati, 1962.

The publication of two lectures delivered in memory of Louise Taft Semple. A general survey, of which the most valuable part is to be found in Professor Blegen's present opinion on the problems involved. He states it as his view that the real destruction of Mycenae coincided with the transition from LH. III B to LH. III C. See below, under Gla.

N. K. SANDARS. *AJA*, lxvii. 117 ff. and Pls. 21-28. *Later Aegean Bronze Swords.*

This long article assembles all the known material, and now, alongside Dr. Catling's articles on the Naue II swords, a complete survey of the swords used by the Mycenaeans is available.

H. W. CATLING. *Op. Ath.* iv. 129 ff. *Patterns of Settlement in Bronze Age Cyprus.*

A very useful survey; general remarks on the LC. III period will be found on pp. 145 f.

Additional information on sites already known

Mycenae. The Mycenae Tablets, iii. Edited by J. Chadwick. (Transactions of the American Philosophical Society. N.S. vol. 52, Part 7, 1962).

As well as the record of tablets recently found at Mycenae, this volume gives an account of excavations in the West House (Dr. Verdhelis), in the House of the Oil Merchant and in the House of the Sphinxes (Mrs. French), and in the Citadel House (Lord William

Taylour). The LH. III B pottery found in these excavations is well illustrated, and thus a most valuable addition to our settlement material, especially with regard to the stratification in the Citadel House, which was destroyed by a violent fire. Note should be made of the two-handled jug with strainer spout found in the West House (op. cit., p. 21, Fig. 21) which must be the earliest of its kind yet known.

Tiryns. H. Müller-Karpe, *Germania*, xl. 255 ff. and 273, fig. 8.

This article contains a comparison of the Tiryns helmet (cf. Pl. 24*a*) with one from Pass Lueg, in the Salzburg district.

G. S. Kirk, *The Songs of Homer*, Pl. 4, *b* illustrates the stirrup jar found with the helmet.

Argos. P. Courbin, *Stratigraphie et Stratigraphie* (Études Archéologiques, pp. 59 ff.).

A detailed stratigraphical report of excavations of which a preliminary report appears in *BCH*, lxxxi. 647 ff. and *BCH*, lxxxiii. 762 ff. Protogeometric kilns were found in close proximity to a sub-Mycenaean grave (it appears to be a cist tomb, cf. op. cit., p. 62, Fig. 1) and to Protogeometric cist tombs, and the area continued to be used for burials at least down to sub-Geometric times. One Protogeometric skyphos is illustrated for the first time (op. cit., Fig. 7), and as the excavator says (op. cit., p. 71), it recalls the type of skyphos found in the Protogeometric cemetery on Kos (cf. *PGP*, Pl. 30).

Salamis. C.-G. Styrenius, *Op. Ath.* iv. 103 ff.

A full account, with excellent photographs, of the vases and a bronze bowl from the sub-Mycenaean cemetery, originally published by Wide (*AM*, xxxv). The author has identified sixty-three vases, as against Wide's fifty-six.

Gla. C. W. Blegen, The Mycenaean Age, p. 23 reports information from the late Mr. Threpsiadis that the palace 'was abandoned at the close of the pottery phase III B and was never re-inhabited'. Cf. p. 121.

Neleia. D. Theocharis, *Pr.* 1957, p. 67 reports that on this site there was nothing later than LH. III B except for a very small number of LH. III C sherds. He considers, however, that it was inconceivable that the site was deserted before the end of Mycenaean times, especially as there were traces of Protogeometric.

Phaestos. D. Levi, *Ann.* (N.S.) xxiii-xxiv. 397 ff., 467 f., 477 ff.

This report includes accounts of recent Protogeometric and Geometric finds. Illustrations of Protogeometric vases appear on p. 403, Fig. 44, *b*, p. 409, Fig. 51, p. 467, Fig. 139 (probably very late) and p. 499, Fig. 192. It is also reported that 'sub-Mycenaean' pottery was found at Chalava.

Mitropolis-Gortyn. St. Alexiou, *Pr.* 1957, pp. 148 f. and Pl. 75 discusses the figurines from this site, and argues for a date in LM. III B. Cf. p. 189.

Palaikastro. H. W. Sackett, *ILN*, 27 April, 1963, pp. 620 ff. Evidence of occupation in LM. III C. Cf. p. 169.

Old Smyrna. E. Akurgal, *AJA*, lxvi. 369 f. and Pl. 96. A brief discussion of the Protogeometric material from this site; note the illustration of a krater.

Kition. V. Karageorghis, *ILN*, 22 December, 1962, pp. 1012 ff.

A preliminary report of the extremely interesting excavations in progress on this site. The settlement was evidently destroyed at the same time as Enkomi VI, and good ashlar work is found in the reconstruction, as in Enkomi V. Early LH. III C pottery is associated with this rebuilding, but at Kition it appears to have ousted the local Cypriot pottery almost completely (cf. p. 200). There was no further destruction until the time of the earthquake (?) which resulted in Enkomi's desertion, but before this, Granary Class type of pottery had made its appearance, as on other sites in Cyprus. Moreover, the latter disaster was not succeeded by a desertion of this settlement; it was rebuilt and flourished, and thus we have a rare and important instance of continuity. See now *BCH*, lxxxvii. 364 ff.

New Sites

Larisa. Mrs. M. Theocharis, *Thessalika*, iii. 47 ff.

This article records and illustrates Mycenaean finds in the area; some of the pottery is considered to be LH. III B-C in date.

Argissa (west of Larisa). H. Rachoviti-Gourgioti, *Thessalika*, iii. 25 ff. The description of a Protogeometric plate.

Homolion (at the north entrance of the Tempe valley). D. Theocharis, *BCH*, lxxxvi. 792.

Report of a Protogeometric cemetery. Rock-built tombs containing well-preserved skeletons, bronze fibulae showing northern influences, skyphoi and gold gems. Dated to 1000–900 B.C.

Iasos. D. Levi, *Ann.* (N.S.) xxiii-xxiv. 505 ff.

The report of Mycenaean material at Iasos (cf. p. 162) is not yet confirmed in this account. The illustrated sherds (op. cit., p. 537, Fig. 50) do not seem necessarily to be earlier than Protogeometric.

Muskebi (near Budrum). G. F. Bass, *AJA*, lxvii. 208.

Report of 'at least six partially destroyed chamber tombs'. The contents included LH. III pottery and faience beads; the vases of one tomb are said to be LH. III C. The full account will be of great interest, as this is an area which has not hitherto produced evidence of Mycenaean occupation, although it is very close to Kos.

Burgaz Tepesi (near Budrum). G. F. Bass, *AJA*, lxvii. 208.

A tholos tomb with dromos and rectangular chamber. Mr. Bass reports that six Protogeometric vases were found in this tomb, and he has most kindly permitted me to say that these comprise a krater, a skyphos with high conical foot, two trefoil-lipped oinochoai, a belly amphora and an amphora with handles from shoulder to base of neck. The style is thoroughly Protogeometric, and closer to the Attic series than are the vases from Kos; concentric circles and semicircles are the main motives of decoration.

Ashdod (Philistia). *Biblical Archaeologist*, xxvi. 31.

Brief report on recent excavations. Philistine pottery, unstratified; a few sherds illustrated on Fig. 13.

SITE INDEX

Sites of marginal relevance have been omitted; with one exception (Medi) no references are given to Appendixes A and B. The most important references are shown in italic figures.

Aetos, settlement, *109* f.; survival of LH. III C pottery types and evidence of Protogeometric pottery, 110; violin-bow fibulae, 55, 110.

Aghios Kosmas, settlement probably mainly abandoned at time of transition LH. III B-C, *112*, *118*; evidence of LH. III C survival, 112, 118.

Agia Triada, evidence for LM. III B and C occupation, *168*; Fringed Style sherds, 171; sanctuary, 168, 190.

Agrilia, cist tombs containing native and Mycenaean pottery, 38 f., *132*, 235; relevance for intruders, 38 f., 259 n. 2.

Amnisos, occupation reported to be continuous, 169, 181.

Amorgos, summary of sporadic LH. III C finds, 147; Close Style sherd, 15, 147.

Amyklai, use as sanctuary in LH. III C, 42, *88* f.; Close Style pottery, 15, 88; animal figurines, 41; Protogeometric pottery showing connexions with Ithaca, 234.

Ancient Elis, slab-covered pit graves containing pottery of early Protogeometric type, 39, *92* f., 234.

Ano Englianos (Pylos), assumed to be Nestor's Pylos, 220 f.; not fortified, 30; palace *megaron* used for religious purposes, 41; destroyed at end of LH. III B, 9, 221; destruction contemporary with second disaster at Mycenae, 222; rarity of LH. III C pottery, *94*; doubt whether tablets are evidence of attack by 223 n. 2.

Anthedon, bronze founder's hoard, possibly LH. III C, 48.

Antissa, slight contact only with Mycenaean world, 160; Grey Ware the characteristic pottery until the eighth century, 255.

Aphaia temple (Aegina), no pottery later than LH. III B, 119; possible use as sanctuary, 119.

Apliki, destroyed and deserted in LC. III, 198; LH. III C pottery rare, 198.

Apollakia, LH. III C vases of latest type, 156.

Argos, description of site, *80* ff.; undisturbed survival until end of LH. III C, 230; evidence of new settlement site after end of LH. III C, 80 ff.; chamber tombs in continuous use throughout LH. III, 81; pit graves perhaps still in use in LH. III C, 33; contemporaneity of latest LH. III C pottery with that of Kerameikos cist tombs, 19; poor quality of small finds, 51; dress pins, 53; votive wheel, 54, 72, 84; arched fibula, 58, 84; tweezers, 59; problem of continuity between chamber tombs and cist tombs, 19; cist tombs contain pottery of Protogeometric type, 19; increase of northern types of skull in cist tombs, 40; eighth century suit of armour, 64.

Arne (Kierion), LH. III sherds, 132; perimeter wall possibly indicating centre of refuge in Mycenaean period, 134, 221.

Asine, general description, *82* ff.; thinly inhabited in LH. III B but with possible large influx in LH. III C 35, 82 f., 226; occupied until end of LH. III C, 82, 230; Granary Class pottery compared with that of Cyprus, 23 f.; building in LH. III C, 31; LH. III C sanctuary with Minoan connexions, 42, 83, 190; cist tombs and pit graves of Mycenaean period, 33; poor quality of LH. III C small finds, 51; Protogeometric cist tombs, 39, 83 f.; hand-made pottery in these tombs perhaps introduced by new arrivals, 260 n. 1.

Askalon, LH. III B and Philistine pottery separated by destruction level, 213; Philistine bowl compared with LH. III C bowl at Sinda, 209.

Assarlik, earliest pottery in tombs resembles Athenian sub-Myc.-Protogeometric, 21, 162, 254; cremation practised, 71.

Astakos, evidence of contact with Mycenaean world, 102.

Asteri, LH. III B occupation perhaps continuing into early LH. III C, 88.

Atchana, latest pre-destruction pottery LH. III B, 208; settlement probably destroyed by Land and Sea Raiders, 207, 238.

Athens, Acropolis, defences strengthened at end of LH. III B, 30, 113, 221; desertion of North Slope houses and building of fountain at time of transition LH. III B-C, 113; pottery from North Slope houses, 7, 9, 113; pottery from fountain deposit, including Close Style and Granary Class, 113, *117* f.; scarcity of Granary Class, 116; bronze founder's hoard, 48 f.; cruciform dagger from hoard, 68.

——, Mycenaean chamber tombs and pit graves, 33 f., 113.

——, Kerameikos sub-Mycenaean cemetery, cist tombs and pit graves, 37; contemporary with end of LH. III C, *17* ff.; characteristic features, *116*, *119*; pottery, *119*; northern types of skull, 40; dress pins, 53; iron pins, 54, 70; violin-bow fibulae, 56; arched fibulae, 58; tombs associated with intruders, 37, 231; contemporary with later stage of Perati cemetery, 232; bottle with possible Cypriot connexions, 27.

——, Protogeometric cemetery, bottle with possible Cypriot connexions, 27; stag, 41; shield-bosses, 65; hand-made figurines, 260.

Atsidadhais, report of Mycenaean 'goddess' figurines, 184; child pithos burials perhaps of LM. III C date, 184, 187 n. 5.

SITE INDEX

Ayia Irini (Cyprus), destroyed and abandoned in LC. III A, 198; small sanctuary of early CG date, 202.

Ayia Irini (Kea), LH. III C sanctuary and evidence of later use, *44*, 147, 244.

Ayios Andreas, occupation in LH. III B but later continuation uncertain, *90* f.; small jar of sub-Mycenaean character, 91.

Ayios Stefanos, slight evidence of LH. III C occupation, 88.

Ayios Vasilios, important settlement in LH. III B, but no LH. III C yet identified, 90.

Berbati, abandoned towards end of LH. III B, 77, 221.

Beth Shan, links with Egypt and Aegean but almost complete absence of Philistine pottery, 213.

Burgaz Tepesi (near Budrum), tholos tomb containing Protogeometric vases, Addenda.

Cave of Pan, Mycenaean cult spot not subsequently used until fifth century, 43.

Chalandritsa, tumulus-covered cist tombs of Geometric date, 39, 101, 234.

Chauchitsa, one Mycenaean sherd, 140; later cist tombs, 38, 142.

Clazomenae, Mycenaean sherds, 161.

Colophon, tholos tomb containing unrecorded Mycenaean pottery, 33, 161.

Corinth, *see* Old Corinth.

Delos, evidence for Mycenaean sanctuaries and probable subsequent continuity of worship, *44* ff., 244; evidence of occupation in LH. III C, *148* f.

Delphi, general discussion of settlement and tombs, *122* ff.; LH. III C occupation, 123, 226, 251; LH. III C pottery, 15, 16 n. 2, *123* ff.; possible ceramic link with Achaea, 100, 227; evidence for Mycenaean sanctuary, 43 f., 123 f.; violin-bow fibula, 55.

Dendra (Midea), LH. III A panoply, 62 ff.; slight evidence of occupation in LH. III C, 77; doubt cast on identification of gold object as part of arched fibula, 55.

Derveni (Aigeira), tombs with features similar to those of Kephallenia, 86; violin-bow fibula, 56, 86.

Derveni (Keryneia), Late Protogeometric pithos burial, 22 n. 3, 39, *101*; type of burial paralleled in Elis and Messenia, 101; ceramic connexions with Ithaca, 101, 234.

Diakata, LH. III C cemetery and contents, *104* ff.; Close Style type of pottery, 106; multiple-loop fibula, 57; short sword with rounded shoulders, 69.

Diasela, tombs still in use in LH. III C, 92.

Dictaean Cave, bronze tools, 49; violin-bow fibulae, 55; multiple-loop fibula, 57; knives and daggers of European type, 60, 69, 190; Fringed Style tankard, 176.

Dimini, cist tombs with LH. III B pottery, 33, *129*.

Dodona, knife of North-western Greek type, 60.

Dreros, sub-Minoan tholos tomb and contents, 184 f.

Elateia, knife of North-western Greek type, 60.

Eleusis, survival of MH. cist tombs into LH. III, 33, *114*; LH. III sanctuary, 43, *114* f.; likelihood of break in occupation after beginning of LH. III C, 115.

Emborio, cist tombs of LH. III B date, 33, 159; establishment of settlement in LH. III C, *159*, 228; discussion of pottery, 159; destruction late in LH. III C, 159, 233.

Enkomi, general survey, 22 ff., *197* f.; strengthening of fortification in thirteenth century, 197; Naue II sword in Swedish tomb 18, 68, 196; destruction of level VI at end of LC. II, 197; evidence for survival of LH. III B pottery later than in Aegean, 238; level V rebuilding characterized by early LH. III C pottery and fine ashlar construction, 22 f., 197, 199 n. 3, 229 f.; destruction of level V in LC. III A, 198, 200; appearance of Granary Class type of pottery from level III onwards, 23, 201, 236; desertion at or before end of LC. III B, 198; deposits of bronze objects, 48 f.; continuance of bronze industry during LC. III, 200, 203; introduction of iron in level IV, 25 f.; iron knife with bronze rivets from level I, 26, 61; tombs contain local ware only, 201; scarabs of Ramesses III contemporary with levels IV—II, 201, *240*; violin-bow fibula, 55.

Epidaurus (Apollo Maleatas), evidence of cult place in LH. III, 42 f., *78*.

Episkopi (Ierapetras), LM. III B cemetery, 170; Octopus Style stirrup jar, 7.

Erganos, LM. III B-C tomb, 177.

Eutresis, fortified settlement perhaps used as centre of refuge, 30, *120*, 221; probably deserted at time of transition LH. III B-C, 120, 221; desertion connected with northern invasion, 251.

Galaxidi, vases of LH. III C or later date, 125.

Gazi, LM. III B or C sanctuary, 189.

Gla, fortified stronghold destroyed at end of LH. III B, *120* f., 221, Addenda; desertion linked with invasion from North, 251.

Gortyn, new settlement in LM. III C, accompanied by appearance of non-Minoan type of pottery, 32, *183*, 193, 235; violin-bow fibula, 56; arched fibulae, 58.

Gournia, occupied not later than LM. III B, 169; Octopus Style sherd, 7; shrine, 189; pithos burial, 187 n. 5.

Gremnos, discussion of reported continuity LH. III B to Protogeometric, 133 f.

Gribiana, lanceolate spearhead, 66.

Halos, Protogeometric cist tombs as evidence for new arrivals, 38, 138, 259.

Hama, cremation cemetery, 71 n. 4; iron knife with bronze rivets, 26 n. 1, 61.

Ialysos, general description of LH. III chamber tombs, *152* f.; pottery, 7 f., 12 f.; ceramic links with Naxos and Perati, 155; influence of Granary Class slight, 155; cremation associated with inhumation, paralleled on Kos and at Perati, *157*, 228; stirrup jar of Minoan type, 175; high quality of LH. III C small finds, 156; scarabs, 52; iron bracelet, 70 f., 157; weapons, 68 n. 6, 156 n. 4; cemeteries abandoned before end of LH. III C, 157, 233.

Iasos, report of Mycenaean and sub-Mycenaean pottery, 162, but cf. Addenda.

SITE INDEX

Idalion, fortified acropolis deserted before end of LC. III B, 198, 201; small sanctuary in early CG, 201 f.; tomb containing pottery of very late LH. III C type, 24; ceramic link with Crete, 26.

Iolkos, survey of evidence, *128* f.; palace destroyed and settlement abandoned in LH. III C, 9, 128, 227, 250; subsequent re-occupation, and significance of persistence of Mycenaean type of architecture and pottery into Protogeometric period, 31 f., 34, *136* f., 234 ff., 243 n. 1, 255; Protogeometric cist tombs and their significance, 38, 235, 259; problems of relative chronology, *136* f.; violin-bow fibula, 56; arched fibula, 58.

Iria, evidence from one house of occupation at time of transition LH. III B-C, 78.

Isthmia, defence wall against invasion built in LH. III B, 30, *85*, 221; slight evidence of settlement in LH. III C 85.

Itea district, tombs and settlement indicating some occupation in LH. III C, 126; vase of Achaean type, 126, 227.

Kafkania, cist tombs of Mycenaean date?, 33, 39, *92*.

Kalbaki, cist tombs with native pottery, dated by dagger to late LH. III B, 37 f., *102*, 231 f.; importance as possible source of groups later moving south, 37 f. 231 f.; lanceolate spearhead, 66.

Kallithea, greaves, 62 f., 98; Naue II swords, 98.

Kalochorio, terracotta head similar to one from Asine, 190.

Kalymnos, tombs used in LH. III B and C, *154*; Granary Class influence, 16, 155 f.; Octopus Style stirrup jar, 161.

Kameiros, LH. III tombs, *153*; Close Style stirrup jar, 6; influence of Granary Class, 155; abandoned before end of LH. III C, 157.

Kapakli, significance of tholos tomb used in Protogeometric and later periods, 129, 235.

Kaphirio, report of LH. III, sub-Mycenaean and Protogeometric occupation, 95.

Karpathos, contents of tombs and Minoan connexions, 154; cruciform dagger of LH. III B date, 68.

Karphi, general review of LM. III C—sub-Minoan settlement, sanctuary and tombs, *172* ff.; appearance and significance of *megaron*, 32, 172; scarcity of non-Minoan pottery, 173, 192, 235; links with Cyprus, 27; bronze implements, 49; dress pins, 53; violin-bow fibulae, 55 f.; arched fibulae, 58; problem of date of desertion of site, 175.

Katarraktis, tholos tombs and settlement probably LH. III B, 97 f.

Katsamba, settlement occupied until early LM. III C, 169, 181; LM. III C shrine, 189.

Kavousi, tholos tombs and sub-Minoan pottery, 187; shield-boss, 66; iron weapons, 191.

Kazanli, sherds of LH. III A or B type, 205.

Kefala, settlement destroyed in LM. III B, 168 f., 229.

Kition, continuous occupation LC. III to CG, 198 and Addenda; significance of wavy-line pottery from well, 24, 202, 240; Minoan sherd from well compared with Mouliana krater, 27.

Klauss (Achaea), tombs with LH. III C pottery and Naue II sword, 98 f.

Knossos, Palace area, occupation in LM. III B, 169; Shrine of Double Axes, 169, 189; slight evidence of occupation in LM. III C, 179; sub-Minoan shrine in underground Spring Chamber, 180, 193.

——, Zapher Papoura cemetery, not used later than LM. III B, 192; daggers, 69.

——, Mavrospelio cemetery, Octopus Style stirrup jar, 179.

——, Gypsades cemetery, sub-Minoan tombs and contents, *180*; importance of pottery for chronology, 26, 28; iron knife with bronze rivets, 26, 61, 180; dress pins, 53, 180; sealstones and beads, 180, 190; LH. III C influence, 180.

——, Agios Ioannis sub-Minoan tomb, bronze pin with ivory head, 53.

——, Kephala tholos tomb secondary deposits, Fringed Style and Granary Class type of pottery, 179.

——, Fortetsa cemetery, possible cremation in sub-Minoan tomb Π, 187; iron knife with bronze rivets in Late Protogeometric context, 61.

Kokkinochomata, report of Protogeometric pottery, 96.

Kokkolata, cemetery apparently not used later than LH. III B, 103.

Kolonna (Aegina), tombs, no evidence later than LH. III B, 119.

Korakou, general description, *85* f.; undisturbed occupation into LH. III C, 85, 226; Close Style vase, 15 n. 1; violin-bow fibula, 55, 86; apparently abandoned in LH. III C, 86.

Kos, Serraglio Mycenaean settlement, undisturbed occupation into LH. III C, *153*, 227; unfortified, 30; Late Protogeometric cist tombs above settlement, 153; possibly the burials of first Dorian settlers, 253 f.

——, Langada and Eleones cemeteries, *153*; instance of cremation paralleled at Ialysos and Perati, 153, 157, 223; Naue II sword, 157; abandoned before end of LH. III C, 233.

Kouklia, presumed continuous occupation from LC. III to CG, 198, 201 f.; Mycenaean influence in ivories, 199.

Kourion, Bamboula settlement, LC. III occupation but no LH. III pottery found, 198; discussion of chronological problems, 202 f.

——, Kaloriziki cemetery, continuous use from LC. III to CG, 201; appearance of Mycenaean type of chamber tomb in LC. III B, 203; ceramic comparisons with Crete and Athens, 26 f.; use of cremation, 71, 204; shield-bosses, 66; sceptre, 204, 236; fibulae and pins, 204 n. 2.

Kourtes, probable survival of sub-Minoan features, 182.

Kozani, Early Iron Age cist tombs evidence for intruders from North, 38, 139 n. 5, 145, 259.

Krisa, fortified settlement destroyed at end of LH. III B, 30, *125*, 221; destruction linked with invasion from North, 221, 251.

Ktouri, discussion of settlement pottery, *131* f.; Mycenaean(?) perimeter wall possibly suggesting centre of refuge, 134, 221.

Kydonia, chamber tombs, 168; LM. III B Octopus Style stirrup jar, 7.

Lakkithra, general description of LH. III C cemetery and finds, *104* ff.; sword with cast-hilt, 69 n. 3.

Lapithos, continued use of cemetery from LC. III to CG, 198; Mycenaean type of chamber tomb found in LC. III B–CG. IA, 203; fibulae and pins, 204 n. 2.

Larisa (Hermos), one Mycenaean sherd recorded, 161.

Leporano (S. Italy), LH. III C pottery found, 215.

Liliana, LM. III B—sub-Minoan cemetery, *183*; instance of cremation, 187; glass paste ornaments, 190.

Lipari, small amount of LH. III C pottery, 215.

Livatho, tombs with LH. III C pottery, 103.

Maa, LC. III fort probably destroyed and deserted in this period, 198; masonry resembles that of Enkomi level V, 197.

Mallia, re-occupation settlement LM. III A–C(?), *169*; character of pottery, 170 f.; uncertainty of date of destruction, 169, 235; violin–bow fibula, 56, 169, 171.

Malthi, occupied during LH. III C, *94*; kylix stems suggest link with Kephallenia, 94; iron dagger and knife, 94.

Marmariani, Mycenaean settlement, 133; significance of Protogeometric tholos tombs containing handmade pottery of Macedonian type, 22, *137* f., 244, 255.

Mavrovouni, possible occupation in early LH. III C, 90; Protogeometric vases found nearby, 90 n. 5.

Mazarakata, LH. III C cemetery and finds, including jewellery and violin-bow fibulae, 103.

Menelaion, probably destroyed late in LH. III B, *88*, 221.

Metaxata, description of LH. III C cemetery and contents, 104 ff.; LH. III B survivals, 104; violin-bow fibulae, 104; lanceolate spearheads, 67, 104.

Midea, *see* Dendra.

Milatos, LM. III B tombs, 169; stirrup jars as possible evidence of overlap between LM. III B and LH. III C, 7 172, 176; stirrup jar of early Fringed Style, 169, 177.

Miletus, evidence summarized, *162* f.; identified with Hittite Millawanda, 219; fortified in LH. III B, 162; undisturbed occupation into LH. III C, 227; ceramic links with Dodecanese, 162; destroyed before end of LH. III C, 21, 162; earliest re-occupation pottery linked with sub-Myc.-Protogeometric pottery of Athens, 21, 163, 233; connexion of re-occupation settlement with Ionian migration, 254.

Mitropolis, shrine of LM. III B or earlier date, *168*, 189 and Addenda.

Modi, description of contents of Late Protogeometric cemetery, *267* f.; kantharoi, 27; iron weapons, 191.

Monemvasia, chamber tombs used in LH. III C, and significance of pottery as indicating Aegean contacts, 89.

Mouliana, LM. III C tombs, review of evidence, *177*; cremation and inhumation in tomb A, *188*; bowl of Granary Class type, 16 n. 2, 177; shield depicted on krater, 65; shield-bosses, 65, 72; lanceolate spearhead, 67; sword with cast-hilt, 69 n. 3.

Mouriatadha, review of evidence, *93* f.; possible sanctuary, 42, 93; difficulty of dating time of destruction, 93 f.

Muskebi (near Budrum), Mycenaean chamber tombs, Addenda.

Mycenae, Settlement, summary of evidence, *73* ff. and Addenda; capital of Mycenaean empire, 219; first destruction during course of LH. III B, 4, 74, 250; second and major destruction at end of LH. III B, 4, 9, 74 ff., 221; revival after second destruction, 226; third and final destruction, involving Granary, 17, 73 ff., 230; destruction of Granary dated *c.* 1150 or later, 241; causes and effects of destructions, 230, 236 f., 250 f.; survival after final destruction, 75; LH. III B ivories, 47; winged-axe mould, 57; Levantine amphora, 69; bronze founder's hoards, dated towards end of LH. III B, 48 f.; swords from hoards, 68 f.; corslets and shields on Warrior Vase, 63; shrine in palace and possible significance of later superimposed temple, 41 f.

——, Tombs, chamber tombs used in LH. III C, *75*; poor quality of LH. III C small finds, 51; LH. III C pithos burial, larnax burial and cist tomb, 36, 75; later Protogeometric cist tombs sunk in ruins of Mycenaean houses, 39 f., 75; violin-bow fibulae, 55, 57.

Myrsini, cemetery used LM. III A-C, 170; discussion of LM. III B and C pottery, 178; Naue II sword, 178, 190.

Nauplia, evidence of occupation in LH. III C, 80.

Naxos, settlement at Grotta possibly continuous LH. III A to Geometric, *149* f.; contents of chamber tombs predominantly LH. III C, 35, *150*; cremation, 151; child pit burial, 151; LH. III C ceramic connexions with Attica and Dodecanese, 115, 150 f., 228; Naue II sword in LH. III C context, 151; iron dagger in LH. III C context, 70, 151; later burials not in chamber tombs, but earliest contemporary with sub-Mycenaean Athens, 151, 232.

Neleia, occupation not confirmed in LH. III C, 128, cf. Addenda.

Nichoria, settlement destroyed at end of LH. III B, *95*, 221; no proof of LH. III C occupation, 96; cist tombs and pithos burials of Protogeometric date, 39, 96, 234; character of Protogeometric pottery, 96.

Nicosia, occupied in LC. III, 198; decorative motives of LH. III C type sherds paralleled on Philistine pottery, 210, 212.

Old Corinth, evidence of occupation in LH. III B, 85; resettlement perhaps soon before rise of Athenian Protogeometric style, 20, 85; Early Geometric cist tomb, 39.

Old Smyrna, slight evidence only of contact with Mycenaean world, 161.

Olous, burials of LM. III B date, 169; discussion of burial customs and problems of dating, *188* f.; cremations, 188 f.

Olympia, no break in occupation from LH. III onwards, 91; LH. III C occupation, 91.

Orchomenos, inhabited in LH. III B, 120; casual find of sub-Mycenaean vase, 120.

Palaikastro, occupied not later than LM. III B, *169*, but cf. Addenda for evidence of LM. III C occupation; stirrup jar used as evidence of possible overlap between LM. III B and LH. III C, 7, 176.

Palaiokastro (Arcadia), chamber tombs used in LH. III C, 92.

Palaiokastro (Thessaly), cist tomb of Protogeometric date, evidence of intrusive group, 38, 138, 259.

Palaiopyrgo, pithos burials of Protogeometric date, 39, 92.

Palaiopyryi, important settlement flourishing in LH. III B, no LH. III C yet identified, 90.

Panagia, tombs of Protogeometric date containing pottery of sub-Minoan type, 184; iron weapons, 184, 191.

Parga, tholos tomb with native pottery, LH. III B sherds and lanceolate spearhead, 102.

Paroikia, evidence of occupation in LH. III C, 148.

Patele, Early Iron Age settlement, 142.

Pelikata, occupation in LH. III B with possible extension into LH. III C, 108.

Perachora, evidence of occupation in LH. III B and C, 86.

Perati, LH. III C cemetery, review of evidence, *115* f.; significance of site for increase of population in East Attica at time of transition LH. III B-C, 35; desertion of site at end of LH. III C, 116, 232; a few slab-covered pit burials, 20, 36, 115; cremations of similar type to those of Dodecanese, 115, 228; later tombs contemporary with Salamis and Kerameikos cist tombs, 13, 116, 232; main ceramic connexions with Naxos and Dodecanese, 13, *115*, 228; Close Style pottery, 115, 125; Granary Class pottery, 16 n. 2; high quality of small finds, 51; objects of East Mediterranean origin, 52, 116; iron knives with bronze rivets, 26, 61, 70 f.; part of iron pin (?), 54, 70; sword with down-turned handguard, 69 n. 4; violin-bow fibulae, 56; arched fibulae, 58; bronze beaker and tweezers, 59.

Petra, perimeter wall of great extent, possibly Mycenaean 134, 221.

Phaestos, evidence for occupation in LM. III B, 168; new settlement after beginning of LM. III C, 32, *182* f.; appearance of non-Minoan type of pottery in new settlement, 182 f., 193, 235; Fringed Style sherds, 171, 182; sub-Minoan tomb containing arched fibulae, *183* f.; violin-bow fibula in Protogeometric tomb, 56; cremation replaces inhumation after appearance of Protogeometric pottery, 188.

Pharai, cist tombs of Geometric period, 39, 101.

Pharsala, LH. III B vases from tomb, 131.

Pherae, post-Mycenaean cist tombs, 132.

Photoula (Praesos), early LM. III C tholos tomb and contents, 177 f., cremation associated with inhumation, 177, 188; bronze pin, 53, 178.

Phylakopi, settlement occupied into LH. III C but deserted in this period, *148*, 227; Peschiera dagger, 69.

Pigadhes, destroyed and abandoned in LC. III, 168; LH. III C pottery rare, 198.

Pitane, Octopus Style stirrup jar similar to one from Kalymnos, 161, 228.

Polis, cult site occupied in LH. III C, *108* f.; bronze founder's hoard (?), 48 n. 2; lanceolate spearhead, 67; ceramic connexions with Kephallenia, 108 f.

Praesos, *see* Photoula.

Prinias, evidence of LM. III C or sub-Minoan shrine, 182, 190.

Prostovitsa, extensive LH. III C cemetery, 98.

Prosymna, probable abandonment at end of LH. III B, 77 f., 221.

Pteleon, tholos tombs built or re-used in LH. III C, 34; review of pottery and other objects, *130* f.; probable link with Achaea, 130, 227.

Pylos, *see* Ano Englianos.

Rakhmani, discussion of Mycenaean sherds associated with pottery of Marmariani type, *133*, 138.

Ras Shamra (Ugarit), discussion of relevant evidence, 207 f.; destruction to be dated not earlier than 1191 B.C. consequently due to Land and Sea Raiders, 207, 238; significance of context of sword with cartouche of Merneptah, 207 f., 239 f.

Retziouni, cist tombs with hand-made vases of Marmariani type associated with sub-Mycenaean(?) amphoriskos, 38, *133*, 138; significance of tombs for intrusive group, 138, 259.

Salamis, sub-Mycenaean cist tomb and pit grave cemetery associated with new arrivals, 37, 231, 252; relative chronology, 17 ff., 232, characteristic features, *116*; review of pottery and small finds, *119* and Addenda; absence of 'goddess' figurines, 41; dress pins, 53; arched fibulae, 58.

Samos, evidence of Mycenaean occupation slight, 158; presumed from other evidence to have been inhabited by Mycenaeans in LH. III C, 228.

Saratse, contact with Mycenaean world in LH. III B and perhaps into LH. III C, 140.

Sardis, single Mycenaean sherd, 160.

Scoglio del Tonno, probable settlement of group of Mycenaeans into LH. III C, *215*; Octopus Style sherds, 228.

Scutari, Naue II sword, 70 n. 1.

Sinda, destroyed at end of LC. II, 197, 229; rebuilding characterized by much early LH. III C pottery and masonry similar to that of Enkomi level V, 23, 197 ff., 229; Close Style type of pottery, 16 n. 1; second destruction in LC. III A soon followed by abandonment, 198, 200.

Skyros, slight evidence only of Mycenaean habitation, 138 f.; shield-boss of Protogeometric date, 65.

Sparta, sporadic Mycenaean sherds not later than LH. III B, 88; violin-bow fibula from Orthia temple, 55.

Stenos, LH. III B occupation, possibly also in LH. III C, 126.

Tarsus, small Mycenaean settlement, dated to transition LH. III B-C, *205* f.; settlers perhaps refugees from Greek Mainland, 222, 236; rarity of monochrome bowls, 206; Octopus Style sherd, 206, 228; ceramic links with Athens, 117, 206; settlement deserted before Iron Age, 206.

Tegea, Mycenaean and Protogeometric pottery from sanctuary of Alea Athena, *87*; report of tholos tombs, 87.

Tell Abu Hawam, discussion of chronological difficulties involved in attributing destruction to Land and Sea Raiders, 208.

Tell Fara, Philistine pottery similar to early LH. III C found in Cyprus, 209, 212; earliest Philistine pottery associated with sherd bearing cartouche of Seti II, 213.

Tell Sukas, no Mycenaean pottery found later than LH. III B; reasonable attribution of destruction to Land and Sea Raiders, 208, 238.

Thebes, settlement destroyed in LH. III A, 121, 220; chamber tombs establish occupation in LH. III C, 121, 226; violin-bow fibulae, 55, 121; significance of sub-Mycenaean vases in later cist tombs, 20, 38, 121 f., 231.

Theotokou, cist tombs (sub-Myc. to Geometric) indication of newcomers, 38, 259; sub-Mycenaean lekythos, 22, 138.

Therapnai, violin-bow fibula, 55.

Thermi, later stages of Mycenaean pottery not found, 160.

Thouria, report of Protogeometric pottery, 96.

Tiryns, fortified settlement destroyed at end of LH. III B (= second destruction at Mycenae), 4, 9, 79, 221 f.; no evidence of settlement by invaders at this time, 251; slight occupation in LH. III C, 79; 'Treasure', 48, 68 n. 2; sub-Myc. and Protogeometric pit graves and cist tombs (above earlier settlement), 39 f., 79 f.; bronze helmet, shield-boss and spearhead, and iron dagger from early pit grave, *80*, 84; helmet, 64 f., 72; shield-boss, 65; violin-bow fibula, 55.

Torre Castelluccia (S. Italy), LH. III C pottery, 215.

Tragana, re-use of tholos tomb in LH. III C, 34, *95*; Close Style type of pottery, 16 n. 1; unusual bowl shape paralleled at Athens, Emborio and Tarsus, 95, 117 n. 6.

Trikkala, LH. III B-C sherds, 132.

Troy, review of relevant evidence, *163* ff.; VII*a* Priam's city, 164, 249; LH. III B but no LH. III C pottery in VII*a*, 164; LH. III C pottery of Granary Class type found in both VII*b* 1 and VII*b* 2, 164 f.

Trypa-Vromousa, cemetery, slight continuity into LH. III C, 122.

Tylissos, occupied in LM. III B, 169; cremation burial assigned to Protogeometric period, 182.

Vardaroftsa, evidence for LH. III B and LH. III C pottery, *141*; LH. III C pottery survives destruction layer and perhaps continues to be imitated after end of style further south, 141.

Vardhates, unorthodox type of cist tomb, pottery dated LH. III B-C, 38, *126*.

Vardino, Mycenaean pottery in reasonable quantity, 140; violin-bow fibula beneath burnt stratum, 56, 142.

Vasilike, tholos tomb of LM. III B-C date, 176 f.

Vergina, Early Iron Age cemetery with cist tombs and pithos burials, 38 f.; types of tombs and bronze objects indicate intrusive group from North, 259; distinctive hand-made pottery, *143*, 145; pyxides of Mycenaean type, 144; Protogeometric vases, *143*; possible eleventh-century date of tomb C (arched fibula, bronze Naue II sword, no iron), *145*.

Volimidhia, tombs probably not used later than LH. III B, 95; comparison of tomb construction with that found at Metaxata, 104.

Volimnos, Protogeometric and Geometric pottery, 96.

Voula, cemetery in use till transition LH. III B-C, 112; LH. III pit graves, 33.

Vourvatsi, cemetery in use until early LH. III C, 112.

Vrokastro, evidence for LM. III B occupation, 169; review of evidence for LM. III C and later occupation, *185* ff.; apparently simultaneous use of cremation and inhumation, 188; stirrup jar of type found at Milatos and Karphi, 186; violin-bow fibula, 55, 185 f.; arched fibulae, 58; iron knife with bronze rivets, 26, 61, 186, 191; shield-boss, 65; necklaces of Minoan type, 190.

Zygouries, destroyed at end of LH. III B, *84*, 221.

GENERAL INDEX

Aeolian migration, traditional account of the migration, 247 f.; absence of confirmatory archaeological evidence, 255.

Ahhiyawa, probably to be equated with the Mycenaean world, 4, 218 f.; King of Ahhiyawa in West Asia Minor soon after the mid-thirteenth century, 220.

Alasia, district devastated by Land and Sea Raiders, identified as Cyprus, 237 f.

Arzawa, district devastated by Land and Sea Raiders, located in West Asia Minor, 237 f.

Boeotians, traditional account of displacement by Thessalians and subsequent move to Boeotia twenty years before Dorian invasion, 247, 250; probably of North-western origin, 247; archaeological evidence insufficient either to confirm or deny their arrival in Boeotia, 251.

Cremation, instances of, in Mycenaean and Minoan contexts, 71; area of origin and manner of introduction to Aegean world as yet unknown, 71.

Depopulation, at end of LH. III B, generally on Mainland south of Thessaly, 221 ff., 251 f.; in Argolid, 4 f., 77 ff.; in Laconia, 34 f., 90; in Messenia, 34 f., 97; in Elis, 97; in West Attica, 35, 112 ff.

——, during LM. III A and B in Crete (slight only), 167, 170, 191, 229.

——, during LC. III in Cyprus, 198.

Destructions, on Greek Mainland, in LH. III A, see *Site Index*, Thebes; during LH. III B, see *Site Index*, Mycenae; at end of LH. III B, see *Site Index*, Krisa, Gla, Zygouries, Mycenae, Tiryns, Menelaion, Nichoria, Ano Englianos; during LH. III C, see *Site Index*, Mycenae, Iolkos.

——, in Eastern Aegean, during LH. III C, see *Site Index*, Emborio, Miletus.

——, in Crete, during LM. III B, see *Site Index*, Kefala; during LM. III B or C, see *Site Index*, Mallia.

——, in Cyprus, at end of LC. II, see *Site Index*, Enkomi, Sinda; during LC. III A, see *Site Index*, Enkomi, Sinda, Apliki, Ayia Irini, Pigadhes, Maa(?).

Dorians, linked through their kings with Heracles, 246; traditional account of invasion and settlement of Peloponnese and subsequent moves across South Aegean, 247 f.; invasion and settlement of Peloponnese dated by Thucydides eighty years after the fall of Troy, 250; radical differences between traditional account and archaeological evidence, 251 ff.

Hittite documents, referring to Ahhiyawa, 4, 218 f.; the significance of the Tavagalavas letter with regard to the situation in Millawanda (Miletus), 219 f.; record of King of Ahhiyawa waging war in Western Asia Minor, 220.

Increase in population in LH. III C, general remarks, 222 f.; in Achaea, 98, 100; in Kephallenia, 107; in East Attica, 112, 115; at Asine, 82 f.

Ionian migration, traditional account of, 246, 247; movement occasioned by earlier invasions, 247 f.; archaeological evidence confirms traditional date of migration, but raises doubts on connexion with Dorian invasion, 254.

Iron, introduced to Aegean from East Mediterranean, 25, 70; first found at Enkomi in level IV and thereafter in common use, 25, 200; iron objects found in LH. III C contexts, 70 f.; knowledge how to work iron probably not before Protogeometric period in the Aegean, 70.

Native elements within Mycenaean territory, in Kephallenia, 104 f., 107; in Thessaly, 135.

New settlers (Mycenaeans), possibly in Crete during LH. III C, 193 f., 235 f.; in Cyprus at beginning of LH. III C, 198 ff.; in Cyprus after destruction of Granary at Mycenae, 23 ff., 203; at Tarsus at beginning of LH. III C or rather earlier, 205 f.; see also under *Increase in population*.

——(non-Mycenaeans), probably recognizable in users of cist tombs and pithos burials, 18, 37 ff., 234 f., 259; cist tombs of LH. III B date at Kalbaki suggest possible area of origin, 37 f., 231 f.; distribution of cist tombs and pithos burials, 37 ff.; significance of archaeological evidence in relation to dialect distribution and to traditional account, 252 ff.; northern types of skull at Argos and Athens confirm origin of intruders, 40; Macedonians moving into North Thessaly recognizable from their pottery, 234 f., 250, 259.

Relative chronology, LM. III B overlaps the beginning of LH. III C, 7 f.; sub-Mycenaean co-extensive with most of later phase of LH. III C, 17 ff., 28 n. 1; sub-Minoan in part co-extensive with the later phase of LH. III C, 15, 180; LC. II B and LH. III B end at about the same time, 23; LH. III B in East Mediterranean overlaps beginning of LH. III C in the Aegean, 197, 208, 238; LC. III A = early LH. III C, 23, 198 f.; LC. III B = Granary Class (later phase of LH. III C), 23 f., 201 f.; some sub-Minoan earlier than the end of sub-Mycenaean in Athens, 28; sub-Minoan in part contemporary with LC. III B, 26 f., 180; transition LC. III B-CG. IA to be equated with transition sub-Myc.-PG in Athens, 27 f., 241; early Philistine pottery reflects not quite the earliest stage of LH. III C, 209 ff., 212, 237 f.

Spartan kings, descended from Heracles, 246; genealogies used as basis for traditional chronology, 248 f.; doubt cast on authenticity of average length of reigns, 256.

Survival, Minoan features, tombs and burial customs, 187, 193; religious customs, 189 f., 193.
——, Mycenaean features, pottery, 243; architecture (at Iolkos only), 243 n. 1; tholos tombs, 34, 244; religious practices on Delos and Kea(?), 244.
Thessalians, traditional account of move from Northwest into Thessaly, 247; archaeological evidence suggests infiltration into Thessaly from twelfth century onwards, 234 f., 250.
Trojan War, archaeological reasons for dating the war soon after the middle of the thirteenth century, 220 f.; focal point of tradition, and dates assigned by tradition, 248; most reliable traditional dates confirmed by contemporary evidence, 249.

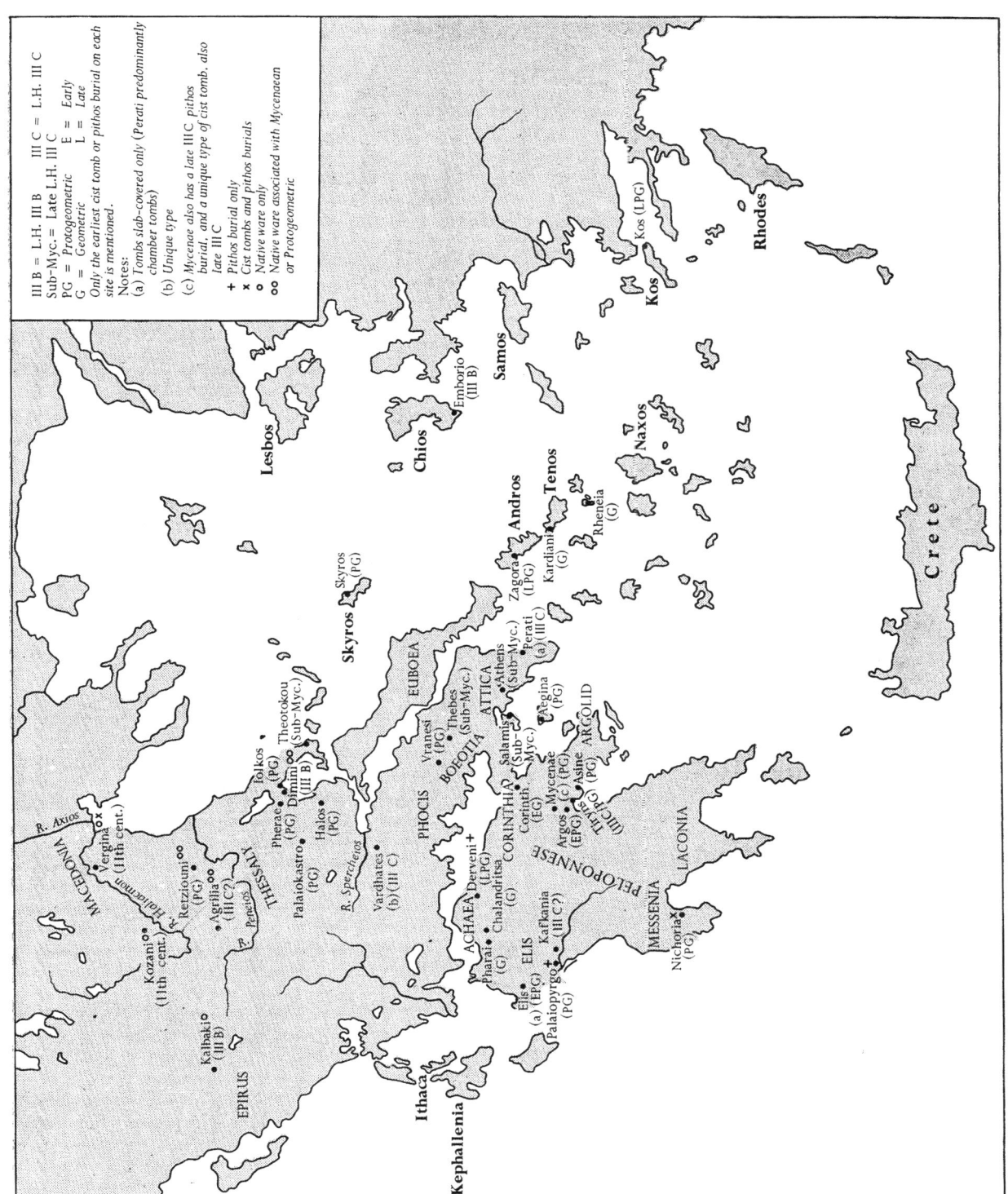

THE DISTRIBUTION OF EARLY CIST TOMBS AND PITHOS BURIALS

PLATE 1

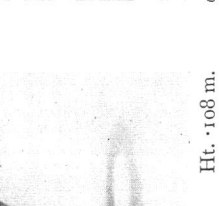

Ht. ·170 m. *b.*
Ht. ·108 m. *d.*
Ht. ·152 m. *a.*
Ht. ·108 m. *c.*

LH. III B VASES

a and *d.* IALYSOS. *b.* HALA SULTAN TEKKE, CYPRUS. *c.* KALYMNOS

PLATE 2

a. Ht. ·234 m.

b. Ht. ·182 m.

c. Ht. ·09 m.

d. Ht. ·21 m.

STIRRUP JARS, IALYSOS
a and *b*, L.H. III B.   *c* and *d*, L.H. III B-C

PLATE 3

a. Ht. ·235 m.

b. Ht. ·32 m.

c. Ht. ·16 m.

d. Ht. ·105 m.

a. LH. III C CLOSE STYLE STIRRUP JAR, ASINE
b-d. VASES FROM KAMEIROS TOMB 48

PLATE 4

a. Ht. ·40 m.

b. Ht. ·28 m.

c. Ht. ·07 m.

d. Ht. ·22 m.

LH. III C CLOSE STYLE VASES, MYCENAE

PLATE 5

Scale 1:6

LH. III C VASES AND SMALL OBJECTS FROM IALYSOS TOMB 84

PLATE 6

a.   Ht. ·23 m.

b.   Ht. *c.* ·24 m.

c.   Ht. ·327 m.

d.   Ht. *c.* ·175 m

OCTOPUS STYLE STIRRUP JARS
a. MOULIANA.   *b.* NAXOS.   *c* and *d.* PERATI

PLATE 7

a.   Ht. (to rim) ·093 m.

b.   Ht. (to rim) ·148 m.

c.   Ht. ·19 m.

d.   Ht. *c.* ·20 m.

LH. III C VASES
a and *c*. IALYSOS.   *b*. PERATI.   *d*. NAXOS

PLATE 8

LH. III C KRATERS, KEPHALLENIA

PLATE 9

a.
Ht. ·19 m.

b.

a. LH. IIIB KYLIX, KALYMNOS
b. LH. IIIC KYLIKES, KEPHALLENIA

PLATE 10

a. Ht. unknown b. Ht. ·46 m.

c. Ht. ·261 m. d. Ht. ·284 m.

e. Ht. ·165 m. f. Ht. ·221 m.

LH. III C VASES FROM SITES IN ACHAEA

Scale 1 : 2

LM. III C FRINGED STYLE
PYXIS PATTERNS, KARPHI

PLATE 12

GRANARY CLASS VASES, MYCENAE

Scale 2 : 5

PLATE 13

Scale 2 : 5

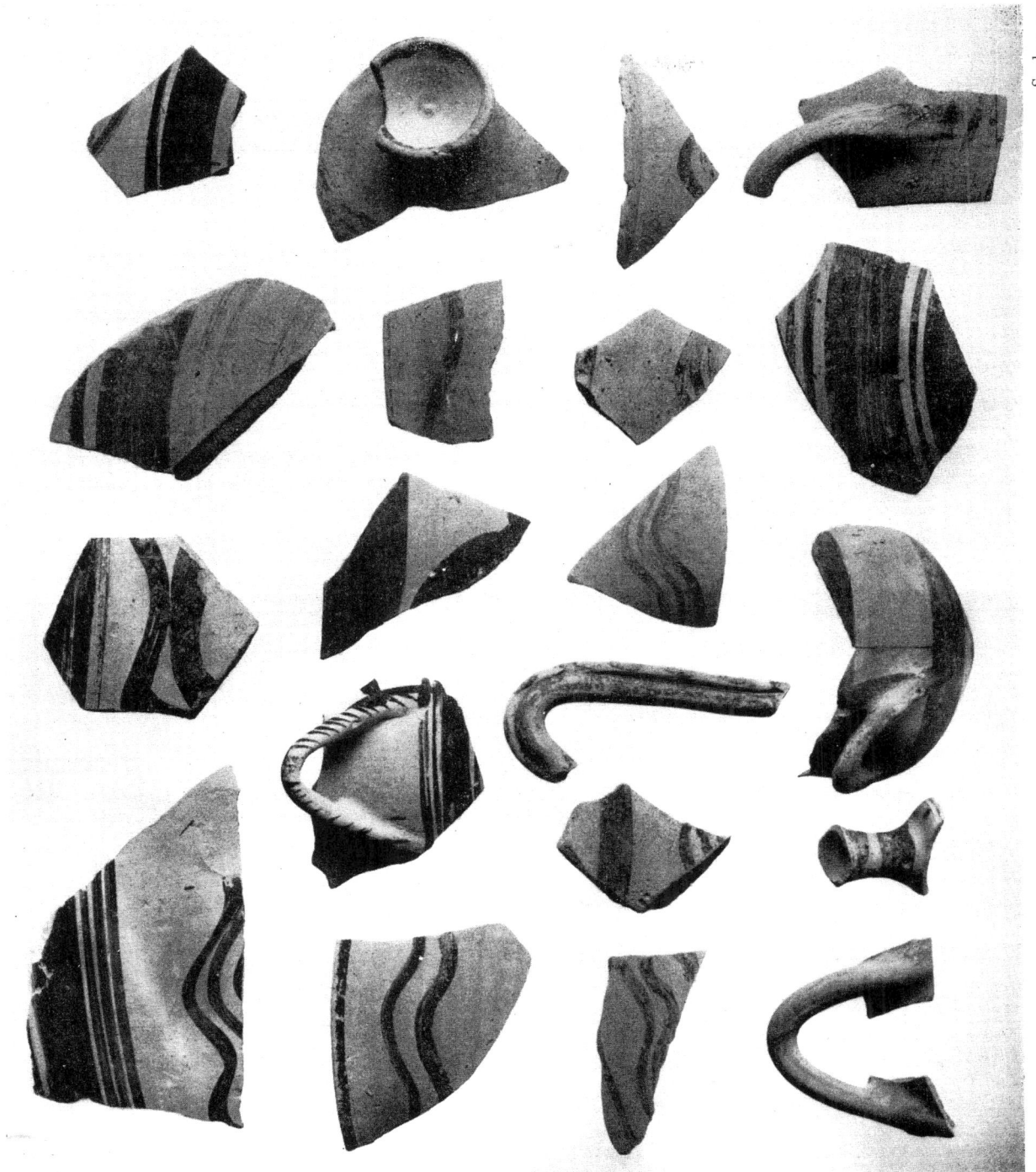

SHERDS, KITION

PLATE 14

a. Ht. ·153 m.

b. Ht. ·20 m.

c. Ht. ·08 m.

d. Ht. ·078 m.

SUB-MYCENAEAN VASES, KERAMEIKOS

PLATE 15

a.   Ht. ·111 m.

b.   Ht. ·082 m.

c.   Ht. not known

d.   Ht. ·088 m.

a and *b*. SUB-MYCENAEAN LEKYTHOS AND CUP, KERAMEIKOS
c. SUB-MYCENAEAN LEKYTHOS, NAXOS
d. CG. I A CUP, CYPRUS

PLATE 16

a. Ht. ·255 m.   *b.* Ht. ·270 m.

c. Ht. ·097 m.   *d.* Ht. ·121 m.

a and *b*. LC. III B BOTTLES, KALORIZIKI (CYPRUS)
c. SUB-MYCENAEAN BOTTLE, KERAMEIKOS.   *d.* EARLY PG. BOTTLE,
ATHENS, ACROPOLIS SLOPE

PLATE 17

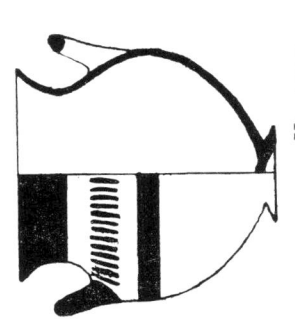

Ht. ·391 m.

Ht. ·096 m.

Ht. ·134 m.

Ht. ·20 m.

a.   b.   c.   d.

a and *b*. SUB-MINOAN AMPHORISKOS AND KANTHAROS, KARPHI
c. LH. III C AMPHORA, PERATI.   *d*. LC. III B–CG. I A AMPHORA, CYPRUS

PLATE 18

a.   Ht. ·24 m.   *b.*   Ht. ·147 m.

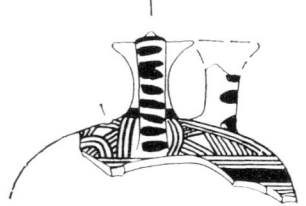

c.   Ht. ·129 m.   *d.*   Ht. as preserved ·075 m.   *e.*   Ht. ·114 m.

LATE STIRRUP JARS
a. LC. III B, CYPRUS.   *b.* LC. III B, CYPRUS?   *c.* LC. III B, KOUKLIA (CYPRUS)
d. SUB-MINOAN, KNOSSOS.   *e.* LH. III C, ARGOS

PLATE 19

Ht. ·145 m.

Ht. ·23 m.

b.

Ht. ·09 m.

Ht. ·088 m.

d.

PHILISTINE VASES

PLATE 20

MYCENAEAN JEWELLERY
a. IALYSOS? *b-d.* MYCENAE. *e.* PROSYMNA

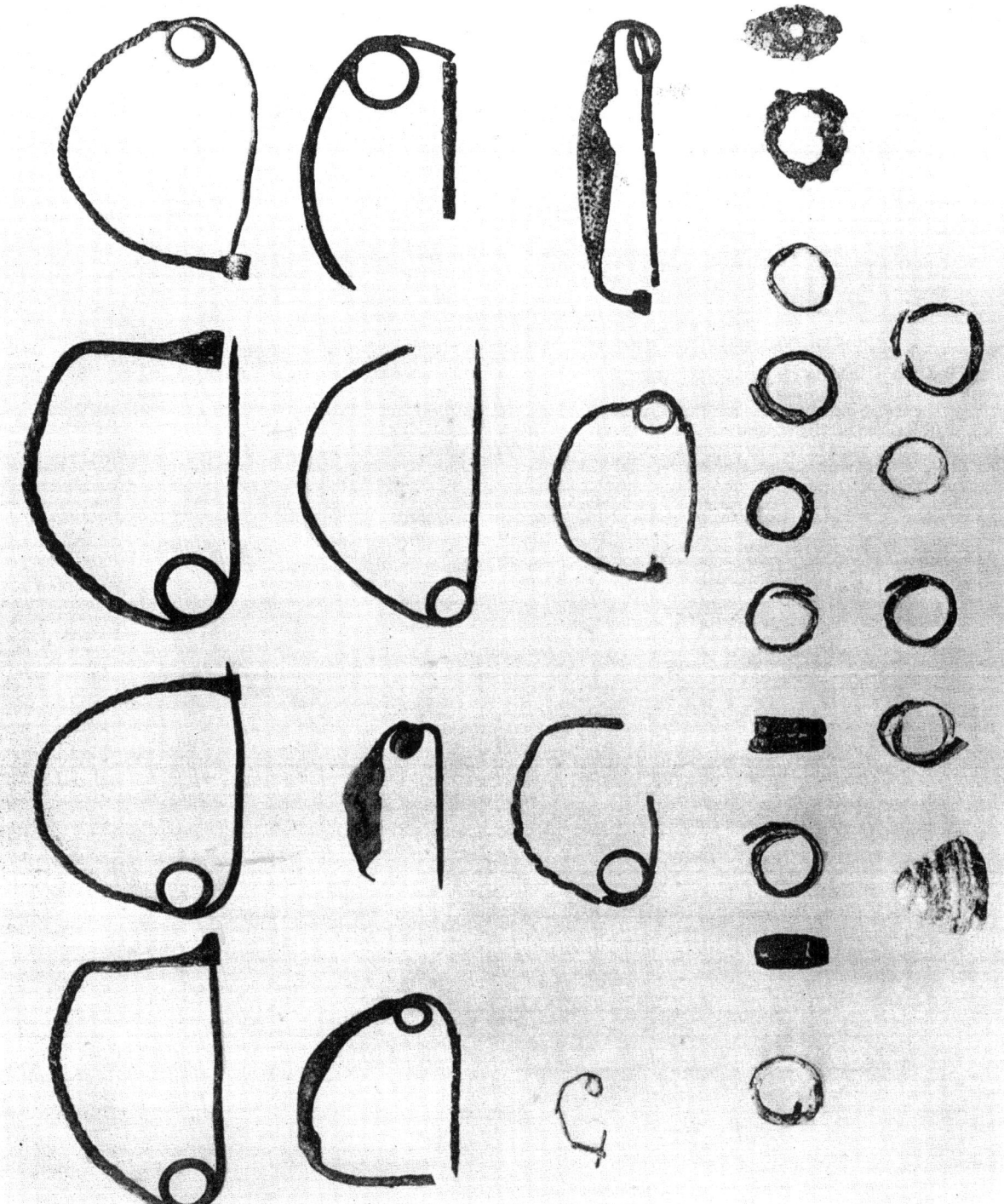

PLATE 21

Scale 2 : 3

SMALL FINDS FROM KERAMEIKOS SUB-MYCENAEAN TOMB 108

PLATE 22

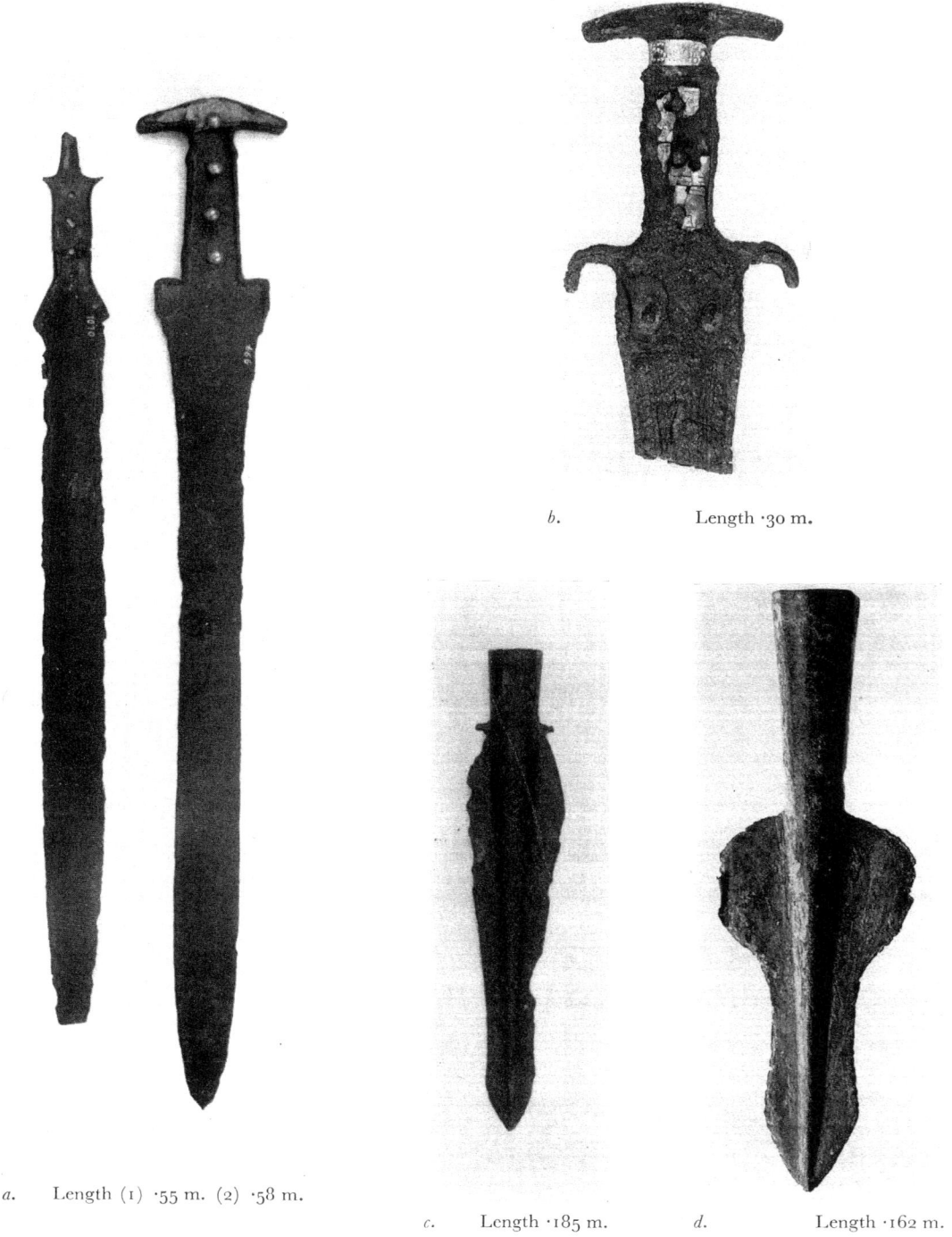

a. Length (1) ·55 m. (2) ·58 m.

b. Length ·30 m.

c. Length ·185 m.   *d.* Length ·162 m.

SWORDS.   *a.* MOULIANA.   *b.* PERATI
SPEARHEADS.   *c.* MOULIANA.   *d.* 'NEAR THEBES'

PLATE 23

a.   Ht. ·34 m. Dm. ·174 m.

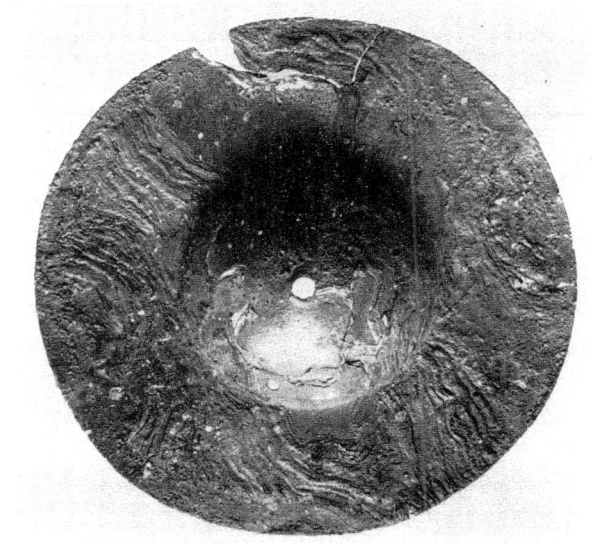
b.   Dm. ·114 m.

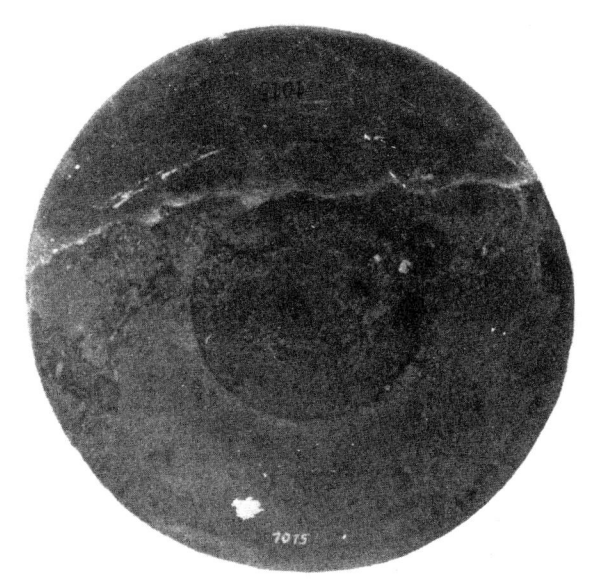
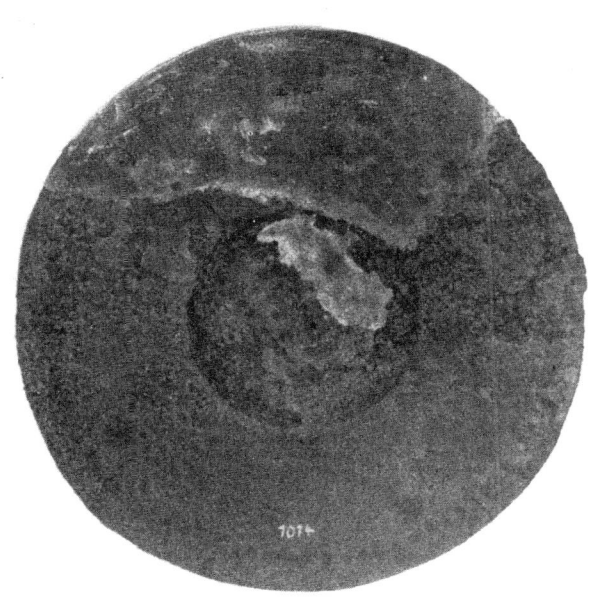
c.   Dms. ·19 m.

SHIELD-BOSSES
a and *b*. KERAMEIKOS (PG).   *c*. MOULIANA

PLATE 24

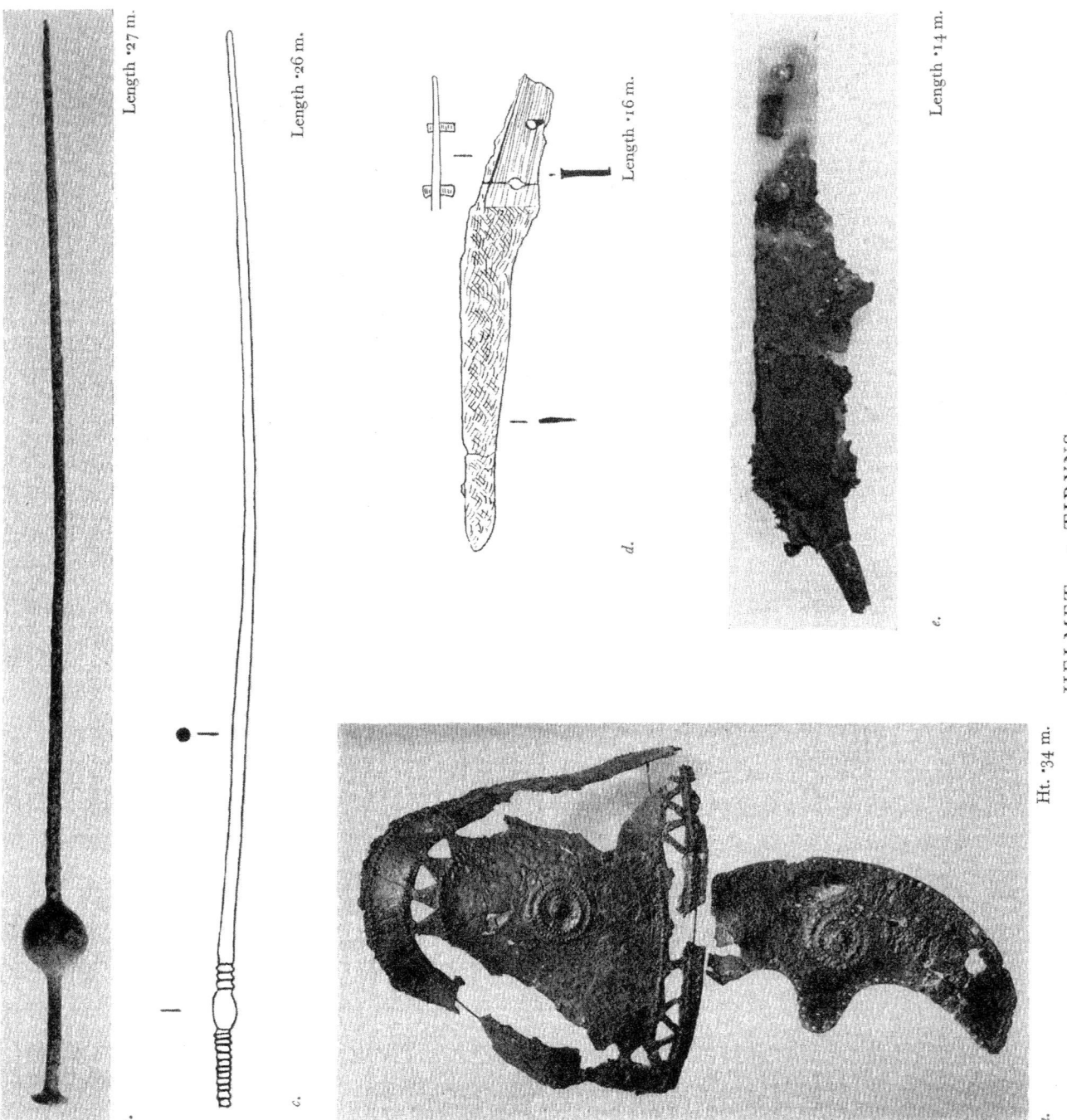

HELMET. *a.* TIRYNS
DRESS PINS. *b.* UNKNOWN PROVENIENCE. *c.* KNOSSOS

Printed in Great Britain
by Amazon